A HISTORY OF TECHNOLOGY
&
INVENTION

Progress Through the Ages

VOLUME III

The Expansion of Mechanization
1725–1860

Contributors to This Work

JEAN-BAPTISTE ACHE, Lecturer, National Museum of Arts and Crafts, Part Five, Chapter 1

MAURICE AUDIN, master printer, Director of the Lyon Museum of Printing, Part Eight

ARTHUR BIREMBAUT, civil engineer of the Mines Administration, Part Six, Chapter 2

PHILIP W. BISHOP, formerly Head Curator, Department of Arts and Manufactures, National Museum of History and Technology, Smithsonian Institution, Part Nine, Chapter 2

MAURICE DAUMAS, Director, Museum of the National Conservatory of Arts and Crafts, Part One (collaborator); Part Two, Chapters 1 and 3, Chapter 5 (collaborator); Part Three, Chapters 1, 2, 3, and 4 (collaborator), Chapters 5 and 6; Part Five, Chapter 2; Part Six, Chapter 4

MARGUERITE DUBUISSON, Director, the Museum of Knitwear, Part Seven, Chapter 3

WALTER ENDREI, engineer, Budapest, Part Seven, Chapter 1 (collaborator)

DANIEL FAUCHER, Honorary Dean, Faculty of Letters, Toulouse, corresponding member of the Institute of France, Part Six, Chapter 1

ANDRÉ GARANGER, I.C.F., former director of the Association of French Builders of Machine Tools, Part Ten, Chapter 2

BERTRAND GILLE, professor, Faculty of Letters and Humanities, Clermont-Ferrand, Part Six, Chapter 3

PAUL GILLE, Chief Engineer of Marine Construction (E.R.), Part One (collaborator); Part Three, Chapters 1, 2, 3, and 4 (collaborator); Part Four

ARMAND MACHABEY, doctor, University of Paris, Chief of Department of Research and Documentation of the Service of Measuring Instruments, Ministry of Industry, Part Ten, Chapter 5 (collaborator)

PIERRE MESNAGE, director, National College of Chronometry and Mechanics, University of Besançon, Part Ten, Chapter 4

JACQUES PAYEN, archivist and palaeographer, Director of Studies, College of Applied Advanced Research, Part One, Chapter 2 (collaborator); Part Seven, Chapters 1 and 2 (collaborator)

JEAN PILISI, textile engineer, graduate of E.N.S.A.I.T. (Roubaix), editor-in-chief of *The Textile Industry*, Part Seven, Chapter 2 (collaborator)

PAUL R. SCHWARTZ, administrator of the Museum of Textile Printing (Mulhouse), Part Seven, Chapter 4

S. W. SHUKHARDIN, Institute of the History of Science and Technology, Moscow, Part Nine, Chapter 1

With the collaboration of the Center for the Documentation of the History of Technology

A HISTORY OF TECHNOLOGY
&
INVENTION

Progress Through the Ages

VOLUME III

The Expansion of Mechanization

1725–1860

EDITED AND WITH AN INTRODUCTION BY

MAURICE DAUMAS

TRANSLATED BY

EILEEN B. HENNESSY

CROWN PUBLISHERS, INC.   NEW YORK

English Language Publishers' Note

The publishers of the English language edition of this volume wish to express their gratitude to Philip W. Bishop, formerly of the Smithsonian Institution's Museum of History and Technology, now of London, England, for his generous and most valuable service as consultant in the extensive and arduous process of preparing this translation. The fact that this edition required further orientation to American experience and therefore the incorporation of the appropriate research presented additional problems in interpretation and translation, and Dr. Bishop's professional concern has been an enormous strength to us.

We wish also to thank Edwin Battison, of the Smithsonian Institution's National Museum of History and Technology, for valuable critical comments on the material in Part One, Chapter 2, and Part Two, Chapters 1–4; and Dr. David Jeremy, formerly Research Fellow at the Smithsonian Institution and now of Westcliff-on-Sea, England, and editor of the valuable publication *Henry Wansey and His American Journal,* 1970, Philadelphia, Pa., American Philosophical Society, for his comments on Part Seven, Chapters 1–4.

The reader is referred to the bibliography on page 572 of Volume I for useful references to current English language material.

ORIGINALLY PUBLISHED AS *Histoire Générale des Techniques,*
UNDER THE DIRECTION OF MAURICE DAUMAS.
©1968 BY PRESSES UNIVERSITAIRES DE FRANCE

ENGLISH TRANSLATION ©1979 BY CROWN PUBLISHERS, INC.
PRINTED IN THE UNITED STATES OF AMERICA
PUBLISHED SIMULTANEOUSLY IN CANADA BY GENERAL PUBLISHING COMPANY LIMITED

Library of Congress Cataloging in Publication Data

Daumas, Maurice, ed.
  A history of technology & invention.
  Translation of Histoire générale des techniques.
  Includes bibliographies.
  CONTENTS.—v. 1. The origins of technological
civilization.—v. 2. The first stages of mechanization.—v.3. The expansion of
mechanization.
  1. Technology—History. I. Title.
T15.D2613   609   71-93403
ISBN 0-517-52037-0 (v. 3)

CONTENTS

Introduction. By Maurice Daumas 1

PART ONE

METHODS OF PRODUCING POWER
By MAURICE DAUMAS and PAUL GILLE   17

CHAPTER 1: *Traditional Sources of Power*   19

Windmills 19
Waterwheels 24
Water Turbines 29

CHAPTER 2: *The Steam Engine*   39

The Atmospheric Engine 39
The Condensing Engine 44
The Double-acting Engine 50
The Progress of the Steam Engine 58
The Steam Engine in France 70

CHAPTER 3: *Mechanical Power and Its Measurement*   81

   Bibliography 89

PART TWO

THE MACHINE INDUSTRIES   91

CHAPTER 1: *Mechanical Factors in Industrial Progress*
By MAURICE DAUMAS   92

CHAPTER 2: *Industrial Mechanization* By ANDRÉ GARANGER   101

First Experiments and Successes 101
Nineteenth-Century Machine-Tool Builders 105
The Invention and Evolution of Machine Tools 113

CHAPTER 3: *Light Machinery and the Beginnings of Automation*
By MAURICE DAUMAS   160

CHAPTER 4: *The Measurement of Time*
By PIERRE MESNAGE   182

v

CHAPTER 5: *Standardized Measuring Systems and the Beginnings of Precision Mechanics*
By MAURICE DAUMAS and ARMAND MACHABEY   198

Early Linear Measures 198
The Organization of the Metric System 203
Progress in Manufacturing Precision Instruments 211
Diffusion and Revision of the Metric System 222
The Evolution of Measuring Instruments 226
    Bibliography 231

PART THREE

TRANSPORTATION AND COMMUNICATION   233

CHAPTER 1: *Roads, Bridges, and Road Transport*
By MAURICE DAUMAS and PAUL GILLE   235

Road Building 235
From Stone to Iron Bridges 242
Road Transport 257

CHAPTER 2: *Rivers, Canals, and Ports*
By MAURICE DAUMAS and PAUL GILLE   271

Canals 272
Ports 276
Dry Docks 281
Lighthouses 282
Lightships 289
Dredges 289

CHAPTER 3: *Ships and Navigation*
By MAURICE DAUMAS and PAUL GILLE   291

Sailing Vessels 291
Steamships 298
The Evolution of Marine Steam Engines 318
Raw Materials 322
The Techniques and Instrumentation of Navigation 327

CHAPTER 4: *Railroads*   332

Tracks 332
Steam Traction 338
The Development of Railroads 359

CHAPTER 5: *Lighter-Than-Air Craft: The First Steps*
By MAURICE DAUMAS   369

CHAPTER 6: *The Birth of the Telegraph*
By MAURICE DAUMAS   376

Visual Telegraphy 376
Electric Telegraphy 378
    Bibliography 390

PART FOUR

MILITARY TECHNIQUES
By PAUL GILLE   391

CHAPTER 1: *Fortifications*   392

CHAPTER 2: *Land Artillery*   399

CHAPTER 3: *Naval Artillery*   406

CHAPTER 4: *Portable Weapons*   414

CHAPTER 5: *Ballistics*   422

    Bibliography 430

PART FIVE

CONSTRUCTING AND EQUIPPING URBAN BUILDINGS   431

CHAPTER 1: *Construction and Architecture*
By JEAN-BAPTISTE ACHE   432

Old and New Techniques 432
The Use of Iron 434
Wooden Structures 447
The Beginnings of Reinforced Concrete 448
The Architectural Consequences of Construction Techniques 451

CHAPTER 2: *Domestic Comfort and Sanitation*
By MAURICE DAUMAS   453

Water: Supply and Drainage 454
Lighting 460
Heating 467
    Bibliography 472

PART SIX

THE EXTRACTION AND EXPLOITATION OF NATURAL RESOURCES   473

CHAPTER 1: *The Evolution of Agricultural Techniques*
By DANIEL FAUCHER   474

The Revolution in Cultivation 474
The New Agriculture 486

CHAPTER 2: *The Mining Industry*
By ARTHUR BIREMBAUT   505

Progress to the End of the Eighteenth Century 505
Progress of Mining Techniques to 1860 518

CHAPTER 3: *The Evolution of Metallurgy*
By BERTRAND GILLE — 527

The English Technical Revolution 531
The First Half of the Nineteenth Century 542
The Nonferrous Metals 553

CHAPTER 4: *The Rise of the Heavy Chemical Industry*
By MAURICE DAUMAS — 556

Bibliography 580

PART SEVEN

THE TEXTILE INDUSTRIES — 581

CHAPTER 1: *The Spinning of Textile Fibers*
By WALTER EUDIER and JACQUES PAYEN — 583

CHAPTER 2: *Weaving and Mechanical Finishing*
By JACQUES PAYEN and JEAN PILISI — 599

CHAPTER 3: *Hosiery*
By MARGUERITE DUBUISSON — 619

CHAPTER 4: *Textile Printing*
By PAUL R. SCHWARTZ — 633

Bibliography 653

PART EIGHT

TECHNIQUES OF EXPRESSION — 655

CHAPTER 1: *Printing*
By MAURICE AUDIN — 656

The Gutenberg Press 656
Printing for the Blind 662
The Cylinder Used in Typographic Printing 665
The Mechanical Press 666

CHAPTER 2: *Methods Derived from Typography* — 671

Stereotyping 671
The History of Stereotyping 675
Stereography 679
The Printing of Music 688

CHAPTER 3: *The Evolution of Mechanized Printing Techniques* — 689

Relief Printing 690
Intaglio Printing 696
Flat-Surface Printing 699

Color Engraving 701
Relief Printing (Embossing) 702
Conclusion 703
    Bibliography 705

PART NINE

THE SPREAD OF TECHNICAL PROGRESS   707

CHAPTER 1: *The Development of Technology in Russia (1700–1850)*
    By S. W. SHUKHARDIN   709

CHAPTER 2: *The Introduction of Modern Technology in the New World*
    By PHILIP W. BISHOP   722

The Establishment of the First Large Industries (1800–1850) 725
    Bibliography 733

GENERAL BIBLIOGRAPHY 734
INDEX 735

INTRODUCTION

T HE EXPANSION OF mechanization constitutes the fundamental event of the period to which this volume of *A History of Technology & Invention* is devoted; that is, from approximately 1725–1740 to 1850–1860. During this period of less than a century and a half there appeared all the characteristics of the industrial civilization in which we are now living. Such major events as the independence of the United States and later of the former Spanish and Portuguese possessions in Central and South America, the French Revolution and the European wars, and the revolutions that shook Europe between 1830 and 1850 all brought about or paved the way for the great political, economic, and social transformations out of which the modern world was born. It was not by chance that during this same period the technical means available to man for the needs of his industries underwent equally spectacular upheavals. Their mutation was favored by certain economic and social factors that have often been analyzed. The progress of technology itself contributed a new element to the economic evolution of the countries of Western Europe during the first half of the nineteenth century—by giving a modern face to industrial production, it determined the appearance of the social structures that were established in these countries.

The primacy of mechanization   It is not incorrect to see in the expansion of mechanization the primary cause of all these transformations. The use of machines to substitute for more powerful and faster methods of production in place of manual labor had already become widespread during the seventeenth century, as outlined in the introduction to Volume II. But up to the mid-eighteenth century it still seemed as if the machine's domain was limited and that the variety of its forms and uses could not be developed at will. Beginning with the second half of the eighteenth century, the opposite was true. Already, at the beginning of the century, with the development of the steam, or "atmospheric," engine, the first mechanical means of producing work had appeared. The machine was placed at man's service no longer to capture and distribute the natural power of the winds and streams but to utilize the power that man could create artificially by a heat source. So began the conquest of the sources of artificial power that has continued to be pursued down to our age. From its early stages it made obligatory the development and transformation of industrial mechanics, which in less than a century taught man to work with other materials, to make increasingly less use of wood, and to use metals.

In the same period, and apparently without any direct connection with the invention of the steam engine, the spinning and weaving of the principal textile fibers then in use—silk, wool, cotton, flax—were gradually mechanized. Not only

1

were machines able to eliminate the hand labor of spinners but their operation was also made automatic, along with that of the traditional crafts of the weavers. The appearance of mechanization in the textile industry gave rise to the development of factories in which, beginning at the end of the century, the power that was at first supplied by the waterwheel came progressively to be produced by the steam engine. This new type of factory, anticipating those of the nineteenth century, drew upon a supply of labor that had been made available in Great Britain, the country initiating these changes, by the transformations then taking place in agriculture.

General factors   In less than a century the open-fields system, which guaranteed each small landowner the opportunity of cultivating his own parcel of land, surrounded but without fences by those of his fellows, was replaced, under pressure from the large landowners, by a system of enclosures. For the needs of livestock breeding, which was greatly extended (chiefly with a view toward increasing the production of wool), the individual parcels had to be sold, willingly or otherwise. The vast estates thus created were then surrounded by fences. The small landowners had formerly supplemented the resources won from their land by working at home for the manufacturers, who supplied them with wool or cotton and later collected the woven cloth or fabrics. As a result of their exploitation by merchants, these craftsmen had for the most part already lost the independence of their craft. Their migration toward the factory workshops was the direct consequence of agrarian reform. They were joined by the great mass of landless men who had formerly eked out a meager income from the animals they had pastured on the community or common lands now enclosed within fences.

During this period, agricultural techniques underwent other transformations, thanks to some British gentlemen-farmers. The changes chiefly concerned methods of rotation, fertilization, and drainage but did not yet involve the introduction of mechanization, which did not appear until after the middle of the nineteenth century, on the initiative of American manufacturers. But the evolution of agriculture, first in Great Britain and then in several Continental countries, was one of the decisive factors in the development of industrial mechanization, thanks to the release of a supply of labor that had to ensure its livelihood by placing itself at the service of the manufacturers.

The textile industry was not alone in attracting these new workers. Small wares, hardware, and the mechanical trades experienced a similar development because of the prosperity of Great Britain's international trade, despite the vicissitudes of the American Revolution and later the blockade during the Napoleonic wars. This development itself made obligatory a reconstruction of heavy industry, chiefly in the mining and steel industries and in mechanical engineering. The latter was actually to begin to develop in the first quarter of the nineteenth century, at the same time that a new branch of activity, construction in metal, was making its appearance. To the distant markets available to Great Britain's maritime commerce was added the growth of domestic consumption caused by the demographic growth that began in that country in the eighteenth century. This growth, moreover, was not limited to Great Britain but also manifested itself on the Continent, and as soon as the period of military and political upheavals was over, the same phenomena produced the same effects. Industry based on modern technology developed in countries like France, the Netherlands, Belgium after its independence, and Germany, where the repercussions of the French Revolution had opened the way for the rise of capitalism. Then, from the mid-nineteenth century on, it was to spread over the entire European continent.

Although talented technicians had appeared in the United States at the beginning of the nineteenth century, the industrialization of this country did not accelerate until after the Civil War.

Industrial factors Other, purely technical, factors contributed to the flowering of industrial development in England in the last two decades of the eighteenth century. The atmospheric steam engine invented by Newcomen and Calley, after the experiments of Thomas Savery, was put into service because it filled a precise need: that of pumping water out of mines from depths for which the classic installations of pumps operated by horsepower or waterwheels were becoming inadequate. More precisely, the steam engine met, first, the needs of the tin and copper mines in Cornwall. By a chain of consequences that seems to be the general rule in the march of technical progress, its wider use in Great Britain and its appearance on the Continent encouraged the development of coal mining, which until then had evoked but little economic and industrial interest.

By the end of the seventeenth century, deforestation had reached such an advanced stage that it was beginning to arouse concern for the supply of fuel and materials for such wood-consuming industries as glassmaking, metallurgy, and naval construction. By about the middle of the eighteenth century, England had to resort to the Scandinavian countries for spars long enough for the masts of ships. Coal was already replacing wood in the glassmakers' kilns and in furnaces for reducing nonferrous ores, particularly those of copper. Almost from the birth of the steam engine, coal was used to heat its boilers. The efforts of more than thirty years by the masters of the Derby forge had resulted early in the eighteenth century in the successful use of coke to make cast iron. Coke-operated blast furnaces assured a growing production of cast iron at the very moment when the building of steam engines was beginning to call for increasingly large quantities of this material. Toward the end of the century, the process of refining cast iron in puddling furnaces began to transform iron, which had remained a relatively scarce and expensive material since the origins of metallurgy, into an abundant substance available for numerous uses.

The exploitation of coal deposits and the growth of iron smelting gave a new impetus to the mining industry, an impetus that during the nineteenth century was to require the improvement and development of the industry's technical equipment. The numerous innovations that between approximately 1760 and 1830 gradually transformed these various branches of industry were closely linked to the development of industrial mechanics; that is, to the progress achieved in the art of building machines. The classic, and very characteristic, example of John Wilkinson's boring mill, which enabled Watt to obtain a satisfactory steam tightness between the piston and the cylinder of his new condensing engine, amply demonstrates how technical progress forms a unity from various elements brought together by forces that make them interdependent. The various industries needed other modern equipment in addition to the steam engine, and mechanical engineering was stimulated to supply them with it precisely because it had access to a bigger supply of metals whose qualities were better known and more uniform than formerly.

Mechanical engineering To achieve this, mechanical engineering had to solve several problems arising from the need for heavy-duty components, for lifting and handling equipment, for apparatus for foundries and rolling mills, or for completely new kinds of material like the first cast-iron rails for the railroads serving the mines. Shortly thereafter, the use of cast iron by English engineers for bridge construction required still another adaptation of equipment. But the most delicate problem to be solved was that of precision.

Wilkinson's boring mill came to be invented solely because of the skill of a practicing technician who, like Watt, had a special aptitude for mechanical invention. Before Wilkinson, in France Jacques de Vaucanson (1709–1782) had demonstrated the same qualities. From the historical point of view, Wilkinson's best piece of work as a mechanic is still the invention of the toolholder on a carriage moved by a screw and mounted on a prismatic bed applied to an industrial lathe and drilling machine. But these two machine tools, constructed for a definite purpose, namely the building of automatic machines for weaving silk, remained practically unknown. A different fate awaited the slide lathe, reinvented concurrently around the end of the century by the Englishman Henry Maudslay (1771–1831) and an American, D. Wilkinson (not to be confused with the aforementioned Englishman, John Wilkinson), because its reappearance occurred within a more sophisticated technical and economic context.

Meanwhile, another path had brought light machinery to a degree of precision with origins found, at the beginning of the eighteenth century, in clockmaking. It was from this industry that the makers of surveying and astronomical instruments borrowed methods and tools in order to create the first precision machines originating from the genius of the Englishman Jesse Ramsden. The machine for dividing circles, which Ramsden invented at the cost of a supreme effort (between 1770 and 1780), filled a particular need: the mass production of instruments for nautical astronomy, which were needed in increasingly large numbers by navigators. In France, a generation of less brilliant but equally effectual engineers, of whom Nicolas Fortin and Joseph Lenoir were the best representatives, invented, together with the astronomers and geometers of the Académie des Sciences, the precision instruments that alone made possible the establishment of the bases of the metric system. This splendid undertaking, begun in the early hours of the French Revolution in the general spirit of reform animating the men of that time, was a response not only to immediate needs but also to an intelligent appreciation of the future demands of scientific, industrial, and commercial activity.

Only later did the methods of light, precision mechanics become an indispensable adjunct to the heavy industries of mechanical engineering. But long before the precision lathe became indispensable in the workshops of the late nineteenth century, the machine tool had become, during the first half of that century, a basic component of industrial equipment.

Not only did the construction of various types of machine tools that appeared within the half century give rise to a new branch of industry, but soon almost every contemporary industry became transformed. The use of machine tools increased the quantity and quality of production in such basic industries as sheet metal working, nail making, and screw cutting, and made possible the assembly-line production of machines for carding, spinning, and weaving, which until the early nineteenth century were still poor in strength and performance. Mechanization transformed such industries as papermaking, which for six or seven centuries had been based on unchanging techniques, and the new chemical industries such as those of artificial soda, acids, illuminating gas, and stearic acid, which required new mixers, crushers, pumps, and filter presses.

Lastly, the expansion of mechanization was decidedly encouraged in the steam engine's adaptation to industrial processes and to transportation. After 1800, when the patents of Watt and Boulton came into the public domain, the conservative influence of the inventor and the factory owner, which had been maintained for twenty-five years in defense of their personal profit, was eliminated. Only then was the construction of steam engines really able to begin. Watt's brilliant collaborators and the younger generation of engineers, who had long been bridled, were able to give free rein to their inventive spirits. The design of Watt's engine quickly became outmoded as expansion, high compression, and double expansion were introduced. Locomotives and steam boats appeared in the course of this development. This new stage demanded a new effort of production and adaptation on the part of mechanical engineering, which thus entered its golden age.

Toward the acceleration of progress When we consider this period, which extends from the mid-eighteenth century to the middle of the nineteenth, we cannot fail to be struck by the fact that not only did the actual inventions follow each other at an increasingly rapid rate but that almost all of them led to industrial innovations that together completely transformed the bases for the evolution of our civilization. Such fecundity is due to the fact that at each stage the economic, social, and demographic evolution created a particularly receptive situation. Whether we consider the steam engine (in its first form or with the improvements that Watt and his successors made to it); the process of making cast iron with coke and wrought iron in the puddling furnace; the method of producing spinning machines and weaving looms, slide lathes, the hydraulic press, milling and boring machines; or the mechanical propulsion of boats and locomotives, the inorganic chemical industry and (slightly later) the distillation of coal for the production of illuminating gas, each of these developments responded more or less directly to the need to expand production in order to satisfy an increasingly active trade stimulated by ever-growing consumption. As a consequence, the new technical methods favored urban concentration, which itself required more powerful and faster means of transportation for exchanging raw materials and finished products and for supplying the cities. As the cities grew, they provided a market for new lighting methods and called for new supply and distribution systems for water and illuminating gas as well as for the removal of waste, projects that in turn encouraged the transformation of traditional industries that until then had been held to limited activity.

The interaction of technical progress with economic and social evolution is a constant factor in the history of our civilization. For millennia, then centuries, this interaction occurred so slowly as to leave the observer with the impression that earlier ages lived in a state of almost permanent equilibrium. Beginning with the first half of the sixteenth century the process began to undergo a visible acceleration, the rhythm of which slowly increased until around the last quarter of the eighteenth century. But until then, the methods and the level of industrial production retained a classical character with which the events of the first half of the nineteenth century contrast profoundly.

The reader will be able to note throughout this volume that similar phenomena recur in the various aspects of technical progress during the period under discussion. Despite a certain drive of the inventive spirit, progress seems at first to have clashed with the stability of a fund of knowledge common to technology and economics that was sufficient for the needs of the period. And even before this period, most of the major inventions for which it is famous had had short-lived predecessors. For example, the use of the rolling mill, which dates at least from the Renaissance, was extremely slow to take hold in the heavy-metallurgy industry: by the mid-eighteenth century it had only recently been partially adopted by the copper- and lead-working industries, and in iron metallurgy its use was exceptional.

A perfect illustration of this technico-economic stability is the unchanging content of the technical books of the period. Numerous treatises repeated a scarcely modernized common body of knowledge inherited from sixteenth- and seventeenth-century works, which themselves had borrowed a great deal from the writings of versatile authors in earlier periods. These handbooks often retained through their successive editions a style of writing that remained unchanged throughout the eighteenth century. The famous *Dictionnaire universel de commerce* of Savary des Bruslons, which includes the best historical source material not only on commercial methods and land and maritime trade but also on methods of production and machine construction, was compiled at the end of the seventeenth century. For more than a half century it retained its full value for the men of that time; the last edition dates from 1759–1765. Other works enjoyed an even more astonishing longevity, as for example those of the military engineer Bernard Forest de Belidor, whose most famous work, *Architecture hydraulique,* was first published in 1737–1753 and was partially reedited by Navier in 1819. *La Science des ingénieurs,* the first edition of which dates from 1729, was republished unchanged in the nineteenth century and its last edition appeared in German in 1857/58.

Although the evolution of technology became less deliberate, it did not yet favor the immediate success of new inventions, which nevertheless seem to have exercised an increasingly persistent pressure. This is evidenced by the renewed difficulties of various inventors who attempted to mechanize various operations of the textile industry after the end of the sixteenth century. Witness also the long efforts, which lasted for no less than a half century, to produce cast iron with coke to a level of industrial exploitability, and the long and difficult gestation of the steam engine, which extended over almost a century.

Yet the period did not reject these novelties as the preceding century had done, although they were accepted reluctantly. The technical level had visibly improved, which made possible the invention of machines and the elaboration of methods sufficiently perfected to make them usable. Then, suddenly, around 1780–1790, a breakthrough seems to have been made: technical progress found a favorable environment in which to develop. This environment was provided by the eighteenth-century society of the country dominating international trade and in which, given population pressure on the one hand and agrarian reform on the other, a profound social evolution was beginning to take shape: Great Britain. Now that these factors were exerting their complementary influences within this vast movement, techniques of every type benefited from the accelerating evolution of these factors. This acceleration, which was partly blocked until after 1815 by Continental and maritime wars, was to go on after the second quarter of the nineteenth century and has continued to manifest itself down to our own time.

The concept of the Industrial Revolution It is this rapid evolution, specifically British in origin, that has been designated by the term *Industrial Revolution*. This expression, already coined by the end of the eighteenth century, was, after being used by several historians, sociologists, and economists, readapted in 1881 by the first Arnold Toynbee. The idea of an industrial revolution was definitively established by Paul Mantoux in a work published first in 1906 under the title *La révolution industrielle au XVIIIe siècle*. Although it has been revised and supplemented in the course of its various editions (the last ones dating from 1959 for the French edition and 1962 for the English), it is nevertheless a work conceived and written more than seventy years ago. Since then we have been able to modify our viewpoint regarding the evolution of technology during the twentieth century and its effects upon the structure of our civilization. At the time when Mantoux was preparing his work, the development of technology in the second half of the nineteenth century was still too recent to permit proper analysis. The changes that had then transformed technology and industry were seen as the consequences of the Industrial Revolution, to which a period was assigned that was then not much more than sixty or seventy years earlier, namely 1830–1840 to 1900. It was impossible in Mantoux's time to foresee that these transformations were to continue permanently and at an increasingly rapid rate. In comparison with these changes, the pace of the period then known as the Industrial Revolution, namely 1760 to 1830, seems very modest.

The generation working and thinking in the era of 1880 to 1900 felt that the civilization it knew had achieved a level of perfection that would be difficult to surpass. From this resulted a sense of stability, which naturally influenced the manner of judging the period immediately preceding it. This state of mind persisted until the beginning of the First World War, and it is in this context that Mantoux developed an idea that had been born in the previous century.

Mantoux's analysis of the economic and social history of this period in England is excellent and elicits no criticism. He correctly evaluates the influence of the technical factors that at that time concerned the textile industry, metalworking, and the production of power in England. The concept of an industrial revolution seemed attractive and was generally adopted. After Mantoux the concept gave rise to a number of works, some of which repeated and developed the same themes, whereas others seriously weakened the fundamental bases of the classical idea.

The opening and closing dates of the British Industrial Revolution have been the subject of long discussion. Contemporary historians have extended the terminal phase to 1830 or 1840, though Mantoux held with 1800. The most vigorous criticisms of the traditional concept have been formulated by the American economic historian John U. Nef, who prefers (and rightly so, it seems) to fix the initial period as being in the 1780s (more precisely, in 1785) rather than in 1760, and feels that we have not yet lived through the end of the period. In addition, Nef dates the preliminary stages of the Industrial Revolution from as early as the end of the sixteenth century. These concepts are completely justified and greatly weaken the classical idea as it is now (somewhat academically) accepted.

In any event, and even if we accept the vigorous reservations expressed by Nef in this regard, it does not appear that the use of the term *Industrial Revolution* can be troublesome insofar as it permits us to designate conveniently a complex phenomenon in which technical progress played a major role and which affected a particular country—Great Britain—at a particular period, roughly the last quarter of the eighteenth century and the first quarter of the nineteenth. For greater convenience, historians have retained the term *Middle Ages* to designate a historical period, the knowledge of which has been completely reappraised during the last few decades.

However, the use of the term *Industrial Revolution* to designate the phase of industrialization in various countries of the world, a phenomenon that occurred everywhere following the industrialization of Great Britain, is difficult to accept. It would be tolerable in the case of France when we are studying the first half of the nineteenth century, but it must be rejected when we consider the countries of Central and Eastern Europe. From the economic point of view, the phenomena possibly have several characteristics in common, but from the social and technical points of view, they are completely different. In particular, no other country was, like Great Britain in the era 1780–1800, such a coherent and autonomous center of invention and innovation. Industrialization (and by this we mean both the appearance of modern methods of production and the laying of railroads and distribution of electric power) was accomplished by adopting certain inventions from the innovative countries and assimilating these borrowed elements in a complete enough fashion to permit the country in question to become an innovator in its turn. In this context it is difficult to claim that an industrial revolution occurred at the end of the nineteenth century in the United States, and it would be erroneous to speak of an industrial revolution in connection with China or an African country in the second half of the twentieth century.

The myth of a technical revolution

To return to the subject under discussion, and in order to understand fully the period considered in this volume, we must also be careful to avoid a confusion that has become so common in our time that we employ the terms *industrial revolution* and *technical revolution* to designate the same phenomenon.

For the reasons mentioned above, early twentieth-century authors can be excused for having created this confusion, but it is difficult to accept today. In particular, the series of inventions in the eighteenth century now appear to us to originate in the traditional process that governed the evolution of technology from its origins until around the middle of the last century. Concerning the textile industry, for example, if we consider the history of the inventions to which it owes its mechanization we see that a century and a half sometimes elapsed between the first experiments that led to the invention of the machines and their being put to use in industry. When inventions seem to succeed rapidly, as in the case of Sir Richard Arkwright's water frame or James Hargreaves's jenny, we can find antecedents for them that date from the last quarter of the seventeenth century. The use of coke in metallurgy was thus the result of efforts continuously pursued from the end of the sixteenth or beginning of the seventeenth century until after the middle of the eighteenth century. We have already noted that the history of the steam engine begins almost a century before Watt, but a general acceptance of this source of power did not come about in industry until a quarter century after the work of the famous Scottish engineer. Only a rather casual presentation of the history of these inventions can give the impression that they were sufficiently close in time to produce an impact at a given date.

In the history of technology, invention is in truth only very rarely reduced to being a single event credited to a single person. It is a complex operation that before leading to industrial innovations benefits from a period of experimentation that is sometimes several centuries long, is accumulated from generation to generation, and is one in which individuals separated by time and space almost always participate. It reaches fruition only when the age permits it to. This requires the conjunction of a certain number of cultural and social factors and an attainment by the society in which it is to appear of an indispensable level of maturity. As we come closer to contemporary periods, this process becomes increasingly rapid. In the eighteenth century this rhythm unquestionably accelerated, in comparison with the preceding century, but the phenomenon cannot be called a technical revolution.

To be convinced of this it suffices to observe the rhythm of technology's evolution after the period to which the name *Industrial Revolution* has been given. Then we see that the acceleration continued to manifest itself, affecting both the evolution of machines already known at the end of the eighteenth century (the steam engine and machine tools) and new inventions as well. The water turbine became established within some thirty years, the inorganic chemical industry was built up in forty years on completely new foundations, the production of illuminating gas became widespread in the same length of time. Before 1850, electric telegraphy took hold in several countries within a period of about fifteen years. Thus, the evolution of technology between 1820 and 1850 revolutionized the physical appearance of the industrialized countries more profoundly than it had done between 1760 and 1820. After this date the rhythm of evolution continued to increase with the development of new processes for the preparation of steel, the appearance of the synthetic chemical industry, the industrial production of electricity, and the invention of the internal combustion engine, to such a point that some authors do not hesitate to speak of new industrial revolutions. Nevertheless, they do not provide a satisfactory analysis of the events about whose history they are writing.

Science and technology   Another error in the classical conception of the
Industrial Revolution is to place the beginning of
the scientific era of the progress of technology at the same point in time. We have
already broached this subject in the introduction to the preceding volume by
showing how relations between science and technology were established, beginning in the sixteenth century. We have demonstrated how these relations became
closer in the seventeenth century and at the beginning of the eighteenth, and how
at that moment a joint domain, which for the sake of convenience we have called
technology, was formed.

Regarding the inventions generally associated with the Industrial Revolution,
it would be erroneous to believe that they were a new and unexpected manifestation of the contribution of the period's scientific knowledge to the progress of
technology. The manner in which these inventions were conceived, investigated,
and realized does not indicate that research methods superior to those known to
their predecessors were available to the inventors of this generation. In particular,
preliminary study of the results to be obtained and analysis of the effective devices
spring solely from sheer empiricism. An attempt has been made to point to Watt's
work as demonstrating the first fruitful liaisons between science and technology.
Everything that has been written on this subject is completely exaggerated. There
is no doubt that Watt was an educated man, but one may ask if his intellectual
development did not come from the success of his first steam engine, through
which he acquired social position and contact with a coterie of friends in Birmingham, rather than his development being the consequence solely of knowledge
acquired from contact with the professors of Glasgow University. In the environment in which Watt worked at the beginning of his career as a repairer of scientific
instruments at this university, he was able to acquire rigorous intellectual habits
and pragmatic standards of judgment, and these qualities served him well. But if
we consider the scientific knowledge of the period from 1750 to 1770, we may ask
which elements of this knowledge helped him to overcome inadequacies of his
inventive talent. As far as science is concerned, he was in approximately the same
situation as Papin, Savery, and Newcomen after the works of Otto von Guericke
and the discovery of the vacuum.

The fact is that Watt was concerned with a single problem and his success was
due in part to his restricted objective. Other men of his time and place would have
been capable of doing the same work, but no other single man could have
accomplished all of it. There was, for example, Watt's contemporary John
Smeaton whose name reappears in several chapters of this volume. He had
received a better education than Watt but his technical training was the same. He
pursued many projects, built civil engineering works, and made experimental
studies of the output of waterwheels and windmills. He attempted to perfect the
atmospheric steam engine but could not anticipate the solutions Watt was able to
discover, undoubtedly because he did not have fifteen to twenty-five years to
devote to this research. If the requisite knowledge had been available, perhaps
Smeaton would have been the inventor of the condensing steam engine.

In reality, the steam engine, like the internal combustion engine a century
later, was born without the assistance of science. Very much to the contrary, it was
the increased use of the steam engine that encouraged the scientific studies that

were to open the field of thermodynamics. An engineer of Spanish origin, Bétancourt y Molina was perhaps the first to attempt a theoretical study of the steam engine, in the closing years of the eighteenth century. This was followed by a number of treatises by technicians such as Rumford's on the boring of cannons and those of Séguin. The point of departure for the investigations of Sadi Carnot is unquestionably the operation of the steam engine; his famous book *Réflexions sur la puissance motrice du feu (Thoughts on the Motive Power of Heat)*, published in 1824, laid the first foundations of a new science.

It was during this period that the systematic study of engines began to acquire a certain importance. In Part Two we shall see how a particular problem (that of cutting gears), which by the middle of the eighteenth century had received satisfactory theoretical solutions, was still done empirically by builders in the first quarter of the nineteenth century. In fact, a homogeneous science of machinery did not begin to develop until the second half of the nineteenth century.

Science began to exert an influence on technology in a fairly general and sustained manner only after the period to which the name Industrial Revolution has been assigned. Chemistry furnishes the most conclusive example, in the works of J.-L. Gay-Lussac on sulfuric acid and of Eugène Chevreul on fats. The distillation of coal by William Murdock and Philippe Lebon to obtain illuminating gas brought about, on the one hand, the appearance of a new branch of chemical science—organic chemistry—and on the other offered industry new products to exploit. Thus, even before the discovery of the first synthetic dyes, the chemical industry was the most scientifically advanced one.

Before the close of the first half of the nineteenth century, another example appears that is still more characteristic of the interdependence of science and technology in modern progress. I refer to the direct applications of electromagnetism hardly more than a few years after the work of Ampère and Faraday. In 1828 the latter described the principle of the electric motor, and four years later Pixii, a French builder, following instructions by Ampère, made the first machine to supply alternating and direct current. Several years later, the first electric telegraphs came into operation.

The invention of the electric telegraph, much more so than of the steam engine, is an example typical of modern invention, which requires the interaction of the most diverse resources and rapidly increases in scope, continuously evolving and bringing new problems before the scientifically curious. Occasionally the solutions to some of these problems appear, profiting almost immediately from the results of laboratory research. With the telegraph appears one of the most spectacular characteristics of contemporary technology: the rapidity of its conception, exploitation, and development. In short, this is the kind of process that suddenly introduces important modifications in the living conditions of entire peoples at each stage of its development.

The technician These rapid and quite spectacular beginnings heralded equally decisive events that illustrate the history of technology in the twentieth century, to be discussed in the next volume. Meanwhile, we should not get the impression that, beginning in a certain time, technical progress was achieved in sudden spurts independent of their historical context. Let us recall that for the period under discussion it was the steady progress of industrial mechanics that continued to be the dominant factor and that if it had not acquired new methods of action at this time, the history of technology would have been quite different from the one we know.

In this context, the craftsman retained his full importance for a long time. The leaders of industry, and their workers, who had no training in science, only very slowly made way for engineers trained in technical schools. This transformation of technical personnel is another of the most characteristic features of the period. Eighteenth-century English engineers were self-taught in technology. At that time no opportunities for specialized instruction existed, and apprenticeship was on a person-to-person basis, ensuring the perpetuation of traditional methods. For a long time (at least since the sixteenth century) the millwright had been the most accomplished technician. Skilled in woodworking, with brass and iron work as sidelines, he was responsible for all fairly large-scale projects and for the maintenance of machinery and works of art. When he possessed a somewhat more highly developed sense of mechanics, he became an inventor and innovator. Men like Swaim Renkin, who distinguished himself not only by his achievement of the famous great wheel at Marly but also by pumping and drainage installations at other sites, and the Swede Christopher Pohlem are the best representatives of these craftsmen, to whom machinery owes two centuries of its progress. Several other branches of technical activity required specialized personnel, but their training had been acquired under the same circumstances. In Germany and Hungary the mining industry had long had expert workers who had been born and raised in their environment. The schools of mining, which had been in existence more or less continuously since the Renaissance, furnished only a relatively rudimentary training. The most gifted among their pupils, or individuals who were better favored by social conditions, rose to a higher level solely through their experience.

In France public works were not carried out under the direction of qualified engineers until after the middle of the eighteenth century, after the foundation by Trudaine of the first technical school for engineers in the world, the École des Ponts et Chaussées (School of Bridges and Roads). In every other industrial activity projects were directed by experienced men whose primary concern was to maintain the prosperity of their establishments and who were distrustful of innovations likely to endanger that prosperity should they fail. Still, there were among them some more enterprising spirits who attempted to learn and to apply their knowledge to promote new ideas. Often they were rich landowners, generally members of the nobility, who were able to invest some money in new experiments. Réaumur in eighteenth-century France is a fairly good example of this kind of individual. At that time in France certain factory inspectors played a by no means negligible role as innovators.

In England, Savery, Newcomen, and the technicians who perfected the first model of the steam engine belonged in the category of millwrights. The various inventions in the textile industry were for the most part due either to amateurs endowed with a genius for tinkering or to men in the business who realized the advantage of mechanizing a given operation and who possessed sufficient skill in their fingertips to succeed more or less effectively. Side by side with them, one man, Richard Arkwright, achieved great fame in his time, thanks to the success of his projects. He had a special genius for business and unscrupulously pirated others' inventions. But there was also a large number of manufacturers with farsighted views and sufficiently acute judgment to do useful work. For example, there were Roebuck, the first to give Watt financial support, and Holker, who was lured to France, where he was responsible for a number of major industrial innovations.

Engineers and their training Around the middle of the eighteenth century there appeared a new category of technician to whom Great Britain owed the new technical bases of industrial activity. Those who inaugurated this were men in quite diversified fields like John Smeaton, the first to assume the title of civil engineer, and John Dollond, who raised the craft of scientific instrument making to the status of a national industry.

Their successors, chief among them Watt, were the first engineers to specialize in a definite field. It was not by chance that in this period Great Britain possessed a particularly brilliant generation of mechanicians and builders, a large number of whom were Scottish. In this volume we shall see the importance their work assumed and how they caused a decline in traditional technology in the modern world. None of them had received higher professional training; every one of them had trained according to the traditional method, by practicing his craft. All of them, however, possessed such abilities that they were more than qualified craftsmen like their predecessors; by their example they pioneered a new type of superior, high-level technician. This new tradition was continued in Great Britain after their departure from the scene. Men like Maudslay, Stephenson, and Brunel, who succeeded them, ensured England's primacy in technical progress for another half century.

It is certain that all these men were more or less well treated by the society within which they lived and worked. The prestige then enjoyed in England by industrial technology, and the support given it by manufacturers and capitalists, was unequaled in any other country. Although science was in this period more distinguished in France than in England, the French technicians, some of whom might have been as brilliant as their English colleagues, were far from enjoying a comparable social position. Dollond and Smeaton became members of the Royal Society, as did many others around the mid-eighteenth century. The prestige of an instrument maker like Jesse Ramsden was completely different from the esteem accorded in France to a man like Nicolas Fortin. Not until the end of the eighteenth century did the highly talented Joseph Lenoir become the first craftsman-member of a French scientific group, the Bureau des Longitudes.

After the Napoleonic wars, when industrial mechanics began its rise in France, its first servants were men of the stature of English engineers in the preceding generation. Those who became heads of major enterprises—Calla, Cavé, and Farcot—trained themselves and shaped their destiny with their own hands. But the technicians' environment had already improved greatly after the creation of the École Polytechnique and the principal naval schools of instruction. These schools, intended (especially during the Empire) for the training of skilled workers for the public services and the army, did not immediately supply engineers to private industry. We know that those who were educated there included the greatest French mathematicians, physicists, chemists, astronomers, and engineers of the first half of the nineteenth century. Although in general they did not engage in industrial activity, they exerted a direct influence on the training of French technicians. In fact, pupils of Monge and Hachette contributed to a rapid revival of technical literature. They prepared manuals that were accessible to men of average education, sources that had until then been sorely lacking. It was they who developed that new discipline between pure science and the practice of the technicians, called engineering by the English, but in what has gone before, for lack of a French equivalent, we have called technology. In the same period, moreover, a similar literature was also being born in England. The appearance, development, and constant growth of this literature put into concrete form the transformation of technological research that had been achieved, under the pressure of events, during the decades that closed the eighteenth century and opened the nineteenth.

As early as the Empire period, advanced instruction given in the schools born of the French Revolution was complemented by a more general instruction entrusted to the École des Arts et Métiers. In this way groups of skilled workers needed by heavy modern industry and the public services, the technical nature of which was constantly growing, were rapidly trained. In this regard, among the facts most characteristic of the first half of the nineteenth century we should recall the part played in the creation of railroad networks by numerous graduates of the École Polytechnique (some of whom were among the leaders of the Saint-Simonian movement) who thought, by favoring contacts between individuals, to put their knowledge at the service of their social convictions. Following the French lead, all the European countries and the United States established a teaching system intended to train engineers on various levels. In Great Britain, where the engineers maintained a relatively closed circle and kept control over the sharing of knowledge, a system of higher instruction was not inaugurated until the end of the first half of the century.

The growth of professional instruction, which included pure science, rapidly bore fruit. Science and technology, which had until then (notwithstanding what has been said on this topic) followed quite distinct paths, began to complement each other. Nevertheless, we should not deceive ourselves but should continue to reject the too generally repeated statement that technology springs from application of the sciences. As early as the nineteenth century, the relationship between them had already taken a more complex turn. Engineering assumed a position between science and technology as an intermediary for a relationship developing in both directions. The examples mentioned—the heat engine and thermodynamics, the distillation of coal and organic chemistry, electromagnetism and the electric telegraph—are in this regard very conclusive. These phenomena have become accentuated in the course of time from this period down to our own day, and we shall have occasion to return to this subject in the next volume.

The conception and plan of this work The preceding discussion has made possible a general outline of the conditions under which the progress of technology, whose history is detailed in this volume, was achieved. Undoubtedly, the history of technology should not be limited solely to the history of inventions. During the period discussed here, perhaps more than in earlier epochs, economic, social, and political factors exerted a permanent influence on the development of technical progress. We have already had occasion to explain why we have not accorded them a larger place. Among the branches of history, the history of technology is still too recent to permit of easy synthesis. In particular, too many facts concerning the genesis of the technical foundations of our civilization are still so poorly known that in a first general history it is indispensable first to draw up a balance sheet of what is known, and above all to try to grasp the originality of all the major technical inventions and their interdependence. An attempt to understand how at each period the special knowledge of engineers was exercised in order to surpass the level of the achievements of their age seemed to us equally indispensable. This is the deliberately attempted goal we set at the beginning; we have continued to pursue it during the preparation of this volume.

We have retained the method of exposition adopted in the second part of the preceding volume, that is, a division by main branches of activities, which best corresponds to the period under discussion. However, since most of the outstanding events of this period occurred within a relatively limited geographical area, we wished to avoid giving the impression that the technical world was limited to a handful of European countries, particularly Great Britain. The last part of this volume gives a brief outline of the contemporary achievements of Russia and the United States. It thus constitutes a transition to the fourth and last volume in this series, in which the horizon of the technical world widens to include all the continents.

MAURICE DAUMAS

PART ONE
METHODS
OF PRODUCING POWER

THE SUBJECT OF this section is one of the most important in the history of technology during the period to which this volume is devoted. The creation of the first artificial source of power was the fruit of a long effort that for all practical purposes continued into the middle of the nineteenth century after the endeavors at the end of the seventeenth. The importance of James Watt's work, which falls at almost exactly the midpoint of this period, is common knowledge, but the value of the inventions that preceded his work must not be underestimated. Moreover, by Watt's being the first to adapt steam successfully to the production of rotary power, he opened an era of improvement in the steam engine (an era in which he himself did not participate) that lasted until a time quite near our own. But we may say that by the middle of the nineteenth century all possible means of improvement had been tried and adopted. Although the steam engine had not yet attained its ultimate degree of development, its significant evolution was complete by the period at which this volume ends.

However, it must not be thought that traditional sources of power lost their usefulness immediately. The remainder of this history will show how waterpower continued to maintain its importance in modern civilization. Long before the appearance of Fourneyron's turbine, there was continued development of waterpower through the introduction of improved waterwheels, as will be seen in one of the following chapters.

Wind power was by no means a negligible additional source of power in certain regions and for certain specific uses down to and including our own age. The mechanical methods available in the nineteenth century even made possible the fitting of lighter and more flexible components to traditional mills, which have not yet completely disappeared from the rural scene in some countries.

CHAPTER 1

TRADITIONAL SOURCES OF POWER

WINDMILLS

The persistence of tradition

Until the beginning of the twentieth century, windmills continued to play a major role in numerous areas of Europe, especially on the coasts of the North and Baltic seas. On all the other continents their use remained perhaps more widespread than in the industrialized countries of Europe and, later, America. But it was primarily in the latter countries that the most persistent efforts were made to improve their structure and operation.

The use of metal to build windmills began at the start of the second half of the eighteenth century. John Smeaton was perhaps the first to order the use of cast iron to consolidate and reinforce the classic wooden framework. In the same period, around 1745, his compatriot Edmund Lee introduced the automatic fantail, which was intended to orient the axis of the sails to the direction of the wind. However, the practical use of this device posed mechanical construction problems that industry was hardly in a position to solve properly before the second half of the nineteenth century.

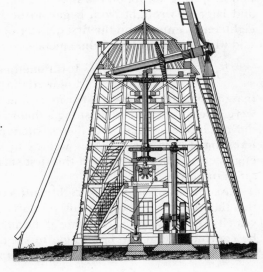

FIG. 1. Windmill with revolving cap. Constructed by Hallette around 1830.

Down to this time, then, windmills continued to retain for the most part their traditional appearance, which was hardly an improvement over that of the eighteenth century. The two models in use were still the windmill with a revolving cap (Figure 1) and the post-mill. Some fairly late works, for example, Laboulaye's *Dictionnaire des manufactures,* in 1891, still showed diagrams of mills almost identical with those constructed one and even two centuries earlier (Figure 2).

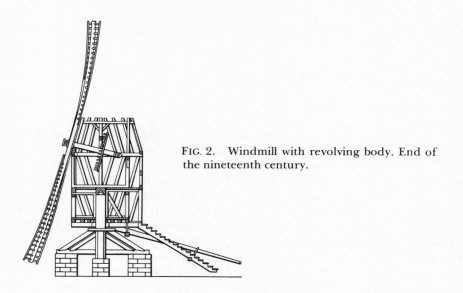

FIG. 2.   Windmill with revolving body. End of the nineteenth century.

Gears continued to be made of wood, to traditional designs, until the beginning of the nineteenth century. The result was a considerable loss of power in transmission. It has been calculated that the output of a mid-seventeenth-century mill supplying 40 hp. on the shaft did not exceed 39 percent. Gears of cast iron, and later of wrought iron, began to be introduced in the last quarter of the eighteenth century and the first quarter of the nineteenth. However, it cannot be said with certainty at what time metal completely replaced wood in these devices.

Theoretical research   It is nonetheless true that this type of construction followed the progress of industrial engineering and that this progress was rapid. For more than a half century numerous experiments were directed first to establishing a theory of windmills. Although these projects did not influence their actual construction, they are nevertheless extremely interesting, for in this field, as well as in several others within the purview of engineering, they constituted the first stages of a technology that industry was quick to utilize.

At the beginning of the eighteenth century Antoine Parent had calculated that the wind exerted on the sails of mills a force proportional to the square of its velocity and the square of the sine of the angle at which it struck the sails. From this he concluded that the best angle to set the surface of sails in relation to the direction of the wind was 54° 44′. This factor had been accepted without question by millwrights of the time. One by one Daniel Bernoulli, Colin MacLaurin, then Jean d'Alembert took up the problem, considering the rotational velocity of the sails (which Parent had ignored) and trying to calculate how the angle of the surface to the direction of the wind should vary in relation to speed. The shape of the sails was also the object of calculations by Leonhard Euler and d'Alembert.

Shortly after 1750, John Smeaton devoted himself to experimental research on these topics. The English engineer used windmill sails the axle of which was attached to an arm that could be rotated by means of a spindle (Figure 3). In this way sails of various shapes and sizes could be tried. Charles de Coulomb was to

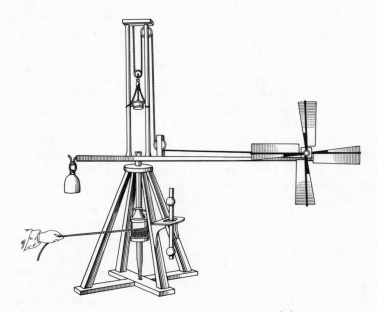

FIG. 3.   Smeaton's experimental model.

repeat these kinds of experiments around 1780 with a similar device. The two experimenters arrived at similar conclusions, rediscovering the mathematical findings of MacLaurin and Euler, which introduced the cube of the wind velocity into the calculations and determined the variation in the angle of the sails. But at the same time, this research showed that by trial and error the technicians had found the best solutions for the shapes and sizes of sails before the theoreticians had. The flared shape of the sails of Dutch windmills, with their concave shape and warped surface, proved practically and theoretically to be the one providing the optimum drive.

Development in the nineteenth century

During the next half century, Navier, Borgnis, and Gaspard Coriolis concentrated one after the other on perfecting the theory of windmills. But in 1845 the results of Smeaton and Coulomb were still accepted by Jean-Victor Poncelet, who again noted that the most favorable shape was that of Dutch mills.

After the beginning of the nineteenth century, however, metal construction of windmills gradually led to new shapes, which were widely utilized (under the name *aeolian*) at the end of the nineteenth century and in our own time, until rural electrification made it possible to replace them with electric motors.

The history of this invention is not very well known, for it consists of a series of minor accomplishments and experiments abandoned and then resumed by inventors who did not know of the attempts of their predecessors. This history constitutes a fairly characteristic example of the progress of light machinery during the nineteenth century.

"Panemonian" mills   In the early years of the nineteenth century we find a certain interest in mills with a vertical axis that were then designated by the name *panemonian*. This type of mill had a kind of wheel placed on a vertical axle. The vanes, attached vertically to the edge of the wheel, were cone shaped. The wind exerted a stronger force on the concave than on the convex side, and thus the net driving force exerted by the wind was the difference between these two effects. Other ingenious minds invented models of vertical mills on which the vanes disappeared when they were positioned contrary to the direction of the wind. These devices generally involved complications in construction and operation, which always prevented the horizontal mills from giving satisfactory results. Since in theory this type of device was likely to have more operating days per year than mills with a horizontal axis (the vertical mill), experiments were repeatedly made until the early years of our century, but they were never followed by practical applications.

"Aeolian" mills   In our time, only mills with horizontal or slightly inclined shafts have been widely used to supply power to pump water from wells and to supply rural dwellings.

As mentioned, these devices were perfected thanks to a succession of contributions, especially in the second half of the nineteenth century. At a very early date these mills were built entirely of iron. The vanes, made of thin sheet metal, were fixed on a metal shaft and were equipped with devices (generally consisting of springs or tension systems) for varying their angle in relation to the wind direction proportionate to their velocity of rotation. A centrifugal governor permitted automatic control of these variations as well as limiting the speed of rotation during a period of strong wind. The tail was also the object of a great variety of empirical tests that made it possible to find the most satisfactory solutions.

In this respect it is interesting to mention, by way of example, a device (Figure 4) probably constructed about the middle of the nineteenth century by an inventor named Delamolère. The tail consists of a small windmill positioned in such a way that the main sails break the force of the wind on it when they are facing into the wind. If the wind's direction changes, the small mill is made to rotate and its axle drives a pinion that gears into a stationary toothed wheel. The windmill is thus automatically kept into the wind. In addition, the position of the sails on their axes is controlled by a centrifugal governor whose fly-balls swing out when the rotational velocity of the sails increases with wind velocity. It is evident that this device already presents all the characteristics of a feedback control.

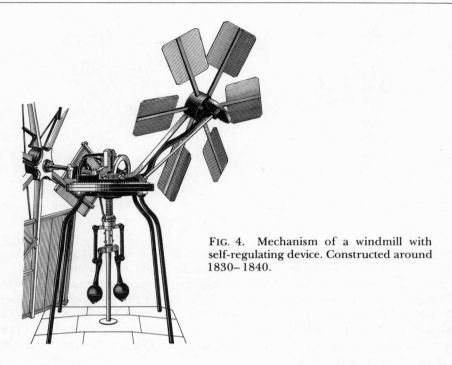

FIG. 4. Mechanism of a windmill with self-regulating device. Constructed around 1830–1840.

Mills of this type operated lift and force pumps by a crank fixed to their shaft. The pump chamber rested on flanges that permitted it to turn about its vertical axis when the position of the driving crankshaft changed. Such devices (Figure 5) were known by 1830. Later an attempt was made to vary the stroke of the piston in relation to the wind velocity, in order to regulate the work of the pump according

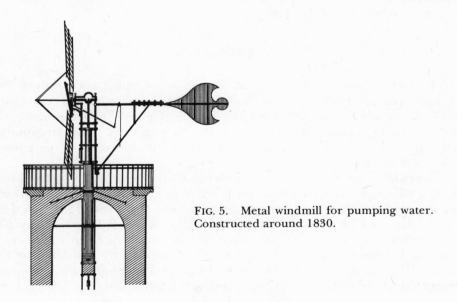

FIG. 5. Metal windmill for pumping water. Constructed around 1830.

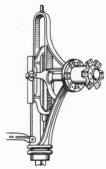

FIG. 6. Wind pump with La Hire gear.   FIG. 7. Pumping mechanism with cog-wheels and crankshaft.

to the power supplied by the windmill. In this case a centrifugal governor controlled the movement of the stops that limited the stroke of the piston.

Finally, we might mention that the last improvements in general use at the beginning of the twentieth century involved converting the rotational movement of the windmill's axis into the alternating movement of the pump's piston rod. The crank had been abandoned in favor of gear trains, for example one by La Hire (Figure 6), and a double gear with articulated links (Figure 7), which gave the transmission greater flexibility.

With this stage it seems clear that the destiny of the windmill had been completely fulfilled. Details of this final phase are still lacking, but from this quickly outlined development we can see that it is a perfect illustration of the process of collective invention so characteristic of efforts in the last century to make the best possible use of a traditional mechanism for specific purposes, with the help of the techniques that modern light engineering made available to inventors and builders of the time.

WATERWHEELS

The use of waterpower acquired all the more importance during the eighteenth century when an expansion of industry occurred before the steam engine was capable of providing a ready source of power. England being the leader in waterpower at this time, it was British engineers (John Smeaton in particular) who devoted themselves to perfecting the operation of the known kinds of water mills.

Waterwheels powered foundries, grindstones, sawmills, and forge bellows. Spinning mills were set up in hilly regions where streams flowed rapidly. Treadmills operated by horses, oxen, or even dogs continued to be used for a long time in areas that had no streams. When the height of the fall was inadequate, Newcomen-type steam engines were used to raise the water from a lower to a higher level of the millrace, but no factory of any importance could be built far from a sufficiently powerful stream where the ground's configuration permitted creating a small dam. For this reason, in the eighteenth century the valleys of the

Pennine Hills were the scene of a major industrial concentration, which lost much of its importance when steam power became available.

All this explains why during this period many engineers and mathematicians devoted much effort to establishing a satisfactory theory of waterwheels and to improving their output.

The first goal was not achieved in the eighteenth century, for until the beginning of the nineteenth none of the theoretical views proposed were satisfactory. But the construction and operation of waterwheels were appreciably improved. A short time later the introduction of turbines offered new possibilities for the use of waterpower.

Tests and theoretical research   The science of fluid mechanics took its first theoretical steps at the end of the seventeenth century, and during the following century the science of hydraulics began to undergo a certain amount of development. Research by mathematicians and experimenters was directed toward analyzing the operating conditions of waterwheels and to comparing the advantages of the three known varieties—undershot, breast, and overshot wheels. Only later did researchers begin to become interested in impulse wheels.

Although mills with horizontal wheels (that is, with vertical shafts) had been known since the earliest use of waterpower, vertical wheels seem to have been the type most frequently used. The simplest was the wheel with flat paddles driven by the water's current (Figure 8), and it was upon this type that the first observations and calculations were made, the latter being aimed at determining the pressure exerted by the water on the blades. Mariotte, Newton, and several other engineers (including Bernoulli in 1727) were interested in this problem and performed experiments to determine what weight carried by a lever or pulley balanced the

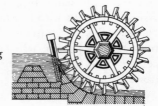

FIG. 8. Breast wheel with flat wooden paddles. Beginning of the nineteenth century.

pressure of the water on the blades. From these experiments they concluded that the pressure exerted on the blades was proportional to the square of the relative velocity of the current in relation to the velocity at the circumference of the wheel. For almost a half century the rule formulated by Parent—namely that the maximum effect was obtained when the speed of the center of action of the paddles was equal to one-third the speed of the current—was accepted as correct.

This rule was abandoned after Smeaton's experiments of 1752 and 1753 and Charles de Borda's work in 1767. As in the case of the windmill, Smeaton designed an experimental device to study waterwheels. He was able to vary the speed and volume of the current and measure the effects by means of a rope over a pulley, one end being attached to the shaft of the wheel, the other holding a weight. In

France during the same period Charles Bossut was using a similar device, and like Smeaton he found that the maximum effect was obtained when the speed of the wheel was equal to two-fifths the speed of the current. Lastly, Borda demonstrated that the force was proportional to the velocity of the water and not to its square, and that the maximum effect was obtained when the velocity of the wheel was equal to half the speed of the current.

Other factors were also the object of long discussion and research. An attempt was made to determine what width of millrace was the most favorable in relation to the width of the wheel, what should be the angle of the blades on the shaft, and what their spacing should be (that is, how many blades should be used to obtain the best output), and what portion of the blade should be immersed in water at its lowest point.

Technical improvements   The evolution of these theoretical ideas had no direct effect, however, on the construction and installation of the wheels, which continued to be done according to a time-honored tradition that evolved very slowly until approximately the end of the eighteenth century. Thereafter, improvements came more rapidly, especially when cast iron and later wrought iron began to be used. John Smeaton was primarily responsible for this progress. The name of this English engineer is associated with the construction of the third Eddystone Lighthouse, in 1755, with the digging of the Forth and Clyde canal, numerous civil engineering works, with studies on machinery, and with improvements he made on Newcomen's steam engine. Smeaton also installed numerous waterwheels. It was he who in 1769 built the first wheel with a cast-iron axle, for the Carron forge. This test was not conclusive, because the brittleness of cast iron caused the axle to break in freezing temperatures.

During the second half of the eighteenth century there appeared increasing numbers of large-diameter wheels, of which the machine at Marly had been the sole example for a long time. Among others, the large installation at London Bridge was put into operation in 1768 and functioned until 1817, when it was replaced by iron wheels. The English engineers John Rennie and M. I. Brunel built the first large wheels with iron shafts, around the end of the eighteenth century and the beginning of the nineteenth. Shortly thereafter, wood was abandoned for the industrial production of waterwheels, especially when the use of overshot wheels became general. Poncelet's wheel, which in the period under consideration showed the ultimate improvement in undershot wheels, was made completely of iron.

Poncelet's work on undershot wheels dates from 1828. By theoretical studies the famous engineer established a method for improving the output of undershot wheels, which even under the best installation conditions was only 30 percent of the available power of the waterfall. In particular, Poncelet demonstrated that power losses caused by the impact of water on the vanes could be eliminated by giving the vanes a curved shape (Figure 9). He calculated the most effective curve of the vanes, the profile and arrangement of the sluice gate, the radius of the wheel, and the width of the rim bearing the vanes that would permit the best use of the water's effect on the curved vanes while still retaining the advantage of undershot wheels—their speed of rotation, which was greater than that of breast wheels and overshot wheels. Poncelet carefully studied all the other elements that

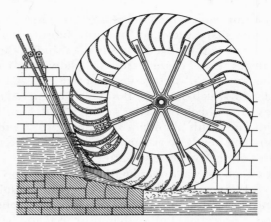

FIG. 9.   Poncelet's wheel.

made it possible to improve output. He determined that the profile of the bottom of the millrace should follow the wheel's profile for a certain distance downstream from the vertical line passing through the wheel's axis, to ensure the discharge of water from the curved vanes at the most advantageous point in the wheel's revolution. All these factors combined to make it possible to double the output of undershot wheels. However, the construction of this type of wheel was not within the capabilities of all builders at the time when Poncelet's work became known. The wheel was built completely of metal and consisted of eight cast-iron sections assembled around the axis, and sheet metal vanes. The output of a wheel did not reach the hoped-for figure unless Poncelet's design was faithfully followed. Apparently, it was not until around 1850 that all the construction difficulties were finally overcome.

Overshot wheels　　　The breast wheel and the overshot wheel substituted buckets for the flat vanes. It is impossible to say with certainty what the origin was of these two types of wheels. Undoubtedly, the use of a channel to direct the water current toward the wheel's blades gradually led to using part of a waterfall to make the water's weight act on the blades. Before the end of the seventeenth century, no attempt seems to have been made to

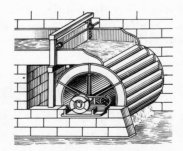

FIG. 10.   Overshot wheel with wooden buckets. Beginning of the nineteenth century.

FIG. 11.   Metal overshot wheel.

promote any widespread use of buckets. Their construction, even in the triangular trough shape they kept until the substitution of metal for wood, was more complicated and thus more costly than that of the flat blades. In addition, their advantages were not understood. Belidor felt that, on the contrary, the use of buckets was less advantageous than that of blades, and he recommended breast wheels with which the water flow would be curved toward the bottom to follow the shape of the wheel. In Navier's edition of Belidor's *Architecture hydraulique,* which he published with abundant notes in 1819, he felt that the carelessness of the famous engineer's treatment of overshot wheels had had unfortunate consequences on the systems built after his time.

Désaguliers was undoubtedly the first to express a differing opinion. According to him, buckets made it possible to obtain results ten times greater than those obtained by blades. In 1754 Deparcieux gained more precise ideas by experimenting with a waterfall of more than four feet, and he also recognized that the effect was greater as the speed of the wheel decreased. This conclusion was confirmed the following year by Leonhard Euler, who was no doubt the first to establish a clear-cut distinction among three categories of wheels, according to whether they worked as the result of the effects of impact, the weight of the water, or in reaction to the water. As in the case of overshot wheels, Smeaton and Borda contributed the most definite ideas of the period. The former discovered experimentally that the overshot wheel made it possible to obtain results double those of wheels with flat blades. Borda established that the maximum effect was achieved when the speed of the wheel was equal to half the velocity of the water falling into the buckets. Numerous problems continued to be debated, particularly those of determining what minimum speed should be set for the wheels, what maximum speed should be fixed for the capacity of the buckets, and how the millrace should be shaped so that the buckets on their downward passage would or would not be immersed in the stream. In 1819 Navier pointed out that in practice breast wheels and overshot wheels should be no less than about 16 feet in diameter and that the diameter should be increased relative to the height of the fall in such a way as to keep the ratio of the wheel's speed to that of the water at 1:2. He tells us that wheels of this type were built whose diameter was as much as 49 feet. At this period these were still wooden wheels with iron hubs. To the hub was attached a gear whose radius was one-third or one-half the radius of the wheel; it served to drive the machine to be operated.

Shortly before the middle of the century a new type of breast wheel (Figure 12) was invented by the French engineer Sagebien. This wheel differed from classic waterwheels in that the vanes were not positioned radially. The inventor of

Fig. 12.   Sagebien's wheel.

this device calculated the angle of the blades so they entered the water at an angle of 45° to the surface. Thus the water filled the spaces between blades without a shock and came out at the bottom of the channel without making waves. This arrangement made it possible to increase the output of breast wheels with flat blades from 60–70 percent to 80–90 percent. Sagebien's metal wheel was quickly adopted for a great number of hydraulic installations.

Metal construction   In France the first wheels constructed entirely of metal appeared around 1830. At this date a wheel with a radius of more than 21 feet was installed at the Sèvres factory by John Hall. The buckets were made of sheet iron, the spokes were wrought iron, and the rim, journals, and shaft were cast iron. On such wheels the driving gear was located on the wheel's rim, which made it possible to obtain a considerable reduction ratio in the gears.

Around the middle of the nineteenth century, the construction and operation of wheels had reached a degree of perfection not to be surpassed thereafter. The practice as well as theoretical study of hydrodynamics had made possible the best use of waterfalls by means of vertical wheels. For each type of wheel, the layout of the millrace, the size of the circumference, the shape and number of the buckets, and the automatic control of the water flow were perfectly determined and fixed. From now on the efforts of hydraulic engineers would be brought to bear on the development of turbines, the first models of which had already come into use.

WATER TURBINES

Many other improvements could still have been made in vertical waterwheel installations after the development through the middle of the nineteenth century, but it seems that these improvements would not have been capable of appreciably transforming the efficiency of this method of developing the power of streams. Builders realized the advantages and disadvantages of the systems in use. Around this period one Armengaud, a French engineer famous for his knowledge in this field, wrote in his *Traité des moteurs hydrauliques:* "They [vertical wheels] have the advantage of low maintenance costs, ease of repair, and a low breakdown rate. In truth, it is frequently enough to replace a few blades and tighten a few bolts, and in this way they operate for years at a stretch without any repairs." On the other hand, these installations were cumbersome, the wheels turned relatively slowly, and such wheels were unusable in midwinter. Even bucket wheels, whether overshot or breast wheels, whose useful possibilities were more extensive and whose efficiency was greater, presented disadvantages of the same type, which it was impossible to avoid.

Despite increasing numbers of steam engines gradually put into service in France after the Napoleonic wars, the need for waterpower continued to grow. More precisely, the numbers and development of industrial establishments continued to be closely dependent on the growth of usable waterpower. Since France possessed abundant waterways with extremely varied flows, it was natural that, under the pressure of industrial expansion, more attention was paid in that country to the possibility of creating a type of hydraulic engine that would meet new needs. The Société d'Encouragement pour l'industrie nationale promoted this innovation by its offer in 1826 of a prize of 6,000 francs for the large-scale application of water turbines in factories and mills.

The word *turbine* was invented by a mining engineer and professor named Burdin at the École de Saint-Étienne. This new word designated a type of horizontal waterwheel Burdin had designed two years earlier.

The scoop wheel We know that horizontal wheels had been in existence since the origin of water mills, but they had not in fact been used except under special circumstances. In France their use does not seem to have spread beyond the southern regions.

Since the scoop wheel's axis was vertical, a millstone could be fixed to its upper portion without additional transmission gearing. Thus the scoop, or "Pyreneean" wheel, was suitable for small individual installations. Its production, which required only the skill of an artisan, spread throughout diverse geographical regions without major variations. It has come down to our own day in the form of the Arab spinning wheel (Figure 13). The water, obtained from a waterfall or a brook with a rapid current, was led either through a trough hollowed out of wood or through a flume, to give a greater impulse to the blades, which were carved in the shape of a spoon. The wheel's axle was turned at a relatively rapid speed, certainly the feature that caught the attention of engineers in the beginning of the nineteenth century.

Tub wheels Tub wheels were suitable for larger installations on dams where the fall was not very great, especially on fairly wide streams with a reasonably swift current. The famous Basacle mills at Toulouse, described by Belidor in the first edition of his *Architecture hydraulique*, are always mentioned as an example. This type of mill, examples of which were to be found on the river Aude and on the Pau, appears to have been used particularly in the south of France. Like the earlier models, the use of tub wheels was not as widespread as that of vertical wheels, but they continued in service well into our time. The wheel, always carved out of wood, consisted of a cylindrical axle, on which helicoidal paddles were attached, and an outer rim (Figure 14). It was placed at the bottom of a masonry pit several inches deep. The water was carried to the upper portion by a flume that gradually narrowed so that the speed of the flow increased toward the entrance to the tub. The water turned the wheel by passing through it from top to bottom. This type of wheel, whose efficiency suggests turbines of the early period, presented the same advantage of turning at a

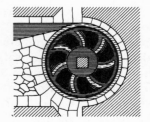

FIG. 13.   Spoon wheel.   FIG. 14.   Tub wheel (plan).

relatively high speed but had the further advantage of being immersed in the current, which in large part averted the risk of being made inoperable by freezing. These characteristics caught millwrights' attention as they came about.

Ball-bearing devices were probably employed, for the first time, to facilitate the rotation of the horizontal wheels, though at what time it is difficult to determine with any accuracy. Marble ball bearings between 3 and 4 inches in diameter, placed in the circular grooves of two wooden disks, were used for this purpose.

The output of traditional horizontal wheels did not exceed 25 percent and could even be as low as between 12 and 15 percent, as at the Basacle mill.

The principle of the reaction wheel

The transition from horizontal wheels to turbines seems to have come about indirectly. During the eighteenth century several engineers, in particular Leonhard Euler and his son, studied how to use the principle of the reaction wheel to construct a reaction motor. A drawing of a device consisting of a tube rolled around a cylinder appears as early as in Branca's work. Désaguliers described another system (Figure 15), which we owe to the Englishman Barker, this time a genuine adaptation of the reaction wheel. Slightly later (around 1750), a German, Segner, thought of constructing a reaction wheel with several horizontal branches arranged like spokes at the base of a vertical cylinder.

The most important contribution of this period was one made by the Eulers, who in a paper published in 1754 described a device inspired by Segner's. Euler's wheel consisted of a cylindrical drum positioned on top of a conical one (Figure 16). The top drum, which acted as a reservoir, was stationary; water passing through it flowed into the conical drum through a series of curved tubes. The bottom drum was supported on a vertical rotating shaft that was turned by the effect of water acting against it as it emerged at the bottom from curved tubes similar to those in the upper portion. The chief merit of the Eulers' paper lies not in the description and theory of this machine (which, except for one attempt by Burdin, was not put to use) but in the fact that it proposes the use of a stationary reservoir that ensures the distribution of the in-flowing water over the entire surface of the wheel at once and a device for its discharge around the entire periphery.

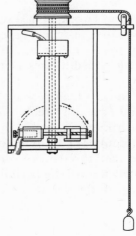

FIG. 15.   Barker's water engine (from Désaguliers).

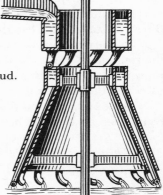

FIG. 16. Euler's wheel, as reconstructed by Armengaud.

The last attempt to apply the principle of the reaction wheel was Mannoury d'Ectot's "hydraulic lever" (Figure 17), patented in 1807. The device consisted of a vertical inlet tube whose lower portion was curved in such a way as to direct the water into the reaction wheel from the bottom; the two reaction tubes were curved in the shape of joined symmetrical S-shaped involutes in relation to the vertical axle that supported them. This shape ensured the most effective discharge of the water. Although this device was described for a long time in treatises on physics, no practical application of it was ever made.

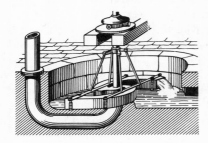

FIG. 17. Mannoury d'Ectot's wheel.

Burdin's work   Around 1820 to 1824, Burdin, always mentioned as the predecessor (or more precisely the inspirer) of Fourneyron's work, built several installations in the department of Puy-de-Dôme with hydraulic machines based on Euler's wheel. The first was part of the equipment of the Ardres mill; thus Burdin's engine was known under this name for some time. Burdin himself described the machine of the Pont-Gibaud mills, in 1833.

Burdin's wheel repeated the basic plan of Euler's, but in a form better adapted to the work required of it. Water admitted through an upper reservoir flowed through inclined pipes into a rotor consisting of a horizontal annular casing (Figure 18). It flowed out through inclined nozzles made of sheet iron and held between two flanges. Burdin had thought of having these nozzles discharge alternately toward the periphery and the inside. He insisted several times on the advantage of this device, which made it possible to avoid, at the point of outflow, turbulence detrimental to the output. Tests with the Prony brake showed that the Pont-Gibaud machine had an output of 67 percent of the available power.

In response to the competition sponsored by the Société d'Encouragement, Burdin presented a paper on horizontal wheels in which he abandoned Euler's principle. This paper is the source of both the name and the conception of the centrifugal turbine that Benoît Fourneyron was to construct. It is evident that the entire story of attempts to develop the reaction wheel is linked with the history of turbines only by the fact that, having attempted to develop a horizontal wheel, Burdin suggested its transformation into a turbine.

The turbine he described (Figure 19) consists of a stationary reservoir within a revolving casing. The reservoir and the casing are equipped with vertical guide vanes whose arrangement and profile were carefully designed so that the water flowing through the openings left for that purpose would cause a reaction on the movable component. Burdin noted that this type of turbine can function when submerged and it causes no loss of head.

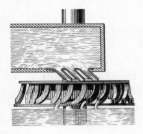

FIG. 18.   Burdin's wheel, used at the Pont-Gibaud mills. Before 1827.

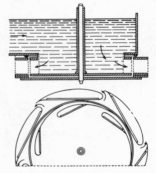
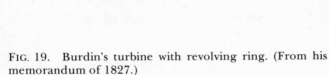

FIG. 19.   Burdin's turbine with revolving ring. (From his memorandum of 1827.)

The description of this turbine takes up only one page of the paper in which Burdin studied the general conditions of use of horizontal wheels and discussed the possible applications of the theoretical studies published by Borda and Navier in 1767 and 1819 respectively. Since he suggested no practical solution for the construction of turbines, the Société d'Encouragement awarded him a medal of the value of 2,000 francs only, and left the subject open to competition. Several years later, Fourneyron presented the results of his work, which won him the Société's prize in 1833.

Fourneyron's early work   It is undeniable that Benoît Fourneyron's work is based on the training he had received from Burdin at the school of mines in Saint-Étienne. In 1821 Fourneyron, then nineteen, became an engineer at the forges of Pont-sur-Lognon (Doubs), and was thereby led to take an interest in improving hydraulic engines. The waterwheel in this factory provided an inadequate drive for the rolling mill with which the manufacturers proposed to make tinplate. In 1827 Fourneyron operated an experimental 6 hp. turbine under a fall of 4 feet 8 inches. In 1830 he installed a second experimental turbine under a fall of between 10 and 20 feet to operate a centrifugal blowing engine at the Fraisans forge in the Jura, and almost immediately thereafter installed a second, 50 hp., turbine in the same establishment.

In 1833 Fourneyron, who had taken out a patent in 1832, presented a paper to the Société d'Encouragement in which he described these three turbines and outlined a general theory of these new types of engines.

According to the general diagram given by Burdin, Fourneyron's turbines consisted of a stationary circular reservoir placed inside the rotor. The water thus flowed from inside to outside and from top to bottom (Figure 20). But Fourneyron had also examined a system that was the exact opposite of the one he had adopted in his first industrial installations, in which the intake piping introduced the water at the bottom, directing the flow from bottom to top. He does not appear to have used this system thereafter.

In addition to the special shape of the vanes, the angle of which could be varied with the amount of fall, even in its early stage Fourneyron's turbine possessed the characteristics of an engine that could be used industrially (Figure 21). The turbine was housed in a large cast-iron cylinder closed at the top by a cover; the inlet pipe opened into the side of the cylinder. (After trying wooden pipes, Fourneyron quickly replaced them with cast-iron ones.) The cylinder, containing a sluice that could be controlled by an external crank, was placed on top of the reservoir. The revolving wheel was submerged in the masonry tailrace, to the bottom of which was fixed the socket supporting the shaft of the wheel. This

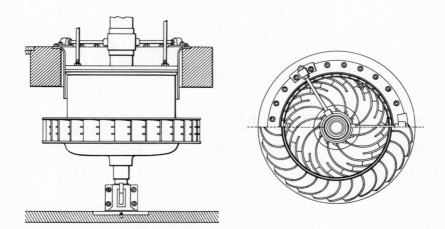

FIG. 20.   Principle of the operation of Fourneyron's turbine. *Left:* Exterior view of the guide case and the rotor. *Right:* Projection of the blades of the guide case (*center*) and the rotor forming the outer ring.

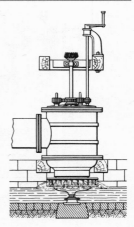

FIG. 21. First model of Fourneyron's turbine used in industry.

shaft extended upward and left the reservoir through a stuffing box. There was a bevel gear on its upper portion that engaged that of the transmission shaft.

A series of tests was made on the Pont-sur-Lognon turbine, the first to be put into service. Measurements made with the Prony brake gave varying outputs of between 51 and 88 percent, depending on the operating conditions; in practice, the yield must have been on the order of 70 percent.

Early development of turbines

The blessing of the Société d'Encouragement established Fourneyron's reputation. In the next few years he installed several other turbines, which used increasingly higher heads. In 1837/38 he equipped two falls of 360 and 380 feet respectively at St. Blazien in the Black Forest. He had installed a supply pipe 550 yards long, at the bottom of which the pressure reached 11 atmospheres. The turbine's rotor measured only 12 inches and weighed just 38½ pounds. The actual power was 60 hp., the useful effect exceeded 80 percent, and the wheel revolved at a speed of 2,300 rpm. For that period, this could be considered a major achievement. Not until thirty years later did Aristide Bergès, regarded as an innovator in the use of high heads, equip a fall that had a 666-foot drop.

For the spinning mill at Augsburg, Fourneyron built turbines whose output was 220 hp. In 1843—that is, ten years after the publication of his paper—129 factories and mills had been built or enlarged, thanks to Fourneyron's turbines, in France, Germany, Austria, Italy, Poland, and even Mexico.

After Fourneyron, other builders—Cadiat in 1839, Callon in 1840, Huot in 1852—tried to construct turbines similar to his, but they did not enjoy the same success.

Shortly after Fourneyron two other engineers, Fontaine-Baron and Jonval, created turbines that again used the principle of the vertical flow of water, as in the old tub wheels. At the time, these turbines were called overshot ones because the water came in through the top of the casing.

In the same period, and for several years thereafter, studies were made of the construction of centrifugal turbines supplied from the bottom, as in one of the models tried out by Fourneyron. This type was called an undershot turbine, a name that fell into disuse, however.

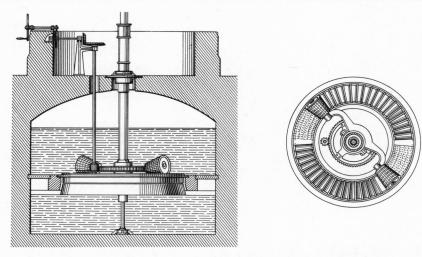

FIG. 22.   Fontaine-Baron turbine, constructed by Brault, after modification of the guide vanes system.

*Fontaine-Baron's
axial turbine*

The turbine Fontaine-Baron patented in 1840, which was built three years later by the firm of Fromont & Sons in Chartres, consisted basically of two horizontal casings with vanes for the passage of the water (Figure 22). The upper casing, which was stationary, acted as a reservoir; the lower one, supported by the central vertical axle, acted as the rotor. The sluice device, which was quite complicated, demonstrates the progress made by the machine industry in the previous few years. In Fourneyron's turbine the sluice system consisted of a ring placed inside the reservoir and in which there were vertical openings. The water's flow was regulated by causing this ring to pivot several degrees. In Fontaine's turbine each blade in the reservoir had a small sluice capable of up-and-down movement (Figure 23), which when lowered closed the opening next to the blade on which it was located. These gates could be controlled simultaneously by a device with wheels and an endless chain. A short time later the builder eliminated these adjustable sluices, the control of which must have been quite uncertain, and

FIG. 23. *Left:* Original type of blade used on the Fontaine turbine. *Right:* Simplified vane. In both diagrams the blades in the upper portion are those of the guide case; those in the lower portion are the blades of the rotor.

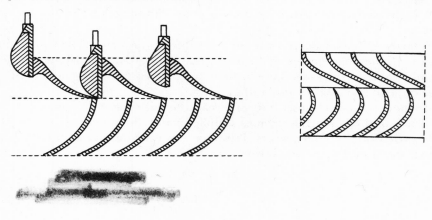

replaced the system with another in which thin sheets of brass unrolled in a circular arc above the reservoir to the width necessary to achieve the desired reduction in the rate of flow, as can be seen in Figure 22. In Fontaine's turbine the power of the water entering the wheel was completely a function of its velocity; during its passage through the wheel the pressure of the water remained unchanged.

The Jonval-Koechlin reaction turbine
Contemporary with Fontaine's turbine, another type of axial turbine came about as the result of a theoretical error made by one of the inventors, Jonval, but corrected and developed by André Koechlin, a Mulhouse manufacturer. In Jonval's 1841 patent he diagramed a turbine consisting of a vaned rotor placed in the neck of a vertical conduit. This driving wheel turned above a stationary wheel with convex blades and a sluice gate was placed at the opening of the tailrace (Figure 24). This arrangement (exactly the opposite of Fourneyron's and Fontaine's turbines) was determined by the principle that the rate of flow through the turbine was to remain constant, which made it possible to place the driving wheel at any position in the fall without losing the benefit of the power corresponding to the total height of the fall. Jonval also had the idea that water acted on the wheel at a velocity that was accelerated by reducing the diameter of the conduit.

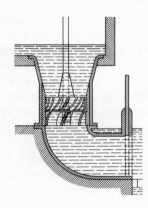

FIG. 24.   Jonval turbine (after the patent of 1841).

In 1843 André Koechlin, having acquired Jonval's rights, realized that if constricting the conduit was favorable to the operation of the turbine, the velocity of the water was as well a function of the difference in level between the headrace and the tailrace. Koechlin realized the possibility of placing the driving wheel at any level of the fall if the water flow remained constant beneath and above the wheel and if the wheel was located less than 33 feet above the tailrace. With these corrected principles Koechlin decided to build an industrial turbine in which the driving wheel had above it a reservoir with stationary blades, with a sluice still located in the lower portion of the outlet cylinder (Figure 25). These engines, known as Jonval-Koechlin turbines, were quickly used to equip falls ranging from 10 to 16 feet in height. In 1855 Fourneyron gave the outlet cylinder the form of a diffuser capable of recovering a large part of the water's remaining kinetic energy. In the second half of the nineteenth century, reaction turbines were to undergo still more very tangible improvements.

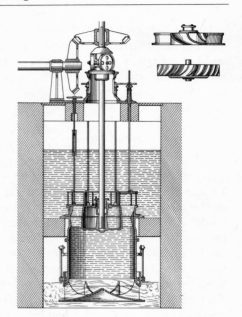

FIG. 25. Jonval-Koechlin turbine. *Upper right:* detail drawing of the blades of the guide case *(top)* and rotor *(bottom).*

The limited distribution of turbines The various types of turbines invented during the 1830s and 1840s were immediately put into service and furnished a new method of developing water-power by making use of waterways that heretofore could not be employed. Numerous improvements were thereafter made on these turbines, and other models inspired by one or the other were quickly developed. During the second half of the nineteenth century the construction of water turbines was to develop greatly, but at the date at which we are temporarily concluding this discussion, despite the fact that turbines had been quite favorably received and were already regarded as engines with a future, specialists still valued the services rendered by vertical waterwheels, which were not about to disappear. In 1858 Armengaud wrote that "it is good to note . . . that in many cases the turbine has not yet succeeded in giving an output equal to that achieved with a good overshot wheel or a well-installed breast wheel."

At this time the construction of turbines was still a specialty of the French. A report on the 1851 Exhibition in London, which mentions the presentation of a double turbine by Fontaine-Baron, points out that this type of hydraulic engine was unknown in England. A report on the 1855 Paris Exhibition mentions only French builders and a Tyrolean engineer, one Fenbach, who was cited for presenting a turbine in which water passed from the outside to the inside of a revolving wheel and which seemed to anticipate various models that began to be developed after the end of the century. Water was directed by a flume to a single point on the wheel, the vanes of which were shaped like the buckets on Poncelet's wheels. General Morin, who awarded a second-class medal to this turbine, had this to say of it: "We lacked results of experiments on this wheel, but we should be grateful to Mr. Fenbach for having partly realized the idea of a French scientist [Poncelet] in order to introduce a new turbine system to industry in his country."

CHAPTER 2

THE STEAM ENGINE

I N THE preceding volume we saw the first steps in the development of heat engines that could be used as a source of driving power, from sporadic attempts by the Marquis of Worcester and Denis Papin to Savery's achievements. Although the latter's engine contributed a solution to the problem of lifting water mechanically and contributed particularly to that of pumping water out of mines, it had its disadvantages. It is impossible to say whether Savery inspired the inventors who were at almost the same time to introduce definitively industrial uses of the steam engine.

THE ATMOSPHERIC ENGINE

Research by
Newcomen and Calley

It is chiefly to Thomas Newcomen that we owe the fulfillment of the first stage. We possess very few biographical details on this man, whose name is linked with the beginning of the modern era of industrial technology. We know that he was born in Devon at Dartmouth in 1663, that he died in London in 1729, and that he was an ironmonger and tool seller, or rather a blacksmith, in his native city in 1703. At this time he had undoubtedly already begun his attempts to apply the expansive powers of steam to an engine consisting basically of a vertical cylinder in which a piston moved from bottom to top. The cooling of the steam and its condensation allowed the atmospheric pressure, entering through the upper opening of the cylinder, to push the piston back down to the bottom.

We do not know what circumstances led Newcomen to become interested in such a device or whether he began with knowledge of Savery's work. If, as it appears from slightly later evidence, he began his experiments in 1698 (the year Savery took out his patent), he must have been unaware at that time of the latter's invention. On the other hand, he may have been in contact with Robert Hooke, the secretary of the Royal Society, through whom he would undoubtedly have learned of Papin's attempts. This point lends itself to discussion. It is possible that since his work brought him into contact with mining companies, he may have been struck by the high costs of pumping water from mines by horse-driven pumps. From this we can speculate, without any certainty, about the manner in which he devoted himself to the problem of building a steam engine capable of operating drainage pumps. Dickinson has pointed out that Newcomen's engines contain no original invention but simply an intelligent use of devices already known—cylinders, pistons, walking beams, and so on. Newcomen undertook to build his engines with the collaboration of John Calley, a glassblower and plumber who lived in the same city, with whom he was in partnership.

Perfecting the early model Chance may have played a large role in the perfecting of Newcomen's engine, but it seems certain that, thanks to their experiments, Newcomen and Calley discovered the necessary improvements on an early model, which consisted of a small cylinder 7 inches in diameter. The inventors must have encountered difficulties in boring this cylinder. The piston is said to have allowed major leakage despite both the leather covering in which it was enveloped and a layer of water on top, intended to complete the seal. It was observed that if cold water accidentally got into the cylinder when it was filled with steam, internal condensation was accelerated, though other factors could have caused this. The fact is that in the first tests the cylinder was cooled only by an outer cold-water jacket and, a tin-soldered joint having weakened during the engine's operation, cold water entered the cylinder, causing a rapid condensation of steam that made a reaction violent enough to break the chain of the walking beam. Whatever their inspiration, Newcomen and Calley conceived the idea of injecting cold water into the cylinder at the moment when the piston reached the top of its stroke (Figure 26).

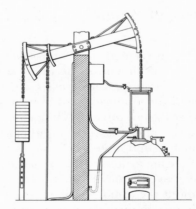

FIG. 26.   Principle of construction and operation of the Newcomen engine (from Tredgold).

Condensation thus being more rapid, the number of piston strokes per minute could be increased. The cooling water and condensation were evacuated through the bottom of the cylinder and returned to the boiler.

Construction of the boiler itself probably presented no particular difficulty. In its early form, and until Smeaton's improvements, it was a large copper vessel capped with a lead dome and placed over a masonry firebox.

The engine's power was developed during the piston's downstroke, under atmospheric pressure, which is why this engine was long known as the "atmospheric" engine. We know that the piston rod was connected by a chain to the end of a walking beam, the other end of which operated the piston of the water pump.

A supplemental pump lifted water to the top of the engine to inject cold water into the cylinder at the desired moment.

Automatic control valves The openings to admit steam on the one hand and to inject cold water on the other were controlled by valves, which in early models were operated manually. The invention of a mechanical device permitting automatic opening and closing of these valves has been attributed to a young worker. The legend of Humphrey Potter is related for the first time by Désaguliers in 1744, following the testimony of Henry Beighton, and was later embellished, but is completely without foundation. Beighton was one of the first engineers to participate in improving Newcomen's engine after it became familiar. It was he who suggested a series of tappets operated by the movement of the walking beam, which controlled the valves. In the very early stages of the use of this engine, several individuals named Potter played different roles, and Désaguliers was probably confused by this.

Use of the engine The first atmospheric engine put into service was undoubtedly one built at or near Dudley Castle, Staffordshire, in 1712. The existence of this engine is definitely known (an engraving of it survives), but no one has been able to discover its exact location. We know that it made 12 strokes per minute and lifted 10 gallons of water at each stroke from a depth of 51 yards, which means, according to Dickinson, that the engine produced 5½ hp. It is possible that prior to this, in 1710, another engine may have been put into service in a Cornish tin mine.

Only in the last portion of their experiments did Newcomen and Calley come into contact with Savery, whose patent covered all uses of fire for pumping. The details of their negotiations are not known, but an agreement must have been reached between them, since at this time Savery's engine had no further chance of success and the only way he could profit from his patent would have been to come to an understanding with his competitors. No patent, in both names or in Newcomen's name alone, is on record.

Matters seem to have progressed very rapidly, for Savery died in 1715 and atmospheric engines were exploited by a kind of company claiming to be the "proprietors" of his patent. Savery and Newcomen are not mentioned as being responsible for the construction of the various engines that quickly came into existence in Great Britain—near Coventry, in Cornwall, in Cumberland, and elsewhere.

Beighton made the first improvements on the engine. In particular, he made the control rods for valves on an engine built near Newcastle-upon-Tyne in 1715. It is to him that we owe the first theoretical studies on the power of steam—in 1717 he published a table showing the relationships between the power of an engine and the diameter of its cylinder. The engine as improved by Beighton retained its original form for several years. Its use spread rapidly throughout the mining districts, being used also to drain swamplands and pump water to supply some cities.

Ten years after the completion of the first atmospheric engine, the first one was built on the Continent, in 1722 in the mining district of Schemnitz (now Stiavnica, in Czechoslovakia). Another was built in 1725 near Liège, and in France the first such engine was installed at Passy in 1726.

In Great Britain the atmospheric, or "fire," engine enjoyed a success that can be regarded as rapid, considering the state of the metallurgical industry at that time. In a half century almost one hundred engines, in increasingly large sizes, had been built and installed. The development of methods for producing cast iron favored progress in the construction of engines and decreased their cost. Cast iron, which was being produced in larger quantities with coke now that the Darby method had been put into operation (around 1730), was in fact substituted for brass in cylinders and progressively for wood in certain other parts. According to Dickinson, in some thirty years the cost of a cylinder thus dropped from £250 to £30.

Perfecting the boiler   The engine's capabilities were improved as experience suggested changes. Thus, for example, the steam supply became more regular thanks to the use of two, three, and even four boilers for a single cylinder. Naturally, changes in the price of coal also played a role in the increasing use of the engines and improvement of their boilers.

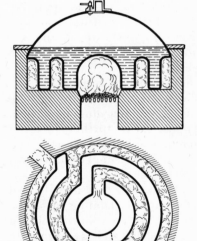

FIG. 27.   Boiler with flues, used in the engine of York Building. 1750. (From Tredgold.)

In early models the firebox was placed directly under the boiler, which led to a great loss of heat. In Cornwall, where the steam engine was immediately and widely put in use, an attempt was made to build boilers with masonry flues in which hot air circulated, but this precursor of the tubular boiler does not appear to have given satisfactory results. Tredgold reproduces a plan and elevation of a boiler built on this principle around 1750 in London (Figure 27) and says that it was the best model of its day. Copper was generally abandoned for the boiler and was replaced by riveted sheets of iron.

Smeaton's research Thus it was on improving the boiler that efforts were concentrated, including those of Smeaton, who played an extremely important role in developing the early Newcomen engine. Various scientists and engineers concerned themselves (prior to or contemporaneously with him) with the technical and theoretical problems raised by the construction and operation of the steam engine. One of them, Francis Blake, a member of the Royal Society, attempted to apply various calculations to the cylinder's dimensions and the results obtained from them. These experiments did not result in any real technical advance, but they undoubtedly helped contemporary thinkers become aware of the problems connected with the new method of producing power that was now available to them. Joseph Black's works on latent heat in 1762, which contributed fundamental scientific principles on the subject, came too early to be of much assistance. Only a profoundly reflective mind like that of James Watt would be able to utilize them, in part, about ten years later.

The improvements Smeaton made to the steam engine remained empirical in nature, a fact that does not lessen their interest. On the contrary, these improvements illustrate the course of invention in every important episode of technical progress. Once the engine had been invented, its use from time to time suggested modifications in form and the addition of devices and accessories which, without modifying the basic principle, increased the engine's effectiveness, and paved the way for a more important phase of its development.

Smeaton began to become interested in the steam engine in 1765. He was the first to build a portable steam engine, of interest also for other reasons. This was, in fact, the first attempt to eliminate the walking beam by using a less cumbersome arrangement, in this case an oscillating wheel. The firebox was equipped with a grate that facilitated its maintenance. In particular, it was placed inside the boiler, whose water supply was preheated by heat from the smokestack (Figure 28). Smeaton was to retain this device in the boilers of the large engines he built later.

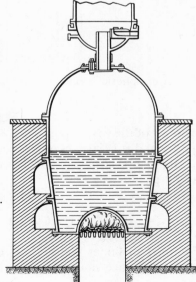

FIG. 28. Smeaton's boiler. Around 1770. (From Bataille.)

With this experimental model Smeaton devoted himself for several years to studies through which he acquired useful information on the qualities of the fuel to be used and a method for varying the engine's power by controlling the injection of cold water in proportion to the output required, and to regulating the performance of the machine. He demonstrated the practicability of lengthening the stroke of the piston in relation to its diameter, identified the maximum load for the piston in order to obtain the best effect during the power stroke, and gave as well the maximum permissible speed. From his data he deduced a new method of building steam engines that differed from earlier models in a great number of details impossible to give here but which constituted an effective adaptation of the engine to the applications required of it. Smeaton obtained considerable flue economy for a higher output. His name remains associated chiefly with the three large engines he built, one at Long Benton near Newcastle in 1772, another at Chasewater in Cornwall in 1775 (Figure 29), and the third at Kronstadt in 1777.

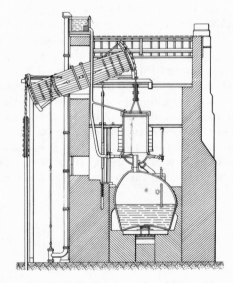

FIG. 29.   Atmospheric engine built by Smeaton in 1775 at Chase-Water. (From Farey.)

The cylinder of the first engine was 52 inches in diameter and it had a stroke of 7 feet; it operated at 12 strokes per minute and produced 41 hp. The cylinder of the second engine was larger—72 inches in diameter. The length of its stroke was 9 feet, and it produced 77 hp.

THE CONDENSING ENGINE

The work of James Watt has often been described, and has even acquired a symbolic significance, not only for the history of technology but also for the history of industrial civilization. The invention of the condensing engine and of the double-acting engine were in truth events of exceptional importance, the effects of which excited all the more interest since Watt was fortunate enough to be able to have his inventions put to use by a shrewd industrialist.

From Newcomen to Watt Unlike Newcomen, who was soon absorbed into the society of his time, Watt enjoyed a long career and reaped the fruits that are more easily won by financial success than by technical achievement. Although Watt's fame was not unfairly earned, it must be said that it influenced the history of the steam engine to the detriment of Newcomen. Watt's name is known to everyone, whereas Newcomen's is known to only a very small number of experts.

The two men and their two destinies are not comparable. But we are justified in asking whether Newcomen's inventive effort was not superior to that of Watt. The atmospheric piston engine would probably have been born in the first quarter or first half of the eighteenth century even if Newcomen had never lived. Nevertheless, it was he who invented the process and found solutions to all the problems raised by its first application. Undoubtedly, he did not invent it alone; perhaps Calley played a greater role in the story than history has recorded. In any case, the result was a discrete invention, and if the atmospheric engine had not been in service for a half century, Watt probably would not have applied himself to transforming it.

Watt's contribution was so personal that we are justified in thinking that the double-acting engine would undoubtedly not have appeared until much later if Watt's idea had not emerged. Imagining a different course of history is always quite artificial, but the viewpoints just discussed reestablish a balance between Newcomen's invention and Watt's, a balance that has been too greatly upset by historical popularization.

Origin of Watt's work James Watt (1736–1819) was the grandson of a mathematician and the son of a merchant in Greenock, Scotland. A boy of delicate health, he received his early education at home, where he learned woodworking, an activity that helped him acquire great manual dexterity. He had successfully resumed his studies when family difficulties forced him in 1754 to seek a trade.

After working for less than a year for a manufacturer of mathematical instruments in London, Watt returned to Glasgow, ill and uncertain of his future. City regulations forbade him to open his own shop to manufacture instruments, but he obtained a position with the University of Glasgow, where he was assigned to the maintenance and repair of the instruments in the physics department. In addition to the security this position offered, it had the advantage of bringing him into contact with a number of young professors, with whom he became friends. Among others, he became acquainted with Joseph Black, who at the age of twenty-eight had just been named professor of chemistry, in 1756.

During the winter of 1763/64 Watt was invited by a Professor Anderson in physics to repair a demonstration model of an atmospheric engine. For Watt this was an opportunity to exercise not only his skill but also his faculties of reflection and observation and to find the point of departure for an extraordinary career.

*The principle of
the condenser*

The engine came from Jonathan Sisson, one of the most famous London instrument makers, and appeared to have no defects in construction. But in operation it could produce only a few piston strokes, because of the quantity of steam consumed.

Watt noted that the steam served first of all to heat the cylinder, which had been cooled during the preceding phase of condensation. Measuring the volume of the steam at atmospheric pressure, he found that it represented 1,800 times the volume of water corresponding to the same quantity of steam. He also noted that for each stroke of the piston the volume of steam needed was four times the volume of the cylinder. This enormous expenditure of steam involved a proportionate expenditure of fuel and did not permit continuous operation of the engine. Watt learned from Black that the transformation of water into steam absorbed a large quantity of heat (in accordance with the principle of latent heat of vaporization, which Black had discovered several years earlier), so he tried to use the heat given off by the steam's condensation to heat the water intended for the boiler. He established that a given volume of water in the form of steam could, during its condensation, heat a volume of cold water six times greater.

In this way Watt was led to believe that in Newcomen's engine a considerable amount of heat was lost without mechanical effect and that this inefficiency resulted from the fact that the steam was condensed inside the cylinder, which was cooled at each working stroke. By his own account, the solution to this problem occurred to him, after several months of reflection, one Sunday in May 1765 during a walk in the outskirts of Glasgow. He realized that steam, being elastic, would escape into an evacuated second vessel at the piston's downstroke if a connection was made between the cylinder and the second vessel, in which the steam would condense. As a result, it was no longer necessary to cool the cylinder. Thus was born Watt's first innovation, a condenser separate from the cylinder.

*A new conception
of the engine*

Several days later Watt constructed an experimental model, the layout of which was like a Newcomen engine in reverse (Figure 30). He did not yet possess much knowledge of industrial machines, and his idea was merely to apply the condenser to a steam-filled cylinder in which a piston moved. This original model, preserved in the Science Museum of London, enabled him to see that his idea was correct, and he worked for two more years to perfect and adapt it to the operating conditions of Newcomen's beam engine. To avoid heat losses in the cylinder he provided a steam jacket and closed it at the top with a cover equipped with a stuffing box for the passage of the piston rod.

Thus, atmospheric pressure no longer played a direct role in the operation of the engine. The piston's downstroke was still caused by a vacuum created in the cylinder by evacuating the steam into the condenser, but the pressure maintained above the piston was the same as that of the steam filling the steam jacket. Moreover, this pressure was about equal to the atmospheric pressure.

Watt applied himself to perfecting the steamtightness of the piston, and he replaced the layer of sealing water with grease or tallow. He placed the condenser below the cylinder and equipped it with a pump that ensured the constant discharge of both the water and the air that entered the cycle with the steam. The

Plate 1. One of the oldest double-acting steam engines, built by Watt; cylinder, valves, steam distribution mechanism, centrifugal governor. London, Science Museum. (Photo Science Museum.)

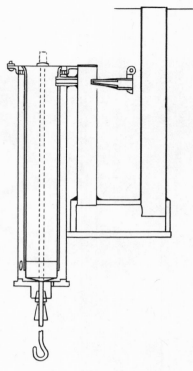

FIG. 30. Diagram of Watt's experimental model (from Dickinson). The atmospheric pressure would be exerted from the bottom, the steam inside the cylinder being forced into the condenser, represented by the horizontal chamber at the right.

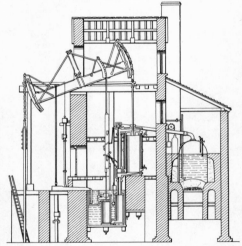

FIG. 31. Watt's single-acting engine (from Farey). On this model, which is the type built industrially in 1788, can be clearly distinguished the condenser with its pump and the steam inlet and discharge mechanism with the system of rods for control of the valves operated by the walking beam.

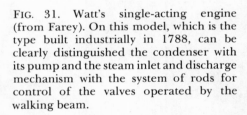

piston rod of this pump was connected to the beam of the steam engine, whose operation was thus made automatic (Figure 31).

The 1769 patent   At the end of this first period of research, Watt took out a patent in which he described in detail five special features of his method for decreasing the amount of fuel used in the steam engine. The first point was to keep the cylinder constantly warm; the second, to use a condenser into which the steam was evacuated; the third, to evacuate the water by using the condenser pump; the fourth, to use steam pressure to act on the piston instead of atmospheric pressure; and the fifth concerned a means of securing the steamtightness of the piston in the cylinder in order to prevent the passage of air and steam.

Watt did not immediately use these five points, but in them we find, in addition to the first major change in the atmospheric engine, the principles that were later to form the basis for the inventions that enabled him to build the double-acting engine.

Industrial construction of the steam engine

Watt was not immediately able to use his 1769 patent. He gave up his trade as an instrument maker in order to devote himself to research on the steam engine. Through the intervention of Joseph Black he had established a partnership with a manufacturer named John Roebuck of Birmingham, who had an interest in the Carron forge. The 1769 patent was taken out in the names of both partners, but in 1773 Roebuck, who was having financial difficulties, made over his interest to Matthew Boulton, who owned the largest factory of that time, in Soho, near Birmingham. It was from this new association that the first large modern enterprise for building steam engines was to be born.

Thanks to the prosperity of his business, which at that time already employed six hundred workers, Boulton was able to devote large sums of money to the final development and building of Watt's engine. A prototype of this engine was already in existence; Watt had constructed it earlier over a mine shaft at Kinneil, near Bowness, to pump out water. Building this early model had given him an opportunity to solve all the problems mentioned above and had led him to take out his 1769 patent. In 1775 Boulton and Watt obtained a twenty-five-year extension of the patent, whose validity was extended also to Scotland, which had its own system of patents.

When the Kinneil engine was dismantled and reassembled at Soho it again served as an experimental model. By 1776 Boulton and Watt had delivered two engines, one with a cylinder 50 inches in diameter, installed at the Bloomfield mines near Tipton. The other, with a 38-inch cylinder, was built for the blower of the furnaces in John Wilkinson's factory at Broseley in Shropshire.

Watt tells us that the construction of these engines was possible thanks only to a boring mill invented by Wilkinson in 1774, the precision of whose operation was such that the deviation in boring did not exceed the thickness of a dime (slightly more than 1 mm.).

A third engine was supplied to a London distillery and a fourth to the Bedworth collieries near Coventry. By 1777 the Cornish mines, which were already using a large number of atmospheric engines, were interested in Watt's condenser, and they quickly became major customers of the Soho plant. At this time the famous agreement governing the conditions of sale of the engine was introduced.

Financial agreements; lawsuits

Having become certain that they were helping their customers make major fuel savings, Boulton and Watt proposed the following arrangement: their engines were delivered and installed free of charge, and users paid only an annual rent of one-third of the fuel saved by replacing the atmospheric engine with the condensing one. Watt invented a counter to register the number of pump strokes, which, together with the easily measured consumption of coal, made it possible to fix the base for the rental. By 1780, seven years after the beginning of the Boulton-Watt partnership, forty condensing engines had been installed, twenty of which were in Cornwall. The sums accruing from the users were continually increasing; their magnitude can be estimated by the fact that the owners of the Chasewater mines offered to purchase the engine outright for a sum of £2,400.

Although the royalties were in proportion to the economies realized by the mine owners, they had increasing difficulty meeting these annual levies and, being unable to break the contracts they had signed, attempted to obtain an annulment of the patents that gave Watt a monopoly on his engines. Thus, until the end of the century Watt had to contend with numerous lawsuits, the decisions of which were in his favor. This also explains why, when Watt found it impossible to use a mechanism like the crankshaft-and-connecting-rod system because it was protected by a patent taken out by another inventor, he found a way to get around the difficulty with an original mechanism of his own.

THE DOUBLE-ACTING ENGINE

The progress of steam engines made another decisive step forward thanks to Watt's invention of a method to obtain rotary motion, which could not be produced by a single-acting engine.

The development of the steam inlet mechanism

Between the two main stages of Watt's inventions, a continuous evolution can be observed. In the industrial production of steam engines it is probable that the condenser as invented by Watt was included only in large models, the price of which did not represent a very high proportion of the total cost. It was for these large engines that Watt perfected a system of induction by which the steam, first drawn into the steam jacket, entered and evacuated through the same opening in the bottom of the cylinder toward the condenser. The latter was connected to a suction pump (Figure 32).

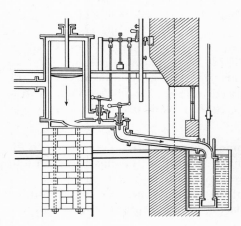

FIG. 32.   Detail of the inlet mechanism of the single-acting engine (from Bataille). Note the steam jacket enveloping the cylinder, and the two valves which control alternately the admission and the escapement through the bottom.

In 1778 Watt conceived the ideas of letting steam enter near the head of the jacket and of extending the inlet pipe downward, parallel to the cylinder. Intake into the cylinder was still from the bottom, and the piston rose under the action of the steam pressure, which took the weight of the beam (Figure 33). The movement of the piston from top to bottom occurred as a result of the vacuum obtained by evacuating the steam into the condenser. Under this arrangement, the driving stroke was still produced according to a principle similar to that of atmospheric engines. The piston's downstroke was assisted by the additional load placed upon it. This pressure, which was around 7 pounds per square inch in Newcomen's machines, had been increased by Watt to almost 10 pounds per square inch.

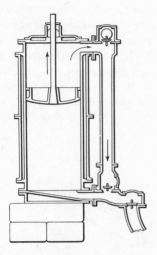
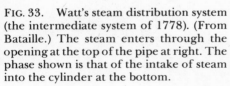
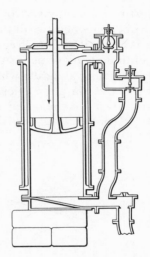

FIG. 33.   Watt's steam distribution system (the intermediate system of 1778). (From Bataille.) The steam enters through the opening at the top of the pipe at right. The phase shown is that of the intake of steam into the cylinder at the bottom.

FIG. 34.   Watt's steam distribution system for the single-acting engine of 1780 (from Bataille). The steam enters at the top of the cylinder, in which a pressure phase is followed by a vacuum phase.

Around 1780 Watt developed a new conception, which no doubt led him to the invention of the double-acting engine: he reversed the operating principle of the engine. Until then, in Newcomen's model as well as in his own, a constant pressure had been maintained above the piston in all phases of operation, whereas below the piston a phase of steam pressure only slightly exceeding atmospheric pressure followed a vacuum phase obtained by condensation either inside or outside the cylinder (Figure 34). In Watt's new concept, constant steam pressure was built up under the piston, but an alternation of pressure and vacuum took place above the piston. This did not yet change the operating principle of the engine, since the piston was raised by steam pressure at the moment when a vacuum was created above it by evacuating the steam through a set of valves toward the condenser. This device does not seem to have been satisfactory, nor does Watt appear to have used it in this form. But it constituted a very clear-cut advance in the thinking of Watt who had, since 1769, wanted to build a steam engine to produce rotary movement.

Numerous other inventors and experimenters were more or less assiduously pursuing the same goal in the same period, but it is striking that, before Watt, none of them thought of making the steam work alternately on both surfaces of the piston.

Experiments by other inventors   In 1724 a German engineer, Jakob Leupold, published a drawing of an engine consisting of two Newcomen-type cylinders supplied with steam by a four-way cock that operated two pistons alternately (Figure 35). This engine is in reality the first example given for the use of steam at a pressure higher than that of the atmosphere, namely two or three atmospheres, but the arrangement of its two alternate beams, each of which controlled a water pump, was suggestive of a device to give continuous movement. A little later (in 1736), Jonathan Hulls conceived the idea of turning a paddle wheel in a continuous movement through ratchet wheels driven by an atmospheric engine (Figure 36). One wheel turned in a direction contrary to the other during the power stroke of the engine and was driven by a counterweight in the opposite direction during the idle period.

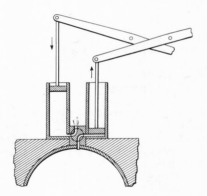

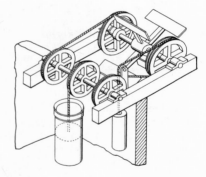

FIG. 35. Leopold's atmospheric engine (after Tredgold) 1724.

FIG. 36. Jonathan Hull's atmospheric engine, 1706 (after Tredgold).

Thereafter, Keane Fitzgerald in 1759, John Stewart in 1777, Matthew Washbrough in 1779, and James Pickard in 1780 in turn thought of various devices to obtain continuous movement with the help of the atmospheric engine. Even after Watt, builders like Thompson in 1793 and Sherrats in 1794 built double-acting engines using the principle of the atmospheric engine. For this purpose they made use of two cylinders operating alternately. In Thompson's model the cylinders were positioned one above the other and drove the same beam, whose opposite end was equipped with a crankshaft that drove a toothed wheel, which engaged with a pinion placed in the center of a large flywheel. In

Sherrats's model the two cylinders were placed side by side, the extension of the piston rods forming a rack that engaged each side of a toothed wheel, following the principle of the double-acting air pumps being built in this period.

To conclude this discussion of attempts to compete with Watt's engine, mention must be made of E. Cartwright's experiment of 1797 (Figure 37), for it indicates an extremely ingenious inventive spirit on the part of its creator. The

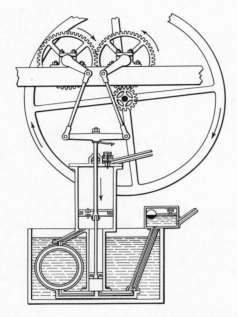

FIG. 37.   Cartwright's rotary engine working in a closed circuit, 1797 (after Bataille).

principle consisted of causing fluid (whether water or steam) to circulate inside the engine, without any connection with the outside. The steam worked on the upper face of the piston. Movement was transmitted by the piston rod to two gear wheels by means of a double crank and connecting rod system attached to a single crossrod. Continuous rotation was ensured by a large flywheel. As ingenious as Cartwright's engine may have been, it did not have a very long life.

The principle of the double-acting engine   Watt himself had thought in 1769 of using two single-acting engines and two crankshafts acting alternately on a single wheel. After elaborating his conception of the single-acting engine, he conceived the idea of supplying steam to the top and bottom of the cylinder, thus applying it alternately on the two faces of the piston. In this case two problems presented themselves: that of converting the alternating movement of the beam head into rotary movement, and that of connecting the piston rod to the other end of the beam.

The planetary gear   Concerning the first problem, the crankshaft-and-connecting-rod system had just been patented in 1779 by Matthew Washbrough and in 1780 by James Pickard. It is even probable that the first of these patents had been taken out as the result of information

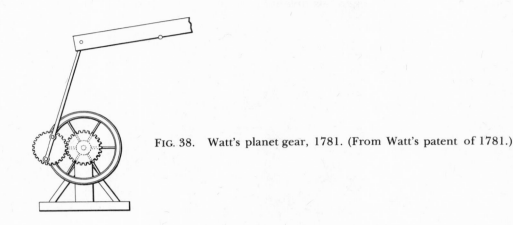

FIG. 38.   Watt's planet gear, 1781. (From Watt's patent of 1781.)

leaked by one of Watt's employees. Watt found a way to get around this patent by inventing a device using an epicyclic gear train (Figure 38), known by the name *Watt's sun and planet gear*, which he patented in 1781.

Watt's work with parallel motion   Watt made various attempts to modify the connection of the piston rod with the beam head. The connection could no longer consist of a flexible chain resting on a circular arc of the beam, as had been used in single-acting

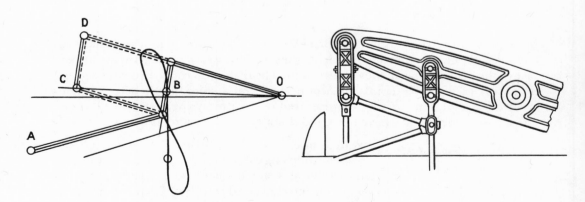

FIG. 39.   Watt's parallel motion of 1784—principle and construction."O" is the center of oscillation of the beam; "A" is a stationary point on the body of the engine. "B" and "C", at which the piston rods are pivoted, describe elliptical trajectories, which are perceptibly straight when "D" (the head of the beam) describes an arc.

engines; it had to be rigid so as to exert power in both directions. Watt also tried to use a rack, but without much success. In 1784 he patented the device of jointed levers known as Watt's parallel motion (Figure 39).

The cutoff valve   Meanwhile, in 1782, Watt had taken out a patent covering the principle of the double-acting engine at the same time as one on the use of a cutoff valve. Until then, steam pressure had been used in all engines to exert a continuous thrust on the piston for the entire duration of its stroke. In 1769 Watt thought that the steam supply could be stopped before the end of the piston stroke and its expansion could be utilized for the last portion of the stroke. In this way he expected to absorb the shock of the piston as it reached the end of its stroke. Later he realized that although the total power of the engine was decreased in this way, the result was nevertheless an economy in steam and hence in fuel to produce the same amount of work. In 1778 he returned to this idea and attempted to apply it; he included it in his 1782 patent.

The governor   Lastly, in 1787 Watt completed this brilliant series of inventions with the speed governor (Figure 40). This consisted of a spindle supporting a conical pendulum with two balls, which was rotated by a drive belt from the engine. Separating the balls by centrifugal force activated a lever that limited the opening of the valves controlling the flow of steam to the cylinders.

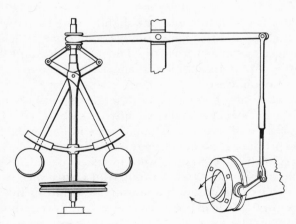

FIG. 40.   Governor with fly-balls. 1784. The spreading apart of the balls under the action of centrifugal force reduces the opening of the valve.

Watt was unable to have this device patented because it had been used before him, in a more primitive form, in grain mills. There is a description of it in Robert Stuart's *A Descriptive History of the Steam Engine* (London, 1824).

The first double-acting engine was built in 1783, but the most fully developed example was installed in 1784 at the Albion mills in London.

The engines turned out by the Soho factory after this date remained for all

practical purposes unsurpassed for almost fifty years, despite modifications in
their construction, such as replacing the wood in the beam with cast iron, and
adopting a slide valve to control the steam flow, and a crankshaft and connecting
rod to transmit rotary motion to the driveshaft (Figure 41).

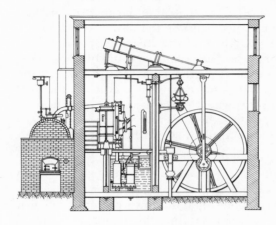

FIG. 41. Double-acting rotative engine as built by Boulton and Watt between 1787 and 1800 (from Farey).

*The industrial uses
of steam*

The success of steam engines in the Boulton and
Watt period is well known. In twenty-seven years of
collaboration (1773–1800), the two manufacturers
built approximately five hundred engines, slightly more than one-third of which
were pumping engines, the rest being double-acting ones. Dickinson estimates
that the engines developed an average of 15 hp. each, which for the Soho factory
would represent 7,500 hp. in addition to all the indigenous methods of power
production available to industry up to this period.

After 1800, when all of Watt's patents simultaneously entered the public
domain, the building of steam engines expanded greatly. Tredgold estimates that
in 1817 the cotton mills of Great Britain and Ireland had at their disposal more
than 20,000 hp. produced by steam engines and that in 1825, in the city of
Glasgow and its suburbs, 310 engines were in existence, including 68 on steam
boats. There is no question but that without Watt's work such progress in using
steam as a power source would not have occurred within such a short period of
time. The changes in the British economy that resulted from this invention have
often been described. The steam engine was not the sole reason for the birth of
modern industry, but it contributed to a considerable degree.

The nature of Watt's work

Some have seen in Watt's work the opening of a new
era in the development of technology through
direct application of scientific knowledge, but it seems that the importance of the
scientific character of Watt's research has been greatly exaggerated. The fact that
he knew of Joseph Black's discovery of the latent heat of steam undoubtedly
helped him understand why the condensation of steam inside a cylinder resulted
in a waste of fuel. But though Watt's experiments were the fruit of an original
attempt at logical investigation, they were not followed by the application of

scientific knowledge at any high level, even considering the state of science at the time. His experiments revealed his adoption of a method deriving from the scientific spirit, rather than the use of scientific knowledge as such. In this same period, in other areas (for example, in navigation, surveying, and public works), a great deal of more advanced scientific information was widely used, and it is here that we are able to discern the marriage of science and technology. It was not until

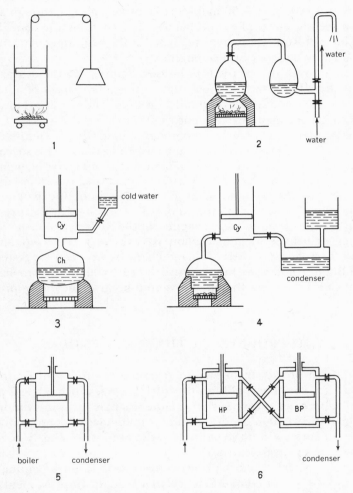

FIG. 42. Various phases in the development of the steam engine, from the end of the seventeenth century to the beginning of the nineteenth century. 1. Production of steam in the cylinder in order to raise the piston (Papin); 2. Production of steam in a boiler. The steam is used in a separate vessel to draw in and force toward the water to be pumped, in an alternating action of intake and condensation of the steam (Savery); 3. Use of steam to raise a piston whose driving stroke is then obtained by condensation in the cylinder (Newcomen); 4. Discharge of steam toward a condenser which is separate from the cylinder (Watt, 1769); 5. Double action of the steam on the two faces of the piston in a completely closed cylinder (Watt, 1784); 6. Use of double expansion of the steam by means of one high-pressure and one low-pressure cylinder (Woolf, 1803).

the first half of the nineteenth century, and especially with the growing use of high-pressure boilers, that the problem of the behavior of steam in engines had its scientific study. The first works to introduce the methods of mathematical physics in the study of heat engines, namely the works of Béthencourt, were still very pragmatic in character.

The generation of English mechanics and engineers who at the time of Watt or immediately after him built the various types of steam engines employed in industry between 1800 and 1850 had little scientific training, though all of them had a special feeling for applied mechanics. In their time, the contributions of Dalton, and later of Rumford, can be regarded as the beginning of a long chain of research that led to a theory of heat engines.

Lastly, though all the credit for the development of the steam engine is generally attributed to Watt, it must not be forgotten that its industrial and commercial success was due to Boulton. It was his qualities as head of a business, his daring and his perseverance that ensured Watt's success.

The special protection obtained from Parliament, which extended the life of the first patents for twenty-five years, was a factor essential to this success. On the other hand, Parliament inhibited improvements that could have been made to the steam engine during that period by Watt's competitors, as well as invention of other types that appeared as soon as the monopoly of the patents expired. Although the types built by Boulton and Watt continued to be produced for almost a half century without basic changes, in the early years of the nineteenth century other principles of construction were in fact perfected and quickly applied in industry. Some of these principles had already been suggested, even by associates of Boulton and Watt, but their use was ruled out by the two manufacturers, who stuck to the models they had invented because they were protected by their patents.

THE PROGRESS OF THE STEAM ENGINE

The evolution of the steam engine after the beginning of the nineteenth century is due first to the use of high-pressure boilers, which made it possible to apply the principle of steam expansion in either a single- or twin-cylinder engine; second, to the improvement of certain important details of construction, such as control of the steam flow and the packing of the pistons; and lastly, to the almost exclusive use of metal instead of wood.

The various aspects of this progress are closely interdependent, for the engine very rapidly increased in efficiency, thanks to the improvement of certain of its controls, progress in the construction of boilers, and the design of less cumbersome forms.

Trevithick's high-pressure engines   As we have seen earlier, Leupold had described in 1724 an engine that utilized a steam pressure higher than atmospheric pressure. The first construction of a high-pressure engine was due to Richard Trevithick, who seems to have begun his experiments around 1797. Trevithick's aim was to build a portable engine that could propel a carriage. For this purpose he created a cylindrical

Plate 2. Rowlandson's drawing of Trevithick's locomotive of 1808. Association of American Railroads

boiler inside of which he placed the firebox. He eliminated the condenser but offset the disadvantages of this by also eliminating the auxiliary pump used to remove water and air. The single-acting cylinder was installed in one end of the boiler so that it was kept hot. Moreover, this engine was one of the first models in which the walking beam was replaced by a crosshead that moved along a slide bar, with a connecting rod that rotated a shaft through a crank. Trevithick's undertaking seems to have encountered a certain number of difficulties. He pursued it, with Andrew Vivian, for several years, and in 1805 made the first experiment with steam traction on a railroad, an event to which we shall return.

Oliver Evans   In Philadelphia at the same time (1804), the engineer Oliver Evans built a high-pressure engine (Figure 43) that operated for several years. It consisted of a vertical double-acting cylinder without a condenser. The piston rod was topped with a connecting rod that turned a crank on the hub of a flywheel. The valve gear consisted of three-way cocks whose opening and closing were controlled by the rotation of the flywheel.

Evans's efforts met with indifference on the part of his compatriots. He seems to have been an inventor with a daring, fertile mind ahead of his time. His shop

Plate 3. Steam engine installed at a coal mine; England, circa 1790. Anonymous painting. Walker Art Gallery, Liverpool. (Photo Walker Art Gallery.)

functioned until 1819, when it was destroyed by fire, while Evans was on his deathbed in New York. In the United States, the construction of steam engines was not to begin its growth until later.

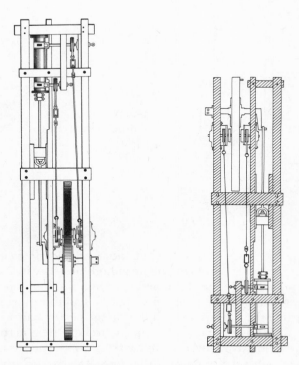

FIG. 43.   High-pressure engine of Oliver Evans. (Diagram from the original drawing by Evans.)

Hornblower's reciprocating compound engine

The first attempt to use the expansion of steam seems to have been by Jonathan Hornblower, who in 1781 took out a patent for a twin-cylinder engine (Figure 44), the conception of which, he claimed, dated from 1776. In fact, this engine relied heavily on the principles that Watt was just then applying. It was a single-acting engine. Steam entered at boiler pressure into the smaller cylinder and by expansion into the large cylinder. The power stroke took place during the descent of the pistons, which received the steam supply from above. The discharge into the condenser took place at the bottom of the large cylinder. In the ascent of the pistons the steam passed from one side of the pistons to the other through side cocks.

At this time Watt was able to oppose the development of this engine. (Somewhat later he himself used the expansion principle in his own engines.) In 1798 Hornblower was granted another patent for a device using the same principle. In the long run, his engine proved to be less efficient than Watt's single-acting engine. Still, the idea of using steam at a relatively high pressure had been conceived simultaneously with the application of the principle of expansion.

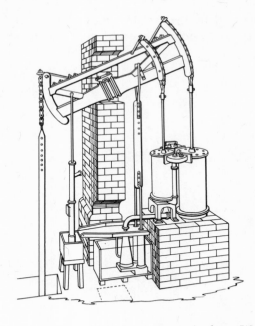

FIG. 44.   Single-acting engine with two cyl-inders, utilizing the expansion of steam. Hornblower, 1781 (from Bataille).

Arthur Woolf   Arthur Woolf adapted Hornblower's process by utilizing steam at high pressure in the smaller cylin-der. The development of Woolf's double-expansion (or compound) engine was laborious. His first patent dates from 1803, but he had to experiment for a long time before adjusting the sizes of the cylinders to the performance required of the steam at various distinct pressures. He appears to have held erroneous concep-tions that prevented him from successfully carrying out the necessary calculations, so it was not until after several failures that he succeeded around 1811 in con-structing a type of engine that made it possible to reduce the fuel consumption by one-half of that required in one of Watt's engines.

The construction of his engine was undertaken in Great Britain. His partner, Edwards, emigrated to France in 1815, and thereafter the Chaillot plants also began to construct these engines (Figure 45). The double-expansion engine seems

FIG. 45. Woolf's double-expansion engine built by Edwards, around 1815 – 1820.

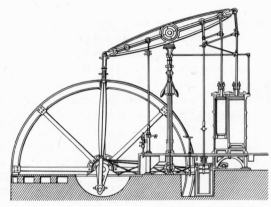

to have met with greater success on the Continent than in Great Britain, where it was late in developing.

Boilers The use of high-pressure steam, whether in single-cylinder engines without a condenser or in twin-cylinder engines, was particularly dependent on the invention of new types of boilers.

Boulton and Watt had put into use a boiler with a large chamber, rectangular in cross section, the top of which was shaped like a dome (Figure 46). The bottom was concave and ensured complete use of the heat from the firebox. Later, cylindrical boilers known either as French boilers or Lancashire boilers were used, and efforts at improvement were concentrated on the water supply and the design of the firebox (Figure 47). During the period from 1825 to 1830, smoke-consumption devices and revolving grates were already beginning to be applied.

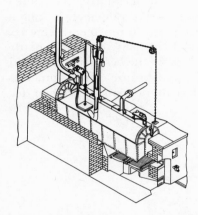

FIG. 46. Domed boiler, of the type built at the beginning of the nineteenth century. (From Tredgold.) (Note the feed system controlled by a float valve.)

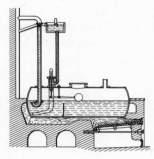

FIG. 47. Cylindrical boiler. Beginning of the nineteenth century. (From Tredgold.)

Beginning in the first quarter of the nineteenth century, several inventors constructed various types of tubular boilers. Woolf in particular had invented a large multiple-tube boiler, which he developed successfully. As we shall see, tubular boilers, and especially those with flues, developed extensively as soon as steam was applied to transportation methods.

Improving the general design of steam engines The evolution of the steam engine after 1800 was concerned with the general design of the classical beam engine, and this development quickly resulted in variations in the supporting structures, the kinds of which rapidly took many forms.

The most important modifications of the beam engine resulted from the introduction of a cast-iron framing on which the various parts of the engine were constructed. This addition, which was quickly adopted, was no doubt invented by

Matthew Murray around 1802. This framework was later changed and expanded along particular lines. Around the middle of the century, all the lower controls for Watt-type engines were encased in an iron chamber mounted on the framework and surrounded by a metal flooring on which workmen could move around.

As soon as cast iron became available at lower prices, the traditional wooden walking beam and columns were replaced by metal. Wrought iron began to be substituted in part for cast iron around 1810 to 1820. But both iron products continued to be employed simultaneously, depending on the type of engine being built and the load to be imposed on the various parts. Around the middle of the nineteenth century, wrought iron and cast iron were used in roughly equal amounts, but later they both gradually gave way to steel.

Around 1840 to 1850, conscious industrial design appeared for the first time in modern technology. Although certain types of atmospheric engines (particularly those in Smeaton's time, and even Watt's engines) achieved a certain elegance of design that was not lacking in grandeur, it was the use of cast iron that made it possible to satisfy a desire for industrial aesthetics that was completely lacking in metallurgical construction during the first quarter of the nineteenth century. Fluted cast-iron columns and their capitals, which formed the pillars of the engines produced by factories after around 1840, offer the best example of this (Figure 48). Even the addition of certain brass and bronze parts—brackets, bearings, lubricators, nameplates—added (perhaps unintentionally) to their decorative effect.

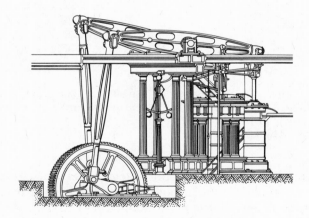

FIG. 48.   200 hp. steam engine driving a winch. About 1850. (From Bataille.)

Output and machining of parts It has not been adequately demonstrated that the growth in the number of steam engines and especially of their types encouraged development in the machining of a great variety of parts. But the situation may have been exactly the opposite, it having been the progress of industrial mechanics that made it possible to develop the steam engine. Not only did the early models of walking beams and connecting rods change rapidly; the invention of new forms for traditional parts and especially of supplemental parts for new uses also continued at an accelerated pace during the first thirty or forty years of the nineteenth century. Axles, clamps, beam supports, couplings, cranks, pulleys, slideways, and bedplates became standardized items in the metalworking shops, permitting manufacturers to make the traditional forms of the engine more flexible and to devise numerous solutions to problems arising when the steam engine was applied to increasingly extensive uses.

The development of pistons Naturally, the engine's basic components also underwent significant development. For example, the shape and especially the construction of the piston were modified to meet the introduction of high pressures. Watt had been obliged to adapt the shape of the piston in single-acting engines to double-acting engines. He used a packing of hemp and tallow, held by a junk ring, which was retained for almost a century in low-pressure engines. In 1797 Edmund Cartwright was the first to use a metal packing, using antifriction metal, and in 1816 John Barton introduced piston rings held against the inner wall of the cylinder by springs (Figure 49).

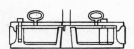 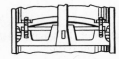 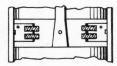

FIG. 49.   Evolution of the piston. *Left to right:* Pistons with hemp jacket, with metal jacket, with rings.

The steam supply Valves and valve gear also stimulated inventors' imaginations. In the earliest engines the inlet and exhaust passages were equipped with cocks whose operation was at first controlled manually; later, drop-type valves operated by tappets were used. The first improvement was suggested by Leupold, whose four-way valve simplified the arrangement of the pipes and cocks. The multiple-cock valve (Figure 50) was employed quite frequently; Maudslay improved its construction, and as late as the nineteenth century Cavé used it in his reciprocating engines.

FIG. 50.   Four-way cock for distribution of steam in a double-acting engine.

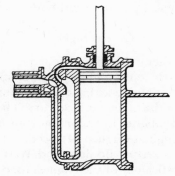

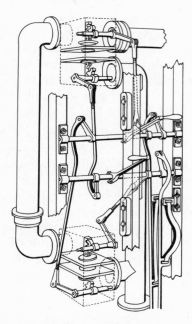

FIG. 51.   Operating rods of the valves in the rotary engine built by Boulton and Watt for the Albion mills in London, 1784. (From Bataille.)

As we have seen, it was Watt who introduced a sophisticated use of valves (Figure 51). The invention of the slide valve by Murdock in 1799 did not eliminate the use of drop valves, which continued to be the best adapted to pumping engines not having a rotating shaft (Figure 52). In 1801 Murray conceived the idea of controlling slide valves, which had an alternating linear movement, by means of an eccentric gear fixed on the shaft of rotating engines. This method was the simplest of those devised, starting for example from the walking beam. Murray also simplified the D valve conceived by Murdock. After him appeared a succession of designs for slide valves adaptable to engines of various capacities and to the expansion and nonexpansion types (Figure 53). The complementary components of the slide valve were developed especially for regulating and reversing locomotives. This subject will be discussed further in the chapter devoted to the early development of railroads.

Cornish engines The beam engine continued to be used especially to pump water and hoist coal and ore from mines. In other industries, other types of engines quickly replaced the beam engine, particularly to economize on floor space.

Single-acting engines continued to be used for drainage until around the end of the nineteenth century. They were designed to achieve the lowest possible cost of operation and maintenance. The development of this type, known as Cornish engines (Figure 54), occurred during the first ten or fifteen years of the century.

After Boulton and Watt had retired from business, it was found that the efficiency of the engines used in the great tin and copper mines of Cornwall was

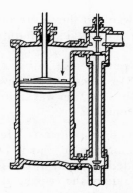
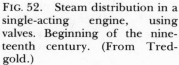
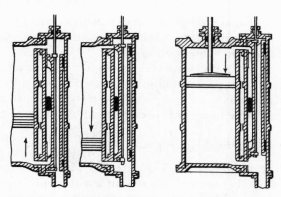

FIG. 52.   Steam distribution in a single-acting engine, using valves. Beginning of the nineteenth century. (From Tredgold.)

FIG. 53.   Steam distribution in a double-acting engine, using slide valves. (From Tredgold.)

lower than it should have been. In 1811 mine owners became concerned about this situation and ordered an inquiry into the operation of their engines. Publication of this report encouraged builders to improve their manufacture. Among them, Woolf and Trevithick made the greatest contribution to the development of heavy-duty pumping engines. The engines giving the best results were condensing engines, which operated at high pressure and by expansion for nine-tenths of the stroke. According to conditions, however, double-acting engines were also employed, and even atmospheric engines remained in use for some time. The

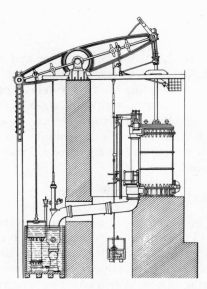

FIG. 54.   Example of Cornish engine built around the middle of the nineteenth century. (From Jullien.)

principal change in these machines was that as time went on they were made increasingly larger. They were almost universally adopted for drainage pumping and water distribution.

Woolf's twin-cylinder engine was not immediately put into use, nor was the plunger piston engine introduced by Trevithick after 1815. These two types were not able to compete with the classic Cornish engine, which in sum was simply a modified and improved version of Watt's single-acting engine.

Maudslay's engines The most important modification was Henry Maudslay's complete elimination of the walking beam around 1807 (Figure 55). The piston rod was guided vertically by two slide bars, between which was an antifriction wheel at each side of the crosshead. At each side of the crosshead there was also a connecting rod that operated the crankshaft beneath the cylinder. This type, known as the table engine, quickly came into widespread use and inspired the development of a series of vertical engines that could be installed easily in a factory building.

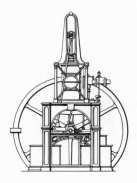

FIG. 55.   Maudslay's engine with vertical cylinder and double connecting rod. After 1807. (From Tredgold)

Short-beam engines of the "grasshopper" type and Maudslay's connecting-rod type were especially designed for steamships.

Maudslay's engine, representing the first widely accepted elimination of the beam in engines, resulted in more direct application of power. Around 1820 to 1830, numerous other models of direct-acting engines were tried more or less successfully by English, French, and American builders, using methods consisting of linking the piston rod directly to a connecting rod the other end of which was connected to the crankshaft.

The oscillating cylinder One engine appearing at this time offered great advantages. Its principle consisted of making the cylinder itself oscillate by having it supported on two trunnions upon which it could pivot. In this way the piston rod, pivoting directly on the crankshaft, made it possible to eliminate the crosshead, guides, and connecting rod.

Murdock had already suggested a device of this type to Boulton and Watt, but it seems that at that time it was difficult to machine trunnions satisfactorily. Moreover, the steam feed had to be adapted to the oscillating cylinder. In 1815 Manby secured a patent for such a device.

Joseph Maudslay (the son of Henry) and John Penn overcame the principal difficulties, and practicable engines began to be installed around 1827, at first in small cargo ships. Later they were being built with a power of several hundred hp. for large steamships.

In France this type of engine received special attention after 1825, Cavé building 120 between 1830 and 1840 (Figure 56).

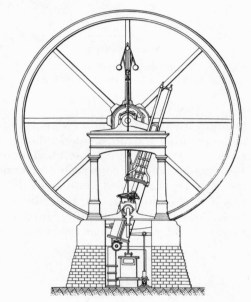

FIG. 56.   Engine with oscillating cylinder, built by Cavé. Around 1830. (From Jullien.) Distribution of steam is done through the axis of oscillation of the cylinder.

The oscillating engine continued to be used extensively until around 1850, but as it was relatively fragile and subject to heavy wear and tear its popularity declined after that date.

Horizontal engines

Normal development led to engines with horizontal cylinders, which appeared during the first quarter of the nineteenth century. William Symington was probably the first to construct such an engine (in 1802), whose external appearance suggested that of Henry Maudslay's vertical engine. However, for all practical purposes the horizontal engine (Figure 57) was not built before 1825. It found its most obvious use in railroad locomotives, and it was during the second quarter of the nineteenth century that it began to be put to effective use. Its employment in factories as a stationary engine did not become significant until around the middle of the century.

Experiments with rotating engines

At that period the types constructed had run the gamut from the vertical engine to the horizontal one by way of a certain number with inclined cylinders. It should be pointed out that from the end of the eighteenth century numerous attempts were made to apply steam to rotating engines. By this should

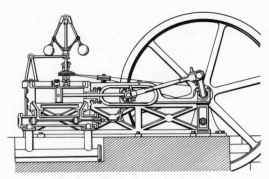

FIG. 57.   Example of horizontal industrial engine, with crankshaft and connecting rod. Built around 1828 by Taylor. (From Armengaud.)

be understood that inventors were trying to use steam not to operate a piston but to cause either a drum-shaped cylinder or a paddle wheel within a cylinder to revolve on its axle. Watt himself had mentioned this method of using steam in his 1769 patent, and he constructed several prototypes (Figure 58). These experiments were abandoned because of difficulties in construction and operation, which the methods of the time did not allow him to overcome. After him, Hornblower in 1798 and 1807, Murdock in 1799, and a certain number of other English builders made many experiments in succeeding years.

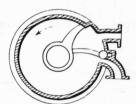

FIG. 58.   Diagram of Watt's rotary engine.

Thus, during the first half of the nineteenth century numerous models of rotating engines appeared one after the other, after applying very different principles, but for all practical purposes they did not find continuous application in industry during this period.

THE STEAM ENGINE IN FRANCE

Newcomen's steam engine became known in France some fifteen years after its appearance. During the eighteenth century its use was to grow, but very slowly. On the other hand, Watt's first engines were received around 1780 with a great deal of curiosity. These were single-acting types and, for reasons discussed later, familiarity with double-acting rotating engines came only just before the French Revolution. Until 1815, circumstances for their introduction were unfavorable,

Plate 4. The Chaillot steam pump in 1781, at the time of installation. Watercolor by Matthaus Halm. French National Library, Print Collection. (Photo Ph. Brossé - P. U. F.)

for two reasons: industry was hardly flourishing and war and national policy obviously restricted industrial exchanges with England. Moreover, the small number of French builders at the time prevented large-scale development. After 1815, industrial and commercial contacts with England were resumed, and France quickly set about making up for lost time. This was accomplished by the early years of the reign of Louis-Philippe. Important theoretical and technical innovations were to occur during this period.

The atmospheric engine (1726–1779) — In 1726 two Englishmen, May and Meyer, installed a steam pump at Passy. One Bosfrond may have installed a second one at Cachan the following year. Although approved by the Académie des Sciences, their success seems to have been short lived.

The first genuinely useful practical application occurred in 1732 at the Fresnes mine near Condé. The name of one Pierre Mathieu is vaguely associated with this engine. It is not certain whether he built it himself, based on observations made in England, or if he may have employed an Englishman to build it. In any event, the engine was described in 1737 by Belidor in his *Architecture hydraulique*.

In that same year an engine was installed at the Anzin (Nord) collieries, and another was put in service in 1749 at the Littry collieries eight miles from Bayeux. By 1753 three engines were working at the mines of Saint-Georges-Chatelaison in Anjou, followed by ones in Montrelais (not far from Ancenis) and Aniche. In Flanders such engines were used after 1763 near Dunkirk to drain water from the polders. By 1756 the number of engines at Anzin had increased to four.

It appears that by 1750 it was possible to build these engines successfully in France. We know the name of one shop, that of Nicolas Focq of Maubeuge.

In royal residences, small steam-powered pumps were used to supply water to parks and gardens. We may sum up the situation by saying that these installations remained few and scattered, but interest in the invention was in general very keen in circles that prided themselves on being enlightened.

Attempts at improvements or simplification followed, such as those suggested by Moura and Gensanne in 1740 and 1744. There were also premature attempts to apply the engine to locomotion and navigation, details of which will be found in another chapter: Cugnot's steam wagon (1770), and steam boats by d'Auxiron (1773), Jacques-Constantin Périer (1775), and Claude Jouffroy d'Abbans (1778 and 1783).

The condensing engine (1779–1781)

Jacques-Constantin Périer (1742–1818) attempted in 1775 to apply Newcomen's engine to a boat. It was he who was to introduce into France the new steam engine that Watt had in the meantime completely transformed.

Périer and his brother and collaborator Augustin Charles were mechanics in the service of the duke of Orléans and were on familiar terms with the duke and his son, the duke of Chartres. At a very early date Périer had become interested in steam engines and had in particular closely followed d'Auxiron's 1773 experiments. After his own failure he undoubtedly felt that the time was not ripe for steam navigation (which was very true), and he conceived a project for supplying Paris with water by means of steam pumps. Here he was back in safe territory, since such an installation had already been operating in London for some time.

At first Périer planned to use Newcomen engines only. But during a visit in the fall of 1777 to John Wilkinson's factory at Broseley to order some cast-iron pipe he learned of Watt's engine and of the 75 percent savings in fuel it made possible.

Périer attempted to acquire one through Wilkinson, who was not so stupid as to infringe upon a patent which had just been extended by a special law. Wilkinson contacted Watt, and Périer then needed only to communicate with him. Making use of contacts in France, Watt quickly was granted a fifteen-year license for that country, in April 1778. Finally Périer, who had returned to England, negotiated with Watt and Boulton in February 1779.

Delivery was made in the following months, the special parts being made at Soho while the remainder of the engine was built on the spot at Chaillot, the site of the future steam engine and the place to which Périer had moved his entire mechanical engineering enterprise in the fall of 1778. The engine began operating successfully in August 1781 and continued to do so until the time of the Second Empire. It was a single-acting steam engine with a cylinder 63 inches in diameter, making 10 strokes a minute, and capable of lifting 57,600 hogsheads of water to a height of 110 feet in 24 hours. A second similar engine was soon installed next to the first one.

Watt and Boulton had asked £24,000 for the rights to use the two engines, with an equal amount to be paid upon each issue of stock by the Compagnie des Eaux. In actual fact the sum of £48,000 was paid, which was very little, given that Watt and Boulton usually asked for a rent equal to the value of the coal saved by their engine.

Périer never claimed to have invented condensing engines, but he immediately began to build them, disregarding the 1778 license. For this reason Watt and Boulton, who came to France in 1786, filed claims that in fact came to nothing, but the exact nature of them has been misunderstood. Moreover, it should be pointed out that, given the international practices of the period, such behavior does not indicate any particular unscrupulousness on the part of the French engineer but shows, on the contrary, his feeling of a civic duty to be performed.

The Chaillot foundry　　The Chaillot foundry, thus created by chance, was to become the first large French mechanical engineering shop. Driving power was supplied to the foundry by a steam pump that fed overshot wheels, the classical method used during the period prior to the double-acting engine.

Chaillot's production was at first concentrated on steam engines, but all the usual large-scale foundry work was later added. During the French Revolution Chaillot was the primary producer of artillery, employing up to two hundred workers. During Watt's 1786 visit he was unable to conceal his admiration and admitted that Périer made steam engines quite well.

The nature of Chaillot's production necessitated developing certain machine tools practically unknown in France until then. Near the classic tilt hammer and two large lathes, the Chaillot installation is said to have included a machine for boring cylinders, a precision lathe for the rollers of the rolling mill, and lastly a multiple-boring machine for cannons. Having perfected the technique of boring, the Périer brothers succeeded in performing it in a single operation. At Chaillot there were also subsidiary shops for cabinetwork and boilermaking. At the height of the Terror, during the time when artillery was being produced as a matter of patriotism, people came to admire the foundry's traveling crane, which was regarded as a masterpiece of ingenuity.

Among the notable achievements at Chaillot, mention should be made of other single-acting steam engines installed at Le Gros-Caillou several years after the original ones; a steam drill press for Indret; later, all the machines for the Oberkampf establishment at Jouy; a submarine and a steam engine for Fulton; the first French hydraulic presses, and so on.

Le Creusot foundry, whose first pig was cast in December 1785, had been created under the name of Périer-Bettinger & Company. The equipment certainly owed a great deal to Périer. In any case, Chaillot supplied the rolling mills. Steam engines played an important role in the new foundry, being installed to pump out nearby mines as well as to operate blowing machines for the blast furnaces. Waterwheels were used for the boring machines, but for the tilt hammers an attempt was made to obtain direct rotation from the single-acting engine, using large-diameter flywheels. The experiment failed, and it was necessary to return to the waterwheel. It seems clear that one of the Le Creusot steam engines did not come from Chaillot but was purchased from Watt. It is certain, in any event, that, all told, Watt filled only two orders for France prior to 1800, one being the 1779 order already mentioned and the other being for a foundry whose name is not known.

Prior to 1783 the abbot of Arnal had installed steam mills at Nîmes, using an engine supplied by Périer. Here again it was merely a question of pumping water to operate a waterwheel.

The double-acting rotating engine (1788–1790)

As we have seen, the need to obtain rotational movement was becoming increasingly urgent in industry. In addition to metallurgy and flour milling there were spinning mills, which were expanding greatly in this period. Watt had solved the problem in 1783/84, but after that date he refused to reveal any information to foreigners.

A scientist, the marquis de Béthencourt, having been politely shown the door at Soho in 1788, apparently decided to play the part of an industrial spy. Having observed over the top of a wall the operation of an already installed engine, he guessed its principle and communicated his conclusions to the Académie des Sciences, in a paper supported by illustrations, in December 1789. Périer was a friend of the marquis and was certainly already in on the secret, for in April he had requested and obtained a license to build steam mills in the Paris area. In 1790 he installed a steam-operated flour mill with the first double-acting rotating engines built in France. Needless to say, they had been built in the Chaillot shops.

The first French cotton mill to have a steam engine was the mill built after 1787 by Foxlow at Orléans, for the duke of Orleans. The engine was not installed until 1791. This application nevertheless remained exceptional. At the Saint-Lubin spinning mill, which Périer himself founded during the French Revolution, the river Avre continued to be the only source of power.

Stagnation during the Revolutionary and Empire periods

The last years of the *ancien régime* had already been poor years for the Périer brothers, speculators having gained control of the stock of the Compagnie des Eaux. During the Revolution, progress ground to a complete halt. The mill installations undoubtedly continued to operate, but though the gun machinery proliferated, it was at the expense of the other equipment, which was converted to weapons production. In any case, no new engines were built, and some, like those at Montrelais, were abandoned.

During the Directory and Consulate periods, such publications as the *Journal des Mines* and the *Annales des Arts et Manufactures,* soon joined by the *Bulletin de la Société d'Encouragement pour l'industrie nationale,* sought to make English prototypes better known. This was difficult, since their documentation was reduced to sources that were deliberately vague, such as *Nicholson's Journal* and others. Various French inventors suggested new systems, but they had had little experience and consequently met with little success.

Yet there remained a need for a small engine, which was to lead later to the appearance of the internal combustion engine. In 1806 the Société d'Encouragement opened a competition for a small engine to deliver about 7,235,000 foot-

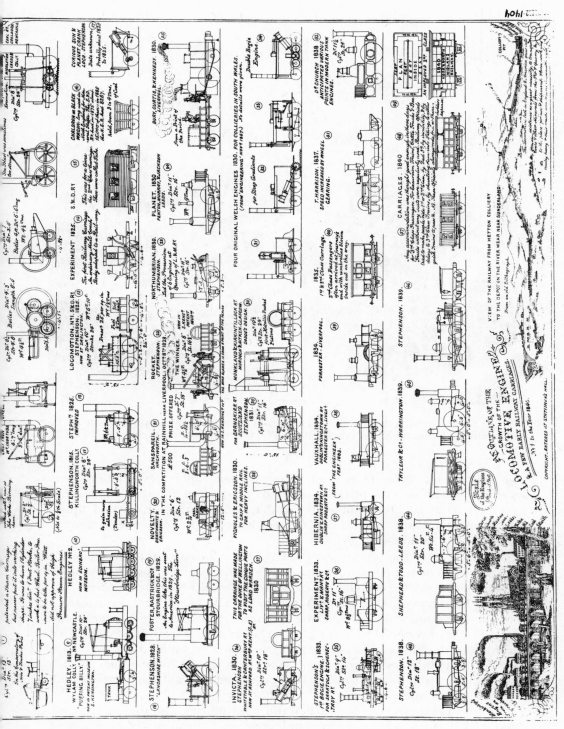

Plate 5. An outline of the growth of the locomotive engine, 1771–1840. Drawing by T. West, 1886. Library of Congress

Plate 6.   General view of the foundry at Le Creusot, circa 1806. By the kind permission of the Société des Forges et Ateliers du Creusot. (Photo Forges et Ateliers du Creusot.)

pounds of work in 12 hours, at a cost of no more than 7.50 francs. Charles Albert and Louis Martin won the prize in 1809. The production of this engine was not successful, because of the economic crisis that heralded the end of the Empire. Like many others, the builder, Albert, went bankrupt in 1812. The mechanic, Martin, will be mentioned later.

At the turn of the century the Périer brothers invented their machine for hoisting coal, a new application of the double-acting engine. Until then winches operated by horse-driven whims had been used, for which Anzin maintained four hundred horses, at a cost of 200,000 francs annually. The Périers constructed a very useful engine without a walking beam, by employing the system of two toothed wheels invented by Cartwright, instead of a crankshaft. In 1800 the first coal-hoisting machine was installed at the Littry collieries; a second was installed in 1802, an example followed first by Anzin, then by others. At Anzin twenty-one pits were equipped with this device in 1810. At this time Périer claimed to have built more than forty units.

Despite these efforts, the situation did not compare with that in England. Around 1810 the number of engines in France was estimated to be hardly more than about two hundred, the majority of which came of course from Chaillot.

Unfortunately, this establishment was never to recover the prosperity of its early years. For a long time its main work had been filling government orders, for which virtually no payments were made. An 1808 contract to install steam pumps at Marly came to nothing, because Périer was unable to deliver the engines. In succeeding years, however, he received several advances, totaling 600,000 francs. Old, ill, and disillusioned, Périer did not sell his factory until a few months before his death, practically a ruined man, in 1818.

Other shops were opened from time to time. We have little information about their business, which must have remained very limited. There was one such establishment at Beauchamp (Haute-Saône), which was managed by Ramus, a former official at Le Creusot, and another at Choisy-sur-Seine, managed by Courrejollet. Boury, a pupil of Périer who established himself in Lyon, built double-acting engines for drainage and hoisting in mines.

Practice and theory at the time of the Restoration   The engines built until 1815 were not only very few in number but were also of a completely outdated type not appreciably different from those being built by Watt some thirty years earlier. The improvement of using only metal in their construction remained unknown. Some major innovations—the eccentric gear, the slide valve, and the centrifugal governor—were perhaps not completely unknown: Martin had tried a slide valve supply system in his 1809 engine, and Hachette had described the governor in 1811, but it can be said that these devices continued to be disregarded.

The situation changed immediately after the fall of the Empire. The first major event was the arrival in France in 1815 of the Englishman Edwards, Woolf's former collaborator, who after several years took over the Chaillot shops. He brought with him a double-expansion engine and soon built several hundred examples. Edwards became a naturalized French citizen. The Anzin collieries purchased a part of his patent from him and established an engine shop.

Several years afterward two other builders, Aitken and Steel, settled in Paris and opened a shop at La Gare, where they constructed triple-expansion engines equipped with Brunton's smokeless firebox. This system does not seem to have been a great success. Aitken and Steel also built the low-pressure, double-acting engines developed by Watt. Another shop, opened near Charenton by Manby Wilson, was also constructing these engines.

These shops also supplied the Trevithick high-pressure engines without condensers. Cordier and Casalis, former pupils at the École des Arts et Métiers in Chalôns, attempted to perfect the system, simplifying it by eliminating the double-acting principle.

In 1828 the smallest engines were of 2 hp. Those built according to the Watt specifications by Aitken cost 7,300 francs, the compound engines turned out by Edwards's factory cost 8,500 francs, and Aitken's triple-expansion engines cost 12,000 francs. The high-pressure Trevithick-type engines cost 6,600 francs. The highest-powered engines (120 hp.) cost 129,000 francs for the Watt-system engines supplied by Aitken, 130,000 francs for the double-expansion engines of Edwards, 149,000 francs for the triple-expansion engines of Aitken and Steel, and 127,000 francs for the Trevithick-system engines. Here we can see the first signs of competition.

Under the Restoration, plans for a steam pump for Marly, which had remained in abeyance under the Empire, came to a head. The engine installed under Louis XIV was stopped at the end of August 1817 and temporary pumps were put into service. A new design was presented in 1818 and accepted in 1820. Meanwhile, the mechanic entrusted with the construction (the same Louis Martin who had been awarded a prize by the Société d'Encouragement in 1809) had in 1819 toured English factories in the company of Hachette, an instructor at the École Polytechnique, and Cécile, director of the Marly waterworks. The new engine, of the Watt type, was built at Le Creusot in 1823, and the new installation at Marly was completed in 1826.

It was also under the Restoration that the first theoretical research was done in France on the operation of heat engines. This is not the place to discuss either the content or the fate, with its incalculable consequences, of the treatise published by Sadi Carnot in 1824 under the title *Réflexions sur la puissance motrice du feu*. On the other hand, these experiments on the expansive force of steam should be mentioned as belonging more specifically to the field of technology.

Béthencourt seems to have been the first to concern himself with measuring the elastic force of steam as a function of temperature. He designed a simple apparatus and presented some results of his research to the Academy in 1790. Dalton took up the same project in 1802 and drew up a table which, though very complete, dealt only with temperatures between 0° and 100°C.

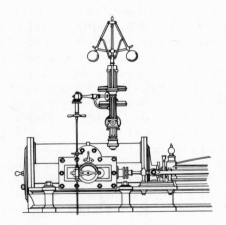

FIG. 59.   Farcot's variable-expansion engine. (From Armengaud.)

At first the use of boilers was unregulated. Then, on October 29, 1823, Louis XVIII approved an ordinance, the first of its kind, requiring a preliminary hydraulic test at five times the pressure normally used, the affixing of a copper test plate supplied by the mint, and installation of safety plugs that would melt at a temperature corresponding to the test plate on the boiler.

It then was realized that these temperatures were unknown. The Academy was consulted and it ordered the famous series of tests carried out by Arago and Dulong, the results of which were published in November 1829. The two physi-

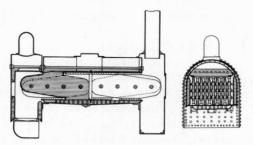

FIG. 60. Hallette's boiler. Patent of October 9, 1835. Shaded areas indicate the sections filled with water. This drawing from the patent shows a locomotive boiler, but the Hallette boiler was applied to stationary engines.

cists made measurements effective up to a pressure of 24 atmospheres, for which they found a temperature of 224.2°C.

By 1830 it had become possible to build some fifty steam engines a year in France. At that time there were in the country only seventy-one steam boats in all—tugboats, packets, and cargo boats. During the reign of Louis-Philippe, the development under way for the past fifteen years entered an accelerated phase. The number of builders increased so considerably that it becomes impossible to think of mentioning them all.

One of the most important was Joseph Farcot, who on October 22, 1836, patented the first steam-supply system embodying the idea of variable expansion using a governor (Figure 59). This invention is often ascribed to Corliss, who rediscovered it independently in the United States some ten years later but whose engine did not become well known in Europe until the reign of Napoleon III. In 1835 the Hallette boiler (Figure 60) appeared, to remain in use until after 1850, with the appearance of the Belleville multiple-tube explosionproof steam generator (Figure 61). On the other hand, a machine as convenient as the steam-

FIG. 61. Belleville's multiple-tube boiler (from the patent of 1850). In the upper portion can be seen the complete network of tubes. In the lower portion are the tube sections with their junction boxes.

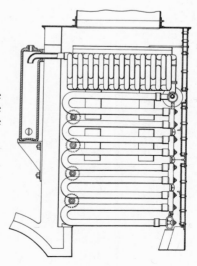

powered carriage remained completely unknown; Calla did not introduce it into England until after 1851.

In 1852 France had 6,080 engines, with a total power of 75,518 hp. In the following decade their number increased to 22,513, with a total power of 617,890 hp. In reality, then, providing industry with power was the work of the Second Empire, but between 1815 and 1850 France unveiled and developed several ideas most significant for the future adaptation of steam power. It is nevertheless true that on the whole this first half century, technically speaking, appears more as a prolongation of the eighteenth century than as the beginning of a new era. This new epoch began after 1850.

The period between 1830 and 1850 also witnessed the birth of railroads and the real beginnings of steam navigation. These applications posed problems in adapting engines to their new roles. The result was numerous improvements and a more rapid development of engines. Further details of this process will be found in a later chapter.

CHAPTER 3

MECHANICAL POWER AND ITS MEASUREMENT

Theory and practice   The construction and use of steam engines gradually brought to the forefront of the engineers' and
manufacturers' preoccupations new ideas whose nature and importance could not
until then have been suspected. The source of mechanical power now available to
industry was the first to be created entirely by man, who constantly sought a means
to control it completely and to direct it according to his needs and will. Even before
the fiftieth anniversary of Newcomen's first heat engine, engineers had already
realized that empirical methods were no longer sufficient. It was becoming necessary for them to invent methods of measurement and techniques of calculation
that would enable them to use these measurements not only to control the
operation of the engine but also to conceive effective improvements.

It has frequently been said that the steam engine inaugurated the modern
age, in which science and technology were becoming increasingly complementary.
This is correct, but in a sense exactly contrary to the one generally given it. It was
not science that brought forth, or even simply aided, the various inventions that
made it possible to use steam as a power source. Rather it was the experience of
these inventions that led to the birth and development of a new field for scientific
exploration.

Throughout the eighteenth century a long series of efforts had been made by
a growing number of technicians to extract the basic ideas that would serve as a
basis for mathematical procedures adaptable to this new field. But these procedures remained too rudimentary during this time to be a very effective system,
and so the progress of steam engines was attained almost exclusively through trial
and error.

The science of thermodynamics, the genesis of which is outlined in Renée
Taton's *Science in the Twentieth Century* (London: Thames and Hudson, 1966), was
born during the first half of the nineteenth century only after the use of heat
engines became general. Not until the following half century did it become a
reliable guide for building engines.

Newcomen's rule   For more than a century the steam engine was used
almost exclusively to operate water pumps. It had
been built for this purpose, and when it became necessary to define the work
capacity of the first examples, it seemed obvious to evaluate it in terms of the
weight of water that could be lifted within a given period of time. It was necessary

81

to take into account the variables—the diameter of the cylinder, the stroke of the piston in length and time, and the pressure exerted on it—in order to try to calculate how the power would vary when one or more of these characteristics was modified.

The first attempts were made with the help of arbitrary formulas. We do not know how Newcomen established the rule he used, described by Désaguliers, probably on the testimony of Beighton.

> From the Diameter [of the cylinder] squar'd he cut off the last Figure, calling the Figure on the left Hand long Hundreds, and writing a Cypher on the right Hand, call'd the Number on that Side, Pounds; and this he reckon'd pretty exact as a Mean, or rather when the Barometer stood at 30 and the Air was Heavy.

As enigmatic as this method of evaluation may seem, we find in it two ideas that were to be retained for a long time for atmospheric engines.

The round inch   The first is that of the square of the diameter of the cylinder divided by ten. In the conceptions of that time, and in terms of the English system of measurement, Newcomen was thus dividing the cylinder's cross section into ten "round inches" and expressing the pressure exerted on the piston in "long Hundreds" per round inch. A pressure of 12 pounds per round inch corresponded to a pressure of 15.3 pounds per square inch.

The round inch was probably used in calculations for only a few decades. In the periods of Smeaton and Watt it seems to have been no longer taken into consideration. However, in his *Treatise on the Steam Engine,* published in 1827, John Farey regrets that the square inch was commonly substituted for it: "The area of the cylinder in round inches can be obtained merely by squaring the diameter of the circle in inches . . . but if we ask for the area in square inches, the square of the diameter must be multiplied by 0.7854." This remark is characteristic of the empiricism that still governed all calculations on the steam engine and was not to disappear completely for a long time to come.

Pressure on the piston   The second idea is that of the pressure exerted on the piston. In Newcomen's engine atmospheric pressure powered the driving stroke, which had to overcome all the loads brought to bear on the surface of the piston: the weight of the water to be lifted, the inertia of the walking beam, the residual pressure of uncondensed steam and, especially, the friction between all moving parts of the engine and the water pumps. Newcomen's estimates, which added 25 to 33 percent to his calculations for friction, were too high. The mechanic Beighton, one of the first to develop the heat engine shortly after it was put into effective operation, defined the load on the piston at 8 pounds per square inch. This figure, later the object of numerous experiments and long discussions, was reduced to 7 and even 6 pounds. During the extended experiments Smeaton performed in 1767 with his first small 1-hp. engine, he found a value for this pressure that was close to Beighton's, and he chose the figure of 7½ pounds. Later, for their 1778 condensing engines Watt and Boulton adopted the figure of 7 pounds per square inch.

Methods of calculating power as a function of the several factors remained very imprecise for some forty years. For a time, calculations were made solely in terms of the diameter of the cylinder and the dimensions of the pumps, ignoring the number of strokes per minute and the length of the stroke. Thus it was impossible to calculate the quantity of water lifted to a given height in a given time, which according to Farey is "the exact measure of the mechanical power of a machine."

John Smeaton was the first to introduce a certain system into these calculations, the formula for which still remained quite complex. He made experiments on several atmospheric engines in order to determine their output, which he estimated from the amount of fuel consumed to raise a certain quantity of water to a given height.

In an engine with a cylinder 10 inches (254 mm.) in diameter and with a stroke of 3 feet (915 mm.), he found that by burning one bushel (84 pounds) of coal he could lift 2,919,017 pounds of water to a height of 1 foot. Horsepower was still unknown as a unit of work, but it has been calculated that Smeaton's results correspond to a consumption of 55 pounds per horsepower-hour.

In his big Long Benton engine, Smeaton found an available power corresponding to approximately 40 hp., with an actual pressure on the piston of 7½ pounds per square inch. The boiler produced 7.88 pounds of steam for each pound of fuel.

The output of the engines built before Smeaton was extremely variable. In 1787, on 57 engines in use near Newcastle, Smeaton found an average output of 5,590,000 pounds lifted to a height of one foot with one bushel of coal, with a maximum of 7,444,000 and a minimum of 3,220,000 pounds, which in pounds of coal per horsepower corresponds to a maximum of 50.7 pounds, a minimum of 22 pounds, and an average of 29.32 pounds.

In the appendix to Price's *Mineralogia cornubiensis* (1778), we read that

> The invention by Mr. Newcomen of the heat engine has enabled us to give our mines a depth double that which could be attained with all the other machines . . . but the enormous consumption of fuel by these engines absorbs a great portion of the profits of our mines, for each heat engine of any size burns 3,000 pounds of coal a year. . . . This is an expenditure so great that it is practically prohibitive.

But Smeaton had already succeeded in decreasing the consumption of coal by one-half.

In 1772 he published a table giving the equivalent of all the characteristics that would have to be calculated to build and operate engines with cylinders having diameters between 10 and 72 inches: the dimensions of the cylinder, movement of the piston, characteristics of the boiler, conditions under which water was to be injected, the quantity of coal used per hour, and lastly the mechanical power.

In calculating the last factor he introduced a unit known as the cylindrical inch foot, equivalent to 0.341 pounds of water; that is, the quantity of water lifted one foot per minute by a cylinder one inch in diameter. For example, the power of an engine having a cylinder with a 52-inch diameter and which made 11½ strokes per minute with a piston stroke of 7 feet 4 inches was 4,104,672 cyl.-in.-ft. per minute.

Although in principle Smeaton's tables were used to determine one factor in relation to the others, their special purpose was to estimate the consumption of coal as a function of the engine's power. In Smeaton's table there is one column giving the consumption of coal per hour (7.4 bushels in the case of the 52-inch engine) and another giving the work done per minute for a consumption of one bushel per hour—555,000 cyl.-in.-ft. in the example given.

The consumption of coal It is easily seen that these figures were not simple to handle. In addition, calculations were all the more uncertain because the weight of the bushel varied according to the place and time, and the quality of the coal had to be taken into consideration. In Smeaton's time the weight of the bushel was 88 pounds, but several years later it was only 84 pounds.

Smeaton drew up his table of fuel consumption on the basis of the best Newcastle coal. In 1778 Boulton and Watt used Wednesbury coal for their calculations, but when they began to deliver engines to Cornish mines they suggested a bushel of Swansea coal as the basis for comparison.

We have seen that Boulton and Watt based their royalties for the pumping engine with a condenser on the savings in coal as compared with that of an atmospheric engine, so that after 1778 the problem of valuing the coal burned for a given amount of work became more important.

The comparisons made by Watt were with atmospheric engines in use before the improved types built by Smeaton after 1772. Smeaton himself made highly detailed observations intended to promote Watt's engine, which he regarded as an extremely useful invention. He found that it consumed half as much coal as his own engines at Long Benton and Chasewater. Since at equal power the latter themselves consumed half as much coal as an ordinary atmospheric engine, the actual economy obtained by Watt was 75 percent.

In 1778 Watt expected to lift with his condensing engine 500,000 cubic feet of water to a height of one foot, with a consumption of one hundredweight (112 English pounds avoirdupois) of Wednesbury coal. But the experiments demonstrated that his forecasts were too optimistic.

In the same year, Boulton gave the following rule for calculating the consumption of coal: figure the volume in cubic feet of the space traversed at each stroke of the piston, and multiply this volume by the pressure in pounds avoirdupois per square inch of the piston. The result will be the weight of coal in pounds that will be consumed during 1,800 strokes of the engine. Assuming a pressure of 7 pounds per square inch, this rule gives a quantity of approximately 21.75 million pounds of water lifted one foot by a bushel of coal.

In its form and in the manner by which it was fixed, this rule was not far removed from those used for several decades before this. During the first thirty years of the nineteenth century similar rules, derived from the same empiricism, were used to calculate the power of the atmospheric single- and double-acting engines with a condenser.

Horsepower as a unit of power

However, when double-acting engines began to be built, a definition of their power became more important than an estimate of the comparative fuel consumption. The first engines were sold to London breweries, which were using horse-driven whims. Watt was asked to tell his future clients exactly how many horses the engine would replace. He then carried out several experiments and discovered that a horse of a given breed moving at an average speed of 2½ miles per hour could lift 150 pounds to a height of 220 feet per minute by means of a rope over a pulley. Watt calculated that the power supplied corresponded to raising 33,000 pounds (528 cubic feet) of water to a height of one foot in a minute. In 1784 Boulton and Watt suggested this as the unit of power under the name *horsepower*.

Doubts about horsepower

The very idea of horsepower and its value was long disputed. As this figure exceeded by about one-third the power of a real horse, for which the figure of 22,000 rather than 33,000 pounds was given, long discussions ensued. Boulton and Watt replied that they had made their experiments with the strongest horses used in the breweries. They also attempted to use the argument that horses could not work more than eight hours per day, whereas in theory the engine's working time was unlimited, which justified adopting a higher value for the unit.

The value of the horsepower given by Boulton and Watt was not published in a printed text until 1805. This value, reduced to one second, became 33,000/60 = 550 pounds lifted one foot in one second. The value of 542.6 pounds was also used during the first half of the nineteenth century in England. In France too, for a long time, builders adopted varying values for horsepower. Not until around 1850 was it generally accepted as being equal to 75 kilogram-meters/second (instead of 76, for the sake of simplification). However, the problem had not yet been definitively settled, as we are about to see.

Calculating power

The power (F) developed on the piston of an alternating engine is arrived at by:

Area of the piston × Speed × Average Pressure on the piston or, in terms of the number of revolutions (in minutes):

(1)
$$F = \frac{\pi}{4} \times D^2 \times C \times \frac{N}{60} \times p$$

With his unit of 33,000 foot-pounds per minute, Watt arrived at a very simple formula for calculating the power of his engines. He took the average pressure of 7 pounds per square inch of piston surface, which gave him (with the diameter of the piston measured in inches) the speed of the piston (V) in feet per minute:

$$7 \; \frac{\frac{1}{4}\pi \; D^2 V}{33,000}$$

by adopting the approximate value of $\pi = 22/7$

$$\frac{7 \times 22/7 \times D^2V}{4 \times 33,000} = \frac{D^2V}{6,000}$$

and in seconds: D^2V^1 (V^1 being the piston speed in feet per second).

In metric units, this would be $\frac{100}{3.491}$ D^2 C N p, in hp. of 75 kgm. In Watt's engines operating on atmospheric pressure,

$$p = 0.4919$$

The formula for power became:

(2) $$F = \frac{D^2 \, C \, N}{0.592} \text{ for one cylinder}$$

Watt had agreed that atmospheric pressure should not be exceeded in the boilers, and the engine operated solely on the vacuum of the condenser: the value of 0.4919 was the average ordinate of the diagram taken from the indicator with the expansion generally accepted.

Nominal horsepower   When the pressure in the boilers is raised, the mean pressure "p" on the piston increases. If formula (2) is always used, it becomes incorrect as a statement of the power in hp. of 75 kgm.

It would continue to be correct if a higher unit were used. Thus, the term *nominal horsepower* has been established for the hp. given by formula (2), which had a fixed number for the average pressure on the piston, despite a higher pressure "p," and while retaining formula (2), which is independent of the actual pressure "p."

Formula (2) indicates what was then called nominal horsepower. For example, let us consider a Second Empire ship—the *Louis XIV*—whose engine had the following characteristics:

$$D = 1.759 \text{ meters} \quad C = 1.065 \quad p^1 = 1.119 \text{ kg.} \quad N = 53$$

Its power in hp. of 75 kgm/s. is 679.7; that is, 680 hp. The application of formula (2) gives us: Nominal power = 296.4 nominal hp.; thus, in this case the nominal hp. would have an actual power of $\frac{680}{296.4} = 229$ kgm/s.

As steam pressure rose in the boilers, nominal hps. of between 150 and 200 kgm/s. were obtained, whence the confusion that persists in all documents bearing only the words, "Engine of X . . . nominal hp.," without any indication of the equivalent power of these horses.

To avoid error, official documents often indicated (in addition to the nominal power) "power in horses of 75 kgm." (consequently, different from the nominal power), or power indicated, which signifies that the pressure on the piston was measured by means of this indicator, showing that formula (1) had been applied with the real (indicated) pressure. It was thus a power in horses of 75 kgm.

This continual variation in the nominal hp. (100 to 300) also prevented any one power from being declared official. Around 1870 it was finally decided that henceforth only horses of 75 kgm. would be used, in order to avoid ambiguity, but they were not accorded a definite official character.

Auxiliary equipment   As the construction of the steam engine improved, the number of its component parts multiplied, which to a certain extent gradually simplified and clarified the construction. In addition to the mechanical parts of the machine as such and the necessary corrections, engineers and manufacturers found themselves obliged by the last quarter of the eighteenth century either to invent or to adapt appliances for control, measurement, and safety. The manner in which the operating principle, and the design of these devices evolved is in itself as characteristic of the progress of industrial technology as are the great moments of creative invention.

It can reasonably be asked to what extent the absence of these small improvements slowed down the development of the steam engine in the period between Newcomen and Watt, and whether the appearance of this equipment was due simply to the major inventions of the century or to a state of maturity reached by the engineering industries. It is certain that by creating new needs, the steam engine considerably accelerated the development of complementary activities in the first half of the nineteenth century. The capacity for machine finishing was being developed and strengthened, leading to rapid abandonment of craft methods and calling upon the inventive spirits of a constantly growing number of mechanics.

It is not possible here to review all the inventions of secondary importance that, beginning around 1780, constantly provided new impetus for the evolution of the steam engine. Two or three examples suffice to pinpoint more precisely the direction of this evolution.

The counter   In order to determine a relationship between the work performed by a pumping engine and the fuel consumed, it was indispensable to know the number of piston strokes made in a certain period of time. For this purpose Watt attached a counter to the walking beam. Its construction and improvement were inspired by indicators used on certain odometers in which toothed wheels meshed and caused needles to move around dials indicating tens, hundreds, and thousands of revolutions. The wheels' movement was operated at each stroke by the oscillations of a small pendulum.

The use of the counter was already a regular feature on Cornish engines at the time of the 1811 inquiry into the operating conditions of these engines. As late as the middle of the nineteenth century, the use of this counter had apparently not yet been abandoned.

The indicator   The counter could be used only to estimate the work of an engine whose characteristics were thoroughly known and remained constant. With the use of the expansive power of steam it became necessary to use another device to measure the engine's work.

In his 1782 patent Watt gave a diagram of the piston's work by drawing on the face of the engine's cylinder a graph illustrating the expansion curve (Figure 62). The indicator he later invented was inspired by this demonstration model. This apparatus consisted of a small auxiliary cylinder connected to the body of the driving cylinder. In the former was a carefully adjusted piston constantly balanced by steam pressure and a spiral spring. The end of the piston rod moved directly in relation to variations in pressure. It was a collaborator of Watt, one Southern, who put the indicator into service in 1796. He had added a recording device consisting of a small board with a sheet of paper that moved horizontally with each stroke of the engine (Figure 63).

The use of the indicator, which made it possible to obtain a diagramatic record of the work performed, spread rapidly. Around 1840 the board was replaced by a revolving cylinder. Other devices appeared one after the other from this time on, most of them based on the principle of Watt's indicator.

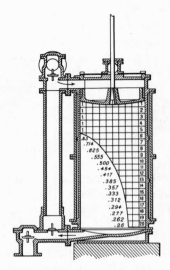

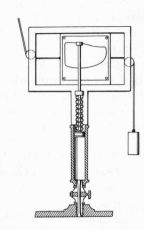

FIG. 62　Diagram of an expansion engine, from Watt's 1782 patent (from Bataille).

FIG. 63.　Watt's pressure indicator (from Tredgold).

Manometers　The need to control steam pressure in a boiler led to the appearance of a new measuring instrument that rapidly came into general use. Because the first engines functioned at a pressure close to atmospheric pressure, the first device used (in imitation of Watt's) was a manometer consisting of a vertical tube open at both ends immersed through a stuffing box into a closed container of mercury. The upper end of the container was connected to the boiler.

With the use of high pressure came manometers closed at the top. The air isolated above the mercury was compressed as a result of the mercury's movement so that it dissolved in the metal, and the readings of the manometric tube were quickly changed. Manufacturers returned to the earlier model, increasing the length of its tube so that the mercury column could balance the pressure in the boiler. These instruments were cumbersome and, since they were made of crystal in order to eliminate heat expansion, they were also very fragile, as well as being difficult to read.

Several variations on this manometer became available. One type, with a float, took the form of a metal U-shaped tube. Another had two tubes whose sections were dissimilar, and a third was a differential manometer using mercury and water. Several French manufacturers—Desbordes, Galy-Cazalat, Decoudun, Richard—made their early reputations with these inventions.

All these devices quickly fell into disuse when in 1849 the French mechanic Eugène Bourdon began manufacturing the metal manometer that has borne his name ever since. Bourdon used a tube flattened on one side so that it could be rolled into a spiral and closed off in a point at one end. This end had a needle that moved over a graduated dial, with the other end being connected to the boiler. Variations in pressure distorted the tube slightly by changing the diameter of the coil.

The origin of the metal manometer is not well known. It appears that the invention cannot be attributed to Bourdon himself. He may have made his first experiments in 1843, adapting for this purpose a metal bellows invented by a certain Raulin four years earlier. In 1851 he exhibited this instrument for the first time, in London. By this time Vidi had already invented his aneroid barometer, which was also based on the elasticity of metal. In 1855 Tresca wrote that "the metal manometer, now known under the name 'Bourdon manometer,' is to be credited to the Prussian Schinz, who worked for a long time in France. . . . Still, it is to Mr. Bourdon that we owe the general, practical development of this instrument."

BIBLIOGRAPHY

ARMENGAUD, Senior. *Traité théorique et pratique des moteurs à vapeur.* Paris, 1861-1862.

BARTON, D. B. *The Cornish Beam Engine.* Penzance, 1966.

BATAILLE, E. M. *Traité des machines à vapeur.* Paris, 1847-1849.

BELIDOR. *Architecture hydraulique.* Paris. 1737-1739, and the revision (of the first part only) by NAVIER. Paris, 1819.

DICKINSON, H. W. *James Watt, Engineer and Artist.* Cambridge, 1936.

———. *Matthew Boulton.* Cambridge, 1937.

———. *A Short History of the Steam Engine.* Cambridge, 1937.

FAREY, John. *A Treatise on the Steam Engine, historical, practical and descriptive.* London, 1827.

Machines motrices et réceptrices. Catalogue du Musée du Conservatoire National des Arts et Métiers. Paris, 1952.

PRONY, R. *Nouvelle architecture hydraulique.* 2 vols. Paris, 1790-1796.

ROLT, L. T. C. *Thomas Newcomen, The Prehistory of the Steam Engine.* London, 1963.

TREDGOLD, Th. *Traité des machines à vapeur.* Translation and notes by F.-N. Millet. Paris, 1838.

PART TWO
THE MACHINE INDUSTRIES

CHAPTER 1

MECHANICAL FACTORS IN INDUSTRIAL PROGRESS

T HE EXPANSION OF mechanization can be regarded as the fundamental cir-
cumstance in the period of the history of technology that is the subject of this
volume. It is not easy to determine when it began, because the movement was
complex, many facts not yet being known, and the reasons for it are obscure.

Economic factors undeniably exerted a profound influence upon this expansion. Until now these are the only factors that have been studied adequately, but
the importance of the technical factors should not be underestimated. Indeed, if
technology had not reached a certain stage of maturity, it could not have been
capable of meeting, and perhaps even stimulating, the demands of the economy.
Just as a constant pressure developed between the economic and the technical
factors, reciprocal influences within the latter restrained or accelerated progress
depending on the circumstances.

The primacy of
industrial machinery
This tangle of interactions has not yet been
thoroughly unraveled, but there is no doubt that the
appearance of machine industries in their modern
form during the first half of the nineteenth century had decisive repercussions on
all aspects of industry—spinning, weaving, chemical products, metallurgy, and
mining—as well as on all other techniques for the use and equipment of space,
communication and transportation, and cultivation and exploitation of natural
resources. The outlets that the machine industry opened up by making increased
production capacities available to other industries, combined with new methods of
production that these industries increasingly brought in by virtue of their own
progress, provided the conditions most favorable for the rapid increase in the rate
of the machine industries' quantitative, and especially qualitative, development.

The invention of the steam engine and its improvement to the point where it
became a universally usable source of energy was, as we have seen, a rather long
story. The process, begun in the last quarter of the seventeenth century, ended
only around the middle of the first half of the nineteenth. If a century and a half
had to be devoted to this invention, it was because for much of this time engineering was incapable of solving the problems posed by the building of new engines
and their components. It was not until around the beginning of the nineteenth
century that this stage was reached and the use of the steam engine became truly
general.

The difficulties that inventors of the steam engine and the first modern machine tools had to overcome caused them to realize that only the development of a theory of mechanics, then nonexistent, could give them the means for general solutions. The concept of the machine was still extremely vague. Inventing, building, and perfecting machines was a genuine art, in the old meaning of the term, pervaded by empiricism. No analytical and comparative study of the various parts of machines had been attempted, nor could it be, until several theoretical propositions emerged to give it a foundation.

The period between 1780 and 1820 was particularly decisive in this regard. Despite the major political and military upheavals that absorbed most of the energy expended during these forty years, the mechanics' activity continued, and quite important new ideas began to emerge.

Definition of the machine   A clear distinction was established between the machine as a unity, with its own technology for which a theory had to be developed, and the mechanisms by means of which movements were transmitted. Although these two ideas were now distinguished, a definition of the machine was to be sought for a long time before a satisfactory formula could be found. From the time of Leupold, who attempted this at the beginning of the eighteenth century, down to Reuleaux and his contemporaries of the last quarter of the nineteenth century, many definitions were suggested.

Leupold's 1724 definition was quite a good one, considering the period: "A machine is an artificial arrangement by means of which we are able to perform a beneficial movement, that is, to move something with economy of time and energy, which would not be possible in any other manner."

Nineteenth-century authors sought to eliminate the vagueness of this definition, sometimes by taking into account relationships either between the speed of the motor and of the connected system, or between the source of power and the movement.

Ampère's 1830 formula, "the machine is a tool with the help of which it is possible to change the direction and speed of a given movement," was, because of its brevity, too vague to serve as a basis for analytical studies. A definition by Robert Willis in 1840 took into consideration the nature of the internal forces and stated the problem more precisely. Laboulaye (1849), Haton de La Goupillère (1864), Poncelet (1867), and finally Reuleaux (1875), among many others, formulated definitions whose diversity clearly shows that it was difficult to establish this concept. Reuleaux's definition was expressed thus: "A machine is an assembly of resistant bodies disposed in such a way as to oblige natural mechanical forces to act by introducing precise movements."

Around the mid-nineteenth century, engineering as a new science was beginning to find its theoretical bases, or at least to demarcate its field fairly clearly. The history of this science has not yet been studied, and in the present state of our knowledge we can do no more than point out a few fragmentary facts suggestive of its nature.

One of the most important such facts concerns the distinction between the theory of motive power and that of the transmission of the forces intended to produce motion.

The study and classification of mechanisms

The theory of motive power became more or less consistent only around the middle of the nineteenth century. Poncelet's works were among those that made the greatest contribution. In particular, it was he who (in 1826) introduced the term *work* into technical literature. The first attempts at the end of the eighteenth century to evolve a theory were short-lived. Sadi Carnot's famous paper, published in 1824, *Réflexions sur la puissance motrice du feu,* went unnoticed at the time. It was not known and appreciated until Clapeyron wrote a long commentary on it ten years later and until the first elements of thermodynamics had been defined by Mayer, Thomson, and Clausius.

The study of mechanisms began during this same period. As early as the closing years of the eighteenth century, Monge sought to isolate the theory of mechanisms from general mechanics. His teaching program at the newly created École Polytechnique revealed the need for a classification that Hachette was in turn to complete and teach. Monge's theory was based on the idea that the function of a machine was to transform one motion into another, so he established four main classes of movements that resulted in ten different classes of mechanisms.

This classification, propagated by the École Polytechnique, was adopted fairly generally, since it seemed for the first time to introduce a semblance of scientific analysis into this field. But it had the defect of not giving a sufficiently strict definition of the mechanisms to be assigned to each class, so that great confusion continued to reign. The extension of Monge's classification in 1806 by Lanz and Béthencourt, who increased the number of classes to twenty-one, did not remove its shortcomings. A more rational attempt by Borgnis in 1818 did not succeed in breaking the influence of Monge's classification. Some of Borgnis's conceptions were adopted later and more successfully by Poncelet.

In his *Essai sur la philosophie des sciences,* published in 1834, Ampère introduced for the first time the word *kinematic* to designate the scientific study of motion. The principles set forth by Ampère were followed by the English professor of applied mechanics Robert Willis, who in his treatise *Principles of Mechanism,* in 1841, supplied a classification of mechanisms based on the relationships between the speed and direction of the motion provided and the motion to be produced. These relationships could be constant or variable for both, or one could be constant and the other variable. Three main classes were thus defined, among which were distributed Monge's classes based on the principle of converting one motion into another. With the work of Willis, the analysis of mechanisms and the scientific study of their nature laid the foundations of the science of kinematics.

The name of the new science appeared shortly thereafter, in 1849, in the title of Charles de Laboulaye's work *Traité de cinématique théorique et pratique.* In fact, though, much uncertainty and confusion still reigned in this field, and despite the efforts of a succession of authors, Monge's concepts had scarcely been upset. For some time to come, engineers like Bélanger and Haton de La Goupillère failed to overcome the difficulties impeding all progress in theory. It was not till 1875 that Franz Reuleaux opened new avenues, without, however, completely achieving his objectives. The analytical portion of his *Cinématique théorique,* published that year, was the most constructive one. Isolating the subject from the problems of constructing machines and of dynamics, he brought kinematics back within the framework of a mathematical discipline. It was he who defined ideas that were later to be of great use to geometrical kinematics, involving, for example, pairs of components and the kinematic chain.

Reuleaux was less successful when he devised a complete symbolism for the components of mechanisms and their relationships, with which he hoped to develop an analytical geometry of kinematics. He objected to earlier theories as having been of no use in the invention of new mechanisms. Even his extremely complex symbolism failed to make it possible to undertake works of synthesis.

Despite deceptive appearances, this research (which was continued for almost a century) was far from negligible; quite the reverse. It led to a search for the bases of a science that was of a completely new character, and in fact it was due to these efforts that this goal was reached in the twentieth century. These results had consequences of prime importance for the rise of industrial techniques in general.

When engineering undertook to resolve less general problems by mathematical methods, it arrived at concrete results more rapidly, though not without effort.

The making of gears In the preceding volume we discussed the first approaches to the geometrical problem of cutting gears. At the time, experts were not yet capable of understanding the solutions whose theory had been outlined by eighteenth-century geometers. Moreover, they had no need to go beyond empirical procedures. In the last years of the eighteenth century the development of waterpower and the gradual introduction of the double-acting steam engine began to change the conditions under which power was transmitted. Wheels and gear trains had to be made of metal in order to connect the more powerful engines to the heavier machines to be operated. In addition, it became increasingly necessary to improve tolerances and reduce the clatter of the old gears, in order to maintain regularity in the speed of machine tools, whose work was becoming more precise.

In accordance with these needs the theoretical and practical study of gears became, in the space of a quarter century, a fundamental condition for the progress of applied mechanics. Till now the history of technology has not sufficiently stressed the importance of this problem in the early stages of modern mechanization.

Nor were these early problems easily solved. In the first stage a certain number of writers, particularly English ones, attempted to popularize the eighteenth-century geometers' ideas of the use of mechanics. Possibly the first work, John Imison's *The School of Arts,* published around 1787, recommended the epicycloidal form for gear teeth. The text, reissued in 1803, was adopted in part by John Hawkins, who in 1806 published under the title (quite novel for the time) *Teeth of Wheels,* the translation of the memoirs of one Camus. Imison's work, popularized and made known through these three successive editions, had a definite influence on the development of gear cutting, though it contained an editor's error, the word *diameter* being used for *radius* in one sentence. But theory still mattered little to the machinists who found in Imison's work an empirical method for preparing a brass pattern from which the gears could be cast. This procedure was used for some thirty years.

The use of cast iron made it possible to make, cheaply, wheels and pinions for machines and transmissions. The working faces of the crude cast pieces were then corrected by filing or grinding so that they were brought to a satisfactory condition.

The geometrical study of gear teeth — Much was written on gears during the first forty years of the nineteenth century. Most of these writings were at first very practical and quite empirical in nature. The ideas emerging during the preceding century had not yet been sufficiently exploited and developed to lead to a definite theory. Moreover, mechanics and shop foremen to whom these works were addressed wanted procedures rather than basic theoretical ideas, which they would not have been able to understand or apply.

Most works on mechanics came from the pens of English writers like James White and Robertson Buchanan. In 1808 White took out a patent for a helical gear inspired by a type of gear described by Robert Hooke in 1666 (Figure 1). The latter consisted of a stack of coaxial cogged wheels staggered at a uniform angle.

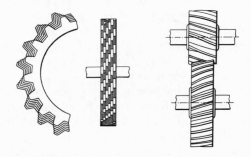

FIG. 1. *Left:* Principle of Hooke's stepped gear. *Right:* White's helical gear.

This design involved less friction than a spur gear, because of the continuity of the action of one of these composite gears upon the other. In his work *Century of Inventions,* published in 1822, White described the helical gear as well as the herringbone gear formed by two helical threads with symmetrical pitch. Herringbone gears were adopted by manufacturers only much later.

Technical literature developed rapidly, providing expanding opportunities to discuss the profiles and proportions of gear teeth most effective in good transmission. A debate concerning the epicycloidal and involute forms was carried on for almost twenty-five years. In 1827 Poncelet demonstrated the advantage of involute gears in ensuring a more even distribution of stresses on the teeth. In 1837 Hawkins studied the proportions between the length and the thickness of the teeth, the width of the space, the manner in which the teeth engaged one another, and the most favorable value for the angle of pressure.

Robert Willis's 1841 treatise must be considered as one of the most important of its time. In addition to the attempt at classification mentioned before, it

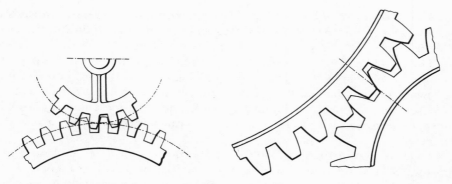

FIG. 2. *Left:* Toothed wheels with straight flanks. *Right:* Toothed wheels with an involute profile.

FIG. 3. A bevel gear. Compare this gear, whose construction was common in the nineteenth century, with those shown on pp. 279–81 of Volume II.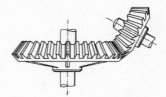

included earlier studies on the profiles of teeth and the manner of laying out their outlines. His analysis of this problem was the most thorough study yet published. Willis also gave the reasons why the profile of involute teeth was generally more advantageous than the epicycloidal. But he was more than a theorist, for he invented the odontograph, a device making it possible to lay out the profiles of involute teeth in a practical way, and he provided numerical tables for making ordinary gears with their tolerances.

The practical result of this first period of research using applied geometry was the abandonment of straight-toothed profiles in favor of those determined by geometric curves ensuring minimum play and shock, and the best angle of pressure. In particular, the value of 14½°, recommended by Willis for the angle of pressure, was generally accepted. The controversy over the two profiles—epicycloidal versus involute—was not then resolved, and was to be continued until the end of the nineteenth century. A more or less modified empiricism survived in the builders' shops till just before 1850. R. Woodbury reports that an inquiry by Hawkins revealed that in 1842 only one engineer, the American Joseph Saxton, could make truly epicycloidal gear teeth. Several years earlier he had constructed a machine to cut such gears, but only for clocks or similar small mechanisms.

Transmitting power over distance In spite of the slowness with which geometrical theories penetrated industrial practice, engineering enjoyed a rapid growth during the first half of the nineteenth century, as can be seen in the chapters devoted to the emergence of modern machine tools or of machines for spinning, weaving, knitting, printing, and so on. The use of new types of power sources and the increase of transmission mechanisms completely transformed factories' equipment and the interior layout of shops.

The problem of gears arose in transmitting motion to the various parts of a machine, from the power source to the working part. In the preceding century, even when a single shaft such as that of a waterwheel or a horse-driven treadmill drove several machines, the lantern gear was the only one known and used to transmit energy to each machine. Power was transmitted over only a very short distance.

As early as the first half of the nineteenth century, power began to be transmitted over a greater distance as the number of machines increased. The power source, whether a steam engine or water (wheel or turbine), became a center driving all the machines in a large shop and even all the shops of a factory.

Transmission shafts were now installed above machines and through the length of shops. These shafts were fitted with pulleys, one of which received motion from the shaft of the power source, while the others transmitted the motion to the shafts of each machine to be operated (Figure 4).

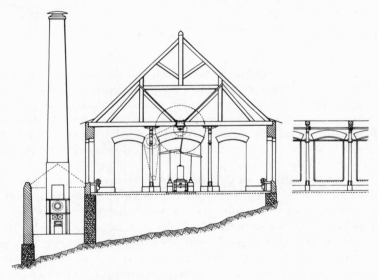

FIG. 4.   Distribution of driving power at the Indret factory in 1834. *Left:* The boiler room. *Center:* Twin-cylinder steam engine. *Right:* Transmission shafts on pedestal blocks and bearings.

Pulleys, belts, and cables

We have seen that lathes and grinding wheels in seventeenth- and eighteenth-century shops were sometimes operated in this fashion. The hemp and aloe ropes inherited from this period were at first used in factories at the beginning of the nineteenth century, and even much later, when the power to be transmitted was still relatively weak (Figure 5). The pulleys had a deep enough V groove to exert pressure on the cable sufficient to prevent its slipping.

As soon as the power to be transmitted began to rise to the value of one or more horsepower, ropes were replaced by flat leather belts, the ends of which were joined by hooks or nails. Grooved pulleys were replaced by pulleys with either flat or slightly convex rims to prevent the belt from leaving the driving surface (Figure 6). The best conditions for the use of pulleys and belts were quickly

FIG. 5. Transmission by rope and grooved pulleys.

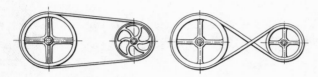

FIG. 6. Transmission by belts and pulleys with flat fellies.

determined. It was learned how to give belts the tension necessary to avoid slippage, either by slightly shifting the receiving shaft (that is, the machine that supported it) by means of tension screws or by placing against the loop a belt tightener consisting of a weighted wheel (Figure 7).

A clutch system consisting of a metal bridle with which the belt could be slid onto a loose pulley was soon invented. A system of very long metal shafts and cast-iron pillow blocks and brackets was developed without difficulty (Figure 8).

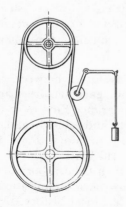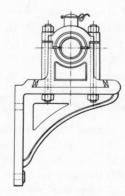

FIG. 8. Bracket and pillow block for a transmission shaft. At the top is a lubricating wick.

FIG. 7. Belt-tightener with tension wheel.

Hooke's coupling, or Cardan joint, which until then had been used only in light machinery, such as chronometry and instruments for astronomy and navigation, was adapted to industrial machinery. This made it possible to ensure power transmission without fluctuating torque between two shafts that were not precisely aligned.

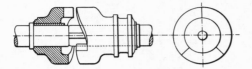

FIG. 9.   Clutch for a transmission shaft.

FIG. 10.   Cross section of a cable made of metal wires twisted around a vegetable-fiber core.

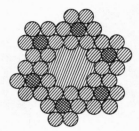

   In fairly large factories it was necessary to distribute power to several buildings, for which teledynamic cables of metal wire came into use. The appearance of these methods gave rise to important mathematical studies and also to improving certain wiredrawing techniques. The drawing of metal wire was gradually perfected between 1830 and 1850. Cables of drawn and cold-hammered wires were not very flexible and at first could be used only for static fasteners such as ships' stays. An attempt was made to render them more flexible by annealing, but this caused them to lose their advantageous high coefficient of elasticity resulting from drawing.

   Even before 1850, cables of drawn, nonannealed wire were successfully made, formed from strands of thin wires spun around a core of vegetable fiber (Figure 10). These cables were used at that time for outside transmission over grooved pulleys.

Modern factories and shops   All these methods, developed between approximately 1825 and 1850, gave factories and their shops the general appearance they were to retain for almost a century. Transmission systems using belts and cables began to disappear when electric power replaced individual steam generators, which occurred during the period between the First and Second World Wars.

   It is indispensable to draw attention to the variety of factors, both theoretical and practical, that governed the expansion of industrial mechanization. It was these factors that gave a special character to the technical history of modern large-scale industry during the first half of the nineteenth century.

CHAPTER 2

INDUSTRIAL MECHANIZATION

FIRST EXPERIMENTS AND SUCCESSES

I N VOLUME II we saw that as early as the sixteenth century it was possible to perform certain operations for transforming metals with the help of machines that lessened the worker's effort, increased the precision of his work, and made possible operations that he would not have been able to perform manually.

Although early machines had in two or three centuries reached almost all shops and many factories, their use was limited till around the middle of the eighteenth century. Lathes were used only to make small objets d'art, clock movements, and mathematical instruments. Steel and iron were occasionally worked on lathes, but brass was the metal most easily turned.

Large machines were in use only in a limited way. Apart from hydraulically driven trip-hammers used to forge large pieces of iron, the only large industrial machines were rolling mills and boring machines for drilling cannons.

The sudden development of industrial mechanization from the end of the eighteenth century is attributable to numerous causes. The economic factors have been frequently studied and are well known, but they were able to attain their full effect only to the extent that the techniques for transformation of energy as a whole had matured. Moreover, the quality and abundance of available materials had to meet the builders' needs. Finally, it was possible to think of building machines and increasing their number only if the power sources to operate them also increased and became capable of supplying steady and cheap energy. It was this conjunction of technical factors that gave birth to the modern heavy machinery industry, under the circumstances described below.

The planing machine,
slide lathe,
and screw-cutting lathe
Around the mid-eighteenth century most of the methods for working metals—turning, drilling, boring, milling, rolling, shearing, forging, and so on—were already in existence, but dressing flat surfaces was still being done with chisel and file.

The performance of the planing machine built by Focq in 1751, the first machine intended to eliminate this manual work, was very poor, and it was necessary to wait several decades for a planing machine worthy of the name.

At the same time, around 1751, Jacques de Vaucanson (1709–1782) built the first metal slide lathe, with a carriage that moved parallel to the axis of the centers.

However, as with the planing machine, probably only one model of this remarkable invention was built, and thus it must be regarded as a prototype whose industrial use was most likely restricted to building textile machines by the same inventor.

The same was certainly true for Senot's astonishing screw-cutting lathe (1795), which was much advanced over David Wilkinson's American lathe (1798) and Henry Maudslay's English one (1797) but whose use is unfortunately unknown. These three machines confirm the statement of the American professor J. W. Roe that "for the lathe, as for the planing machine, the French were pioneers."

The invention of lathes in the space of a half century foreshadowed the use that the most skilled builders were to make of mechanics and the new machine-tool industry that was to emerge, thanks to their successive inventions. The origins of modern industrial techniques are thus found quite far back in the eighteenth century. The first machines had only a very limited use, because they were moved

Plate 7. Screw-cutting lathe by Senot (1795). Paris, Musée du Conservatoire national des Arts et Métiers. (Photo Ph. Brossé - P. U. F.)

only by the worker's muscle power. For example, in the same period John Wilkinson's boring machine was operated by waterpower. The historical importance of this machine has already been stressed—its construction was essential to building the first examples of Watt's steam engines. As the result of a sequence we find constantly repeated in the history of technology, the availability of the double-acting engine brought to manufacturing a new power source and permitted an increase in the number of machine tools.

Whereas the first experiments were by French engineers, the industrial phase of invention and development was the work of an extraordinary generation of English engineers. It can be asked whether these men were created by their age or whether, conversely, their exceptional qualities gave this period its new character. Whatever the answer, it is obvious that the fact that they existed and worked in such large numbers and with such imagination during a mere fifty years exerted a considerable influence on the evolution of our civilization.

The first industrial machine tools

In 1775 John Wilkinson, an ironmaster well known for producing cannons, invented a device to bore steam engine cylinders that made it possible to make accurate bores by supporting the boring bar at each end by a backrest. The superiority of this system over those known earlier is obvious: the tool worked parallel to the axis of an inflexible spindle, producing a cylindrical surface.

It had now become possible to machine Watt's steam cylinder, and in 1776 his partner, Boulton, wrote: "Mr. Wilkinson hath bored us several cylinders, almost without error; that of 50 inches diam[ete]r, doth not err the thickness of an old shilling in no part."

Because for some twenty years Wilkinson cast and bored all of Boulton and Watt's cylinders, his machine can be considered the first industrial machine tool. With it opened an era—the age of the machine—that would revolutionize the world in only a few decades.

Under the pressure of growing needs, another genuine machine tool, Maudslay's screw-cutting lathe, was to be born just before the close of the eighteenth century, in 1797–1799. This machine (discussed later, in the section on lathes) was the work of the first great mechanic, who was thereafter to build many other machines but whose greatest merit is perhaps that he trained four of the most famous English builders, the creators of the machine-tool industry: Clement, Nasmyth, Roberts, and Whitworth.

England, on the verge of bankruptcy in 1783 after the signing of the Treaty of Versailles, gradually recovered, despite enormous difficulties such as those created by the Continental blockade. With the coming of the nineteenth century England saw opening before her a long period of prosperity that was to assure her world supremacy.

Special machines

The discussion thus far contains nothing that could lead us to believe that a search was being made for methods directly concerned with the amount of work to be done or methods capable of making the work of men, women, and children less arduous.

Vaucanson was probably the first to have these objectives in mind when he invented the chain bearing his name, around the mid-eighteenth century. To make it he conceived the idea of a machine that he ordered from one Rosa, at 11 rue des Lions-Saint-Paul in Paris, and that was probably intended specifically for building his textile machines, as also were his famous slide lathe and horizontal drilling machine.

A short time later two Americans, Jacob Perkins in 1795 and Jesse Reed in 1811, took out patents respectively for machines to cut nails and to shape nail heads at the same time.

Numerous improvements were thereafter made on this type of machine, bearing the names of the American James White (1811) and the Frenchman Lemire, a father-and-son team. They undertook, in 1819 at the Clairvaux Forge in the Jura, industrial production of wire tacks, following methods patented in 1806 by the Japy brothers at Colmar for striking the heads of nails and wood screws.

The Japy family were particularly prolific inventors. On March 17, 1799, Frédéric Japy, a clockmaker at Beaucourt in Haut-Rhin, obtained a patent for "various machines suited for simplifying and decreasing the labor in clock-making." Clocks no longer needed to be made in a craftsman's shop but in a factory, employing unskilled labor.

These machines consisted of:

—a machine to cut brass, the tool being a "milling cutter with a saw edge." This machine, "which did seven times more work than the earlier methods," cut strips of brass.

—a punch "for cutting all kinds of objects." This was a hollow punch, used to cut pieces out of strips of steel or brass. It could be used to mark the positions of holes on plates. "A single worker, solely by hammering, turned out his parts as quickly as the spectator could count them."

—a lathe to turn the plates of watches. The inventor wrote that "a worker, or even a 12-year-old child operating the lathe, and a cripple turning the wheel of the lathe" made sixty large plates and an equal number of small ones in one hour.

—a machine to cut wheels, from brass or steel, which cut 3,000 teeth in two minutes.

—a lathe or "machine for making round or square pillars." The worker could "easily produce 700 pillars per day, with an unskilled laborer (or a child) turning the wheel."

—a "machine to make balance wheels"; a small lever-operated screw press, which cut balance wheels out of a strip of brass at a single blow, at the rate of 500 wheels per day.

—a "machine for straight drilling"; a small horizontal bow drill to drill holes in objects held in a vise.

—a "machine for riveting the pillars to watch plates," which could be operated by a child.

—a "machine to cut the slot for the pallet stone." This tool was a "slotting file" pulled by a chain and a crank. This system "permitted no variation and avoided the risks of incorrect filing, which frequently occurred under the old, time-consuming method."

—a "machine for slotting screws." Here again the tool was a slotting file. A single worker, "who in most cases was only a 12-year-old child, slotted 5,000 screws a day."

Such a collection of small machines simultaneously designed and built for a single product is a marvelous example of what could already be undertaken by ingenious manufacturers when sufficient markets were available for their products.

Two similar cases, Bramah and Brunel, are known in England in the same period. Joseph Bramah (1748–1814) had in 1784 invented a lock that was a great success. Since hand labor was neither sufficiently accurate nor productive for its manufacture, with Maudslay's help Bramah developed the machines necessary for quantity production. He also built a hydraulic press and a wood-planing machine with twenty-eight tools mounted on a vertical spindle, a principle similar to the one he may have used for milling certain parts of his locks.

Marc Brunel was born at Hacqueville in the Department of Eure in 1769. After serving for six years in the Royal Navy he left for the United States, where he was chief engineer for New York City. In 1799 he left the United States for England, where he remained until his death. There he designed a group of machines to replace the hand production of wooden tackle blocks used in large numbers on the British Navy's sailing ships. With Maudslay he then built a series of 44 different machines that made it possible to replace 100 skilled workers with 10 unskilled workers.

Cutting tools   Although they were still very crude, the principal cutting tools were already known and in use before 1800: tools for lathes and planing machines, drills, borers, screw taps, and milling cutters.

Three gear-milling cutters made by Vaucanson around 1780 have often been described. They have very fine teeth, probably produced by a chisel, for cutting the teeth of pinions for clocks. These cutters were purchased around 1895 by the American builders Brown and Sharpe for their company museum.

Similar tools for the same type of work had been made even earlier, around 1760, by Hulot. Diderot's *Encyclopédie* gives definitions for the various cutters employed not only by clockmakers but also by gunsmiths.

The circular saw also existed, even before the invention of the true "endless saw" credited to A. C. Albert of Paris, whose patent is dated September 1799. Although artificial grinding wheels were not to appear until later, we have seen that much use was made of the natural sandstone grinding wheel, and polishing with oil and emery was known.

The shapes of the drills and borers used as early as Biringuccio's time to bore and ream cannons are known. Collado's *Manual de artilleria* (Milan, 1592) contains drawings of reamers and screw taps, and Monge (in his *L'art de fondre les canons* of 1793) illustrates the drills whose use he was recommending.

Such were in general the machines and tools used for metalworking at the end of the eighteenth century. They were still slow and lacked precision, but in them were united the elements that were to make possible the astonishing progress in the next century.

NINETEENTH-CENTURY MACHINE-TOOL BUILDERS

For all practical purposes, the machine age begins with the nineteenth century. Thanks to steam, which made it possible to establish shops far from waterways and near sources of raw materials and labor, new industries were created whose expansion required increasingly numerous, powerful, and diversified machine tools.

After Watt's patent came into the public domain in 1800, more came to build steam engines, resulting in increased production, which after 1802 was directed toward high-pressure engines that were less cumbersome, more economical, and thus superior to Watt's engine. In 1810 there were already 5,000 steam engines in service in England; twelve years later there were 10,000, for a total of 200,000 hp.

Paralleling this development, British iron production increased, reaching 500,000 tons. [This should be 250,000 tons of pig iron.—Ed.] This figure, for 1807, contrasts with 32,200 in Prussia and 48,000 in the United States.

In that same year Robert Fulton built his first boat with two side paddle wheels, the *Clermont*. Nine years later a steamboat service was inaugurated on the Thames, and in 1819 the first Atlantic crossing by steamship was made.

In 1814 only lathes, drilling machines, and boring machines existed. Plane surfaces were still being produced by hand, a costly and inaccurate method. It is said that lack of a machine tool to plane guide ways accurately was the occasion for Watt's invention of parallel motion.

It was sixty-six years after Focq's 1751 machine before the first planer with two uprights, a stationary tool, and movable bed appeared.

The first English tool builders

Without forgetting Bramah, already mentioned, and Jeremy Bentham (1757–1831), we believe that Maudslay, one of Bentham's pupils, was the father of the English machine-tool industry.

Henry Maudslay (1771–1831) worked first in Bramah's shop, where he became a foreman at nineteen. For eight years they together designed machine tools, particularly the slide lathe and the hydraulic press, discussed later.

Maudslay then settled in London, about 1798, in a shop where from 1802 to 1808 the greater part of his energies was devoted to constructing block-making machinery designed by Brunel for the mass production of the pulley blocks mentioned earlier. Here between 1797 and 1799 he built his famous small screw-cutting lathe, and then other machine tools and machines of all kinds, as well as numerous steam engines, including the first marine ones.

One of Maudslay's pupils was Richard Roberts (1789–1864), a particularly prolific inventor who in 1817 constructed a small planing machine (to be discussed later) with two uprights and a stationary tool. He invented the back-geared headstock for lathes and built machines for boring, cutting gears, and for drilling and slotting, and is believed to be the inventor of the mortising machine. Around 1825 he went into partnership with Sharp in the firm of Sharp, Roberts & Co.

After working first for Bramah and then Maudslay, in 1817 Joseph Clement (1779–1844) set up a small shop in which he never employed more than about thirty persons (Maudslay employed several hundred). In 1820 Clement built his first planing machine, then built another, larger model, discussed later in the section devoted to planing machines. Clement was greatly interested in the problems of screw cutting. He perfected the screw-cutting lathe and produced drawplates and screw taps. In this regard he probably influenced Whitworth, who worked for him for a time before going to work for Maudslay.

Another, equally famous, pupil of Maudslay was James Nasmyth (1808–1890). Nasmyth distinguished himself at the age of nineteen by making a steam car that reportedly was driven around the streets of Edinburgh for several months before being put out of order by the poor condition of the roads.

In 1826 Nasmyth invented a "steam arm," originally intended for machining to shape the bosses of control levers, with the help of a circular planing device. This machine was less cumbersome and faster than the planing machine (which Decoster was later to transform into a shaper), but Nasmyth's chief claim to fame is that the invention of the steam hammer is generally attributed to him. We shall show that this can rightly be claimed by a French builder.

Maudslay's most brilliant pupil was incontestably Joseph Whitworth (1803–1887). In 1825, at the age of twenty-two, Whitworth went to work in Maudslay's shop, where he remained for eight years before going into business for himself in Manchester. By this time the principal machine tools for which there was a need had already been invented. Whitworth could do no more than develop them, and in fact he did more or less perfect them all. He added to the slide lathe the automatic cross-feed and to the shaper the quick return movement. The superiority of Whitworth's machines derived essentially from their quality, which so clearly exceeded that of their competitors that at the Great Exposition of 1851 in London a special class had to be established for them.

The foregoing discussion has given a general view of the work of Maudslay and his pupils. However, an outline of the beginnings of English industry would be incomplete without mentioning Fox and Bodmer.

James Fox contributed to perfecting the slide lathe, for it is to him that we owe the feed shaft, the rack, and the bedways of narrow profile. He built other machines, notably (in 1820) a planing machine that was not as large as Clement's but was nevertheless capable of planing pieces 10 feet 6 inches long and 22 inches wide.

Johann Bodmer, born in Zurich in 1786, cannot be considered apart from the first British builders, because after settling permanently in England in 1833 he invented the vertical lathe (which he called a circular planer) and the planer with a single upright.

By the mid-nineteenth century English industry was at the peak of its power. The first railroad line between Liverpool and Manchester was put into service in 1830. Twenty years later the total railroad trackage had risen from eighty-three to more than six thousand miles, and the rolling stock included several thousand locomotives. As early as 1836, tens of thousands of steam engines were in operation practically everywhere, and the appearance of portable steam engines after 1841 was to increase their number considerably. Steam navigation and, at the same time, the construction of iron vessels and war ships was also developing. The first ironclad ship was launched in 1842.

In the field of mechanical engineering, England's superiority was rapidly translated into important exports to countries who were also seeking to become industrialized, the United States, France, and Germany in particular.

The first French builders   At the beginning of the nineteenth century there were only a few shops for machine construction in France. It was not until around 1820 that the first English machine tools were imported by the naval dockyards, by such factories as Le Creusot and Fourchambault, and by manufacturers like Pihet, Cail, Gouin, and others. These establishments used and then began to construct them, to the point that at the Paris Exposition of 1834 there were several stands displaying French-built machine tools. The École Royale d'Arts et Métiers of Angers exhibited, according to one report, "a carefully built boring machine," which won a bronze medal. The Châlons school won a silver medal for a tapping machine and a planing machine.

Among the pioneers of French construction three names are especially important: Calla, Decoster, and Cavé.

In 1788 Étienne Calla (1760–1835), a pupil and friend of Vaucanson, established in Paris a factory to make machines for spinning mills. Here he produced in particular his mechanical loom, for which he received a gold medal in 1827. According to Hachette, it was here in 1800 that he may have built for Fulton, according to the latter's designs and under his direction, an experimental high-pressure steam engine.

In 1820 Calla set up a foundry at 18 rue du Faubourg-Poissonnière (he later moved to No. 92), where he turned out major artistic works like the doors and screens for the church of Saint Vincent de Paul and fountains like the one in the Place Louvois. This foundry was later transformed into a shop to build machines.

François Calla (1802–1884) took over the management of the business from his father in 1835. At the age of twenty-three he had successfully collaborated in reorganizing the Châtellerault munitions factory, where he installed a grinding shop, a fitter's shop, and a forge with a bellows and tilt hammers.

Calla admired the best English builders of the time, and in most cases he took his inspiration from the machines of Nasmyth, Sharp, and Whitworth, adapting them to the requirements of his compatriots, just as he introduced into France the use of Whitworth's calipers and gauges, which were responsible for the high quality and reputation of Calla's products.

Jules Gaudry says that during a trip to Manchester Calla met Whitworth, who at first welcomed him ungraciously, accusing him of copying his machines.

> "What do you expect?" Calla told him. "Wishing to do a good job, I found no way of doing differently from you!" "It's true," answered Whitworth, extending his hand, "your copies are worthy of the inventions, and I gain by being popularized by you in France, a country whose esteem I value highly. Take what you like from my shop, and let's be good friends."
>
> From that day forward they were very close, and Whitworth did not build a new machine without taking Calla into his confidence, making him the representative of his interests in France. There was even talk of establishing a branch at Calla's factory for the production of the famous Whitworth cannon. But the time was not ripe in France for ordering entire artillery from private industry.

Around 1849, having transferred his shops to La Chapelle, Calla was building machine tools of all kinds and sizes. Among the most important machines he supplied to the state arsenal, mention is made of a lathe with an 11-foot faceplate for the naval establishment at Indret; for the arsenal at Toulon a lathe whose centers were 5 feet high, with a faceplate 9 feet in diameter and a bed 46 feet long, and a total weight of 100 tons, and a planing machine 16½ feet wide, 36 feet long, and equipped with four tools. In the same establishment he had already installed, in 1835, a very large mechanical sawmill that was completely novel in its conception.

François Calla respected and was respected by his workers. He built three free schools and a social welfare center at La Chapelle-Saint-Denis. A distinguished economist, he was a member of the Chamber of Commerce and the General Council of Manufactures, and was one of the founders of the Comptoir d'Escompte (Discount Bank).

Pierre Decoster (1806–1861) left his native Belgium at the age of fourteen for Paris, where he became an apprentice in the shop of one Saulnier, a mechanic in the Popincourt quarter, who built steam engines. In 1839, at 9 rue Stanislas in Montparnasse, he set up machine shops where he undertook production of machine tools, textile machines, and transmission gearing.

In a catalog published in 1847 Decoster expressed himself, with a touch of vanity, as follows:

> After a series of uninterrupted projects spread over eight very busy years, I acquired in this area of machine construction—I do not hesitate to say it—an experience that has enabled me to observe and avoid the shoals on which one often comes to grief when one is starting out.
>
> Since 1840 I have been supplying a great number of machine tools of all kinds and sizes to a large number of engineers.
>
> Machine tools, which barely ten years ago were limited to ordinary lathes, a few planing machines, and a few boring machines, have proliferated prodigiously, and today include a great number of mechanical operations which used to be performed with considerable difficulty by hand at unheard-of cost; they make it possible to carry out large-scale projects which it would have been impossible to undertake without these powerful means.

The list of machines built by Decoster includes slide lathes, machines for drilling, boring, mortising, planing, milling, gear cutting, shearing, chamfering, bending, and so on. At the time, he enjoyed a certain success with his planing machines with a movable tool and a stationary support for large objects, a type of machine already in use for about a decade in England, as in France.

In his catalog Decoster goes on to explain that

> having followed the construction of the machines in the largest factories in England, I was able to recognize the merit of the best tools in use, the conditions they fulfilled, and the advantages they offered. Upon returning to France I decided, when I founded my firm, on the production of several of the machine tools which I have since then built, chiefly planing machines with a pivoting tool to work in both directions; except that instead of making the object move, I preferred (and rightly so) to make the tool move, because, as everyone has observed, the machine then occupies less space, is lighter and less costly, and therefore more suitable to the majority of the French machine shops.

Decoster was mistaken about the method of use of average-sized and large planing machines, but it was he who combined the vise directly with the shaper to form the shaping planer. Although several builders in France preceded him in producing machine tools, he nevertheless deserves a place in the forefront of pioneers in this industry.

François Cavé was born on September 12, 1794, to poor agricultural laborers in the village of Mesnil, on the northern boundary of the Department of Oise in Picardy. At the age of seventeen, with the limited education it was possible to acquire in a village at the time, Cavé walked the seventy-two miles to Paris to complete his apprenticeship as a cabinetmaker.

He worked under miserable conditions until his military service in 1812. In 1814 he returned to his native village but soon left it again, once more on foot, for the capital. A miserable life was resumed on inadequate wages.

Cavé was in fact a born mechanic. He began his career in the shop of one John Collier, a builder of English origin, in the rue Richer. Later, in a spinning mill in the Clignancourt quarter where he had begun as a foreman, he suggested to his employer that a steam engine be built to replace a defective one.

The result was the invention, in 1825, of a steam engine with reciprocating cylinders, and Cavé's decision to set up his own shop near the Porte Saint-Antoine. He was unsuccessful at first, but by hard work he succeeded in overcoming the difficulties constantly confronting him.

The reciprocating machine had been so coldly received by the industrial world that at the 1827 Exposition it received only honorable mention. According to one report, it offered no advantage other than "moderate cost and reduction in size."

Seven years later, at the 1834 Exposition, the language was quite different. The builder won the first gold medal, and the king, upon hearing the jury's report, bestowed on him forthwith the cross of Chevalier of the Legion of Honor.

Cavé expanded his shops at 216 rue du Faubourg-Saint-Denis in 1826. To equip them he designed and made all the machine tools he needed, even the most important ones, with the exception of two filing machines purchased from Calla.

Cavé soon became involved in naval construction. In 1828 he built the engine for the *Courrier,* the ship that linked Calais with Dover at the then-considerable speed of 13 knots per hour, and which for the first time had "wheels with jointed or 'feathering' paddles that collapsed as they rose in order not to lift the water."

Thereafter, his shops turned out 100 to 120 hp. tugs for navigation on the Seine, and ships intended for service on the Rhine. One of the latter appears in his accounts for June 1842 under the heading "Iron boat, called Rhine tugboat. Cost of construction: 42,190 francs; sale price: 48,519.36 francs."

In 1832 the Ministry of the Navy gave Cavé an order for two 180-hp. steam engines.

> They were the most powerful constructed to date in France. Where was one to find the tools necessary for such a project? Powerful boring mills were needed, and heavy hammers to forge the shafts destined to transmit power; the assembly of the parts also required new tools. M. Cavé perfected his [punch] and, by an addition as simple as it was ingenious, made it capable of cutting out iron rods and large sheets of metal. He then invented a beautiful machine for planing metals, which made it possible to work, mortise and plane the part, and which, operating at very high speed, moreover provided the facility for cold shaping the elbows of cranks with much greater economy than by hot forging. Then the shafts had to be made. M. Cavé was never at a loss when it was a question of inventing new and better combinations.

It was then that Cavé built first the tilt hammer, then the steam hammer, to be discussed in its own section. He also built a planing machine 10 feet wide and 42⅔ feet long that had eight independent tools and a table and was equipped with an auxiliary device for boring, as well as a radial drill that was "one of the most beautiful drills known," according to Jules Gaudry.

In 1843 Cavé accepted a contract to build one million contemporary francs worth of equipment provided he be given the order for four 450-hp. engines for steam frigates ordered by the French navy. He succeeded brilliantly and reduced the delivery time. From the shops of Cavé, who was sometimes called the French Stephenson, came numerous locomotives in seven different models, between 1837 and 1855.

In the field of machine tools Cavé not only designed all those he needed but also built tools for numerous machine shops: lathes, planing, vertical mortising and reaming machines, drills, machines to work sheet iron, forge equipment, and so on.

On June 11, 1836, he applied for a five-year inventor's patent for "a machine operated directly by steam or any expansible gas, and intended to replace the screw-press, the drop hammer, and all similar machines." The drawing included in the file depicts a punching machine. The patent was granted on November 19, 1836.

This patent may also have been applied to the steam hammer that in his forge replaced a manual hammer requiring the services of twenty-four men, as well as a combination machine to punch and rivet plates for boilers.

The adolescent who on March 20, 1811, had entered through the Saint-Denis gate into a Paris joyously celebrating the birth of the King of Rome and who, fifteen years later was to set up on the same spot a factory for machine construction employing 1,000 persons and covering an area of 8,000 square yards is one of the creators of the French machine industry. He died in March 1875 at the age of eighty-one, after a remarkably hardworking and honest life.

Some other French builders in the first half of the nineteenth century must also be mentioned. The *Établissement de constructions mécaniques* in Strasbourg introduced machine tools into the program of its new shops at Graffenstaden in 1841. Hallette established his factory at Arras toward the end of the Empire period, recruiting some of his workers from among the prisoners of war interned in that city, among whom were English smiths and craftsmen. By alleviating their plight he kept them in his service and built marine engines and machine tools, including a planing machine with a table, which was the largest of that period, being 49½ feet long and 16½ feet wide. The builders who participated in the Paris Exposition of 1849 included, in addition to those already mentioned, Huguenin, Ducommun, and Dubied of Mulhouse, Derosne and Cail of Paris, and Stehelin of Bitschwiller.

The first American builders American industry could not get started until the Revolutionary War (1775–1783) introduced political and economic liberty.

Great Britain, perhaps disturbed by the colonies' potential for industrial development, obstructed any growth of American industry by imposing customs duties favoring English products, and domestic taxes on American ones.

After the victorious conclusion of the Revolution, the American government in turn raised customs barriers to protect its industries, which were encouraged by the extraordinary expansion of cotton cultivation. For its part, the British Parliament passed a law in 1785 forbidding emigration of mechanics as well as exportation of machine tools, their models, and plans. The United States was thus forced to use its own resources to develop its own equipment.

At the end of the eighteenth century this equipment was certainly still poorer and more rudimentary than that of the other large countries, and it underwent few improvements during the first half of the nineteenth century. The examples we possess of an American invention worthy of note are the screw-cutting lathe, for which David Wilkinson received a patent on December 14, 1798, and, in the field of specialized production, the making of nails cut out of sheet metal, for which Perkins around 1795 used machines probably of his own conception.

In 1819 Blanchard patented his copying lathe, to produce large quantities of rifle butts at the arms plant in Springfield, Massachusetts.

When Baldwin wanted to make his first locomotive, in 1832, he had to overcome enormous production difficulties, since he did not have the necessary machines. For example, the cylinders of this locomotive had to be bored with a manually operated tool. Thereafter, Baldwin had to build his own boring mills indispensable to his work, which included the production of fourteen locomotives in 1835 and forty in 1836.

The first planing machine could not be imported from England until 1828. Slightly later, around 1830, Gay and Silver built a well-known American planing machine for their own use. It was an extremely clumsy device mounted on a granite base, on which slide bars were added so that the table could be pulled in one direction or the other by a chain. During the same period, these builders also constructed lathes that again had stone beds. The beds of the Putnam Company machines were wooden, as were those produced by Samuel Flagg in Worcester. The latter had strips of cast iron attached to act as slide bars. Around 1841 Gay and Silver built a horizontal milling machine.

During the same period the first American metal lathes appeared, being produced in particular by Shephard, Lathe and Co. and the Fitchburg shops. Not until the second half of the nineteenth century were the machine tools that made the reputations of American builders produced at an increasingly rapid rate.

The first German builders   After their studies or apprenticeships, the first German builders of machine tools served a training period in English factories, as the Frenchmen Calla and Decoster had done earlier. This was the experience of Richard Hartmann in 1845 as well as of Anton Collet, who while in England met Otto Engelhard, later his partner.

The German machine-tool industry began to take form only around 1860, and thus after the period covered in this volume. The first specimens worth comparing with the best English designs were exhibited at the Universal Exposition in London in 1862. By and large they were submitted by builders in the Chemnitz area, the most famous of whom, along with Hartmann, was Johann Zimmermann.

In a book he wrote in 1867 to describe a selection of sixty of the best machine tools of the period, a certain Reverend Hart of Karlsruhe mentions only four

German models. The genuine beginnings of an industry that was thereafter to make rapid progress dates from this period.

THE INVENTION AND EVOLUTION OF MACHINE TOOLS

The lathe For the reasons indicated above, the lathe, whose origin dates back to earliest antiquity, was obliged to wait a long time before being put to industrial use. In fact, the first all-metal lathes did not appear until around the middle of the eighteenth century. But these were very exceptional, for wooden lathes continued to be used for another half century. It was impossible to obtain adequate precision and production with these simple lathes. The only improvements made to them were gradually replacing wooden parts with metal components (particularly headstocks and toolholders), and adding iron spindles and bronze bearings.

Vaucanson's slide lathe The first metal lathes are owned and on exhibit by
(1751) the Musée du Conservatoire national des Arts et Métiers in Paris. The oldest is one built around 1751 by Jacques de Vaucanson (Figure 11). It was a slide lathe; that is, it was built for the cylindrical turning of metal pieces approximately 3 feet long and up to a foot in diameter.

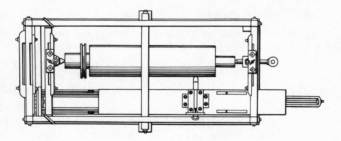

FIG. 11.   Vaucanson's slide lathe, around 1751.

This lathe consists of a frame of square-sectioned iron bars. It supports the bed on which the tool carriage moves and, at each end, the two centers between which the object to be turned is mounted.

The bed's guideways are two iron bars 1½ inches in cross section, inclined in such a way that the carriage slides on surfaces inclined at a 45° angle.

This solution is the first attempt at prismatic guide bars, since adopted by the great majority of lathe builders to obtain greater precision of machining and to reduce wear on the slide bars.

The carriage is of bronze. On its upper portion it has a cross slide on which the toolholder can be moved by a screw. Its longitudinal movement is likewise obtained by a screw placed between the two slide bars on the bed, which can be

Plate 8. Slide lathe with iron frame, by Vaucanson (circa 1751). End view. Paris, Musée du Conservatoire national des Arts et Métiers. (Photo Ph. Brossé - P. U. F.)

turned with a crank located at either end. Maudslay adopted the same arrangement fifty years later.

The two centers that held the material to be worked are independent. Their vertical movement is fairly wide, since the maximum diameter of the pieces accepted is close to a foot; on the other hand, their horizontal adjustment can be varied by only a few centimeters. From this we can deduce that Vaucanson designed this lathe to turn cylinders for his looms, all of which were the same length.

The inventor's ingenuity permits us to believe that continuous movement of the object being machined was produced by a pulley and a crank-operated flywheel.

Thus, by the middle of the eighteenth century an all-metal lathe had been designed and built that for the first time presented two remarkable features: carriage movement parallel to the axis of the centers, and guidance of this movement on prismatic slide bars.

Vaucanson's lathe is thus the first slide lathe and, most significantly, it establishes priority for the invention of the tool carriage with guided movement. On all the lathes discussed earlier, as on those built down to the beginning of the nineteenth century, the principal parts were made of wood, and the work done by the tool (given the absence of any device to hold it stationary) depended solely on the worker's strength and skill.

This lathe dates from approximately 1751, because starting around this time Vaucanson invented the machines that, in addition to his automatic ones, won him fame: a silk reeler, a mill to throw silk, an automatic loom, and a loom to make patterned fabrics.

To obtain better performance of his silk-throwing machine, Vaucanson invented a special warp and the machine to operate it. It is also reasonable to believe that he invented his slide lathe and the horizontal drilling machine, also preserved in the Musée des Arts et Métiers, for the special machining of certain components of his textile machines.

Screw-threading lathes　　Like the first development of the slide mechanism, the first screw-threading device is a French achievement. It is embodied in Senot's 1795 lathe, exhibited next to Vaucanson's. In the fifteenth century Leonardo da Vinci had sketched the principle of threading by reproduction. Long after him, other inventors had the same idea. Jacques Besson's lathe dates from 1569 (see Volume II, page 266), and we know that a French guilloching lathe of 1740 exhibited in London was able to thread by means of patterns. Moreover, an illustration in a 1741 French book depicts a small, hand-operated bench lathe that is very original in that the part to be threaded and the lead screw are turned simultaneously by a series of gears rather than with a rope, as on Besson's lathe. The tool rest, being one piece with the lead screw, reproduces its thread correctly.

Senot's lathe (1795)　　In 1795 Senot applied the same idea. He built a lathe like Vaucanson's, completely of metal, consisting of a frame holding the principal parts of the machine, namely,

—the stationary headstock, with its spindle turning in self-oiling pillow blocks. At one end was the chuck to hold and feed the part to be threaded. The other end had a swing frame, which transmitted the movement of the spindle to the lead screw by a train of interchangeable wheels;

—the tailstock, which could be moved on the frame according to the length of the parts to be machined;

—the tool carriage, fed by the lead screw;

—fixed and following adjustable backrests.

The idea of using a swing frame to obtain different pitches with the same lead screw was to be adopted later by Maudslay, often regarded as the inventor of this device as well as of the mechanical movement of the tool carriage, an idea used a half century earlier by Vaucanson.

Feeding the workpiece by a chuck with several locking screws, and maintaining it in position with a multiple-jawed steady work rest were also new ideas that were not adopted until much later.

Maudslay's lathe (1800)　　We have said that Maudslay can be regarded as the first builder of machine tools for industrial use. It was in Bramah's shop that, in 1794, he conceived the idea of making a lathe with a tool carriage. He was probably unaware of the earlier French inventions mentioned in the *Encyclopédie,* for his toolholder was integral with the movable

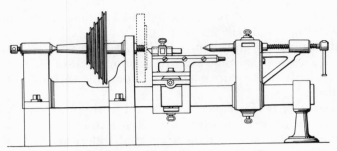

FIG. 12.   Maudslay's slide-and-finishing lathe, 1800.

tailstock. Because of this, as it worked, the tool moved away from the tailstock and came closer to the stationary headstock, thus increasing its misalignment and working under increasingly poor conditions.

At the age of twenty-six Maudslay opened the shop that in 1799 turned out his first screw-cutting lathe (on exhibit in the Science Museum in London), on which he separated the toolholder from the movable tailstock. This is a bench lathe whose centers are 1½ inches high. It has a bed 3 feet long consisting of two prismatic iron bars on which the tool carriage is mounted. The stationary headstock (which is on the right, not the left, as at present) and the tailstock are supported by only the back bar.

The carriage is controlled by a bronze lead screw with a square thread. The lead screw has a diameter of one inch, a lead of one-quarter inch, and is supported between the bars, as in Vaucanson's and Senot's lathes.

The spindle, which had a dog-chuck plate, was turned manually by a crank, the motion being communicated to the lead screw by gears.

The main defect of this machine was that the lead screw and its nut had to be changed in order to obtain a different thread. Maudslay eliminated this defect around 1799 by reinventing (for he probably was not aware of its existence) the arrangement devised five years earlier by Senot, using change gears.

It should also be noted that though Senot's lathe is a very sturdy machine with a large capacity, Maudslay's second lathe (which like the first is preserved in the Science Museum) is a bench model, manually controlled and with flat slide bars, using 28 change wheels with between 15 and 50 teeth.

Naturally, Maudslay later built larger models. On one of them, for an astronomical instrument, he threaded a screw 5 feet long and 2 inches in diameter, with a pitch of 50 threads per inch. Thus the nut, which was 12 inches long, had 600 threads.

David Wilkinson's lathe (1798)   At approximately the same time as Senot and Maudslay, an American named David Wilkinson (not to be confused with the Englishman John Wilkinson, already mentioned) also invented a screw-cutting lathe. (The same observation concerning an invention born almost simultaneously in places very distant from each other can be made for other machines, particularly for the steam hammer.)

Like Maudslay, he definitely did not know of Senot's lathe, and was certainly unaware of Leonardo da Vinci's drawing of a lathe with a continuous movement reproducing the threads of a lead screw on a cylindrical rod.

The lathe designed by David Wilkinson appears not to have been built, but a drawing of it, accompanying the patent taken out on December 14, 1798, indicates that it is similar to the others in principle, although the arrangement for moving the tool carriage by a lateral lead screw is clearly inferior to the one with a center lead screw.

David Wilkinson's lathe was driven directly by a waterwheel. Its carriage moved along the bed with the help of three rollers traveling on three slide bars. As in Maudslay's first lathe, it was necessary to change the lead screw to obtain different pitches. The total length of the machine was 18 feet.

The patent came into the public domain, but its value was officially recognized fifty years later by Congress, which in 1848 awarded the inventor a grant of ten thousand dollars.

Various types of ordinary lathes

By the beginning of the nineteenth century, as we have seen, the basic principles of turning and screw cutting were known. Much time was to pass, however, before they were generally applied. In 1848, for example, lathes were still classified as follows:

1. The simple center lathe, "intended chiefly for turning wood or small objects of brass, iron or cast iron, provided that their diameter did not exceed 60 or 80 mm.";
2. The center lathe with single and double gears, on which "it was possible to obtain speeds suited for turning objects of any metal, the limit being fixed by the diameter of these objects and the dimensions and power of the machine";
3. The face lathe, which, being larger and having "a well combined multiplication of gears, made it possible to turn large pieces. This type of lathe was generally complemented by a carriage support by means of which it was possible not only to perform the turning of parts but also to bore with all the accuracy desirable";
4. The slide lathe, "on which the part turned or bored itself once it had been placed between its centers and the tool adjusted." It was this type of lathe, built in all sizes, that became most widely adopted, because it offered in particular "the advantage, so important for the owner of a factory, that it need not be operated by a skilled worker; the most unqualified man could learn to operate it in a very short space of time. . . . Most slide lathes are nowadays equipped with a reversing screw [lead screw] and gears that make it possible to thread screws of various sizes and pitches; this increases their use and makes them still more valuable for shops doing custom work."

At a time when lathes with wooden beds were still numerous, Armengaud stressed the exceptional value of a carriage that moved parallel to the axis of the centers, as on Maudslay's lathe of 1795–1797 and on Vaucanson's, fifty years earlier.

Eliminating dependence on a worker's manual skill and strength, these remarkable improvements, which were later applied to other machines, made it possible to eliminate the human factor in cylindrical turning. Formerly, to obtain a good surface the worker had been obliged to hold his tool's handle firmly in both hands, leaning on a stationary support and moving it longitudinally and transversally as evenly as he could.

Improvements on metal lathes   Maudslay's first lathes were small bench lathes, and he was probably not in a position to build larger ones until he was able to install a planing machine in his shop.

No other planing machine had been built, since Focq's 1751 machine, until in 1817 Roberts built (by hand) his.

In the same year Roberts built the first large metal lathe, which he used until 1854. It was thereafter used until the end of the century by Beyer, Peacock and Company, who then donated it to the Science Museum in London.

In addition to its size (9½ inches high at the centers and 6 feet long between them), which gave it great possibilities in use, Roberts' lathe had several new features: a bed with two guide rails, one flat and the other prismatic, and a headstock with a four-stage cone pulley and a train of gear wheels controlling a device to vary the almost continuous changes in the traversing speed. The spindle was mounted on cylindrical bearings and the carriage was moved in both directions automatically along the length of the bed by the lead screw.

Fox made other improvements on the slide lathe, including a feed shaft complemented by a rack feed, which was an attempt to achieve rigidity in a carriage sliding along iron I bars (Figure 13).

There is a model of a lathe made by this builder in the Musée des Arts et Métiers in Paris. The original, built around 1830, may have been one of the first large English machine tools imported into France. Its bed, cast in a single piece, was 23 feet long and 2⅓ feet wide. It was similar to the preceding lathe but differed from it particularly in the fact that the feed shaft was driven more simply, by means of two two-speed cone pulleys and a belt.

Clement, the best designer of his time, conceived a device to engage the lead screw by a dog clutch, later applied by Fairbairn.

Whitworth's lathe of 1835 combined all the improvements credited to English builders, with the addition of an automatic cross-feed tool. The famous mechanic

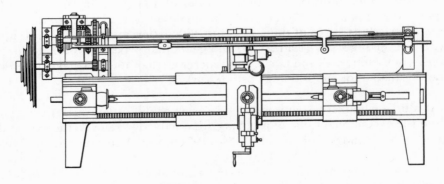

FIG. 13.   Fox's slide lathe, around 1814. The tool-rest carriage is pulled by a rack.

had thus built a lathe whose layout and component parts were thereafter to undergo few modifications until the invention of speed-change gearboxes.

The lathe and the drill being the most commonly used machine tools, several builders began to produce them in the principal industrial centers of France, generally taking their inspiration from English models.

Vaucanson's originality in designing prismatic slide bars was followed by that of two Parisian mechanics, Gengembre and Saulnier the elder, who hoped to replace the ordinary bed with "two horizontal columns, turned in perfectly cylindrical form." It was said that this arrangement offered "the advantage of making the construction of the machine easier by allowing all corrections to be made on the lathe, whereas in the English system the dressed parts could be made only with the planing machine or by the hand of a fitter." The experiment was not successful.

Decoster, whose production program was very extensive, built several slide lathe prototypes. The heights of their centers ranged from 7 inches to 2 feet; the smallest models had 4 cutting speeds, the largest 18.

Decoster's catalog suggests that he invented the following backrest, but we know that this useful accessory had appeared already in 1795 on Senot's screw-cutting lathe.

By 1850, the end of the period under consideration, machine shops already possessed many simple lathes without carriages, on which it was necessary to work with a hook tool. But the slide and screw-cutting lathe was becoming increasingly familiar, and more and more builders were undertaking its production in all sizes.

In naval construction, in particular, shafts of constantly increasing diameter and length were being demanded. We have already mentioned the very large lathe, with a total weight of 100 tons, delivered by Calla to the Toulon shipyard. The builder had adapted to it a device to drive the faceplate by an internal crown gear, allowing more teeth to be engaged on the drive pinion. Thus it was possible to make cuts 2 inches wide and 16 inches thick on pieces of wrought iron.

Conditions for use   It was recommended not to exceed the cutting speed of 6 inches per second in the case of malleable cast iron, and between 8 and 8½ inches for wrought iron.

One builder adopted the following formula:

	Per second	*Per minute*
Steel	3 inches	10 feet
Iron	7½ inches	26¼ feet
Malleable cast iron	6 inches	19⅔ feet
Copper and bronze	14 inches	46 feet

The tool usually advanced .016 inches for each revolution of the spindle for wrought iron, cast iron, and copper, but it was accepted that since this depended on the nature of the work, it could be varied within quite wide limits, from .8 to .08 inches.

These results were considered very satisfactory; with iron they were even regarded as remarkable, "because the tool, being constantly moistened by drops of water made to fall on it, was not likely to overheat."

On center lathes (that is, lathes without a carriage and with a stationary tool support), "it was necessary to turn manually with the hook tool; the speed at the circumference of the object could be noticeably increased, because the tool did not remain long in contact with the metal, it was driven less deeply into the material, and a slight movement of the hand moreover removed the cuttings very easily."

Face lathes Gap lathes were the first answer to the problem of machining large-diameter objects. When these lathes proved inadequate, simple ones consisting basically of a headstock with a very high center were built. One of the oldest and best known of these was the one built by Maudslay around 1830. It had a faceplate 9 feet in diameter, in front of which was a channel 19⅔ feet deep to permit turning the rims and boring the hubs of large flywheels. A rod to bore steam-engine cylinders with a maximum diameter of 9¾ feet could also be mounted on this lathe.

Vertical lathes The first vertical facing lathe was patented in 1839 by Bodmer, who called it a circular planing machine. This machine (Figure 14) was never built, but had some interesting features. Its faceplate was controlled by an internal toothed crown wheel and was guided by a circular V guide rail.

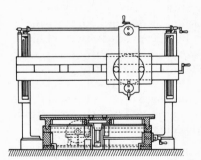

FIG. 14. First vertical lathe with two upright columns, 1839. J. G. Bodmer called it a circular planer.

Automatic lathes Whitworth built an automatic lathe for large-quantity production of wood screws, for which he took out a patent in 1835. His lathe already had some features that were not adopted until several years later by American builders: a feed bar, locking by clamps in a tapering socket, and a camshaft.

In a complementary 1839 patent, Whitworth describes a double-friction cone to reverse the movement of the spindle, as well as a round cam operating the feed bar.

Wheel lathes The machining of certain components for railroad rolling stock, which was difficult to do on the machines of the time, led to building special machines. The period around 1840 saw the invention of lathes to machine the wheels of locomotives and cars, both mounted on axles and unmounted.

Basically, the lathe was composed of a massive cast-iron bed, a heavy

Plate 9. Lincoln lathe. Smithsonian Institution

headstock and a tailstock with a chuck toothed on the inside, and two pivoting tool supports. A rack system permitted moving the tailstock (or movable poppet) for the emplacement of the mounted axle.

Originally, the centers bore all the weight and they quickly worked loose. To eliminate this, Decoster took out a patent on June 17, 1847, for "improvements made on large lathes, and chiefly on those intended for turning the wheels of locomotives and cars." On the bed he provided supports whose height could be regulated. The axle was placed on these supports, which now served only to center it. In this way both wheels could be turned simultaneously.

The threading machine and the tapping machine   In the early days of machine building, the consumption of bolts and nuts was so small that every mechanic had to make those he needed. There was a complete lack of uniformity in sizes, shapes, and pitch of the threads. Each bolt and nut formed a unique pair not comparable with its neighbors, so that it was necessary to put a special mark on each bolt and its corresponding nut to show that they belonged to each other.

Between 1800 and 1810, Maudslay pioneered attempts to standardize threading. He improved the screw dies and taps then in existence and developed a series of taps with uniform dimensions, ranging from the smallest (for clockmakers) to taps as large as 6 inches, with differences in diameters of 1/16 or 1/8 of an inch, depending on the size.

We know that Maudslay had considerable influence on Whitworth, whose work resulted in the adoption in 1841 of the so-called Whitworth proportions and genuine standardization. However, its adoption required many years, in spite of efforts by the navy and railroad companies. Around 1850 one could still read the following:

> It is not natural that the owner of a machine built in Paris, for example, should be obliged, when it is in operation 100 or 200 miles from the capital, to turn to the builder himself when a bolt or nut is missing, or to repair drills, taps, and bearings because he is unable to find the corresponding object in his locality.

Meanwhile attention was being paid to improving thread cutting. In France the importance of this problem led the Société d'Encouragement pour l'industrie nationale, to offer, in 1836, two prizes of 1,000 francs each for research on tools suitable for replacing the ordinary taps and dies. In the following year a Parisian mechanic and steam-engine builder, Achille Rouffet, partly solved the problem and was awarded a silver medal.

The grand prize was won by Waldeck with his system of screw plates for cutting square and V threads. A second prize was awarded to him also in 1840 for a tap with a variable diameter.

Meanwhile, in 1838, a locksmith named Gouet had conceived the idea of a tap with four bearings. Two tap systems were presented at the Exposition of 1839. One had three bearings, two of which were of metal and faced the third, which served simply as a guide and could be of wood. The other system included four diametrically opposed bearings that were brought together by turning the rim of the screw plate.

In that same year one de La Morinière (who will also be mentioned in the section on planing machines) designed an expandable tap, which was intended to replace a series of individual ones of various diameters, to eliminate machining accidents following a breakage of tools in an excessively deep cut, to tap cast iron more easily and, finally, to facilitate tool grinding. This tap for large diameters was made by Mariotte at Le Havre.

Threading a bolt 1½ to 2 inches in diameter with a manual tap required the strenuous effort of at least two men. In the case of a tap equipped with bearings one worker sufficed, whereas with a machine the bulk of his work was eliminated.

One of the first machines for threading bolts and screws, built by Decoster, was equipped with a tap with three bearings. Two speeds permitted the threading of small and large diameters, the higher speed being obtained by direct drive from the spindle, the slower one by a gear train. The bearings were moved by operating a lever. This machine was simpler and less expensive than the English machines of the period—in 1847 its price was 1,200 francs.

The boring mill   In our discussion of gun construction in Volume II we referred to the vital role of the horizontal and vertical machines used to bore and ream cannons. We then noted that the industrialization of the steam engine might have been delayed for many years if Smeaton's grossly inaccurate horizontal machine had not been replaced by that of John Wilkinson, an ironmaster near Bersham in Chester, for boring of cylinders, because these mills had scarcely been modified for centuries.

For example, in 1725 there was a famous factory in a London suburb. The machines it used had cutters consisting of iron drums with six or eight blades fixed in slots on their rims. The object to be machined was placed on a carriage with rollers, which was moved on wooden rails by a winch. The weight of the cutter and its bar caused the tools to work on only the lower portion of the object, so that it had to be pivoted 90° after each cut, only to obtain what was in the final analysis a poor result.

Smeaton's boring mill (1775)   In 1769 Smeaton tried to solve this machining problem by supporting the end of the toolholder by a small carriage carrying a deadweight. In this way the blades no longer worked solely on the lower portion of the cylinder but over the entire surface. This device did not prevent the tool, which was not guided and which remained free throughout the entire operation, from working by following the irregularities produced in the casting.

Wilkinson's boring mill (1775)   In 1775 John Wilkinson perfected his horizontal boring mill suitable to machine the cylinder of Watt's steam engine (Figure 15) with a degree of precision adequate for that period.

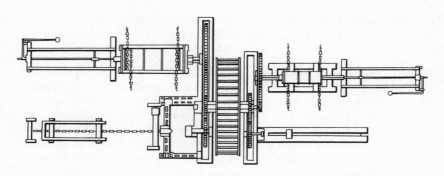

FIG. 15. Wilkinson's horizontal boring mill, 1775. The machine is operated by the water-wheel in the center; gear trains transmit the motion to four work areas. *Top left:* Boring cylinders for steam engines. *Bottom left:* Lathe for pistons. *Top right:* Boring of pump cylinders. *Bottom right:* Lathe for trueing piston rods. (From the reconstruction by the Science Museum.)

Wilkinson notably reinforced the diameter of the boring bar and eliminated the overhang on Smeaton's boring bar by supporting its end on a backrest. The tool was a ring on which the cutting blades, two for rough cutting and one for finishing, were attached. The feed movement (approximately .06 inches for each revolution of the spindle) was provided by a rack and pinion.

The use of horizontal boring machines with a boring bar of a fixed height spread and they continued to be built for a long time, even after the First World War.

Vertical boring mills　　When large cylinders were seamed on a horizontal machine it was difficult—indeed, almost impossible—to obtain a sufficiently accurate cut. If the material were too thin (especially in the case of the air cylinders used in blowing engines), the weight of the object itself caused distortion. Even with the greatest precautions, the cylinder could become slightly out of round.

Vertical machines offered a means to avoid this, provided the cylinder was correctly located and care was taken not to distort it by gripping it too tightly. The design of these machines had to permit vertical movement of the seaming bar.

The French builders who around 1840 received an order for steam engines for the first transatlantic liners had to complement their inadequate horizontal boring mills with vertical ones. On these machines, in which the object was also stationary, the toolholder had two movements: continuous rotation and perpendicular. The first was in proportion to the diameter and nature of the object; the second, always very slow, depended on the quality of finish desired, the sturdiness of the machine and tools, and the amount of power available.

The boring mill built by Cavé around 1840 for his own needs (that is, to bore cylinders with diameters of as much as 6½ feet) had an unusual feature in that it was placed in a masonry pit some 21 feet deep and 13 feet in diameter that was covered by a platform at ground level. Potential purchasers were assured that this arrangement economized space and "protected the various parts of the mechanism from variations in temperature."

The advantages of easier location of the workpiece and economy of labor were also claimed for this type of machine. In this regard, a document of the time stated:

> Since the machine works alone as soon as the object has been located and the operation of the tool has been adjusted, an ordinary laborer can operate the machine. When the pieces are fairly thick (and it is rare that they are less than several centimeters thick), with a little practice such a man can easily operate two such machines simultaneously. If to these advantages we add the ability, by the simple addition of a special device, to plane the outside surfaces of the objects which have been bored, we can say without hesitation that such a machine becomes indispensable in machine shops.

Decoster, who also built boring mills, added to them a movable side support whose height could be varied, which was intended for turning external cylindrical parts, such as the flanges on reciprocating cylinders of steam engines. Such a machine, which could bore a diameter of 8 feet 2 inches for an equal height, weighed 14 tons and cost 8,000 francs in 1847.

However, the use of these machines, whether vertical or horizontal, remained limited to simple operations like those done with a drill or lathe on small objects. Experience over a period of time revealed their defects, which were partly remedied by increasing their speed and, most notably, by adding to the horizontal models a table whose height could be varied. These models then (around the middle of the nineteenth century) became capable not only of boring but also of milling and drilling.

The planing machine   A method to replace the difficult hand labor necessary to produce plane surfaces with the chisel and
file was sought for a long time.

We know that a machine built by Villons in 1716 performed a similar operation, to make musket barrels with a tool that was already called a milling cutter, a
kind of rotary file. Before being hot rolled, strips of iron drawn out by hammering
were milled in the same way that a piece of wood is planed on a planing machine,
but since the object was hand held, both precision and output were low.

The absence of sufficiently powerful and accurate boring machines forced
manufacturers of pumps, for example, to build the pump chambers by assembling
iron staves and banding them, as was done for vats. Each stave had to be shaped
first with a hammer on an anvil to give it the desired curve. The edges were then
filed down to make the level that allowed the staves to be overlapped.

Focq's planing machine   A mechanic from Maubeuge, Nicolas Focq, built a
machine for planing metal as one planed wood
(Figure 16), described in 1751 in the *Recueil des machines et inventions approuvées par
l'Académie des Sciences.* The operator moved the tool horizontally across the piece
by means of a crank. Material was cut on the return stroke as well as the initial one
by "a crescent-shaped tool which cuts with the end of its horns" (Figure 17). The
tool was held in a tool rest that was "pulled by its ends with the help of a strong
rope" along a horizontal bar acting as its support and guide.

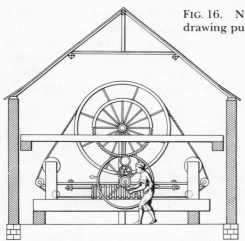

FIG. 16.   Nicolas Focq's planing machine,
drawing published in 1751.

FIG. 17.   The plane on Focq's machine.

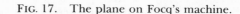
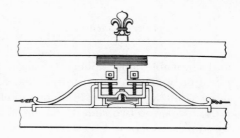

The same machine was also used to finish the assembled staves by planing the
inside of the pump chamber, which could be up to 10 feet long and 4 feet in
diameter.

Caillon's planing machine   At the beginning of the nineteenth century, a Pari-
(1805)   sian locksmith named Caillon, whose shop was lo-
cated at 82 rue Saint-Martin, built for his own use a
machine to plane pieces of iron of all lengths and with widths up to 9½ inches and
thicknesses to 3¼ inches.

This machine consisted essentially of a table traversed by a screw integral with the tool rest, which moved along the object to be worked. The screw was moved by a belt and two reversing pulleys. With a lever the workman controlled one or the other pulley and reversed the direction of the tool's movement.

Caillon's planing machine won honorable mention at the Paris Exposition of 1806 and thanks to several improvements, a silver medal in 1819. Between Focq and Caillon, more than a half century had passed, during which surfaces still continued to be dressed by hand. Projects of this type were, moreover, confined to small objects. But the development of mechanical production stimulated the evolution of several models which, like the earlier ones, were manually operated but in some cases already had the general appearance of modern planing machines.

The invention of the planing machine may be claimed by six English builders: Bentham, Bramah, Matthew Murray, James Fox, Joseph Clement, and Richard Roberts.

In a patent he took out in 1793 Bentham may have described a planing machine. Bramah may have done the same in 1802, and Matthew Murray (born around 1765) is believed to have built a small planing machine, supposedly to machine the slide valves of steam engines. In 1814 it was being used in a locked room the workers were forbidden to enter.

Fox's planing machine (1814) In the same year James Fox, already mentioned in connection with his improvements to the slide lathe, built a planing machine for his textile equipment. It remained in operation until 1859. Its control and reversing mechanism for the table seems to have been adopted later by Clement. Fox built a larger model for the same purpose in 1821, which was capable of planing objects 10 feet long and some 2 feet wide. In 1820 George Rennie built a planing machine on which the movement of the table was controlled by a screw. Its pivoting tool rest allowed the tool to work during its return stroke as well as its traversing stroke.

Roberts's planing machine (1817) Focq and Caillon held the workpiece stationary and caused the tool to move, but English builders adopted the opposite solution of a stationary tool and a movable table. Roberts's design followed that of his predecessors in his 1817 machine built of metal entirely by hand. It included a bed on which was mounted a table 52 inches long and 11 inches wide, moved manually by means of a chain and cross pin along two slide bars, one flat and the other a V bar; and two vertical standards joined by a crossbar on which the tool rest carriage with its graduated plate could traverse.

This small machine, which is very remarkable for the period, is preserved in the Science Museum in London.

Clement's planing machine (1820) Roberts was closely followed by Clement, who had worked for three years for Bramah, then Maudslay. Having set up his own shop, he built in 1820 a similar machine. A few years later Clement built a second planing machine that for more than ten years was the largest in England. It had the advantage of being able to work with two tools, one on the traversing and the other on the return movement of the table. The table, which traveled slowly on rollers over a masonry base, was moved by one man (or two, when it was operating at full capacity). It operated day and night for a long time and brought its inventor a substantial income.

Planing machines with a movable tool

The overall length of a machine with a stationary tool had to be approximately double that of the table so that the table would not overhang. This disadvantage was avoided in planes with stationary worktables, a feature that also offered the possibility of machining pieces that were very heavy or too high to pass under the toolholder crossbar of machines with a movable table.

On the other hand, adjusting the height of the tool in relation to the object was a long and difficult process, the vertical movement of the table and tool being limited. But the principal defect of the system, and the one that caused it to be gradually abandoned, lay in the fact that the tool had a tendency to lift the crossbar during the work, which was detrimental to output and accuracy.

For a long time it was claimed that this criticism was not justified and that, for example, the large machine built by Mariotte for the Indret shops made cuttings "2 inches wide and four to five times that number in length, and .04 inches thick almost everywhere" in cast iron. It seems certain, though, that the tool too often chattered, which became unacceptable as demand increased for more cutting power and quality.

De La Morinière's planing machine (1834)

In 1834 the planing machine with a stationary worktable was invented by De La Morinière. This engineer, then manager of the Manufacture des Glaces de Saint-Gobain, needed to dress a casting table 13 feet long, almost 10 feet wide, and weighing 12 tons, for floating plate glass.

There were no planing machines of these dimensions in France at that time. De La Morinière, being of the opinion that for bulky, flat, heavy objects it was better to leave the object stationary and make the tool movable, designed and had constructed a planing machine with a stationary worktable, a prototype of those still in existence (in very small numbers, it is true) for doing similar work, like planing armor plates. This type of machine was originally extremely simple.

The casting table was supported on two low brick walls and was enclosed in a wooden frame that carried two metal bars of the type used for banding wheels to act as a track for the planer.

The planer consisted of a traveling gantry crane on which the toolholder could move transversely like the carriage of a traveling bridge, to work over the entire width of the table. The machine was moved manually, by means of crossbars, on the shaft of which were two pinions engaging endless chains. The experiments having been satisfactory, an actual machine was designed, a model of which, now on exhibit in the Musée du Conservatoire national des Arts et Métiers, reveals the basic principles of its construction.

The crossbar is moved, by means of two endless chains and a reversing device, on two V guide rails fixed to two tall uprights. Two toolholders permit working in both directions, and in addition both tool rests can be tilted. The table is supported by screw jacks to shift vertically the objects to be tooled. Lastly, the mechanism is placed in a pit so that the slide bars are at ground level.

De La Morinière ordered from Cavé two large tables, which were to be delivered completely finished, and explained his method, which Cavé followed to build a similar machine for his own shops, replacing the two driving chains with racks and pinions.

De La Morinière later returned to the navy and was assigned to install shops in the shipyards of Cherbourg, Indret, Rochefort, and Toulon, which had pieces 30 feet long to be planed. Orders for the large planing machines were given to Mariotte, who was opposed to using racks, "which in contrast to the use of chains offer only disadvantages, and are expensive."

Other builders imitated Cavé and Mariotte. Some, like Decoster and Pauwels, adopted the system of traction by internal chains; others (like Farcot) copied Mariotte, with chains on the outside of the table. Still others, like Pihet, preferred the racks recommended by Cavé. This type of machine soon became known as the French planing machine, to distinguish it from the planer with a stationary tool and movable table, to which the English by and large remained faithful and which they quickly perfected.

Whitworth's planing machines (1835)

Joseph Whitworth attached great importance to machining flat and cylindrical surfaces as perfectly as possible, and the quality of his work was such that at the great Exhibition of 1851 in London his machine tools were considered so superior as to offer unfair competition with other exhibitors.

His first planing machine, patented in 1835, had a stationary worktable and a traveling tool similar to that of de La Morinière, but better designed. The tool rest crossrod moved on the frame with the help of rollers. Its movement was obtained by two screws with elongated threads pulling each end of this crossrod. The tool rest pivoted automatically each time it reached the end of its stroke, causing the tool to work in both directions.

Whitworth also built planing machines with a stationary tool and movable table (Figure 18), for which in 1835 he took out the first patent. One of them (whose capacity was not very great, since its table was only about 4 feet long and approximately 15 inches wide) is preserved, like Roberts's, in the Science Museum in London. It represents noteworthy improvements in comparison with earlier

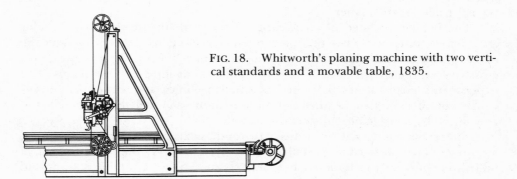

FIG. 18.   Whitworth's planing machine with two vertical standards and a movable table, 1835.

machines with stationary tools. It is no longer driven manually but by a strap and stationary and free pulleys; the direction of operation is automatically reversed by adjustable stops fixed to the table. The table, with T grooves, is moved along V slide bars by a screw in its axis. The crossrod is supported on two vertical standards and is moved up and down manually by two vertical screws controlled simultaneously by level gears. The tool rest carriage can be tilted, and the tool rest itself pivots, as on Whitworth's machine with a stationary table, in order to plane in both directions.

Characteristics of these models

The table here provides some idea of the various models built around 1845 by a French builder and of the principal characteristics of the machines most in demand.

Model number	Length of bed	Surface of table	Price in francs	Remarks
1	7 ft. 6 in.	4 ft. × 10 in.	1,500	Has stationary tool and movable bed
2	13 ft.	8 ft. × 1 ft. 4 in.	2,500	
3	14 ft. 9 in.	9 ft. × 1 ft. 8 in.	3,000	
4	16 ft. 3 in.	10 ft. × 2 ft. 4 in.	4,000	
5	10 ft.	8¾ ft. × 3 ft. 4 in.	4,000	Has movable tool and stationary bed
6	15 ft.	13 ft. × 4¼ ft.	5,500	
7	19 ft. 6 in.	17½ ft. × 5¼ ft.	6,500	
8	24 ft.	22¼ ft. × 6½ ft.	7,500	

Conditions of use

In cutting cast iron, the cutting speed of the planing machines varied between 3 and 4 inches per second, or 15¾ and 19⅔ feet per minute, with a feed of between .015 and .04 inch at each stroke of the tool.

Let us imagine that we have to plane a sheet 6¼ feet long and 6¾ inches wide, or 3.5 sq. ft., at a speed of 3 inches per second. On a machine with a rotating tool allowing it to work in both directions, the stroke of the tool must be approximately 7.2 feet to permit the tool to free itself and pivot each time it reaches the end of its stroke. It is easy to calculate that planing the sheet in question needed some 8 hours with such a machine; that is, a working day of 11 hours, allowing time for mounting and removing the object and for preparing, adjusting, and sharpening the tools.

As the use of planing machines grew, the invoice price per square centimeter of surface planed gradually decreased from 2 to 1.5, then 1 centime, around 1850. Using this last figure, planing the cast-iron piece in our example cost the customer 35 francs. The cost to the entrepreneur was as follows:

Day's wages of the worker (in Paris)	4 francs
Cost of power (steam engine)	3
Cost of tools	2
Interest and amortization on the machine (10% of 8,000 francs for 1/365 year)	2.20
Miscellaneous expenses	3.80
Total	15 francs

The contemporary document from which we have taken these figures concludes by saying, "Thus the work of the machine, when well done and well supervised, can easily bring in a net profit of 20 francs per day, presuming that it is constantly working and that one does not want to overwork it."

As for overworking the machine, we are informed that "in such machines, the resistance offered by the tool at work is sometimes no more than 1/10 hp., and can rise, depending on the quantity of metal to be removed, to a maximum of 4/10 or 5/10 hp."

Other types of planing machines Machines with stationary tools and movable tables seemed, at least in the beginning, to be best suited to machining objects that were neither too large nor too heavy; but experience showed that machines with stationary worktables had inadequate output and accuracy. Other solutions thus had to be found.

In 1839 Bodmer applied for a patent for a planing machine with a single vertical post and stationary tool, and for his vertical lathe with two vertical posts. Neither machine is believed to have been built.

Bodmer's planing machine with a single vertical post (or open frame) consisted essentially of the following components:

— A strong post able to move transversely on a bed perpendicular to the one that held the table;
— A tool carriage that could be oriented in various directions and that moved vertically and transversely on the post;
— A table in the form of a hollow box whose upper face and one side had T grooves and that slid along its bed on two V slide bars positioned at different heights to eliminate any rocking movement.

Bodmer's idea made no impression on contemporary builders, for it was not taken up until several decades later.

Lateral planing machines were built to replace the machines with stationary tables to a certain extent for machining heavy, bulky objects on which the surface to be finished was long but narrow. The objects were attached to platforms with T grooves, or to a stationary table. The toolholder moved over a table placed laterally. The table was similar to that of a filing machine with a movable head, but its axis was traversed by a screw providing the traversing and returning movements of the tool.

In certain types of work it was occasionally necessary to plane not horizontal faces, as above, but lateral ones of bulky objects. Strange planing machines were therefore designed whose slide bars were attached vertically to a wall. Instead of being horizontal, the cross slide on which the tool carriage moved was therefore vertical. The apparatus was simple, but it is easy to imagine that it was completely lacking in rigidity and that the accuracy of the work under such conditions was minimal, despite the slow cutting speed. Such a machine was in service for a long time in the shops of the Soho foundry near Birmingham.

The shaping machine Planing surfaces too small to be machined economically on planing machines led to the development of machines similar to planers, that is, with alternating movement and a chisel but with smaller dimensions. The idea originated in England. Instead of a stationary tool and a moving workpiece, the opposite solution was adopted: the tool was fixed to a carriage with an alternating traversing stroke, the piece being attached to a table with a longitudinal feed. The stroke and the feed were of course adjustable.

Nasmyth's shaping machine   The first machine of this type was probably one built by Nasmyth in 1836, on which the tool rest slide was controlled by an exterior crank; the table advanced automatically each time the tool returned to its starting point.

This machine, which was intended "to replace working with the cold chisel by adding to it, thanks to the smoothness it made possible, the finish of the file," was then known as Nasmyth's steel arm.

Shaping machines with a   When it was necessary to machine large or heavy
movable carriage and   objects, the table had to be fixed and the tool fed by
stationary table   moving the carriage along a bed long enough to
hold the workpiece. One or more tables could then
be attached to this bed and made to support two or even three carriages. This considerably increased the capacity and output of the machine.

For a long time these machines were known as movable-head shaping machines, the head consisting of the carriage and the tool rest slide.

Shaping machines with a   One of the most important first improvements to
stationary carriage and   shaping machines was providing for a quick return
movable table   of the tool, as on the planing machine. This was the
work of Whitworth (Figures 19 and 20).

Two other British machine builders, Sharp and Stewart, caused the crank moving the toolholder to operate along the latter's axis rather than being offset as in Nasmyth and Whitworth's designs. They also introduced a graduated scale on the bed to facilitate measuring the movement of the table or tool.

In Stockholm, Bolinder adopted an arrangement (later abandoned) that

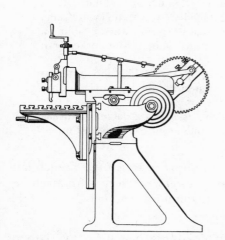

FIG. 19.   Whitworth's shaping machine, with a device for the automatic lowering of the tool; around 1840.

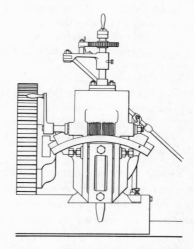

FIG. 20.   Tool head of Whitworth's shaping machine. It could be oriented in different directions.

consisted of adding, on a shaping machine with a long bed, a means of longitudinal planing in addition to the ordinary transverse planing. The carriage now had two tool rests, one that could work perpendicular to the bed, the other parallel. The carriage was driven slowly or rapidly, as necessary, to move the bed along.

Just as there were two types of planing machines, there were also two kinds of shaping machines, depending on the size or weight of the objects to be machined. The table was movable in small machines so that the tool could operate over its entire width, whereas in large machines, since the object could not be moved, it was the carriage slide mechanism (i.e., the head) that was movable.

The Decoster shaping machine (1846)   For planing small objects, Decoster was the first to conceive of considerably reducing the time needed to attach a workpiece to the table by using a vise with parallel jaws (Figure 21). Decoster explains the process in his catalog.

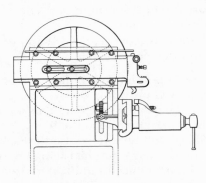

FIG. 21.   Decoster's shaping machine.

The filing machine is remarkable for its simplicity, the rapidity with which it operates, and the invaluable addition of the vise clamp, which is attached to it in order to tighten the object to be planed immediately, with no loss of time.

This filing machine is, in fact, very unusual in various ways, enabling a quantity of small objects, which are found so often in shops, to be worked with very great speed.

With such tools, it is understandable that the use of files and cutters is becoming extremely rare, and that in the greatest number of cases they are completely eliminated.

This shaping machine system, for which I took out a patent, naturally gave me the idea to make similar devices with milling cutters, with continuous rotation, and so on.

So was born the name *shaping machine (étau-limeur)*, which the French language has retained ever since. The term *shaper (limeuse)* was reserved for machines with a movable head, whose use was moreover to diminish gradually as use of the planer and the milling cutter increased.

Operating conditions   When Decoster took out a patent for his shaping machine in 1846, iron was being planed over short lengths at the speed of 4 (10 cm) to 5 inches per second (20 to 24 feet per minute).

In general, a feed of .004 to .006 inch for each stroke of the tool was considered normal, depending on the nature of the metal, the finish desired, and especially the dressing of the cutter. With a very sharp cutter it was possible to increase the feed to .008 of a millimeter and thus to plane, with a stroke of 4 inches, a surface of from one-third to one-half a square yard per day. Taking into consideration that the process involved small objects that generally had to be planed on several sides, repeated mounting and removal of the object as well as tool dressing were necessary.

This output was regarded as "considerable when compared with that of even the most skilled worker, and all the more economical in that it eliminated the use of cold chisels, files, and hammers." The document being quoted adds that "completely assembled, with the wooden frame on which it rests, this machine sells for 1,000 francs in the builder's shop."

*The vertical
shaping machine*

The first such machine was probably built by Roberts in England soon after the planing machine and before the shaping machine, probably around 1825.

Some ten years later, French builders began to build simple machines with a deep gooseneck frame carrying the toolholder, which could not be tilted and was controlled by a disk crank.

The models built by Derosne and Cail, like Decoster's, had a round table that moved lengthwise, sideways, and in a circle. Its movement was either manual or automatic, depending on the size of the machine as defined by the stroke of the tool. For example, the principle characteristics of the Decoster vertical shaping machines were as follows:

Model no.	Stroke of tool	φ to be machined	φ of the plate	Price in francs	Weight in lbs.
1	14 in.	6 ft. 8 in.	4 ft.	8,000	14,740
3	6 in.	3 ft. 4 in.	2 ft.	3,000	
4	5½ in.	1 ft. 8 in.	1 ft. 6 in.	3,500	2,310
5	4 in.	1 ft. 5½ in.	11 in.	1,000	

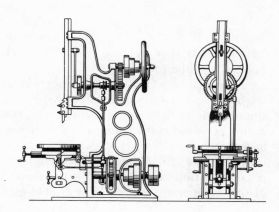

FIG. 22. Lowell Bements, mortising machine with a circular plate, 1845.

Model 4 had a single column and a toolholder mounted on each side, one working on a circular disk and the other on a rectangular table. This arrangement of two opposing heads was not retained.

Machines to cut grooves in bores can be compared with these mortising machines. They too had a tool with alternating vertical movement, an exception being Maudslay's horizontal machine built at the beginning of the nineteenth century for his own use. Moreover, on these machines (known more simply as slotting machines) the toolholder and the control device are placed under the workpiece, over which the tool is drawn—exactly the reverse of the arrangement with the mortising machine. The chief advantage of this arrangement is that it takes large-diameter objects, especially wheels and pulleys.

The milling machine   The milling cutter is an ancient tool. Historians disagree on its origin, some favoring the file, others the drill. The *Encyclopédie* itself equivocates, describing the fraise for the har-quebusier's flashpan as "a piece of steel as large and round as an acorn, with a rough surface like a file" and the clockmakers' milling cutter as "a kind of drill."

We have already mentioned that Villons's 1716 machine milled the flats and edges of iron strips to be rolled as rifle barrels. Its inventor speaks of the milling cutter as a tool already in existence, which he may simply have put to a special use. On the other hand, it is certain that this tool was fitted to other machines during the eighteenth century.

The Musée du Conservatoire national des Arts et Métiers has pictures of cutters used on Hulot's 1760 machine for slotting wheels (i.e., cutting gear teeth), of cutters by Vaucanson (1770), and also of a machine (1720) made to cut them, the cutter turning on its axis after each stroke of the hammer on the chisel. In his *Essai sur l'horlogerie* (1763), Berthoud gives a description and drawing for another machine to cut milling cutters, shaping fraises, using a cutter instead of a cold chisel.

Applications of this tool, which were for a long time limited to handwork, did not change quickly. Bramah may have used a milling cutter with a vertical spindle to machine the bodies of the locks he was making in London around 1790, but the first milling machine with a table to which to attach the workpiece was not built until a century after Villons's machine, by the American Simeon North.

Eli Whitney's   Eli Whitney invented the cotton gin, which was to *milling machine (1818)*   have such a great influence on the development of the textile industries in the United States. Around 1815 he established a gun factory in Connecticut and invented, three years later, a milling machine for rifle parts.

This machine (Figure 23) is approximately 18 inches high and 2½ feet long. Its frame is a solid wooden block supported by four wrought-iron feet. The spindle, whose diameter is slightly more than 2½ inches, ran in bearings in two housings bolted to the frame and was driven by a pulley approximately 20 inches in diameter.

The table, which has disappeared, moved lengthwise between a guide block last on the frame and another V-shaped one on the front table bracket. Movement of this table was obtained by a double-grooved pulley attached to the spindle

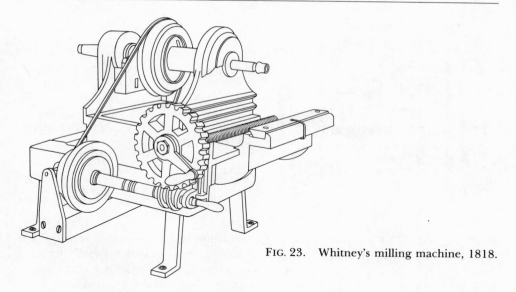

FIG. 23.   Whitney's milling machine, 1818.

between the two bearings and connected by a round belt to a similar pulley mounted on a shaft with a brass worm gear. The shaft could be raised or lowered to engage (or disengage) this gear with a wrought-iron worm gear controlling the movement of the table. Movement could thus be effected automatically or manually by a crank. The height was adjusted by blocks placed under the workpiece.

The Gay and Silver milling machine (1830)   The Gay and Silver machine shop was established around 1830 to produce textile machines and machine tools. Whitney's machine obviously inspired these other American machine builders. Their model, made entirely of metal, was much sturdier than Whitney's and had in addition a tool carriage capable of limited vertical movement, which greatly facilitated adjusting the tool. Frederick W. Howe served his apprenticeship with Gay and Silver before becoming one of the best American engineers.

The milling machine of Robbins and Lawrence (1848)   Howe went to work for Robbins and Lawrence as a designer and quickly rose to be chief engineer. He too took his inspiration from earlier designs, and around 1848 he built a machine (Figure 24) that still bore a strange resemblance to the Whitney and Gay and Silver machines but that had improvements making it stronger and more accurate. It was controlled by a three-speed cone pulley connected by a gear to the spindle. The spindle-holder carriage moved vertically while the table moved lengthwise, also controlled by a three-speed cone pulley. It was possible to move the table sideways by hand, and it had a vise to hold the pieces to be milled.

Other milling machines   Except for Decoster, early French builders of machine tools appear not to have built milling machines.

In his 1847 catalog Decoster includes a picture of a "profile milling machine"

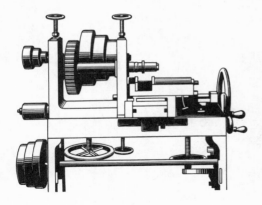

FIG. 24. Horizontal milling machine by Robbins and Lawrence, 1848. Drawing by Frederik W. Howe.

that weighed 1,364 pounds. This simple machine has a horizontal spindle that turns in a cast-iron support bolted to a strong frame, with a possibility of a transverse adjustment of a few fractions of an inch. Control is by a three-speed cone pulley and two straight pinions: the shaft of one of the pinions extends to receive a pulley that supplies the longitudinal movement of the worktable. This slide has a vise similar to that of the shaping machine by the same builder, in which the object is held after it has been adjusted to the proper height.

This milling machine was certainly designed around 1840, and we are justified in thinking that it inspired a Le Havre mechanic named Nillus, who in 1847 built a similar machine. His model, however, had a certain number of improvements, the most important being a strong bracket that moved vertically, carrying a table with longitudinal and transversal T grooves, and controlled manually by a screw and crank.

According to a technical publication of the time, this milling machine may have been made to the specifications of an English engineer named Paul, who is supposed to have designed from memory a machine he had observed in England, where the simple milling machine had been in use for almost twenty years. The fact is that in 1829 Maudslay had built a machine designed by Nasmyth to mill the hexagonal faces of nuts and bolts, an operation formerly done with the file.

The use of milling spread slowly, however, because it was impossible to exceed a cutting speed of 16½ feet per minute in cast iron without causing excessive heating and wear to the tool. The production, tempering, and sharpening of this tool were difficult. The shape of its teeth required a rational design, and its use required machines that were more powerful, stronger, more stable, and had more regular movement than did turning, planing, and drilling machines. Until the beginning of the second half of the nineteenth century, then, its use in Europe was regarded as difficult and expensive. Whitworth himself did not undertake to build milling machines until after 1850.

It was in fact the Americans who launched the milling machine and who developed it to such a point that they long maintained supremacy in this field.

The drilling machine   Together with the lathe, the drilling machine is one of the oldest machines known; Homer mentions its existence in the *Odyssey*. Its construction, like that of the lathe, evolved little in the course of centuries. Clockmakers built very simple bench models that were operated manually by crank or treadle, but these were only to drill small-diameter holes, generally in thin, soft metals.

This category includes Vaucanson's horizontal drill (Figure 25), which, like his lathe, can be examined in the Musée du Conservatoire national des Arts et Métiers. Basically, it consists of a spindle carriage that can be moved longitudinally (approximately two feet) on a table formed by two square-sectioned iron bars inclined at a 45° angle, exactly like the carriage on Vaucanson's lathe, and similarly controlled by a central vernier screw. The spindle itself slides vertically on two cylindrical vertical columns, again by means of a central vernier screw. Its rotary movement and feed are manual.

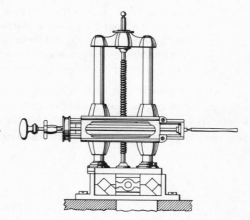

FIG. 25.   Horizontal drill by Vaucanson.

Rudimentary boring machines were used for larger holes, but only rarely, and then for special projects like the cannons mentioned earlier. For sheet metal and even cast iron, punches of tempered steel were used in punch presses.

There are no historical milestones in the development of the drill comparable with those of the lathe (Vaucanson, 1751; Senot, 1795; Maudslay, 1797), the boring mill (J. Wilkinson, 1775), and the planing machine (Focq, 1751). The need for machines specially adapted for drilling seems to have made itself felt rather late. Just as the beds of the first lathes were of wood, in the first vertical drilling machines the spindle carriage was bolted to a wooden post.

Around 1840 many American machines were being built in this form. One of them, whose capacity was one-quarter of an inch, was operated by a three-speed cone pulley that gave its spindle a maximum speed of 150 rpm. The height of the spindle was fixed, but the table could be raised and lowered by a pinion, a rack, and a lever.

Machines with a metal column or upright gradually appeared, and sturdier designs were developed whose capacity, speed, and precision steadily increased, especially when the twist drill, invented by the American Morse, replaced the flat, forked bit.

Numerous types of drills, which differed on the whole only slightly from each other, were produced by English and French builders in the first half of the nineteenth century (Figure 26). The French machines were reputed to be generally lighter than their competitors, the price of raw materials being considerably higher in France than in Great Britain. One Parisian model was described in this way:

> This vertical drilling machine can be placed in any corner of the shop; the bedplate is strong enough to eliminate the need to anchor it at the top. Its plate is movable; it not only moves up and down to come closer to the ground but is also adjustable around the axis of the pillar in order to move off-center or to clear completely the vertical line of the drill holder. It is equipped with a system of movable jaws that allow the clamping and precise centering of the object to be drilled. The movement of the toolholder is transmitted by belts, with the help of reversing pulleys and appropriate gears. Lastly, the pressure or rectilinear movement of the drill holder is effected by a feed screw that acts directly on the shaft, and by a manually operated gear train. Thus, the pressure depends not on the machine but on the operator, who can regulate it at will, increasing or decreasing it according to the nature of the material, the precision of the opening desired, and the speed with which he must operate.

This obviously simple machine (perhaps too light and too weak for a drilling capacity of between one and two inches) should not be compared with a Whitworth drill of the same capacity, which was heavier and more highly developed and cost approximately 3,500 francs instead of 1,000.

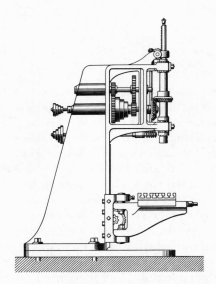

FIG. 26.   Whitworth's vertical drill, 1835.

The need soon arose for machines that could drill holes in increasingly bulky and heavy objects, as for example in locomotive fireboxes, in which a large number of holes had to be drilled on several faces without the workpiece being moved. This led to the development of the radial drill with pivoting arms, attached to the walls or columns of the shop, and carrying a spindle that was capable under these conditions of drilling at any point on a large surface.

One of the first radial drills put into service in France, on the Orléans railroad, came from Sharp & Company of Manchester. This drill's arm was carried on a vertical column attached to a wall.

Later, radial drills were built that could be installed anywhere in a shop (Figure 27). One of them, in service in the shops of the Lyon railroad, had been built by Calla to a Whitworth design. We know that Jules Gaudry admired one built for Cavé for his own needs.

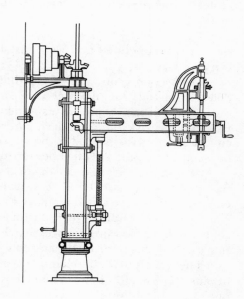

FIG. 27. Radial drill, 1848. The four speeds of rotation of the drill are supplied by the steps of the cone pulley attached to the wall. Vertical movement of the arm along the column and horizontal movement of the drill holder are obtained by screw and crank.

This type of machine was included in Decoster's project. In addition to his four models of ordinary vertical drills, it had included two radial drills—one with a 3¼-foot arm, weighing 5,500 pounds, and valued at 2,500 francs, the other with a 6½-foot arm and costing 6,000 francs.

These machines, which were derived from the first models, had very simple mechanisms. Because they were built without bedplates, and since the bases of their columns were cemented into the ground, their tops had to be secured to the shop's ceiling.

Cutting speeds of the drilling machines were lower than speeds for the lathe and planer. On the average, it was

        8 feet 2 inches per minute in steel
     10 feet 6 inches per minute in wrought iron
     14 feet 9 inches per minute in cast iron
     28 feet   per minute in copper

Improvements were later made in the rigidity of the machine, since the growing use of twist drills permitted constantly increasing cutting and feeding speeds.

The grinding machine and polishing machine

The use of the sandstone grinding wheel is very old. The foregoing discussion has described some examples of polishing operations with the grinding wheel.

Thereafter, in line with the development of machine construction and increased production and precision, a more clear-cut distinction came to be made between trimming, grinding, and polishing (truing was not to appear until much later). Around 1830, a distinction was made between "sharpening wheels as such, used simply to sharpen the tools of the turner, planer, or fitter, e.g., chisels, hook tools, tempered steel drills, etc."; and "wheels for grinding down or polishing metal surfaces."

The former, which were small, were of hard sandstone. In most cases they were treadle operated and were installed in various places in a shop, near the workers' stations.

The second group, called grinding mills, were larger machines. They were driven from the general power source in the factory and were grouped together in one section of the shop or in a special building. Some were of soft sandstone for preliminary work, others of hard sandstone for finishing, and their velocity at the circumference was judged to be considerable because it "sometimes exceeded between 23 feet and 26¼ feet per second"; that is, less than 1,640 feet per minute!

Grinding wheels of metal or sheet metal were also used, "with the addition of fine damp sand," as well as "cast-iron, horizontal wheels dressed with tin and emery," which were called lapidary's mills.

The faces of well-tempered iron grinding wheels had hatchings cut with the cold chisel. These were not crosshatchings as on files, but were "straight, equal, precise, and sharp for the clean removal of cuttings or scrapings."

The wheels used, for example around 1760 by "pointers" to grind the points of pins, were small. They were 3 inches in diameter and 1½ inches wide, and each one of them could put points on some 300,000 pins before being recut.

In some cases, composition grinding wheels were used to polish objects. These were generally "grinding wheels of hardwood, whose surface was impregnated with powdered pumice stone, emery, colcothar (red peroxide of iron), or jewelers' rouge, and putty powder applied by means of tallow." The speed of these grinding wheels could attain 650 yards per minute.

To obtain a still better result, the final polishing operation was done with wooden grinding wheels faced with buffalo hide coated with colcothar. These mills revolved at speeds of between 1,300 and 1,500 yards per minute.

Despite the relative slowness of these speeds, accidents caused by sandstone grinding wheels breaking were frequent, and efforts were made to develop artificial stones that were more homogeneous and solid.

Exact information on the origin of the artificial grinding wheel is lacking. According to Karmarsch, the first ones, called emery wheels, may have been made in England around 1840; it is certain, though, that in 1842 the Frenchman Malbec made an artificial grinding wheel by agglomerating quartz with shellac. He took out a patent the same year, and it appears that his invention had genuine value, since in 1843 the French government ordered him to set up a factory at the national armaments manufacturing center at Châtellerault. This was modeled after the one just built at Paris, probably by Youf, the purchaser of the patent and owner of the shop Aux Forges de Vulcain.

After 1850 the use first of grinding, then truing, machines rapidly became widespread, with numerous improvements being made to the wheel in both the abrasive and binding materials.

Gear-cutting machines   We saw earlier that clockmakers were, as early as the beginning of the seventeenth century, the first to invent and use machines for cutting, or slotting, the wheels and pinions of gears. Two centuries later similar but larger machines were developed to cut wheels for industrial gears. The structure of these machines had not been in any way modified: the iron frame that served as a general housing was preserved, the workpiece was mounted on the same axis as the divided plate, and the chisel or cutter was operated by a crank.

A machine with a worm screw was developed to cut wheels with any number of teeth.

Plate 10. "National factory. Manufacture by English methods of good cast steel razors, equal to those of Sheffields [*sic*] in England." Engraving published in Paris at the end of the eighteenth century. Paris, Musée du Conservatoire national des Arts et Métiers. (Photo Ph. Brossé - P. U. F.)

The cutting tools had the advantage of being relatively simple and easy to make and sharpen. They were similar to those of the planing and mortising machines and were in most cases mounted on a shaft that provided rotary and feed movements.

The tools were made in the form of the space between the teeth, but the precision of their content needed to be no greater than that of the work performed, which in the final analysis was no more than a crude rough cut. An attempt was made to replace them with milling cutters.

Milling cutters to cut gear teeth consisted of a "piece of steel ending in a kind of rose countersink bit, the profile of which was that of the spaces between the teeth."

> This rose countersink bit was cut by furrows inclined relative to the axis, and thus seemed to consist of a series of knives grouped around a single axis. Turning rapidly and being moved along the rim of a wheel, operating in the direction of the axis of the crown gear, this tool cut the latter, leaving an empty space whose section was that of the bit, that is, the curve desired.

Making steel milling cutters was expensive. In 1840 the price could go as high as 40 francs apiece for a three-inch cutter with a diameter. Tempering in particular was a very delicate process; the pieces often got out of shape and even split during this operation. Sharpening was also difficult with the methods then available.

Platform machines   Gear teeth were more precise on this type of machine because the platform itself made greater precision possible. This was so either because of the combination of gears used or because carefully graduated plate was used, the diameter of which was as large as possible to reduce errors of division.

Pihet built machines of this type, with an index plate of 3¼ feet. Several served in his Paris shops, one of which was described in 1827 in the magazine *L'Industriel.* The same description of platform machines serves for Saulnier's machines to "divide toothed wheels of wood or cast iron, whether conical or cylindrical," and for Piat's machines.

On April 10, 1829, a father-and-son team named Glavet, mechanics at Metz, took out a patent for a machine to cut spur and conical gears by planing, using a template.

Cartier's machines   Cartier, a flour mill engineer who had to cut many gears, began in 1838 to build dividing-plate machines of various sizes (one had a plate 8 feet in diameter, the largest in France then), which could cut cylindrical and conical gears.

The gear to be cut was fixed horizontally to a vertical mandrel carried by the dividing plate. The division was done by a series of perforated disks having a number of perforations corresponding to the number of teeth to be cut.

The tool cut either vertically (in the case of spur gears) or obliquely (bevel gears), being tilted in the latter case by the adjustable toolholder.

To work wood or soft metals, the cutter arbor turned between 1,500 and 2,000 rpm. Usually there would be at least two passes for spur gears and four for bevel gears.

For cast iron and wrought iron it was necessary to use shaped tools with a single edge or milling cutters with many edges of cast steel. Their profile was intended to cut two sides of a straight tooth simultaneously, or the single side of a conical tooth, but at a much slower speed, the tool rotating at no more than 80 or 90 rpm.

Small-diameter gears were cut in two passes, a rough milling cut and a finishing operation. Three operations were needed to cut large spur gears and four for bevel gears.

Operating conditions   On a Cartier machine, two and a half 11-hour workdays (including setting-up time) were required to cut a pinion of malleable cast iron 2 feet 1½ inches in diameter with 63 teeth 5½ inches wide. The tool was operated manually by a crank.

The price of the cutting was established as follows:

Salary of the worker: 2½ days @ 4 francs	10.00 francs
Salary of the laborer turning the crank, @ 2.50 francs	6.25
Maintenance expenses and depreciation of tools and machine	7.50
Total	23.75 francs

The same work done manually required at least 11 days, and sometimes 12 or 13, depending on the skill of the worker. He was paid .95 francs per tooth, was supplied with the necessary cold chisels and files, and the wheel was laid out with the teeth marked on both sides. Using a chisel he had to cut the two sides and the root contour of each tooth, rough plane them with a rasp and then a lastard file, and finally finish them off with the smooth or semismooth file.

Thus the cost of 63 teeth came to .95 × 63 = 59.85 francs, to which was added 5.15 francs for the tools, making a total of 65 francs (that is, slightly more than 1 franc per tooth), as contrasted with 38 centimes for machine work. Moreover, in mechanical cutting it was not necessary to lay out the teeth beforehand.

Whitworth's machine (1835)   Gear-cutting machines were built by the English, the most famous one being Whitworth's. The general layout of this machine, patented in 1835, was the opposite of the machines discussed above. The blank to be cut was placed on a horizontal mandrel, the toolholder was vertical and could be oriented on the horizontal and vertical planes, and the tool was a shaped cutter.

The principal movements (the movement of the carriage holding the blank and the feed of the tool) were automatic to the point that the worker's labor was reduced to operating the dividing apparatus, which consisted of a train of gears.

Decoster's machine (1843)   The Parisian builder Decoster took out a fifteen-year inventor's patent in October 1843 for an improvement to his gear-cutting machines. He called it a universal divider, but it does not appear to have been entirely successful.

His catalog showed several machine models. Some, like Cartier's, had dividing plates with a vertical mandrel to hold the blank and a horizontal shaft for the cutter. Machines with plates 2 feet in diameter cost 1,200 francs, although another model with a 3¼-foot plate weighed 3,960 pounds and cost 2,000 francs.

Three other models were built for larger wheels. They were simple machines, comparable to a face lathe, in which the circumference of the plate, which had a large number of notches, seems to have served as a divider. The blank to be cut was probably mounted on the spindle in front of the plate, and the tool rest was perhaps replaced by a device driving a shaped cutter that worked on a horizontal plane. The largest model, with a divider 6½ feet in diameter, weighed 6,600 pounds and cost 4,000 francs.

This series of machines was complemented by another, equally simple, series for cutting racks.

The mechanical punch press

This machine derives, naturally, from the hand-operated punch and the stamp press, used to stamp out rough blanks in all shapes from metal strips for further finishing.

In the second half of the eighteenth century a farrier in the small city of Smithfield, Rhode Island, named Orziel Wilkinson, observed that nails could be made by cutting up scrap iron and making points with the file.

He designed a small blanking press, which could hold tools of different sizes; it was attached to an oak plank and was operated by stirrup. The machine formed a kind of wooden horse on which he placed his eight-year-old son, who in playing on it cut out the nails. This press may have been the first machine of this type built in the United States. To complement it, the same Wilkinson may have built a rolling mill in 1794, but no trace of a patent has been found for these two machines.

On July 21, 1829, a patent was granted to G. Daracott of Boston for a power-driven press to stamp out copper parts. In October of the same year R. Macomber obtained a patent for a spring press. Between 1829 and 1871, nineteen other patents were granted in the United States for flywheel presses.

The screw press

The coining of money led to the birth of at least three machine tools: the rolling mill, the stamping mill, and the screw press. These machines, designed, like many others, by Leonardo da Vinci, are among the oldest in existence.

The invention of the screw press has been attributed to the famous Paris engraver and coiner Nicolas Briot, ca. 1615; but this is incorrect. He was preceded by approximately a half century by the German inventor Schwab, and by almost a century by the famous Florentine engraver, sculptor, and goldsmith Benvenuto Cellini.

Around 1530, in order to strike bronze medals with the effigy of Pope Clement VII, Cellini used a press with a lever six Italian *bracchia* (13 feet) long, for he had noticed that throwing this lever as quickly as possible produced better impressions.

The manually operated screw press, a simple machine, underwent few modifications over the centuries. Briot made the striking die independent of the rotary movement of the screw and aligned the die with guide rods. Boulton built for the London mint a fairly complicated device mechanically controlled that was disappointingly unproductive, as was the system based on wedges or friction pulleys that was patented on December 30, 1858, by Mme. Delachaussée.

Cheret built a machine for the Paris mint in 1861, adopting an idea a Parisian piano builder named Penzoldt had had in 1836, namely to replace an excessively rigid positive control on a centrifugal dryer with a friction system. A model of Cheret's invention on a scale of 1:10 is in the Musée du Conservatoire national des Arts et Métiers. It consists of a flywheel with a leather-covered rim mounted on the end of the screw. Two vertical plates, fixed to the horizontal control shaft and driven by stationary and loose pulleys, bear on and turn the flywheel and move the screw down or up as desired. This design is still common on friction presses.

Here we may note that the coining of money led to the use of the drop hammer, whose output was superior to that of the screw press. It was used in the Paris mint beginning in 1791 to mint copper coins of the Republic.

The drawbench   Until the middle of the sixteenth century, wire was generally drawn manually, by pulling it through a series of dies of decreasing sizes.

In the seventeenth century the equipment of the drawing shops was improved by using machines that were still very simple but that were operated by an external power source. Drawing became a relatively important industry, for it worked iron, copper, gold, silver, and their alloys.

Here is Frémont's account of how precious metals were drawn.

> The metal, which was cast in an ingot by the founder, was first forged on the anvil and brought to the diameter of a broom. This forged ingot underwent a first drawing through the drawing frame to reduce it from the diameter of a broom to the diameter of a cane by passing it through a die called a caliber. This reduction in diameter required approximately eight or ten drawings through holes of decreasing diameters, with the effort of eight workers operating four levers.
>
> This first drawing of the ingot was done not in the drawing shop but at the "laboratory of the royal drawing frame," a public office which alone had the right to possess and use the drawing frame and to apply quality marks. The ingot was then brought to the drawer, who filed it down to eliminate the forge scale remaining, and cut it in two parts, which were again returned to the drawing frame laboratory to be drawn through approximately 40 holes of the die as such (all the other dies have a special name). After its passage through the die the coil that had been brought down to the diameter of a cane was reduced to the diameter of a writing pen; the work of four men operating the levers of the drawing frame sufficed to obtain this result.
>
> The third drawing of the coil was done on the drawing bench, by passing it through some 20 holes of decreasing size in a third die frame called the ras; the labor of two workers was required for this. The wire, which was now reduced from the diameter of a writing pen to the diameter of a tag of a lace, was submitted to the fourth drawing on the drawing bench, by a single worker called a feeder. The die plate, which had approximately 20 holes, was now called a *pregaton,* and the wire was reduced to a dimension known as a *gavette.*
>
> The fifth drawing was done on mills for drawing the *gavette,* with dies known as *gavette* dies.
>
> Finally, the *gavette,* a wire already greatly reduced in diameter, was taken by turners, who brought it down to a diameter less than that of a hair by passing it through dies called drawing irons. The wire was now called *or trait.*

There were three different sizes of *or trait:* superfine ordinary, superfine fine, and finally the smallest, the *trait lancé.*

These holes were obtained by first closing the metal of the die by hammering with a small hammer. The eye was calibrated and polished by driving in a sharply pointed awl. In this way the holes were shrunk and repolished successively with similar, increasingly fine, points. The *or trait,* when reduced to this extreme point of fineness, must have passed through more than 140 holes in the caliber, die, ras, pregaton, gavette dies and drawing irons. At each passage through a new hole it was rubbed with fresh wax to reduce the friction.

The drawing of gold and silver has been given as an example, but that of brass and iron was done in the same manner, with the help of very similar dies and benches. The *Encyclopédie* shows those used by the pin maker, the locksmith who turned out French window fastenings, and the craftsman who made tubes by brazing copper plates wrapped around iron rods, the diameter of which was equal to the inside diameter of the tube. And Blakey made a die to give steel wires the profile of small clock pinions (mentioned in 1744 in the *Recueil des machines approuvées par l'Académie des Sciences*).

Imperfections in the production of screws were still so numerous at the beginning of the nineteenth century that the Société d'Encouragement pour l'industrie nationale felt obliged to offer a prize in order to encourage improvements. Rods of crude wrought iron were generally used, the unequal diameter of which made threading difficult and defective. A partial solution was found by passing these rods through a calibrating operation on a drawing bench.

In this way, or so we learn from his patent request of March 22, 1806, "Louis Japy succeeded in inventing a machine able to draw iron and other metals to very considerable lengths, without any imprint of pliers, or other inequalities; this machine was in service in the drawing shop of M. Migeon, ironmaster at Grand-Villars."

The drawbench underwent few modifications thereafter, the overall concept of this machine remaining extremely simple.

Forge material

As early as the end of the eighteenth century, steam was applied to operate the forge hammer mechanically.

On April 28, 1784, James Watt patented a forge hammer in which the hammer head was raised by a steam-operated piston and dropped by its own weight. Twenty-two years later, in a patent of June 6, 1806, William Deverell proposed to increase the speed of the drop by compressing the air in the upper portion of the cylinder. These two patents were not applied, and some thirty years passed before the first steam-operated power hammer was put into service.

The mechanical hammer

In the meantime, existing machines were improved. The use of crank-operated mechanical hammers (or tilt hammers) to shape pieces of average size became general, and during the first half of the nineteenth century a large number of hammers, called side hammers, were built of cast iron. The camshaft was no longer powered directly by a waterwheel but by a transmission gear.

The steam hammer   However, the appearance of the steam hammer did not suddenly eliminate the use of trip-hammers, for they continued in use for several decades, operated by a steam engine. After building one for his shops at Le Havre, Mariotte undertook to produce them and delivered several to the French navy. He mounted the steam engine and the tilt hammer on the same cast-iron base. A system of springs brought about the dropping of the hammer. The structure weighed approximately 11,000 pounds, and we know that at the time (1845) it was worth approximately 5,000 francs. Mariotte also built smaller models in which the weight of the hammer head did not exceed 44 pounds and the cylinder of the steam engine had a diameter of only 4 inches.

The power hammer   The invention of the steam power hammer is generally attributed to Nasmyth, in 1841. However, such a machine was already in operation in 1836 in Paris, in the shops of François Cavé. He had installed a tilt hammer, with a reversing beam acting as a spring in an immense housing. Twenty-four men rotated the camshaft. Cavé decided to replace these men by a 16-hp. oscillating steam engine.

On June 11, 1836, Cavé applied for the five-year patent already mentioned, to apply a single-acting steam cylinder to a hammer, a stamping machine, or any other similar machine. He then designed his steam hammer, built it, and made improvements that led E. Jonveaux to write that "it operates between two well-finished slide rods, rising and dropping with perfect regularity, without any deviation; the speed and extent of the rising and dropping movements are varied as desired by the action of the steam."

Cavé made other, similar hammers, the most powerful of which, operated by a 40-hp. steam engine, forged 20-ton shafts (Figure 28). Nasmyth took up Watt's idea only in 1839, without developing it.

In the same year F. Bourdon was required to solve the problems of forging large-diameter shafts and heavy parts for transatlantic ships that the Schneider brothers had contracted to build. Bourdon devised a steam hammer he called the *pilon,* a name that has remained attached to this machine. Unlike Nasmyth at this time, he was not content to make a simple sketch but made a complete study that became known to the naval engineers charged with the factory control of government contracts (notably Mimerel, Bertrand, and Paulin). Moreover, he built a small-scale model, which has been preserved, on which he made initial experiments that were ultimately satisfactory.

The Schneider brothers hesitated for a long time before giving the order to build the pilon. Not until several months later, in 1840, was it finally built by Le Creusot factories. It was put into service at the beginning of 1841 in their shops, where, according to Poncelet, General Robert saw it in operation. A five-year patent was requested on October 11 of that year.

Surviving letters dated May 19 and May 23, 1840, prove that Bourdon's design had been completed by this time, since he was strenuously insisting to his employers that it be built. Eugene Schneider and Bourdon made a trip to England two months later, in July 1840.

In Nasmyth's absence, Gaskell is supposed to have shown the visitors his

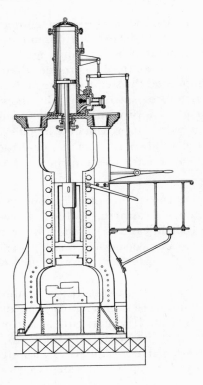

FIG. 28. Cavé's steam hammer, 1848.

partner's catalog of drawings, most notably the sketch of a power hammer, dated November 24, 1839. "They were greatly impressed by it, and carefully noted the drawing and all its details," writes J. W. Roe, whose statement is based on Nasmyth's autobiography. He explains, moreover, that the English builder, paying a return visit to Le Creusot factories in April 1842, is supposed to have noticed the power hammer operating there and may have taken out a patent several weeks later, on June 9, 1842, to protect his rights.

In a paper published in August 1884 by the Société des ingénieurs civils de France, G. Boutmy related in great detail the story of Bourdon's invention, with which he was thoroughly familiar, because for many years he had been the direct collaborator of the famous engineer to whom we owe other important inventions.

Very simply, Boutmy tells what he saw and heard during Nasmyth's visit to Le Creusot in April 1842, and the sincerity of his narrative is beyond doubt. We can only regret, with him, the polemic engaged in by Nasmyth on the occasion of the Exposition of 1844 (at which the Schneider brothers exhibited one of their power hammers) to claim the exclusive priority to this invention. In the course of this he "permitted the printing by his historiographer of imaginary events detrimental to the memory of his French colleague, and which, despite their benevolent form, tend to insinuate that the latter merely profited by the information supplied by the hero of the book."

Bourdon's first power hammer had a head of 5,500 pounds and a fall of 6½ feet. It consisted of 4 cast-iron columns braced by and supporting a plate on which the steam cylinder rested. The hammer slid between these columns, which were strengthened by 4 braces, also of cast iron (see Part 6, Chapter 3, on metallurgy).

Numerous repairs were made on this machine, whose construction proved to be too weak when called upon to induce shocks of hitherto undreamt of intensity. While damage to the machine was being repaired, the various components were reinforced so well that when Nasmyth saw the pilon in April 1842 it was operating in satisfactory fashion. The Schneider brothers reminded Nasmyth and Gaskell of this on October 12, 1843, in a long letter describing all the circumstances of the invention and the relationships between the two companies.

Power hammers with 2½- and 3-ton heads began to be built in 1842 by Le Creusot factories for the naval shipyards at Rochefort, Guérigny, and Fourchambault. These machines were used exclusively for forging heavy equipment such as shafts and crankshafts, large cranks, and connecting rods for engines. Bourdon decided to extend the application of power hammers to stamping, which made it possible to make pieces with complicated shapes that formerly had to be made of cast iron or wrought iron. He now designed a new hammer with a 3,960-pound head that had a fall of 5¼ feet. Its vertical standards dovetailed to the anvil block instead of being independent of it as in earlier models.

Lastly, Bourdon built a still smaller model having a 2,200-pound head with a fall of 3¼ feet and anvil block, standards, and base cast in a single piece. It was used to produce nuts and bolts, hinges, small fittings for wagons, and similar items.

By the time Schneider's five-year patent expired in 1846, Bourdon had perfected the various models of his machine that his experience acquired in forging and stamping had led him to build for emerging industries, particularly those of naval and railroad construction.

From then on the weight and fall of the heads continued to increase, and at the Exposition of 1849 Michel Chevalier, the official reporter, found a power hammer with an 8,800-pound head completely remarkable. But much better hammers were soon to be made.

The rolling mill The origin of the rolling mill is not known, but we know that in the form of two parallel cylinders with smooth or grooved surfaces it was commonly used as early as the fifteenth century to work soft metals. The preparation of blanks to strike coins, of strips of precious metals for goldsmiths, and of tin and lead sheets was done with a rolling mill operated by a hand crank. From its first use, smooth and grooved cylinders were used in complementary fashion. A sequence of smooth cylinders rolled the metal into strips with the desired thickness and a sequence of grooved cylinders cut these strips into rods of a given length. Cylinders with grooves whose depths diminished from one side to the other were probably in use at a very early period. Passing a metal rod through each groove in the order of the diminishing sections permitted the gradual reduction of the bar's section.

Combining in a single stand a smooth cylinder and a grooved one enabled goldsmiths to make specially shaped pieces.

The rolling mill was used to work iron as early as the sixteenth century. This innovation appears to have occurred first in the Liège area and in Germany, then to have spread to England during the seventeenth century, and then to Sweden. It was first used for working small iron rods to make needles. An installation included a rolling frame with smooth iron cylinders and a slitting frame with grooved cylinders and steel cutting edges.

In the sixteenth century, iron was first passed through the rolling mill, then was probably slit by shears with blades operated by a waterwheel. Slitting mills for copper and zinc were similarly equipped and were to remain so until the end of the eighteenth century. The slitting mill with rollers may not have been put into use until the first quarter of the seventeenth century, when waterpower may first have been employed to operate it. Until then the smooth-cylinder mills had been manually operated.

In these installations only the cylinders were of metal; all the housings and gear trains were of wood. Iron was passed first through the rolling mill, then through the slitting mill, after it had been reheated in a special furnace to about 850°C. Because of the nature of these machines, until around the end of the eighteenth century their use remained limited to small objects, to rods approximately 18 inches long with a section of approximately 0.16 square inches. All ironworking was done with the tilt hammer or hand hammers.

It was in lead working that the rolling mill was first used on a major scale, beginning in the first quarter of the eighteenth century. The *Recueil des machines approuvées par l'Académie des Sciences* for 1729 gives a description of a rolling mill built by Fayolle for large sheets of lead. By the end of the century rolling mills strong enough to roll brass sheets could be built. Romilly's large rolling mill, established in 1782, is shown in Diderot's *Encyclopédie*.

Around 1751 a Parisian manufacturer, the ironworker Chopitel, wishing to produce shaped iron bars, built a hot-rolling mill at Essonne near Corbeil. It consisted of two heavy iron cylinders operated by a waterwheel. The cylinders were grooved so that they could turn out the molded metal components that Chopitel used for stairways, balconies, balustrades, window frames, and other articles ordered from him.

Henry Cort was perhaps the first in England to use large rolling and slitting mills for which he was granted a patent in 1783. But it seems clear that his installations still differed very little from those described and illustrated by Swedenborg in 1734 and Emerson in 1758 (Figure 29). Undoubtedly, the lantern gears had been replaced by metal pinions quite similar to those used on rolling mills from the beginning of the nineteenth century onward. The drawings ac-

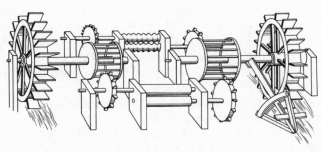

FIG. 29.   Rolling and slitting mill, mid-eighteenth century (from Emerson).

companying Part 6, Chapter 2, on metallurgy show that the housings of rolling and slitting mills were placed face to face in the eighteenth century and side by side in the first half of the nineteenth. Around 1840 the rolling train began to be built with housings lined up face to face, but in the middle of the century this arrangement, which later predominated, was still rare.

In 1791 Jamain and Poncelet, of Sedan, built large rolling mills to produce sheet iron and steel plates. As its use grew, and until the beginning of the nineteenth century, the rolling mill was developed by the Englishmen Keane Fitzgerald (1758) and Washbrough (1779), and the Frenchman Droz (1783/84), a Parisian mechanic and medal engraver.

These improvements, intended to give greater regularity and precision of operation, together with the power furnished by increasingly larger sources (notably the steam engine), caused the use of the rolling mill to spread rapidly, especially after it became capable of producing rails (which conditioned the creation and development of the railroads) and shaped iron rods for metal frameworks.

The hydraulic press The principle of the hydraulic press is described in a treatise published by Pascal in 1650. But almost a century and a half passed before the machine itself was built. In 1796 Bramah took out a patent in London for a machine that could press cotton, paper, fodder, and the like. Its principal component was a piston that compressed water in a pump chamber. The shape of the piston's cylinder was such that the tighter the seal, the greater its pressure on the water; but then the piston seized up. The problem of watertightness was not solved until Bramah conceived the idea of using a joint of fulled leather mounted over a metal disk.

The Périer brothers were building hydraulic presses (Figure 30) in their Chaillot factory, probably several years later. In 1797 they took out a patent that mentions Bramah's invention and in 1812 they described a press they built for a cloth factory at Ternaux. The large piston, with a section of 108½ sq. in., developed a pressure of approximately 24 lbs. per sq. in. The upper plate was at first stationary, but later, when the length of the stroke became too great, both plates were made movable.

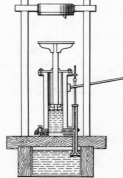

FIG. 30.   Hydraulic press built by the Périer brothers, 1812.

A little later, in 1824, Hallette, already mentioned, built a press to extract oil. A system of valves made it more flexible and economical, it was claimed, than other types. Later, probably beginning in 1840, Cavé also produced these presses, achieving pressures in the neighborhood of 1,000 tons.

In the same period, the hydraulic press began to be used to work lead, which gave Fox the idea in 1847 of trying to use this press to forge other metals. But this type of work was not done until 1860, by the Austrian engineer Haswell, at the Staats-Bahn Forge in Vienna.

In the meantime the idea of using this machine to key and especially unkey locomotive and carriage wheels and axles had been developed, the screw presses used until then having become inadequate. A model exhibited by the house of Stehelin & Cie of Bitschwiller was shown at the Exposition of 1849. It was purchased for 5,200 francs (crane included) for the shops of the Lyon railroad.

In any event, for a long time to come, use of the hydraulic press was the exception, reserved for operations requiring great power, and because the jobs to be done were generally infrequent and much too slow and costly, amortizing the cost of the installation was difficult.

Sheet-metal machines   The working of sheet metal, especially for plates for steam boilers and ships' hulls, rapidly became widespread.

Louis Lemaître began his career as a foreman in the shop owned by his brother-in-law, Cavé, and later established a large factory at La Chapelle-Saint-Denis, outside Paris, which specialized in working sheet metal. In a letter to a Mr. Rochet dated January 22, 1845, Lemaître gives this information about the materials and methods used and the funds that must be invested for naval construction.

Outfitting a sheet-metal shop capable of building ships can vary to an infinite degree. Nevertheless, you must spend approximately 20,000 F if it is to be properly equipped. The principal tools are the following:

A steam-powered shear and its carriage	6,000 F
A mechanical punch and its carriage	6,000 F
A pair of hand punches	1,000 F
Bellows, anvils, small anvils, hammers, drills, etc.	7,000 F
Total	20,000 F

Riverboats could be built with 10,000 F worth of equipment. You could also spend 150,000 F, if you wanted to build ships of from 2 to 400 hp., considering that you must have a complete set of heavy blacksmith's equipment for forging the keel, the sternpost and the stem.

The thickness of the metal sheets used in ship building varies between 3 and 18 mm., depending on the size and the use for which they are intended. For riverboats of up to 40 hp., 4-mm. sheets are used for the sides and 5- to 6-mm. sheets for the bottom. Ships of greater power intended for the same purpose require sheets ranging up to 8 mm. For seagoing vessels, sheets no less than 9 mm. thick are used for the sides of certain ships, and sheets of 11 to 12 mm. for the bottoms, for vessels of 100 to 125 hp. For vessels of 3 to 400 hp., sheets of 12 to 15 and even 16 mm. would be used. The cost is 1.25 F per kilogram, exclusive of the framework.

The punch and the shear　　The first machines intended for these purposes were generally operated by hand with long, powerful levers, or by waterpower when it was possible to build the machines near a stream. In France, Pihet (one of the inventors of gear-cutting machines) was one of the first to manufacture a machine that in addition to punching thick sheets of metal could also cut and punch iron bars, to make square or hexagonal nuts. These machines may have allowed him to reduce considerably the cost of certain operations and so to acquire large markets. For example, the report on the Exposition of 1834 mentions that at this time Établissement Pihet & Cie employed 500 workers and that after the Revolution of 1830 they produced, among other things, 120,000 rifles and 600 iron beds.

Cavé's punch shears　　This famous French mechanic has already been mentioned several times. A drawing attached to the patent application Cavé submitted on June 11, 1836, for a "machine operated directly by steam" depicts a punch he installed in his factory. The capacity of this machine permitted him easily to pierce holes 15 to 18 mm. in diameter in 10-, 12-, and 15-mm. thick sheets, and 18- and 20-mm. holes in iron bars 20 to 25 mm. thick. On occasion 25-mm. wheel tires were pierced with a 23-mm. punch. Cavé soon remodeled this machine into a punch shears by providing for the installation of either a toolholder and punch or a shear (Figure 31).

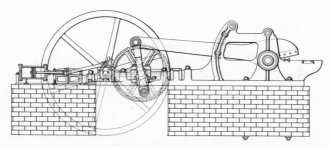

Fig. 31.　Calla's lever-operated shears, 1845.

Calla's punch shears　　Calla designed another improvement, in his machines, which were controlled by pulley and eccentric cams. The operator inserted a pivoting chock between the beam and the toolholder or blade holder in order to engage the descending movement of the slide. When the chock was withdrawn, the pulley continued to turn and the beam to oscillate, but it was no longer activating the toolholder, which thus remained motionless.

Other shears　　The production of other models with continuous movement was undertaken by most French and English machine-tool builders. Some of these models were controlled by eccentrics or crankshafts, others directly by the piston of a steam engine.

Decoster, for example, supplied two eccentric-type models. One could shear through 300-mm. wide sheets of metal 14 mm. thick; its price was 3,000 francs. The other was able to cut 650-mm. sheets 18 mm. thick, and sold for 4,500 francs. Three punches and two blades were included as part of the equipment.

Steam-operated models, which naturally were the most powerful, were used for heavy work in railroad construction shops, shipyards, and large metallurgical plants. The guillotine shear was not developed until the second half of the nineteenth century.

The riveting machine Riveting arrived with railroads, shipbuilding, boilermaking, and metal structures. For instance, the Britannia Bridge, for railroads, built by Robert Stephenson between 1846 and 1850, required no less than two million rivets totaling 900 tons. It was thus necessary to invent appropriate riveting machines, some of which worked by strokes, others by continuous pressure.

The Fairbairn riveter It will be seen later that Durenne applied continuous pressure of a die to form rivet heads. William Fairbairn, a Manchester boilermaker, adopted the same mechanical method to do the actual riveting and patented a riveter (Figure 32) in 1838. His desire to make significant economies in labor costs had led him to invent this machine, which struck one blow every eight seconds, leaving only four seconds to shift the object and position the rivet correctly between the dies. Using this mechanical method it was possible to apply 10 to 12 times as many rivets as by hand.

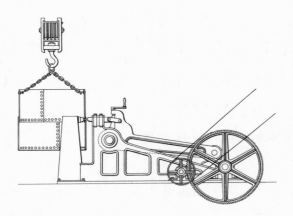

FIG. 32. Fairbairn's riveting machine, 1838.

A Fairbairn riveting machine was imported into France by Hallette of Arras and was purchased by J. J. Mayer & Cie in Mulhouse. Mayer perfected it by adding a clutch system that permitted the machine to be stopped quickly when a rivet was poorly positioned, something hitherto impossible.

The price of the machine, approximately 11,000 francs, was very high for that period. It was difficult to operate, its application was quite limited, and the placing of rivets was not perfect. But the idea of mechanical riveting had been launched, and it caught the attention of several builders. Two French models, by Lemaître and the Schneider brothers, were built for the Exhibition of 1844.

The Lemaître riveter   The first steam-operated riveting machine was built
in 1844 by Cavé, using data supplied by his brother-
in-law, Louis Lemaître. The latter may have been inspired by Cavé's 1836 punch
and the 1838 Fairbairn riveter, but the advantage of Lemaître's machine (a model
of which is displayed in the Musée du Conservatoire national des Arts et Métiers)
was that it could punch before riveting, and it gave the operator time to locate his
rivet correctly. Lemaître took out a ten-year patent in France and in England a
caveat valid until May 1845, which he attempted to sell for 30,000 francs.

The swan-neck housing of this riveter had two slightly offset slides, each
activated by a lever moved directly by a steam-driven piston (Figure 33). On one
slide was a holder for the punch, on the other a die holder for riveting. Prerolled
sheets of iron or copper were placed on a double-beaked anvil. Work done by this
method was excellent, because the edges of the sheet were tightly pressed together
before the operation.

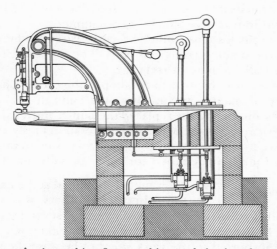

FIG. 33. Lemaître's machine for punching and riveting sheet metal, 1845.

On January 6, 1845, Lemaître was able to write to one Golez that

> I do not make a practice of guaranteeing my boilers, considering that this
> is not done. This would require the firemen to be more careful, so as not to
> allow them to burn, as occasionally happens. All I guarantee is that my work is
> more perfect than that of others, considering that I have manufacturing
> methods no one else has, methods which won the gold medal for me at the last
> Exposition.

Lemaître invented and then put into production another machine that made
it possible to rivet tubes as much as 23 feet in length, with a diameter up to one
foot. This problem, long regarded as insoluble, was thus successfully solved,
particularly in the production of long cylindrical beams made of sheet metal for a
metal bridge Lemaître had been commissioned to build. Later this machine was
used to produce smokestacks from sheet metal, such as those used on steamboats.

Operation of the machines   Before these machines appeared, riveting was done by hand, requiring a team of three men and one child, whose job it was to carry the rivets and place them in the appropriate holes.

The Lemaître machine pierced holes 22 mm. in diameter in forged-iron plates 12 mm. thick, using a steam pressure of 5.4 atmospheres in the boiler. The slide valve admitting steam to the cylinder had to be opened very quickly to punch holes properly, for if this operation was performed too slowly the punch hammered on the plate without cutting through it.

Lemaître estimated that with three men and two children operating his punch riveter it was possible in an 11-hour day to make 400 holes in sheets 10 to 11 mm. thick and to insert 400 rivets 10 to 19 mm. in diameter. The same team working by hand could have made only 80 to 130 rivetings in the same period on plates in which the holes had been pierced beforehand.

It may be noted that at this time mechanical production of rivets was not yet considered necessary, for a blacksmith could produce 220 pounds of rivets per day, cutting them from heated rods of the desired diameter and forming heads on them with a die and four or five blows with a hammer.

For many years small shops could be seen in Paris in which workmen clustered around a forge shaping rivets and bolts. The fire was blown by a bellows operated by a dog walking in a squirrel cage.

In 1836 Antoine Durenne, who had a shop in the rue de Charenton in Paris, conceived the idea of manufacturing rivets mechanically by using one of his punching machines, on which a die replaced the punch and a nailhead shaper the bolster. But as is evident, this was merely an adaptation to this type of work of a machine already in existence. Around 1850 in Manchester an Englishman named Haley built the first machine designed and built specially for this purpose.

The Schneider riveter   Another model, exhibited at the Exposition of 1844 by the Schneider brothers, was also operated by steam, which as we may remember had been in use for several years to operate the power hammer at Le Creusot factory. This riveter was mounted on four rollers so that it could be transported to the work site, but because the steam boiler was independent of the machine, the necessary piping system limited its movements.

As with the Lemaître riveter, the advantage of the Schneider riveter over Fairbairn's was that the tool came into operation only when the rivet was correctly located. Moreover, using a toggle joint resulted in much greater power at the end of the stroke than was available at the top of it, at a considerable economy of steam. A final and most important point was that pressure could be maintained on the rivet as long as seemed necessary.

The Lemaître and Schneider riveting machines first used fabricating boilers that were later commonly used in other metal construction.

Bending machines   Machines replaced manual bending in the first half of the nineteenth century.

Small machines with three horizontal cylinders were used to shape metal wheel tires. The diameter of the circle desired was adjusted by changing the distance between the cylinders. Around 1835 a Parisian wheelwright named E. Philippe replaced this system with large horizontal wheels around which he turned the strips to be bent.

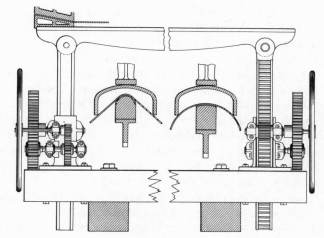

FIG. 34. Lemaître's machine for bending sheet metal, 1848.

The shaping of plates for boilers and tanks was done similarly but on a larger scale. Cavé built two manually operated machines for his shops. One consisted of a movable vertical roller that was made by levers to revolve around another, stronger, stationary roller while pressing on the plates. The second machine consisted of two long horizontal rollers between which the plate was passed. It received pressure from a third roller lowered into position by two large levers.

These machines were simple but nevertheless defective. They were improved by Pihet in particular, who built several of them, with rollers 100 inches long, for the Royal Navy.

Bending by shaping   Heavy boilermaking involved producing bottoms for boilers and tanks. In Cavé's shop this work was done by a kind of steam hammer, the head of which fell on a swage of the desired shape. Some English machines consisted of a convex swage and a concave die between which the red-hot sheet of metal was squeezed by a pressure screw.

Toward the end of the first half of the nineteenth century the Établissements Cail & Cie, which at this time was already specializing in equipment for sugar refineries, had assigned its engineer, Houel, to build a power hammer with a steel head, which was raised by a cam and fell on an anvil or spherical die holding the copper boiler. A workman had to shift the boiler constantly in order to subject every part of it to the tool's action.

Bending by stamping   Certain techniques for stamping resembled those used for bending by shaping. On May 28, 1838, Louis Japy, a clockmaker and mechanic in Berne, a suburb of Seloncourt in Doubs, had obtained a ten-year patent for a mechanical drop hammer. On February 19, 1842, he applied for another patent for a stamping system adapted to this drop hammer or to a balance beam or a press. Its purpose was to "stamp iron and copper sheets, that is, kitchen articles of iron or copper." Stamping was normally done in a single action with one annealing, but deeper objects, like casseroles, required two stampings and two annealings. During the operation the workpieces were held by rings screwed on manually. An attempt was soon made to eliminate this detail by inventing mechanical clamping.

Another stamping method was invented by one Jean Palmer, a mechanic with a shop at 16 rue Montmorency in Paris. He probably would have remained unknown except that the invention of his "caliper with screw and circular vernier" was produced in the United States. On September 7, 1848, this invention was the subject of an application for a fifteen-year patent for tools called calipers that used screws to determine the exact thickness of sheets of metal. The merits of this invention had not yet been recognized when Messrs. Brown and Lucien Sharpe, who had come from the United States to present their first universal milling machine, discovered this new tool at the Paris Exposition of 1867 and immediately realized its value. They took home a Palmer tool, made several modifications in it, and began to manufacture it as the micrometer caliper. Somewhat later Sharpe expressed his satisfaction at having learned of this invention and thus having found a practical method for reading one-thousandths of an inch.

Jean Palmer's work on the stamping and drawing of metals led him to take out a series of patents, the first being dated November 25, 1848, and the last March 13, 1852.

Deep stampings were begun on screw presses. Since these presses had a limited range, the fabrication was completed by drawing, which caused operating problems and also resulted in numerous rejects when the stamped objects were subjected to the action of the drawbench. Palmer built a machine that was a combination of the two earlier models but which we shall not discuss, since it was not finally developed until after the period covered in this book.

The machine age   If man is a tool-making animal, as Carlyle wrote, his ability to make tools is dependent above all on the power that operates them.

Prior to when the steam engine was adapted to industrial work, the genuine machine tool did not exist because there was no reason for it to exist.

Baron Thénard, chairman of the jury for the Ninth Exposition of French Industry that opened on May 1, 1839, "in the main square of the Champs-Elysées," declared that "the art of using motive power, the most marvelous conquest that it has been granted to man to make (the creation of the heat engine), will give him almost infinite power."

The machine age had begun. In the same period the editor of *Moniteur industriel* wrote that "today the primary industry of the people is not the use but the making of machines. A country's power of production is in direct proportion to its machines."

The machine tool was the father of the first heat engine and indeed the father of all these machines. One after the other the machine tools needed were invented and built, widening the scope of the various machine industries.

By the close of the first half of the nineteenth century these various machine industries were already numerous in Great Britain, where they had had the most development, and English industry was at the peak of its power. In Whitworth and his colleagues England had the best builders of machine tools and the best manufacturers of tools. Its progress later slackened, whereas in the New World the equipping of a new and extremely rich country was to create new needs and techniques.

Whitworth visited North America in 1853 and was profoundly impressed. Upon his return he remarked that "the supply of labor is relatively small, but this lack is compensated for by a very large use of machinery in every branch of industry. The remarkable prosperity of the United States is due chiefly to this intensive use of mechanization."

In the field of machine tools as in many others the acceleration of progress was to be most rapid on the western shores of the Atlantic. The development of manufactures and an increase in series of parts to be machined were to make it economically feasible to use old tools such as the milling cutter and new tools such as the artificial grinding wheel, twist drill and spindle, first on simple machines, then on semiautomatic models, and finally on automatic machines whose power would be increased by electricity.

By 1850 all the components for such a burst of activity were combined.

CHAPTER 3

LIGHT MACHINERY AND THE BEGINNINGS OF AUTOMATION

A MONG THEIR other consequences, the rise of the heavy metallurgical and machine industries and the spreading use of steam engines encouraged the rapid development of a new type of industry, light machinery, which had begun to emerge during the last two decades in the eighteenth century.

The origins and importance of light machinery Still older antecedents could in fact be found for light machinery. Clockmaking had for several centuries been preparing the technical conditions for precision mechanics, which developed from the small-craft shops of scientific instrument builders. For a long time numerous small factories had been using traditional but primitive mechanical methods. The camshaft, driven by a waterwheel, transmitted enough power to various places in shops to operate hammers, drop stamps, and presses, which made it possible to shape ordinary objects and tools more quickly and with less effort. Even though there was scope for the craftsman's imagination and inventiveness, the means remained limited until construction materials became more suitable, until cast iron, wrought iron, brass, and copper were more easily available, and until the resources of industrial machinery were more widely accessible.

Thus there was no significant development in this field until the first half of the nineteenth century, and it was chiefly between 1825 and 1850 that methods of industrial production began to be noticeably affected by it.

The phenomenon is important, for with it began a gradual change in the traditional conditions of human work and existence. The use of light machinery spread to extremely varied areas of activity. It required only machine tools of modest size, adapted to the operations to be performed, and also only limited power. Gradually, machinery that made possible the rapid and accurate performance of professional work that previously was often slow and painstaking became available to individuals and small shops. It permitted not only faster and cheaper production of common objects but also industrial production of mechanical devices to facilitate or eliminate certain monotonous everyday tasks.

The rise of mechanization This mechanization of professional and domestic activities—one of the most striking characteristics of contemporary civilization—became general only toward the end of the last century, but the stream of inventions that led to the present stage of development had its origins between 1800 and 1850.

160

It involved products as diversified as portable firearms and electric telegraph equipment (discussed in later chapters), food and clothing, playthings, and many others.

The first household appliances, such as meat grinders, were in use around 1850. At this time machines were being used to weigh, mold, and wrap chocolate without individual handling. In food preparation plants choppers, blenders, and other machines were operated by steam, which also supplied heat for processing, making possible an improvement in the quality and quantity of products. In baking the mechanical kneader made its appearance but to a lesser extent, because over half the bread consumed in France was made at home. Around 1845 a cork-making machine, which included a cutter, drill, and turner, was producing 200,000 corks a day. In that same year Thomas Delarue and E. Hill of London developed a machine to fold envelopes, which was rapidly copied. Another machine, used in 1849 for the same purpose in Paris, folded 4,000 envelopes an hour.

Production of brass pins had been mechanized early in the nineteenth century by various members of the Jeker family in Germany and France. The making of fasteners for clothing and other uses went through the same transformation later. In 1843 two Parisian manufacturers, Gingembre and Damiron, invented a machine capable of making a fastener in a single movement of the brass wire. Several years later they were running a factory with 80 steam-powered machines, were employing 600 workers, and were producing between 1,800 and 2,000 pounds of fasteners a day. This example, among others, shows clearly the rapidity with which these branches of industry were accepting the new methods that technological progress was creating in a world ready to receive them.

The sewing machine   The history of the sewing machine is an even better illustration showing the force of mechanization's expansion outside the heavy-machinery industry or, more precisely, it is a prime example of the heavy-machinery consequences of industry's progress.

Imagination was not enough to ensure industrial success for an invention as complex, relatively, as the sewing machine. As soon as technology could approach with some confidence the difficulties it had to overcome, the mechanization of sewing attracted inventors. The first attempts tried to imitate mechanically the movements of an ordinary needle, by a system of pincers that caused it to go through the fabric in both directions. In 1804 a French patent was taken out for such a machine by Thomas Stone and James Henderson. Despite its lack of success, inventors were still persisting in trying to apply this system forty years later. One improvement used a needle pointed at each end, with an eye at the center. In 1834 Josué Heilmann used such a needle on an embroidering machine that operated successfully, but when other American and French inventors attempted to use it for mechanical sewing they were unable to obtain satisfactory results. Whereas for embroidery the slow operating speed was compensated for by increasing the number of needles on the machine's carriage, with sewing only a single needle could be used on each machine, so that time was lost rather than gained.

Heilmann's embroidering machine was produced industrially by a well-known nineteenth-century English builder of textile machines, Thomas Houldsworth of Manchester. The carriages holding the needles were guided by a

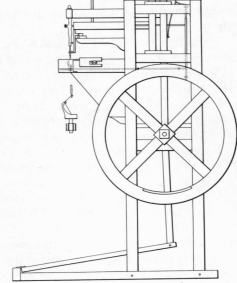

FIG. 35. "Sew-embroiderer" of Thimonnier and Ferrand, from the 1830 patent. Detail under the needle plate machine shows the pivoting part that makes the chain stitch.

pantograph that allowed repetition of the embroidery design. One worker guided the pantograph, two were in charge of the carriages, and two more were kept busy threading spare needles. Such a machine could be used only in factory production. The development of domestic sewing machines required using a continuous thread and especially the back-and-forth motion of a single needle, which merely pierced and returned from the fabric without itself going entirely through it.

Thimonnier's machine   Barthélemy Thimonnier (1793–1857), the first to apply this system, called his machine a sew-embroiderer, but this was simply a chance combination of words. His invention preceded Heilmann's by several years, who probably never heard of Thimonnier prior to his own invention. Moreover, the two machines had nothing in common. On Thimonnier's sew-embroiderer the needle, held vertically above the table on which the fabric was laid, worked from top to bottom (as on all succeeding machines), but it was in reality a kind of embroidery hook. It passed through the fabric, caught the thread stretched out horizontally beneath the fabric, and pulled it through in a loop; its second stitch formed a chain stitch with the first loop. The stitch was knotted under the table by a small vertical rod with an eye in its upper end, through which the thread passed. This rod made a revolution around the needle when it was at the bottom of its stroke (Figure 35).

Thimonnier tried to build his device during 1828 and 1829. A tailor and the son of a modest family, he had no mechanical training, and it is all the more remarkable that his inventive mind turned to an effective solution. But perfecting the first model benefited from the help of one Ferrand, an assistant at the École des Mines de Saint-Étienne. The 1830 patent was taken out in both men's names.

Various difficulties prevented them from developing it satisfactorily. Fifteen years later, Thimonnier was helped by a Lyon manufacturer named Magnin, who

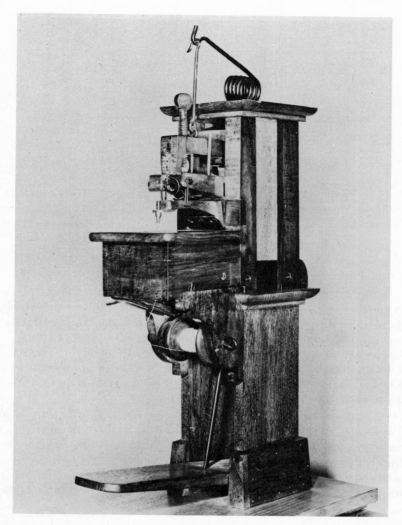

Plate 11. Thimonnier's sewing machine, for making the chain stitch in accordance with the system patented in 1830. Paris, Musée du Conservatoire national des Arts et Métiers. (Photo René-Jacques, Paris.)

simplified the device and won for it a certain reputation as an embroidering machine. The chain-stitch machine had already been outclassed by the lock-stitch sewing machine, which had been invented in the United States as early as 1834.

The double-thread sewing machine   The first idea for this type of machine came from Walter Hunt in 1834, but the first practical example, built by another inventor, Elias Howe, Jr., dates from only 1846. As developed and patented in France in 1855, Howe's machine used two continuous threads. The thread under the fabric passed through the eye near the tip of the needle. A bobbin with a back-and-forth motion, placed above the fabric, fed a second thread into the loop made by the first one when the tip of the needle penetrated the fabric (Figure 36).

The lock-stitch machine immediately enjoyed a great success in the United States. Several manufacturers began to build simplified or improved models that differed from each other in various details. Over a period of several years rival

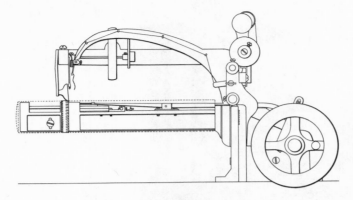

Fig. 36. Elias Howe, Jr.'s, sewing machine, from the French 1855 patent.

makers perfected the chain-stitch type concurrently with the lock-stitch model, though its speed never reached that of the lock-stitch one. Moreover, chain-stitch seams unraveled along their entire length as soon as the thread broke.

Howe's patent was developed in England after 1846 and in France beginning in 1854. Thanks to the superiority of the American industry's production methods, for several decades it far surpassed the industries of the Old World, even that of England, in producing sewing machines.

The evolution of the sewing machine came about slowly, without any profound upheaval, following this early stage. Its development paralleled that of the materials for construction and machine tools. The lock-stitch system was by far the most highly developed. Chain-stitch systems using one or two threads continued to exist for special purposes only. The double-thread chain-stitch machine was built for the first time in 1851 by the New York firm of Grover & Baker.

Plate 12.   Interior of I. M. Singer & Co.'s sewing machine manufactory, New York City. From *U.S. Magazine* I, September 15, 1854. Smithsonian Institution

Mechanical writing   It was natural that mechanical methods should be sought to shorten or eliminate the manual actions by which certain mental processes were expressed concretely. The performance of music had long been mechanized in a more or less rudimentary fashion, as will be discussed later, and the idea of mechanizing writing and mathematical calculations (the practice of which dates from the origins of civilization) must have tempted inventors. If they did not immediately succeed, it was because they had no notion of mechanics and no experience in this line, an inadequacy that gave them sufficient presumption to devote themselves to enterprises that at that time were doomed to failure. But the fact that these attempts were made at all testifies to the needs of the new machanical civilization and to the necessity of removing certain barriers. Craftsmen, conscious of the limits of their art, had to be stimulated by ambitions free from all traditions.

Reproducing handwriting by mechanical means was tried as early as the eighteenth century, but was not yet used for the purpose of helping professional copyists. Some of these early inventors were simply following the contemporary appetite for building automata that would imitate human gestures as closely as possible. Like the mechanical musicians of Vaucanson, Kintzing, and Jacquet-Droz, the writing automata (discussed later) were simple programed machines. The writer built by von Knaus of Vienna and the "little boy writing" by Pierre Jacquet-Droz, which are still in existence, enable us to relate them to the other automata of this period, which was indeed the golden age of this strange art.

Other inventors sought to enable blind people to write mechanically. Some of the results are listed by Ernst Martin, who in 1934 published the only detailed history of the writing machine that we have. The earliest attempt listed by this author is that of the Englishman Henry Mill in 1713. Others were those of the Frenchman Pingeron (1780) and the Italians Pellegrino Turri (1808) and Pietro Conti (1823).

The first attempts to write more rapidly by means of a suitable mechanism began around 1830. In 1829 William Austin Burt of Detroit built such a machine, a reproduction of which is in the Smithsonian Institution, Washington, D.C. We

a ä	o ö	n	s sch
i e	u ü	d t	l
w	b p	ij ch z	ckq g
m	f v	r ck	h

FIG. 37. Principle of the keyboard of the Baron de Drais's stenotype machine. *Below:* Striking code for one-quarter of the keyboard, 1832.

also have a letter written with it. Two years later Baron de Drais (whose name has been popularized by legend, though strictly speaking he was not the inventor of that ancestor of the bicycle called the *draisienne*) had built to his order a key-type machine that wrote not letters but combinations of signs—it was probably the first model of a stenotype machine. The four quarters of a square could be struck in black or white, giving sixteen different combinations of the letters of the alphabet (Figure 37).

First experiments with writing machines The invention of a writing machine by the Marseille printer Xavier Progin is better known, because his 1840 patent has been preserved. Basically, the machine (Figure 38) consisted of a large wheel whose rim had interchangeable belts on which the characters were engraved in relief. The letters were also shown on the edge of the wheel so they could be located easily by the operator. The wheel was turned manually and held in striking position by a locking device. The paper was pressed with a lever against the character to be printed. The principle of this device has been adopted in our own time in the form of a movable, interchangeable type ball that replaces the array of characters on the classic machine.

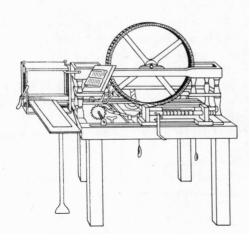

FIG. 38. Xavier Progin's writing machine, the so-called Proginographe, 1840.

Slightly later, in 1843, the American Charles Thurber arranged long rods in the form of a reel, an arrangement that anticipates the circular disposition of type bars in the first Remington machines, the basic mechanism of which was invented in 1867 by Sholes and Glidden. The machine was intended for composing the sheets of stereotypy then used in printing; it could be used for musical notation and possibly for mechanical writing. The inventor pointed out that it could write as quickly as the human hand.

From then on inventions followed at irregular intervals and at an increasingly rapid pace for some thirty years. It is difficult to know to what extent each inventor was inspired or guided by the experiments of others. Even if we suppose that each experiment was known in the country where it occurred, information about it was probably very limited and did not cross linguistic frontiers. Numerous experiments were made in many countries, and we are justified in believing that they

Plate 13. Rolling-mills of Lendersdorfer, near Düren, 1838. Painting by Carl Schütz. Leopold Hoesch Museum, Düren. (Photo Rheinisches Bildarchiv, Cologne.)

remained independent of each other. This demonstrates that the problem was beginning to come to a head and illustrates quite well the process of development and perfection of a given invention when the technical and economic conditions have become adequate.

More than ten attempts to perfect the writing machine before 1850 can be enumerated, including those of Dujardin at Lille in 1838, Perrot (the inventor of the *perrotine,* a machine to print fabrics) at Rouen in 1839, Pierre Foucauld at Corbeil in 1843 and, most significantly, the work of Giuseppe Ravizza (1811– 1885).

A keyboard to strike the characters appeared on several machines invented during the time when Ravizza was trying to build his own mechanism, between 1830 and 1855, the year the patent was registered. Ravizza used it ignorant of his contemporaries' research, but his special contribution is inventing a system to transmit movement through jointed levers that controlled simultaneously striking the characters and advancing the paper (Figure 39). This design anticipated the one that Sholes, Glidden, and Soulé built ten or twelve years later and that was developed by the Remington firm when completed and perfected. With his *cembalo-scrivano,* or writing tympanum, Ravizza had found a technical solution to the problem of mechanical writing. However, he was unable to bring the tech-

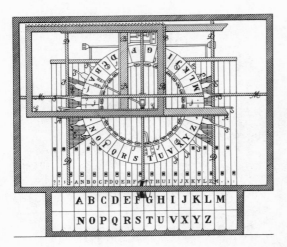

FIG. 39. Giuseppe Ravizza's *cembalo-scrivano* ("tympanum for writing"), 1855.

nique into production; more than twenty years were to pass before that stage was reached. The firm of E. Remington and Sons, of Ilion, New York, began to produce these machines successfully in 1873.

The problem of mechanizing mathematical calculations
Mechanizing mathematical calculations was a longer venture, both presenting less difficulty (if one limited oneself to the two basic operations of addition and subtraction) and much more, if one's ambition extended to mechanizing more complex operations such as division and extracting square roots. A machine to add and subtract could have been put into service as early as the first quarter of the eighteenth century, because the principle of the machine had been worked out and the technical difficulties could have been easily overcome. The machine could have even been used easily for simple multiplication, with a large multiplicand and a multiplier of several dozen units. But more than a century and a half elapsed and far more complex machines were invented before mechanical calculation came into common use. This long gestation period is explained only by the fact that society had no need for such calculations and that building adding machines did not encourage any commercial market.

People who performed mathematical calculations had available to them nonmechanical procedures such as logarithms, rules, tables, or counters, which they were accustomed to use and were sufficient for their needs. However, the temptation to mechanize these mental operations became so strong between the early seventeenth century and early nineteenth that achievements in this line compelled the public to take an interest. In the second half of the nineteenth century the calculating machine began to impose itself upon the public's attention.

Schickard's machine
The adding and subtracting machine invented by Blaise Pascal is often cited, too generously, as the prototype of mechanical calculators. The truth is that Pascal's machine was probably not the first to be built, and, moreover, did not produce very remarkable offspring.

The German mathematician and astronomer Wilhelm Schickard (1592–

1635) of Tübingen seems to have been the first to conceive, and was certainly the first to build, a machine making it possible to perform the four mathematical operations mechanically. This invention went unnoticed in its own time and remained unknown until lately. Recent publication of Kepler's complete works brought to light some notes that enabled several authors to describe and interpret Schickard's machine. It was built at the end of 1623 and destroyed in a fire several months later; only a rough sketch (Figure 40) and a few notes on its design now remain. We need only note that Schickard conceived and put into concrete form before Pascal a device to carry over automatically the tens, hundreds, and so on.

The concept of such a device led men to envision the mechanical performance of arithmetical operations. It is quite easy, in fact, to inscribe a number using a toothed wheel whose rotation makes the corresponding number appear in an opening in a plate over a disk or rotating cylinder. By turning the wheel as many additional units as desired, the numbered disk advances the same number of units and an addition is made; the addition of a series of equal numbers is equivalent to a multiplication. Rotating the wheel in the opposite direction during the second stage of the operation mechanically achieves a subtraction and likewise

Plate 14. The Hallette shops at Arras (before 1848). Lithograph by Cuvillier. French National Library, Print Collection. (Photo Documentation Française, Paris.)

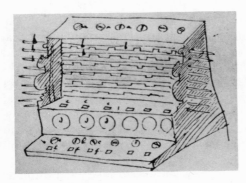

FIG. 40. Drawing by Schickard showing the general form of his 1623 calculating machine.

for division. Placing several such wheels side by side allows the user to note from right to left the units, tens, hundreds, and so on. The difficulty was in making devices to allow carrying the tens leftward from wheel to wheel. This difficulty, which now seems insignificant, was such an obstacle, given the mechanical methods of the first half of the seventeenth century, that the very conception of a mechanism of this nature seemed impossible.

Clock works achieved continuous motion with the help of reduction trains. The same was true of revolution counters and pedometers when the first ones were built, around the end of the seventeenth century. The oldest known mechanism allowing tens to be carried is that invented by Pascal, to whom Schickard's machine was completely unknown.

Pascal's adding machine Pascal had the first model of his adding machine built between 1642 and 1645 (Figure 41). Many anecdotes, both true and false, have been told about this episode. It is not known how many models were built nor how many sold (at a price of 100 *livres*). One of the eight machines still in existence is dated 1652. Those that can now be examined are all of the same type and are, surprisingly, of poor construction. The works consist of lantern gears, which were habitually used in this period in large machines, cranes, treadmills, and windmills that were intended to overcome strong resistances. The quality of the finish is far inferior to that of a good clock of the time. The essential component, the carry-over mechanism, is quite heavy as conceived and meshes poorly into the pegs on the lantern gear it is supposed to control (Figure 42). In addition, tens are carried simultaneously from wheel to wheel when the wheels register the number 9. The machines had 6 or 8 wheels (4 or 6 digits plus *sous* and *deniers*), and so the strain of transmission was high enough to prevent carry-overs from being transferred and to cause the machine to jam when several wheels stood at the number 9.

For all practical purposes the adding machine was not accepted. Even if Pascal had turned to a better mechanic than was his clockmaker in Rouen, it is unlikely that his invention would have aroused much interest.

However, the idea of mechanizing mathematical operations had been put into concrete form, demonstrating that this was not a completely utopian idea. Although Schickard's experiment had borne no results, Pascal's was known and frequently commented upon. A prototype of this machine, given by Canon Périer, Pascal's nephew, to the Académie des Sciences in 1711, was described in the *Recueil*

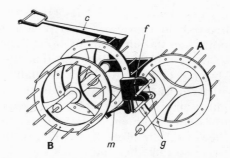

FIG. 41. Pascal's adding machine. *Top:* View of the mechanism. *Bottom:* The cover removed.

FIG. 42. Pinwheels and carry-over mechanism for carrying the tens in Pascal's machine.

des machines approuvées par l'Académie des Sciences in 1746, and Diderot was later to give more detailed information about it in the first volume of the *Encyclopédie*. We know that Pascal himself went to the trouble of sending models of his machine to several important people. Thus, it could be discussed from personal knowledge, and people did not fail to make reference to this invention, as to all the deeds and writings of a man as famous as Pascal. The truth is that if the machine has become part of history, it is not because of Pascal's ability in applied mechanics but rather because it was the work of such an exceptional man.

Mechanical addition and subtraction

Other machines built on this model attracted no attention, though we have descriptions and sometimes copies of them. Their workings are often more complicated than was Pascal's, and insofar as we are able to judge while allowing for deterioration through time, they could not have produced much better results.

However, one machine (which is in the collections of the Conservatoire des Arts et Métiers, and which seems incorrectly attributed to Lépine) still performs satisfactorily. Its general design is the same as Pascal's machine, but the transmission devices are built not with lantern gears but with toothed wheels similar to those cut by clockmakers. Carrying the tens is done ingeniously and simply by a train of gears that has, for each ten digits, a wheel with only one tooth out of ten. The device is designed so that the transmitting wheels all turn in the same direction. The recording is done not with a stylet but with small rods projecting in front of the box, each having a pinion that turns the corresponding wheel of the accumulator.

This machine by an unknown inventor, built apparently around the middle of the eighteenth century at the latest, shows that a good solution for the problem of mechanizing mathematical calculations—at least as far as addition, subtraction, and simple multiplication were concerned—had been found by this time.

The Leibniz multiplying machine

Another mechanical solution had been suggested by Leibniz as early as 1673, but he was unable to finish building his machine, which never operated correctly. He publicized its principle and even presented the model to the learned societies of various countries, but its description was not published until 1710 and then only in a review of limited circulation, the *Miscellanea berolinensia*. Thus, its reputation was far from attaining that of Pascal's machine.

It is easy to understand that the technology of Leibniz's period was not advanced enough to allow a mechanism of such a modern conception to be built satisfactorily. Leibniz's device in fact anticipates those that enabled nineteenth-century mechanics to make the calculating machine a useful instrument. It consists of toothed pinions placed horizontally side by side and corresponding to the wheels of the totaling device (Figure 43). The teeth on each pinion are of unequal length so that their movement along their axle makes it possible to select the number of teeth that will be engaged on the register wheel in a single revolution. It is thus possible, in a single operation and after the pinion gears of the units, tens, hundreds, and so on have been appropriately moved, to cause all the digits of the number (the multiplicand, for example) to be registered and to appear in the sighting holes of the totaling device.

FIG. 43.   Mechanism of Leibniz's multiplier.

Furthermore, if this device is stationary, the part that forms the register and the transfer mechanism (in the latter case the pinions with unequal teeth) is able to shift as a unit along the totaler. In this way multiplication is done as in a written operation. The operator registers the units digit, turns the mechanism, and the first product appears in the totaler. He shifts the carriage one place to the left, registers the tens digit, and operating the mechanism makes the second product appear, and so on.

The Thomas arithmometer   It is striking that this solution was revived in a very precise way a century and a half later to produce with more reliable means the first widely used calculating machine, by Charles Henry Thomas.

The inventor, a chevalier of the Legion of Honor who adopted the name Thomas de Colmar, registered his patent in 1820. He was manager of an insurance company in Paris, and there is no doubt that his professional concerns stimulated him to use his mechanical talent in this experiment. The suggestion that he could have seen the model of Leibniz's machine, then preserved at Hanover, is possible but not very likely, as the existence of this machine was not well known at that time. (Dr. Roth, who invented an adding and multiplying machine a short time later, and who in 1843 published a list of the various inventions since Pascal and Leibniz, was unaware of its existence.)

It is not known who built the first Thomas machines. For a century the system

Plate 15. Anchor forge, probably circa 1836, at Bristol. Painting by William James Muller. City Art Gallery, Bristol. (Photo City Art Gallery.)

was developed, under the name *arithmometer* and with various improvements, by various manufacturers.

Its general design is that of the Leibniz machine, except that the registering and carrying device is stationary, whereas the totaler and its gears can be lifted on hinges like a cover, and can slide transversally.

The original 1820 model (Figure 44) had three digits on the register and six on the totaler. The register consisted of three cylinders with grooves of varying lengths on their active faces so as to establish a toothed scale ranging from 0 to 9. A toothed wheel could be moved along each cylinder by using a small button moving along a slide. The button was positioned on the upper face of the platen by divisions from 0 to 9 on a small scale. A number with a maximum of three digits registered in this fashion was carried on the totaler by an ingenious device: a fourth cylinder parallel to the others and connected with them by a gear train and a ratchet wheel. A pull on a ribbon wound around the fourth cylinder caused the entire mechanism to function.

A fifth and final cylinder to the left had nine notches arranged in a spiral over its surface. By a spring drum this cylinder controlled the return of the register mechanism after the ribbon had been activated, but its chief purpose was to determine whether the operations the user desired to perform were addition or multiplication. If its slide was placed on the first notch, at number 1 on its index,

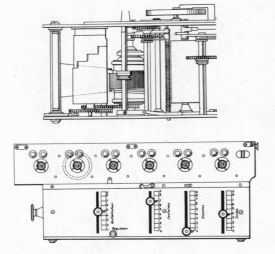

FIG. 44. Thomas de Colmar's arithmometer, 1820. *Below:* The machine viewed from above. *Top:* Detail of the operating mechanism. At left can be seen the cylinder for the factors of multiplication, then the barrel drum and the ribbon, and finally the first cylinder of the register.

the machine added the numbers introduced through the register. To multiply, the operator introduced the multiplicand and registered it on the totaler by pulling the ribbon, then placed the slide of the multiplier cylinder opposite the units digit of the multiplier, and pulled the ribbon to record the first product. Then he repeated this operation with the tens digit of the multiplier after moving the totaler carriage one digit to the right, and the same for the hundreds.

The dials of the totaler were graduated from 0 to 9 on each of their half circles and in the opposite direction had a double graduation on an inside circle. One series of these graduations was used in adding and multiplying, the other in subtracting and dividing, depending on the sighting slits moved by the operator.

Thomas also solved numerous operating problems, which ensured that the machine produced the most precise results possible and eliminated accidental errors. In particular, pressure springs eliminated all effects of inertia that would have caused the dials to go beyond the proper position. Carrying the tens, the thorniest problem on all earlier machines, was now done progressively rather than simultaneously, the forward movement being transferred fractionally from wheel to wheel of the totaler. In addition, the register's cylinders were grooved on only half of their surface and so turned freely while the carrying was being done.

The machine proved immediately to be perfectly dependable and usable for all four calculating functions. Thomas continued to refine it for almost thirty years. He improved the system of blocking the components by introducing a stop motion and he replaced the ribbon and the multiplying cylinder with a crank having a register dial, which made it possible to count the revolutions and know the multiplication factor applied. Thomas added control dials for the numbers introduced in the register. Finally, clearing the total, which was done in the 1820 model by a milled button for each dial, was mechanized by a double spring rack that brought all the dials back to zero simultaneously.

Naturally, Thomas increased the number of stages on his machine. The models built by Payen around 1848 generally had 6 digits in the register and 10 in the totaler. For the Exposition of 1855 Thomas had a model built that was 6½ feet long and had 30 numbers.

Roth's machines Having been awarded a prize by the Société d'Encouragement pour l'industrie nationale, the arithmometer quickly enjoyed a certain fame and led to other inventions. In 1828 a round adding machine, reminiscent of an instrument built in England in 1812 by John Goss, was constructed by an inventor named Lagrous. In 1843, after several years of research, Dr. Roth developed a linear adding machine (Figure 45), for which he had devised an effective system for successively carrying the tens. He used a trigger on each wheel applied by a spring on an eccentric cam. At each return to zero the trigger fell back toward the center of the cam and caused the next wheel to move forward, during which time a catch provided a blocking action. In 1841 Roth also built two models of a round, four-function calculator,

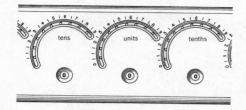

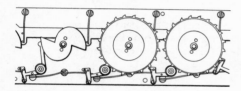

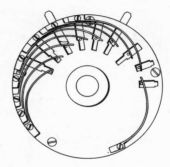

FIG. 45. Roth's adding machine. *Top:* The upper platen and the register dials. *Bottom:* Internal mechanism with carryover mechanism for the tens.

FIG. 46. One of the pinions of the driving device in Roth's circular calculating machine. A cam (not shown) pressed on the tongue of each tooth and controlled its movement.

but, having gone blind (according to M. Flad) he was not able to finish developing it. For this machine Roth applied an idea published as early as 1709 by the Italian Poleni. The pinion gears on the driving device had variously sized teeth, that is, they slipped into a notch in the pinion gear under the pressure of a central cam, on whose perimeter they were supported by springs (Figure 46). The principle of variable teeth was readopted by the Russian Odhner in 1875.

The arithmaurel The most remarkable achievement of this period was the arithmometer designed by Maurel and perfected by Jayet in 1849. The two inventors adopted the Thomas system, but the cylinders of the register were arranged on a single axle by lengthening them successively. Registering the multiplicand was done by moving graduated levers, which each brought a toothed indexing wheel into the proper position on the grooved cylinders. The machine calculated the product while the multiplier was being registered on needle dials. The arithmaurel, remarkable in its conception,

Plate 16. The Alexis Godillot factories. Supplies for the army. The hall of the central factory: stamping. Engraving taken from Turgan, *Les Grandes Usines,* Paris, 1881. (Photo Alain Doyère - Conservatoire national des Arts et Métiers.)

performed in a few seconds multiplications with products as high as 100 million less one and divided numbers of this size by divisors lower than 10,000. But the transmission mechanism was very complex and delicate. The machine was built by Winnerl, an excellent maker of marine chronometers. The fragile and costly arithmaurel was never commercially produced.

Difference engines

The ambitions of mathematicians and mechanics were now turning toward more complex problems. The English mathematician Babbage tried for many years to build machines capable of performing higher calculations such as establishing astronomical tables. Starting in 1812 he drew up plans for a machine to give the various terms of a series by differences. He went quite far with these plans and with constructing the machine, but when faced with sizable expenditures and dwindling research funds he was forced to abandon his experiment, around 1835. Babbage later tried to build a machine that would perform any series of calculations on any number, but as with the first experiment, the analytical engine was not completed before his death.

As early as 1834 a Swede named Georg Scheutz conceived the principle of the difference engine. With the help of his son Edvard he worked out a complete set of plans and had it built in 1853 by a Stockholm mechanic named Bergstrom. This machine, which won a medal of honor at the Exposition of 1855, made it possible to calculate logarithms and mathematical and astronomical tables and printed the results. This is undoubtedly the first recording calculator ever built, only two models of which were constructed.

By their very nature these machines could not find a wide use. In the mid-nineteenth century the calculator generally used, the Thomas arithmometer, does not appear to have been in great demand. In 1820 the inventor himself believed it would not lessen the work load of professionals, but he did think it could be used for checking at the end of a day, as for example in accounting services, where a clerk could be assigned to operate it. At the Exposition of 1855, at which the Thomas arithmometer and the arithmaurel each received only honorable mention, a reporter noted that these machines were not widely used yet in business.

Automation and mechanization   With the arithmometer we have an example of automation that has undergone major developments in our time. To be sure, there is nothing here at first glance to compare with the means that electromagnetism and electronics have placed at man's service since 1942, the date Aiken's Mark I machine was put into operation at Harvard, but this process, which in reality had begun centuries earlier, reached a new phase at the beginning of the last century. Although man was still forced to operate manually the calculating machines existing around 1850, he was freed from certain mental operations that the machine performed for him, having only to record the figures and receive the result.

Mechanization does not always involve automation. Thus, lathes, milling cutters, planers, and molding presses, which at this period were already highly perfected, had no elements yet of automation. A worker had to operate the machines and be responsible for the quality of the product. However, some mechanical processes were already performing automatically at a certain phase of operation without intervention by the worker. Such actions were still limited in scope and result; even in our own period the automatic machine can produce only what it is made to do with the information given it. There is no thinking machine, and undoubtedly there never will be one, to the extent that unlimited initiative can be expected from it.

The elements of automation available in the middle of the last century are worth analyzing, for they enable us to understand the progress of techniques shaping our present-day civilization, in which an obsession with automation has become dominant because it is profitable.

Early origins of automatic machines   The oldest automatic machine for industrial use that can be cited is undoubtedly the one to divide circles built by the English engineer Jesse Ramsden in 1773. A touch on the treadle turned the dividing plate to the necessary angle, allowing the scriber to engrave the division on the limb. The worker took no part in the essential operation of feeding and tracing, and the exactness of the division was not dependent on his skill. It would even have been possible to think of supplying power to the machine by a hydraulic hammer, for example, in which case no human intervention would have been needed to divide a graduated circle.

In reality, numerous automatic activities had been obtained from various machines long before the eighteenth century. A certain amount of automation in the beginning can be attributed to the powder, paper, tanning, and fulling mills operated by camshafts driven by waterwheels. Here we are, to be sure, at the limits of the historical notion of automation, but this concept is not erroneous insofar as we can accept an evolution of the methods that led from this point to true automation.

The types of mills just mentioned came into use in the Middle Ages. Around the end of the fourteenth century appeared, somewhat mysteriously, the mechanical clock. In the verge escapement with a crown wheel that regulates the falling of the clock's driving weight we already have an automatic mechanism to divide time into equal intervals. But from its earliest stages clockmaking created a mechanism unquestionably automatic in character: the snail, which controlled hammers striking the bells to sound the hours. Although the verge merely repeats the same movement as long as it is supplied with the necessary driving power, the sounding mechanism carries out a program fixed for it in advance, since the number of blows struck changes with the hours. We might easily mention now the arrays of jointed figurines that struck the public clocks as early as the fifteenth century, but this did not lead to the birth of industrial automation.

Musical devices   There is greater justification for mentioning the mechanical musical devices that flourished somewhat later, toward the end of the Renaissance, when the art of gardening was developed and the writings of Alexandrian engineers were disseminated by printing. In the latter could be found descriptions of the use of waterpower to produce musical sounds in a series of pipes. But the effects then obtainable from the pipes were varied all the more by adopting from industrial installations the camshaft to control valves in the pipes. From this time on the art, and later the industry, of recorded music was to develop in a continuous line broken only by the use of the ear trumpet and the sound diaphragm, then by electroacoustics and finally magnetic tapes. Along the way a large number of completely automatic programed devices were popularized.

The art of hydraulic organs was lost during the seventeenth century, but the rudimentary camshaft had been considerably refined. The simple cam had been replaced by straight or curved metal rods forming the tongues of cylinders in music boxes, which were to enjoy an increasing vogue at the end of the eighteenth century.

In the meantime came a series of crank-operated organs and flutes in organs designed to teach canaries to sing and later in the barrel organ which became very popular in the last century. Finally, a spring drum and a pendulum fusee borrowed from the art of clockmaking made these mechanisms completely automatic (Figure 47). Moving a catch set the mechanism in operation as bellows blew air into the pipes and pins operated the valves in a preset order to perform the chosen piece of music. Finally, the drum with points made a slight endwise movement and was then ready to perform a new air. When all the pieces had been played, a spring pushed the cylinder back into its original position and the playing could begin again. Mechanical organs at the end of the eighteenth century (by Kintzing) and the beginning of the nineteenth (by Davrainville) had cylinders with five recorded

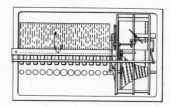

Fig. 47.   Organ mechanism with cylinder and spring.

melodies. These organs were sold with a series of three or five cylinders, making an entire repertory of recorded music available to the music lover.

The pin barrel   Recording was actually a matter of reconstructing the music from the score, which gave a more artificial character to the music of these devices than is the case with our modern records and tapes. By "more artificial" should be understood "more mechanical" and even "more automatic," since the melody was recorded without benefit of a performing musician. Writers in the sixteenth and seventeenth centuries described methods for recording music on cylinders. Although these methods are experimental in nature, they are, strictly speaking, the first techniques for preparing a program to control the action of a machine. In 1775 the Reverend Engramelle published a more theoretical method from which came methods used industrially down to our own time.

The music-box industry became increasingly prosperous from the moment Antoine Favre, a clockmaker in Geneva, invented a metal comb with vibrating teeth (Figure 48) and created a new category of mechanical music in addition to the automatic playing of carillons and organs. Yet in these devices the pin barrel continued to be the essential component on which the melodies were recorded.

The pin barrel, complemented by cam profiles, also became the major element in the magnificent automatic figures, generally in the form of musicians, built in the eighteenth century, ranging from Vaucanson's German flute player (which brought to life a statue by Coysevox) down to the harpsichord player of Jacquet-Droz and Leschot (1773) and the famous dulcimer player by Kintzing (1785). Around 1780 Jacquet-Droz applied a cam profile to control the movements of a piston to vary the pitch of a whistle pipe, and he succeeded in reproducing with astonishing fidelity the songs of certain birds. Singing birds produced by Swiss workshops enjoyed a great vogue during the first half of the nineteenth century. They all contained, in miniature, a programed automating apparatus that could already have been adapted to industrial uses if the need had been felt. In truth it was felt: the automatic lathe for making rifle butts by the American mechanic Blanchard is little more than a transposition of this type.

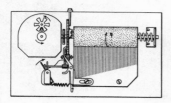

Fig. 48.   Music box with a metal comb.

The perforated disk   Every possible effect was won from the pin barrel, of which the cylinder music pieces from the second half of the nineteenth century offer numerous and varied examples. Beginning in 1880 there appeared in Leipzig a new category of musical device in which the drum was replaced by a perforated metal disk. The lips of the perforations caused the teeth in the metal comb to vibrate. Shortly thereafter appeared the first phonographs, for which the music was recorded in grooves cut on wax during a performance. Thanks to its acoustic factors, the music box was greatly simplified and its possibilities were expanded, but the barrel and then the disk remained the principal components.

The concepts of automation found in the music box are not the only ones discernible during the two or three centuries preceding the development of modern automation. We find definite examples in eighteenth-century guilloching and reproducing lathes. The rosette of the guilloching lathe, on which a follower rested and whose depth or surface profile determined the oscillations of the lathe's mandrel, already anticipates the profiles to be placed later on machine tools. The same is true of the jointed devices controlled by spring drums that enabled the engraving on a medal to be automatically reproduced. The reproducing lathes by Nartov, Peter the Great's mechanic, are among the oldest known developments of this principle in existence.

The perforated card   Lastly, attention should be called to the fact that one of the basic elements of modern automation, the perforated card, is an invention of the seventeenth century. When Bouchon and Falcon used perforated cards to replace the drawboys of the knotted cords on

Plate 17.   Blast furnaces at Marchiennes au Pont—general view. The Company of Rolling Mills, Blast Furnaces, Forges and Foundries at Providence. Engraving taken from Turgan, *Les Grandes Usines,* Paris, 1882. (Photo Alain Doyère-Conservatoire national des Arts et Métiers.)

drawlooms to weave patterned silk fabrics, they were probably inspired by seventeenth-century methods for marking the cylinders of hydraulic organs. Prior to the time of Reverend Engramelle, who succeeded in perforating the cylinders directly, perforating was done first on sheets of paper laid flat, which were then glued to the cylinder. The transition from these perforated strips to perforated cards to make the drawing automatic was made during the first quarter of the eighteenth century. One century later Jacquard completed the system with a mechanism having rods, which quickly came into general use.

Music boxes, in turn, benefited from this technique. In 1892 the Gavioli brothers invented a pneumatic device that allowed barrel organs to be operated by perforated cardboard strips. Shortly thereafter, perforated rolls of paper were adapted to player pianos. Pianolas, making possible the automatic playing of classical music pieces performed by the best pianists, are still being built.

Even before these developments occurred, the perforated card had been adapted to analyzing major statistics. The American statistician Hollerith designed this adaptation to help in analyzing the eleventh decennial census of the population of the United States, carried out in 1890.

It would be dangerous to draw firm conclusions from this rapid general survey of the genesis of modern automation techniques. The history of this subject is still too little known to permit our affirming that certain relationships were in fact generated. It can reveal only that, like all the other techniques forming the foundations of our civilization, the technique of automation, seemingly the most recent one and one that appears to certain superficial observers to have been born only in recent decades, possesses deep roots in the centuries preceding our own.

CHAPTER 4

THE MEASUREMENT OF TIME

T ECHNOLOGY AS PRESENTED in this volume covers roughly the period from 1750 to 1850, but with clockmaking we cannot conform strictly to these limits. The most recent limit of the period will certainly be the mid-nineteenth century, which for two reasons forms a natural break in this history: first, the appearance of the electric clock in 1840, the early experiments with which were short-lived then but are of rich promise now. Second, the mid-nineteenth century forms a break because it was a period in which planned production began to win out over trial-and-error methods after long struggles whose birth and growth over more than a century we are about to see. Indeed, to place the beginning of this study in context we shall have to go back rather far, for in the field of clockmaking the eighteenth century forms a unit beginning considerably before 1700. In reality it started around 1680, when the pendulum clock and the balance-spring watch, based on models by Huygens, began to replace the older forms.

The building of clocks Although Huygens's innovations were revolutionary from the scientific point of view, they changed nothing regarding clockmaking and its methods. However, demand was growing as early as the first years of the eighteenth century, and the rigid framework of the old crafts seemed incapable of coping with it. For this reason innovative minds made repeated efforts to establish factories capable of large-scale production. Many attempts ended in failure. Sully (1680–1728) saw his factory at Versailles swept away in 1718 by Law's financial debacle, and the Royal Manufactory, founded in 1787 and managed by Romilly (1714–1794), did not survive the first disturbances of the French Revolution. The national works, created in 1793 at Besançon by the Swiss Megevand (1754–1814), did not long withstand financial anarchy and demagogy, but it remained as the basis for the clockmaking industry of Besançon. The enterprise established by Voltaire at Ferney in 1770 (which was more of a business establishment than a factory) enjoyed a rapid success thanks to the incomparable public relations expert who was its moving spirit, but prosperity was followed several years later by losses, and the venture was dissolved. In contrast, total success came to the factory founded in 1772 by Frédéric Japy (1749–1812) near Montbéliard. He simply gathered together factory workers, placing at their disposal machines of his own invention that achieved a considerable increase in productivity. In 1795 production was close to 3,300 movement blanks per month, at a cost of 6.50 francs each. In 1801 the factory had 300 employees and was turning out 8,460 blanks per month, slightly more than one per worker per day, at a cost close to 2.50 francs. Production was constantly increasing, reaching 25,000 per month in 1813, and the cost fell to less than two francs each. But movement blanks are not movements, the latter being evaluated at approximately double the value. These prices can be compared with the breakdown of a gross price of 36 *livres* for the movement, which it was proposed to fix in 1776. It is thus possible to confirm a figure for the monthly output of the early watch factories. At the same time the case represented slightly more than half a day's work, so we can say that thereafter the production time of a watch was that needed for its finishing and adjustment. But this time can vary within extremely broad limits, depending on the care taken and the degree of precision sought.

Plate 18. Watch factory work room, Waltham, Massachusetts. Smithsonian Institution, Collection of Business Americana

Numerous treatises on clockmaking, notably the illustrations in Thiout's *Traité* (published in 1741) and those of the *Encyclopédie,* supply us with excellent information on early clockmaking techniques. By this time the clockmaker's equipment was quite varied, including a great many instruments lumped together under the name *tools,* from the simplest chisel to the most complicated machine. Next to devices as old as civilization—the bow to turn a drill, for example—we find small, manually operated machines for milling and planing, which already foreshadow semiautomatic machinery, with very complex movements and very fine adjustments, each designed for a clearly defined operation. The most remarkable are the slotting machines designed to divide and cut the teeth of wheels and pinions, tools for setting up escapements, for cutting fusees, and for shaping various parts of the escapement cylinder. The variety was all the greater because many master mechanics invented or adapted for their own use tools for which they have left no descriptions. The purposes of many of these objects (among the small number surviving in collections) are today difficult to explain. Information on machines invented by Japy and others is less accessible because it is contained in inadequately illustrated patents that made their first appearance in France around 1800.

The first half of the nineteenth century was occupied by a struggle between inventors trying to impose mechanization and the general body of the profession seeking to perpetuate quasi-manual production methods. The latter were able to increase production volume and decrease its cost only by hasty and careless work, omitting significant improvements that are always costly in the beginning. At the same time, the craft was losing its status and becoming less remunerative. Neglecting the craft's traditions coincided with the emergence of a day-laboring class. Downgrading the worker brought about a deterioration in the quality of the work. Such a situation never stabilizes itself and can be resolved only by the disappearance of the activity in question or by radical changes. For a long time the innovators chiefly experienced failures. One of the most remarkable innovators of this period was the Swiss Pierre-Frédéric Ingold (1787–1878), a former employee or Breguet who succeeded in having several of his inventions put into practice. But he did not succeed in overcoming the clockmakers' opposition to his machines, and after disappointments in Paris and London he emigrated to New York in 1844. There he finally found the necessary support, and it was from the New World that mechanical clock production returned after 1880.

In this respect, then, the entire period under consideration, and especially the first half of the nineteenth century, was a gestation period paving the way for the modern clockmaking industry, at the cost of many difficulties. But concerning clocks and watches themselves, it was a period of expansion, exhibiting the emergence, development, and finally the triumph of mechanical clockmaking on the basis of the sound and substantial principles laid down by Huygens.

Escapements Throughout this story, invention is constantly bursting forth and reasserting itself. In the early period the initiative comes for the most part from the master clockmakers. Beginning in approximately 1680, we witness patient and thorough experiments (extending over more than a century and finally crowned by complete success) to modify the old crown-wheel escapement to adapt it to the pendulum and balance wheel and thus take full advantage of their regulating qualities.

The crown-wheel escapement was well suited to the foliot, which had to be impelled in each direction while accompanying its movement. In contrast, the pendulum (like the balance wheel with a hairspring) alters the direction of its own movement, thanks to its inertia. Not only does it need no assistance, it must also be left as free as possible, requiring only a very slight push to maintain its movement.

This was the starting point of the search for a "free" escapement that would ensure continuous movement without loss from operating disturbances. This was an exacting ideal that was not achieved (insofar as this is possible) until very recently. In this search a prodigious number of escapements were invented and tried, including many unknown to us. Only a few of these mechanisms have had a more or less significant life, and for observers looking back to see the entire picture of the progress accomplished, they are milestones on the road toward the free escapement. This escapement is found (without prejudice to several rare and highly perfected mechanisms reserved for observatory clocks) in its two principal modern versions: the lever, which is universally employed in watches, and the spring detent, used for marine chronometers.

If it is possible to trace after the event an abridged version of the evolution of escapements, the first innovators who modified the crown-wheel escapement did so by trial and error. Naturally, it is impossible within the limited scope of the present volume to pause at every stage and mention names other than those of the principle pioneers and inventors. London was at first the leading center for invention. Robert Hooke (1635–1703) and William Clement (who was still alive in 1699) made profound modifications in the escapement as a whole. In 1666 Hooke proposed that the two principal pieces become flat and their axes parallel, a project that in Clement's hands became a practical device. The crown wheel became the escape wheel, and the verge and its pallets became the escapement (Figure 49). The device was perfected by George Graham (1673–1751) around 1715. The Graham deadbeat, or recoilless escapement, is one of the major inventions in clockmaking—it is still in use and was used until around 1900 for the most precise astronomical clocks.

The principle of the deadbeat escapement (Figure 50) lies in sliding the anchor that is coupled with the pendulum on the wheel it holds motionless during

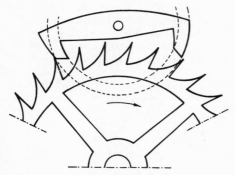

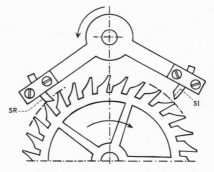

FIG. 49. Recoil anchor escapement. At each oscillation the anchor receives an impulse from the teeth, followed by a very slight recoil of the wheel when the pallet of the anchor penetrates more deeply between the teeth.

FIG. 50. Deadbeat escapement. The inclined, or "impulse," surfaces (SI) of the anchor receive impulses from the teeth, which then slip tangentially on the "dead" faces (SR).

"locking," which occupies the greatest portion of the periodic time. When the wheel escapes (and with it the entire train, causing the hand to move forward one step) it gives the pendulum the necessary impulse.

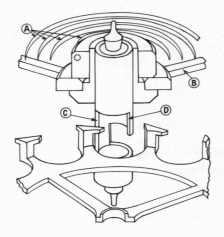

FIG. 51. Cylinder escapement. A: Hairspring; B: Balance wheel; C: Lip for entrance of the teeth of the wheel giving the pulse to the cylinder. The inside face of the cylinder slips on the teeth during the moment of inertia; D: Exit lip. (From a drawing by R. Chaléat.)

Now the same principle had to be applied to watches, as Graham himself did in 1725 with the invention of the cylinder escapement (Figure 51). This is an empty cylinder mounted directly on the staff of the balance wheel, which plays the role of the deadbeat anchor. It ensures the moment of inertia in the works when a tooth on the escape wheel slips over its surface, then allows it to escape upon receiving the driving impulse.

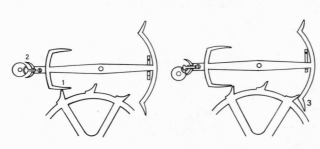

FIG. 52. A more developed form of the Mudge anchor escapement. The impulse faces and deadbeat phases are on two different parts of the anchor. *Left:* The anchor receives the impulse from the toothed wheel at 1 and transmits it to the balance wheel through 2. *Right:* The toothed wheel is at rest (3), and the balance wheel continues its movement.

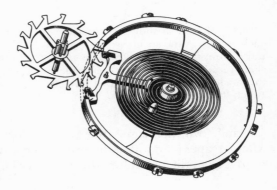

FIG. 53. Modern form of anchor escapement for a watch (from a drawing by R. Souzongno).

Although they represented considerable progress, deadbeat escapements had one serious defect: friction by the balance wheel or pendulum on the pallet throughout the entire inertia phase of the train was minimal when the parts were well polished and new, but in the long run this friction was a major cause of breakdowns.

When Thomas Mudge (1715–1794) of London invented the detached lever escapement around 1755, he undoubtedly did not know he had just made the greatest genuinely technological invention in the history of clockmaking. In this escapement the anchor is an intermediate part between the train and the balance wheel. It ensures the moment of inertia of the train, during which time it is itself completely motionless. The balance wheel is connected with the anchor for only two very brief moments at each half oscillation: first to disengage the train to let it take one step forward, then to receive the impulse through the anchor. In contrast to other devices, the anchor escapement must have been redesigned many times since Mudge's primitive conception of it, and it is only in our age that it has acquired its present form (Figures 52 and 53). By virtue of its numerous functions, which follow each other at very short intervals, this device (the quintessence of the clockmaker's art) poses difficult problems not only for theoreticians but also for experimental mechanics. (A complete and detailed theory of the functions of the anchor escapement did not really exist prior to the work of the Reverend R. Chaléat of Besançon, *Annales de chronométrie*, 1959).

The clockmakers of Mudge's time, and the inventor himself (who in his entire life built only about twenty anchor watches) did not suspect the true nature of the progress this step represented. Even the cylinder escapement, though simpler, was still beyond the capacities and comprehension of the average craftsman. The cylinder escapement eliminated the verge escapement only around the middle of the nineteenth century, and not until the twentieth century was it in turn superseded by the anchor escapement. This most instructive example shows the long periods of maturation between the birth of an invention by its originator and its full exploitation by industry. Just as it requires certain physicochemical conditions to produce crystals in a solution and to ensure their growth, so also are completely new intellectual, technical, and social conditions required to spread the use of an invention that may have existed as a prototype for many years.

Despite its influence, the anchor escapement was not the only direction pursued by clockmaking. Another path was opened in France after 1748 by Pierre Le Roy (1717–1785), when he invented a "free" escapement that in some respects reached theoretical perfection. This escapement was a single-beat type; that is, the balance wheel received an impulse in one direction of its movement but not when it returned to the same position in reversing its movement. This condition is necessary (but far from sufficient) if we are to hope that there will be no disturbance in the movement. Le Roy's escapement, remarkable in its conception but more questionable in its execution, seems to have been applied only in the two marine watches built around 1765 (Figure 56), which contained many extremely interesting inventions. It is finally Ferdinand Berthoud (1727–1807), John Arnold (1736–1799), and Thomas Earnshaw (1749–1829) who share the credit for perfecting the escapement always used in chronometers, where performance requirements are carried to the extreme (Figure 54). This single-beat escapement is called a detent escapement, after the part to which is assigned the most delicate

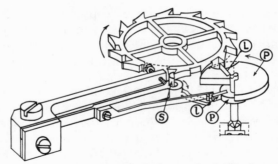

FIG. 54.   Detent escapement. The axle of the balance wheel (not shown) has a double plate, P. The small cam (I) releases the wheel at rest at S, in the direction indicated by the arrow. This is followed by the impulse on the large cam (L). Upon the following oscillation, when the plate returns in the opposite direction the small cam I, acting on the spring R, does not effect the release (from a drawing by R. Chaléat).

operation, that of ensuring the detachment of the balance wheel in the proper direction and its free movement in the opposite direction. But despite its use in chronometers, this escapement has never been successfully adapted to pocket watches (apart from construction difficulties and its very high price), because of its lack of operating reliability in the various positions and the shocks to which pocket watches are always subject. Such reliability is achieved in the highest degree by modern forms of the anchor escapement.

Compensating for heat   It is evident that clockmakers did not turn their attention first to the escapement and then to other problems; all the improvements moved together, though not at the same pace, some pushing others away. Thus, the development of escapements, and more generally an approach to precision in clocks, revealed more subtle and indiscernible defects in the early clocks. The most important were rate changes attributable to changes in temperature.

After having long denied this influence, Huygens finally realized its reality, but being of the opinion that temperature affects the dimensions and elasticity of all metals equally, he believed the defect could not be remedied and he lost confidence in the future of his own inventions, especially the spiral spring. In the last years of his life he devoted great, but unsuccessful, efforts to a search for new regulating components. The discovery attributable to Hooke, that metals have different coefficients of expansion, opened the way for compensating devices, which stimulated the imaginations of inventors. These devices are innumerable, the best known being Graham's mercury pendulum (1721) and the bimetallic grid pendulum (Figure 55) by John Harrison (1693–1776), apparently invented as early as 1726. In the former the expansion of mercury forming the pendulum weight tends to raise the center of oscillation, which is compensated for by lengthening the pendulum rod. Until the invention of the iron-nickel alloy invar in 1900 this was the best device available. Numerous bimetallic devices were invented in France between 1730 and 1760 independent of the Harrison pendulum, whose construction had not then been disclosed. Among the inventors of these devices was Julian Le Roy (1686–1759), Pierre's father. The objective in all these combinations is to maintain the center of oscillation in a fixed position by acting on the weight through levers moved by different expansions of steel and brass rods. Because of the numerous points of articulation and the unavoidable frictions, their operation is always irregular and they lack reliability no matter how much care is taken in their construction. This is why not one of them predates the mid-nineteenth century. In contrast, the bimetallic strips (Figure 54) in which two metals are soldered and on which temperature variations impose constant distortions are still an important element in modern technology, even (and especially) outside the clockmaking industry. Bimetallic strips also seem to be due to Harrison, who introduced them for the first time into his 1760 chronometer, in which the two metals were simply riveted tightly together; we are not certain who was the first person to succeed in soldering them. The theory of bimetallic strips was explained by Yvon Villarceau in 1863.

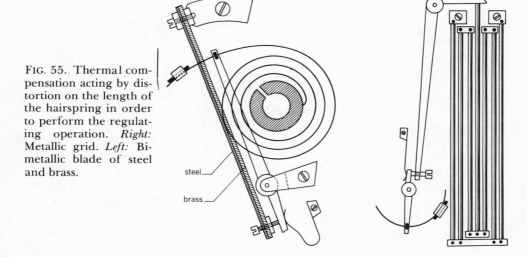

FIG. 55. Thermal compensation acting by distortion on the length of the hairspring in order to perform the regulating operation. *Right:* Metallic grid. *Left:* Bimetallic blade of steel and brass.

steel

brass

Compensating pendulums made a strong impression on contemporary thinkers, who quite correctly saw in them the first example of a natural phenomenon overcome by applying its own characteristics. We can view this device as the ancestor of all the feedback mechanisms whose already considerable importance continues to grow.

Compensating for heat with the hairspring posed a more difficult problem, a genuinely satisfactory solution for which was to be supplied only by modern metallurgy in the form of elinvar, an alloy with invariable elasticity. Although pocket watches in the eighteenth century were not sufficiently accurate to raise the question very frequently, in contrast it was of supreme importance for marine watches. At first an attempt was made by Harrison to affect the length of the spiral spring by a bimetallic grid, then by a bimetallic strip (Harrison in 1760, followed by Berthoud). Meanwhile, Pierre Le Roy invented a compensating balance wheel equipped with small glass phials containing alcohol and mercury. Subsequently, Earnshaw devised the bimetallic balance wheel compensator, which was constantly improved throughout the nineteenth century and part of the twentieth, as for example the Ditisheim balance wheels in 1923.

Isochronism   As early as the mid-eighteenth century, the progress to date confronted clockmakers engaged in the problems of chronometry with the issue of a lack of isochronism in the hairspring. The nature of this problem was completely different because it was linked to the laws of elasticity and its complete solution required methods of mathematical analysis nonexistent at the time. This did not prevent major improvements from being made, improvements that were the fruit of judiciously applied empiricism and intuition. Pierre Le Roy discovered an improvement produced by a hairspring with a number of complete turns plus a quarter turn. Arnold was the first to demonstrate the role of the terminal curves of the hairspring. Breguet invented the type of hairspring bearing his name, in which the last turn is raised above the plane of the others. This device, always used in well-constructed watches, is aimed at giving the last turn all the space needed to assume its shape as desired. Despite these early improvements, around 1850 the isochronism problem had not yet been resolved. This issue has now been dealt with to a great extent, but the problem is nevertheless still present.

The history of the watch   This account of how the main functions of timekeeping instruments developed gives no real idea of their active evolution. To outline this development is difficult because of the interaction of scientific, technical, artistic, economic, and social factors.

Let us begin with the watch, which by the eighteenth century already appeared to man as the vigilant and tireless companion of every moment. Long a valued object, coveted by the poor, the symbol of a certain social position, its use had spread widely through broad strata of society. Widely differing types existed, from the very modest copper "onion" watch to elegant gold ones in various colors embellished with enamels and diamonds. Mechanically their general construction was much the same: rewinding was done by opening the case and using a key, a fusee was present, and there was a balance wheel protected by an engraved balance cock. There was an escapement generally of the verge type, though it was sometimes a cylinder, hook, or duplex type (these being other forms of deadbeat escapements), and there were, very rarely, anchor or detent escapements in scientific pieces. But watches did not yet have jeweled pivots, even when expensively and carefully built. The first pierced rubies, drilled in London in 1704 by Nicolas Fatio de Duillier (1664–1753) of Geneva, were an English monopoly for a long time. Breguet's influence spread their use, which continued to expand into modern times. Above a certain price level, the eighteenth-century watch had a repeater mechanism that struck the hour at night by repeating, as desired, the hour and the quarter passed. Minute repeaters made in the nineteenth century struck the minutes elapsed since the last quarter hour. The initial price of a silver watch was between three and four *louis*, that of a gold repeating watch between 20 and 40 *louis*, whereas a luxury watch cost far more than 1,000 *livres*.

One general feature of the watch's development was a gradual reduction in the thickness of its movement. The first watches, which were as high as they were broad, were reminiscent of their ancestor the tower clock. The clockmaker's skill succeeded later in housing the same basic components by limiting the spread of the two platens between which the mechanism was assembled. As for the diameter, the eighteenth century produced charming small watches set in a ring, but sixteenth-century masters had already successfully built astoundingly delicate masterpieces of miniaturization.

The old civilization was unaware of contrast between the ornamental and the functional; everything in the watch, as in furniture and weapons, was both ornate and functional. In these minuscule objects style manifested itself with as much vigor as in large structures. Watches thus successively followed the fashions of the Louis XIV, Regency, Louis XV, rococo, Louis XVI, Directory, and romantic periods. Between the latter two styles, there was the Breguet style, a unique exception, created and imposed by the master clockmaker.

Around the end of the century, the genius of Abraham-Louis Breguet (1747–1823) brought the aristocratic watch to a perfection never before achieved. Breguet, born in Neuchâtel, remains preeminent among Parisian watchmakers. After more than a century and a half his watches still function perfectly, provided they have received normal maintenance—they are the pride of their owners, for Breguet's watches have never been and never will be equaled. They reflect not only the refinement of a technique by a craftsman of genius who avoided no difficulty, but particularly reflect a society in which the propertied class did not count the money it spent for personal objects, particularly for watches. Breguet watches are laid out in infinitely varied ways. There are some related layouts that were built on the same general design, but no two are identical, with the exception of the group known as the subscription series. Every known complexity is found in them, in particular the "perpetual" automatic calendars that take into account leap years and the inequality of the months. The anchor escapement is often used, contrary to customs of the time, and also used are pierced rubies, temperature compensating devices, and antishock devices, which Breguet called parachutes, to protect the balance staff.

Among so many marvels, our attention is particularly attracted by the perpetual, or self-winding, watches that are automatically rewound by the wearer's movements. Their invention, dated between 1770 and 1775, must be attributed to Abraham-Louis Perrelet (1729–1826), a native of the Swiss city of Le Locle. Breguet and various craftsmen in the mountains around Neuchâtel began to build them regularly after 1780. The principle was even then that used today: rewinding is done by a weight pivoting around an axle offset from its center of gravity, the rotations winding the mainspring through a ratchet mechanism.

Breguet watches are admirably constructed, for this master watchmaker employed the best workers of his time. Their craftsmanship combined richness and sobriety with inimitable taste and an individuality impossible to forget once one has seen it at close range. It must be noted that these masterpieces cost fortunes: a beautiful watch cost between 3,000 and 5,000 francs, probably equivalent to some 20,000 francs today.

The subscription watch was the proletarian member of the Breguet family. This thick silver watch with an enamel dial and, strangely, only a single hand, which permitted a reading to within two or three minutes of the correct time, still cost around 400 francs.

Not everything that bears the name *Breguet* on the face or movement comes from the hand of this famous watchmaker. Authentic Breguets are identified by their number, which must correspond to that still carefully preserved in the company records at its headquarters, where a list of their successive owners can be traced.

Once Breguet was gone, decadence set in; or so, at least, many people have believed and written. But things are not so simple. Certainly the technicians are not to be despised; Breguet's competitors showed that they were able to work as well as he as they continued his line. We need only mention Oudin, a former Breguet employee.

What disappeared was the customers. The middle-class purchaser now supplanting the aristocrat was not disposed to waste a fortune on watches and trinkets. This would have been the end of luxury watchmaking except for the reappearance from time to time of a patron or eccentric who can still, let us note, find artists to satisfy his requirements.

In any event, around 1800 for the ordinary watch and 1840 for all categories (with some honorable exceptions), watchmaking became routine: a commonplace mechanism, no complexities, hasty construction, a heavy case, and poor decoration or tasteless imitation of the earlier style.

Pendulum clocks and regulators

Whatever Breguet's influence through the watches he built, it is especially with the pendulum clock that the eighteenth century appears as the golden age of clockmaking. We may distinguish between pendulum clocks placed on mantelpieces, hanging clocks placed on walls, hung on brackets, or, more importantly, on a matching pendant, and the pendulum clock, a piece of furniture placed directly on the floor. All these models played an important role among eighteenth-century furnishings.

When simple, pendulum clocks were elegant and carefully made, but for the Court and the great lords there was no limit to their ornateness. Collectors from every country vie for possession of eighteenth-century pendulum clocks, of which many are still on the market, but it is the public collections that offer inexhaustible opportunities to admire them. In France the national palaces, the Louvre, and the Conservatoire national des Arts et Métiers house the main collections. In Great Britain, outside of the royal palaces there is the Wallace Collection. Quite large collections are also to be seen in Germany, Austria, Italy, Spain, and elsewhere.

Mantel and wall clocks are excellent timepieces, to be sure, but one's interest turns first to their decorative details. It is beyond our subject to describe this aspect. Every type is offered, from the exuberant fantasies of the rococo style down to the supremely elegant sobriety of the Louis XVI style in its last expressions. Clocks with automatic features, carillons, and organs display unlimited richness and fantasy.

Regulators can be classified in two ways. What counts for some is, above all, their cabinetwork and bronze fittings. They are sometimes signed by the greatest cabinetmakers or founders. Others seek primarily scientific examples: their always refined decoration is discreet, emphasizing the mechanism and particularly the pendulum. The latter—proportioned, built, finished, and polished with the greatest care—is always compensated in most cases by a gridiron or bimetallic leven, which majestically beats the seconds. Its swing is not very great, rarely surpassing four degrees, so it is practically isochronous. The suspension, either knife-edge or a delicate spring, is the object of special care. The escapement is generally a Graham deadbeat anchor.

The mechanism often includes several intricacies, the most common being that it indicates true solar time next to mean time. This requires a bit of explanation. We know that the apparent movement of the sun is not uniform, so that solar days are unequal and at each true noon (occurring as the sun passes over the meridian) it is necessary to add a certain number of minutes (called time equation) to find mean noon time. The time equation is zero near the equinoxes and solstices, but between them it reaches alternately a maximum of four positive or negative values, the largest being close to 17 minutes. The time equation can thus be plotted by a cam with a profile in somewhat the shape of a bean and making one revolution per year. By a train of epicycloidal gears a roller traveling on this cam controls an additional hand that indicates solar time. This made it possible to set the clock by referring to a meridian without making any calculations and to conform to the ideal of agreement with the sun.

The most famous eighteenth-century regulator builders were Jean-André Lepaute (1720–1798) and his brother Jean-Baptiste (1727–1803), Ferdinand Berthoud, Robert Robin (1742–1809), and Antide Janvier (1751–1835).

Some regulators give calendar information, but clocks giving astronomical information (the rising and setting of the sun, phases of the moon, and eclipses) and planetary clocks especially form a separate class whose undisputed master is Antide Janvier, a native of Franc-Comtois. Very beautiful pieces by him can be seen in the Musée du Conservatoire national des Arts et Métiers, the Besançon Museum, and the Musée Paul Dupuy in Toulouse. His two masterpieces had varying fates. One was a complete planetary clock (including all the planets, even Uranus, which had recently been discovered), giving detailed information on the moon's phases and its principal irregularities, useful in calculating eclipses, as well as giving the same information on Jupiter and its satellites. Janvier's other masterpiece predicted (quite unreliably, however) the hours of the tides by combining knowledge of solar and lunar movements. One clock, perhaps the most luxurious ever built, made for Louis XVI and placed in his office at the Tuileries in 1789, was destroyed by fire in 1871 and nothing remains of it. But the other, completed in 1800, still exists and functions perfectly since being restored in 1956; it is in a private collection in France.

Beginning about 1800 the pendulum clock and the regulator evolved differently. The Empire clock continued the tradition of noble decoration. Gilded bronze often yielded to black-patinated bronze in making Egyptian or Roman-style caryatids, according to the taste of the period. But the noble pendulum clock was extremely expensive and was beyond middle-class taste so it was rapidly supplanted by the small, incidental pendulum clock. Some of these clocks are very amusing and even quite pretty—romanticism brought with it the troubadour and cathedral clock styles that were unexpectedly whimsical, such as a certain windmill in the Musée des Arts Décoratifs whose sails bristle with gothic hooks. But this genre declined rapidly, and as early as 1840 we must definitely speak of the pendulum clock as being decadent. The movements in so-called Parisian pendulum clocks are still carefully built, but they look dishearteningly uniform, and the complexities and extra functions that contributed so much to the charm and individuality of old pendulum clocks have disappeared. Without questioning the efforts or merits of the Second Empire decorators and bronze founders, it must be said that most of their production, as for its artistic value, became practically worthless.

During the first half of the nineteenth century there was no break in the continuity of styles in regulators, whose design and construction achieved perfection. Austere designs, extremely sober decoration, and frequent use of ebony and dark woods give them a solemn appearance. We should specially mention mantelpiece regulators, built on the same principles as long-case regulators but having pendulums that beat half seconds, and thus being four times shorter. Some of them, built between 1800 and 1850, were given constant-force escapements. These extremely ingenious and complex mechanisms provided true intellectual pleasure to those who thoroughly understood their operation; their effectiveness in regulating clocks is only theoretical. They are apparently a manifestation of the baroque spirit in mechanics.

The last descendants of the classic regulator are found in observatory clocks built until around 1880 and even 1900. The name of Auguste Fenon, director of the École d'Horologerie at Besançon, is associated with them. Today, these pendulum clocks, relieved of their timekeeping role but carefully maintained and in perfect operating condition, are the letters patent of nobility for the institutions that have preserved them.

Public clocks

Monumental clockmaking is a special field. The starting point for the entire clockmaking art, it enjoyed its first golden age in the sixteenth century, when municipal governments considered themselves honor bound to install in some prominent position a clock surpassing those of rival cities.

The nineteenth century is another remarkable period for these clocks, because of interesting technical developments on the one hand and brilliant achievements by individuals on the other. In Great Britain especially, much was done to improve the accuracy and reliability of large public clocks. These efforts included inventing new escapements and mechanisms to control the indicator components so as to defy bad weather. The name of Edmund Beckett Denison, later Lord Grimthorpe (1816–1905) is associated with the famous Big Ben clock in the Parliament tower at Westminster Palace (1859).

Several amazing clocks built in France in the nineteenth century are noteworthy for serving no useful purpose. They exhibit all the technological resources of their age, but the spirit animating them is medieval. There is first the clock in Strasbourg Cathedral, designed by Jean-Baptiste Schwilgué (1776–1856) and completed in 1842. It was the successor to a magnificent sixteenth-century clock, and major parts of the housing (*edifice* would be a better word) that shelter it come from its predecessor. Its program of calendar and astronomical information is prodigious: it automatically computes the date of Easter according to Gregorian rules, taking into consideration nonperiodic peculiarities, a unique feature that would require a thick volume to describe it. The achievements of Auguste-Lucien

Vérité (1806–1887) at Besançon in 1860 and then in his native city of Beauvais in 1869 are two versions of a design inspired by Schwilgué and Janvier but with different layouts. Monumental astronomical clocks are still being built occasionally here and there, but after the clocks we have mentioned this genre is particularly difficult to revive.

Marine chronometers   This outline of how the clock's functions (escapements, compensators, isochronism) evolved has occasionally mentioned the marine chronometer. Its invention was the fruit of persistent efforts over more than a century, and it is hardly an exaggeration to speak of the epic of marine chronometry. To go into detail would exceed the scope of this chapter, but it is necessary to outline it briefly.

Determining longitude at sea by observing solar time, preferably at noon, and comparing it with the time at zero meridian as read on the chronometer, is a very old idea often attributed to Gemma Frisius (1508–1558). For lack of a reliable portable chronometer, this method was long considered utopian, a feeling reinforced by Huygens's own lack of success in this area. In 1714, however, the British Parliament offered a prize of ten thousand pounds sterling to anyone who would measure longitude at sea to within less than one degree, and the prize would be twenty thousand pounds if the error was less than a half degree. Contemporary technology made it possible to attack if not solve the problem. All the century's great clockmakers tested their inventive faculties, and even more their tenacity, on difficulties in which the snares laid by man were unsurpassed by those laid by nature.

John Harrison dominates the English scene on this question. With unwearying stubbornness over forty years he built successively four different chronometers. The first three followed an unworkable formula. But the fourth model, radically different, finally won the prize, in 1765, though not without the ill will of the Commission on Longitudes. The National Maritime Museum at Greenwich renders the great pioneer worthy homage by displaying his four chronometers

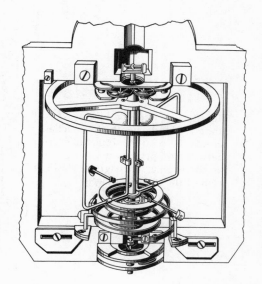

FIG. 56. Marine chronometer by Le Roy. The mechanism is shown without the dial and hands. The horizontal balance wheel and tube-and-ball device forming the thermal compensation system can be distinguished.

not only as capable of working but actually working on certain days. (They were restored in 1935 by Commander Gould.)

An equal amount of work was done in France on chronometers, and from a distance we can admire the builders' rivalry among whom are Pierre Le Roy and Ferdinand Berthoud, the former being more daring, the latter more methodical. The culmination of the competition was voyages made by Royal Navy ships in 1767, 1768, 1771, and 1772 to test the two types of instruments separately and together, with excellent results that would have been worthy of the English prize. It is regrettable that the scientific rivalry of these two great clockmakers gradually degenerated into a personal quarrel full of recriminations and bitterness. Today it would be impossible to champion one against the other, but two points must be noted: the unquestionable priority of Le Roy in inventing the detached escapement (Figure 57) and Berthoud's tireless perseverance from the first experiments in 1760 until sturdy, reliable, and reproducible chronometers were achieved. It is thrilling to experience physically the stages in this progress by seeing the series of marine chronometers in the Musée du Conservatoire national des Arts et Métiers. First is a monstrous and almost useless chronometer, but there follow three series of chronometers, and the "longitude watch," Number 52 in the third series (dated 1793), already has many features of current marine chronometers.

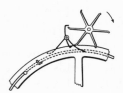

FIG. 57.   Detached escapement of Le Roy's chronometer.

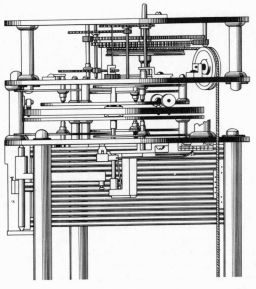

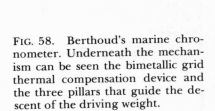

FIG. 58.   Berthoud's marine chronometer. Underneath the mechanism can be seen the bimetallic grid thermal compensation device and the three pillars that guide the descent of the driving weight.

Simultaneously with England's naval leadership, the preeminence of her chronometry was asserting itself in the closing years of the eighteenth century. One essential factor in this preeminence was the use of pierced rubies and hard stones. In the hands first of Arnold, who in 1782 patented the first model of terminal curves (for helical springs), and then Earnshaw, this admirable instrument acquired its final form. After 1800, in fact, there were no further revolutionary changes in the chronometer's general appearance. The mahogany box, the massive brass case suspended from gimbals, and the arrangement of the mechanism are as immutable as British tradition. The work of perfecting the device continued throughout the nineteenth century, being henceforth brought to bear on the regulating component, the balance wheel-hairspring combination.

Harrison's chronometer Number 4 was subject (rarely, it is true) to gains of 10 seconds per day. The daily deviation of an 1800 chronometer could be as much as 5 seconds, but today it is less than 0.05 of a second a day—two centuries, two decimal places.

CHAPTER 5

STANDARDIZED MEASURING SYSTEMS
AND THE BEGINNINGS OF PRECISION MECHANICS

EARLY LINEAR MEASURES

*Various values
for the foot*
Until the decimal metric system was established, the foot was for all practical purposes the basic unit of linear measurement. Documents and comparison tables both before and after the eighteenth century, and a metrological study of examples, reveal a great variety of values for this unit. The diversity is only apparent, however, for in numerous cases the lengths of various feet seem to derive from the Roman foot, approximately 11.76 inches. (This at least is what appears from studies by Guilhiermoz and from examining extant objects.) It is possible to classify these measurement units into ten categories, each related to the Roman foot.

Each category in the table below is designated by both a letter and a number for the sake of simplifying discussion; so, R1, for example, stands for the Roman foot.

Foot	*Designation*	*Equivalent*	*Examples: foot of*
Roman foot of 16 digits ("finger's breadth")	R1	.294 m.	
15 Roman digits	R2	.275 m.	Brussels
16/15 of R1	R3	.314 m.	Leyden, Besançon
18/16 of R1	R4	.330 m.	Burgundy
6/5 of R1	R5	.353 m.	Chartres
"Neo-Roman"	R'1	.298 m.	Ghent, Courtray
24/25 of R'1	R'2	.286 m.	Lorraine, Antwerp
15 digits of R'1	R'3	.279 m.	Mechlin, Castille
6/5 of R'2	R'4	.343 m.	Lyon
6/5 of R'1	R'5	.358 m.	Comté de Burgundy

The actual sizes of the measuring rods representing these units obviously fluctuated around these values, without departing too far from them, with any exception being due, for example, to defective stamping. In any event, the foregoing classification includes many values and offers the advantage of introducing some clarity into a field that is quite confused.

Formerly, long feet bore the same *manual* foot, as for example R4, R5, R'4 and R'5. This ancient designation was still used in the eighteenth century in Turin, for example, where the *piede manuale* measured .3425 m. (R'4).

Subdivisions of the foot   The foot was divided into 12 inches (*oncie* in Italy, at Turin, Milan, and other cities) and the inch into 12 *lignes* (8 *achtel* in Hamburg), the *ligne* into 10 or 12 parts or points (12 *atomi* in Italian cities such as Alexandria, where the *trabuc* (2.860 m.) was equal to 6 feet, the foot being 12 *oncie* or 144 points or 1,728 *atomi*).

Although duodecimal numeration was most common, decimal division of linear measurements was also used, as in Lorraine, for example, where the foot of .286 m. was subdivided into 10 inches, 100 *lignes,* or 1,000 points. Sometimes the division was mixed: in Hamburg the surveyors' foot (R3) consisted of 12 inches, 120 *lignes,* and 1,200 parts.

Surveyors' measures   Large measuring units consisted of a variable number of feet. The (fathom) *toise* and the *canne* (an expression common in southern regions) were generally composed of 6 feet. The Parisian *toise* was 6 feet of .3248 m., or 1.949 m., and the Montpellier *canne* was 6 R4, or 1.98 m., whereas the Hamburg *klafter* was 6 R'2, or 1.719 m. There were exceptions, however—the *toise* of the Comté de Burgundy was 7 R'5, or 2.506 m.

The *canne* was habitually divided into *pans, palmes,* or *empans.* In principle the *pan* was equivalent to three-quarters of a foot, and was subdivided into inches (or *menus* or *oncies*), *lignes,* and points. In Toulouse,

1 *canne* = 8 *pans* = 64 inches = 512 *lignes* = 4,096 points.

We can find other combinations, illustrated by the two *cannes* used in Genoa. One contains 10 *palmes* of .249 m. each (2.49 m.), while the other, the surveyors' *canne,* contains 12 *palmes* (2.99 m.). Surveyors elsewhere used measures with variable dimensions, with such names as *verge, perche, gaule, corde, chaîne,* and so on.

In Paris several *perches* were current with sizes fluctuating between 18 and 20 royal feet (5.8464 m. to 7.1456 m.). In Burgundy the *perche* was equal to 9.5 R4 (3.13 m.), whereas the Antwerp *verge* had 20 R'2 (5.736 m.), the Mechlin one consisted of 20 R'3 (5.56 m.), and that of Courtray had 10 R'1 (2.977 m.). In Madrid the *cuerda* (*corde,* rope) was equal to 33 long *palmes* of .2087 m. (6.89 m.), but in Palermo the *cordo* of 128 *palmi* each .2581 m. long equaled 33.06 m. In the Department of Morbihan the *gaule* was eight Parisian feet (2.598 m.) and the surveyors' chain was 24 feet (7.796 m.). Many more examples could easily be given.

Textile measures   The ell generally consisted of 2, 2.5, or 3 feet. The ell in Provins or ell used in the area called the Fairs of Champagne was 2.5 R4, or 3 R2 = .825 m. The Castilian ell (a contemporary of the Provins ell) consisted of 3 R'1 = .837 m. In Paris the ell (actually a double ell) was 1.188 m. (4 R'1), as is indicated by the 1554 standard preserved in the Conservatoire national des Arts et Métiers.

The Venetian *braccio* (fathom), used to measure woolen goods, measured .683 m. and was very close to the Bruges ell, which (at least in the fourteenth century) measured approximately .685 m., a value very close to 2.5 R2. In Florence the term *braccio* was applied to two measures differing in their use and size: the *braccio di panno* (wool fathom) of .584 m. (approximately 2 R1) and the *braccio di terra* (land fathom) of .548 m. (2 R2).

Linear measures for land and ocean The fathom was current in many countries. In Denmark, Norway, and Sweden it bore the names *favn,* *kaun,* and *famnar* and was equivalent to 6 feet (*fot*) R′1 or 1.78 m. in Sweden and 6 Rhineland feet (*fod*) R3 or 1.88 m. in the other two countries. Old and more recently reproduced maps from these countries have depths expressed in fathoms. In England the fathom is equal to six English feet or two yards.

To measure land and sea distances, the pace, league, mile, and so on were also commonly employed. Here are several examples:

> Land distances: In Paris the mile consisted of 1,000 *toises* (1.949 km.). Since 1766 the league (*lieue*) was equal to 4,800 *pas* (paces), each equal to 5 feet (6.680 km.). In Lisbon there were 18 leagues to a degree (6.173 km.), while in Germany 15 were counted to the degree (7.408 km.). In England the statute mile, still in use in various countries, is equal to 1,760 yards (1.6093 km.).
> Ocean distances: The nautical mile in France, one-third the nautical league of 20 to the degree, equals 1.852 km. In 1906 it was adopted by 22 governments.

Other countries use English units: the nautical mile (varying from 1.843 km. to 1.862 km. depending on the latitude), the foot (.3048 m.), and the fathom (1.8288 m.).

Agricultural measures The terms designating agricultural measures and their corresponding values are so varied that within the narrow limits of this work it is possible only to touch upon the subject.

Surveyors and geometers used measures with various values—the *verge, canne, perche,* and so on—and expressed the results of their measurements in square *verges, cannes, perches.* But peasants, undoubtedly because of their permanent contact with nature, had a relatively subjective method of evaluation. Land areas were expressed in terms of the fertility of the soil, the amount of effort made to cultivate them, the quantity of seed necessary to sow them, the length of time needed for the work, and the like.

This explains the use of picturesque expressions that reflect these qualitative and quantitative characteristics. For example, the *journal* (*tage-werk* or *morgen* in German) is that part of a terrain that can be plowed in the course of a day's (*jour*) work. *Boisselée* or *boisseau* designates areas sown with a *boisseau* (bushel), *staio* (the Italian bushel), or *setier* (approximately eight pints) of seed. Certain measures such as the *acre* and *arpent* (roughly equal to an acre) were widely used. The term *acre* is commonly used in Normandy and is current in Great Britain, Germany, and elsewhere. The *arpent* is so deeply rooted in French history that it is still locally (and illegally) used.

Variations in agricultural measures from one region to another could be considerable. The Paris *arpent* fluctuated between approximately 51 and 65 *ares* (an *are* was equal to 100 square meters or 1,080 square feet), the Normandy *acre* between 34 and 97 *ares.* The Picardy *journal* fluctuated between 26 and 27 *ares,* and in certain southern towns even went as high as 120 *ares.*

Standards of measurement The standards for linear measure are generally metal rulers. Long tradition decreed that they be publicly displayed, so they were embedded in the walls of certain buildings — churches, the town hall, and the like. However, these prototypes were sometimes engraved in stone, as was, for example, the ell of Sabugal in Portugal in the thirteenth century, the gauges engraved in the walls of Strasbourg Cathedral, and so on.

Displaying the standards enabled consumers and manufacturers to refer to them easily and also made it possible to prevent fraud, which, given the proximity of these "justices of the peace," was easy to disclose and prove. But on a technical level the opinion of the metrologist is very different. The standard being by definition the basic element for comparison, it must be protected from any possible alteration, and its public display is thus contrary to this technical demand. In this regard the Parisian *toise* discussed in Volume II is a typical example.

Viewed from our standpoint, standards of ancient metrology appear quite arbitrary; but they undoubtedly sufficed for a commercial system less demanding of accuracy than ours is today.

Most specimens of linear measures that have survived, that is, standards and copies of them, are end measures meaning that their length is defined as the distance between their end faces, in contrast to point or line measures, in which points or lines marked on the rule indicate the standard length. These measures were subdivided by notches that were engraved with a heated engraving tool and were thus quite crude. So the results of measuring contained a large amount of uncertainty.

The subdivisions of wooden measures are frequently represented by copper nails with filed-down heads, a procedure employed to mark off the arms on wooden Roman scales.

The limits of precision In the eighteenth century the cooperation of scientists and manufacturers contributed to improving the metrological qualities of the measures. For example, the "Peruvian" fathom *(toise)* marks a stage in the evolution of scientific metrology begun by seventeenth-century scientists. This fathom, the permanent referent for the geodesic operations of Delambre and Méchain, was examined at the International Bureau of Weights and Measures from 1887 to 1890. The results of the comparisons were as follows:

End fathom	1.949090 m.
Point fathom	1.949001 m.

These two values correspond within .1 mm. This seems to be the best tolerance achievable in 1735 and even in the second half of the eighteenth century, since the caliber of weapons could be verified with the Gribeauval star gauge to within .1 mm., or $1/25$ ligne of the Parisian foot. It will be noted that, at the beginning of the eighteenth century, tables listing calibers of cannons and balls rarely mention values less than ⅛ *ligne* (.3 mm.). In the seventeenth century it was believed possible to measure $1/12$ *ligne* (.2 mm.) by using transversals, whose principle has already been explained. Those who could have guaranteed this measurement would have been extremely optimistic. Even the *Encyclopédie,* in the article on the pendulum, implies that ¼ *ligne* (approximately .55 mm.) seems to constitute a limit difficult to exceed in comparing linear measures.

As techniques of division were perfected, systematic use of verniers made it possible to push back the limits of precision. We shall see how the inventors of the metric system put the vernier to use, notably, adapting it to Lenoir's first comparator for linear measures, which made it possible to achieve precision of .02 mm. The comparator was to be called upon to play an extremely important role in dimensional metrology as soon as the problem of interchangeability of parts was introduced to industry. This problem may perhaps have originated in weapons factories and in particular with the *Tables de construction* established by Lieutenant-General Gribeauval between 1764 and 1789.

Interesting information appears earlier, for example, in the *Traité d'artillerie* of Surirey de Saint-Rémi in 1707. This shows a trend toward standardizing calipers, undoubtedly an approximate standardization but one indispensable in this field. Finally, a still older example is that of the shipyard at Venice, which in the thirteenth century employed 16,000 workers capable of building, "with the help of prefabricated parts, a galley in one day." In our opinion this is a striking example. An organization of such scope presupposes teams of engineers and specialized workers, as well as assembly-line production of measured parts.

There was obviously no question of achieving accuracy as small as the micron. The problem under discussion may have been solved in 1803 by Vacheron and Leschot with a comparator accurate to the micron (one thousandth of a millimeter), used in their factory until 1888.

The precision of linear measurement took another step forward on Sep-

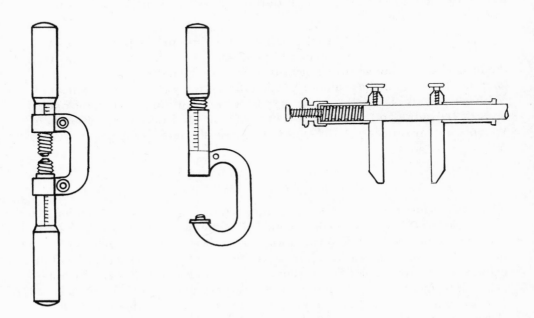

FIG. 59.   Screw-type gauge and gauge with circular vernier, patented in 1858 by Palmer.

tember 7, 1858, when the Frenchman Palmer was granted patent No. 7518 for inventing a gauge "with a screw and circular vernier." The principle of this well-known scale depends on the use of a micrometric screw. The Palmer micrometer was adapted to the sliding caliper in order to measure internal diameters of apertures and for similar purposes. In 1894 the gauge was applied to Hartmann's automatic recording comparator used in the International Bureau of Weights and Measures, a device that provided a way to adjust industrial end standards to within half a micron.

The table below, summarizing the foregoing information, shows that in linear measurement precision appeared only at the end of the nineteenth century, a thousand times greater than it had been in the seventeenth century. This is a brilliant performance.

Period	Accuracy	Remarks
Seventeenth and beginning of eighteenth centuries	.5 mm.	Mersenne, Picard, *Table des calibres d'artillerie* (1707)
1631		Invention of the vernier
1735	.1 mm. (1/25 *ligne*)	"Peruvian" fathom
1789	.1 mm.	Gribeauval star gauge (for artillery caliber)
1790–1799	.02 mm.	Borda platinum rules; Lenoir comparator with verniers
1839		Commercial meter (metal: tolerance + .2 mm.)
1842	.01	Invention of the Palmer micrometer
1876	.01	Improved Gribeauval star gauge
1894	.0005	Hartmann comparator

THE ORGANIZATION OF THE METRIC SYSTEM

Attempts at unification   The need to create a universal measurement system, which had barely been recognized at the end of the seventeenth century, became increasingly evident as the eighteenth century wore on. In France the monarchy attempted to substitute Parisian units for local ones. In 1766 eighty copies of the "Peruvian" fathom (the standard for the Parisian fathom), accompanied by replicas of the ell and the *poids de marc* (a unit of weight) were distributed to the provincial parliaments and sent abroad.

Setting up a universal standard still appeared impossible, or at least very remote. Comparisons between the standards in use in France and in England were nevertheless established. In 1742 George Graham ordered copies made by Jonathan Sisson of the standard yard (now held in the Tower of London) and by Samuel Read of the troy and avoirdupois pounds. These copies were sent to Paris, where the Académie des Sciences assigned du Fay and Abbot Nollet to make comparisons with foreign standards. The length of the Parisian half fathom was marked on one of the English standards, which was then returned to London along with two *poids de marc* weights.

In Volume II we saw that at a very early date scientists proposed adopting as a universal measure the length of a pendulum beating the second. But the fact that this length varies with latitude made it difficult to decide on a length acceptable to all countries. La Condamine, and after him Condorcet, suggested taking as the standard of reference the length of this pendulum at the latitude of 45°, measured at sea level. Work was to begin under Turgot in 1775, but the fall of the comptroller-general prevented this. But even if the principle of this reform had been adopted, it is practically certain that it would never have spread to any great extent. Substituting a uniform measuring system for all the traditional local units would have run counter to too many ancestral habits on all levels of society and in every country for it to have any chance of being accepted in normal times. The vicissitudes of the metric system during its first forty years were to prove this adequately.

The principle of the natural unit   The period of the French Revolution created circumstances favorable to realizing a unified system of weights and measures. The decision to do so was officially made by the National Assembly on May 8, 1790, following a report by Talleyrand. Because of the difficulties created by the Revolution, this project could be successfully carried out only after long and painful efforts, and it was not until 1799 that standards for the meter, kilogram, and liter—the bases of the new metric system—were deposited in the National Archives.

The ones promoting this reform were the mathematicians, astronomers, and geometers of the Académie who, in accordance with the idea formulated long ago, had at first envisaged taking as the basic unit the length of the simple pendulum beating the second at a given latitude. Great Britain and the United States were sounded out on the prospect of joining in the preparatory work toward the reform, but the Académie's scientists quickly abandoned the idea of basing the linear unit on the pendulum, and the two Anglo-Saxon countries did not collaborate. The Académie's committee decided to derive a natural unit of measure from the quarter segment of the earth's meridian, and for this purpose to measure the meridian arc between Dunkirk and Barcelona. The Paris meridian had already been measured twice, in 1670 by Picard and in 1740 by Abbot Lacaille. Actually, however, French scientists wished to profit from the occasion to resolve an old dispute about the exact shape of the earth, and measuring such a long meridian arc would furnish them with the necessary information.

Other factors made it possible to undertake these major projects. At this time there were in France several highly skilled instrument makers who built devices precise enough to perform successfully the operations proposed. There were available to the committee in particular Borda's repeating circle, built by Étienne Lenoir, and the large precision balance built by Fortin for Lavoisier. As the work progressed, these were supplemented by comparators, rules to measure bases, and various other devices that could be invented only through collaboration by physicists and workers who had for a long time given much consideration to such problems.

The creators of the metric system The final plan was adopted by the National Assembly on March 30, 1791. The Académie des Sciences set up five committees for the various projects planned: triangulating and determining latitudes, measuring the base and the length of the seconds pendulum, weight of a known volume of water, and comparing provincial measures with Parisian ones.

The makeup of these committees quickly changed, because of events that followed. The most important scientists in this work were Méchain and Delambre on the first two committees, Borda and Cassini for the third, Lavoisier and Haüy for the fourth, and Tillet and Brisson for the fifth. A central committee, originally including Borda, Condorcet, Lagrange, and Lavoisier, was named a little later to direct all operations.

After the Académie was suppressed, this group of scientists continued its work under the name Temporary Committee on Weights and Measures, a temporary bureau substituted in 1795. A bureau of weights and measures, created in February 1796, later (during the Directory period) completed the work and granted approval for the operations.

Provisional standards A certain number of decisions were made even before the various measurements were begun. In particular, the principle of dividing measures into decimal units was adopted and studies on terminology were begun, a problem that gave rise to numerous disputes. A law of April 7, 1795, established the nomenclature later adopted, but this underwent various attempts to modify it before it was finally made obligatory by an 1839 ordinance.

A 1793 law temporarily established the equivalences of the new and old units while awaiting the definitions decided upon. The meter was thus provisionally fixed at 3 feet 11.44 *lignes* of the Académie's fathom, the *grave* (kilogram) at 2 pounds 5 *gros* 49 grains of so-called *pile de Charlemagne*, or "Charlemagne stack" (defined later). It was decided to establish temporary standards and send them to all *départements*.

The provisional meter was calculated from the measurement of the meridian made in 1740 by Lacaille. A comparison of the meter and the Académie's fathom was then made by Lenoir with the help of a comparator he built especially for this project (Figure 65). It consisted of four brass measuring rods calculated to be approximately as long as the meter, which were compared by being placed end to end with two of Lenoir's iron fathom rules that had first been compared with the Académie's fathom. This comparison technique was extremely delicate, involving supplementary devices built by Lenoir that were most precise.

Determining the kilogram Measuring the unit of weight was still more difficult. It was first done by Haüy and Lavoisier and was repeated in 1799 by Lefèvre-Gineau and Fabroni. The Académie had decided that the unit of weight would be the weight of a cubic decimeter of distilled water weighed in a vacuum at the temperature of melting ice. The kilogram's weight was to be determined according to the well-known Archimedes' principle that a body immersed in a fluid that does not alter it loses weight by an amount equal to that of the fluid displaced. A cylindrical body was selected to facilitate shaping it and calculating its volume. An instrument maker, Nicolas Fortin, was given the task of making three upright cylinders and adjusting them to the volume determined, for which he built a comparator of his own invention. He was ordered to build other balances based on Lavoisier's model (Figure 60) for the Committee on Weights and Measures. A cylinder was also used later by Lefèvre-Gineau.

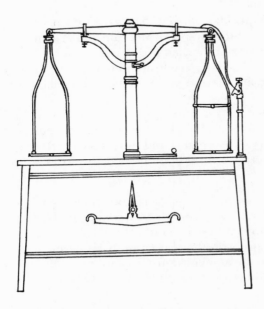

FIG. 60.   Diagram of the model of Fortin's scale used for determining the kilogram.

Discussions on the value of the kilogram

No report describing the experiments of either Lavoisier and Haüy or Lefèvre-Gineau and Fabrioni exists; only the results have been preserved. One reason Lefèvre-Gineau's verification was probably necessary was because the kilogram determined by his predecessors had been established on the basis of the provisional value for the meter. When Delambre and Méchain finished their geodesic operations, and the official value of the meter was known, it was .144 *ligne* shorter than the provisional meter calculated in 1793, so the value of the kilogram had to be modified. But it is also possible that a certain confusion had arisen concerning the exact value of the old *poids de marc* units used.

The standards used were those contained in the stack of 50 marcs known as the *pile de Charlemagne*, or "Charlemagne stack," which under the *ancien régime* had been preserved at the mint and had probably served since the sixteenth century in some measure as a national standard (see Volume II, Plate 27).

The stack consists of thirteen small conical brass buckets nested inside each other, each of which constitutes a weight standard. Starting with the smallest, we find first a one-*gros* standard (the *gros-plein*), which fits exactly into a bucket also weighing precisely one *gros*. The latter fits into a double *gros*, followed by the quadruple *gros*, then the ounce, the double ounce, and so on. The largest bucket weighs 14 *marcs*, and its immediate predecessor weighs 8. The stack is so conceived that each bucket (up to the 8-*marc* one) has a cubic capacity weighing exactly the same as itself; that is, the 8-*marc* bucket when full weighs 16 *marcs*. The twelfth piece is a bucket weighing 14 *marcs,* and the thirteenth is the container, itself weighing 20 *marcs,* making a total of 50 *marcs* for the complete stack. In particular the 1-*marc* bucket (the *marc creux,* or hollow *marc*) contains seven pieces nested inside each other, which together constitute the *marc plein* (full *marc*). Calculations by Tillet in 1770 had demonstrated that the weight of the *marc plein* was less than that of the *marc creux,* and a *marc moyen* (average *marc*) had been calculated in order to compensate for this difference.

This example shows what confusion concerning the exact value of the various standards could prevail under the old system, although it was not as much as one might think—actually, each piece in the Charlemagne stack was regarded as a standard. When the metric system was developed this concept was improved by simplifying the diverse weight standards and by adopting as a basis for the system a single standard for each class of measures—the meter and the kilogram—and relating all other measures to them. But at the time the Committee on Weights and Measures was making its studies it was still possible to take three different *marc* weights as bases for comparison to determine the kilogram.

M. Birembaut has noted that what happened in effect is that Lavoisier must have used the *marc creux,* but his results must have been interpreted with the *marc moyen.* This is undoubtedly the second reason why Lefèvre-Gineau was ordered to make another calculation.

There was also a third reason. The Lavoisier-Haüy result had been reached at 0°C., but in the course of the study it was found that the maximum density of water is at 4°, not 0°. The second experiment was performed at 4°.

Such was the nature of the problems that physicists and instrument makers had to cope with in order to establish the bases for the metric system.

Determining the length of the meter, that is, measuring the quarter segment of one of the earth's meridians, required more classic operations. Triangulation had by now been systematically used for a century, and Méchain and Cassini in particular had just united the triangulation network of France with that of England.

Triangulation operations Triangulating the meridian was done by Delambre and his assistants between Dunkirk and Rodez in 1792–1797 and by Méchain and his aides between Rodez and Barcelona in 1792–1798. Each team had two Lenoir repeating circles (Figure 61), an astronomical telescope, pendulums, barometers, thermometers, graphometers, levels, and cases of mathematical instruments. The survey began with measuring a base between Melun and Lieusaint, and another was measured between Vernet and Salces in the eastern Pyrenees. The length of these two bases for the entire triangulation had to be ascertained very precisely. Lenoir was given the task of making the necessary measuring rods, which were of platinum and measured 12 feet (approximately 4 meters) in length. They were covered with a copper sheath attached to them at one end only; at the other was a vernier with which to read the difference in expansion of the two metals in relation to the temperature. In addition each platinum rod had at one end a small graduated scale in a groove (Figure 62), for measuring the precise interval between the large rules when they were placed end to end during the survey (Figure 63). These geodesic measures were subjected to studies of thermal expansion and their lengths were compared.

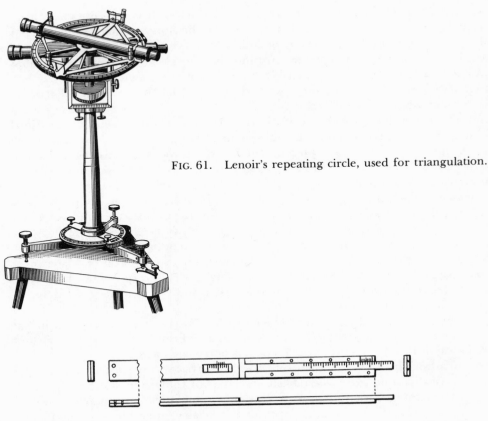

FIG. 61.   Lenoir's repeating circle, used for triangulation.

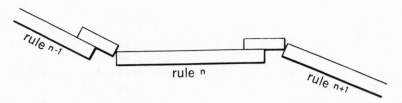

FIG. 62.   End of platinum measuring rods for measuring bases in triangulation.

FIG. 63.   Use of measuring rods linked together by their small sliding rules.

One of them was taken as a standard and compared with the Peruvian fathom. These computations were done on a Lenoir comparator giving a precision of 1/100,000 of a fathom or 1/116 of a *ligne*.

The entire triangulation operation involved measuring 115 triangles. In 36 of them the errors in observing the three angles taken together totaled less than one second, and the greatest error did not exceed five seconds (Figure 64).

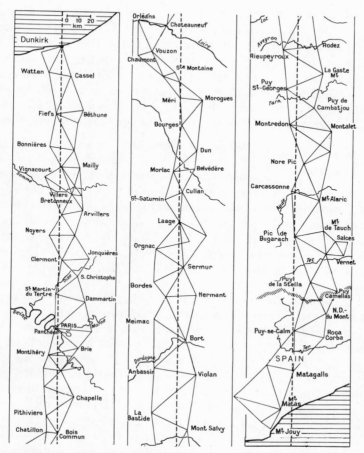

FIG. 64.   Triangulation of the meridian from Dunkirk to Barcelona.

Final approval of the survey

All the observations by the geodesists were collected in Paris at the end of 1798, and the final operations were entrusted by the government of the Directory to a committee that included the French scientists Borda, Brisson, Coulomb, Darcet, Haüy, Lagrange, Laplace, Lefèvre-Gineau, Méchain, and Prony, as well as various foreign scientists. One group of scientists was detailed to make a new comparison of the rules for measuring bases of triangles with fathoms. These comparisons confirmed those made at the beginning of the survey. Another group had to make the calculations and verifications relative to the geodesic operations and determine the official length of the meter. In particular, the exact lengths of the two bases, the values of the angles of each triangle, astronomical observations, azimuth, and latitude were established and carefully recalculated. The length of the quarter meridian was established by giving the flattening of the earth a value derived from the Dunkirk-Barcelona arc and measurement of the arc by La Condamine in Peru. The distance from the pole to the equator was found to be equal to 5,130,740 fathoms, from which the official meter was fixed at 3 feet 11 *lignes* 296 (instead of the 3 feet 11 *lignes* 442 as earlier calculated).

Lastly, a third group of scientists was charged with determining the official value for the unit of weight. It was on this occasion that Lefèvre-Gineau did the experiment described above. The cubic decimeter of distilled water at 4° was found to be equal to 18,827.15 grains, the average weight of the total Charlemagne stack (here, reference to the *creux, plein,* or *moyen marc* was abandoned). The official kilogram was slightly lighter (−.735 gr.) than the provisional *grave.*

Establishing the official standards of 1799
While the committee of scientists was making its final calculations, the official standards for the meter and kilogram were being formulated. In earlier years a number of temporary standards had been set up. Other experts in addition to Lenoir and Fortin, the instrument makers to whom creating the most delicate instruments and parts had been entrusted, were called upon: Fourché, the scale adjuster at the mint, the brothers Joseph and François Dumotiez, well-known makers of physics instruments, the mechanic Jean Merklein, famous for the lathes he built for Louis XVI, and Jecker and Kutsch, well known for their dividing machines.

Deriving values for the official meter and kilogram was an operation requiring high precision. This is the first time that platinum, a metal known in Europe for only a half century and previously regarded as merely a curiosity, was used for a utilitarian purpose. Because of its high melting point it had not been possible to reduce it except into a material that was not very homogeneous. Utilizing a hydrogen torch for the first time, Lavoisier succeeded in melting it and making it more uniform. The first in France to learn how to work platinum was a Parisian goldsmith, Marc-Étienne Janety. He had settled in Marseille during the Terror but was recalled to Paris in September 1795 and ordered to build four measuring rods and four platinum cylinders to be adjusted by Lenoir and Fortin respectively.

In order to adjust the official prototype of the meter, the committee wished to obtain an accuracy of 1/1,000 *ligne.* Lenoir adapted to his comparator an elbowed index that reduced the small differences of length to be measured, to facilitate reading (Figure 65). Twelve iron meters were provided, which were compared

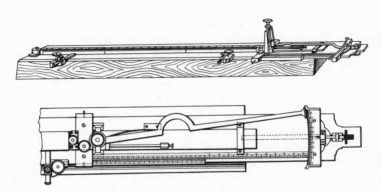

FIG. 65.   Lenoir's comparator for making the official standards for the meter.

with each other and with two of Janety's platinum measuring rods. Then, using Borda's method, these fourteen meters were taken four by four, placed end to end, and compared with the double fathoms (or no doubt to one of them—the control standard—which had been used to measure the bases at the beginning of the survey). This series of comparisons required making a supplementary piece to assure that the length of the double fathom was equal to that of the four meters placed end to end. In order accurately to measure the length of this piece, which was to be 45 *lignes* 18 in length, nineteen identical copies were made of it, which were placed end to end and compared with the fathom. This detail helps us understand the complexity of these operations and the extreme care with which each was performed in order to achieve the highest possible degree of precision. Thus the iron meter Number 2 was recognized as being the most accurate, and served as a standard of comparison for all the others. "They were all found to be so exactly equal," the report tells us, "that they were distributed, without distinction and without regard to their numbers, among the committee members." The platinum meter adopted as the prototype particularly was verified with the iron meter Number 2.

Although the original idea had been to define the official length of the meter as the distance between two lines marked on a metal rule, the final prototype was an end meter, a flat platinum measuring rod whose total length was adjusted exactly to the length of the meter.

We have no details of how the platinum cylinder that was to become the standard prototype of the kilogram was adjusted. This was done by Nicolas Fortin, using a comparator with a movable stop—perhaps the same one he had built in 1791. Fortin first made a hollow brass cylinder against which he adjusted the platinum cylinder.

The two standards, for the meter and the kilogram, were deposited in the National Archives on June 22, 1799, after they had been presented to the legislative body. This date marks the end of the long series of projects necessary to establish the bases of the metric system. It can also be seen as the date on which (for the first time in France) it was recognized that manufacturing techniques were as important to the success of this project as were the ideas of the scientists. In fact, Lenoir and Fortin were permitted to sign the official report, together with the French and foreign scientists forming the committee.

PROGRESS IN MANUFACTURING PRECISION INSTRUMENTS

The problem of basic standards and the principle of a system of universal measures could be solved during the second half of the eighteenth century only because of progress made during that time in methods of making certain instruments. Accurate measurement, of angles especially, made it possible directly and indirectly to increase the precision of dimensional metrology.

Mathematical instruments   Various crafts used certain specific instruments for measuring, drawing, and calculating. The form of these, unchanged for centuries, survive down to our own times in some cases. The so-called mathematical instruments—dividers, the compass with a pencil point, the compass for drawing lines, and protractors and rulers—were in common use by the end of the sixteenth century. During the seventeenth century they acquired their quasi-final form. It is almost impossible to discover their prior history. They were sold in cases that were often decorated.

Special compasses were developed during the same period to meet the needs of draftsmen, engravers, cartographers, astronomers, and topographers. Among the most widely used was the beam compass, composed of a wooden or metal beam along which slid two needle holders whose position was fixed by a screw. Until the nineteenth century they were produced in all sizes. The compass for tracing ellipses, which derived from the beam compass, was less widely used. The three-legged compass, use of which seems to have been quite widespread in the seventeenth century, was thereafter employed only by sculptors.

Other compasses derived from early forms dating probably from the increasing use of cannons. These were, first, the outside caliper (Figure 66), a kind of scissors with twin legs curved so as to measure the diameters of spheres and cylinders. Other models had legs bent outward to measure the internal diameters of pipes and gun bores without being impeded by the raised edges.

The reducing compass (Figure 66), sometimes called a proportional divider, was a four-pointed compass composed of two intersecting flat legs. A sliding locknut moved up and down a slot in the center of each leg. This made it possible to vary the proportional separation of the two points on each side. Scales on the flat sides of the legs enabled the user to determine the relationship. This type of compass, which had undoubtedly been known as early as the sixteenth century, eliminated the need to calculate the relationship between two dimensions and allowed solving other problems of the same type.

The proportional divider   Workers in many crafts had little practice in dealing with numbers, an operation all the more difficult because the subdivisions of units of measurement originated in various systems with differing degrees of complexity. The need to do the greatest number of jobs possible without difficult calculations assured the success of the proportional

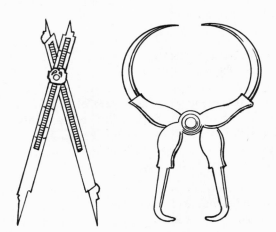

FIG. 66. *Left:* A reducing compass. *Right:* Outside calipers; shapes current in the first half of the eighteenth century.

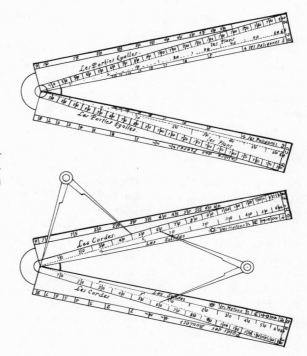

FIG. 67. Proportional divider
Below: Transferring a measurement proportional to an arc with a divider.

divider. This instrument (which must not be confused with the reducing compass) was conceived around the end of the sixteenth century. The first descriptions of it were published in 1606 by Galileo, then in 1607 by Baldassare Capra of Padua, who claimed that he had been making such instruments for almost ten years. It quickly became a classic instrument that was the object of numerous descriptions and treatises until around the middle of the eighteenth century. Then its use seems to have gradually declined, no doubt because the technicians who used it were receiving better training, until it was finally phased out at the beginning of the nineteenth century with the spread of the decimal system. A proportional divider designed solely for the needs of clockmakers was in use until around the end of the nineteenth century.

The proportional divider (Figure 67) evolved very little between its birth and its disappearance, a period of slightly more than two centuries. It consisted of two flat equal-sized rulers joined at one of their ends by a flat hinge that made it possible to open out the compass completely so it formed a perfectly straight, continuous ruler. This type of hinge is very characteristic of the construction of certain seventeenth- and eighteenth-century measuring instruments and particularly of folding rulers. The center of the hinge was the starting point for a series of straight lines engraved on each face of the legs and diverging fanwise to the opposite ends of the legs.

These lines had various scales repeated symmetrically on the corresponding faces of each leg. The six basic scales were those of equal parts, planes, chords, solids, polygons, and metals. And on one face or another there were usually scales for sines and tangents, calibers of cannons, weights of balls, and several others.

By using a divider to mark certain intervals or distances between openings on appropriate scales, the proportional divider solved numerous problems in arithmetic, geometry, triangulation, weight relationships according to the dimensions or densities of metals, powder charges, and the like.

The principle of the proportional divider may be compared to that of instruments used chiefly for topographical measurements, such as the trigonum and the sliding square. But these do not appear to have been used after the beginning of the eighteenth century.

Measuring angles   Another category of instruments used extensively for a long time included those for sighting and for measuring angles. Their origin goes back to even the earliest periods of astronomical observation, but it was definitely for topographical surveying and leveling that the various models were originally developed. The origins of these instruments are still uncertain and date from a period much earlier than that covered by this volume, but it is interesting to note that there is good reason to believe that most of them derived from certain practices current in daily life. This is true, for example, of the cross-staff, also known as the Jacob's staff, one of the oldest sighting instruments, which came from a simple staff to which untutored villagers or geometers had learned to add a crossbar (Figure 68). Certain engravings by Sebastian Munster, a versatile German writer in the first half of the sixteenth century, show soldiers using their pikes as cross-staffs to measure the size of a piece of land or the height of a tower.

The shadow scale (Figure 69) probably also has a popular origin. But it was perfected by mathematicians as early as the Moslem period.

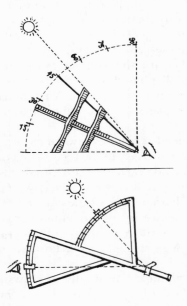

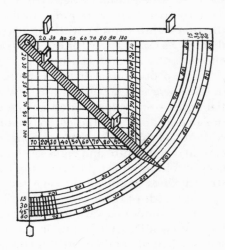

FIG. 69. Quadrant with shadow scale for measuring heights by sightings.

FIG. 68. *Top:* Cross-staff. *Bottom:* Davis quadrant.

The cross-staff and shadow scale produced two groups of descendants that were originally distinct but ultimately combined to become one when modern navigational instrument production was developed in the second half of the seventeenth century.

Like all first models of instruments that appeared quite early, the cross-staff was at first of quite complex construction, because its builders tried to make it serve a number of purposes. But by the seventeenth century it was used only in nautical astronomy and acquired a simpler form. This was the first instrument involving the idea of "shooting the sun" by turning one's back to it. The observation was made by using the shadow of the slide on the pointer. The Davis quadrant, conceived by an English navigator of the same name, already combined a straight pointer, which played the same role as the cross-staff, and segments of a circle with sliding sights (Figure 68). The observation was made with the sun at the observer's back as with the cross-staff; hence the name *backstaff*. The use of this instrument was still widespread in the second half of the eighteenth century after the cross-staff had disappeared.

The shadow scale was in fact the early method of graduating instruments that consisted of a brass disk or quarter disk. These instruments, equipped with a holding ring, were suspended or held vertically at the end of the arm. An alidade that moved around the center of the circle and that had a sight at each end was used for sighting. Quite rapidly, probably during the Middle Ages, the limb of these instruments was divided into degrees and half and quarter degrees in imitation of the graduated circles used by astronomers from earliest times.

These circular instruments were made lighter, in the form of circles and quadrants. In this case the shadow scale disappeared and only the division of the limb into degrees was used. One of the oldest instruments of this type, used extensively by navigators during the Renaissance, was the mariner's astrolabe, a simple graduated circle having an alidade with sights. One of its two right-angled diameters represented the horizon; the other divided the upper semicircle into two quarter circles, each divided into 90°. This simple instrument was widely used and was still being made in the middle of the eighteenth century.

The true astrolabe, which had its golden age between the thirteenth and sixteenth centuries, was a much more scientific instrument. It consisted essentially of a plane projection of a map of the heavens that could pivot above a stereographic projection of the earth. It was never more than a luxury and a prestige instrument that found no practical use.

The graphometer The use of circular instruments by geometers and surveyors began to increase in the sixteenth century. The one that came to be the most widely used, the graphometer, was invented in almost its final form by Philippe Danfrie in 1597. Basically it consisted of a graduated semicircle diameter with a stationary alidade on its diameter and a mobile alidade pivoting around its center (Figure 70). Each alidade had two sights, with those of the mobile alidade passing between those of the stationary one. When positioned on a tripod with a swivel joint, the graphometer made it possible to measure accurately the angle separating any two points on the terrain.

The graphometer was certainly the most frequently used surveying instrument from the middle of the seventeenth century to the middle of the nineteenth.

FIG. 70. Graphometer with sights. Mid-eighteenth century. The alidade with sights was later replaced by an eyepiece with an achromatic objective.

FIG. 71. *Cercle hollandais,* or surveyor's circle, mid-eighteenth century.

Being built in large numbers, it benefited from all the improvements often intended for instruments from which greater precision was required and whose use was popularized, such as sights with crosshairs, methods of setting and dividing borders, a bevel on the alidade to increase the accuracy of the reading, shape, and mounting of the rotating pivot, and lastly the use of the vernier.

The surveyor's circle (Figure 71), known as the *cercle hollandais,* or Dutch circle, began to be generally used during the seventeenth century. It had four stationary sights at 90° angles and a pivoting alidade with sights.

The theodolite Next to these relatively simple instruments, at a fairly early period (undoubtedly around the middle of the sixteenth century) there appeared devices consisting of combinations of graduated rules joined to one another or of a horizontal disk with an alidade holding a vertical half circle that could pivot around its center. Such an instrument was described for the first time in 1571, under the name *theodolite,* by Leonard and Thomas Digges. It made it possible to measure directly the angular distances of two points (two stars, for example) at different altitudes. Despite progress in its construction, the theodolite continued to exist for approximately two centuries without any modification in its structure. Moreover, it was little used. Only during the last quarter of the eighteenth century did it begin to be generally adopted, when the great English builder Jesse Ramsden transformed it into a precision instrument with achromatic eyepieces (Figure 72). The favorable reaction that greeted it in Great Britain led to its introduction, at the beginning of the nineteenth century, on the Continent, where Gambey in France and Reichenbach in Germany first built theodolites.

Large astronomical instruments This was the general picture, toward the end of the seventeenth century, of instruments to measure angles that were being built by specialized instrument shops, the most famous establishments being the English ones. There were also well-known works in France, Italy, Germany, and central Europe.

To the instruments mentioned above we should add those used by astronomers. But these instruments were still being produced in quantities too small to give

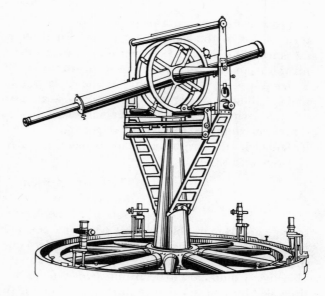

FIG. 72. Ramsden's large precision theodolite, a type of construction common around 1790.

rise to a genuine industry the way instruments for navigation and topography had. Great instrument makers had appeared at the peak of Moslem civilization, but the art seems to have been lost in Western civilization for several centuries. Astronomers like Tycho Brahe and Kepler at the end of the sixteenth and beginning of the seventeenth centuries brought about a rebirth of instrument making. Inventors began to construct quadrants and large segments for which the technique of dividing limbs was perfected. We owe the method of subdividing by transversals to Tycho Brahe. The instruments of this great Danish astronomer (some of which are preserved in the Narodni Technike Museum in Prague) measured to about 3¼ feet of radius and were for a very long time regarded as the most important instruments ever made, since as late as the seventeenth century quadrants of more than 3 to 4 feet were rare. Until around the middle of the eighteenth century constructing a quadrant with a radius of between 6½ and 8 feet was considered a difficult and even ruinous enterprise for the man who undertook it.

Large mural circles were employed in observatories only after Roemer, then working in Paris, devised the method of observation by reflection. Its use became general only in the closing years of the eighteenth century with the adoption of eyepieces having an achromatic objective.

The adaptation of eyepieces to instruments The invention of optical instruments at the beginning of the seventeenth century (see Volume II, pages 268–69) had no influence for almost seventy years on the construction of instruments for measuring angles. In their early stages compound eyepieces were used only in precision astronomy, and until the beginning of the nineteenth century the compound microscope generally gave no better images than a simple microscope or magnifying glass.

Only when the first micrometers (in particular Auzout's, see Volume II, p. 315) became known was it possible to think of mounting eyepieces on the circles and quadrants used in astronomy. The first such experiment successfully performed was by the astronomer Picard. In 1669, having been given the task of measuring the length of the meridian between Paris and Amiens, Picard ordered for this triangulation a quadrant with a radius of 38 inches and a segment of 18°, each equipped with two eyepieces, one replacing the stationary and the other the mobile alidade. After this almost all large astronomical instruments were equipped with eyepieces, but the small-radius instruments used by navigators and surveyors continued to have the classic sights. The short-focus eyepieces were too irregular in their sphericity and especially their chromatism to replace the alidades with sights.

The problem of achromatism — The method of building achromatic objectives was discovered in 1757 by the English engineer John Dollond. The history of this discovery is quite strange and remarkable. In his *Treatise on Optics* (1704) Newton stated that it was impossible to make achromatic objectives by combining two lenses possessing different indices of refraction. He demonstrated that the focal length of such objectives would have to be infinite. Newton's authority was such that this opinion prevailed for almost a half century, and when the first achromatic objectives were built in 1733 in spite of his theory, they went unnoticed. Dollond carried on a discussion with Euler in 1752 and 1753, defending Newton's theory against Euler's ideas. However, after receiving from a Swedish professor a demonstration showing the incorrect geometry of Newton's theory, Dollond also built achromatic objectives, consisting of a crown lens and a flint lens. He took out a patent from which his firm alone profited for fifteen years, winning judgments against English competitors who, relying on various precedents, tried to break this monopoly.

When Dollond's patent expired, the production of achromatic objectives remained a privilege of English lens makers. Crown or ordinary opticians' glass was readily obtainable in all countries, but this was not true of flint. For a half century this heavy crystal with clearly defined characteristics was successfully prepared only by certain English glassworks with skills kept secret. Around the end of the eighteenth century, these skills were lost even in England, which was suffering from a shortage of flint. Not until the beginning of the nineteenth century did the production of flint make some progress in France, when the systematic studies of a French glassmaker, d'Artigues, enabled him to produce after 1811 a steady supply of satisfactory flint. In Germany, the physicist Fraunhofer went into partnership around the same time with the Swiss glassmaker P.-L. Guinand and established an optical glass industry that continued to develop steadily during the nineteenth century.

Reflecting instruments — Between 1730 and 1785 the instruments of navigational astronomy and geodesy underwent a profound evolution, marked by the appearance of certain reflecting instruments that modified the method of "shooting the stars" with the cross-staff and Davis quadrant but did not completely abandon their principle. Robert Hooke in 1666 and Newton in 1699 had already described the method of using two mirrors on a graduated segment to measure the angular distance between two stars or the height of one star above the horizon. The two mirrors' images were made to coincide on the stationary mirror by shifting the alidade whose center held the second, mobile mirror that reflected one of the images. But it was the English astronomer Hadley who, unaware of these precedents, described in 1731 two types of octants, one of which was generally adopted a little later.

Around 1750 the octants in use were still quite bulky, having a radius of 30 inches, and were built of wood and brass or iron and brass. Slightly later they were cast in brass in a single piece, with a smaller radius. The established angle being 60°, the instrument became known as a sextant. It was quickly perfected and equipped with a small achromatic eyepiece, a reversing screw, and a vernier. As early as 1788–1790 it had acquired the form it was to retain until modern times (Figure 73). The Davis quadrant made it possible to measure the altitude of a star to within five or six minutes, the 1750 octant to within a minute or half minute. However, for several decades the makers had to search for a way to set the two surfaces of the small mirrors perfectly parallel; at the beginning of the nineteenth century this difficulty had not yet been completely overcome.

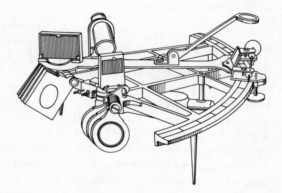

FIG. 73. Sextant for marine astronomy. Construction typical of around 1800.

Octants and sextants were objects commonly for sale when in 1772 the French naval officer and physicist J.-C. de Borda conceived of improving the reflection method by using a complete circle equipped with an eyepiece and two mirrors, which made it possible to remeasure the same angle several times without returning to zero, by coincidence of the images in the collimator of the eyepiece. Thus any error due to the device itself was offset by being distributed among the number of times the measurements were repeated. Actually, Borda had merely made more practical a reflecting circle device invented twenty years earlier by the German astronomer Tobias Mayer but publicized only in 1767. Mayer's circle was less convenient to use than the sextant, because of certain defects.

Borda's reflecting circle was quickly adopted by navigators from the Continental countries, whereas the English remained faithful to the sextant for maritime use and the theodolite for surveying (Figure 74). In 1784 the French worker who had built Borda's circle, Étienne Lenoir, devised a repeating circle with two eyepieces, which he built technically perfect and so ensured the success of Méchain and Delambre's triangulations to measure the meridian from Dunkirk to

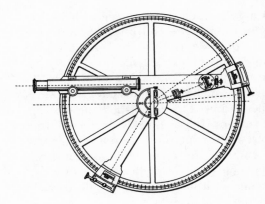

FIG. 74. Borda reflecting circle for marine astronomy.

Barcelona. Several years later the English makers lost their supremacy in this art, in which they had almost continuously been leaders in the great progress achieved in less than one century.

Progress in astronomical instruments The techniques of making instruments for angular measurement cleared the way for the machine age earlier than for the building of industrial machinery. Constant pressure throughout the entire eighteenth century between consumers' demands and production methods had been the determining factor in transforming this highly specialized industry, which at the end of the seventeenth century was still using traditional craft methods. This pressure affected both the search for quality and the need to increase production. The requirements of navigators, surveyors, and topographers grew steadily, but they would not have been sufficient of themselves to bring about the qualitative progress in techniques that was imposed by the demands of astronomers.

The production of large astronomical instruments was completely transformed in a half century, thanks to several specially talented English builders—George Graham, Jonathan Sisson, John Bird, and Jesse Ramsden. Graham's reputation was established between 1720 and 1730; Ramsden died in 1800.

At the beginning of this period quadrants and segments consisted of metal rods flattened by hammering and assembled with screws and dowels. Brass alloyed with iron was used for the graduated portion of the circle, for the alidade, and so on. But distortions produced by heat were larger because of the different coefficients of expansion of the two metals. Bird was the first to begin using only brass—even rolled brass—for all parts, including those used for assembly. Not until 1787 did Cassini think of making a mural quadrant with a radius of eight feet by casting it in a single piece. The events of the Revolution prevented him from carrying out the experiment, which had gone quite far, but it opened a path that was later developed.

The invention of mechanical dividers In the same period the English workshops solved a large number of construction problems to eliminate all the defects of large instruments: journals and rotational devices, the shape of the alidade, counterbalancing, suspension, and so on. But the problem that occupied minds and talents for the longest time was that of dividing graduated limbs. Since the problem arose this had been done with the divider and beam compass. But two difficulties had to be solved: the geometrical division of segments, and engraving the dividing lines.

Geometrical division presented the difficulty that a 90° arc cannot be evenly bisected into degrees. For a long time empirical procedures were used, the least satisfactory of which was transferring a universal model onto the limb to be divided. Graham and Bird invented geometrical procedures that were more accurate. Engraving the line was improved by using better hammer-hardened metals in their production. In the second half of the eighteenth century rolled brass gave still better results. Efforts were also made to improve the tools used by workers.

As early as the second quarter of the eighteenth century the makers were beginning to seek a method to perform divisions by machine so as to eliminate human error and increase low-cost production, especially for small navigational instruments. The clockmaker's dividing platform was then in common use. An English clockmaker, Henry Hindley of York, built the first machine for dividing circles around 1739 by adapting the machine for cutting the wheels used in clocks.

Between 1765 and 1768 the duke of Chaulnes built a machine to divide circles and another to divide straight lines. For the first time this French scientist used the microscope for marking. The apparatus concerned with the scriber and its movements was ingenious. An attempt to move the platform by a tangent screw did not give the hoped-for results, for it was not yet possible to cut screws with an invariable thread.

After trying for thirteen years, from 1760 to 1773, the great inventor Jesse Ramsden succeeded in building the first dividing machine applicable to industry (Figure 75). For this purpose he had to invent a lathe to thread the lead screw that was to drive the platform. (Details of this work are given in Volume II, pp. 276–278.) He used a screw with a cutting thread to cut the teeth of the platform, an operation done in discontinuous fractions corresponding to nine out of ten teeth of the wheel so as to distribute the inevitable error over the entire circumfer-

FIG. 75. First machine for dividing the limbs of instruments, built by Ramsden in 1773.

ence. The platform was designed to hold the dividing instrument. The regularity of its teeth as well as the invariability of the lead screw's thread were the essential factors in the machine's precision. Ramsden had to invent other ingenious devices, in particular those having to do with the driving treadle, which reversed by means of a spring drum, and a device that automatically released the scriber. A touch on the treadle by the worker caused a limited-feed movement of the platform by the tangent screw and activated the scriber. The entire mechanism was so well conceived that the discernible error in the feed was less than 10″. The machine made it possible to divide a sextant into degrees and 1/6 of a degree (that is, 10′) in about a half hour. As a result, the cost of small instruments was noticeably decreased.

The invention of Ramsden's machine can be regarded as marking the end of a period of adaptation by the instrumentation industry that paved the way for the precision light-instrument industry, which proved so important for the development of modern industrial techniques at the end of the nineteenth century.

Other dividing machines were built by the best workshops: in England by Edward Troughton, in France by Mégnié, Riché, Fortin, Jecker, and in Germany by Reichenbach. Gambey was the first to build a machine for dividing large-diameter astronomical circles. The spread of the metric system required rapid proliferation of standard rules in France, and the use of the dividing engine helped in this. This in turn increased the demand for the machines and so accelerated their development.

DIFFUSION AND REVISION OF THE METRIC SYSTEM

The difficulties of the metric system

The use of the metric system encountered public ill will from the very beginning. Even while the preliminary research was being done, many doubts were expressed on the advisability of making its use mandatory. It appears that the official proclamation of the standards did nothing to eliminate these difficulties. One of the first enactments of the Consulate, the law of December 10, 1799, officially approved the meter and the kilogram, which were declared the official standards for linear measures and measures of weight throughout the Republic. But less than a year later, a law of November 4, 1800, already compromised the ordained principles of nomenclature and permitted using the old names of measures in place of the new ones. This law, intended to facilitate spreading the new system, began to introduce the first confusion, since it permitted the use, for example, of the terms *pound* for kilogram, *bushel* for decaliter, and so on. A second, much more serious, blow to the metric system was struck by a decree of February 12, 1812, which permitted the commercial use of measuring and weighing instruments showing equivalences between the old and modern units. Although the official system continued to be taught in schools, this appears to have been an attempt to adapt the system to earlier practices; the experiment was to last for ten years. A complementary order indicated, for example, that a dimension equal to 2 meters, to be called a fathom, would be divided into 6 feet, and the measurement of fabrics could be done with a 12-decimeter measure called the ell, and so on. The debasement of the system was rapid, spreading to the units of weight and volume.

The metric system legally imposed; its dissemination outside France

The decimal metric system was restored to its initial purity in various stages. In 1825 the decimal system of weights and measures that had been suppressed in 1816 was reinstated. An 1837 law reestablished the entire system, effective January 1, 1840. The institution of the Service of Weights and Measures dates from this time; 364 inspection bureaus were then in existence, though not all of them were provided with complete sets of metric standards.

The creation of customary measures had involved sending new standards for the fathom, ell, bushel, and pound to the *départements* in 1813. Substituting metric standards for these customary ones was begun in 1840, and from this time on the use of this system in France and later other countries continued to spread. In 1840 only Belgium, the Netherlands, and Luxembourg had adopted it. France undertook to publicize and propagate the system in other countries. The government ordered from the French instrument maker Gambey thirty sets of brass measures, a proportion of which were sent to the leading European countries. The international exhibitions in London in 1851 and in Paris in 1855 and 1867 stimulated a change of opinion in favor of the metric system, but as yet few countries had adopted it. The metric system became obligatory in Chile in 1848, Cuba in 1849, Colombia in 1854, Spain and the Philippines in 1860, Italy in 1861, and Brazil in 1862. Its use was authorized in several other countries, such as the United States, Great Britain, Prussia, and the North German Confederation.

Preliminaries of revision

Almost simultaneously, the academies of science in Paris and Saint Petersburg, as well as the Geodesic Association, adopted resolutions that raised the problem of the international dissemination of metric system standards. The increase in the number of copies of the standard meter made it absolutely necessary to consider replacing the end standard with a line standard and consider forming an international body to undertake making copies for the countries requesting them, to relieve the French government of such an international responsibility.

The Académie des Sciences formed a committee calling itself the French Section of the International Commission on the Meter that first met on September 1, 1869. So began the work of revising the metric system, which led to the creation of the International Bureau of Weights and Measures.

The French Section proceeded to examine the meter and kilogram deposited in the National Archives and studied the question of the material to be used for making the new standard. The 1799 standard, made of platinum, actually contained a certain percentage of iridium, for at that time there was no known method for completely purifying platinum. It was felt that the future standard should also be made of the same alloy, containing 10 percent iridium, so that its coefficient of expansion would be close to that of the first standard.

During these deliberations the problem of what comparator to use was examined, as well as that of how to construct a cold chamber, for the plan was to perform the comparisons at a temperature of 0°C.

The problem of international standards

This preliminary work was presented to the International Commission on the Meter, convened by the French government on August 8, 1870. Twenty-four governments had agreed to participate, but some were not represented because of the Franco-Prussian War that had just begun. These meetings accepted the National Archives' meter as the basic unit for establishing an international standard.

The Committee on Preparatory Research was formed, which until 1872 continued the work begun by the French Section. In particular, a more exhaustive examination was made of the meter and kilogram in the archives. A decision was made to use a comparator with longitudinal movement for determining line meters and a comparator with transverse movement and two microscopes for comparing line meters with the archives' meter. It was decided that comparisons of length would be performed at 0°C. and of the weights in a vacuum. Comparing an end rule with a line rule is quite delicate because of difficulties in aligning precisely the ends of an end rule. Optical procedures introduced by the French physicist Fizeau were adopted that eliminated rubbing the end faces of the rule with the parts of an ordinary comparator and made it possible to obtain greater accuracy. But the application of Fizeau's method was to raise certain difficulties, which were, however, corrected during the work.

Preparing the platinum-iridium alloy

At the same time the Committee on Preparatory Research examined at length the problem of preparing the alloy from which the standards would be made. Although the metallurgy of platinum and of the metals in platinum ore had made great progress, especially with the school of French chemists working around Sainte-Claire Deville and Henri Debray, it was still not possible to obtain pure platinum (and still less iridium) in quantities large enough to produce all the standards required.

A certain portion of the platinum was prepared in France, but the committee ordered a supply of platinum and iridium from an English manufacturer, Matthey, and Sainte-Claire Deville himself prepared, from materials of various origins, the quantity of iridium that was lacking. The separation of iridium, done in the laboratory of the École Normale, was extremely difficult, and Sainte-Claire Deville and his colleagues had to invent special methods to achieve it. Later they had to solve another problem, that of obtaining in a single casting an ingot of platinum-iridium alloy sufficiently large to permit production of all the standards desired. This decision had been made to guarantee that the metal in the different standards would be uniform in all of them.

Casting a 550-pound mass of the alloy involved inventing a special furnace heated with a coal-gas and hydrogen torch. After various tests the final casting of the ingot was done on May 13, 1874, at the Conservatoire national des Arts et Métiers. An ingot of 236 kg. was obtained with the shape of a plate 1.14 m. long, .78 m. wide, and .080 m. thick. The alloy obtained was given the name Conservatoire alloy or 1874 alloy. Later its composition again gave rise to many discussions, for it was realized that its density was not as high as that of a sample of the alloy prepared earlier under excellent conditions. This difference in density resulted from the accidental introduction of traces of impurities, in particular several milligrams of iron and ruthenium. It was eventually decided to use the Conservatoire alloy to establish the prototypes, but individual governments were allowed to choose between receiving a standard made from this alloy or one from another alloy ordered from the Matthey firm.

Establishing the international prototype for the meter

The problem of the shape of the standard meter was the object of an extremely detailed study resulting in the decision to adopt the X profile (Figure 76) suggested by the French instrument maker Tresca. While Sainte-Claire Deville and Debray were busy with the production of the alloy ingot, Tresca arranged for tests of various materials to determine the best method of drawing out the shape for the official standards. After casting, the Farcot firm forged and sectioned the ingot into rods 25 mm. thick. The bars were drawn under the direction of Gueldry, director of the Forges d'Audincourt, who had made the preliminary tests.

FIG. 76. X profiles of the international standards of the 1875 meter. *Left:* Line standard. *Right:* End standard.

Since it had been decided that at the request of the various governments either line or end standards would be made, decisions still had to be made on the profiles for the ends of the end standards. But such details were not the only ones posing problems for the scientists and experimenters. From these problems we can judge the extreme care taken to create international and national prototypes of the meter and kilogram that would be completely satisfactory.

These initiatives toward making the metric system a universal system of measurement were possible only because of new techniques developed during the nineteenth century and more particularly because of improved instruments for precision measurement.

The international convention on the meter

A diplomatic convention held in 1875 to approve the work done in the preceding years decided to create the International Bureau of Weights and Measures to maintain the official standards of the meter and kilogram. This work continued for several years.

It must be remembered that representatives of all countries agreed to consider the length of the National Archives' meter as the universal reference that would never again be brought into question. On several occasions during the international meetings the question was raised about whether to relate geodesic measurements, the fundamental basis of the international system of measures, to a natural measurement more precise than the one calculated at the end of the eighteenth century. This idea was ultimately dropped, and the definition of the meter became the one known for nearly a century, based on the distances between lines on an accepted standard bar of platinum.

The modern definition of the meter   However, at this time Maxwell suggested linking the platinum standard to the wavelength of a given luminous radiation. Wavelength measurements were performed in 1892 and 1893 by Michelson and Benoit on the light emitted by cadmium, and the length of the meter was linked to the wavelength of three radiations of cadmium. It was finally the eleventh conference on weights and measures, held in 1960, that adopted the definition of the meter presently in effect. According to this definition, the meter is the length equal to 1,650,753.73 times the wavelength of the red orange radiation given off under certain conditions by an isotope of krypton.

THE EVOLUTION OF MEASURING INSTRUMENTS

The creation and gradual application of the metric system had immediate consequences on the production of measuring instruments, standards to measure lengths, and weights to calculate masses.

The construction and characteristics of these instruments were defined by law and thus were duplicated uniformly. A July 16, 1839 law fixed the norms that had to be met by instruments subject to government control. This law indicates the technical possibilities then available for their production, possibilities that did not develop until automatic measuring instruments came into common use in modern times.

In the nineteenth century and even later, the legal effect of the meter standard and its multiples and of the series of weights was spread largely by illustrations known to everyone.

The standardization of meters and their multiples   After 1840 jointed wooden or metal meter rules, called folding meters, were made. They consisted of five sections, each 20 centimeters long and divided into centimeters and millimeters. Similarly, double meters were made on the same design and were used more and more frequently. The decameter was made in the form of tapes or chains; in the latter case, the characteristics of the links were specified by law. In addition, the acceptable tolerances were defined as follows: for wooden meters, + 1 mm. or 10^{-3} in relative value, and for metal meters + .2 mm. or 2×10^{-4} in relative value.

The standardization of weights   The change was perhaps more profound regarding the series of weights (Figure 77). Their shapes, sizes, and abbreviations, as well as tolerances, were legally fixed. Cast-iron weights, established in a series from 50 kg. to 500 g., were to be shaped like a truncated pyramid, which in itself was not new, since it had already been used for weights in the old systems (Figure 78). Making and using one-kilogram weights and subdivisions thereof in cone shapes was authorized, but for practical purposes this souvenir of the old stacks of weights disappeared rapidly,

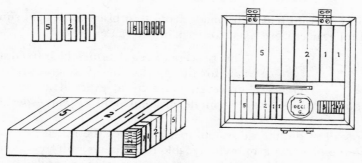

FIG. 77.   Box of parallelepiped weights weighing a total of one kilogram, and subdivided. First model, ca. 1800.

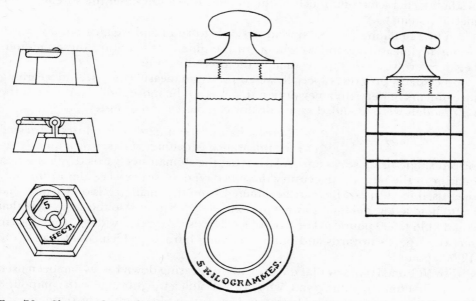

FIG. 78.   Shapes of common weights set by a law in 1839. *Left:* Cast-iron weight. *Right:* Copper weights.

which proves that the builders and specialists had succeeded in systematically creating new forms that were more practical to handle. Cylindrical weights were in particular employed with increasing frequency.

The shapes of copper weights were undecided prior to the metric system, not having the characteristics fixed by decree in 1839. The old weights had been made in the greatest variety of shapes, some of them cylindrical. The great novelty of the legislation concerning the metric system is that it imposed certain shapes and sizes for the entire series of copper weights from 20 kg. to 1 mg. The law even specified the production methods; for example, copper weights could be hollow or solid, molded or cut out, but weights of 20 grams and over had to be cut out, and weights of less than one gram had to be made from thin brass blades cut square. The length and tolerances were fixed for each of the values.

Results of applying the metric system

This process of regulation, which fixed all the details for the production of weights and measures, answered perfectly to every daily and industrial need until our own time. The 1946 modernization of the system respected its basic principles.

The spread of the metric system met a need of the nineteenth century by standardizing and making interchangeable those items industry required with increasing frequency. Industrial forms themselves evolved, probably under the influence of the geometrical and utilitarian shapes decreed for measuring instruments. There is probably a relationship between the poverty of the industrial aesthetics characterizing much of the nineteenth century and the spread of the metric system.

The regulating process spread not only to rules and weights but also to all means for measuring and weighing. In the nineteenth century these methods began to evolve more rapidly than in the preceding one.

Technical progress especially aided precision measurements. And weighing instruments underwent an evolution that was all the more significant in that the new models were intended especially for commerce and industry.

Counter scales

The first half of the nineteenth century witnessed the appearance of counter scales, which quickly replaced single-beam scales and in large part the Roman steelyards. Until the first quarter of the nineteenth century these two types of scales were almost the only ones used in business. Beam scales ranged from the small precision balance that could hold a few *gros* (one *gros* = approximately 3.8 grams) to the large scale that could hold 6,000 pounds. The sizes of steelyards also varied widely, from ones in service in port shipyards and public weighing bureaus, which could take up to 12,000 pounds.

In Volume II we saw that the principle of gearing down forces had been used for the first time by John Wyatt, who in 1741 built a weighbridge with compound levers. The use of compound beams and levers to build weighing instruments was to reduce considerably the use of the classic types of scales and even bring about the disappearance of some of them.

The Roberval scale, the principle of which was known in the seventeenth century, was not produced industrially until the first half of the nineteenth century; its use was legally authorized on December 5, 1840. It consisted of a system of jointed members supporting the platforms, thanks to which the results of weighing are independent of the position of the load on the platform. This system made it possible to build the first counterweighted machine, which was convenient to handle and came into widespread use as soon as the new cylindrical copper weights were available.

A second type of counterweighted scale was built by Béranger in 1840 (Figure 79). It consisted basically of a combination of an equal-armed beam (double or single) and an articulated system of levers reminiscent of that in platform scales. The sensitivity of this scale is theoretically comparable to that of the equal-armed beam scale. The use of Béranger's scale spread quite rapidly.

FIG. 79.   Counter scale of the Roberval type,
built by Béranger in 1840.

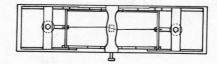

Other models, like Giraud's and the Phanzeder scale, which are variants of
the Béranger scale, then appeared. The former is no longer in use, but certain
automatic scales have used its mechanism.

Weighbridges   The invention of various types of weighbridges to
weigh large masses led to the disappearance of the
large beam scales and steelyards of earlier centuries. In 1822 Aloise Quintenz, a
Strasbourg mechanic, took out an inventor's patent for a platform weighbridge
conceived with a gearing-down system (Figure 80). Quintenz had the original idea

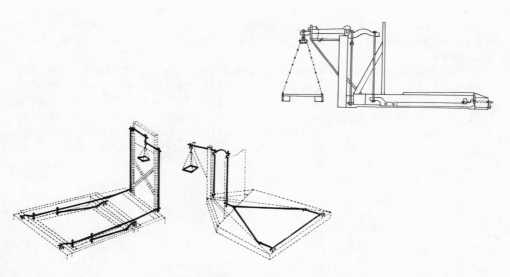

FIG. 80.   Diagrams of weighbridges designed by Quintenz. *Top:* Elevation of an 1822
weighbridge. *Bottom, left:* Early model of centesimal weighbridge, with four supporting
points for the table. *Bottom, right:* Model of the decimal weighbridge that was finally
adopted. Note the three supporting points.

of using a beam with two connections, to which the load was transmitted by a triangular lever and the platform itself. He devised this weighbridge so that the weight placed on the platform was balanced by a mass 100 times or 10 times lighter on the beam. These weighbridges, known by the names *centesimal weighbridge* and *decimal weighbridge,* came quickly into use in commercial and industrial establishments, especially the decimal weighbridge.

In 1835 Béranger invented a Roman weighbridge of a now familiar type. Béranger's innovation consisted in adapting a steelyard arm with a slider to a platform weighbridge in order to weigh large masses (Figure 81). This invention enjoyed great success because moving a slider on a graduated rod replaced lengthy handling of weights. Weighbridges capable of dealing with 10, 50, 100,

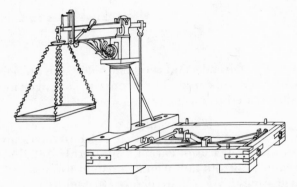

FIG. 81.   Weighbridge with table and steelyard arm, invented by Béranger.

and more tons were later invented using this principle. Counterweighted machines and baby-weighing scales in universal use were also built for weights of less than 50 kg.

These inventions are based on very simple principles known long before the nineteenth century, but they were not invented until this period, probably to meet very precise needs: an increase in the number of operations and in the weights handled in business and industry. We are also justified in believing that prior to this time there was not available the type of steel capable of giving these machines sufficient sensitivity. It must be noted that the methods of constructing common weighing machines was completely transformed, for the first time in perhaps millennia, in the space of a few decades.

BIBLIOGRAPHY

Annuaire du Bureau des Longitudes.

ARMENGAUD, Senior. *Le portefeuille des machines.* Paris, 1848-1861.

BERGERON, *Manuel du tourneur.* 2nd ed. Paris, 1816.

BERNARD, E. *Revue générale des machines-outils.* Paris, 1887.

BIGOURDAN. *Le système métrique des poids et mesures.* Paris, 1901.

BIREMBAUT, Arthur. "Les deux déterminations de l'unité de masse du système métrique," in *Revue d'Histoire des Sciences,* XII, 1959, pp. 25-54.

BOUTMY, G. *François Bourdon et le marteau-pilon.* Paris, 1884.

BUXBAUM, B. *Beiträge zur geschichte der Technik und Industrie.* B. 9th, 10th, and 11th editions, 1919-1921.

CHRÉTIEN, J. *Nouveau manuel complet des machines-outils.* Paris, 1866.

DAUMAS, Maurice. *Les instruments scientifiques aux XVIIe et XVIIIe siècles.* Paris, 1953.

DELAMBRE, J. B. *Base du système métrique.* Paris, 1806.

DOYON, André, and LIAIGRE, Lucien. *Jacques Vaucanson, mécanicien de génie.* Paris, 1966.

EUDE. *Histoire documentaire de la mécanique française.* Paris, 1902.

GARANGER, André. *Petite histoire d'une grande industrie.* Paris, 1960.

GAUDRY, J. *Notice sur François Cavé.* Paris, 1875.

Horlogerie, Catalogue du Musée du Conservatoire National des Arts et Métiers. Paris, 1949.

MACHABEY, Armand, Jr. *Mémoire sur l'histoire de la balance et de la balancerie.* N.p.n.d., 1950.

——. *Histoire des poids et mesures depuis le XIIIe siècle.* Troyes, 1960.

Mécanique. Catalogue du Musée du Conservatoire National des Arts et Métiers. Paris, 1956.

NEDOLUMA, Alois. "Geschichte der Werkzeuge und Werkzeugmaschinen," in *Blätter fur Technikgeschichte,* 22, 1960, and 23, 1961.

Poids et mesures. Métrologie. Catalogue du Musée du Conservatoire National des Arts et Métiers. Paris, 1941.

QUILE, Humphrey. *John Harrison, The Man Who Found Longitude.* London, 1966.

ROE, J. W. *English and American Tool Builders.* New Haven, 1916.

Le système métrique décimal, sa création en France, son évolution, ses progrès. Paris, 1930.

VALICOURT, de. *Nouveau manuel complet du tourneur.* Paris, 1858.

WITTMANN, Karl. *Die Entwicklung der Drehbank.* Berlin, 1942.

WOODBURY, Robert S. *History of the Gear-Cutting Machine.* Cambridge, Mass., 1958.

——. *History of the Grinding Machine.* Cambridge, Mass., 1959.

——. *History of the Lathe.* Cleveland, 1961.

——. *History of the Milling Machine.* Cambridge, Mass., 1960.

PART THREE

TRANSPORTATION AND COMMUNICATION

Plate 19. A late eighteenth-century road. Painting by Demarne. Paris, Louvre Museum. (Photo Giraudon, Paris.)

CHAPTER 1

ROADS, BRIDGES, AND ROAD TRANSPORT

ROAD BUILDING

H IGHWAYS, THE INDISPENSABLE foundation for transportation and communication, were for a long time unsuited for what was required of them because
of their poorly constructed surfacing. Paved roads were still not usual in the
eighteenth century, a time that saw a heavy increase in transportation. Hence the
need to provide more solid foundations and a more resistant and uniform surface
became increasingly urgent.

Bridge and highway engineers In France the necessity of creating a general highway network was understood as early as the first half
of the eighteenth century, and organizations for
building and maintaining highways were set up. Daniel Trudaine, the general
administrator of highways in 1737, and his son Philibert efficiently undertook this
work. They organized the École des Ponts et Chaussées (School of Bridges and
Highways) in 1747, which trained the necessary technical personnel and from
which came many engineers whose fame as builders became universal. But construction techniques made only slow progress.

Mention should be made of work done by Turgot's collaborators. He was the
administrator of the individual taxing authority in Limoges in 1761 and built 160
leagues of roads in the Limoges and Brive area. His chief engineer, Pierre
Trésaguet, particularly distinguished himself and was assigned to Paris in 1764 as
inspector general of public works.

When builders before Trésaguet's time wanted a solid road they first had to
put down a layer of stones of varying thickness piled up in no particular order.
This made a road surface that was cambered, uneven, and broke up easily. Poorly
drained, the surface also offered great resistance to wheeled vehicles. Trésaguet
laid his roads on beds of fieldstone set on edge and covered with a layer of gravel.
A traveler named Arthur Young admired them, noting that they were not uneven
or dusty and that they had a compact surface made of crushed granite. Outside
Turgot's area the use of this technique did not spread rapidly.

Turgot had to reorganize the highway administration, and abolished the
corvée (forced labor) in 1776. But the financial difficulties of the period delayed
the construction of a satisfactory road network. During the Revolutionary and
later the Empire periods, funds were lacking to renovate and consolidate the
highway system.

Degradation of the roads   Military necessities led to opening new roads to give convoys access to theaters of operation, as for example the Simplon route, completed between 1801 and 1805. But maintenance continued to be very uncertain, and in all the diaries of the time we find references to the difficulties of travel and road transportation.

Notes by one Marbot, who made long journeys in the emperor's courier service, are very informative. In 1806 he wrote, "At this time the roads in Prussia were not yet macadamized. One almost always traveled at a walking pace on shifting sands into which carriages sank deeply, raising unbearable clouds of dust." And in 1807 he noted that "for as long as we were in the dreadful country of Poland, where no macadamized road existed, as many as twelve and sixteen horses were required to pull the carriage through the quagmires and swamps in the middle of which we traveled, and even then the carriage traveled at a walking pace."

The techniques of road building made their first progress in England for economic reasons. The resulting improvements began to be applied after 1830, first in Belgium and then in France.

In England during the eighteenth century there was no lack of attempts to improve roads. As early as 1715, General Wade, who was ordered to disarm the Highlanders after their rebellion, used his troops to improve roads and build bridges.

John Metcalf (1717–1810), of Knaresborough, nicknamed Jack the Blind Man, devoted his efforts to constructing better roads and built numerous thoroughfares in the north of England. Despite his infirmity he was able skillfully to lay out good roads through mountainous areas.

Surfacing techniques remained unreliable, and transportation continued to be difficult throughout the eighteenth century. In 1714 Ralph Thoresby related in his journal that the coach from Hull to York operated only in summer. Daniel Defoe, the author of *Robinson Crusoe,* considered the roads around Leeds impassable, with excessive gradients and broken surfaces that made travel dangerous. In 1770 Arthur Young spoke of the "infernal roads" between Preston and Wigan, and in all of England in general, "where you run the risk of breaking your neck and legs." Potholes full of mud and as much as four feet deep were filled with stones carelessly thrown in.

This great deterioration was blamed on narrow carriage wheels, but experiments with wide-wheeled carriages showed that four horses were needed to pull these vehicles, whereas two horses sufficed for ones with narrow wheels.

McAdam   Finally, intelligent engineers, John Loudon McAdam (1756–1836) and Thomas Telford (1757–1834), undertook the study of road construction.

A committee studying how to improve toll roads asked the advice of McAdam, who was in charge of maintaining the roads of Ayrshire. He set forth his ideas in a book, *Remarks on the Present System of Road-Making* (1816), in which he argued for a solid, smooth, artificial surface on which carriages could roll easily. He recommended using coarsely cut stones that would bond together by pressure and be even more firmly fixed in place by carriage wheels (Figure 1).

This idea was completely opposed to the earlier one of using round stones

FIG. 1. Macadam roadway consisting of three layers of stones two inches in diameter. Each layer is four inches thick.

and gravel, which were forced out by carriage wheels as the road became worn, making holes that gradually grew deeper. But the McAdam system produced a road that became increasingly packed and hard under the pressure of carriage wheels. Incidentally, rollers to pack down road surfaces did not appear until around 1840.

In the final analysis this system was an application of Trésaguet's 1764 method used first in France, then in Sweden and Switzerland. But McAdam was the first to apply it in England and to understand that the road surface was more important for easy movement than were wheel rim widths. McAdam methodically tested various sizes of crushed stones, which he classified into three categories: those that could fit into one's mouth, those weighing six ounces, and those that could pass through a two-inch ring.

Thomas Telford Telford, the son of a Dumfriesshire shepherd and apprentice to a master mason and quarryman, started his career by cutting stone destined for the new Somerset House in the Strand for the famous architects the Adam brothers. He became supervisor of public works for Shropshire, where he devoted his attention to bridges and roads, which he found to be in deplorable condition. In 1793 he was assigned to build the Ellesmere Canal in Wales and in 1802 was sent to the north of Scotland to improve the roads and build new bridges. In 1812 he left Scotland, continuing to build roads in England and Wales. At this time there were no schools for civil engineers in Great Britain, and men like Telford got their training from personal experience.

Telford described the ideal road as straight and level, with a hard, smooth surface, and he realized that to achieve this ideal the most important condition was to obtain hardness in the paving surface. He also recognized that stones thrown into mud did not hold and that under pressure from wheels the mud rose to the surface, especially in rainy weather. It was absolutely necessary to have a reliable foundation for the road, for which he used stones laid down by hand, the broadest side facing down and covered with other stones to make a uniform mass. This was actually the same principle as the one applicable to houses, in which the foundation is the most important element.

Telford established precise rules for new-road construction. First he advised using maps and surveying to lay out the route, which until then had been laid out without preliminary topographic study. He fixed at approximately 3 percent (1:35) the gradient that would allow coaches to drive safely. On main roads the gradient should be limited to 2.5 percent (1:40). The road should be raised three or four feet above the surrounding land so its surface would be fully exposed to the wind and sun. The road should not be flat, to allow water to flow off. Streams made detours necessary; the road should go around them if they were too wide. It could be more economical to build a bridge than to go too far upstream. Swamps should be avoided by detours or be crossed by an embankment or causeway built on substantial pilings.

Telford's common-sense rule to seek the shortest distance and avoid unnecessary gradients was not always internally consistent. His other recommendations were widely followed later: avoid crossing cities by building detours or bypasses and give the authority the eminent domain right to cross private property.

Telford gave detailed instructions for building road foundations and surfaces. The foundation was constructed of crushed stones laid in beds each 4 inches thick and rolled until a base of 12 inches was obtained. The spaces between broken stones were filled with stone chips and the base was covered with a bed of fine gravel.

The surfacing could be of various types (Figure 2): either paving stones 8 inches by 6 inches; crushed stones small enough to pass through a 2½-inch ring and packed down like the base, or gravel and stones packed down by rolling.

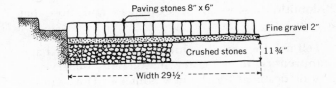

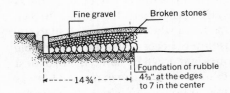

FIG. 2.   Telford's system of surfacing roadways. *Top:* Surfacing of paving stones. *Center, left:* Macadam surfacing. *Center, right:* Pebble surfacing. *Bottom:* Surfacing of fine gravel and broken stone on a foundation of rubble.

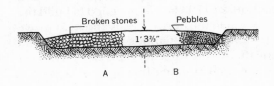

Studies and experiments made in England in the first quarter of the nineteenth century made it possible to establish solid roads, setting examples followed on the Continent after 1830. The technique of macadamizing roads was now stabilized for about the next century.

New research methods   This period is characterized by an important change in the methods of handling problems raised by road building and maintenance. An attempt was made to substitute research based on mathematical methods for the traditional empiricism. In France the engineers of the Department of Bridges and Highways began to establish the bases for these calculations, without always arriving at uniform results.

The principal problem concerned the draft, or pulling power of the horses, and the resistance opposed to this effort by the vehicle, the size of its wheels, the grade of the road, and the nature of the road surface. The work applied by one horse also had to be defined. This definition depended on a large number of variable factors that were difficult to determine by indisputable rules: the breed of horse, its weight, its load, the conditions under which it worked. The first studies on this subject were made by La Hire in 1699. He found that on level ground a horse pulls a load equal to that pulled by seven men, but in the mountains the load is equivalent to that of three men.

The question was taken up again in the nineteenth century by numerous engineers. Tredgold gave a table showing speeds of a horse without harness or load in terms of the duration of its trip. Coulomb found that on level ground a horse can pull 1,540 pounds for a distance of 24 miles in one day. Between 1830 and 1840 Rumford, Dupin, Hachette, Navier, and later numerous Bridges and Highways Department engineers attempted to calculate the work done by one horse, but the results remained uncertain.

Hauling of vehicles   The radius and width of wheels was also the subject of many studies during the same period. As early as 1757 Richard Lowell Edgeworth had given numerical coefficients for the draft of vehicles. He determined that wheels with conical or inclined axles tended to damage the roads, as a result of the uneven velocities of their rims, and he recommended straight, cylindrical wheels and spindles. In 1811 Rumford claimed an advantage for wheels with wide fellies, and in 1813 Gerstner studied the relationship between the kind of surface and the width of the fellies.

In France the most important work was done slightly later. In 1832 Schwilgué established a table of ratios between the weight of vehicles, the width of their rims, and the pay load transported. In the same year Coriolis published studies on the various resistances during movement, and a study of carriage springs as well. He attempted to determine the effects of different grades and to establish a coefficient of moving friction, taking into consideration the nature of the terrain, friction in the axles, and the location of the carriage's center of gravity. The type of surface, the dimensions and shape of the wheel, and the shape of its rims were taken into consideration to determine the friction attributable solely to the terrain.

Coriolis's results were regarded as very acceptable in the nineteenth century for they were close to those obtained experimentally by Arthur Morin in 1838. Morin, an officer in the Engineers' Corps, invented a relatively simple dynamometric apparatus (Figure 3) that was sufficient to study the many problems of applied mechanics. The resistance of vehicles, he found, was in inverse proportion to the diameter of the wheels. Almost at the same time another experimenter, one Dupuit, applied the square root of the diameter of the wheels. For all practical purposes the difference between the two findings was negligible, for the diameter of the vehicle wheels was close to one yard.

The two authors came to opposite conclusions concerning the effects of vehicles' speed on their resistance. Morin felt that the resistance increased with

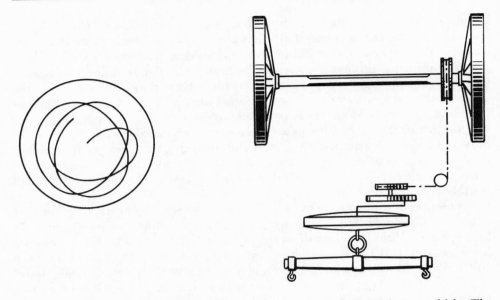

FIG. 3. Morin dynamometer applied to study the draft of horsedrawn vehicles. The recording mechanism attached to the whipple-tree consists of a spring component with a pencil point that traces a line varying with the force of traction on the surface of a disc rotated by the wheel shaft. *Left:* Curve obtained during trial runs.

speed whatever the surface of the road, but for Dupuit the resistance was independent of speed on paved roads. Toward the end of the century the Bridges and Highways Department engineers justified Dupuit.

Attention was also given to the wear and tear that vehicles caused on roads. A commission appointed in 1816 to study the effects of a horse's speed on the various surfaces made known its conclusions in 1828. On paved roads a walk was more detrimental than a trot, but the opposite was noted on surfaces of packed paving blocks.

These results did not in themselves represent remarkable or definitive additions to knowledge, but the research is quite important from the historical point of view because it testifies to a departure from the empiricism that had from the very beginning been the builder's sole guide, and with good reason. Although the mathematical background had not yet developed, the new direction had been clearly defined and was slowly to develop.

Laying out and building roads
The methods used in other aspects of road building had more reliable, experimental bases. The problem of laying out routes made great progress around 1840. A method to compare economically the various alternatives for a given route, published in 1841 by a Bridges and Highways Department engineer named Favier, was quite widely applied during the nineteenth century. Topographical surveys became generally used. Numerous studies attempted to solve the problems of laying out and building roads, and several of them involved calculating cuts and fills. In 1836 Coriolis published five volumes of tables on this subject.

Dupuit-put into use an instrument with a small graduated wheel to estimate the surfaces of embankments. The planimeter first invented in 1827 by one Oppikofer of Berne made it possible to calculate areas geometrically, but it was seldom used, since work methods at the time did not require it. Not until after the invention of the Amsler model (later perfected by Coradi) in 1854 was the planimeter used as a working tool.

Thus, toward the middle of the century, reliable methods were beginning to find acceptance and general rules began to serve as a basis for construction projects. It was accepted without argument that gradients should be limited to 3 percent and curves to a radius of 164 feet. The importance of a road's degree of exposure and of the solidity of its substructure had finally been demonstrated, and it was agreed that the surface be made of hard materials bonded together. The various types of surfaces were well known, as were roads' proportions, their crowns, and the dimensions of drainage ditches and their sides (Figure 4).

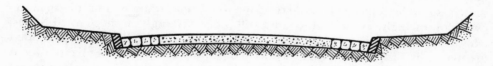

FIG. 4. *Top:* Profile of paved road with gutters at each side, around 1860–1880. *Bottom:* Profile of embanked road with single sidewalk, around 1860–1880.

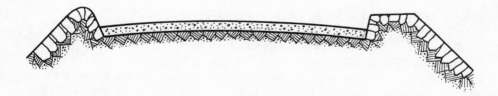

The equipment used to lay out roads began to evolve gradually in the 1840s. The item most characteristic of this evolution was the new compressor roller, then pulled by horses. This roller, used by Polonceau in 1844, was a cylinder between large tubs that could be filled with stones gradually to increase the weight of the vehicle by as much as three to six tons as the paving materials became packed down (Figure 5). Soon the roller came to be pulled by a steam engine, then was finally

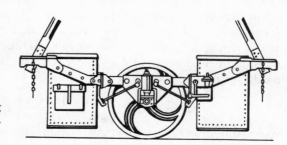

FIG. 5. Road roller for consolidating metal. The tubs are filled with stones. Mid-nineteenth century.

equipped with an engine of its own and became the steam road roller of modern times, with the steam engine later being replaced by a diesel one.

A new type of surface, bitumen, appeared shortly before the middle of the century and was almost universally used until modern times. Bitumen was extracted from asphalt selected according to the qualities of the material and the use to be made of it. Asphalt itself was also used, for bitumen was believed to increase adhesion in hot weather.

The influence of railroads   The network of major long-distance roads was extended and perfected in almost every civilized country between about 1830 and 1880, but then the development of railroads stopped this growth. In France, for example, it was found at the end of the century that the national highways had remained unchanged and in the same condition as in 1867. But regional and local highways had on the other hand experienced more development. Long-distance haulage had decreased in importance during this period and had even disappeared in some cases to be replaced by local trucking to railroad stations. This phase in the evolution of highways was illustrated still more strikingly in the United States, where during the nineteenth-century period when inhabited areas expanded greatly, railroads preceded highways as new ground breakers. The abandonment of long-distance highway use later continued until World War II, until the internal combustion engine (especially the diesel engine) could be used in vehicles capable of transporting goods over long distances.

FROM STONE TO IRON BRIDGES

The eighteenth century was the great age of stone bridges; the nineteenth, of metal bridges. The development of construction techniques for stone bridges was chiefly the work of French engineers, whereas the introduction of metal bridges and their rapidly improved construction were due to a particularly brilliant generation of British engineers.

Wooden bridges   Rapid changes in bridge building occurred around the middle of the eighteenth century, but, naturally, construction methods from earlier times were not abruptly abandoned. Many bridges were still built of wood. Even when cast iron and then wrought iron began to be used in large quantities, wood was still used for some parts. New knowledge about the strength of materials made possible a better use of wood, but even though it still remained a frequently used material, it generally stopped during the eighteenth century being the main material used for major permanent projects, for reasons of construction and maintenance economy. One of the last wooden bridges built in France was the Morand Bridge over the Rhône at Lyon in 1775. During the nineteenth century and even later, wood continued to be used for the roadway and trusses of bridges resting on masonry pillars (Figure 6).

Stone bridges   The eighteenth century was an age of great activity and progress in France. Medieval bridges still survived, and in several cities ornate bridges had been built during the Renaissance.

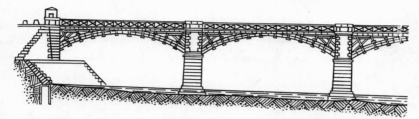

FIG. 6. Ivry bridge. Trusses and roadbed of wood. Early nineteenth century.

But both types, in most cases with poor foundations, were undermined by floods and fell into ruin in the seventeenth century, so much reconstruction was undertaken.

The first major work of this time was the Tuileries Bridge, or Pont Royal, for which J. Hardouin-Mansard called in one of the Roman brothers, a good builder from Maestricht, the Netherlands. The bridge was built on the boldest lines and was, according to de Dartein, of unshakable solidity.

The building of bridges was begun: by Gabriel at Blois (1716); and by Hupeau at Orléans (1751). Bayeux began the bridge at Tours (1764) that was completed by de Voglie. That at Nantes, begun by Hupeau after 1755, was finished by Perronet (1757–1765), who made an investigation of the difficulties experienced in the construction and so developed new methods.

Until then, whether at Blois, Tours, or Nantes, the basic technique remained the same—the use of a depressed arch (see Volume II, p. 357) and thick piers. From a theory of unknown origins and from their own experience earlier builders had deduced that in order to withstand the sideways thrust of an arch, piers had to have a thickness equal to one-fifth of the opening. All arches and piers, including those of the Nantes Bridge, were laid out in this manner.

The bridge of Blois has eleven arches with spans increasing in width toward the center of the bridge (Figure 7). The bonding and decoration of the stone are carefully executed, but the setting out of the arches is still simple, consisting of three arcs struck from three centers, the spring having an arch with a small radius and the center being closed with an arch of a greater radius (Figure 8). This is the three-centered arch in thirds; all three arches have an opening of 60°. The bridge is hog backed, the center arch being the highest and widest. The change in the curvature of the arches, which at first glance is indiscernible, is not pleasing when noticed.

The bridge at Tours differs greatly from the Blois and Nantes bridges, for its roadway is horizontal and all the arches have the same span. It was thought that the pier foundations' stability could be ensured by building them in caissons on pilings driven five or six feet below low-water level.

The thickness of the piers is still equal to one-fifth the span of the arches, which have a more complicated outline than those of the Blois Bridge. There are eleven concentric circles with radii increasing from the haunches to the crown, which gives the arches a curve that, though it still has a three-centered shape, is much more regular (Figure 9), the increase in the curves being almost imperceptible.

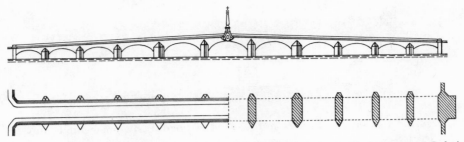

FIG. 7.   Plan and elevation of the bridge at Blois, built over the Loire by Jacques Gabriel and Pitrou between 1716 and 1724.

FIG. 8.   Central arch of the bridge at Blois. Diagram of the vault.

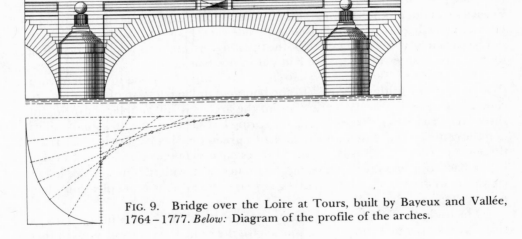

FIG. 9.   Bridge over the Loire at Tours, built by Bayeux and Vallée, 1764–1777. *Below:* Diagram of the profile of the arches.

Difficulties in building foundations in sandbanks along the Loire caused errors, erosion, and breaks in several arches one after the other. They were finally strengthened in the twentieth century with injections of cement. In 1774 it was noted that the eighth pier and its adjacent arches were sinking, and in 1776 the fourth arch collapsed during construction. In a 1789 disaster four arches collapsed, in 1835 the parapets fell, breaking the voussoirs of the ninth, tenth, and eleventh arches.

An investigation of these difficulties revealed cavities in the foundations of the ninth and tenth piers. In 1836 injections of pure hydraulic lime were made, and a general revetment was built to prevent water as it passed under the bridge from carrying away the sand and undermining the foundations, which were not sufficiently deep.

Perronet   Bridge-building techniques were transformed after the middle of the eighteenth century, thanks in particular to J.-Rodolphe Perronet (1708–1794), the son of a Swiss officer in the French service. In 1725 he started work in the architectural offices of the City of Paris, joined the Department of Bridges and Highways in 1735, and was made an instructor of draftsmen in an office established by Daniel Trudaine. This office later became the École des Ponts et Chaussées (School of Civil Engineering), which became famous through the names of de Cessart, de Chézy, Gauthey, de Prony, and Lecreulx.

In 1763 Perronet was called upon to complete the Nantes Bridge, whose construction was running into difficulties (Figure 10). As usual, the piers were built with a thickness one-fifth the span of the center arch (24 feet for 120), which should have resisted the thrust of the contiguous arches. Westminster Bridge in London had been built similarly between 1730 and 1750 on piers whose thickness was one-fifth of the spans.

But at Nantes this rule failed; an arch built without being buttressed by its neighbor caused the pier to lean. It was necessary to dismantle the arch under construction, lay the centerings of the neighboring arches, and continue with them as quickly as possible so they could support each other. It was impossible to increase the thickness of the piers, because the point was to so improve the flow of water by increasing the size of the opening.

The study of rivers and their flow began to be more methodically pursued at this time. A hydraulics engineer, du Buat, derived from his experiments a formula

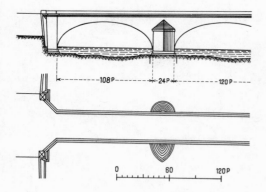

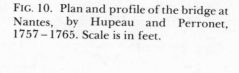

FIG. 10. Plan and profile of the bridge at Nantes, by Hupeau and Perronet, 1757–1765. Scale is in feet.

FIG. 11. Diagram of the stresses exerted on piers by bridge vaults.

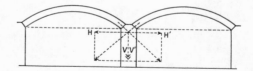

later improved by de Prony to account for the rate of flow, seasonal irregularities, and the effect of freshets in certain streams. A reduction in the thickness of piers began to be considered, but it was feared they would no longer be able to sustain the thrust of a single adjacent arch. Perronet deliberately adopted this plan, however, and in his bridges had to build his scaffolding and construct all the arches simultaneously.

Under these conditions it was no longer necessary to respect the old limits on the rise of the arch, which could now be extended and laid out on a single arc, thereby raising the spring and leaving a wider passage for the water. At the same time the wider arc made it possible to lower the surface of the bridge and to eliminate, or at least reduce, the access gradients.

From then on the piers were required merely to support the vertical component of the stresses (Figure 11). The horizontal thrusts were transmitted from one arch to the next, canceling each other out, or their differences were carried over onto the abutments. Thus the mass of the piers could be considerably reduced.

New conceptions   These ideas were rigorously applied to the Neuilly Bridge, built between 1766 and 1774 by Perronet and de Chézy, and then to the Sainte-Maxence Bridge on the Oise. In his first design for the Neuilly Bridge (Figure 12) Perronet had piers with sections shaped so as to facilitate the flow of water. He ultimately adopted grouped columns, which gave the Neuilly Bridge its characteristic appearance and fame (Figure 13).

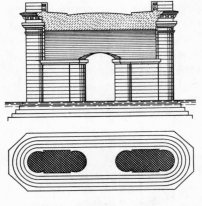

FIG. 12.   Perronet's plan for the piers of the Pont de Neuilly.

FIG. 13.   Pont de Neuilly, built by Perronet and Chézy in 1766–1774.

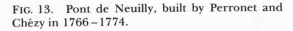

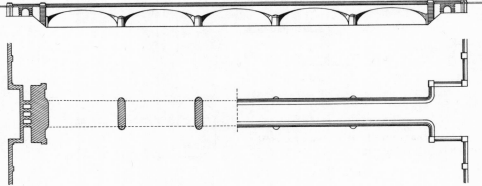

The depression of the arches, planned at 1:12 but carried out at 1:11.2, surpassed all earlier bridges in daring—the Ponte Vecchio in Florence had a depression of only 1:7. The thickness of the piers (retained at Tours at 1:5) was reduced to 1:12.44 of the opening. (Neuilly was 1:9.23.)

There was no lack of critics for this audacity, but Trudaine supported Perronet and his projects were carried out. Perronet maintained that it was possible to go even further. The bridge of Saint-Dié, designed by his pupil Lecreulx, was to have a depressed arch of 1:18. The projecting heads now supported only the footpaths and could be flattened still more; connected with the principal arches by "cow horns" they became a platband rather than an arc. Perronet strongly approved of this design, which gave the appearance of a flat platform, in his opinion the ideal conception of a bridge.

The critics, who however unjustified were numerous, caused Perronet to hesitate in building the Pont de la Concorde (1786–1791). The first design, based on that of the Pont-Sainte-Maxence, aroused vigorous opposition. To achieve his objective while preserving the principles to which he was most devoted, he agreed to adopt piers of a more classical section, with a less obvious depression of the arches. The thickness of the piers was once again to be 1:7.8–1:8.5, according to a decision reached on February 25, 1787. This was a partial return to the old practices (Figure 14). Perronet, with the support available to him, could have persisted in his initial design, but in order to complete the work more quickly he preferred to make concessions while preserving the general appearance he had conceived. The flattening was reduced to 1:10.4–1:13.3, so the roadway was not absolutely flat but rose slightly up to the center.

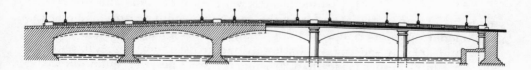

FIG. 14.   Pont de la Concorde in Paris, built by Perronet and Demoustier, 1786–1791. Broken lines in shaded portion at left show the first design of the profile.

It must be added that Perronet attached great importance to solid, careful construction, using only the best materials from well-known quarries. The foundations were solid, the blocks used in the piers were larger, and the joints were even, ranging from 7 to 9 mm.

The cut stones were mounted on quoins and the joints filled with cement mortar. The joints of the arches were slightly larger.

Émiland-Marie Gauthey   Gauthey (1732–1806) is the logical successor to Perronet in the evolution of bridge building. He has perhaps remained somewhat in the shadow of his illustrious predecessor, but his more diversified activity clearly marks the evolution of bridge-building techniques in the late eighteenth century and early nineteenth.

Gauthey, Perronet's pupil at the School of Civil Engineering, was penniless, but he immediately distinguished himself and was hired without delay as an instructor, which assured him of a salary. After two years of schooling he became deputy engineer in 1758 in Burgundy, where in 1763 he was actively concerned with studies on canals, in Saône-Yonne. We next find him involved in discussions on major construction projects such as the Sainte-Geneviève church.

The most characteristic of his works were his methodical studies on the strength of materials and his comparisons of stones from various quarries. These studies enabled him to calculate more accurately thicknesses, effects of joints, adherence of mortars, and friction of stones.

Without going as far as his successor Vicat, Gauthey analyzed calcareous and chalk rocks, hydrated limes and natural cements, pozzolanas and trass, and recognized the importance of their high silica and aluminum content. He also discovered the possibility of using ashes. Navier, who published his works, says, "M. Gauthey wished to assemble into a single body doctrines of which his predecessors' books offered only applications, and no one could add anything necessary to develop a complete theory."

In 1782, the year he became chief engineer for the province of Burgundy, he built the quays of Chalon and obtained approval of plans for the Canal du Centre, which Perronet at first opposed before accepting Gauthey's judgment.

His outstanding works, in addition to his studies on the Panthéon (Sainte-Geneviève), the Chalon quays, and the canal projects, are the bridge of Navilly over the Doubs and the church at Givry, in the construction of which he applied all his ideas on the resistance of stones and the weight of arches.

London's bridges   In eighteenth-century England the builders of stone bridges were not innovators, but the French engineer's example was taken up by the early nineteenth century. Among the great builders of this period were John Rennie and his son and Thomas Telford.

Until 1750 only one bridge, London Bridge, crossed the Thames in London. This thirteenth-century bridge had 20 semicircular arches, the center one being almost 69 feet. It was 925 feet long and 26 feet wide but had become inadequate because of the growth of traffic.

A second bridge, Westminster, was built between 1738 and 1750 by the Swiss Charles Labeleye. It was 1,327 feet long, 44 feet wide, and had 15 major arches with spans decreasing in width out toward the ends—the center arch had a span of 75 feet, but those on the banks had spans of only 25 feet. In the nineteenth century it was decided that the large number of arches hindered traffic, so between 1854 and 1862 the bridge was rebuilt in iron, with only 7 arches and a width of 98 feet.

A third bridge, Blackfriars, was built from 1750 to 1769 by Robert Mylne. Between 1811 and 1817 John Rennie constructed Waterloo Bridge, which Canova called the most noble bridge in the world. It was the first bridge in London to be built with a flat roadway, on 9 semielliptical granite arches. The arches, all equal, had openings of 120 feet and rested on piers 20 feet thick (30 feet at their bases) built on piles one foot in diameter. We see that in this bridge, built at the beginning of the nineteenth century, the builders were still using a ratio of six for the thickness of the piers to the opening of the arches, which was a far cry from the daring of Perronet and his pupils. The road was 28 feet wide, bordered with sidewalks 7 feet wide.

Plate 20.   The building of the Waterloo Bridge, begun by John Rennie in 1811. Engraving. (Photo Radio Times Hulton Picture Library, London.)

Plate 21.   The de-centering of an arch of the Pont de Neuilly. Preliminary painting by Hubert Robert. Formerly in the Cailleux Collection, Paris. (Photo Ph. Brossé.)

Between 1815 and 1819 Rennie built Southwark Bridge, the first metal bridge over the Thames (see Cast-iron bridges).

Between 1824 and 1831 London Bridge was rebuilt 164 feet upstream from its first site. The design was by George Rennie under his father's direction and was built by his brother, John, Jr. It consisted of 5 granite arches with spans ranging from 151 feet for the center arch to 130 feet for the end ones and remained in service unchanged for more than a century.

In these masonry works the British builders showed less audacity than did French engineers and paid less attention to style. The engineer who came closest to French design standards was Thomas Telford, who was inspired by the Neuilly Bridge in planning the bridge he built over the Severn near Gloucester.

Cast-iron bridges   In their use first of cast iron, then of wrought iron, British engineers demonstrated great boldness in their designs and achievements and completely transformed the art of bridge building. The first cast-iron bridge was built by John Wilkinson and Abraham Darby (the third of that name) from 1776 to 1779 to replace the ferry crossing the Severn near the Darby foundry at Coalbrookdale (Figure 15). The roadway was

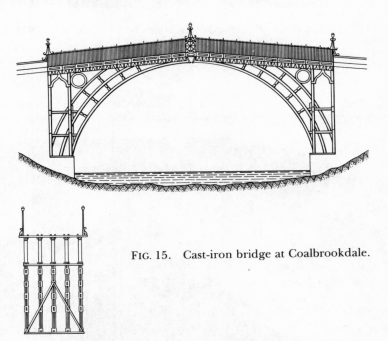

FIG. 15.   Cast-iron bridge at Coalbrookdale.

supported by an arch composed of 5 cast-iron ribs with spans of 99 feet at a height of approximately 49 feet. The ribs were cast in half arches at the Darby foundry, the most important casting project performed in this period. The bridge (which is still in place) gave its name to the locality, Ironbridge.

Several other cast-iron bridges were erected in the following years. One of them was built by Roland Burdon in 1796 over the Wear, near Sunderland, in northeastern England. Its metal arch had a span of 236 feet. The first design has been attributed (probably incorrectly) to Thomas Paine, the revolutionary.

Thomas Telford began quite early to use cast iron in constructing his bridges, his first such being built over the Severn at Buildwas. With its span of 130 feet it was for Telford a preliminary test for more important projects. In the early nineteenth century he made generous use of cast iron to build two aqueducts at Chirk and Pont Cysyllte, which were part of the canal system developed in northern Wales. In the first aqueduct the arches were built of stone, the bed of the canal being formed with sheets of cast iron. The Pont Cysyllte aqueduct was built on 19 cast-iron arches resting on masonry piers, and the canal bed was also of metal.

Techniques of building highway bridges were quickly refined. Southwark Bridge in London had three arches, a center one of 240 feet and two side arches with spans of 210 feet, laid on 24-foot piers, so the ratio of the piers' thickness to the opening of the arches was 1:10. It had 8 assemblies of segmental iron ribs 8 feet deep at the springs and 6 feet at the keystone, and 2¾ inches thick, with 4-inch U-shaped flanges. The bridge, built between 1815 and 1819, remained intact until 1913.

The cast-iron Pont d'Austerlitz in Paris, built between 1804 and 1806, showed a very bold technique. The sections were assembled with iron angles that fitted into slots left by the casting process (Figure 16). In the Sunderland Bridge, built several years earlier, the builders had used iron rods that were also embedded in grooves in the sections. On the Tewkesbury Bridge Telford used pieces shaped like a Saint Andrew's cross and bolted to hold the arches together.

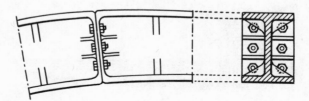

FIG. 16. Connection of two cast-iron sections of the Pont d'Austerlitz in Paris.

The most beautiful achievement of this time was the Pont du Carrousel in Paris, built by Polonceau in 1831–1834. He employed cast-iron arches made in sections and assembled by contact. In order to stiffen the ties used to attach them he gave them ribs identical to those reinforcing the chords. The sections were in two parts bolted together to form a tube and contained a wooden core formed of tarred timbers .4 inch thick and between 33 and 66 feet long (Figure 17). This bracing eliminated vibrations of the arch when the sections were being mounted. The cast-iron parts for the arches were between 1¼ and 1⅓ inches thick. The bridge's three arches had equal spans of 156 feet and a rise of 16 feet (Figure 18). The roadway was of wood (Figure 19).

Polonceau gave the Pont du Carrousel a special elegance by filling the spandrels with concentric circles (Figure 18). On other bridges the spandrels consisted of simple uprights with round lower portions fitted into sockets in the arch. The rings of Polonceau's spandrels had H sections into which the iron ties of the tubes fitted. This arrangement made for a better weight distribution (Figure 20). Contact was provided by small cast-iron bobbins connected by flat iron ties on the lower portion of the rings (Figure 21).

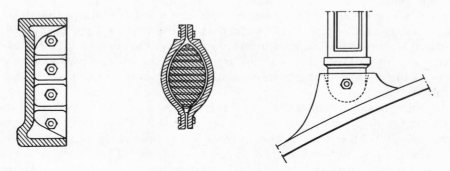

FIG. 17. Construction technique of cast-iron bridges built by Polonceau. *Left:* Gothic U-shaped end arc. *Center:* Tubular section with wooden core. *Right:* Attaching a spandrel to the arch.

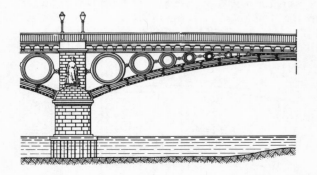

FIG. 18. Cast-iron spandrel of the Pont du Carrousel.

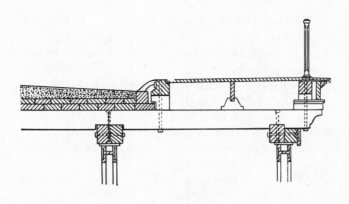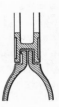

FIG. 19. Wooden roadway of the Pont du Carrousel, resting on cast-iron spandrels.

FIG. 20. Section of Polonceau's ring spandrels.

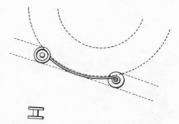

FIG. 21. Cast-iron spools supporting the rings and held together with a strip of iron. *Below:* Section of a spool.

Cast iron was used for large bridges, such as the Solférino (1858) and Saint-Louis (1877) bridges in Paris, until the second half of the nineteenth century. But as soon as the puddling process of making wrought iron permitted the production of fairly large pieces of iron this metal was used for a large number of bridges. The first wrought-iron bridge was the Pont des Arts in Paris (1802–1804). At this time it was not yet possible to use large iron girders, so the Pont des Arts was simply a footbridge with a light framework of rectangular-sectioned iron bars.

Not until forty years later did the iron industry produce wrought-iron girders for large projects. From this time on the art of using metal frameworks for constructing covered markets, docks, and bridges developed very rapidly.

Iron bridges   The first iron bridge, the tunnel bridge designed by Robert Stephenson for the railroad line to cross the Menai Strait in northwestern Wales, was built before midcentury (Figure 22). This bridge consisted of two parallel metal tubes with polygonal sections, each carrying one railroad track. It had four spans, two supported on the small island of Brittania, which gave its name to the bridge. The two end spans were 230 feet long, the center ones being 459 feet. In the years before the bridge was completed in 1850 its design had given rise to many experimental models on the scale of 1:6 built by Stephenson with the help of metallurgist William Fairbairn and mathematician Eaton Hodgkinson. It was a question of determining precisely the relative sizes of the girders forming the upper part of the bridge and those making up the lower portion as a factor of iron's resistance to expansion being greater than its resistance to contraction. Because of the experimental work required, the construction methods used, and its high cost, the Britannia Bridge remained until the early years of our century the most imposing bridge successfully completed.

Another type of iron bridge was designed in the years just before 1850, the first examples of which were undertaken by Isambard Kingdom Brunel. The first of these truss bridges with latticed stiffening were the Windsor, Chepstow, and Saltash bridges built by Brunel for the Great Western Railway. This British engineer designed stiffening trusses used to support the roadway by chains. The trusses of Chepstow Bridge have tubes with circular cross sections, whereas those of the Saltash Bridge (Figure 23) have oval sections. Their spans are, respectively, 298½ feet and 459 feet. The last of these truss bridges, the Royal Albert, which crossed the Tamar at Saltash near Plymouth, was opened in May 1859, shortly before Brunel's death.

The construction of iron bridges had reached its most brilliant period. Industrial adaptation of the Bessemer process was now beginning, and before the end of

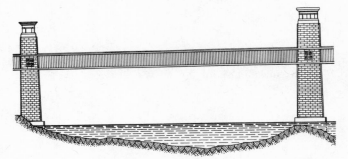

FIG. 22. Britannia Bridge, built by Robert Stephenson.

FIG. 23. Saltash Bridge on the South Devon Railway, built by Brunel over an estuary seven miles from Plymouth.

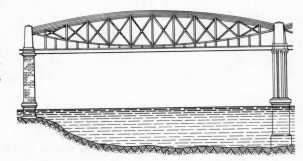

the nineteenth century steel, which became increasingly available, almost completely replaced wrought iron and cast iron.

Suspension bridges The use of metal made possible still another solution for bridging broad spans: the suspension bridge. The principle of this type of bridge had long been known, but it had been used only for light footbridges, which had to be rebuilt frequently. The production of iron chains developed in England at the beginning of the nineteenth century; a patent for chains with flat wrought-iron links was taken out by Samuel Brown in 1817. Progress also in wire drawing made strong metal cables available to builders. Such cables were used by the Séguin brothers, the first to build suspension bridges in France.

But the first great achievement was that of Thomas Telford, who built a bridge (Figure 24) suspended from metal chains to span the Menai Strait separating Anglesey Island from Wales, on the London-Holyhead road. Its construction was approved in 1819 and it was opened to traffic in 1826. Stephenson's bridge for the Chester-Holyhead railroad was built alongside it twenty-five years later.

Telford's suspension bridge had a span of 580 feet. The chains were combined in groups of four, each chain formed ten-foot bars made into links flattened at the ends and assembled with bolts. The road, 30 feet wide, was suspended from the chains by vertical rods at 5-foot intervals. It was later necessary to reinforce the roadway's rigidity to prevent it from swaying in strong winds. At this time such an undertaking required of its creator not only engineering talents on a high order

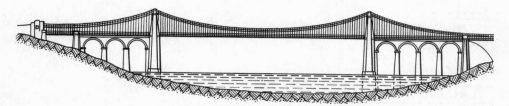

FIG. 24. Menai Bridge, an iron suspension bridge built by Telford.

but also the qualities of a manager to organize the production of components and plan the work on the building site. The success of such an important and novel work on top of his earlier work won Telford a substantial reputation.

The contributions of Marc and Camille Séguin were contemporary with Telford's work—their first suspension bridge was built over the Rhône between Tain and Tournon in 1824. The two brothers had previously built a small experimental footbridge 53 feet long at a minimal cost (50 contemporary francs), which enabled them to perfect construction details. They then proceeded boldly to construct the bridge over the Rhône, which had a gap of 656 feet.

The system was very light and simple. The cables, of iron wire, were supported by pylons on the riverbanks and, when there were several spans, on intermediate pillars (Figure 25). The drawn iron wires were capable of supporting

FIG. 25. First bridge suspended from iron cables, built over the Rhône at Tournon in 1825 by the Séguin brothers.

heavy burdens and could thus be very light. Rods attached to cables supported wooden crossties, which in turn supported the wooden deck (Figure 26). The cables were anchored to the riverbanks in solid retaining masses. When there were intermediate piers the cables were carried down into their bases, whose weight held them in place (Figure 27). This type of bridge was inexpensive and was easy to build over long gaps like those of the Rhône and Loire. Numerous examples were built before 1850.

Sometimes chains were used instead of cables, as in the English bridges. The chains usually used were originally in most cases replaced by long links or straight, articulated links (Figure 28). In this way long reaches were bridged. The bridge over the Saane at Fribourg in Switzerland, built between 1832 and 1835 by the French engineer Chaley, was for a long time the largest single-span bridge (869 feet). It remained in use until 1924.

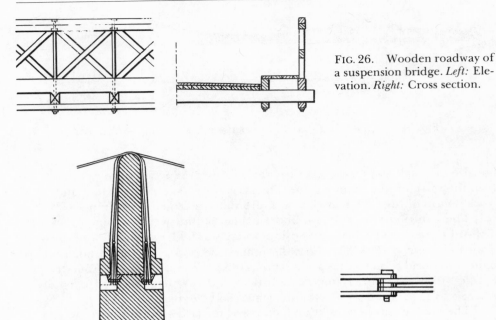

FIG. 26. Wooden roadway of a suspension bridge. *Left:* Elevation. *Right:* Cross section.

FIG. 27. Intermediate pillar of a suspension bridge, with the cables anchored in the base.

FIG. 28. Joint of a metal chain used in English suspension bridges.

Several improvements increased the security of the cable stays, particularly in bridges with several spans. Marc Séguin patented on April 25, 1835 a retaining system for the heads of pylons, using an upper cable extending from head to head as far as the land pylons.

But these light bridges with wooden decks had the defect of being too easily deformed and too elastic. A uniform weight on the entire length of the surface did not modify the parabolic shape of the cable, but an isolated weight caused local distortion of the deck and of the cable, producing a wave effect in the deck when the moving weight shifted. Wind had effects more visible than on masonry or even cast-iron bridges, despite reducing the surfaces exposed to the wind.

Nevertheless, their cheapness, as a result of their lightness and of the possibility of bridging large spans without intermediate piers, led to their frequent use before midcentury. In Paris an attempt was made in 1825 to build such a bridge at the site of the present Pont Alexandre III, but because the land under the left-bank abutment was not compact the construction had to be interrupted. A suspension bridge, the Pont des Invalides, in use until 1856, was built downstream from 1818 to 1829.

Suspension bridges aroused criticism and fear among their users, especially those whose heavy carriages made distressing ruts in the planking. An accident confirmed suspicions as to the stability of these bridges. On April 16, 1850, the Basse-Chaîne Bridge across the Maine River at Angers was crossed by a batallion of the Eleventh Light Infantry Regiment marching in cadence. The rhythm of their march corresponded to the periodic sway of the bridge, resulting in an abnormal amplification of distortion, which broke up the bridge. The entire batallion was hurled into the river, and 223 soldiers and officers perished.

This tragic event discredited light suspension bridges and led to strict regulation of marching troops, who from then on had to break step when crossing bridges. Since it was not specified which bridges were involved, the rule was applied to all bridges.

Beginning about 1850 the construction of these light bridges slowed perceptibly but resumed later with heavier bridges having metal decks and with suspension systems that were more rigid if not totally incapable of buckling.

ROAD TRANSPORT

For all practical purposes, carriage building developed only as new materials were produced by the iron industry on the Continent from about 1800 to 1825. It was also dependent on improvements to the highway system and road surfacing.

These two influences combined to encourage the search for a lighter type of private carriage and for larger vehicles for public transport to the extent that the increase in weight was not proportional to increased capacity.

Vehicle construction The most notable changes involved the axles, suspension, and wheel rims (Figures 29–32). Axles could now be made from a single piece of wrought iron no matter what their length and width, which strengthened them but didn't make the vehicle heavier.

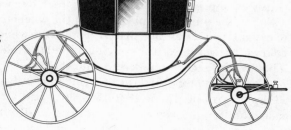

FIG. 29. Mail carriage with spring suspension, 1820–1830.

FIG. 30. Light calash with double suspension. Built in the shops of the Jones brothers, carriage makers in Brussels.

FIG. 31.   Clarence. London livery carriage with a meter for measuring the distances traveled (rear section).

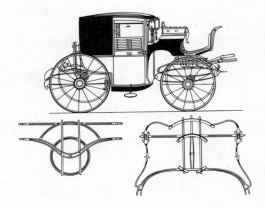

FIG. 32.   Brougham, 1851, with a new system forecarriage. *Left:* Upper side of forecarriage; *Right:* Underside.

The springs and tires could be made of long, continuous strips of rolled iron. Until then the fellies of wheels had been covered with sheets of wrought iron applied one after the other and held in place by screws and nails (Figure 33). Temperature variations caused changes in length and thus stripping and warping of the wheels. The new system, which thereafter became the only one used until modern times, consisted of preparing an iron circle closed by a weld, with a circumference slightly less than the outer circumference of the wheel to be banded. The tire was heated to expand it and was then placed around the wheel and quickly cooled by throwing cold water over it. As it shrank it gripped the felly firmly and assured its strength. The tire was secured by screws into the wood.

In France this method was put into industrial use, probably by a certain Philippe, around 1825–1830. His shop had a certain number of woodworking machines for preparing hubs, spokes, and sections of the fellies, for shaping tenons and drilling their mortises, and for assembling wheels, and also had a furnace for heating tires. All wheelwrights quickly adopted this technique, but with simpler equipment.

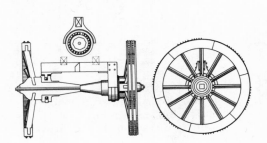

FIG. 33.   Composition of a carriage wheel spindle. *Top:* Ball bearings. *Right:* Banding of the felly with nailed banks of iron, around 1820.

Public transport   After Telford's efforts to improve England's roads
                         at the end of the eighteenth century and when roads
were restored on the Continent after the Napoleonic wars, the organization of
fast, regular transport for travelers and mail became possible. Increased commercial and industrial activities made this necessary. Stagecoaches (Figure 34) were
then put into service, quickly replacing the old, heavy, slow coaches.

Inside the urban centers, which were beginning to spread out, regular public
transport services were also organized during the first half of the nineteenth
century. Pascal's five-*sous* coaches in France had been merely a premature and
short-lived experiment. The omnibus did not appear in Paris until 1828, the first
line being established by Stanislas Baudry following a strange experiment at
Nantes that proved to him a general interest in public vehicles.

A mile from the center of Nantes Baudry owned a flour mill with a steam
engine. He had the idea of opening a public bath to use the surplus hot water

FIG. 34. Parcel-carrying stagecoach, 1825–1850.

FIG. 35. Omnibus with 22 seats: 12 inside, 10 on top, 1830–1840.

collected from the engine's condenser, then thought of a carriage service to attract clients who would otherwise be discouraged by the distance. Vehicles with sixteen seats left regularly from the Place du Pont-aux-Vins (today the Place du Commerce) in the center of the city, the price of the trip being combined with the entrance fee to the bath. The citizens of Nantes used the carriage service in large numbers because of the travel opportunities it offered, but not many of them used the bath. Baudry closed the bath but continued to develop the service, the success of which encouraged him to try the experiment in Paris. The first line he established ran between the Madeleine Church and the Bastille via the Rue de Lancry. The carriages, with fourteen seats and drawn by three horses harnessed abreast, left every quarter hour. Their construction had benefited from the improvements of the period—metal axles and springs and iron-tired wheels gave strength to the vehicles and provided a certain amount of comfort for the passengers. Their success was immediate; between 1828 and 1855 twenty different companies came into being and developed a total of forty omnibus lines (Figure 35). In 1855 they all merged into a single Compagnie Générale des Omnibus.

Steam-powered vehicles   As early as the eighteenth century the development of the steam engine and increased freight traffic encouraged inventors to find ways of applying steam to highway transport and to substitute mechanical power for horses.

We have seen that bad road conditions made transportation burdensome and difficult, and it was thus tempting to increase motive power somehow to offset the inadequacy of teams of horses, but many ideas put forth on this subject did not materialize. In 1759 a Dr. Robinson, then a student at the University of Glasgow, suggested using steam to turn the wheels of carriages. In 1784 Watt gave in one of his patents a description of a condensing engine applicable to carriages, but he recognized that a low-pressure, excessively heavy engine was not usable.

Cugnot's   The first successful steam-powered wagon was built
steam-powered wagon   by the military engineer Joseph Cugnot (1725–1804), whose first model was put into operation in 1770, at a time when the atmospheric engine was still the only type of steam engine known. Cugnot employed two cylinders reversed in relation to the normal arrangement of such heat engines; that is, the open end was at the bottom, the piston rods came out at the bottom, and each connecting rod was jointed to the end of a single walking beam (Figure 36). This arrangement produced alternating piston

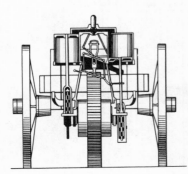

FIG. 36. Frontal view (boiler removed) of the engine of Cugnot's wagon, showing (in profile): the driving wheel, the hub of which supports the entire engine; the two cylinders; underneath the piston rods, the two chains, each connected with a ratchet drive system; the rods that control the operation of the steam inlet valve.

Plate 22. Cugnot's steam dray. Paris, Musée du Conservatoire national des Arts et Métiers. (Photo Ph. Brossé - P. U. F.)

movement and thus automatically controlled the steam inlet to each cylinder. Cugnot's engine did not inject cold water to cause condensation in the cylinders. The engine's movement was derived from a combination of the effects of atmospheric pressure on one piston and the pressure of live steam on the other.

The entire engine as well as firebox and boiler were carried on the front wheel, which provided both power and steering. Each piston stroke from top to bottom caused this wheel to turn through a double ratchet system attached on each side to the axle. A toothed gear made it possible to guide the wagon by a vertical steering column in front of the driver's seat. The rest of the vehicle consisted of a strong truck body of thick wooden beams. The rear portion rested on an axle with two wheels at the side (Figure 37).

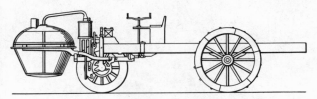

FIG. 37. Cugnot's wagon, profile view. *Front:* The boiler with its firebox. On the front wheel can be seen one of the ratchet-drive systems.

Cugnot's wagon, intended to carry heavy loads for the artillery and military engineering corps, was for its time an ingenious achievement, but it had several major faults. Its platform was unstable because it ran on three wheels only and the heavily laden front wheel hung from a single kingbolt. The boiler emptied quickly and there was no way to supply it with water while it was running, so its output was low. But from a historical point of view this engine is of great importance. Not only does it represent the first mechanical vehicle that succeeded in moving under its own power, but it also had the first successful device for changing the alternating movement of the steam engine into rotary movement, anticipating Watt's inventions by fifteen years.

Even though technically speaking Cugnot's invention could not have the same future as Watt's, his truck could have been put into service after some improvements. The project had been approved by Gribeauval, the artillery general who later invented the type of cannon that gave the Revolutionary and Empire armies their advantage over the artillery of their adversaries. It is useful to note that in 1769 several projects for a mechanical vehicle were presented to Gribeauval almost simultaneously by various inventors, but Cugnot's invention alone was encouraged. The first wagon was an experimental small-scale model of unknown dimensions, but its trials were sufficiently satisfactory to persuade Gribeauval to approve the construction of a full-scale example. The two bronze cylinders and the piston heads were ordered from the Strasbourg foundry, but all the other metal parts were built by a mechanic named Brezin, who assembled the parts and equipped the wagon at the Paris arsenal.

The vehicle was completed in 1771, but the fall of Choiseul, the secretary of state for foreign affairs from 1758 to 1770, had changed the intentions of the ministry, which refused to supply the necessary appropriations for the tests, involving wood for heating and the labor of two men for two days. Thirty years later the same incident was repeated. The director of the arsenal requested authority to destroy the truck, which had not moved from where it had been assembled, and a report from Roland to Bonaparte was not enough to obtain the same appropriation refused by the administration of Louis XV. In 1800 Molard, the first director of the Conservatoire national des Arts et Métiers, had the vehicle transported to the former priory of Saint-Martin-des-Champs, where he installed his collection; it is still there. Thus, the large model of the wagon known to us has never been tried. The legend invented shortly after Cugnot's death, that it was broken to pieces against a wall, is demonstrably false.

Nineteenth-century experiments   Cugnot's machinery was already outmoded when Bonaparte was dissociating himself from the invention by Maria-Theresa's former officer, and other experiments were undertaken in England and the United States. Perhaps the engineers working with Watt would have achieved some results if the great Scottish inventor had then understood the importance of high-pressure engines, but he stuck to his rotary double-acting low-pressure engine, from which he and Boulton thought only of getting maximum profits while it was still protected by patents. Thus, William Murdock was discouraged from pursuing the construction of a steam-powered carriage that could have given satisfactory results for that period (Figure 38).

In 1796/97 Richard Trevithick successfully tested a carriage propelled by a high-pressure engine, the first such model put into operation. The vertical cylinder was encased with the boiler. The piston rod, guided by vertical bars, moved a walking beam, one end of which was jointed to a connecting rod that turned a toothed wheel, which in turn geared into a pinion on the axle of the two driving wheels. In 1802 Trevithick, working with Vivian, built another model of a steam-

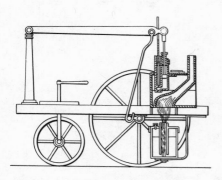

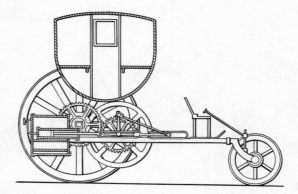

FIG. 38.   Murdock's steam carriage, 1784. The originality of the engine lies in the fact that the gases from the firebox pass through the boiler, in which the steam cylinder is placed.

FIG. 39.   Steam-powered carriage by Richard Trevithick and Andrew Vivian, 1802.

powered vehicle (Figure 39) in which power was transmitted from the horizontal engine to the wheels by a reversing connecting rod. This heavy vehicle with no suspension was unable to withstand the jarring caused by the roads of the time. Cornwall industrialists showed no interest in this novelty. In succeeding years Trevithick successfully operated similar vehicles on rails but met the same indifference.

A Swiss, Isaac de Rivaz of Valais, carried on for almost thirty years interesting experiments that would have been more convincing if he had been less isolated from the milieu of manufacturers and competent engineers. His experiments, begun in 1785, resulted in putting on the road in 1802 a vehicle propelled by a single-acting engine. In 1812 he designed a wagon with a double-acting engine of his own invention, which first operated successfully in 1814 (Figure 40).

In the course of his mechanical investigations Rivaz conceived an ingenious internal-combustion engine (Figure 41), undoubtedly the first one to be built since Huygens's version at the end of the seventeenth century. Between 1804 and 1814 Rivaz tried to improve the performance of this gas engine and use it to propel a vehicle. It was a partial failure. It is now clear that though Rivaz was a pioneer in this field he could not hope at this time to put into concrete form the great dreams of mechanical locomotion he had.

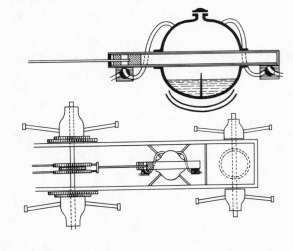

FIG. 40. Steam-powered carriage by de Rivaz, 1814. *Top:* Boiler and horizontal double-acting steam cylinder. *Bottom:* Arrangement of the driving apparatus on the frame.

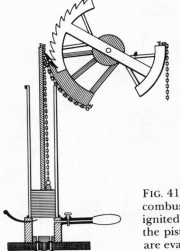

FIG. 41. Internal combustion engine by de Rivaz, 1804. The combustible mixture is introduced through the nozzle at right, ignited by an electric spark between the contact on the left and the piston. During the falling of the weight, the burned gases are evacuated through the valve at the bottom.

In the same period the efforts of Nathan Read and Oliver Evans received no better welcome in the United States. In 1800 Evans drove a steam-operated wagon through the streets of Philadelphia, but thereafter he had to limit the use of his high-pressure engine to stationary installations.

The greatest number of experiments to put a steam-powered locomotive on the road took place between 1820 and 1840, at a time when locomotives were beginning to operate successfully on railway tracks.

In 1805 Obadiah Elliot patented semielliptical and elliptical rolled springs, which made it possible to build light vehicles with better suspension. Most steam carriages in this period had spring suspensions. Gurtney improved boilers and made them lighter, but having no condensers they required water every eight miles. And because the boilers were fabricated from sheets of iron soldered together this resulted in frequent leaks. In 1827 Gurtney proposed a coach steered by a movable axle with two small wheels in front of a four-wheeled vehicle.

Pecqueur and Dietz   In 1828 Onésiphore Pecqueur (1792–1852) patented in France a greatly improved wagon with chains and a differential gear that solved the problem of taking curves (Figure 42). Pecqueur's invention did not pass unnoticed, but though it was often described in nineteenth-century treatises on mechanics, it was not generally applied in practice until gasoline-powered automobiles appeared.

The great pioneer of steam locomotion in France was Charles Dietz (1801–1888), who made trial runs between Paris, Versailles, and Saint-Germain and experimented with a regular service in the summer of 1834. On December 10, 1836, Dietz took out a patent for "a steam carriage, called a tractor, to travel on ordinary roads" (Figure 43). He provided an elastic material to cover the wheel rims and a second, jointed rim to "destroy the bumps on the pavement." Dietz and his father and brother were the only men on the Continent to continue experimenting with road vehicles. Numerous trials were made in England by James and Anderson, Gough, Hanson, and Hancock. The Birmingham steam stagecoach built by Hancock had become well known through a famous engraving.

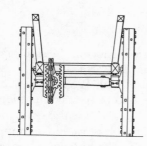

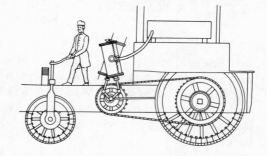

FIG. 42. Pecqueur's application of the differential gear to the rear axle of a carriage, 1822.

FIG. 43. First vehicle by Charles Dietz, patented February 6, 1835. The steam engine consists of two oscillating cylinders.

Pecqueur's ideas were not put into practice. Patents with the same specifications were taken out in England by Hanson in 1830 and Richard Roberts in 1832. In 1833 Roberts built an engine-driven vehicle equipped with a differential.

Around 1840 most English inventors were concentrating on railroads and locomotives, because of the already recognized effectiveness of the system, the profits that manufacturers expected from their development, and the heavy taxes levied on motor-driven road conveyances.

Prejudices and controls   In 1831 a House of Commons Committee was appointed to examine the conditions under which engine-driven vehicles could be used on toll roads. It recognized that such vehicles could travel 10 and even 20 miles an hour, whereas horses could not exceed 4 miles per hour.

Despite this favorable opinion on using the steam engine, it encountered prejudices: fears of the boilers exploding and reactions to its noise and soot. The successes after 1850 of Aveling, Burrell, Garrett, and Rickett in England and Fisher Dudgeon in the United States did not offset the current interest in railroads.

The 1861 Locomotive Act made the taxes on steam-traction highway vehicles uniform with horse-drawn ones but limited the speed of engine-driven vehicles to 10 mph on highways and 5 in cities. The law made obligatory a minimum of two persons to drive and light the vehicle and prohibited the emission of smoke.

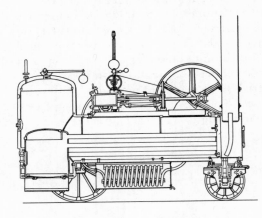

FIG. 44. Highway locomobile built by Cail in 1857. Tubular boiler and condenser. This type of locomobile evolved very little for almost a century.

The only road conveyances developed later were the locomobiles intended to pull agricultural machines and heavy loads (Figure 44), and these were strictly regulated in England. The Red Flag Act of 1865 limited their speed to 4 mph on highways and 2 in towns and villages. Each vehicle had to be accompanied by at least three persons, including one on foot, who had to precede the machine with an unfurled red flag at least 60 yards in front. These restrictions stopped the construction of steam-powered road vehicles in England. The locomobile became simply a practical method of moving a power source (for cutting, threshing, and the like) to the work site. It remained in use until the period between the two world wars—until electricity and the diesel engine were substituted for it.

Plate 23. The London-Birmingham steam coach, invented by Dr. Church in 1833. Color engraving published in Paris. French National Library, Print Collection. (Photo Ph. Brossé - P. U. F.)

Steam-powered automobiles   Inventors were not discouraged; on the Continent and in the United States many of them remained convinced that it was possible to apply a steam engine successfully to highway vehicles. During the second half of the nineteenth century steam-powered automobiles were built and sold for special purposes. Certain of these, notably those by Léon Serpollet, would have proved to be an effective solution to the problem of steam-powered highway transport if the internal combustion engine had not been invented at this time.

Progress in boilers and fireboxes enabled builders in the last quarter of the century to construct vehicles in many sizes, from the single-seater tricycle by Dion-Bouton and Trépardoux and Serpollet's two-seater to heavy vehicles with twelve seats by Amédée Bollée. Bollée, a bell-founder from Le Mans, was a pioneer, the first to build steam carriages able to cover fairly large distances at a steady pace. His most famous achievement was his first vehicle, the *Obéissante* of 1873, which covered 138 miles in 18 hours. Bollée equipped his vehicle with a Field boiler fed by a Giffard injector, used a Stephenson slide valve to control the steam supply, and devised many complicated but effective solutions to problems

FIG. 45. *La Mancelle* (1881), a steam-powered carriage by Amédée Bollée, was one of the most frequently built models. The Field-type boiler is placed in the rear, the two-cylinder steam engine up front. Transmission is by camshaft and differential gear.

of construction and operation. Various other vehicles built until around 1880 enjoyed varying success (Figure 45).

The best results were obtained by Serpollet, who around 1875 invented a boiler system consisting of a flattened tube coiled into a spiral, which caused instantaneous vaporization. In 1890 he went from Paris to Lyon on a three-wheeled vehicle equipped with his steam engine. Afterward he set up a factory in Paris to construct automobiles. Around 1900 it was producing approximately 200 cars annually, vehicles that easily competed with the gasoline cars of the time. In 1903 one of his models, equipped with pneumatic tires, a high-pressure superheating boiler, and a condenser, attained the speed of 80 mph. After Serpollet's death in 1907 the use of steam engines in automobiles disappeared from France for good.

Origin of the bicycle   The bicycle as we know it came into common use at the end of the nineteenth century, when rubber tires were perfected. But two-wheeled vehicles permitting movement along the road dates from a much earlier period. The first ancestor of the bicycle, then called a *célérifère* (from *célérité*, speed), probably dates from the closing years of the seventeenth century. Consisting of a horizontal bar that sometimes represented the body of an animal, it was supported by two wheels of equal height. The cyclist traveled by striking the ground first with one foot, then the other.

This device, which at the beginning was only a toy, nevertheless demonstrated an important mechanical principle: to move a weight by rolling it required less propulsion and permitted more rapid forward movement than did ordinary walking.

This machine was perfected by Baron Drais von Sauerbron, a farmer and engineer in Baden who died in Karlsruhe in 1851. He simplified the *célérifère* (which henceforth bore his name as *draisienne*) and mounted the fork of the front wheel on a spindle that let it turn (Figure 46). Thus the vehicle, still operated by the driver's feet alternately striking the ground, could be easily steered. In 1818 Drais himself exhibited his model in the Tivoli Gardens in Paris. A saddle replaced the bench or frame that had originally served as a seat. The machine was a sensation in England and France. The English followed the design in the hobbyhorse but made it of iron, reducing the weight and giving it more elegant lines.

This fashion was already forgotten when a Parisian locksmith named Ernest Michaux conceived in 1855 the idea of fitting pedals to the hub of the front wheel, which made it possible to drive the vehicle without touching the ground (Figure 47). The Michaux velocipede enjoyed much success during the Second Empire.

FIG. 46. The *draisienne,* a vehicle in use around 1825–1830. The front fork pivots around its vertical axle. The steering consists of a simple straight bar perpendicular to the plane of the figure at the upper end of the axle of the front fork.

The frame was lightened and several other improvements were quickly made: a steel strip carried the seat and rubber rims and a brake shoe were controlled from the steering device by a cord on the back wheel. Production began in England after the war of 1870, which had caused financial difficulties for the Michaux enterprise.

Builders now began to think of attaching the pedals to a crank gear fixed to the center of the vehicle under the frame and of using a chain connecting the toothed pinion on the crank gear to another on the hub of the back wheel. In France the clockmaker André Guilmet designed this arrangement in 1869, and a mechanic named Meyer built the first one (Figure 48).

The next stage in the evolution of the bicycle concerned wheel construction. Between 1870 and 1880 the spokes became thin steel rods held by tension between

FIG. 47. Michaux's velocipede, 1865. The machine has a prop to facilitate starting from a stopped position. The brake on the rear wheel is operated by a cord that rolls around the steering, the bar of which is able to turn around its horizontal axle.

FIG. 48. Meyer's chain bicycle, 1869.

FIG. 49. Rudge's bicycle, 1887. The wheels have steel spokes.

the hub and the rim. This lightweight system made it possible to enlarge the front-wheel diameter of classic velocipedes so as to increase the ratio between the crank gear and the driving wheel. The result was the type of bicycle popularized under the names *grand-bi* in France, *penny-farthing* in England, and *ordinary* in the United States, which enjoyed a certain success as a curiosity piece for twenty to thirty years (Figure 49). For normal use, gearing down by a chain offered great advantages that made possible the commercial development of the bicycle in every country of the world, once final improvements had turned it into a practical and cheap method of individual transportation. The history of the last phase of its development is marked by legal problems and claims of priority. The use of steel ball bearings on a velocipede after 1869 seems clearly attributable to Jules Suriray. Around 1890 Dunlop reinvented pneumatic tires, which Thomson had already conceived in 1845. The Michelin removable pneumatic tire had its first success in 1891 with the victory of Jiel-Laval in the Paris-Brest race.

This invention now seems to us to be associated with a number of picturesque events, but it nevertheless proved of considerable economic and social importance in the opening years of the twentieth century.

CHAPTER 2

RIVERS, CANALS, AND PORTS

I N THE EIGHTEENTH CENTURY rivers were still the most widely used method of reaching the hinterlands and transporting merchandise and travelers, but their flow did not always permit rapid movement, and floods and summer droughts prevented boats from navigating them.

The problem of controlling the flow of streams and rivers was not attacked until mechanical means made dredging effective and methods of building dams and quays had been perfected. Still, in the absence of suitable roads in the eighteenth and even at the beginning of the nineteenth century, rivers made significant transportation possible.

On the Loire, for example, numerous flat-bottomed barges with square sails could be seen traveling up and down the river. They carried wood and coal from the Forez, agricultural products from the Charolais and Bourbonnais regions, grains from Beauce, and wines from Touraine and Anjou, and they brought the products of the Levant and the Americas to the interior of the country. Despite the slowness of the voyage, travelers sometimes preferred the river to the road, which was less safe and more tiring. About 18 miles a day could be covered downstream. The trip from Orléans to Nantes required an average of about 10 days.

The next chapter examines how ocean and river steam navigation was born. In 1832 the first steamboat service between Orléans and Nantes was organized, offering greatly improved transportation. The trip took only two days, but there were accidents and boiler explosions that alarmed the public. Better-designed boats, the *inexplosibles*, were then constructed and restored public confidence. In 1843 more than 100,000 passengers patronized the various navigation companies operating between Moulins and Nantes.

Railroads, which were faster and more regular, dealt a decisive blow to this traffic. Steamboats were abolished and sailing ships now served only for minor local trade in sand and fish. The last steamship company on the Loire suspended operations in 1862.

Steam navigation was introduced on the Seine long before it began on other French rivers. Claude Jouffroy d'Abbans (1751–1832), the first man in France to put a steamboat into service (1783), was not discouraged by difficulties in his early steam navigation experiments. After his return from exile following the French Revolution he resumed his experiments, but not until after 1816 was he able to put them into effect. In that year in Bercy he launched a ship, the *Charles-Philippe,* the prototype for a series of other boats with which a financial group proposed to

271

establish regular service on the Seine. But the royal license granted to Jouffroy did not give him exclusive rights, and the Société Pajol, incorporated at this time, deprived him of any profit from it. Before launching the *Charles-Philippe* this company had imported from London the *Elise,* the first steamship to cross the English Channel. Several months later it made the return journey, after operating for a short time between Rouen and Elbeuf. The first two Seine navigation companies met with serious financial difficulties.

After 1830 public service was established by private companies on all major waterways in France, and in particular on the Seine and its principal tributaries. This period was one of great prosperity for Cavé's firm, which built many river-boats equipped with his steam engine with an oscillating cylinder.

Navigation on the Rhône was still more difficult. This river, an extension of the Saône, offered an exceptional route communicating between the Mediterranean ports and the interior of France. Difficulties in navigating the Rhône were many: periods of low water, instability of the riverbed, gravel banks obstructing its flow, and a swift current. From early times until the use of steamboats became general, towing had been done by teams of horses and oxen. Strings of barges towed like this required 28 to 30 days to travel from Arles to Lyon under the best conditions, and in winter more than two months were sometimes necessary. In the middle of the nineteenth century teams of 30 to 40 horses could still be seen pulling 6 boats carrying a total of 300 to 400 tons. Plans for building a lateral canal, which had long been suggested, were not begun until after 1870.

CANALS

As discussed in Volume II, canals were dug quite early in France, which until the middle of the eighteenth century maintained its lead as the country pioneering in canalization. Construction techniques developed during the seventeenth century—including methods of building locks and aqueducts, reservoirs, catchment basins, siphons for small waterways, and so on—were solidly developed, not to change until modern times.

Despite her lead, France continued to dig canals before and after the period of the Revolutionary and Napoleonic wars. The Canal du Centre at Charolais, constructed under Gauthey's direction in 1783, contributed greatly to the industrial development of the Creusot region. The building of large reservoirs, like that at Torcy (built from 1794 to 1800), which held reserves of 7,062,660 cubic yards of water, was necessary to feed it. This volume was increased to 9,940,040 cubic yards in 1836 and again increased in 1860 and later between 1876 and 1892.

Napoleon added 120 miles of canals—the Saint-Quentin canal and the one between Mons and Condé—to the 600 miles already in existence. In 1821 and 1822 loans were authorized to finish the Rhône-Rhine, Nantes-Brest, Somme, Burgundy, Nivernais, Berry, Ille, and Rance canals. An aqueduct was built on the Armance near Saint-Florentin with five arches each 19 feet wide for a canal 17 feet wide bordered by two towpaths each 8 feet wide.

The Burgundy canal, completed in 1834 over a distance of 148 miles, spanned a change in altitude of more than a half mile between Laroche (Yonne)

Plate 24. *Bound Down the River*. Lithograph by Currier and Ives, 1870. The canal traffic shows steam navigation as against flatboats. Library of Congress

and Saint-Jean-de-Losne (Saône), via the valleys of the Armançon and the Ouche. At 1,241 feet it passed through a tunnel two miles long, and it had a total of 189 locks. This example gives some idea of the size of projects carried out in this period.

The English canal network In 1759 not a single canal had as yet been dug in England, despite the development of industry and the growth of economic activity. The large estuaries which cut deeply into the country, and the fairly flat valleys which linked the various regions provided relatively easy means of communication. Active coastwise shipping facilitated transporting heavy materials. The only canal projects carried out in the first part of the eighteenth century affected some rivers, as for example the Mersey, to improve connections between Liverpool and Manchester.

More intensive exploitation of coal deposits around the mid-eighteenth century changed the economic problem of transportation. It was easy to see that

FIG. 50. Network of the Grand Trunk Canal between Liverpool, Hull, and Bristol. Construction began in 1766.

canals making direct connections would significantly lower the cost of coal to localities where it was used. This was demonstrated by the duke of Bridgewater, the owner of the Worsley mines near Manchester, who in 1759 had a canal dug to connect his mine with Manchester and so develop the mine, which had been difficult because of the high cost of transporting coal by road (9 to 10 shillings per ton for a distance of only 7 miles).

Building the canal was entrusted to James Brindley, an excellent engineer totally lacking in theoretical knowledge. This man, who was later given the task of building the Mersey Canal and then the Grand Trunk Canal, became an excellent adviser to the duke of Bridgewater. He pointed out the disadvantage of using a certain stream, for whose conversion preparations were under way, to link Worsley and Manchester, and he designed a waterway that was level along its entire length.

This first canal, completed in 1761, aroused the admiration of Brindley's contemporaries. Near Worsley it passed directly through the coal deposits, and at the outskirts of Manchester it crossed the Irwell, a tributary of the Mersey, on an aqueduct 39 feet high. No lock had been necessary, in accordance with Brindley's principle.

The two other canals which he built or began before his death in 1772 were constructed on the same principle. The duke of Bridgewater supplied the funds for the Mersey Canal (1766/67), which was a larger undertaking, but the result was the same: the cost of transporting goods was cut in half.

The Grand Trunk Canal from the Mersey to the Trent was intended to link the Irish Sea with the North Sea. It was dug for a distance of 89 miles, during the eleven years from 1766 to 1777. The canal formed the key section of the network that quickly developed to link the Severn and Bristol area in the south to the Mersey and Liverpool and the Humber River and Hull on the North Sea (Figure 50). The network was then completed around Birmingham and was in particular connected with the Thames before the end of the eighteenth century. In the same period similar projects were undertaken in Scotland and Wales, and canal mileage increased rapidly throughout Great Britain.

The economic value of British canals diminished toward the mid-nineteenth century, largely because the railroad network grew as feverishly as had canals after the initial impetus by the duke of Bridgewater. Building the railroad network was also facilitated by the existence of canals, for which the most convenient routes had in every case been selected.

Internal navigation in the United States

The development of steam navigation in the United States led to more communication by waterways. In 1807, to everyone's surprise, Robert Fulton succeeded in traveling up the Hudson as far as Albany and in establishing a regular service to that city, as we shall later see.

Until then, flatboats linked New Orleans and Pittsburgh on the Mississippi and Ohio. Towing was still necessary for upstream traffic. Three to four months were required for the trip, which cost $160, but as soon as steamboats could make this trip the cost fell to $30. By 1825, 125 steamboats were competing with barges on the Mississippi.

Eastern ports needed connections with the Great Lakes in order to keep their business in the North, which was being lost to the South. The Erie Canal from Buffalo on Lake Erie to Albany on the Hudson was opened in 1825. The cost of transportation from New York to Buffalo fell from $100 to $5 and the length of the trip from 20 to 6 days. The development of such cities as Buffalo, Cleveland, Detroit, and Chicago followed. Each state tried to have its own canal in order to obtain increased traffic, but in this rivalry the canals very shortly encountered a new competitor, railroads.

Linking interior means of communication with ports Roads and waterways served to move domestic trade, but they had to be linked with ocean routes for importing and exporting. The possibility of improving a river down to a port or of linking the port with internal networks by a canal had to be considered along with the construction of the port itself.

Well-developed techniques for doing this, the economic possibilities of the regions, and the individual interests of the areas through which the canals passed made it possible to draw up definite plans. Without lingering over developments dependent on the economies of the countries concerned, it is instructive to recall

Plate 25. The canal-bridge at Barton. From an engraving published in 1784. (Photo Radio Times Hulton Picture Library, London.)

the strange attempt to develop the Somme into a major route to penetrate into the heart of France.

The port of Amiens was extremely active until the end of the eighteenth century, despite the difficulties of navigating the Somme, such as the shallows in Picquigny. But in this period these difficulties were still less than those encountered in traveling on bad roads.

The traffic came up from Saint-Valéry, at the mouth of the Somme, bringing with it colonial wares then transported by wagon from Amiens to Paris. The river brought in alcohol and metals and carried away fabrics destined for Spain, Italy, England, Holland, and Germany.

The idea of seeing the Somme assume the role of a great commercial route gained increasing ground. As early as the end of the seventeenth century its users demanded that a continuous waterway be built between the English Channel and Paris, so connecting the Oise with the Somme seemed an easy and inexpensive solution.

Plans were drawn up in 1716 and 1721 and a concession for a canal from Saint-Quentin to the Oise was granted in 1724. But Crozat, one of the promoters, laid out another route during 1729–1731, which followed the low-lying area between Saint-Simon and Fargniers, and the work was carried out.

In 1821 the same ideas were revived. It was expected that this link via the canals and the Somme would take over the trade up the Seine toward Paris. But in fact the condition of the Somme did not permit major traffic, and silting in the bay of the Somme relegated Saint-Valéry to secondary traffic, and the Somme downstream from Amiens was reduced to a subordinate role.

PORTS

From the middle of the eighteenth century two problems in building ports had to be faced: increasing sizes of ships, and the silting up of rivers, which made it more difficult to build ports at their mouths.

Le Havre profited by the silting up of small streams that had earlier caused the disappearance of Lillebonne and destruction of Honfleur. Being closer to the sea, Le Havre could without undue effort cut an entrance channel into the old basin through the alluvium and dredge out a new harbor.

The ports established in deep rias or inlets, as Brest for example, did not yet need dikes to set up well-sheltered harbors; the Brest shipyard easily held its own and continued to develop. Huge buildings were constructed on the banks of the Penfeld, with solid foundations and majestic lines that gave Brest the imposing appearance characteristic of it until 1944: it had workshops, a general warehouse (built 1744–1764), upper and lower ropewalks (1,230 and 1,286 feet long respectively), a hospital, and a jail made necessary because galleys had been abolished.

Elsewhere, hilly windings of the Salou River were leveled and graving docks (a type of dry dock) were dug into the rock. The harbor at Brest, the first constructed in a French military port (1683–1687), was improved several times and enlarged shortly after 1850. When leveled, the flat-topped embankment of the Salou made it possible to construct a small dock there (1822–1827), and after 1858 a double dock 768 feet long with three movable gates able to take two vessels or a single large one. The builders had in mind the dimensions of the *Great Eastern*. On the right bank, almost opposite the old harbor of Brest, the Pontaniou graving docks had already been dug into the rock, from 1742 to 1751 and 1807 to 1820.

The stocks could be seen along the entire length of the Penfeld, with their inclined ramps on which wooden vessels under construction remained for a long time. The boats, there for years at a time, were protected by temporary wooden roofs that sheltered the hulls from the weather.

Lorient

The first port established at the mouth of the Blavet was what is now Port-Louis, a small fortress overlooking the sheltered roadstead in the river. At the beginning of the seventeenth century a number of merchants who were developing the India trade, finding themselves too crowded under the fortress, settled upriver on the right bank of the Scorff, where they were able to spread out on unused land and were more sheltered than at the mouth of the stream. A new Compagnie des Indes was established here in 1664, and by the end of the century the town had 700 families.

By the middle of the eighteenth century the Compagnie had reached its peak of prosperity, owning 35 vessels or frigates and many other ships. The capture of Bengal by the English in 1753 dealt a lethal blow to the Compagnie des Indes, which was abolished in 1769. The port of Lorient and the India Company buildings were repurchased by the king, thus establishing the military shipyard at Lorient.

Buildings erected earlier remained in existence, as for example the general warehouse dating from 1733. Dock No. 1, the Clermont-Tonnerre, was begun in 1822; its 281 feet in length and 75½ feet in width were adequate for wooden ships. It must be noted that instead of building wooden vessels out in the open, Lorient at the beginning of the nineteenth century was building them under a permanent roof laid on 16 granite piers 31 feet high. The stocks were 233 feet long and 82 feet wide.

Activity increased in the port, and the space on the right bank of the Scorff became too crowded; only two small stocks could be built near the covered stocks. The area on the left bank, where the natural slope of the land made it easy to set up several stocks at Caudan, was taken over.

Here, later, the first armored ship with an iron hull was built, the *Couronne,* one of the *Gloire* series. The demands of such new building programs at Caudan required new workshops. Thus the military port was established along its major lines, which remained intact until the bombardments of World War II.

Geographical and political needs led to new ports being planned under conditions less favorable from the point of view of the available site. The construction of the port of Cherbourg, for instance, occupied the end of the eighteenth century and the entire first half of the nineteenth.

Cherbourg

It is possible that after the Roman Conquest Cherbourg may have been a *castellum,* an operating base and site for observing the strait. But the original port was Saint-Martin, a natural cove east of the Cotentin Peninsula, protected from the sea by the cape of La Hague; small boats can still find shelter there today.

This shelter was inadequate for full-sized ships, and the Hogue disaster in 1692, a naval victory by the English and Dutch over the fleet of Tourville, had demonstrated the danger of not having a shelter for a fleet seeking refuge. It was thus necessary to create a sheltered roadstead sufficiently deep to permit entrance by ships of the line.

Vauban's first idea was to build two breakwaters—one a quarter of a mile long at the tip of Le Homet and the other three-quarters of a mile long at Pelée Island. The two embankments would form a screen against winds off the ocean and would leave a channel more than a mile wide between them. Actually, this was a poor scheme, since the depth of the roadstead was too shallow for large vessels, which would have had to remain in the open sea without protection. The project was not carried out, and Vauban limited himself to opening access to a small commercial port able to receive coastal vessels. Docks, locks, and quays were built, but they were of no use to warships.

In 1775 the post captain, one de La Bretonnière, showed the need for a large port with breakwaters built in the deep sea and a roadstead twice as large as envisioned by Vauban. This was an elaborate project, considered at first to be extreme and impossible to build.

However, the major outlines of the project were adopted but modified to form a single breakwater leaving a channel between each end and the mainland. This is the profile of the breakwater still in existence. The problem was to build it, a situation seemingly incommensurate with the technical means then available. The breakwater had to be built at a depth of 67 feet in a sea that was often turbulent.

Similar projects had been built by the Romans but in much shallower depths, as for example the breakwaters in Ostia and Civitavecchia, whose construction Pliny the Younger had observed. They were constructed by throwing stones pell-mell into the sea or by sinking boats filled with stones in order to form a small island or pierheads.

These methods worked only in shallow depths, but even so, Cherbourg tried to use these ancient methods of sinking boats filled with rough stone. It was hoped that sinking an entire fleet would form a strong core covered with *pierres-perdues*. When it had accumulated to low-tide level the superstructure was to be built, of masonry. But the ships' hulks were quickly dislodged by the sea and the stones scattered, without result.

The next idea was to build a segmented breakwater of individual cones made of large, ballasted timberwork sections meeting at their bases but with spaces between their tops (Figure 51). This was the original conception of de Cessart, chief engineer in the comptroller's office in Rouen, who had already made himself famous by overcoming difficulties involved in building the bridge at Tours in 1781.

FIG. 51. Frame cone used by de Cessart in building the Cherbourg dike.

The cones were to have an average height of 66 feet and a diameter of 148 feet at the base and 66 feet at the apex. They were to be filled with stone up to low-tide level, with concrete above that level and up to the top, and on the peak were to have a coping of cut stone. Ninety contiguous cones would have been required, with the large gaps between the cones at sea level to be closed by iron chains to prevent the passage of small boats. This discontinuous breakwater would disseminate the waves' force and ensure calm water in the roadstead.

The first cone was built in Le Havre, then dismantled and shipped to Cherbourg on barges and reassembled in the cove of Chantereyne. The other cones were built on the beach, then set afloat with a girdle of empty barrels, towed to their location, and quickly filled with blocks of stone to send them to the bottom.

It was one of the great attractions of the time, with people coming from everywhere to admire this enormous construction site. The Court and the king paid a visit with due ceremony, and paintings and drawings made this extraordinary work universally known. This publicity led to the common belief that de Cessart's plan had been successful and had made possible the construction of the Cherbourg breakwater.

But this was not the case—it was a failure, even a series of failures. The first caisson, built at Le Havre, was launched on November 8, 1782. Transported to Cherbourg and reassembled there, it was damaged by a violent storm in September 1783, which delayed its emplacement until June 6, 1784. A second caisson, contiguous to the first, was emplaced on July 7, but on August 18 its upper portion was broken up by a storm before it had received its stone ballast, and it was destroyed down to low-tide level.

It was then noticed that the stones dispersed around the broken caisson would make it impossible to submerge a third cone next to the second, and since work could be done only at spring tide, building the breakwater with the planned 90 cones would require 18 to 20 years of work and enormous expense.

It was decided to space the cones at intervals of 30 *toises* (192 feet), then 200 *toises* (1,276 feet), and 18 cones were submerged one after the other at varying intervals. The spaces between cones were filled with stones, abandoning the principle of the grillwork breakwater. Isolated and incompletely filled, most caissons were demolished and the wood was attacked by shipworms and quickly destroyed.

The idea of the caisson system was given up, and in 1789 they were all cut down to low-tide level. A single caisson preserved at the east end of the breakwater to mark the channel was demolished on February 12, 1799. Engineers were obliged to return to the *pierres-perdues* system, which was from then on considered the only method offering a chance of success. The original plan called for an inside slope inclined at a 45° angle and an outer one facing out to sea, with a slope three times its height.

Experience showed which sizes of blocks to use and how storms would change the profiles of the breakwaters, ultimately giving the slopes a shape that would remain stable.

The work was laborious and resulted in many accidents. Workers were knocked down and carried away by the sea; half-finished barracks and batteries were leveled several times by waves. On the fatal night of February 12, 1808, the work crew and troops quartered in the forts were carried away by the sea, and most drowned. But Napoleon was anxious to finish this gigantic project and persisted. It was not completed until 1833.

Plymouth   The construction of the Cherbourg breakwater, which was clearly and openly undertaken with intent to attack England, was watched by the English with apprehension. They began without delay in 1812 to build a breakwater protecting the Plymouth roadstead (Figure 52).

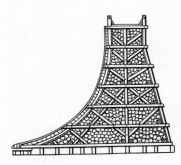

FIG. 52.   A stone and frame dike showing the English system of construction.

This gave rise years later to a controversy over construction methods and costs for the two projects. The English maintained that their methods were more economical and that their project had been better managed, "in strange contrast to the multitude of unforeseen events, the time, and the ostentation involved in the construction at Cherbourg."

In France, Baron Cachin replied with a paper presented to the Académie des Sciences in 1819, which purportedly showed that costs were 8,717 francs per linear meter for the Cherbourg breakwater as against 16,691 francs for the Plymouth one, but it is difficult to vouch for the accuracy of these figures. Cachin more rightly pointed out that the Cherbourg breakwater, whose slopes varied with their elevations, had acquired permanent stability under the impact of successive storms, but the Plymouth one, with a slope uniform on both faces, had not stabilized, despite its being better sheltered from the action of the sea. Experience proved this to be true, for storms caused crumbling of the upper portion and modified the slopes (Figure 53).

The difficulties met with during these projects taught builders much about the action of the sea on works of this nature, for they led to a firm comprehension of the design of the revetments.

The Cherbourg breakwater lies at average depths of from 39 to 43 feet below low-tide marks, and 66 feet above the highest tides. It is approximately 2⅓ miles long at its base and 2-1/5 miles at the peak, and it consists of two branches forming an obtuse angle. It has forts at the center and at each end. Most characteristic from the technical point of view is that no formula was available to estimate the appropriate size of the blocks and stones to be used or of the slopes to be exposed to the sea's action. Despite many experiments a valid theory for the movement of

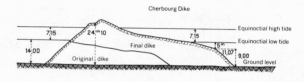

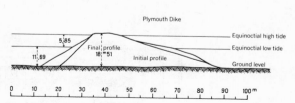

FIG. 53. Comparison of the profiles of the Cherbourg and Plymouth dikes.

water molecules in the waves attacking the structure had not yet been formulated. Gerstner's paper on the movement of molecules and trochoidal shape of the swell remained unknown, and was not rediscovered until after the mid-nineteenth century. Thus, with the projects at Cherbourg and Plymouth trial and error alone demonstrated those contours that would keep their form despite assaults by the sea.

DRY DOCKS

It was easy to build and use docks in Atlantic and Channel ports because of the strong tides; we have mentioned the construction of several docks at Brest, which were cut into the rock. At Cherbourg during the Napoleonic period a dock similarly dug in the ocean floor was filled with water on the occasion of a voyage by Empress Marie-Louise in 1813.

In the Mediterranean the problem was more difficult because of the absence of tides. Given the lack of adequate pumps, it was impossible to operate in the same way as in the north and west of France. The history of the construction of the first dock at Toulon is therefore of special technical interest.

In 1774 the port of Toulon had no dock in which ships could be careened and reconditioned. Every maritime nation had facilities for maintaining vessels: Brest, for instance, had several. But since such facilities depended on the tides, they could be used only at high tide (that is, 10 to 12 days out of the month) and even less in the case of a 90- or 100-gun ship. The problem in the Mediterranean appeared to be insoluble; an attempt to build a dock at Cartagena had been extremely costly and had resulted in failure.

Maurepas had thought of digging a dock at La Seyne, but it would have been necessary to build a fortification. The architect Laurent had suggested digging the dock at Castigneau, which at that time appeared to be somewhat odd, except for the defense of the city and port. One incident demonstrated the urgency of finding a solution. The *Souverain* had been in dry dock for three years, its timbers working loose and the ship itself acquiring a disturbing cant of about 32 inches. It was decided to send the ship to Brest, but it could not withstand a spell of heavy weather and was forced to return to Toulon.

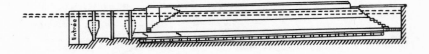

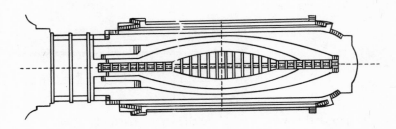

FIG. 54.   Drydock in the port of Toulon, built by Groignard between 1774 and 1778.

Groignard, an engineer and builder since 1754, offered a new suggestion (Figure 54) that was approved by the king in February 1774 and by the naval council in March. Upon being consulted, the Académie des Sciences said that the construction principle had already been applied to a wall at Toulon, to Westminster Bridge in 1750, and to various other works. It involved building the dock in a vast, watertight wooden caisson grounded on the ocean floor. The contract for the construction, using stones from Cassis, was signed on April 7, 1774.

The resistance of the dredged and leveled floor was checked every 3 square feet with a ram weighing 6,600 pounds. The 300-foot-long and 100-foot-wide caisson was built on rafts, then submerged and fixed in place on the floor by 120 pilings. Six months later it showed no signs of either disintegration or deformation.

Complete success crowned this project, with which Groignard's name became associated. The cost of the operation had been 3 million *livres,* whereas at Cartagena 12 million had been wasted.

From records it appears that the construction was not completed until 1778 and that the *Souverain* was the first ship to enter the dock, where its repair work could finally be completed.

LIGHTHOUSES

The eighteenth century saw important improvements in lighthouses, specifically in the construction of their towers and in their lamps, which produced a steadier and brighter light.

Lighthouses such as the Saint Agnes one in the Scilly Isles, built in 1680, still had coal fires, which in this case had burned for more than a hundred years. This primitive, crude system could not be used for lighthouses moored at sea—in the first three Eddystone lighthouses candles were the only alternative.

Smeaton used 24 candles arranged in 2 rows, but even in the clearest weather their range was hardly more than 4 or 5 miles, and it is surprising that in a lighthouse whose construction was so costly it was necessary to use so limited a light source.

The Argand wick lamp   The first burner suitable for use in lighthouses was invented in 1782 by Aimé Argand; it burned oil through a circular burner that passed an air current up its center.

Aimé Argand, of Swiss origin, had come to Paris to study physical and chemical science. He began to analyze the properties of combustion and in 1780 replaced the standard thick, unplaited cotton wick with a flat one held in a perforated circular burner. Air rose through the channel in the center, providing better oil combustion. In addition, Argand placed a metal chimney over his lamp, making it draw faster and giving the flame a more brilliant glow. When it became possible to make heat-resistant glass chimneys Argand substituted them for metal cylinders.

In 1782 Argand presented his device to the Province of Languedoc, which admired this invention that gave a bright light without smoke. In 1783 he offered it to the City of Paris for street lighting but was unsuccessful there and met with no better luck in England. He nevertheless obtained a license in Paris, but his lamp was copied by a pharmacist named Quinquet, whose name rather than that of the true inventor became nationally associated with this invention.

Oil was supplied to the burner from a tank placed at a higher level. Carcel improved this by placing the tank under the burner and using a small pump to feed the oil. The pump was operated by a winch driven by the hot-air current from the chimney.

This invention had important results. First of all, it gave a steady, clearer light than earlier lamps and required only simple maintenance. The light source was more concentrated, which made it possible to use reflectors or lenses to direct the light beam and prevent its being dispersed, giving greater range. In addition— and this is not without importance—the size of the wick and the quantity of oil consumed made it possible to define a lighting unit, since the quantities of light produced could be better defined.

The *carcel*, the first unit to be defined, was decided to be the luminous intensity of a lamp with a burner 12 mm. in diameter, which burned 42 grams of rapeseed oil per hour.

Arago and Augustin Fresnel perfected the Carcel lamp by giving it several concentric wicks. The flame was surrounded with a glass topped by a tinplate pipe that let the draft be quickened and regulated (Figure 55).

Up to ten concentric wicks were placed in later lamps. At first vegetable (colza) or fish oil was burned, and after 1850 mineral oils were used. In England the first such oil burned was a light one produced by distilling Scottish shale.

Optical devices   The oil lamp permitted light to be concentrated into a more powerful beam with parabolic reflectors, which came quickly into use. The lamp was placed at their focal point.

Reflectors had already been used in Mersey lighthouses by 1763, where they were made of small, flat mirrors of silvered glass approximately 1.5 by .5 inches

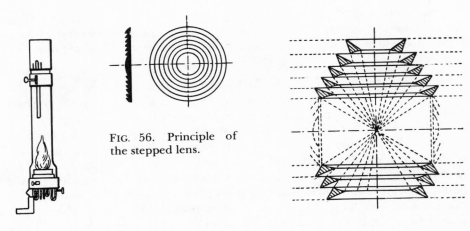

FIG. 56. Principle of
the stepped lens.

FIG. 55. Argand
lamp for lighthouses.

FIG. 57. Fresnel lens; drum
with stationary lights.

arranged tangentially on the theoretical contour of the paraboloid. A few mirrors of this type, with 18-inch openings, are still in use, containing up to 600 of these small facets. The still very primitive lamp used with these reflectors was a burner with a flat wick fed by an oil tank placed behind the reflector. This was the imperfect prototype of the lamps with parabolic reflectors.

The greatest improvement made to the optics of lighthouses was Augustin Fresnel's system designed in 1820 and applied in 1822. This was the dioptric, or refracting, system, which transmitted light better than the catoptric, or reflecting, system of mirrors. The idea had originated with Buffon, who was not able to develop it; Fresnel perfected it, using a system of annular lenses (Figure 56).

When a lamp is placed at the focal point of a lens the light rays are concentrated in a parallel line, forming a ray that collects all the light emitted. But to use the entire field of light a wide-angle lens would be required, whose thickness would absorb too much of the light. Fresnel conceived the idea of using lenses whose thickness decreased toward the center, the outer rings being stepped. This method of grinding lenses eliminated excessive absorption and made the device lighter. Total-reflection prisms were mounted on the outside portions and were arranged in steps above the rings of the lenses in the catadioptic system.

So that a stationary source could emit light in all directions, the glass was assembled around the vertical axis, producing a revolving glass surface that formed the whole optical apparatus (Figure 57).

The first devices designed by Fresnel were formed from small elements with plane surfaces located tangentially to the theoretical profiles. However, complete optics corresponding to the theoretical profiles of the lenses and prisms were soon being built.

In 1782 Lemoyne suggested using lights that flashed at regular intervals, every lighthouse having its distinguishing rhythm. A Swede conceived of rotating screens to cut off the light regularly. But lamps with glass optics provided a better solution. It was sufficient to rotate around the light source an apparatus consisting

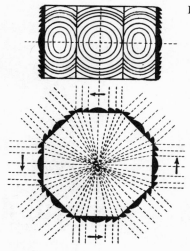

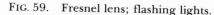

FIG. 58.   Fresnel lens; occulted lights.

FIG. 59.   Fresnel lens; flashing lights.

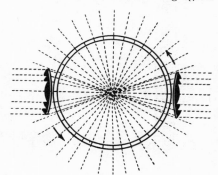

of a crown of stepped lenses with flat inside faces. This concentrated the ray of light through the optic, and the rotation caused the intensity of light to vary regularly in a given direction (Figure 58). Flashing lights were obtained by reducing the crown to two diametrically opposed lenses (Figure 59).

Fresnel's system of oil lamps and optics was a major contribution to the power and regularity of warning lights in lighthouses. Not until after 1850 was the candlepower increased further, by electric-powered lamps.

Before 1850 lighthouses were classified into four or five types, depending on their candlepower. For example, a turning light of the first class was equipped with eight large lenses and the internal diameter of the optical apparatus measured 6 feet; its maximum candlepower was 4,000 *carcels,* and the lamp consumed 750 grams of oil per hour.

Masonry lighthouses   In order to increase the range of the light's beam the light had to be placed at the highest possible point. Thus came the necessity, early recognized, to place the lantern at the top of a tower, which could be set up on a coastline, an island, or an isolated rock, either submerged or projecting. In the first two cases the tower had only to withstand the winds, which are often violent near the sea. In the third case it had to hold up against breakers, so it had to be stronger, since experience had demonstrated the danger of having structures too light.

The tower exposed only to wind could thus be regarded as not noticeably different from ordinary buildings. Accommodations for the keepers were included, either in the tower itself (as at Les Héaux-de-Bréhat, ca. 1840; Figure 60) or in buildings around the tower, as at Barfleur (Figure 61).

If the structure was erected on a cliff high above the water, as at La Hève, the height of the masonry work could be reduced (Figure 62).

It has always been difficult to build towers on isolated rocks that projected little or not at all above the open sea. This technique was worked out especially during the eighteenth century and became more common in the nineteenth,

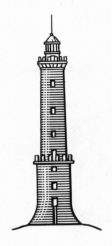

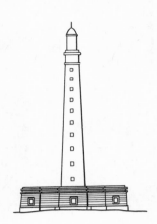

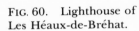

FIG. 60.   Lighthouse of   FIG. 61.   Barfleur lighthouse.   FIG. 62.   La Hève
Les Héaux-de-Bréhat.   lighthouse.

thanks to steamboats to supply construction sites and mechanical devices such as winches and drills.

The building of the various Eddystone lights, described in Volume II, illustrates the difficulties of this type of construction. The first two towers were of wood, and the first was carried away in 1709 after only five years, the second in 1755, after forty-six years.

Within four years a third tower was built, by Smeaton, the first to be guided in this construction by scientific principles. The outline of his tower was hyperbolic, giving the effect of a tree rising out of the earth. It was built entirely of stone assembled by dovetailing and strengthened at each story by an iron girdle embedded in the masonry (Figure 63).

The tower was 85 feet high. It withstood the sea, but the rock began to crumble away under the foundation, so a new lighthouse was built in 1882. Taking into consideration the knowledge available at the time, Smeaton's work, which was different from his predecessors', seems sound.

Smeaton himself realized that the theoretical design of the tower was not the best, "that a stronger wave (the tenth) rose to a height double that of the tower, enveloping it as if with a curtain and hiding it completely."

It has since been appreciated that a sea swell in which wavelengths, differing by one-tenth, were combined, gave rise to a wave motion variable in height with a maximum in every tenth wave.

The Wolf Rock lighthouse, built the same way, receives directly the Atlantic's swells from gales to the southwest and faces the same wave phenomena.

The Bell Rock light, or Inchcape Rock, was built with a similar contour. This tower, marking the approaches to the Firth of Forth and Tay River, became famous at the beginning of the nineteenth century as the first light in Scotland to be built on an isolated rock under such difficult conditions. It was planned by Robert Stephenson, who was inspired by Smeaton's design for Eddystone. The

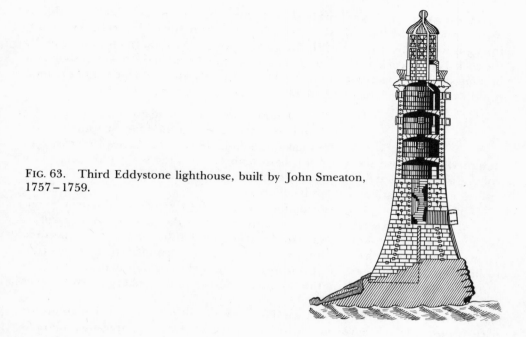

FIG. 63. Third Eddystone lighthouse, built by John Smeaton, 1757–1759.

tower was 115 feet high and Stephenson increased the diameter of the base to 42 feet, which made it possible to have five instead of four rooms there.

The Bell Rock work was even more difficult than at Eddystone, for the rock

Plate 26. Minot's Ledge lighthouse. Lithograph by E. Burrill after A. Frank, 1860. Library of Congress

was above water for only a short period of time, whereas Smeaton had been able to work as soon as the half tide set in. Four years were required for its construction; the light went into service in February 1811. A floating shop moored in front of the rock during work on the foundations was transferred to the tower as soon as it became sheltered from the tides. During the first season of construction the men could work only during a total of 140 hours.

The effects of swell and wind
The contour adopted by Smeaton and repeated by Stephenson was later modified for the fourth Eddystone light, built in 1882 by Sir James Douglas, who designed a solid, strong cylindrical base against which the sea could break. The volume and weight of the tower were considerably increased, and waves reached it only after their first impact had been broken.

Only very incomplete information was available during the nineteenth century on the forces exerted by the wind (and still less by the sea) on masonry works. Because of a lack of coherent wave theory (Gerstner's 1806 theory did not become known until after 1850), very few experiments had determined the force exerted by breakers and the intensity of this force continued to be poorly understood. It was belatedly realized only in the twentieth century that breakers exerted forces greater than did regular waves.

Quite inadequate figures for wind forces were adopted in the calculations for such projects, which gave rise to serious mistakes. One example was Thomas Bouch's bridge over the Tay, which was destroyed by a storm shortly after its construction.

It was recognized only very slowly that wind gusts can produce stresses of 600 pounds and more per square yard on a cylindrical tower, which corresponds to a wind velocity of more than 120 mph. Léonor Fresnel estimated that where lighthouses were built on a rock and subject to wave action, it was necessary to think in terms of a force at least five times greater than the strongest winds. Miscalculations were still being made in the nineteenth century and it was necessary to reinforce lighthouses built on bases that were too narrow, like the Ar-Men one, which had to be reinforced in the twentieth century.

A few figures from Quinette de Rochemont give the construction specifications for the masonry bases of lighthouses and how these specifications evolved during the nineteenth century.

Lighthouse	Date of Completion	Height above the foundation (in meters)	Volume of masonry (in cubic meters)	Ratio of base to height of tower (per meter)
France:				
La Hague	1837	47	1,664	35.4
Les Héaux-de-Bréhat	1840	48.50	1,848	38.1
England:				
Eddystone	1759	23.30	378	16.2
	1882	45.80	1,845	40.3
Bell Rock	1810	34.50	808	22.8
Skerry Were	1843	44.05	1,659	37.6

LIGHTSHIPS

In areas with neither small islands nor a nearby coast, such as in an estuary of a large river or a busy channel, it was necessary to establish a light. In the early seventeenth century a floating light was proposed to be moored near the Goodwin Sands in the English Channel, but at the time it was impossible to build it.

The first lightship was moored at the Nore in 1732. Although at this spot in the Thames estuary it did not appear greatly exposed to the sea, on several occasions it was driven ashore in heavy weather. But the usefulness of this type of lighthouse was nevertheless recognized, and four years later another floating light was placed on Dudgeon Shoal. By the end of the eighteenth century five lights of this type were in service, the most famous being that in North Godwin, then known as North Sand Head.

These were crude devices, usually small remodeled trading vessels of the Dutch type. They carried a lantern with four or six candles hoisted on a mast. At this period no steam propulsion was available and the ship had only two small sails. Therefore, an auxiliary boat stood by in a neighboring port so that in a storm it could assist the lightship and tow it if it was dragging its anchor or severed its cable. At this time anchor cables were made of hemp, iron chains not being introduced until 1820. The first boat specially designed to be a lightship was built between 1820 and 1830. From this initial model new designs and gradual improvements in lightships proceeded down to modern times.

DREDGES

Dredging devices were used early to deepen navigable channels and clear away sandbanks obstructing them. In Volume II we saw that early types of dredges remained in use until some time in the nineteenth century.

In 1744 an English patent was taken out for a dredge that acted like two saber blades in order to scrape the bottom. Dredges with buckets to hold the material scooped up were patented by Richard Liddell in 1753, and in 1755 John Smeaton observed dredges in service. At the end of the eighteenth century the increasing sizes of ships called for deepening channels and for more powerful machines.

The mud mills used in northern Holland in 1780 to deepen and clear the channel to the port of Amsterdam were operated by horses. These boats had flat-bottomed, almost rectangular hulls and a bucket chain passing through a central well. A hand-operated capstan with bars describing a circle 17½ feet in diameter let the operators rotate the dredging chain, which could descend to a depth of 10½ feet. This is the first known bucket dredge.

A horse-powered mill with 4 bars described a circle 23 feet in diameter, permitting 4 horses to be harnessed to it, and a stable on the deck accommodated 3 horses, which leads us to suppose that a total of 7 horses were worked in shifts.

The characteristics of the device show that it was still a very modest one. The pontoon—51 feet long, 29 feet wide, and 10 feet high—had a draft of 2 feet 2 inches and a displacement of 65 tons. Its output was extremely small: 25 cubic yards per hour.

The buckets opened at the bottom, rather than by tipping, as in modern

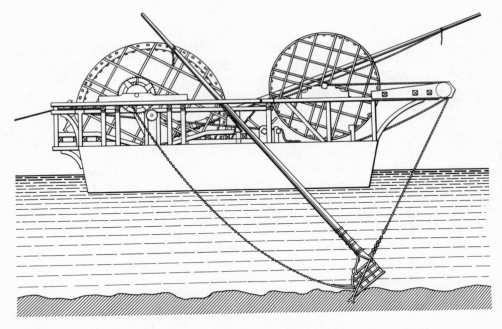

FIG. 64.   Laurent d'Avignon's machine for dredging harbors, 1808.

dredges. The movement was transmitted by means of wooden gears from the axle of the power source to the chain.

This device naturally gave way to steam engines, the first of which dates from 1796. It was equipped with leather bucket scoops and worked in the port of Sunderland. In 1803 a Trevithick dredge was used at the entrance to the East India Company Dock at Blackwall on the Thames. A lateral chain holding the buckets tipped the sand through a hopper and into a barge moored alongside the dredge. Its steam engine was a high-pressure model of 6 pounds and 6 nominal hp., with no condenser. It had a transmission gear using cast-iron pinions and was already a machine of some size—it was 79 feet long at the waterline, the hull was 18 feet wide, its draft was 10 feet, and it could dredge at a depth between 14 and 18 feet. It could raise approximately 180 tons of material in a 7-hour tidal period and seems to have been in service for ten or eleven years.

This was the first of the steam-powered dredges that made it possible to undertake major maritime projects during the nineteenth century.

CHAPTER 3

SHIPS AND NAVIGATION

M AJOR CHANGES in naval technology took place between 1700 and 1850. The lines of hulls and the sails of sailing ships completed the evolution begun in the seventeenth century, and a type of vessel emerging around 1840 to 1850 represented the last stage in this development.

After false starts and trial-and-error experimentation in the first half of the nineteenth century the steam engine began to assume its definitive role as a method of propulsion.

This was also a time when metals (thanks to improved techniques, particularly iron smelting) gradually became more important in ship construction with the use first of wrought iron, then especially of steel, in the second half of the nineteenth century.

SAILING VESSELS

The changes in warships were more significant than those in merchant fleets at this time.

Sizes and shapes of hulls During this period ships of comparable ratings were becoming larger. In England, for example, an 80-gun vessel was as large in 1745 as a 100-gun vessel in 1677. A series of regulations fixed the chief dimensions of warships, which were classified according to the number of their cannons, from 50 to 120. In France there were regulations posted in 1765 (Choiseul), 1786 (de Castries), 1815, and 1837. England published specifications in 1706, 1719, 1733, 1741, and 1745 for 64-gun vessels ranging from 914-tons burden in 1705 to 1,196 tons in 1745.

In France the dimensions for the largest rating (120 guns) increased from 195 feet in length and 53 feet in breadth in 1765 to 210 feet and 57 feet in 1847.

The longevity of wooden ships caused any given one to be kept up for a long time. The *Océan,* for example, built to the plans of Sané and put on the stocks in 1785, was launched in 1790 and, remodeled several times, was still in service in 1842. Regarded as one of the best sailing vessels in the fleet, it was not scrapped until 1855. The lines and structure of the hull were seventeenth century in design.

Warships in Colbert's time had bulging hulls overloaded with decoration. Bows were round and bulky below the waterline and ended in a fairly low cutwater. Behind the prow a transversal bulkhead restricted the decks. The upper gun deck and forecastle were square as a result. The rake of the stem changed from 1:4 around 1665 to 1:7 around 1725, 1:10 around 1740, and 1:14 under Louis XVI.

The hull carried a one- or two-story superstructure. The stern consisted of a vast structure whose cross section resembled that of an ancient lyre. This square stern was changed beginning at the end of the seventeenth century.

The submerged portion of the bottom became rounded and the side strakes worked around to meet the sternpost in a round tuck. In the eighteenth century the stem rose and the stern dropped; the line of the stem was modified if the bulkhead was retained.

Between the forecastle and quarterdeck the sides formed passages, or gangways, between which the upper deck was interrupted. The space thus left was the waist, where the longboat and dinghys were kept. The stern, still square in the tops, had galleries extending over the sides by corbeling that were the heads.

In the nineteenth century the lines of the hull became almost vertical. The bulkhead disappeared and rounded tops connected with the stem. Toward 1840 to 1850 the flat stern was replaced by a round wall surrounding the poop. Gangways were developed after 1770 and at the end of the eighteenth century they closed the waist, thus forming a continuous deck completely covering the upper gun deck.

Masts and sails   The bowsprit gallant, the small mast carried at the end of the bowsprit, a holdover from the seventeenth century, was still in use at the beginning of the next century. It had been installed around 1600 to compensate for the inadequacy of the spritsail as a casting sail to turn the vessel in a following wind. This arrangement, which lacked strength, disappeared around 1720, abandoning the spritsail and replacing it with jibs, which provided the casting effect from then on.

Use of the spritsail itself, which was inconvenient because it filled with water in a heavy sea, disappeared in the second half of the eighteenth century. The development of jibs ultimately compensated for this disappearance.

As early as 1600 topgallant sails had been superimposed upon masts above the topsails. Yet another appeared above the topgallants, a sail seen for the first

FIG. 65. Sail of a man-of-war, late eighteenth century. Square sails: a. Mainsail b. Lower main topsail c. Lower main topgallant d. Upper main topgallant e. Foresail f. Lower foretopsail g. lower foretopgallant h. Upper foretopgallant i. Mizzen topsail k. Mizzen topgallant l. Spritsail m. Bowsprit topsail n. Studdingsail (stunsail) o. Upper main studdingsail p. Lower fore studdingsail q. Foretop studdingsail r. Ringtail

time on the *Royal Sovereign* in 1637, whence the name *royals* given to these sails in England.

The fourth mast, the bonaventure or aftermizzen at the stern, disappeared in the seventeenth century. A triangular sail bent on a lateen yard remained. Above it, for the single remaining mizzenmast had grown taller, a square sail, the mizzen topsail, was rigged.

In the eighteenth century the triangular sail was gradually modified and transformed into a fore-and-aft sail called the spanker, with four nonsymmetrical sides. The forepart of the sail disappeared first; until around 1750 the sail was then held to the mast by a line wrapped around it. Then the yard, which was found to be inconvenient, was replaced by the spar, which gripped the mast with a clamp and came into general use about 1780. The lower edge of the sail was finally bent to a horizontal spar, a long piece of pine wood known as the boom.

In the nineteenth century the desire for speed led to an increase in the amount of sail carried. Above the royals appeared skysails, and at the stern, above the mizzen topsail, appeared the mizzen topgallant and mizzen royal. The bowsprit, extended by a piece of wood, carried as many as four jibs.

Working the sails But the most important modification and the one that profoundly transformed the technique of working the sails was the use of reefs. Volume II discussed how the sail area was reduced by eliminating the small studding sails, or stunsails. This maneuver required hoisting and hauling the yards up and down the mast. Working the reefs consisted of reducing the amount of sail by taking up the sails on the yards. A sailor took in one, two, or three reefs by raising one, two, or three sections of sail. What was impossible with the old sails, which were narrower at the top of the trapezium, now became possible with sails that were almost rectangular. The yard no longer had to be movable. The men worked the sails by supporting themselves against it, leaning over the yard and pulling the sail up against the yard, to which it was lashed by reefs.

Sail working was thus no longer done by lowering the yards but by sending the

FIG. 66. Sails of a man-of-war, late eighteenth century. Staysails: 1. Mainstay 2. Main topmast staysail 3. Middle staysail 4. Main topgallant staysail 5. Flying jib 6. Outer jib 7. Inner jib 8. Fore topmast staysail 9. Mizzen staysail 10. Mizzen topmast staysail 11. Mizzen topgallant staysail 12. Mizzen royal staysail 13. Spanker

crew aloft into the masts. The yards, now stationary, were at first lashed to the mast. Then in the nineteenth century they were fixed by irons or chains, which in normal weather held them in place at the required height. This method of support made it possible to orient the yards according to the wind.

Sails also came to be worked differently. In the sixteenth and seventeenth centuries ships were worked especially with the lower sails, which were taken up from the bottom. When the use of reefs became completely accepted, the large, lower sails were reduced by furling them, sometimes completely, in bad weather or when the ship was preparing for combat. The ship was then sailed with the topsails, the square sails on the topmasts, which were greatly developed and whose area was controlled with reefs.

In good weather all the sails were used and their area was even increased by studding sails. These were no longer the old studding sails attached to the bottoms of the sails but lateral sails attached to small yards that slid on the main yards.

Thus the general silhouette of the vessel was gradually transformed. The ones built from the seventeenth century to the nineteenth became the last examples of sailing vessels.

Warships: frigates We have noted that warships were classified according to the number of guns they carried, the smallest being the 50-gun vessel. Ships carrying fewer than 50 guns were called frigates and were distinguished by special characteristics.

Frigates were fast vessels used either to escort squadrons of the line or for special missions. Their speed permitted them to refuse to fight better-armed vessels, especially as their artillery was weaker not only in terms of the number of pieces carried (40 guns at most) but also was of smaller caliber (12, 8, or 6, whereas ships' guns were of 36, 24, 18, or 12 caliber).

In order to give them greater speed, the ratio of length to breadth was higher with frigates than with ships of the line: 3.6:1 and 3.8:1 for the latter, 4:1 for frigates. Smaller than frigates were corvettes, which at the end of the eighteenth century carried only 20 4-caliber guns.

Construction methods Despite the development of scientific knowledge and the appearance of theoretical treatises such as Bouguer's 1750 study of the stability of ships, experience remained the sole adviser in shipbuilding until the second half of the nineteenth century. Builders' ideas were influenced by their natural traditions, as in England, where they relied on tried-and-true designs. Until the end of the eighteenth century there were no standard works offering theories applicable to naval construction.

Even though France was more responsive to scientific doctrines, the French were unable to solve every problem, even in the nineteenth century. Duhamel du Monceau, who founded the École des Constructeurs in 1765, still had little confidence in applied mathematics and preferred to study the characteristics of ships that had been the most successful and use them as examples for new building.

The lines of hulls were in effect not calculated. Although regulations fixed the main dimensions for each class of ship, they went no further. No standards were imposed on builders, who laid out the lines each in his own way, adopting those he believed to be best. Thus Sané, a great builder whose activity extended over monarchy, republic, and empire and whose hull designs were justly famous, was entrusted with designing prototypes for the various classes of ships. But shipbuilders did not follow them exactly, preferring their traditional plans, which they adapted to the general dimensions imposed on them. Some French builders, like the Ozanne brothers, were most successful in building fast craft, but their influence was limited.

Many French ships, which were famous for their hull lines, were captured by the English and integrated into the British fleet, which thus had a significant proportion of French vessels (especially vessels with 80 guns) in its squadrons.

Although the English were not slow to copy French hulls, they did not blindly follow their techniques but adapted them to their own requirements. This was especially true of frigates. Frigate hulls were built in France with narrow bows, the waterlines forming a sharper angle at the stem than was the case with English ships. These faster ships often proved superior to English frigates in maneuverability and in combat. Indeed, the contrast between two technical approaches can be seen here. The English ship, larger in the bow, rose better on swells and was more seaworthy, and the French ship, with its finer bow lines, cut into the swells but was less seaworthy in heavy seas.

According to whether one wanted a more seaworthy vessel or a more maneuverable war machine, one or the other form was adopted or criticized. For example, the lines of the English frigate *Endymion* had been copied in 1797 from a captured French ship, the *Pomone*. English builders made several modifications to it, and the construction details were wholly English. The *Endymion* proved to be one of the fastest ships in the British navy and was for a long time part of the fleet, not scrapped until 1860.

Razee vessels   As mentioned, frigates were armed with fewer and smaller-caliber guns than were ships of the line. It was difficult if not impossible for them to engage more heavily armed ships in battle. To deal with this disadvantage a new type of vessel was developed, the razee. The upper gun deck, with the entire corresponding upper part of the hull, bridge, and gunwales of the ship of the line, were eliminated. The lower gun deck was retained and was equipped with the most powerful guns.

A type of ship with valuable qualities was thus developed. It had a smaller displacement and the position of the lower gun deck was raised in relation to the waterline so that the portholes could be left open in a heavy sea and the guns fired in any weather. The hull was slimmer and the new vessel could make greater speed, since the rigging still carried the same amount of sail as the older type. In this way a well-armed stout frigate with very good seagoing qualities was developed. An example is the English vessel *Eagle*, built in 1804 and armed like a vessel of 74. In 1832 it was transformed into a razee, which became a 50-gun frigate by eliminating the upper gun deck.

Coastal navigation   Coastal navigation in the merchant navy became increasingly active. The difference between the cost of transportation by sea and land was considerable. Shipping a load of wood from Bristol to Chatham, which cost 16 shillings by boat, cost 5 shillings a mile by road.

Boats were able to carry a much larger load at lower cost offsetting port taxes and the hazards of navigation. This coastal navigation used undistinguished small boats with a capacity of less than 100 tons—brigs, schooners, and cutters.

Packet boats   We have little exact information on mail and passenger packet boats prior to the eighteenth century. They must have been quite small, judging from the often cited example described in *The Papers of Thomas Bowrey,* published by the Hakluyt Society in 1927. The *Mary Galley,* built in 1704, was a 170-tonner that made the round trip to the East Indies. It carried sail typical of the early seventeenth century: jib, foresail, fore-topsail, mainsail, main topsail, and mizzen. Similar but larger ships appear in London Customs House documents from 1714.

After 1708 the (English) East India Company reported the names and tonnages of its ships. The tonnage, or burden, increased steadily from 400 tons in 1708 to 500 in 1731, 800 in 1775, and 1,200 by the end of the century. Around 1740 it was the custom to design these ships for a tonnage one or two tons less than 500. Those constructed in 1775 had their tonnage increased to approximately 676, then to 720 to 750 tons.

These ships bear a strong resemblance to the 32-gun frigates of the end of the century. Ships of 1,200-ton burdens had almost exactly the same dimensions as the 64-gun frigates, but their armament was weaker, being intended for defense against corsairs and pirates. They carried 56 18-caliber guns, whereas the 64-gun frigates carried 24-caliber guns.

The lower gun deck was nonexistent in merchant ships, but a line of blind portholes was painted on the hull at the level of the lower gun deck, to make an ill-intentioned privateer believe he was in the presence of a well-armed warship.

Ships used in the Atlantic trade, the West Indiamen, were noticeably smaller. In 1755 their displacement measured 300 to 400 tons, and by the end of the century they did not exceed 500 tons. In both cases the absence of heavy artillery freed the entire lower deck, enabling these ships to take a large cargo and provide cabins for passengers.

Progress in mining and transporting coal encouraged the development of a fleet of colliers that plied the Tyne to London, ports in northern Europe, and even as far as the Mediterranean.

In his 1768 and 1780 voyages James Cook sailed in some of these ships outfitted for long journeys, in particular the famous *Endeavour Bark,* the plans of which have been preserved. It was a 366-tonner with very bluff lines, carrying the customary sail of the period.

The clippers and their   In Steel's *Naval Architecture* (1804), we find a 1,257-
evolution in the   tonner intended for the East India trade. It carried
nineteenth century   10 18-caliber guns on the deck and 35 18-caliber
guns on the gun deck. As in the preceding century there was no lower gun deck except for two portholes in the stern to allow the gunners to fire astern. Blind portholes were still painted on the hull to cause would-be attackers to believe the ship was a two-decker armed for war.

In 1838 steamships took their place on the regular Atlantic lines, but sailing ships, faster than eighteenth-century sailing ships, remained in service for a long time to come. There were, for example, the Blackwall frigates of 1838, 835-tonners that reached 1,200 tons by 1742. Speed was obtained by refining the ships' lines—the ratio of length to breadth rose to 4.3:1 in 1844 and 4.7:1 in 1850.

After 1843 Americans began to build 750-ton full-rigged ships, called clippers, renowned for their speed. They enjoyed great popularity during the California gold rush in 1849 and to Australia in 1851 (Figure 67). In England the burdens remained at the 800-ton level, occasionally rising to 1,200, but in the United States they were built as big as 1,800 registered tons.

At this time the China tea trade also led to the use of faster clippers with finer lines. Donald McKay's *Lightning,* built in 1853, had a ratio of length to breadth of 5.5:1.

FIG. 67.   American clipper, around 1850.

A new construction technique appeared toward the middle of the century. In order to increase the sizes of ships and their cargo capacity, wooden hulls began to be replaced by iron ones, which made it possible to trim their lines. The ratio of length to width rose to 6.3:1 and even 6.7:1 in 1870, and tonnage increased from 1,000 to 2,000 tons.

Ships with smaller tonnages naturally continued to be built to transport heavy materials. The early-nineteenth-century colliers continued to be 200- and sometimes 300-tonners. These were originally three-masters, often reduced later to two masts. These two-master brigs had square sails. With their bluff lines they were poor sailors, beating up to windward with difficulty, but with their reduced costs for a small crew they were adequate for the trade in heavy merchandise, which required little speed. Their small size gave them the advantage of being able to travel up rivers and stop at small ports inaccessible to large sailing vessels.

Navigation by sail   The volume of merchandise transported increased considerably between the seventeenth and nineteenth centuries. Modifications in the lines of ships and in their sails made navigation easier and voyages faster.

In the seventeenth century the route to the Indies made use of the northeast trade winds bearing toward Brazil. Then, profiting by the southward-flowing Brazil Current, it joined the westerlies from Cape Horn below the Tropic of Capricorn.

Toward the end of the eighteenth century the use of jibs and the finer lines of vessels made it possible to follow a more direct route via Madeira or the Canaries toward the islands of Cape Verde and Saint Helena and to make the trip via the Cape of Good Hope in three months. With an opposing wind it was possible at the time to beat up to windward at 70°. The actual speed of ships at sea depended on the direction of the winds in relation to the route to be followed and on the nature of the currents encountered.

The crucial importance of a good knowledge of wind patterns and of currents along the main navigation routes had been evident for centuries. This work had been undertaken as early as the fifteenth century by Prince Henry the Navigator and the teams of scholars working under him. These studies, which were expanded to include all the oceans, had a strong influence on the progress of sailing navigation in the eighteenth and nineteenth centuries.

A round trip to the Far East, which in the seventeenth century required 2 years, was reduced to 18 months beginning in the eighteenth century. It was necessary to count on 5 to 6 months of travel in each direction, the remaining 6 months being occupied by the business of the trip. The return voyage had to be timed to coincide with the northeast monsoon in the Indian Ocean to take advantage of winds favorable to east-west travel.

Toward the end of the nineteenth century the techniques of building sailing vessels had reached their peak. Navigation owed its progress to steam propulsion, whose appearance and development are among the most important accomplishments of the last century.

STEAMSHIPS

Naturally, from the very first attempts to use steam as a power source, the idea of using it to propel ships was quickly conceived, but it was much more difficult to apply an engine to a ship than a land vehicle. The size and weight of the engine and the problem of devising a drivetrain raised difficulties that could not easily be overcome in the state of technology at the end of the seventeenth century.

The first experiments   Contrary to a persistent tradition, Denis Papin cannot be credited with building a steam boat. He thought of applying this method of propulsion but never tried it. The confusion results from the fact that he installed in a small boat a system of oar wheels operated not by a steam engine but by a manually turned crank. He traveled down the Fulda River in this in 1707. His boat was indeed broken into pieces by boatmen, but only because Papin had neglected to request the necessary permission from the guild that held the monopoly on navigation for the rivers in this region.

Thomas Savery's engine was totally incapable of being used on a boat, but the Newcomen engine suggested new possibilities. It would take too long to describe in detail all the projects preceding Fulton's work; a short outline of numerous but fruitless experiments will be sufficient.

In 1736 Jonathan Hulls of Gloucestershire took out a patent for a tugboat with a stern paddle wheel. Drawings of it appearing from time to time have led to the belief that it was actually built. The fact is that Hulls simply described his invention in a note and a sketch supplementing his 1737 patent, in which he shows a steam tugboat pulling a ship. The engine was probably an atmospheric engine (the only type known at that time), 30 inches in diameter, with a piston balanced by a weight equal to half the pressure on the piston, which made it possible to obtain continuous action. The driving force was to be transmitted to the axle of a paddle wheel by friction mechanisms. Hulls also proposed using poles operated by cranks and connecting rods to push against the bottom of the stream for propulsion in shallow waters. However, the size and weight of the atmospheric engine made it impossible to build such a device and it was never more than a plan.

In 1763 an American builder, William Henry, succeeded in putting into operation a boat equipped with a steam engine, undoubtedly the first in the world, but it soon sank and the experiment ended here. In 1753 the Académie des Sciences of Paris promoted a competition to search for "methods of supplementing the action of the winds for the movement of ships." Various papers were presented, those of Daniel Bernoulli, Euler, and Abbot Gauthier of Nancy being among the most important. The prize was awarded to Bernoulli, who had logically analyzed the problem based on the Newcomen engine used to circulate water in London. Bernoulli concluded that this 20–25 hp. engine could give a speed of only 2.4 knots. He suggested a device similar to the propeller, to be operated by men or horses. According to Bernoulli the Newcomen engine could offer no advantages over other power sources. Abbot Gauthier suggested a system of paddle wheels, clearly glimpsing in 1754 the advantages of an engine whose steam power would replace a convict gang of 400 men. Here again, the Newcomen engine did not lend itself to such an installation.

Fruitless French experiments In France after 1770 some businessmen and enthusiasts worked for some time on the problem without reaching decisive results. This undertaking was initiated by an artillery officer named Joseph d'Auxiron who was interested in mechanics. He presented a scheme and in May 1772 obtained the promise of a license if he succeeded in demonstrating an actual steam boat. This demonstration was not made, under the conditions stipulated, until the end of the century. D'Auxiron succeeded in selling shares to supply the capital and the boat was built, beginning early in 1773, on the Île aux Cygnes in the Seine at Paris. But building a steam engine presented great difficulties. The mechanical transmission and propulsion parts—paddle wheels and lantern-and-rack gearing—could be built in Paris, but it was necessary to call upon some English manufacturers, Jukes and Coulson, for the steam engine itself. In April 1773 the machinery was installed on the boat, but from then on the work dragged, for unexplained reasons. An accident occurred in September 1774: a heavy weight fell and stove in the hull and the boat sank on the spot. D'Auxiron died shortly thereafter.

In 1775 the best French metallurgist and engineer of the period, J.-C. Périer, attempted to operate a small steam boat on the Seine, but the experiment, about which little is known, was a failure.

At this time, naturally, the only engine available was the atmospheric one, in which steam was condensed in the cylinder at each stroke by injecting cold water. An engine with a separate condenser was not put into service by Watt until 1775 and was not known in France until 1779. D'Auxiron had probably attempted to compensate for the disadvantages of this single-acting engine by using a system of counterweights. Périer, an experienced man, had realized that building a steam boat with the equipment then available, though an attractive proposition on paper, was in fact foolhardy and definitely ruinous. Although he continued energetically building steam engines, and in 1792 introduced the double-acting engine into France, he never attempted to repeat his first—and only—steam boat experiment.

Jouffroy's *precarious achievement* Being less knowledgeable and thus more daring, another officer, Claude Jouffroy d'Abbans (1751– 1832), took over after d'Auxiron's death and re-formed the joint-stock company d'Auxiron had formed. He began to build his first boat on the Doubs, in his native region of Beaune-les-Dames. No definite information exists on this first experiment. In 1782 Jouffroy settled at Vaize and ordered two steam cylinders from Frère-Jean, a well-known founder in Lyon. He placed these 2-foot-diameter cylinders on his boat inclined at a 20° angle so that by means of lantern-and-rack gears the alternating movement of the connecting rods turned a transversal axle with a paddle wheel at each end. To a certain extent this was d'Auxiron's system, but the counterweight was replaced by a second steam cylinder.

This boat was 148 feet long and 15 feet wide, with a 3-foot draft and a displacement of 182 tons. At the beginning of July 1783, Jouffroy succeeded in sailing it on the Saône between Vaize and the Île Barbe. Bolstered by this success, he claimed from the comptroller general the license that had once again been promised to the corporation. The ministry sought advice from the Académie des Sciences, which naturally requested that the boat be tested before its commissioners in Paris. Jouffroy never succeeded in getting together enough money to repeat the trial run and dissension developed among the stockholders so that the corporation was unable to increase its available capital. It quickly became evident that the initial investment had been underestimated, and during 1784 Jouffroy had to stop his work and give up any idea of continuing the enterprise.

Various misconceptions concerning Jouffroy d'Abbans's steam boat have survived down to our own time. Some have seen in the conditions imposed by the Académie des Sciences a maneuver to discredit Jouffroy. The story is commonly repeated that the 1783 boat was equipped with a double-acting engine, but this would make Jouffroy the inventor of this type of engine, which Watt did not build until 1785. Jacques Payen has established the facts as exactly as they can be known from existing original documents. In particular it is incontestable that Jouffroy installed an atmospheric engine that met the demands of the Académie, since by 1783 the condensing engine had been known in France for several years.

Although it is nevertheless true that Jouffroy d'Abbans was the first French builder to operate a steam boat, it is regrettable that he was not better informed about the progress of mechanical engineering in his time and that he was unable to obtain better technical advice and thereby more solid financial backing. Perhaps he could thus have achieved more convincing results and even found an effective solution to the problem when he returned from exile after the Revolution. But this was not to be. It is worth noting that the model preserved in the Musée de la Marine, supposed to be a small-scale copy of the 1776 boat, was not built before the early nineteenth century and that the reconstruction of the famous *Pyroscaphe* built in 1783, done in 1951 with modern methods, is affected by basic errors that have persisted into modern times.

Experiments of the same type were repeated sporadically by amateurs fired with enthusiasm by technology's progress but not well acquainted with the basis of the problem. Among them the most persevering (but no more successful) was the Swiss Isaac de Rivaz, who between 1786 and 1809 persisted in building first a steam vehicle and then a steam boat. Unfortunately, de Rivaz was, like Jouffroy, poorly informed on steam engine progress and mechanics in general and, being a resident of Sion in Valais, Switzerland, was still more isolated than his French colleague from an industrial environment. Although in 1802 he succeeded in operating a steam wagon built under precarious conditions, he failed completely in his attempts at steam navigation. A design by Desblanc, a craftsman and clockmaker from Trévoux on the Saône, was not built full scale but is the only one of this time known to us in detail (Figures 68 and 69). It lets us judge the nature of these enterprises, all of which came up against the fact that industrial mechanics was not yet able to supply effective construction methods.

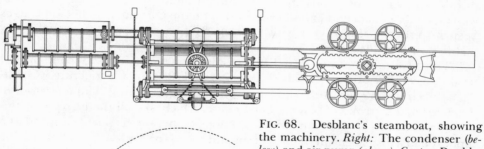

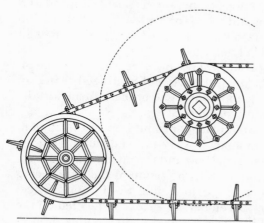

FIG. 68. Desblanc's steamboat, showing the machinery. *Right:* The condenser (*below*) and air pump (*above*). *Center:* Double-acting steam engine with complicated gear for controlling the valves. *Left:* A rack ("La Hire gear") controlled by the piston rod, which gives back-and-forth movement to the four outside wheels that drive the endless chains in Figure 69.

FIG. 69. Desblanc's steamboat. Profile of one of the chains, with its retracting blades.

Losing the lead in the development of steamships, France took no further interest in them during the Revolutionary and Empire periods, since she remained completely isolated from technical progress throughout this quarter century. Instead, England and the United States experimented with and put steamships into service.

Experiments in England and the United States — In Great Britain three partners—Miller, Taylor, and Symington—only the last of whom was an engineer, attempted in 1787 to install a Boulton-and-Watt steam engine on a double-hulled ship that had enough space between them for a paddle wheel, but the power transmission system, made of iron chains, caused serious problems. William Symington perfected it and in 1801 installed one on a steam boat, which inevitably gave Robert Fulton some good ideas. The first boat was 100 feet long, 31 feet wide, and had a draft of 6 feet and a displacement of 250 tons. It made several trips around a small lake in Scotland.

In the United States the experiments of John Fitch and James Rumsey date from the same period. After the Revolutionary War ended on September 5, 1782, the difficulties of transportation over poorly planned and ill-maintained roads naturally drew attention to the navigation possibilities of ocean and river.

In 1784 Fitch and Rumsey submitted to Washington the results of their independent studies, Rumsey seeming to have gone less deeply into the question. Fitch was the first to present feasible plans and projects.

The first project, designed in April 1785, was presented as a prototype with plans to the American Society in Philadelphia on September 17, 1785. The drawings and description no longer exist, but the model survives. This is an engine with an endless chain and paddles suspended on the port side. Fitch had perhaps been inspired by the way in which certain Indian canoes were propelled by paddles on one side.

This early scheme appears to have remained on paper. Fitch's second project used 12 oars placed 6 on each side (Figure 70). In 1786 he made trial runs with this boat, which was 59 feet long and driven by an engine with a cylinder 1 foot in diameter and a stroke of 3 feet. The engine, which like all the engines of this period was a low-compression model, was able to operate the boat at a speed of 3 mph. It had a displacement of only 9 tons and a draft of 3½ feet. In October 1788 it carried 30 passengers from Philadelphia to Burlington, a distance of 20 miles, in 3 hours and 10 minutes, at a speed of 5½ knots.

Fitch attempted to interest various prominent people in regular use of steam boats, but he encountered general disbelief and became discouraged. After an unsuccessful attempt in France, where he took out a patent, he returned to the United States a ruined man and committed suicide.

Rumsey must be mentioned for his attempt at jet propulsion. The boat, built in 1785, was tried out in 1787 on the Potomac. It was equipped with an engine consisting of a pump that sucked up water at the bow and forced it out at the stern (Figure 71). Forward movement was produced by the action of the water being pumped. The boat was a simple structure 18 feet long, 6 feet wide, and 2½ feet deep. Rumsey tried it out in England on December 15, 1792, but he died on the twenty-first. A trial run in February 1793 gave a speed of four knots. Robert Fulton, who knew Rumsey, had followed his experiments, which perhaps led him to take an interest in steam propulsion.

In England in 1801, Lord Dundas, concerned about the number of horses required for towing on canals, had William Symington fit out a small boat, the *Charlotte Dundas,* with a stern paddle wheel. The steam engine consisted of two double-acting cylinders 21½ inches in diameter with a 4-foot stroke placed hori-

FIG. 70.   Fitch's oar-propelled boat, 1787.

FIG. 71.   Rumsey's "jet-propelled" steamboat, 1786.

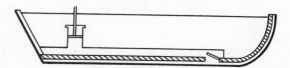

zontally with the boiler between them. The piston rods operated the paddle wheel by a jointed system. In March 1802 the tugboat, which was 56 feet long and 18 feet wide, towed two 70-ton barges for a distance of 19½ miles on a canal in 6 hours. The owners of the canal felt that the economy of not using horses would be offset by the damage caused to the canal banks by the backwash from the paddle wheels. The *Charlotte Dundas* was abandoned in a secluded part of the canal, where it remained until 1861. Fulton had been able to examine the boat and its machinery.

Fulton's early successes   In 1782 Robert Fulton (1765–1815) went to Philadelphia in search of a trade and ultimately became a miniaturist. In late 1786 or early 1787 he sailed for England, where he trained as a mechanic and became an industrial designer. Being of an inquisitive but pragmatic turn of mind, he devoted himself to building canals and various machines. In 1796 he went to France, where he studied machinery with the famous mechanic Étienne Calla (1760–1835), a former pupil of Jacques de Vaucanson.

Fulton began by inventing a submarine, with which he performed several demonstrations, without being able to interest the French government. He also invented methods of underwater attack using explosive devices, the effectiveness of which he proved without arousing the interest of the first consul. Apparently the time was not ripe for undersea warfare, for several years later Fulton had no more success interesting English naval authorities.

Fulton's experiments with steam navigation carried him still further. In Paris he made the acquaintance of the United States ambassador, Robert R. Livingston, who had obtained a license for steam navigation several years earlier from the State of New York. Having no means of using the license, Livingston encouraged Fulton to pursue a project to build a steam boat.

Fulton had undertaken these studies systematically with a view to effective solutions. In particular, he realized that the engines used by his predecessors were unsatisfactory. At this time Desblanc, previously mentioned, had experienced a

Plate 27. Fulton's *Clermont* on the Hudson. Smithsonian Institution

partial failure when he employed retractable blades moving back and forth on an endless chain (Figure 69).

Fulton decided on paddle wheels and tried to calculate mathematically their dimensions, as well as the power and size of the steam engine (Figure 72). Construction of a boat was begun in 1803, thanks to Livingston's help, on the Île aux Cygnes in the Seine. By a curious coincidence an accident occurred like that of thirty years earlier at the same spot, when d'Auxiron's boat sank under the weight of the engine. But Fulton was more fortunate than his predecessor in that he was able to save the engine and install it in another boat.

The boat was 101⅔ feet long at the waterline, 8 feet wide, and 3 feet deep, with a draft of 2 feet. The engine, which came from the shops of the Périer brothers, had a vertical cylinder 3¼ feet in diameter that drove two paddle wheels 11½ feet in diameter. During the first trial run on the Seine, on August 9, 1803, the boat, towing two other boats, maneuvered for an hour and a half, going upstream at a speed estimated at 2,400 *toises* (2.9 knots) per hour. In other tests speeds of 3.58 and 4.5 knots were attained.

Despite this success, Fulton did not succeed in attracting public interest or the attention of the French government, both being preoccupied with military events. Livingston renewed his license from the State of New York in his and Fulton's name. Fulton left France several months later and, stopping off in England, ordered a more powerful steam engine from the factories of Boulton and Watt, to be sent to the United States. He returned to New York on December 8, 1806.

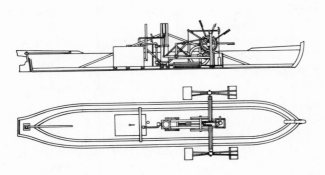

FIG. 72. Design of a steamboat by Fulton in Paris, 1799.

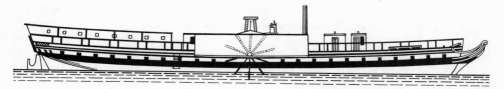

FIG. 73.   Fulton's steamboat, the *Chancellor Livingston,* 1811.

The Clermont *(1807)*   Here, with better backing, he was able to complete the construction of the first steam boat capable of navigating the Hudson. He gave it the name of Livingston's country home built on the banks of the river, Clermont.

The *Clermont* was built in 1807 on the East River in New York City by Charles Browne from plans by Fulton, who made shrewd use of the results of his experiments in France. The new boat had a displacement of 100 tons, was 131 feet long and 9½ feet wide, and had a draft of 2 feet. The engine, which developed 2 hp., consisted of a vertical cylinder 2 feet in diameter. The piston had a 4-foot stroke and a rod connected with a crosshead with its movement guided horizontally on slide rods. This device, reminiscent of the Maudslay engine, was completed by two reversing connecting rods that acted on a walking beam located at the bottom of the cylinder. The other end of the beam transmitted the movement by gears to the shaft of the two paddle wheels, which were 14¾ feet in diameter and each had 8 blades 4 feet 3 inches by 2 feet.

On August 17, 1807, the *Clermont* made its first trial run on the Hudson, from New York to Albany, at a speed of 4.7 knots. It remained in service for the rest of the season. Remodeled during the winter of 1807/08, it resumed service on the Hudson and continued in service for many years. Despite initial reservations by the public, the service settled down and became profitable as other similar boats joined the *Clermont,* Fulton building a total of 19 steam boats. The largest of these was the *Chancellor Livingston* (1811), which was 161 feet long, 33 feet wide, and was equipped with a 60 hp. engine (Figure 73). The last was the *Demologos* (1814). Fulton died on February 24, 1815, at the age of fifty.

Early progress in   The possibility of adapting steam to navigation hav-
steam navigation   ing been demonstrated, steam navigation immediately underwent a rapid expansion on rivers and lakes in the United States.

In England at the same time Henry Bell ordered a boat built for passenger service between Glasgow and Helensburgh. This 28-tonner, built at Port Glasgow, was 84 feet long, 11 feet wide, and had a draft of 4 feet; a large smokestack carried a square sail on a yard. In February 1812 it attained a speed of 6.7 knots. In 1819 Bell put this boat, the *Comet,* into service between the western highlands and Glasgow. It was shipwrecked on December 15, 1820, during one of these trips.

Among the chief proponents of steam navigation must be mentioned those who, contemporaneous with Fulton and after him, continued building steam boats and conducting trial runs in the United States, in particular the Stevenses, John and his son Robert. In 1804 Colonel John Stevens built a boat 67¼ feet long and 17 feet wide with a completely novel layout. A tubular boiler with 100 water tubes 2 inches in diameter and 18 inches long fed a high-compression engine with a cylinder 9¾ inches in diameter and a stroke of 2 feet, which turned a propeller. Stevens also designed a system in which two gear wheels drove twin propellers, and then built a boat propelled by paddle wheels, which he tried out in 1807. (Here he was anticipated by Fulton.)

In 1808 the Stevens family ran one of their boats from New York to Philadelphia. This was the first ocean voyage by a ship whose sole means of propulsion was the steam engine. The trip was a success, even though it was made in a violent gale.

Robert L. Stevens developed the familiar American steam riverboat. His theoretical studies and inventions, in particular his return-tube boiler in 1832, placed him in the forefront of American engineers.

The first steam-powered men-of-war — As soon as the steam engine's ability to propel ships had been demonstrated, its application to warships became logical. Fulton was the first to conceive of a large, powerfully armed ship (Figure 74), which he named the *Demologos* (1814). It was a paddle-wheel ship intended to defend the port of New York against the British fleet, at a time when an incursion by them was feared.

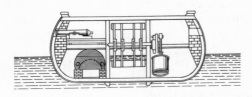

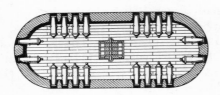

FIG. 74.   Fulton's *Demologos*, 1814.

The *Demologos* was of approximately 2,200 tons displacement and was 154 feet long, 55¾ feet wide, and 20 feet high. An engine with one cylinder 4 feet in diameter and a 5-foot stroke drove a paddle wheel 15¾ feet in diameter and 13¾ feet wide, positioned between two hulls and thus well protected from enemy artillery.

At this time the only idea builders had to increase a ship's protection was to thicken the wooden hull. The sides of the gun deck were five feet thick, sufficient to stop all the solid projectiles of that time.

The artillery consisted of 20 32-pounders from a captured English ship; a set of furnaces to heat cannonballs was installed for firing red-hot broadsides. Later the artillery was increased to 36 32-pounders. The ship was launched in 1814 under the name *Fulton I.* In May 1815 a first trial run gave a speed of 6.4 knots on a 50-mile course and on September 11, with a draft of 11 feet, it gave 5.5 knots. But

Plate 28. Arrival of Queen Victoria at Le Tréport on September 3, 1843. Painting by Isabey (detail). Paris, Musée de la Marine. (Photo Musée de la Marine.)

the War of 1812 between England and the United States had ended with the Treaty of Ghent, signed on December 24, 1814, and, despite the fears of the moment, hostilities did not resume. On June 4, 1829, the *Fulton* of Brooklyn was destroyed by an accidental explosion, with many dead and wounded.

The British admiralty had attempted in 1815 to arm a schooner, the *Congo,* for exploring the Congo. But the trial run was not a success and the engine was removed with its wheels before the departure from Chatham, so the boat made the trip under sail alone. During this period of development for paddle wheelers the admiralty experimented with them for its own purposes. However, they waited until 1821 before giving the famous engineers Brunel and Rennie an order for the first warship, the *Comet,* a 238-ton, 80-hp. vessel launched at Deptford in 1822. In 1821 the admiralty had also acquired the 212-ton, 80-hp. *Monkey,* built at Rotherhithe, which was in fact the first steamship in the British navy.

This vessel was followed by several others, but since they carried only a few light guns they did not constitute a genuine steam-powered military fleet. They were used for postal services, in particular in the Mediterranean, where they made it possible to reduce from 90 to 45 days the length of the round trip between Falmouth and Corfu. The *Black Eagle,* launched in 1831, was 152½ feet long and had a burden of 494 tons B.O.M. (Bulletin officiel de la Marine). It attained 11 knots with a 260-hp. engine. It was built after the French-built *Sphinx.*

The Sphinx *and*   Various unsuccessful trials with small paddle
French vessels   wheelers were carried out in France in 1823, by
                           which time French engine builders had less experi-
ence than did the English, who had better engines. A 160-hp. engine was therefore purchased from Fawcett in Liverpool and an engineer named Hubert built a
corvette, the *Sphinx,* which was launched on August 3, 1829.

This vessel was 151½ feet long, with a hull 24 feet wide. Its draft was 11 feet
and it displaced 177 tons (Figure 75). The engine had two vertical cylinders 4 feet
in diameter with a piston stroke of 4¾ feet. It drove two paddle wheels 7 feet in
diameter with blades 22 inches wide (Figure 76). The wheels were protected by
paddle boxes that increased the beam of the boat to 36 feet. The engine weighed
more than 1,826 pounds and consumed 13 pounds of coal per horsepower-hour.

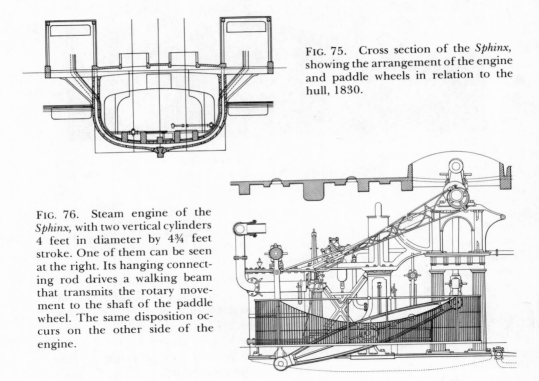

FIG. 75.   Cross section of the *Sphinx,*
showing the arrangement of the engine
and paddle wheels in relation to the
hull, 1830.

FIG. 76.   Steam engine of the
Sphinx, with two vertical cylinders
4 feet in diameter by 4¾ feet
stroke. One of them can be seen
at the right. Its hanging connecting rod drives a walking beam
that transmits the rotary movement to the shaft of the paddle
wheel. The same disposition occurs on the other side of the
engine.

The *Sphinx* had only light artillery: three guns and four 24-caliber carronades. Guns and ammunition together weighed 25 tons. The boat's nautical
qualities were very satisfactory; it attained a maximum speed of 9 knots and an
average speed under steam of 7 knots. It distinguished itself upon its entrance into
service by bringing from Algiers to Toulon the news of the city's capture. Then, in
April-May 1833, it towed the lighter *Lougsor,* whose cargo was the obelisk later
erected in the Place de la Concorde, from Abukir, Egypt, to Toulon and then to Le
Havre. It sank on July 6, 1845, in a shipwreck off the coast of Algeria.

The performance of the *Sphinx* encouraged the French navy to design more powerful ships. As early as 1832 construction was begun on a frigate armed with 15 30-pounder howitzers. This was the *Gomer,* later called the *Descartes,* a 1,474-tonner 233 feet long with a draft of 18 feet and a 450-hp. engine. The wheels were 30 feet in diameter and each had 24 paddles. The speed obtainable was 10 knots at 16 rpm. of the wheels.

It was difficult to increase these dimensions because the wheels, which were fragile and vulnerable in battle, could not be adapted to larger vessels. In addition, the protecting paddle boxes occupied a large area on the side of the ship, reducing the space available for artillery—the *Comet* carried only 16 guns. In order to maintain an armament equivalent to that of a 46-gun sailing frigate, the *Penelope,* launched in 1829 and converted to steam, the English cut the ship in half and, by adding a section of hull in the center, lengthened it by 65 feet. In this way the ship was able to retain an armament of 16 guns. The British admiralty ultimately succeeded in building a powerful paddle-wheel frigate, the HMS *Terrible* (1845). It was a 3,189-tonner (B.O.M. tonnage 1,847) 223 feet long and 42 feet wide, with a 2,059-hp. engine that enabled it to obtain a speed of 10.9 knots. The steam pressure was 2.2 pounds, acting in 4 cylinders that turned the wheels at a speed of 16 rpm.

The driving force of paddle wheels had thus reached a fairly high level but was short of the power needed by a large ship of the line, so in this period the steam-powered fleets were limited to frigates and corvettes. In France, by an ordinance of March 9, 1842, this fleet was to include 20 frigates with 540- or 450-hp. engines, 20 corvettes with 320- or 220-hp. engines, and smaller ships with 160-hp. engines. Conversion of the squadrons of rated ships into steamships had to await the invention of the propeller, around 1845.

Commercial steam navigation   The development of navigation on rivers and lakes in the United States was rapid but required only certain basic designs, since it did not have to be concerned with waves. Hulls were quite low and carried multiple decks for cabins, salons, and the like. Watt's engines were easily adapted to these ships in their primitive form, with the large walking beam at the top of the engine, which fitted easily into large open spaces cut through the decks (Figure 77).

Ocean navigation by steam required other equipment, but it quickly developed, because of its superiority over propulsion by sails and wind. In 1835 the clippers took 35 days to travel from Le Havre to New York and 25 days for the New York-Le Havre trip, thanks to the prevailing westerly winds. Thus there was every incentive to develop a means of freeing ship travel from the problem of contrary winds and calms.

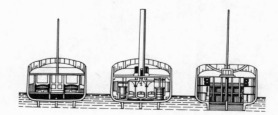

FIG. 77.   Cross sections of the steamboat *London Engineer,* built by Maudslay in 1818.

The first steamship to cross the English Channel was a small boat 52½ feet long, the *Elise,* equipped with a 10-hp. engine, which had just been bought by the Pajol navigation company of Paris. It left London on March 9, 1816, and, after several attempts that were unsuccessful because of the state of the sea, succeeded during the night of March 15–16 in crossing the Channel from Newhaven to Le Havre after 17 hours of rough seas.

The first ship to cross the Atlantic with a steam engine on board was the wooden *Savannah,* built at Corlears Hook in New York (Figure 78). Originally planned as a sailing vessel, a 10-hp. engine was installed with a cylinder 3¼ feet in diameter with a stroke of 5 feet. The cylinder, inclined at a 20° angle, drove (without intermediate gears), a crankshaft connected with the paddle wheels. These wheels, with a diameter of 15 feet, had 10 arms held by a pair of chains and could be folded and stored on the deck in case sails were used. The wheels, turning at 16 rpm., gave a speed of 4 knots. The ship was only 98½ feet long and measured 170 tons, with a draft of approximately 12¾ feet.

The Atlantic crossing was made in May-June 1819, without passengers, but with 75 tons of coal and 25 cords of wood. It left on May 20 and came in sight of the coast of Ireland after 28 days, on June 17, reaching Liverpool on the twentieth. During part of its trip the *Savannah* used her sails. After returning to the United States the engine was dismantled and the vessel returned to sails.

Other crossings followed rapidly the one by the *Savannah:* in 1821 by the English *Rising Star* (122 feet, 70 hp.), in 1823 by the French schooner *Galibi* (118 feet, 50 hp.), in 1825–1827 by the Dutch *Curaçao* (125⅔ feet, 100 hp.), in 1831 by the Canadian *Royal William* (174 feet, 200 hp.). All these crossings were made partly under sail.

After 1837 ships were able to make the Atlantic crossing completely under steam power. The length of the journey was then reduced to 18 days, 10 hours by the *Sirius* and 15 days, 5 hours by the *Great Western.* These two ships, which made the first voyage almost simultaneously in April 1838, had the following characteristics:

	Length	*Beam*	*Draft*	*Engine power*
Sirius	205 feet	25½ feet	14¾ feet	320 hp.
Great Western	233 feet	33½ feet	19⅔ feet	750 hp.

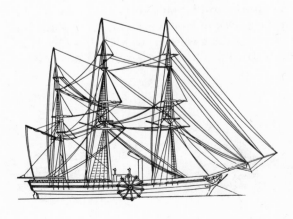

FIG. 78. The *Savannah,* the first boat equipped with a steam engine to cross the Atlantic, in 1818.

Plate 29. Stevens' screw-propelled steamboat made 151 ocean voyages using steam as the sole means of propulsion. Smithsonian Institution

The paddle wheels of the *Sirius* had a diameter of 23⅔ feet; the wheels of the *Great Western* were 28½ feet in diameter. The *Great Western*'s wheels were cycloidal and revolved at 15 rpm.

Passenger accommodations were now much more comfortable than on earlier ships. The *Great Western* was particularly notable for a salon 74 feet long and cabins for 220 passengers and 60 crew.

The *Sirius,* under construction when a steam engine was installed in it, returned to the United States under sail and ended its career as a sailing vessel. But the *Great Western* had been specially built to extend the Great Western Railway line

Plate 30. The "Great Western" on her fifth crossing from Bristol to New York (1838). Painting by Joseph Walter. Bristol, City Art Gallery. (Photo City Art Gallery.)

to the United States. Carefully designed by Isambard K. Brunel and built in Bristol by W. Patterson, it was equipped with a Maudslay engine with two cylinders 6 feet in diameter with a stroke of 7 feet.

The *Great Western* returned to England between May 7 and May 22 and became the first ship to make regular transatlantic crossings. It made 64 voyages between 1838 and 1847, and then put in ten years of service to the West Indies. Transoceanic navigation had thus been established with paddle-wheel steam engines and continued until 1856 with wooden vessels, the last of which was the American ship *Adriatic,* built in New York.

The last paddle-wheel ship was the *Scotia* (1861), built with an iron hull by the Cunard Line. It held the blue ribbon from 1862 to 1867 for the fastest crossing (8 days, 3 hours). It had a displacement of 6,250 tons with a length of 374 feet and a draft of 19⅔ feet. The first ships of the French Compagnie Générale Transatlantique were built in England in the same period.

The propeller   As we have seen, paddle wheels presented serious disadvantages not only for warships but also for commercial navigation—they were too fragile and vulnerable to the action of the sea. The appearance of the screw propeller made possible the development of large ships.

In England, Percy Smith and a Swede, John Ericsson, the inventor of the *Monitor* (then resident in Britain), are frequently mentioned as inventors of the screw propeller, while in France the experiments and failures of Frédéric Sauvage are often mentioned. Between 1800 and 1845 the idea of using screw propellers to drive ships was often suggested and projects were planned.

The truth is that the invention did not suddenly spring at once from a single brain, to be copied by others, thus depriving the inventor of the fruits of his efforts. As early as the eighteenth century several inventors had studied the possibility of using propellers. The following highlights can be mentioned, among others: 1729, a paper by du Quet was read to the Académie des Sciences; 1776, David Bushnell proposed to use screws with two threads and a narrow pitch on his submarine, the *Turtle;* 1785, John Fitch took up the idea of propulsion by propeller (Figure 79); 1800, Robert Fulton, in trials at Le Havre, recognized that windmill vanes were more efficient than the Archimedes' screw.

We find more detailed studies being made between 1800 and 1830. In 1803 a patent was given Charles Dallery, who began constructing a boat but never finished it. In 1804/5 very detailed plans were drawn up by Robert L. Stevens for

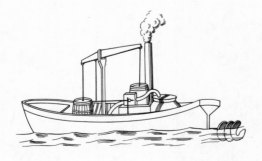

FIG. 79. Fitch's propeller-driven boat, 1796/97 (from an engraving by Baxter and Harley).

the use of single or double propellers. And 1829 saw the designs, tests, and patent of Joseph Ressel of Austria (Figure 80).

These dates clearly show the antecedents to the patents of Sauvage (May 28, 1832) and Smith (1834). But at that time most people could not imagine that a propeller could deliver the same propulsive force as did large paddle wheels.

Frédéric Sauvage and Augustin Normand — Sauvage had persisted in demonstrating the possibilities of the propeller. To this work he devoted all his time and money and wore himself out against the incredulity of his contemporaries. He considered his experiments to be conclusive, but they were made on a small boat. People contended that though the propeller might be adequate to propel a small boat, it could not deliver the power of paddle wheels for large ships. A trial on a ship of sufficient tonnage was necessary to convince the public. At this point Augustin Normand, a well-informed builder who was planning a ship (which became the *Napoléon*), thought that the propeller could be usefully adapted to his project.

Sauvage recommended a type of propeller consisting of a single turn of the spiral. Normand knew of his work and came to an agreement with him, in which

FIG. 80. Joseph Ressel's propeller, patented 1829 (from an 1812 drawing).

FIG. 81. Propeller with one helix and one turn, by Frédéric Sauvage, patented 1832.

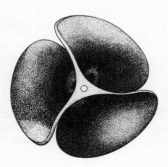

FIG. 82. The Normand and Barnes three-helix propeller. This propeller is the first of eight different models tried out on the *Napoléon* between January and July 1843.

he would bear the costs of a trial run, while reserving the right to modify if necessary the type of propeller. Sauvage could thus prove the effectiveness of helicoid screws without bearing the considerable expense of building and adapting the propeller to a large vessel.

Tests by Normand and an English mechanic named Barnes, a highly competent man, which were carried out with several types of propellers, revealed beyond a shadow of a doubt that propellers with several blades were superior to the helicoid one with one complete spiral (Figure 82). Sauvage protested vigorously, claiming the superiority of his system, and refused to participate in tests performed with designs other than his own. Backed by their agreement with him, which left their hands free, Normand and Barnes abandoned Sauvage's model and, after numerous tests, developed a propeller with several blades, which gave excellent results.

The triumph of the propeller During the same time conclusive trials had taken place in England, first, those of Ericsson and France's Pettit Smith in 1836/37 and later by J. and G. Rennie, which began in 1838. Smith tried a helicoid with several turns (Figure 83). Noting that the output was better when the number of turns was reduced, on the *Archimède* he adopted a propeller with a single turn, and later with two and three blades (Figure 84). These experiments predated those for the *Napoléon* (1843), later renamed the *Corse*.

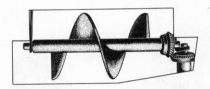

FIG. 83. Francis Pettit Smith's propeller with a single helix and two turns. From his 1836 patent. The same type of propeller had been the object of Dallery's French patent in 1803. The emplacement under the stern had just been patented in 1829 by Ressel. Smith was not aware of the existence of these patents.

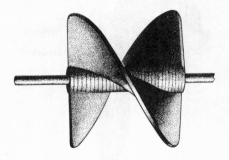

FIG. 84. Twin-helix propeller by Smith, Miller, and Ravenhill. Third propeller of the *Archimède*, 1839.

The most daring innovation was adopting the Smith-Rennie type of propeller on the large *Great Britain*, built in England by W. Patterson in 1842, and substituting it for the paddle wheels originally planned. The advice of I. K. Brunel, engineering adviser of the Great Western Company, which had ordered the ship, was the deciding factor in this choice.

All these results about the ability of propellers to drive large ships seemed conclusive. A spectacular trial run in England confirmed it when the propeller-equipped *Rattler* and the paddle boat *Alecto* were linked by cable and made to pull in opposite directions. The *Rattler* pulled the *Alecto* at 2½ knots, despite its use of paddle wheels. This test confirmed the superiority of the propeller over the paddle wheel.

To return to the *Corse*, built by Augustin Normand, it was one of the largest ships in the French merchant marine at that time. It was 154 feet long and 28 feet wide, with a displacement of 374 tons. The engine had a power of 120 actual (270 indicated) hp. To increase the relative speed of the propeller (the steam engine operated at the slow rate of approximately 33 rpm.), the engine drove a step-up gear consisting of a 125-tooth wheel made of very dry hornbeam wood engaging a 29-tooth cast-iron pinion on the propeller shaft.

Ericsson's design, which had been studied by Delisle earlier (possibly as early as 1823, but more certainly by 1825), consisted of helicoidal blades attached to arms or circles, leaving the center of the propeller open. After trials made between 1829 and 1835 Ericsson took out a patent in July 1836 that was applied in 1837 on the *Francis B. Ogden* (Figure 85). It was tried in France in 1845 on the *Pomone*, a frigate with a displacement of 1,927 tons.

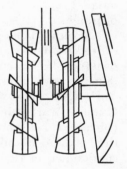

FIG. 85.   Ericsson's propeller, from his 1836 patent. The propeller consists of two drums on a single shaft, each with eight helicoidal segments. The concavities of the segments on one drum are facing forward; those of the segments of the other drum face toward the stern.

In 1847 a solid propeller was substituted for the Ericsson one and its output proved to be noticeably better. This type of propeller, whose superiority had been demonstrated in tests by the *Napoléon* and *Pomone* in France and the *Great Britain* in England, became generally adopted by 1850.

The Great Britain   We must return to I. K. Brunel's design for the *Great Britain,* an achievement remarkable by virtue of his bold adoption of the propeller and his use, for the first time, of iron in ship construction.

The displacement of the ship, launched in 1844, now seems low—only 3,618 tons—but it was one of the biggest of the period. Brunel, who had already built the wooden *Great Western* and had paid great attention to building a strong hull, felt that wood was no longer suitable for the size of the new vessel: a length (between uprights) of 270 feet and an overall length of 318 feet, with a beam of 47½ feet.

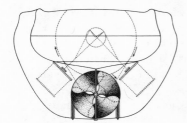

FIG. 86.   Diagram of the arrangement of the engine and propeller in the *Great Britain.*

The *Great Britain* originally had six masts, the first carrying square sails, the five others with lateen sails. Iron plates 18 to 25 mm. thick were used for the keel, and the sides, which were supported by ribs spaced at intervals of 13⅔ inches, were made from sheets 12 to 15 mm. thick. The hull was divided by watertight bulkheads into five compartments. The ship was driven by an engine of 1,500 indicated hp. turning a propeller 15½ feet in diameter. On its trial runs it attained a speed of more than 11 knots (Figure 86).

Its interior accommodations were spacious. There were several salons, the largest being 106⅔ feet by 33 feet. There were 180 cabins for 360 passengers, and the ship could carry 1,200 tons of freight. Its first Atlantic crossing was made in 14 days, 21 hours, at an average speed of 9.3 knots, with 60 passengers and 600 tons of freight.

Several changes reduced the masts to four. On its fifth voyage it ran aground off the Irish coast, where it remained for an entire winter. To protect it Brunel ordered a breakwater and protective fence to be built around it. The hull was not damaged, and after a long period of reconditioning it resumed its service to New York. Later it served on the Australian run, then as a transport ship in the Crimean War, with 1,650 men on board. It was in service until 1881, when it was converted to sail and so used until 1886. Afterward its hull served as a coal depot in the Falkland Islands, where it was still in existence during World War I. It was condemned in 1933 and sunk outside the harbor. Its longevity proves beyond question the strength of the hull built by I. K. Brunel.

Changes in battle fleets   The propellor made it possible to use steam propulsion on large vessels without decreasing the number of guns. The boilers and engines could now be installed in the hold, but it was necessary to compensate for the additional weight placed on the ship. In Volume II we saw that introducing artillery on ships required ballasting to offset the weight of the guns in the tops. The weight of the engine could replace all or part of this ballast. The problem of estimating weight was thus completely solved by installing a steam engine on a ship. All sailing vessels in existing fleets could be converted without modifying the vessels or decreasing their artillery.

Engine power could not be arbitrarily fixed. It was accepted that the weight of an engine was 1,320 pounds per horsepower unit, so that its capacity could easily be calculated by dividing by 1,320 the weight of the ballast it was to replace. For example, for 270 tons the result was 450 hp. Using this formula the conversion would mean ships with a speed of 6 knots, under steam, with a propeller.

In order to increase the engine's power, ships could be lengthened by inserting an additional section of hull in the center. For example, on a ship with a beam of 55¾ feet, a draft of 19⅔ feet, and a ratio of 8 for the surface of the midship frame to that of the rectangle described, it was possible to gain 55¾ × 19⅔ × 0.8, resulting in 80 displacement tons for every yard of additional length. For an increase of 19⅔ feet in length 480 displacement tons are gained. But the hull and accessory parts corresponding to each new section represented 60 percent of the displacement, so the available area was only 0.4 × 480 = 192 tons, or an additional engine weight of approximately 300 hp.

An increase in length of 19⅔ feet thus made it possible to increase the power by 300 hp. and obtain greater speed. For example, instead of 450 hp. for the engine of a ship that had not been lengthened, it was possible to obtain a power of from 700 to 800 hp. and increase the speed from 6 knots to 8 or 9 knots.

From this time on, British and French fleets included ships remodeled for steam. Some were not lengthened, but others were, with an increase in relative speed.

Under the best conditions, however, one could hardly count on speeds of more than 9 knots. But this speed satisfied most navy men, who considered that the design of the battleship was fixed and unchangeable in the form of sailing vessels with a maximum displacement of approximately 5,000 tons. They were convinced that the steam engine was no more than an auxiliary with which to maneuver without sails during battle or in case the ship was becalmed and thought these low speeds perfectly adequate for battleships.

The ideas of Dupuy de Lôme The French engineer Dupuy de Lôme was the first to propose a different approach. Steam was for him the basic means of propulsion. By installing more powerful engines it would be possible to attain speeds of 12 knots. The sail would become a mere auxiliary that could be reduced in size and used only to assist the engine when the wind was favorable.

De Lôme had difficulty getting his views accepted, but they were imposed by the prince de Joinville shortly before the Revolution of 1848. The *Napoléon*, built according to de Lôme's plans, was launched at Le Havre in May 1850 and went to sea in May 1852. It was 233⅔ feet long at the waterline and 53 feet wide, with a draft of 25⅓ feet and a displacement of 5,047 tons. It had 3,411 square yards of sail and was armed with 90 guns.

The sail area, which on earlier ships was 33 times that of the midship frame, was reduced to 28, and was thereafter reduced to 25 times. With its 960 nominal hp., the *Napoléon* achieved a speed of 12.14 knots under steam and 13.86 knots with the help of its sails.

This was the first so-called high-speed vessel whose construction date is important in the history of shipbuilding. This evolution was followed fifteen years later by the adoption of armor plating, which was the beginning of the modern navy.

Dupuy de Lôme had compromised in order to keep the displacement of the *Napoléon* in the vicinity of 5,000 tons. The British navy, which wanted to retain complete superiority in speed, sail, and armament, built considerably larger ships. It began constructing a series of four vessels of the *Victoria* type, a ship launched in 1859 with 130 68-pounders that fired shells, arranged on three decks. Of 6,930 tons displacement, the class had engines of 4,290 indicated hp. and a speed of over 13 knots. It still carried much sail. These ships, which were the last representatives of the three-deckers, disappeared with the coming of armor plate. Their size made it possible to install in them the large quarters favored by admirals—until 1867 the *Victoria* was the flagship of the commander for the Mediterranean squadron.

THE EVOLUTION OF MARINE STEAM ENGINES

One major component of the steam engine is the boiler, which tends on occasion to be overlooked in retracing the history of the use of steam as a source of power. In the case of ships' engines the development of boilers was of prime importance.

The evolution of marine boilers   In its early forms the marine boiler was a simple cylindrical vessel like that of Watt's stationary engines and was enclosed in a brick mass. Symington, who definitely proved his theories, was the first to use a boiler with an internal firebox. Few builders followed his example, and in his *Comet* Henry Bell returned to external heating of a boiler placed in brickwork. When engines developed greater power it was necessary to increase the heating surfaces and place the fireboxes more carefully.

From 1800 to 1845 the ordinary type of boiler was the model with flat walls and an internal firebox with crooked flues to expand the heating surface. The flat surfaces did not withstand pressures well, so they were strengthened by stay bars screwed between the metal faces. Despite this reinforcement, boilers of this type were hardly adequate for internal pressures greater than two pounds.

In the next chapter we shall see how boilers with water tubes and later smoke

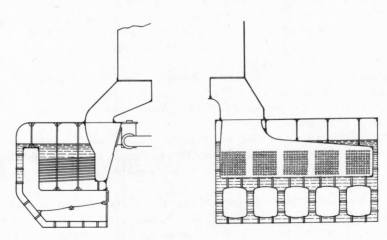

FIG. 87.   Marine boiler for a 600-hp. engine, by John Penn, 1862. *Left:* Vertical transverse cross section. *Right:* Vertical longitudinal cross section.

tubes were developed in locomotives by gradual evolution. The type tried out by the British navy around 1850 was adopted a little later by the merchant marines of every country. Increased steam pressure, which was absolutely necessary for increasingly powerful engines, brought about abandonment of the old boilers with flat surfaces.

Until around 1850 pressures were limited to less than 5½ pounds. Large boilers were fed with salt-laden seawater. The steam discharged from the engine returned to a condenser, where it was mixed with cooling water. The volume of cooling water needed was equal to 20 times the volume of water coming from the condensed steam. Water from the condenser was thus practically as salty as seawater and was also saturated with oil and impurities. So there was no point in returning it to the boilers, which normally had to be fed with water taken directly from the sea.

The water supply As the steam vaporized, the concentration of salts in the boilers increased. From time to time it was necessary to remove the water from the boiler and check its salt content with a graduated hydrometer indicating the point at which the water should be replaced with fresh seawater.

The presence of sulfate of lime in seawater made the danger from precipitations still greater. This salt, whatever its concentration, precipitates at around 140°C. Increasing the speed at which water was recycled did not therefore prevent total precipitation of the sulfate of lime, which formed a deposit on the walls at this temperature. As this deposit became thicker it impeded the cooling action of the water on the metal of the boiler, which ran the risk of burning out, which could bring about damage and explosions. A chart of the pressures and temperatures of live steam shows that this dangerous phenomenon occurs with a steam pressure in the vicinity of 5½ pounds.

Progress in building marine boilers occurred gradually. At first only low-pressure boilers were used in which the internal pressure, the difference between the absolute internal pressure and atmospheric pressure, was very low. The boiler of the *Savannah* (1818) operated at a pressure of 1½ pounds per square inch, but in 1842 that of an oscillating engine had a pressure of only 12⅓ pounds.

Starting at this time an attempt was made to increase pressure while still keeping it below 5½ pounds. These medium-pressure boilers included those of the *Great Britain* (1843) and HMS *Terrible* (1845), both of 2⅓ pounds pressure, the *Atlantic* (1849) at 2⅔ pounds, and the *Washington* (1863), 4 pounds.

The problem of Using fresh water to supply the boiler would have
the condenser eliminated these drawbacks and also retained the
heat absorbed by the removal of hot water from the boiler. But it was impossible to carry on board the enormous quantity of fresh water needed for operating the engines, water that would have been passed through the mixing condenser and discharged into the sea.

The solution was to condense water from the steam in a separate vessel, cooled by the seawater that circulated around it without combining with it, that is, by using a surface condenser. James Watt had thought of this device but had not built one. It was simultaneously worked on by several engineers, without success, until the idea was taken up again by David Napier, then Samuel Hall. These two engineers, working separately, came to the same result.

The first inventors of the system had failed because they had not provided for a large enough surface for condensation or for the quantity of water needed for cooling. This was obtained by numerous brass tubes to circulate the cooling water.

David Napier appears to have built his first surface condenser in 1820/21, but the system was received coolly by ships' engineers. In 1837 Samuel Hall tried out his apparatus, designed in 1833, then tried it out on the *Wilberforce* in 1841. But its tubes were obstructed by the Thames mud brought in with the water stirred up.

From 1837 to 1860 the surface condenser was seldom used despite very satisfactory trials on the HMS *Grappler* (1845) and the *P. and O. St. Mooltan* (1854), on which the boilers and condenser were found to be in perfect condition after 30,000 miles of use. The engineer Edward Humphreys, who had installed them, published these results in 1862. At the same time higher pressures and compound engines with expansion occurring successively in several cylinders were being introduced; thus began the introduction of modern engines.

Until 1850 the use of several cylinders offered no advantages over the engine with one cylinder or several in which expansion occurred in each one, then went directly to the condenser. Multicylinder engines simply were not competitive, because of their low steam pressures and the greater complexity of the engine's components.

The adaptation of Watt's engine — The continuous evolution of marine steam engines between 1800 and 1850 is characterized by the development of many features that differed from one builder to another.

As we have seen, Watt's classic engine could be adapted to paddle-wheel propulsion. For a long time it was used on American riverboats and ferryboats with a large overhead walking beam. To eliminate this unwieldy contrivance an engine with a side walking beam placed at the bottom was developed. Napier introduced a model known as the steeple engine. Inclined cylinders connected directly to the axles of the wheels by connecting rods and cranks were also used.

Paddle-wheel propulsion was specially appropriate for engines of moderate speed corresponding to that needed for the wheel, namely 15 to 16 rpm. The axle of the paddle wheel could thus be driven directly, without the need for gears.

The problem of transmitting power to the propeller — The propeller, when adopted, had to be made to revolve more rapidly than the engine, hence the need for a gear transmission and a reversing control of the propeller shaft below the engine. The layout of the *Rattler* is significant (Figure 88). This ship, with a displacement of 1,078 tons, was equipped with a 437-hp. Maudslay engine. Where what would have been the axle of the paddle wheels was a shaft driven by the engine's crankshafts, which held a large gear wheel that drove a smaller cogwheel on the propeller shaft. The engine had 4 cylinders with a diameter of approximately 3¼ feet and a piston stroke of 4 feet. The inclined cylinders were placed in pairs on each side of the axle. The 4:1 ratio of the diameters of the two toothed wheels made it possible to turn the propeller at 108 rpm with an engine turning at 27 rpm. The boiler still operated at only a low pressure, between ¾ and 1½ pounds.

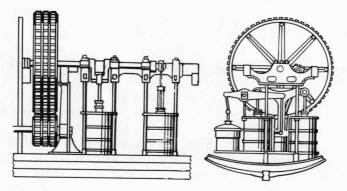

FIG. 88.   The 200-hp., 4-cylinder engine built by Maudslay for the *Rattler*, 1843.

The first engines for the *Great Britain* (1,000 nominal hp.) had 4 cylinders 7⅓ feet in diameter, with a stroke of 6 feet. Increased speed was obtained with a transmission system using chains connecting the gears. The engine rotated at 18 rpm., the propeller at 53 rpm. Steam furnished at 2 to 3 pounds pressure gave 1,500 indicated hp.

After it had run aground and been repaired the *Great Britain* was given a new Penn engine with oscillating cylinders suspended on trunnions, in which the steam inlet system was located. The piston rod served as a connecting rod, making it possible to decrease the size of the engine (Figure 89).

When it was decided to eliminate gearing, the engine had to be made to turn faster, at the speed the propeller required. An original solution to the problem of decreasing the size of the engine was furnished by the English builder Penn, who eliminated the piston rod. Instead, the connecting rod was joined with the piston inside the center of its head.

In France this system was not held in great favor because the large size of the stuffing box, in which the piston head traveled back and forth, caused problems of steamtightness and maintenance difficulties. The gear system was retained for a

FIG. 89.   The 500-hp. engine with two oscillating cylinders built by Penn for the *Great Britain*, 1845.

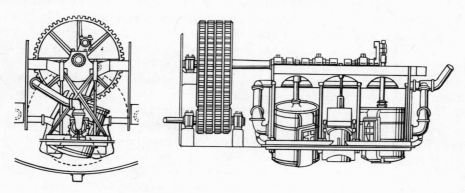

long time, despite its weight and the problems involved in cutting gear teeth. The large wheel had notched crowns in which hardwood teeth were inserted; the small wheel was of cast iron. The meshing of the wooden teeth, despite their geometrically imperfect cutting and the resulting tolerances, was softer, more flexible, and quieter than with a gear system in which the two wheels were metal.

When Dupuy de Lôme presented the first plan for the ship that became the *Napoléon* he used ideas that were far in advance of his time. He designed an iron hull and an engine that turned rapidly enough to drive the propeller shaft directly. The prince of Joinville advised him to abandon the iron hull in order not to offend current opinion. Moreover, he was requested to consult with the Établissement d'Indret, which built the engine with a gear system that let the engine turn at a speed of less than 30 rpm.

Dupuy de Lôme designed an engine equipped with a large wheel with 80 teeth made of mountain ash, which turned a small wheel with 41 teeth. Thus the propeller made 43 revolutions to every 22 by the engine. The four-bladed propeller was 19 feet in diameter and had a pitch of 29 feet.

There were two cylinders 8 feet in diameter, and the stroke of the pistons was 5¼ feet. The results of trial runs by the *Napoléon* in August 1853 were as follows:

Nominal power at 28 rpm (maximum) 900 hp.
Number of revolutions during the trial run 22.54
Normal power 767
Average pressure of indicator diagram 2½ pounds instead of the 1 pound accepted for the nominal power
Pressure indicated on the diagram 1,798 hp.

RAW MATERIALS

Throughout the entire eighteenth century and the first half of the nineteenth the shipbuilding industry used wood almost exclusively. Metals did not assume any importance until after 1850.

The wood supply   The availability of wood was therefore of prime importance in shipbuilding, and in the search for it economic and political questions played a role as important as technical problems.

Wooden planks had to be quite strong and of increasingly large sizes for hulls, keeping pace with the growth in the sizes of ships. Oak, being the wood most suitable for the purpose, was still the most highly prized material; although it presented one serious defect: it ate away iron bolts used to secure the parts. It was therefore necessary to use copper or brass bolts to prevent the connectors from corrosion and destruction.

India supplied the British navy with teak, which had a strength equal to oak's but did not corrode iron the way oak did. But its cost and the difficulties of transporting teak limited its use, especially in the eighteenth century.

It was (and still is) also necessary not to use freshly cut wood, which, being insufficiently dried, rotted very quickly. It had to be drained of its sap by submerging it in water and then letting it dry for a long time in the open air. Plentiful supplies of wood were necessary in order to have available well-dried planks approximately ten years old, including the time for soaking and drying.

Oak was found over a large part of Europe—in France, England, and even in Italy and Sicily. But English oak *(Quercus robur),* which was the most highly valued and the strongest, was preferred.

The necessity for the British navy to increase its shipbuilding during the wars with France in the eighteenth century and the Napoleonic period had impoverished the English forests, which had already been adversely affected by the demands of house builders (for example, to rebuild London in the seventeenth century) and by the demand for wood by charcoal burners supplying the rapidly expanding iron industry.

The use of coal greatly reduced the demand for wood, but the long sea wars created a critical situation—ships were poorly repaired and some were built with wood that rotted quickly. For example, vessels like the *Océan* in France and the 90-gun *Royal William* in England, built in 1719, had a life of almost a century. In contrast, the 110-gun *Queen Charlotte,* under construction in 1810, rotted in 1812 before its launching. In 1805, the year of Trafalgar, repairs to Nelson's *Victory* (1765) cost three times the ship's initial price.

The inadequate dimensions or lack of certain pieces for sternposts—for example, the transom—limited the sizes of ships. In the face of these increased demands the price of wood rose rapidly, especially the price for pieces of exceptional sizes and shapes, and consequently the cost of ships per ton also rose. From five pounds sterling in 1600 it climbed in 1775–1802 to 20 to 21 pounds, in 1803 to 34.5 pounds, and in 1805 (a period of great shortage of wood) to 36 pounds.

In 1804 the price of a load of ordinary oak was 8 pounds, but knee pieces for a gun cost 15.4 pounds. The load, corresponding to 50 cubic feet, was the standard unit of measure for timber. In the case of oak it weighed slightly more than one ton. An 1,800-tonner required 3,000 loads of wood, which when worked was reduced by almost one-half. (This estimate is given by the French author Vial de Clairbois in the navy section of the *Encyclopédie méthodique*'s article on construction lumber.)

A three-rated vessel in England cost roughly 1,000 pounds per gun, so a 74-gun vessel, for example, cost about 70,000 pounds. Half this figure was for timber, one-tenth for masts, one-seventh for the sail and rigging. The remainder, less than a third, was for other equipment and labor. Thus, the price of building lumber was of primary importance; its scarcity and cost were the determining factors in naval construction.

The scarcity of wood for masts   Volume II discussed the sizes necessary for the spars used for the single-piece masts that the English preferred. With the passage of time it became increasingly difficult to find sturdy masts for ships. After United States independence one source of masts was closed to Great Britain, but not for the French and Spanish. It was necessary to fall back on supplies from the Baltic forests, but their trees were smaller. The idea of masts being built up from several pieces of lumber was considered, but England no longer had workers capable of cutting and assembling the sections.

The situation was critical by 1804/5, for masts had to be replaced regularly. Pine, which is excellent from the point of view of strength and flexibility, owes its qualities to the resin it contains. Tree trunks destined to become masts were stored in ditches filled with water, which preserved the resin in the capillaries of the wood. When removed from water the trunks lost their characteristics at the end of 10 or 12 months at most, which required having a considerable stock of replacements. The situation worsened in 1805 when British squadrons had all their large vessels at sea, in squadrons or forces blockading Continental ports. The ships ran the risk of being immobilized when the masts, their strength exhausted, broke and disabled the vessels. Added to accidents caused by gusts of wind was the damage to masts and spars by the "demasting" fire of French sailors.

A considerable effort was made to condition several vessels reinforcing Nelson's fleet. Annihilating the adversaries of the British navy at Trafalgar solved the technical problem at one stroke. The large ships were able to return to British ports and the British navy limited itself to keeping only frigates at sea. The wooden scantlings for repair and construction of hulls and masts were smaller, easier to find, and cheaper for frigates than for larger ships.

Introduction of metal in construction

The use of metal was gradually initiated, at first for special parts, for which it had a particular advantage. In wooden construction the timbers and deck beams were connected by strong crooks, or knees, that were difficult to find. An attempt was sometimes made to bend young oaks to make them grow in the shape of a knee, but the quantity available remained limited and could be obtained only after the many years needed for the trees to grow.

Being costly pieces and cumbersome in the between-decks areas, these knees were easily replaced by iron ones. As early as the time of Pepys (1670), Sir Anthony Deane had thought of using iron joints in the wooden structure, but it was not until the end of the eighteenth century and beginning of the nineteenth that metallurgy was able to supply, in larger quantity and at lower cost, the metal parts that had become indispensable.

Metal knees, stanchions, and the like were used after 1810 on the ships of the East India Company. Iron rings had been adopted as early as 1800 for the hoopings of masts. In 1811 metal appeared to support stays, and it was adopted by the entire British navy.

The stationary standing rigging that held the masts was from then on made of iron cable, which gave greater rigidity to the masts and spars. When the spars were supported by hemp stays they leaned from the windward side and caused the leeward stays to go slack.

The first iron hulls

The use of iron for hulls appeared only in the nineteenth century, and then but deliberately. It was long feared that a crack or tear in the metal wall could not be plugged easily and that the iron vessel, which was much heavier than water, would sink immediately. In this connection great value was placed on the ease of plugging leaks in a wooden bottom, which, even if it filled with water, could float if necessary or would at least sink very slowly.

An iron barge was built in England in 1787 for canal use. After the beginning of the nineteenth century a certain number of iron boats were built in England, but in general it was believed that this type of construction would be limited to canal and river vessels.

In 1822 a builder named Aaron Manby proposed to put the first iron steam boat into service between Paris and Le Havre. To meet objections made at the time he gave the iron hull a wooden sheath to ensure that it would float. A drawing, the only evidence of this strange compromise, shows that the ship had very rudimentary lines.

It seems clear that John Laird was the first, in 1829, to make more general use of iron for steamships. But this was not greeted very favorably, even though it had the advantage of a hull that weighed less than that of wooden vessels.

The slow progress of iron construction Dupuy de Lôme, having been sent to England to study this use of iron, noted in his report on iron vessels dated June 1842 that *Iron Sides,* a sailing ship built in 1838 in Liverpool by Jackson, Gordon & Co., had successfully made three Atlantic crossings between 1839 and 1842 with cotton cargoes. However, it was quite a small boat, barely 98½ feet long, with a displacement of 490 tons. Its very lightweight hull weighed only 24 percent of its displacement.

Brunel's decision to build the *Great Britain* of iron was thus a daring one, but it won the approval of Dupuy de Lôme, who saw in it the possibility of a strong, watertight hull capable of eliminating the startings that were so frequent in wooden hulls. Dupuy de Lôme estimated the weight of this handsome ship at a total of 1,000 tons (or 25.6 percent of the displacement) with a total displacement of 3,900 tons, and with a hull consisting of only 840 tons of iron and 160 tons of wood.

It is astonishing to note that this example was not immediately followed by other builders; but it must be remembered that puddled iron was still expensive and could be supplied only in very small sheets. Shipyards were not equipped for metalworking, although they had equipment and a supply of labor highly specialized in wood construction. This explains why in 1840 the Cunard Line's *Britannia* was built of wood.

Thus Dupuy de Lôme, who favored construction of a large iron battleship, could arrange only for the construction of two small boats, the *Caton* and *Ariel.* The *Caton,* begun in June 1844, was finished in December 1847. It had a displacement of 892 tons, and its engine, which turned at 33 rpm, operated a gear with a ratio of 132–45, or approximately 3:1. The ship was capable of a speed of 10.3 knots, or 11.7 with the help of its sails. The hull was constructed of small sheets of iron 8 feet long by 2 feet wide, varying in thickness from 14 mm. for the bottom to 8 mm. for the upper portions.

Despite the success of the *Great Britain,* the application of iron to battleships was very slow. One of the first iron ships in the British navy was the HMS *Caradoc,* a 576-ton (B.O.M.) gunboat built in 1846/47. Other iron gunboats were constructed in 1851.

The frigate *Dauntless* was built of wood even in 1847. The HMS *Simoon* (1849) was the largest iron battleship, with a displacement of 2,800 tons (B.O.M. 1,980 tons). We have seen that vessels of the *Victoria* type (for example, the 131-gun *Marlborough,* 1850/55, with a displacement of 6,050 tons) were also built of wood. It was felt that wooden walls stood up well under fire from solid balls. Even if the ball came through the walls the damage could be repaired by the ship's carpenters. But metal structures were largely ripped open by the shock of cannonballs (especially if they struck at an angle) and could not be repaired with the equipment at hand. Thus, battleships continued to be built of wood until the danger of broadsides by explosive shells made them too vulnerable. The use of armor plating for protection did not appear until between 1855 and 1860.

Sheathing the hulls   In the last volume we saw that in 1671 Sir Anthony Deane had tried out lead sheathing, repeating the procedure practiced in Roman antiquity. But this technique could not be carried out satisfactorily, and a sheathing of thin pieces of wood continued to be used.

This most inadequate protection was sometimes replaced by studding—the hull was covered with iron nails with large, flat heads placed side by side. Rust eventually connected the heads and covered the hull with a hard shell that prevented shipworms from penetrating it. This made the hull rough and resistant to movement, and, moreover, algae and sea animals could easily attach themselves to it. This technique of studding continued in use especially for stationary buoys, pontoons, and so on, which did not suffer from these disadvantages.

In 1764 the British admiralty ordered experiments made with copper sheathing on a frigate, the *Alarm,* then on small ships, but without great success. Electrolytic reactions between the copper and the iron bolts, the nature of which could not yet be understood, made the cure worse than the disease. In 1783 iron bolts and pins were replaced by copper ones and durable protection was obtained. From then on copper was applied to large merchant ships that had to navigate in tropical waters.

A long article by Pierre-Alexander-Laurent Forfait, a well-known engineer in the Napoleonic era, describes the difficulties experienced in France in adopting copper sheathing. Although it was known in France that the English had made the practice general, trials in 1778 on the *Iphigénie* and in 1779 on the *Gentille* and *Amazone* were not very encouraging. Examining captured English ships enabled the French to study the sheathing technique used in England. Durable sheathings were finally developed with careful use of metals, nails, and application techniques. The great advantage of keeping hulls clean and protecting them against shipworms ultimately led to the general use of this technique.

Scientific procedures for designs and diagrams   In the sixteenth and seventeenth centuries the lines of a ship were plotted from simple sketches that served as construction guides. In the eighteenth century and as early as about 1670 in England the lines of hulls were plotted more accurately with plans that included cross sections. These diagrams made it possible to calculate the displacement and, after Father Pierre Bouguer, to determine the stability of the planned vessel. But until the nineteenth century shipwrights continued to build the frame members of hulls from models they built themselves in yards.

In 1745 Duhamel du Monceau advised making plans in which the sections would be perpendicular to the waterline, in order to relate the design of the hulls to the actual construction. This was tried at Brest but then apparently abandoned. Builders continued to plot the sections perpendicular to the keel, not parallel to the waterline. This was more convenient for shipwrights, who assembled the frames perpendicular to the keel, which was supported by blocks.

Only around 1825 was plotting the hull done in the loft, from which derived the shapes of the framing members. Draftsmen isolated from the shipyards laid out their sections perpendicular to the waterline, an evolution in technique that led to the dominance of design over construction. But the old diagrams continued in use until wooden construction came to an end.

It must also be noted that engines were first described by a fairly detailed general plan showing practically all the parts with their approximate sizes. In the early period of steam-engine construction the shop drew up sketches for the production of individual parts. Not until after the mid-nineteenth century did builders recognize the necessity of first preparing complete specifications with detailed dimensions of the various parts. This led to accurately described dimensions for the parts, working tolerances, and so on.

For a long time to come the inadequate precision of machine tools required the production shop to adjust, in most cases manually with a file, the metal surfaces and parts that fitted together.

THE TECHNIQUES AND INSTRUMENTATION OF NAVIGATION

Until 1486 navigators everywhere were satisfied to remain close to the coast, from which they could find their position. This information was accumulated in charts that then made it possible to determine position in reference to fixed points.

In 1486 Bartholemew Diaz daringly left the coasts behind him, giving the first definite example of navigation on the high seas. But throughout the early period of ocean navigation, all navigators kept their charts secret, whether they were the Portuguese ones for the India route via the Cape or the Spanish ones for their fleets bringing back wealth from the Americas. Cook himself advised his crews to remain silent about the routes their voyages followed in order to keep the rewards of their discoveries for themselves. The charts prepared from the many voyages of discovery were thus reproduced in only small numbers; indeed, the India Council forbade printing them at all. However, it was tempting to obtain the secrets of one's neighbor, and from the sixteenth to the eighteenth centuries the development of navigation helped to spread knowledge and speed progress.

Plotting courses   When land was lost from sight it was necessary to plot one's course between the departure point and the arrival point. This could be done accurately by using charts made according to the method of projection invented in the mid-sixteenth century by a Fleming named Gerhard Kremer (Latinized as Gerardus Mercator) based on a system of increasing the distances between the parallels of latitude.

This projection, which is still used for marine charts, plots the meridians of longitude according to equidistant vertical lines and the parallels of latitude by other lines perpendicular to the verticals and separated from each other by increasingly greater distances as one advances from the equator toward the poles.

In order easily to lay out a course at a fixed angle to the meridians on the globe and corresponding on the chart to a fixed oblique on the meridians, a navigator must have available a gradual divergence of the parallels according to a carefully determined law. Mercator, to whom infinitesimal calculus was not available, could not discover this law. His charts, laid out empirically, were not accurate, and his immediate successors could make only improvements that were themselves empirical. Mercator's charts, published after 1569, were not corrected until 1695, when

Edmund Halley, an astronomer and mathematician, formulated the equation that made it possible to trace the increasing latitudes with accuracy.

By the beginning of the eighteenth century various chart series were available for the use of navigators. At this time charts were edited at the initiative of printers and geographers from information they themselves collected. Colbert had already appreciated the need for hydrographic surveys of coastlines. In 1720 there was founded in Paris a repository of charts and plans, journals and papers on navigation, the embryo of what later became the Hydrographic Service. Twenty years later England and Holland had similar establishments.

In 1773 a decree by the Royal Council established a monopoly for the production and sale of marine charts "in order to protect navigators from the dangerous uncertainty into which they would be thrown by an accumulation of charts that might be published by private persons."

The measurement of speed   With a system available to represent the oceans' surfaces, there were two ways to fix a ship's course, to determine its successive positions during a voyage. Position could be reckoned in terms of the direction and speed of the ship (dead reckoning), or reckoned by taking fixes on the stars, which enabled a navigator to determine the ship's position on the globe from the position of the stars at a given moment.

For centuries the first method, dead reckoning, was the only one that could be used, in which case it was absolutely necessary to estimate the speed and direction of the ship. By judging the wind's strength and the nautical qualities of their vessel, early navigators could acquire experience in estimating their speed. The invention of the ship's log made it possible to measure speed, if still only approximately. The first mention of the log occurs in England in 1577, in a book called *A Regiment for the Sea*, by William Bourne.

In 1643 a certain Reverend Fournier described the log: "For several years the English have been attaching to a knotted line a small oaken blade approximately one foot by five or six inches long." The log is thrown into the sea and, thanks to the water resistance, remains in approximately the same place. By paying out the line attached to it, a navigator could measure the distance traveled in a given length of time. Time was measured with an hourglass because pendulums operate erratically at sea.

Some standard was necessary for this measurement, and the nautical mile, equal to the length of one minute of a meridian arc on the earth's perimeter, was adopted. In the sixteenth century this mile was accepted as being equal to 1,620 meters, a figure confirmed by Edward Wright by measuring an angle of depression in 1589. In 1633 Richard Norwood, measuring by chain a distance of 165 miles on the 0 meridian in London, deduced a length of 1,866 meters for the nautical mile, which was close to the exact distance.

It was realized that the speed measured by the log was inaccurate because the device was dragged along by the ship. Some sailors assisted in paying out the line to lessen the drag of the boat on the log; others used hourglasses that were inaccurate. All this proves how seriously measurements were compromised by inaccuracy.

Using a line with knots spaced at intervals of 120th of a nautical mile (15.43 m.), the number of knots counted in 30 seconds indicates the number of miles traveled in one hour. This precedence led to the convention of measuring a ship's speed in knots, equal to the speed per hour in nautical miles.

Theoretically, the exact length of the nautical mile is

$$\frac{10,000,000}{90° \times 60'} = 1,851.8518 \text{ meters}$$

The round figure of 1,852 has been accepted to simplify the calculations.

Determining a course   Having an at least approximate method to determine the speed of a ship it was also necessary to know its course. A sailing vessel cannot follow a steady course, since a shift in wind direction modifies that of the ship; only a mean course can be determined. This bearing, which today is indicated in degrees, was formerly given in quarters, a quarter being equal to the 32nd part of the circumference of a circle or 11°¼. A course was thus known within only 5 or 6 degrees, and the general route was known with an equal imprecision.

Compasses were still too imperfect to give greater precision. The housing containing the compass rose was not completely nonmagnetic, and the friction of the gimbals impeded movement by the rose. And the declination—the angle between geographic north and magnetic north—was not accurately known. In his 1545 work on navigation a Spanish mathematician named Medina denied the existence of declination, though Columbus had measured it, noting that it varied as one traveled westward. As late as the seventeenth century many pilots shared Medina's mistaken opinion.

The eighteenth century witnessed the appearance of many works on magnets and magnetism, which led to perfecting compasses and increasing their sensitivity. Strongly magnetized needles and nonmagnetic wooden and copper binnacles were used. Precision in reckoning was considerably improved.

Latitude   As early as the eleventh century the Arabs calculated latitude from the height of a star at the instant it passed over the meridian. Astronomical almanacs such as the Alfonsine tables, assembled under Alfonso X of Castile about 1252, gave the declinations of the sun, moon, planets, and brightest stars, which made it possible to determine latitude by measuring the height of a star. For these observations the marine astrolabe, consisting of a simple circle with two perpendicular diameters and an alidade with sights, had been replaced by the cross-staff. The astrolabe, heavy and difficult to maneuver on a ship, gave errors of at least 2 degrees. The cross-staff, or Jacob's staff, was lighter and more convenient to use for observations. From the sixteenth to eighteenth centuries the cross-staff remained in general use. At the same time another instrument came to be employed, the backstaff or Davis quadrant, used with the back to the sun. It was invented by the English navigator John Davis. The measurement of latitude could now be improved to half a degree.

In the eighteenth century notable progress was made with the invention of the octant, from which the modern sextant derives. Newton had demonstrated its principle in 1699 with a drawing of the instrument, but his idea did not become well known until 1742, fifteen years after his death. In 1731 the astronomer Edmund Halley invented and had built another type of octant that quickly came into use. In the same period several astronomers and navigators proposed slightly different models and improvements and the instrument gradually replaced the cross-staff and Davis quadrant. By 1750 the octant made it possible with a clear horizon to reduce the error in measurements of altitude to one or two minutes.

Finally, during the second half of the eighteenth century two other instruments appeared that made possible a great precision in astronomical reckoning. The sextant, perfected by English instrument makers, was simply an improved version of the octant and like it was based on reflecting a ray of light in a mirror in order to double the angle measured. The other, built by the French maker Lenoir, was Borda's repeating circle, which made it possible to multiply the angle measured and reduce sighting errors by the same factor. These instruments have already been described in an earlier chapter (see p. 219). Borda's circle was used by sailors for almost a century, but its use declined during the second half of the nineteenth century in favor of the sextant.

Longitude   The problem of determining longitudes at sea had been raised long before, but at the beginning of the eighteenth century it had not yet been solved and even appeared incapable of solution by simple astronomical observations. Navigators needed to know the time at the meridian of origin at the moment when the time at sea was observed. The difference in these times enabled them to calculate the ship's longitude.

Experience had shown that observing the stars did not allow calculating the time at the meridian of origin. After the discovery of Jupiter's satellites Galileo believed he had such a method, based on the varying moments of occultation or eclipse of the satellites according to the longitude of the place of observation. But this method did not give satisfactory results. Other astronomical procedures were sought, for which it appeared necessary to draw up many tables showing the relative positions of the stars. The Greenwich Observatory was founded by John Flamsteed in 1675 for this purpose.

After the improvements in chronometry by Christian Huygens, clockmakers hoped to build clocks capable of regular operation at sea despite movement by the ship. Such clocks would make it possible to keep the time of the meridian of origin while at sea, and the problem of calculating longitude could then be solved.

The British, by act of Parliament in 1714, created a Bureau of Longitudes whose task it was to examine every invention that might offer a solution to the problem. Large prizes were offered: 10,000 pounds sterling if the error in longitude obtained by the clock presented did not exceed one degree; 15,000 pounds for an error of ¾ of a degree; 20,000 pounds for an error of half a degree. In France the Académie des Sciences of Paris also offered a prize for the same purpose. In the chapter on clockmaking we saw how the Englishman John Harrison was the first to build a satisfactory marine chronometer, while in France the clockmakers Pierre Le Roy and Ferdinand Berthoud were pursuing the same objective. Le Roy having withdrawn from the competition after building a chronometer remarkable in its conception, Berthoud alone attained the goal and in 1773 obtained a license.

Excellent English and French clockmakers (Arnold and Earnshaw, Berthoud, Breguet, and later Motel) quickly gave marine chronometers their final form. This laborious process of invention enabled navigation to make considerable progress in a quarter of a century. Before the appearance of marine chronometers inadequate instrumentation continued to cause considerable errors in nautical calculations.

Correcting geographical errors

In 1741, having "lost his longitude," Admiral George Anson wandered for a month in the Pacific Ocean in search of Juan Fernandez Island. In 1775 the English vessel *Union,* traveling from Cuxhaven, Germany, to Gibraltar, believed from its dead reckoning that it was 40 miles from Cape Finisterre, when it went aground off the Isle de Ré. In 1778 Admiral de Grasse passed to the west of the Bermudas believing he was east of them. In 1782 Admiral Pierre Andre de Suffren would, according to his dead reckoning, have been 30 miles into the interior of Africa, whereas he was not yet in sight of its coasts.

Numerous errors existed in describing the positions of the continents and islands on charts. The positions recorded in 1750 for the east coast of Newfoundland differed by 9 degrees, depending on whether they were taken from English or Dutch charts. In 1765 the coordinates of Iceland were incorrect by 4° longitude and ¾° latitude. At this time it was possible, thanks to more precise observations, to correct the longitude of the Cape of Good Hope, for which the charts had until then been in error by several degrees. Similarly, the longitude of Cape Horn was incorrect by 4 to 5 degrees. The Mediterranean was shown on charts as being more than one-tenth longer than its actual length, even though ships had been sailing through it for thousands of years.

Islands were even more poorly located, often appearing twice on charts. For a long time Saint Helena appeared in duplicate, as did Ascension Island, whose double was still being sought in 1817. On charts from 1800 there were three Galapagos archipelagoes on the same parallel, the two nonexistent groups being 6 and 12 miles west of the true archipelago. Not until the problem of longitude was solved could cartographers and navigators correct their errors.

As early as 1776 François Borda, making a hydrographic survey on the *Boussole,* had on board F. Berthoud's weight-driven clock no. 18 and his spring watch no. 4 (1773). He checked his positions by observations of land altitudes. He remade a very good chart of the route from Cape Spartel off Morocco to Cape Bojador and the Canaries and assigned to Santa Cruz de Tenerife the longitude of 18° 35' 20", today corrected to 18° 34' 31", which represents an error of less than 1 minute of arc.

In 1816 and 1817 Roussin, with the hydrographic engineer Givry on the *Bayadère,* used four of Louis Berthoud's watches on the African coast, and in 1819 he used watches 56 and 94, by the same Berthoud, along the coast of Brazil. He was able to determine that watch no. 56, maintained on the ship at a constant temperature of 30°C., had varied only 0 sec. 45 in 55 days. From March 1816 to September 1817 it was noted on the *Chevrette* in the Mediterranean that watch no. 80 had varied only 6 seconds. With such instruments Commander Gautier was able to determine the longitude of Galita Island within 2', that of Stromboli within less than 1'.

These examples, which could be multiplied, show the progress made in the second half of the eighteenth century by using improved instruments and applying more precise methods of measurement.

CHAPTER 4

RAILROADS

TRACKS

A LTHOUGH RAIL TRANSPORT is now associated with the locomotive—steam, electric, or diesel—it must not be forgotten that its origins lie in early attempts to assist the movement of wheeled vehicles over the ground.

In preceding chapters we have noted the difficulties of moving heavy vehicles over the roads and the exorbitant cost of such transportation. It would have been difficult and extremely costly, especially in mining, to build a network of roads sufficiently strong and well built to bring coal from the face and then haul it to places where it was to be used. The search for a way to improve the situation continued over several centuries.

Wooden rails   The first approach to the problem appears to date from the first half of the sixteenth century, when wagons equipped with wooden wheels traveled on wooden rails.

In the eighteenth century this system, which had not been put into general use, was improved by nailing the rails to regularly spaced oak crossties. In England the crossties were placed 2 feet apart, and the rails were pieces of oak or pine 6 feet long. On such a track a horse could pull a load 3 times heavier than it could on the road. This system spread quickly in England in the Newcastle region, then in the Durham area and in Northumberland, when mining activity was expanding.

Cast-iron rails   Since wooden rails wore out too quickly they were banded with strips of iron. From 1737 to 1767 a series of attempts were made to substitute cast iron for wooden rails, and in 1761 cast iron was widely adopted in Coalbrookdale (Shropshire). Here Abraham Darby had begun to smelt ores with coke. It has been said that since he was producing more cast iron than he could sell he conceived the idea of using it to make rails. He became his own consumer but hoped that other manufacturers would adopt the same idea.

The first trials seem to have presented difficulties, because until then excessively heavy wagons were used. By distributing the loads into small wagons there was less wear on the track. The engineer William Reynolds, one of the owners of Coalbrookdale, made this advance in 1768. He also supplied the cast-iron rail with projecting flanges that held the wheels on the track.

Darby's forecasts were quickly verified. Mine owners in the Newcastle area adopted this arrangement when they realized that a single horse could pull two wagons on cast-iron rails. In 1776 John Curr, manager of the duke of Norfolk's colliery near Sheffield, decided to build a railway to haul coal to the city, but those who were already providing this transportation with wagons or pack horses provoked a riot, removed the wooden rails, and burned them.

Curr rebuilt his track, using cast-iron rails fixed to stone blocks. He thought it would be advantageous to have wagons with iron tires that could move on roads as well as on rails. He used cast-iron bars with ¾-inch flanges on the inside. The wagons were still being pulled by horses. The system spread to South Wales and was installed on the Grand Surrey Iron Railway. The advantages of traction via rails became generally recognized.

In 1720 in the Newcastle area 20,000 horses were pulling wagons, and their number was constantly increasing. One man and one horse were required for each full wagon. On a road with the usual uneven ground the driver had to clear the way and, downhill, apply a brake.

Railways were clearly superior from an economic point of view, but they had to pass over private property, necessitating way leaves and the payment of fees. If private agreement could not be reached, the mine owner was obliged to ask Parliament for an act requiring the owner of the land to let the railway cross his property.

The first act of this kind dates from 1758 for a line near Leeds, but an act allowing construction of a railway that could be used by the general public was not passed until 1801, when the Grand Surrey Iron Railway Company was authorized to construct a line 9½ miles long between Croydon and Wandsworth on the Thames. Any shippers of merchandise could use the rails and necessary horse for traction by paying a fee. The rails of this track had two flanges, upper and lower, which were a logical shape to give them good resistance to flection.

Railways in Le Creusot The same difficulties of transporting the output of mines arose in France as in England. At the time the mining and iron smelting complex at Le Creusot was being built, 2,500 wagons, each drawn by 4 oxen, would have been needed to transport wood and stone. De Wendel thought of bringing wagons and teams of oxen from the Morvan or Lorraine, but fodder was lacking. The administrator of Burgundy was requested to grant grazing rights in the royal forests in 1781 and 1782. Faced with increased demand, prices of wagons rose, from 2 *livres* 10 *sols* to 5 *livres;* a peasant with his oxen could earn 8 to 10 *livres* a day. In 1783 de Wendel obtained an ordinance obliging the owners of draft horses and oxen to supply wagons and animals in sufficient numbers. Thus, when in 1785 the coal mine began to supply the factory steadily, a railway "in the English style" was built (Figure 90).

These roads, with a gradient of 4 to 6 *lignes* per *toise* (4 to 5 mm. per meter) were at first wooden roads. First the terrain was graded to provide a uniform slope. Then the crossties, spaced 3 feet apart, were laid, and lengthwise sleepers or rails were nailed to them with wooden pegs at the same gauge as the wagon wheels. As soon as the foundry began to produce cast iron, bars were cast and fixed to the rails. These, in December 1785, were the first French rails and railroad.

The small wagons had cast-iron wheels with grooves that fitted over the rail. Transportation now became much more economical. On this railroad a horse could pull a load 5 times heavier than the one it could pull on a road.

Between 12 and 15 miles of railroad line were established to link the coal mine

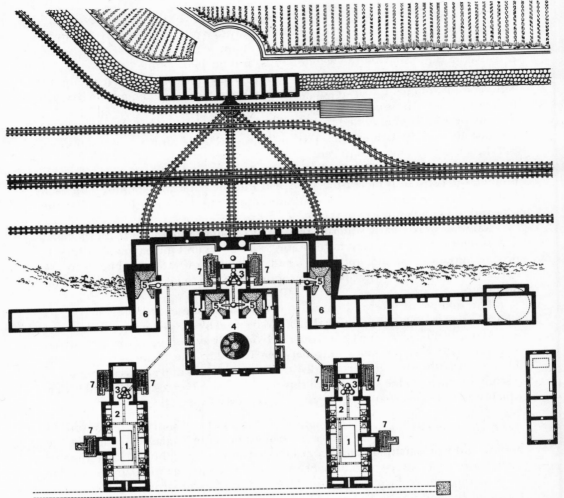

FIG. 90. Rail track layout at Le Creusot factories in 1785. 1. Hammers 2. Forges 3. Bellows 4. Main foundry 5. Blast furnaces 6. Side foundries 7. Boilers.

with the furnaces and connect the various shops. Since the mines were in the nearby hills, the descent was made with loaded wagons, the return trip with empty ones.

The evolution of rails From this point on the shapes of rails evolved rapidly. A bellied rail was used by William Jessop in 1784. Thomas Burns added chairs as supports for the rail ends. In 1789 at the Loughborough Mines Jessop used rails without flanges, but instead the wagon wheels were made with a one-inch projecting flange.

George Stephenson experimented on the behavior of rails under the weight of loaded wagons and saw that they were more seriously damaged by trains traveling at speed. He was led to examine the use of wrought iron made in

Scotland and took out a patent on this subject in 1816. In 1829, for the Liverpool-Manchester railroad he used fish-bellied wrought-iron rails similar in shape to the cast-iron ones.

Stephenson built his first locomotive, the Blucher, in 1814. It was the first one to have flanged wheels and was operated at Killingworth. The railway from Stockton to Darlington had at first been planned with flanged rails for vehicles with ordinary wheels, but Stephenson was so satisfied with his Blucher that he persuaded the railroad's managers to accept rails without flanges and put flanged rims on the cars' wheels.

Plate 31. Steam locomotives of the early George Stephenson model, in service at the coal mines of Hetton around 1820. London, Science Museum, Isaac Brick Collection. (Photo Radio Times Hulton Picture Library, London.)

The ties or rail supports continued to be made of either wood or stone. Gradually, however, the stone supports became replaced by wooden ties, which gave a more flexible track (Figure 91). An attempt was made to replace wooden ties with lengthwise pieces, on bridges or at the ends of lines. But these pieces, a kind of sleeper, presented difficulties in maintenance and replacement, so were later abandoned.

The roadbed and ballast   When after 1828 railroad building became widespread, track construction introduced many new problems impossible to discuss here in detail. Track laying required solutions quite different from those affecting roads, chiefly because of the need to avoid steep gradients and give curves a radius of several hundred yards.

The platform on which rails were to be laid could not be built like roadways. It was necessary simultaneously to provide for firm track on a stable bed and to provide for rapid water drainage from a surface that, unlike that of the roads, could not be cambered. The ballast forming the covering layer had to be both consistent and permeable. At first many different materials were tried, depending on the resources of the regions near the construction sites. Preferences seemed at

FIG. 91. The evolution of rail types.

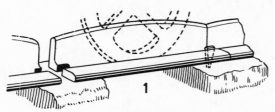

1. Rail used from the Merthyr collieries to Aberdare Junction, around 1800.

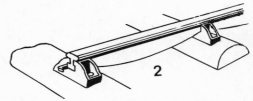

2. Castiron rail reinforced from beneath, 1820–1830.

3. Reverse-U rail in Barlow, England, and the Bordeaux-Sète line.

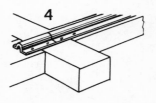

4. Reverse-U rail by Brunel resting on a continuous wooden longitudinal sleeper.

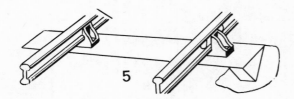

5. Double-headed rail on crossties.

first for sand of a certain composition but lacking that, for a mixture of crushed brick and cinders. The bed of the Darlington road consisted of crushed coal. Crushed flint was not regarded in 1850 as the best ballast.

Track gauge — Another major problem was to standardize the distance between rails, that is, the track gauge. It was solved empirically, for there were no theoretical considerations. As long as railways built in various regions did not connect and the rolling stock did not have to travel from one to another, the problem was not important.

The common practice, dating from the Romans, was to leave a distance of approximately 4 feet 6 inches between wagon wheels. At the Killingworth collieries the gauge of the track was 4 feet 8½ inches. Stephenson built his Blucher for this gauge, so thereafter had no reason to modify it for the other lines he built. But other engineers thought that a wider gap would give trains greater security and permit higher speeds. Brunel, chief engineer for the Great Western Railway, was of this opinion and adopted a gauge of 7 feet ¼ inch. Railroads in eastern counties were built to a gauge of 5 feet.

The Great Western Railway and the Midland Railway met at Gloucester, where the disadvantage of having two different gauges at the junction of two lines became apparent. If this difference were retained, the rolling stock could not pass from one line to the other, requiring the transfer of passengers, baggage, and merchandise and causing a loss of time and costly inconvenience.

Brunel and Stephenson held opposing views and could not come to an understanding. In 1845 Parliament was obliged to appoint a commission to make tests and hear the engineers' arguments. In order to study the problem the commission wished to compare the safety, speed of the trains, and power required of the locomotives in each case.

Trial runs were made in 1845/46 with a Gooch locomotive on a wide-gauge track for passenger trains and a long-boilered Stephenson locomotive on the narrower ("standard" in modern parlance) gauge track. They gave no absolutely conclusive results, but they did appear to show that the wide-gauge track permitted higher speeds and heavier trains, though on the narrower gauge track the locomotives could run more economically. The Great Western locomotive, pulling an 80-ton train, achieved an average speed of 47 mph.

An indescribable chaos reigned during the transfer from one train to the other, with cries of porters looking for their passengers or the coaches. This confusion must have impressed the commission, and rumor even had it that the disorder had been organized by partisans of the narrow-gauge track to obtain a decision in their favor.

What really determined the commission's choice, and what reflects better the practical sense of the English, was comparing the length of the tracks built with each gauge. When the mileage of all the lines already constructed was added up, it appeared that 4 feet 8½ inches had been adopted for a much longer distance. So this gauge was chosen and the Gauge Act of Parliament in 1846 decided that thenceforth any new line would have to be built with this gauge. However, the Great Western Railway continued to use the gauge of 7 feet ¼ inch, but it gradually installed a third rail over its entire network, allowing locomotives of both gauges to circulate everywhere.

France's relations with the Stephensons, who supplied the locomotives for the Saint-Étienne line, and whose plans were adapted for other locomotives, led to the installation of the 4-foot 8½-inch gauge recommended by Stephenson. Most other European countries did the same.

Spain, under the influence of English engineers, used a gauge of 6 Castilian feet (5½ feet). Russia decided on 5 feet and thereafter for political and military reasons did not wish to link up with other European networks. These differences began to be eliminated only in our own period.

STEAM TRACTION

As we have seen in the preceding chapter, experiments with steam-powered traction first concerned road vehicles, but it was on railroads that steam locomotives quickly found their application and increased in number.

As railways developed, the reduced number of horses needed seemed to provide a considerable advantage, but the growth of industrial production and greater demand for coal called for a considerable expansion of the means of transport. Hence the incentive to apply the steam engine. At first only the high-pressure engine without a condenser was available.

Trevithick's first attempts   Richard Trevithick (1771–1833), who became an advocate of using high-pressure steam is unquestionably the pioneer of all locomotive builders. After an 1801 experiment he took out with Andrew Vivian a patent for the steam-powered road carriage discussed earlier. In 1803 Trevithick installed several high-pressure steam engines in the iron works at Penydarran, near Merthyr Tydfil, whose owner, Samuel Homfray, suggested that he build a steam locomotive for the nine-mile track to Navigation House, near Abercynon.

A five-ton locomotive was built that on its first trial run, February 24, 1804, pulled a load of 20 tons at the speed of 5 miles an hour (Figure 92). It made several successive trials and once hauled a load of 25 tons. But because it was too heavy it

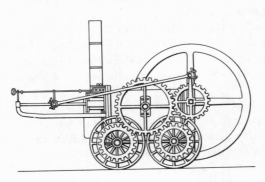

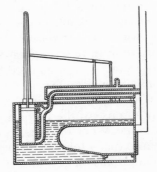

FIG. 92.   First Trevithick locomotive, 1803, tried out at Merthyr Tydfil on February 24, 1804.

FIG. 93.   Boiler of the second locomotive built by Trevithick and Vivian, 1804.

fractured the cast-iron rails and so ended the trials. This proved, nevertheless, that the weight of the engine gave sufficient traction to pull heavy loads.

Trevithick's locomotive had its exhaust through the stack, which gave a better draft to the firebox. Original drawings depicting this first Penydarran locomotive no longer exist, but Trevithick himself says it had a cylinder 8¼ inches in diameter with a 54-inch stroke. In 1804 he is supposed to have built with Vivian a second locomotive (Figure 93).

In 1805 Trevithick designed a new locomotive at Wylam for a railway with wooden rails, which probably was never built. He proposed wheels with projecting flanges and power transmission from a horizontal cylinder through a gear train.

In June and September 1808 he demonstrated an engine weighing 8 tons that moved on a circular track at 12 miles an hour. We have no details of the locomotive, but Trevithick was at that time building stationary engines with reversing connecting rods that he could have mounted on four wheels, with direct connections to the wheels.

In the face of the indifference that greeted these experiments, and the accidents that interrupted them, Trevithick abandoned the problem and left to others the honor of succeeding in this new field.

Various methods of traction
The development of railways for mine transportation continued rapidly, but the question of which traction method to use was still undecided. Although it was evident by 1810 that railroads were superior to roads for moving heavy loads, and though it was also certain that the iron rail was better than the wooden one, the discussion of the best way to have coaches was still open. There were three competing methods: horses, stationary engines (winches) pulling the cars by cables, and steam locomotives. A little later an attempt was even made to combine these different methods on various sections of the same line.

In certain cases horses were used as reinforcements to pull the cars uphill. For the descent the horse could be put into a "dandy" wagon that slid to the bottom of the slope by gravity.

Rack locomotives
In 1829, the year of Stephenson's Rocket, Thomas Brandreth tried out a strange machine in which a horse walked on a moving belt that then turned the wheels of the vehicle. This method was also tried in the United States.

Uncertainty about the performance of locomotives with smooth tires persisted, in spite of Trevithick's demonstration that their traction with the rails was adequate.

In 1811 John Blenkinsop built an engine with a cogwheel bearing on a rack attached to the rail. He estimated that an engine so equipped but weighing less than Trevithick's locomotive could pull a burden five times heavier (Figure 94).

Some colliery railroads were equipped in this fashion, as at the Middleton colliery near Leeds in 1812 and at the Coxloge collieries on the Tyne in 1813. The engines of this type built by Fenton, Murray, and Wood were the first to operate regularly without incident.

The engines were derived from improved Trevithick models, with two vertical double-acting cylinders driving crankshafts set at a right angle. Through

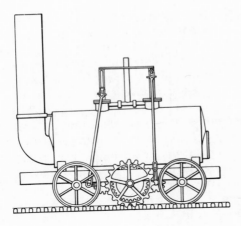

FIG. 94. Blenkinsop locomotive for the Middleton collieries near Leeds, 1811.

gearing the crankshafts turned the cogwheel against the rack. The Leeds engines remained in service only until 1813, but similar engines were used at Clarke's collieries near Wigan from 1815 to 1822.

At the end of 1812 William Hedley, an inspector at the Wylam mines, made test runs with a manually operated vehicle to determine the relation between the weight of an engine and the load it could move from a stationary position. Hedley confirmed Trevithick's results and, after several tests, had an engine built by Timothy Hackworth in 1813. This engine is identified with the 1814 Puffing Billy in the Science Museum (Figure 95). The weight of the engine was too much for the cast-iron rails of the time, so it was converted to eight wheels in 1815 and rebuilt with four wheels in 1830 when stronger rails were available.

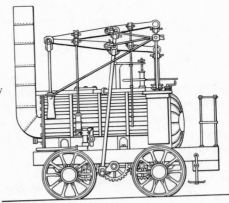

FIG. 95. Puffing Billy, built by William Hedley for the Wylam collieries, 1813.

The first achievements of George Stephenson

The work of George Stephenson began soon thereafter. Born to a poor family in 1781 at Wylam, eight miles west of Newcastle-on-Tyne, he worked in the collieries and learned about the operation of the Newcomen steam engine. In 1812 he became chief mechanic at the Killingworth mines and learned reading,

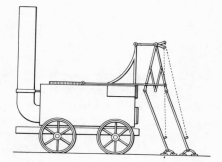

FIG. 96. Locomotive built by Butterly, 1812.

writing, and mathematics in the evenings after long hours of work at the mine.

Having suggested improvements to steam engines, he was permitted to modify them and was assigned workers to assist him. He had seen Blenkinsop and Hedley's locomotive and in 1813 obtained permission to build an engine at Killingworth.

This locomotive had two vertical cylinders 8 inches in diameter with a 2-foot stroke. Each cylinder was connected with an axle and the two axles were coupled by an endless chain. In July 1814 it was able to pull 30 tons—8 times its weight—at a speed of 4 miles an hour on a gradient of 2/900. This was the first locomotive using the simple adherence of its weight on flanged iron rails. These thorough tests resulted in Stephenson, with Ralph Dodds, taking out in 1815 a patent for a new engine built in March 1815 at Killingworth. It had wheels coupled by a connecting rod (Figure 97). This locomotive, Stephenson's Blucher, had previously mentioned three models built, which were mounted on springless axles so that the loads were poorly distributed on the uneven tracks.

In 1815 George Stephenson took out a patent for a suspension system in

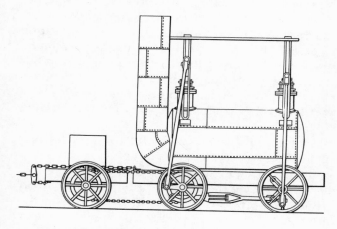

FIG. 97. Locomotive by George Stephenson, built in 1815 for the Killingworth collieries. The wheels are coupled by connecting rods and crankshafts on the axles.

which the pillow blocks of the wheels were supported by pistons to which pressure from the boiler was applied. Several models of this type were constructed from 1816 to 1822 and were able clearly to demonstrate their superiority over horse traction for heavy loads.

*The first
Stockton-Darlington
railway*

The Stockton-Darlington railway, the first one available to the general public, was 12 miles long and opened in 1821. Until then only a few tracks had been installed by mining companies, each for its own transport needs, without any connection between them.

In 1822 George Stephenson was named engineer of the Stockton-Darlington railway. In 1823 a new act gave the railroad permission to carry passengers as well as merchandise and to use locomotives for power.

Anticipating the orders that were to result, George Stephenson and his son Robert, Edward Pease, and Michael Longridge formed a company with Robert as director. This company became the principal center for the development of locomotives for the next twenty years, as well as a training center for engineers.

In the early days of its railroads, passengers were carried in wagons resembling road coaches traveling on rails and pulled by horses. In 1825 Stephenson ordered for this railroad the first passenger carriage, with a capacity of 6 passengers inside and 15 outside. The speed of this vehicle did not exceed 10 miles an hour. The carriage differed from the road coach in that a horse could be harnessed to either end and its wheels were smaller. The price of the trip was one shilling and sixpence inside, one shilling outside.

It was immediately decided to adopt the steam locomotive for merchandise and heavy materials in general. The first locomotive, ordered from Stephenson in September 1824, was put into service in 1825; it was later called Locomotion. It had four wheels coupled with connecting rods. Its weight in working order was 8 tons and it was able to pull 50 tons at a speed of 5 miles an hour on a level track. Three engines of this type were ordered. In the following years various engines were tried on the Stockton-Darlington line, including a four-cylinder model by Robert Wilson of Newcastle in 1825 and a model with horizontal cylinders built by Stephenson in 1827.

A major improvement was made by Timothy Hackworth in 1827 with the Royal George. The cylinders were still vertical but were placed higher and arranged in such a way as to operate a fairly short connecting rod. The heating surface of the boiler was much greater than in earlier engines and the stack gave a greater draft. The six wheels were supported on pillow blocks without springs but with pivoting levers, a design patented by W. Chapman in 1827. The first pillow blocks resting on springs appear to have been applied to locomotive wheels by Nicholas Wood at Killingworth in 1827, contemporary with wheels having wrought-iron tires.

Robert Stephenson was absent from England between 1824 and 1827. Upon his return he and his father applied themselves to serious study of the construction of locomotives with a view toward reducing their weight.

The 1826 act of Parliament authorizing the Liverpool-Manchester railroad stipulated that the engines should not give off smoke. Harry Booth and the Stephensons made experiments and in January 1828 delivered to the Bolton and Leigh railroad an engine tested in June 1828. This engine, the Lancashire Witch, was the first one simplified by Robert Stephenson. It had four coupled wheels with pillow blocks mounted on springs and inclined cylinders driving the front wheels by crank and connecting rod. It weighed 7 tons and pulled a load of 50 tons at a speed of 8 miles an hour on a gradient of 1/440.

Several examples of this engine were built later; it was adopted by Hackworth for several Stockton-Darlington locomotives intended for the coal traffic.

The Manchester-Liverpool line Although the Stockton-Darlington railway provided the occasion for the first trials of locomotives and encouraged the development of practical engines, the Manchester-Liverpool railroad was the first one designed for major traffic and became the first organized transport system.

Traffic had been growing constantly since the end of the eighteenth century, and especially after 1815, between Liverpool (a major port for the importation of cotton) and Manchester, an industrial center for spinning and weaving. Cotton bales were transported either by pack horse or wagon or by waterways, along canals making partial use of the Mersey and Irwell rivers, which were improved and dredged. The toll road had been repaired but wagons carried only a few bales, and a whole day was required for the trip. Canal boats, though they were still small, could be more heavily loaded, but transportation by this means continued to be slow.

The idea of railway transportation took shape in 1824, but not without vigorous opposition from road and boat carriers. Moreover, railroad tracks had to be laid out as straight and over as short a distance as possible, which required expropriating private property. To overcome these difficulties an act of Parliament was necessary, obtained at heavy expense.

Promoters of the railroad met on May 24, 1824, in Liverpool and opened a subscription fund of 300,000 pounds sterling divided into 3,000 shares of 100 pounds each, which was subscribed to by investors from Manchester and Liverpool and landowners between these two cities.

The promoters stressed the various advantages of the project: a shorter distance, travel time of 4 to 5 hours instead of the 36 required by canal, regular service independent of inclement weather, and a noticeably lower cost.

Certain promoters who knew of the Stockton railroad decided to invite George Stephenson to join their undertaking. He laid out the route, at the cost of several difficulties with the inhabitants of the region, especially the farmers. Parliament initially rejected the enabling bill in 1826 but ultimately approved it. The preliminaries had already cost 70,000 pounds.

The construction of the line occasioned the first railroad bridge, a viaduct over the Sankey Valley. A cutting was also dug near Liverpool, at Edge Hill. And the supposedly impassible Chat Moss peat bog — 12 square miles in area and 30 to 33 feet deep in places — had to be crossed.

When work on the line was drawing to a close in 1829 the problem of traction arose. Stephenson and most of the promoters were convinced that the only solution was the steam locomotive, but others believed that stationary engines with winches pulling the wagons by cables were safer. The plan was to install 21 of them along the line, each pulling trains from the preceding station. This system was still used in certain mines as we have seen.

The Rainhill competition (1829) In order to settle this question it was decided to hold a competition, the program of which was published in the Liverpool *Mercury* on May 1, 1829. A prize of 500 pounds was offered in addition to the cost of the engine awarded the prize for

Plate 32.   The Rocket, locomotive by George and Robert Stephenson (1829). London, Science Museum. (Photo Science Museum.)

meeting the conditions set: it had to be of limited weight and able to pull a load equal to three times the weight of the machine at a speed of 10 miles an hour over a track 1½ miles long for 10 round trips.

The Rainhill plateau, not far from Liverpool, where the track was level, was selected for the trial runs scheduled to take place on October 1, 1829. Two points a mile and a half apart were chosen, with an additional length of 220 yards at each end for starting and stopping the locomotives.

Plate 33.   "Puffing Billy," locomotive by William Hedley. London, Science Museum. (Photo Science Museum.)

Five engines entered the competition: Stephenson's Rocket, Novelty by John Braithwaite and John Ericsson, Timothy Hackworth's Sans Pareil, Timothy Burstall's Perseverance, and Thomas Brandreth's horse-drawn Cycloped, which was not accepted for the competition.

The 7.7-ton Novelty and 4.77-ton Sans Pareil achieved speeds of 13.8 and 16 mph respectively but broke down and were unable to complete the tests. The Perseverance reached a speed of only 6 mph and was withdrawn from the competition. Only Stephenson's Rocket finished the tests. Weighing 4.25 tons, it pulled a load of 12.75 tons and attained an average speed of 13.8 mph with a maximum of 24.1 on one stretch. Pulling a light load it reached 31 mph.

Thus, the Rocket was the only locomotive to meet all the conditions, and won the prize. Its success was important for the Stephensons, but it particularly confirmed that the steam locomotive was an adequate method of traction for railroads and that it could attain speeds not even regarded as possible to date. The Rainhill competition proved to be a historic event.

The design of the Rocket has often been attributed to George Stephenson, but in fact it was his son Robert who built it, at Newcastle. The elder Stephenson's attention was absorbed by work on the track. The Rocket was equipped with two inclined cylinders with a 6-inch bore and a 12-inch stroke, driving the front wheels (50 inches in diameter) through connecting rods (Figure 98). The engine's success was due principally to Robert Stephenson's adaptation of the fire-tube boiler, suggested to Stephenson by Henry Booth, the secretary-treasurer of the Liverpool-Manchester Railway. This system had been the subject of various earlier patents. In particular, Marc Séguin had taken out a patent for a fire-tube boiler in France in February 1828 and was the first to make trial runs (in 1827 and 1828) with a view to applying it to locomotives. He had built one before Stephenson, but he appears not to have put it into service until after the Rocket. In any

FIG. 98. The Rocket, 1829, invented and built by George and Robert Stephenson for the Rainhill competition. *Top:* Cross section of the firebox and the fire tube boiler.

case, this was a success for the tubular boiler system, which was to remain the classical type for locomotives for more than a century.

Stephenson had also applied to the Rocket a system in which the exhaust steam was injected at the base of the smokestack, to increase the draft through the firebox. Several devices had been tried out to provide a better draft while avoiding a need for a tall stack. The Novelty of the Rainhill competition had a bellows, and the locomotive built by Séguin had a powerful fan. The system most frequently used was injecting steam coming directly from the boiler, which increased the coal consumption. Trevithick had suggested as early as 1802 that steam be injected from the cylinders, and in 1827 Timothy Hackworth had already applied this idea.

The first railways in France

Although France lagged considerably behind Great Britain in railroad building, it may be of interest to follow the first developments in that country. They show that the primary goal was, as in England, a more economical way to move vehicles. Once the lines were laid, mechanical traction came into use.

One visitor to the mines in Montcenis in 1782 noted that "all the routes are laid out with pieces of wood to which cast-iron flanges are adapted, and the wheels of the carriages hauling the coal bear on these flanges; these wheels are driven so that the wagon cannot deviate and is obliged to follow the route laid out for it, so that a single horse, even if blind, pulls four thousand [pounds] and more without difficulty."

Influenced by publications showing what was being done in England, mine owners requested permission to establish at their own expense a railroad with an inclined roadbed "from the Loire to the Pont de l'Ane, over the Furens River, through the mining territory of Saint-Étienne." The concession was granted by a royal ordinance dated February 26, 1823, because of the advantages to commerce and industry, particularly "to transport the coal being furnished in abundance by the regions traversed." The development company was authorized to collect in perpetuity a tax of .0186 francs per 3,280 feet of distance and per hectolitre (= 2.8378 bushels) of coal and coke or per 110 pounds of material and miscellaneous merchandise. No fares were stipulated for passengers, because no one anticipated then that transporting passengers should be considered.

In June 1824 the Compagnie du Chemin de fer de Saint-Étienne à la Loire was founded and a mining engineer named Beaunier was made director. He ordered that a study be made on a miniature railroad to show the movement of carriages and action of centrifugal force on curves. The railroad was to link Saint-Étienne with the small port of Andrézieux on the Loire, a distance of 9½ miles. The purpose was to find a method of transportation that was more economical than that of wagons traveling by road down to the Loire, where barges could carry the coal farther downstream.

The railroad was planned as a single track, with cast-iron rails resting on chairs made of stone blocks. Traction in level areas was first planned to be done by horses, each pulling 3 wagons each carrying 86 bushels of coal. The carriages were pulled up grades by cable and descended by gravity. This line, the first in France, began operating in 1828.

The journey by barge on the Loire from Andrézieux to Roanne was not without its difficulties—returning upriver was impossible and the downriver trip could be made only a few days a year. Because the boats were used only for the trip downstream and were demolished at Roanne, this added enormously to the cost of transport. Thus, in 1828 a concession was granted to extend the railway 48 miles to as far as Roanne, from which navigation was possible in both directions during most of the year.

Séguin and the Saint-Étienne-Lyon line   During the same period Marc Séguin, the first builder of suspension bridges, proposed building a railroad from Saint-Étienne to Lyon, on which he planned to use steam engines. He had established a navigation service on the Rhône sometime between 1823 and 1825 using a steam boat. On this occasion he had thought of using a boiler that vaporized steam quickly by installing in the boiler's chamber a series of tubes through which passed the hot gases from the firebox. The idea of increasing the heating surface by such an arrangement was not new in itself, since the opposite principle of placing tubes of water in the flow of gases from the firebox had been applied.

Séguin built his first fire-tube boiler for his steam boat. He then took out a patent in 1828 and finally thought of applying it to a locomotive (Figure 99). He had made a trip to England, where he had met Stephenson, who as we have seen had successfully installed a fire-tube boiler in the Rocket. This encounter certainly led to Séguin's decision to introduce locomotives into France.

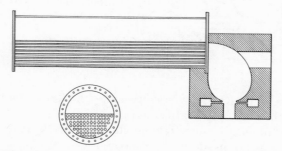

FIG. 99.   Marc Séguin's tubular boiler (from the 1828 patent).

Upon his return he designed a project for a railroad from Saint-Étienne to Lyon, "the safest method and the only one whose realization is feasible . . . the union of the Loire and the Rhône." The enterprise was opened to bids on February 7, 1826. The Séguin brothers and Jean-Baptiste Biot, a famous physicist, obtained the concession, at the cost of .098 francs per kilometric ton.

The cost of building, initially estimated at 1,200,000 francs, rose to 3,000,000 francs, despite all the economies the builders could make. The trip from Saint-Étienne to Lyon via Rive-de-Gier and Givors presented major difficulties for a pioneering undertaking of this kind. It was necessary to build two bridges (one over the Saône) and dig tunnels, the first dug for a railway. Séguin laid out the route with a mining engineer named Brisson, adopting a radius of almost one-third of a mile for the curves and a reduced incline for the grades. In many ways this layout was a remarkable work for the time. The construction of the roadbed was not as satisfactory, because of the engineers' lack of experience in such a new field. The track itself was built of iron rails placed on wooden crossties. The French thus skipped the stage of cast-iron rails and supports made of blocks of stone.

Studying the questions of rolling stock and traction, Séguin wondered if locomotives could be used on all the slopes or if one should not "have recourse to a system of towing similar to that of the towline with a steam engine at a fixed point." In fact, a combination of these two solutions was adopted.

Séguin purchased engines from the Stephenson shops at Newcastle, to be used as models by French builders, though he himself designed a locomotive, which has already been discussed (Figure 100). The characteristics of the two types were as follows:

	Stephenson Model	*Séguin Model*
Total weight	9 tons	4.5 tons
Test boiler pressure	9 pounds	9 pounds
Diameter of wheels	4½ feet	3¾ feet

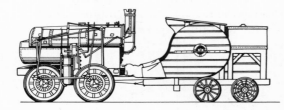

FIG. 100.   The first locomotive with a tubular boiler, by Marc Séguin. Built in 1829 for the Saint-Etienne–Lyon rail-road.

The English locomotive of the type preceding the Rocket had a smokestack 15 feet tall to obtain the necessary draft. Séguin installed a fan that forced air into the firebox, which let him use a short, lightweight smokestack. However, the fan was cumbersome and was not used on other locomotives.

The Séguin engine was a complete success; it built up pressure in 36 minutes and could pull 4 wagons loaded with a total of 15 tons of cast iron. But only one model seems to have been built, and apparently it was not used long in regular service. In the Rive-de-Gier to Givors section, which was completed but not in use in 1830, the locomotive was tried out concurrently with horses. A portion of the downhill trip was made with neither horses nor engines but by gravity only.

The line was opened to traffic in December 1832. In the beginning only coal was transported, but soon a few passengers were accepted, riding in open carriages—frequently the same ones used to carry coal. To avoid accidents the speed was limited to 5 leagues per hour. It was also thought that this would reduce expenses, the engines supposedly being under less strain and thus lasting longer. For the sake of economy, animal traction alone provided five-hour passenger service between Lyon and Saint-Étienne.

In 1834 there were only two locomotives in service, Séguin's and one by

Stephenson. Both were used to haul coal, and railroad authorities still hesitated to use them instead of horses. Two-thirds of the route between Rive-de-Gier and Lyon was served by locomotives by 1838. Completely eliminating horses on August 1, 1844, made possible the 40-mile trip between Lyon and Saint-Étienne in 2 hours and 35 minutes, including stops. But it was reported in 1855 that the wagons full of coal were still descending by gravity between Saint-Étienne and Givors. The locomotive was used only to return the empty wagons.

Although Marc Séguin earned the credit for establishing the first railroad line in France, his career ended there. Shortly thereafter he withdrew from virtually all industrial activity. Increasing the number of railways and extending the lines over long distances was the work of a generation of engineers led by Flachat, Clapeyron, and Perdonnet, who practically had to reconsider all their problems in the light of English experience.

The ultimate success of railroads   The Liverpool-Manchester railroad, four years in its completion, was finished during the summer of 1830. The opening took place on September 15 in the presence of the duke of Wellington and thousands of spectators. The total cost of track, engineering work, engines, and carriages came to 830,000 pounds. The success of the undertaking immediately proved greater than its planners could have hoped. Four hundred passengers a day had been expected, in a very short time 1,000 passengers a day were using the railroad, and additional cars and engines had to be ordered.

From this time on the construction of miles of railroad was undertaken in every country in the world. It is beyond the scope of this history of technology to follow the economic development and financial speculation that resulted; what is important is simply to trace the technical aspects of its evolution.

The evolution of the locomotive   The superiority of the Rocket was due to the arrangement of its tubular boiler, with 25 copper tubes 3 inches in diameter providing a larger heating surface; a separate firebox and smokebox; direct drive, without gears, of the crankshaft by a connecting rod, and finally a better distribution of steam, providing a bigger injection of steam into the cylinder.

However, the Rainhill trials demonstrated to Stephenson that the cylinders were too nearly vertical and that the locomotive became unstable as its speed increased. He modified the Rocket by bringing the cylinders into a more nearly horizontal position. Several engines of the Rocket type were built, but modifications quickly proved to be necessary. In 1840 the Northumbrian, with cylinders of an 11-inch bore and pistons with a stroke of 16 inches, weighed 7.35 tons. The boiler layout was modified so that the firebox, which until then had been outside and behind the boiler, was placed inside it, and the number of fire tubes, which were smaller in diameter, was increased. The Northumbrian profited from experience with the Rocket—its cylinders were placed in an almost horizontal position and the improved tender had a copper-clad buffer in the rear.

A number of engines were built modeled on the 8-ton Planet of 1832 (Figure 101). At the same time Edward Bury, the Stephensons' main competitor, was building similar models, with a steam dome. In 1834 Stephenson introduced the

FIG. 101. Locomotive of the Planet type, built by Robert Stephenson in 1832 for the Liverpool–Manchester railroad.

three-axle Patentee model, on which the center axle, with wheels 5 feet in diameter, was the only driving axle. This engine weighed 11.45 tons.

From then on, cylinders were installed horizontally, except by Timothy Hackworth, who continued to follow the design of his 1824 Novelty. Inclined cylinders were soon completely abandoned.

In 1833 the first locomotive built in England with a bogie or leading truck was sent to the United States by R. Stephenson and Co. This improvement had already been foreseen by William Chapman of Newcastle in 1812. In the United States, Thomas Rogers (1832) and Matthias Baldwin (1834) employed this front swiveling truck on numerous locomotive models of their own construction (Figure 102).

Increased speed   In 1835 the average speed of passenger trains was 20 to 25 mph. I. K. Brunel envisaged bringing the speed up to 35 to 40 mph for the Great Western Railway, with heavier trains and a broad gauge of 7 feet.

FIG. 102. The Lancaster, built by Baldwin for the Charleston-Hamburg railroad, 1834.

To meet this demand the Stephensons built engines with driving wheels 7.8 and even 10 feet in diameter. The North Star, one of the best engines of the time, had 16-inch cylinders with piston strokes of 16 inches, and 7-foot wheels. It weighed 21 tons and had a boiler with a heating surface of 711 square feet. In 1838 it pulled an 80-ton load at 30.5 mph and 45 tons at 38.5 mph. Fifty similar engines were built between 1840 and 1842.

In 1841 Robert Stephenson patented a long-boilered engine designed to increase the heating surface to 800 square feet and thus the heat output. The increase in boiler length, with its increase in power, made it possible to pull heavier trains between 1829 and 1845:

	Length of boiler
1829, Rocket	6 feet
1832, Bury	8 feet
1845, Long-boiler	12 feet

But a swaying movement appeared with the increased length, and nondriving weight-bearing wheels were added at the rear of the locomotive.

Stephenson introduced into France his North Star in 1843 for the Paris-Orléans line (Figure 103). It had a long boiler and three independent axles, the center one bearing the driving wheels. Various French shops copied this model (Figure 104). In particular, a series of locomotives along these general lines was

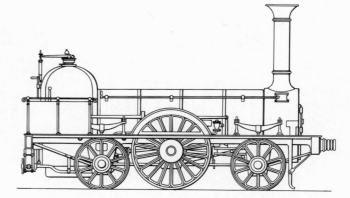

FIG. 103. Locomotive of the North Star type, built by Stephenson for the Paris–Orléans line, 1843.

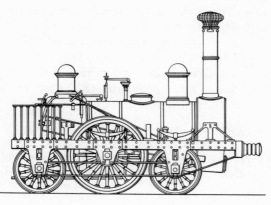

FIG. 104. Locomotive built by Taylor in 1837 for the Paris–Saint-Germain line.

built in 1846 by Derosne and Cail for the Nord railway line in France. They had the following characteristics:

Grate area	9⅔ square feet
Heating surface	775 square feet
Steam pressure	10 psi
Piston diameter	15 inches
Piston stroke	22 inches
Driving wheels' diameter	5¾ feet
Total weight	22 tons
Weight on driving wheels	10 tons

They had a tender that carried 1,838 gallons of water and 4 tons of coal.

Around 1848 Thomas R. Crampton conceived of using larger diameter driving wheels in order to increase speed without increasing the number of revolutions of the engine, but the axle would have been too high to be placed under the boiler, so Crampton put the driving wheels behind the firebox. With this arrangement it was possible even to lower the boiler, which now rested only on smaller wheels (Figure 105).

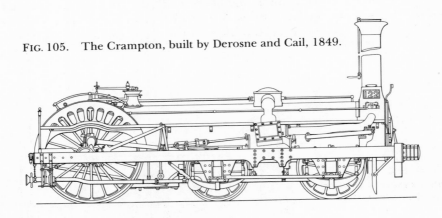

FIG. 105.   The Crampton, built by Derosne and Cail, 1849.

Unable to get his design adopted in England, Crampton went to France, where he had his locomotive built with a very low boiler. (However, the boiler was later raised to the height of other locomotive boilers.) The resulting engine was very satisfactory. It was used in France from 1848 to 1890 to pull fast trains but its driving-wheel weight remained low (10 tons at the beginning) and was held to 13 tons, the safe maximum under the condition of the tracks at the time.

In twenty years the power of engines built in France had increased from an indicated 25 hp. for the Séguin locomotive to 400 hp. for the 1850 Crampton engine.

Steam distribution   So far we have discussed only the evolution of the general structure of locomotives. But its history is much more complicated, for even though the problems of combustion, vaporization, cylinder position, transmission system, and number and diameter wheels were all important factors, many other construction and operating problems had to be solved by builders. Thanks to successive inventions from Stephenson's early attempts to Crampton's work, the locomotive became a powerful and practical source of power. Here by way of example we can mention only the inventions relative to the problem of steam distribution in cylinders.

Steam had to reach each face of the piston alternately, produce the driving effect, and escape into the air. The openings and closings of the inlet and exhaust valves were controlled by a slide valve. In the early days it was flat and controlled by two eccentrics on the driving axle, with a claw lever for reversing (Figure 106).

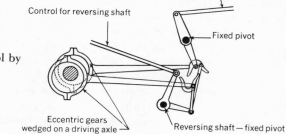

FIG. 106.   Diagram of speed control by eccentric gears with fork.

The Stephenson link motion with straight and crossed bars appeared in 1842. He had thought of connecting the two rods of the distribution system with a slot carrying a sliding block that connected with the head of the valve rod. The link was suspended from a rod that could be raised or lowered, which made it possible to change the position of the link and obtain either a reversing movement or variable steam expansion in the forward direction or when reversing. Many devices with numerous variations on this principle were tried out by builders in every country.

Also in 1842 one Walschaerts, a shop chief for the Belgian railroads, built a distribution system for which he had taken out a patent in 1841 and which shortly thereafter became widespread and used for almost a century. The Walschaerts distribution system, a long-term one, had only one eccentric gear, which formed a right angle with the driving crank. The movement of the slide-valve rod was controlled both by the movement of the link and by that of a rod connected with the piston rod (Figure 107). This seemingly more complicated system had the advantage of providing better control over the movements of the link and of

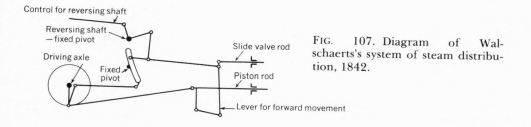

FIG. 107. Diagram of Walschaerts's system of steam distribution, 1842.

eliminating the throttling steam caused by the excessively narrow openings provided by the movement of a simple eccentric gear. The use of steam in the cylinders and the output were both greatly improved, which allowed for the satisfactory development of fast, powerful locomotives.

The evolution of passenger coaches   Improvements in rolling stock were concerned with improving the comfort of passengers. The first cars were only adaptations of coach and stagecoach bodies to the frames of the new vehicles. Passenger cars were then formed by combining several stagecoach compartments. The first, coach-type, cars of the Liverpool-Manchester railroad still looked like the coupe-bodied old stagecoaches. On the roof there was a deck to hold baggage. The second-class carriages were open wagons with benches. In the third-class carriages, which were still cruder wagons, passengers remained standing.

Access was by steps and side doors in 1830. The first carriages specially designed for railroads were built around 1840. They were a logical adaptation of a box on a frame suspended by leaf springs, with buffers and coupling chains. The body and the frame itself were wood.

Beginning about 1850 the increases in speed and load made it necessary to reinforce the wooden frame, and the progress of metallurgy and development of metal rolling made it possible to build all-metal frames.

Comfort was dealt with around 1850 by providing a fairly thick upholstery to deaden the sound of the wheels in the first- and second-class cars. The sound of carriages traveling over paving stones had long since demonstrated the need for interior upholstery.

Interior lighting was done at first with candles, then with oil lamps, which were followed by kerosene lamps, and finally (around 1860) by compressed gas in portable cylinders (Figures 108 and 109).

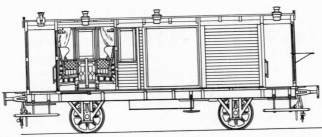

FIG. 108.   Gaslight installation in a passenger car, 1884.

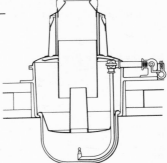

FIG. 109.   Detail of an illuminating lantern using compressed gas, 1884.

Brakes The first wooden rails, which offered great resistance to the wheels, permitted only low speeds, and thus their brakes were at first rudimentary. Later, when cast-iron rails appeared in mines between 1767 and 1776, effective braking methods had to be provided. This was the origin of the first brakes, the principle of which has not changed despite improvements in their construction and control. Tightening brakeshoes on the felly or band of the wheel still makes it possible to use friction to stop the movement of rolling stock.

During the earliest use of steam locomotives when they were still pulling cars representing relatively light loads, they could slow down and stop a train with their own braking. Thereafter it was soon obvious that it was unnecessary to apply a brake on all the cars of a train. Until around 1870 only certain cars on a train were assigned a brakeman, who had to apply the brake at the proper moment.

With the growing weight and speed of trains it was necessary to have more cars with brakemen. Each man had to obey an agreed-upon signal, generally given by the locomotive whistle, to release or apply the brakes. The braking mechanisms—of various types: lever, cam, rack, pin, or screw—made the wheel turned by the brakeman act effectively on the shoe and caused it to exert friction on the wheel rims (Figure 110).

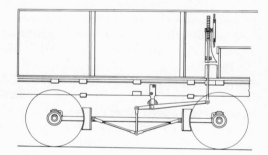

FIG. 110. Wagon brakes, before 1849.

The system of manually braking trains using several brakemen offered various disadvantages, the chief one being delay in responding to signals and a lack of synchronization in operating several brakes on a single train. A system of continuous braking applied by the locomotive itself came only in 1870, providing a solution to this problem that was important for the safety of the trains. Mechanical solutions were not successful. In 1869 George Westinghouse invented a brake control using compressed air, a system introduced into Europe several years later (Figures 111 and 112). In the meantime, the vacuum brake, invented by Smith in 1872, was installed by various companies.

Signaling The first public railroad lines introduced the problem of signaling along the tracks to ensure trains' safety. Trains were run at first simply by sight. By 1837 signaling was being done manually, but train speeds were low and there were few trains in service. Trains could be stopped by showing, on the track or beside it, a signal such as a handheld

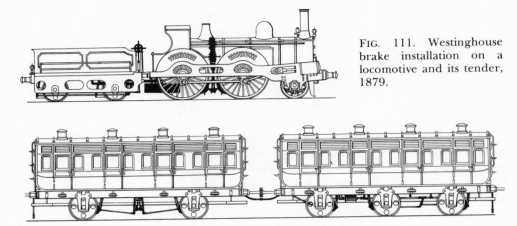

FIG. 111. Westinghouse brake installation on a locomotive and its tender, 1879.

FIG. 112. Westinghouse brake installation on passenger cars, 1879.

red flag or lantern with red lights. These signals are still officially recognized, but they are no longer used except during switching in stations or in unforeseen or emergency situations.

In 1843 permanent, immovable signals were installed at the beginnings of track sections to protect special points such as stations or switches. The first signal was a red disc that could turn on a vertical axis. It was turned edgewise if the track ahead was clear and showed its clearly visible face if the track was occupied.

Hand operation of independent switches and signals was likely to cause errors and thus accidents. To avoid accidents in 1844 one Vignier, an engineer of the Compagnie de l'Ouest, conceived of combining the controls of switches and signals. Switch bolts were connected by rods that prevented signals from indicating a clear track when a switch located farther along the track was not correctly positioned. Conversely, certain switch positions could be obtained only if the position of the signal disc did not oppose the switch's movement through the

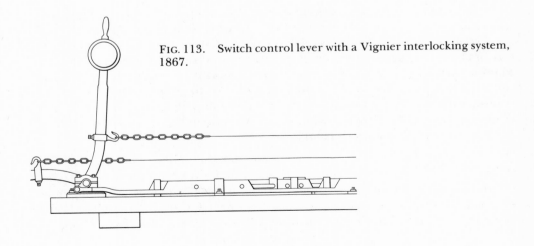

FIG. 113. Switch control lever with a Vignier interlocking system, 1867.

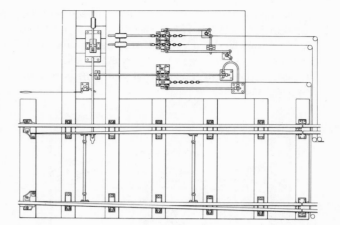

FIG. 114. Vignier inter-
locking system for safety in
switching, 1867.

locking mechanism (Figures 113 and 114). From this time on this interlocking system was developed and perfected, making it possible to avoid the frequent accidents that could easily have occurred, given the increased frequency and speed of trains.

Finally, it should be pointed out that the newborn electric telegraph was immediately used to establish a rapid-communication system between stations. In 1840 a telegraph was used for the first time, on the London-Blackwall line.

Pneumatic railroads As we have seen, from the time the first tracks were installed cars were often pulled by permanent cable-engine stations. The advantage of mobile locomotives over permanent stations rapidly became apparent, but the idea of using permanent stations did not disappear immediately. Certain contemporaries, for example the French physicist François Arago, thought that in the intervals between trains these permanent stations could distribute their unused power in their immediate area, and he tried to encourage their use.

As early as 1810 a Danish engineer named Medhurst suggested a pneumatic system similar to the one now used for postal connections in large cities.

Around 1840 several traction systems were tried based on movement of a piston in a watertight tube between the rails. Pumping stations at points along the line provided the driving force by creating a vacuum in the tube. With this system trains could climb grades that contemporary steam locomotives could not climb.

The first pneumatic railroad was installed between Kingstown and Dalkey in Ireland, a distance of almost 1¾ miles with grades of as much as 17.5 mm. per meter. The installation was built by Clegg and Samuda. This example aroused interest in France for lines with steep grades, and Anatole Mallet was sent to Ireland to investigate the Clegg-Samuda system. On the basis of his favorable report, a law on August 5, 1844, ordered that an experiment be made with this system between Le Pecq and Saint-Germain. The line, opened in 1836, ended at the foot of the Saint-Germain plateau because of the impossibility of climbing such a steep grade. The pneumatic system operated between Le Pecq and Saint-Germain from 1847 to 1862.

A tube with an inside diameter of two feet, split along its upper surface, was laid along the track between the rails. A piston fixed to the frame of the wagon by a metal arm moved back and forth inside this tube (Figure 115). Before and after the wagon passed, the slot was closed by a leather tongue. This flap rose up out of the way during the passage of the arm connecting the piston with the wagon (Figure 116).

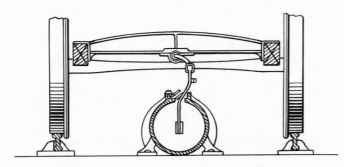

FIG. 115. English atmospheric (suction) system.

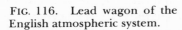

FIG. 116. Lead wagon of the English atmospheric system.

Two stationary 200-hp steam engines installed at Saint-Germain operated lift pumps capable of creating a vacuum of ⅓ of an atmosphere in 3 or 4 minutes. Depending on its weight, a train climbed at a speed between 19 and 42 mph.

Two other pneumatic pump stations were installed, at Nanterre and Chatou. Where the track was level from Nanterre to Le Pecq the corresponding tube was 14 inches in diameter. From Le Pecq to Saint-Germain the grade reached 1⅓ inches per yard and the tube was 2 feet in diameter. Conical junction tubes were needed to connect the tubes with the double pistons, which were of different diameters.

The steam engines worked for only a few minutes per hour, when the trains were passing. The output of the installation, which was complicated and quite fragile, was very low. As early as 1849 it was thought that steam locomotives would be better suited to the traffic. As a result of a study by Flachat, locomotives were built that could pull a 93-ton train from Le Pecq to Saint-Germain, and this system of traction quickly replaced the pneumatic one.

THE DEVELOPMENT OF RAILROADS

In Great Britain   The difficulties experienced in building the first railways in mountainous regions greatly alarmed the public. But the success of the Liverpool-Manchester line created great interest in this new mode of transportation, which it seemed should be available to everyone. The English network spread rapidly. Among the new lines built in the following years, the London-Birmingham line and the Great Western Railway involved some important engineering operations to overcome natural obstacles.

For the Birmingham line, begun in 1832, it was necessary to dig a long cut through the chalk hills at Tring, 30 miles northwest of London. This cut was 2½ miles long and 40 to 50 feet deep. More than 1½ million cubic yards of earth had to be removed, which were used to build up an embankment approximately 15 miles long at Wolverton, across the valley of the Ouse.

The Blisworth cutting also required large earthworks. Over a mile and a half long, and more than 60 feet deep, it was cut through rock, using explosives. The most impressive work for the time was the construction of the Kelsby tunnel, more than 1⅓ miles long. Special methods had to be used to drain water that seeped in during construction. The walls were lined with brick to make them watertight.

Tunnels aroused the distrust of the public, which only reluctantly agreed to venture into them. When a nearly two-mile-long tunnel at Box was opened on the Great Western line between London and Bath many passengers traveled from Box to Corsham by coach to avoid the tunnel section. This fear showed itself in France particularly during the discussions about the route of the Paris-Versailles line. François Arago's famous speech was not totally lacking in common sense, given the technology of the period. Although, contrary to his fears, no locomotive boilers exploded in tunnels, a fatal railroad accident on May 8, 1842, at Meudon, in which the navigator and explorer Jules Dumont d'Urville lost his life, reawakened public fears.

The Great Western Railway was built by I. K. Brunel in accord with his own ideas, and for a long time it remained unique. His engineering works compel admiration by their daring and successful execution, but his adoption of broad gauge caused much debate. The cost per mile to build the Great Western was the highest of all the lines in Great Britain, being over 40 percent greater than the average cost for all British lines as a whole, as estimated in 1850. This cost was higher than that in any other country that had railroads at that time.

Perdonnet gives the following figures for Continental and United States construction, as estimated in 1852 or 1853:

	Average cost per kilometer (in francs)
Great Britain (1850)	570,000
France	390,000
Belgium	270,000
German provinces	201,000
United States	96,500

British railroads were undeniably built with the greatest care and even luxury [strict regulations on routes, fencing, bridges, and so on increased their costs—Ed.] but the early operating results justified the approach. The statistics of the Liverpool-Manchester line show brilliant success from the very beginning.

Years	Number of Passengers	Profits	Freight Tonnage	Profits
1831	445,047	£56,918	108,180	£23,966
1832	356,946	£37,463	159,440	£20,635
1833	386,492	£46,723	194,704	£35,881

The extension of railroads continued in the British Isles rapidly and with a certain amount of disorder. Every commercially active region—and they were numerous and widespread—promoted its private companies to build independent networks. Only after they had been built was thought given to connecting them.

A financial scandal in 1844 cast a certain suspicion on railroad enterprises, but in 1845 Parliament authorized the construction of 1,800 miles of new track, and in 1846 it gave further authorization for 4,620 miles. In 1850 the length of the lines under development was 6,393 miles, far in excess of that on the Continent but representing only slightly more than one-third the length of the railroads in the United States.

Railroads in Europe   On the Continent, despite the initiative of manufacturers who had organized laying the first miles of track around Saint-Étienne, France embarked upon these undertakings slowly and with some caution.

From its emergence as a new kingdom, Belgium appeared to be the most enterprising in this field. After installing a mile-long line to link the Bois-le-Duc collieries with the Mons canal in southwestern Belgium, the government in 1832 developed a unified plan for the entire country and actively began to build. In 1835 the 10-mile-long Brussels-Mechlin line was opened. Mechlin was then linked with Antwerp, Ghent, and Louvain. The northern, eastern, and western parts of the country already had railroads when lines began to be laid in the south after 1840. The program was to be almost completely finished in about 10 years with the building of 375 miles of railway. Around 1850 the system was connected with the lines of northern France, Lille, Douai, and Saint-Quentin, and those of southern Germany, from Liège and Maastricht to Aachen, Cologne, and Dusseldorf.

The dominant economic incentive for this program was not passenger transportation but the movement of goods to and from ports and industrial regions. Thus, no attempt was made to build high-speed lines and rolling stock—for the aim was rather to move heavy trains. Naturally, experience and rolling stock from Britain were most useful, but in 1835 an ironmaster of English origin but of Belgian citizenship, John Cockerill, began to build locomotives in his foundry and machine factory at Seraing near Liège.

A connection was made in 1855 with the Dutch system, which ran from Arnheim through Utrecht, Amsterdam, Leyden, and The Hague to Rotterdam.

Germany was also ahead of France in developing her railroad network. The first line was opened at the end of 1835, between Nuremberg and Furth, then others were begun in succeeding years around Munich, Leipzig, Brunswick, and Berlin. As early as 1840 the German states had 480 miles of railway, whereas

Plate 34. Stationary steam engines installed at Camden for a funicular section of the London-Birmingham line. Engraving taken from F. W. Simmons, *Public works of Great Britain,* 1838. (Photo Radio Times Hulton Picture Library, London.)

France still had only 264 miles. In the 10 years that followed, construction was intensified in Germany as in all European countries, and it began in Austria.

The Engerth locomotive   In Austria the development of railroads was marked in 1851 by a competition to select a locomotive capable of climbing the grades of about 3 percent to cross the 3,215-foot Semmering Pass on the Vienna-Trieste line. A German engineer named Wilhelm Engerth designed for the competition a 10-wheel locomotive with the tender on the same frame (Figure 117). The axle of the tender, upon which the end of the boiler rested, was connected by gears to the last driving axle of the locomotive. Put into service on the Semmering run in 1853, the Engerth locomotive was immediately successful. Its construction was undertaken, with numerous variations, by Cockerill at Seraing and the Ateliers du Creusot in France, and by 1855 more than 400 were in service.

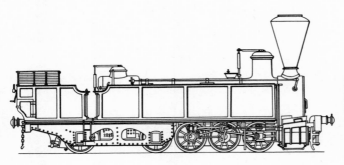

FIG. 117.   The locomotive Engerth, built for the Semmering line.

Studies were begun in 1838 for a line in Switzerland, from Morges on Lake Geneva to Yverdon on Lake Neuchâtel. But the first line built was the Basel-Zurich one, opened in August 1847. A locomotive pulled 7 cars—a total of 76 tons—at 15 mph. The Swiss section of the Strasbourg-Basel line, begun in 1841, was opened in 1844, but the Swiss network did not really begin to develop until after 1850, as in certain other European countries.

Railroad building   In France, after the short lines were built in the *in France*   Saint-Étienne basin, progress occurred fairly slowly. A small network in the Gard region was started in 1836—55 miles long, it connected the coal mining basins of Alès and La Grand'-Combe with Nîmes and Beaucaire. The 1837 opening of the Paris-Saint-Germain line won the railroad's first popular success, and building the Paris-Versailles line along the right bank of the Seine was approved.

Except for the resolutely hostile attitude of the historian Louis-Adolphe Thiers, first president of the Third Republic, the railroad aroused no opposition in principle. Contrary to what has often been written, François Arago proved to be a fervent partisan. In an enthusiastic speech in the Chamber of Deputies he foresaw Parisians taking the train in the morning and returning home in the evening after having made a complete tour of the country. Arago, a member of the political opposition during the government of Louis-Philippe, campaigned to have concessions granted to private companies, fearing that if the government were given the financial means to build railroads itself, it would acquire too much

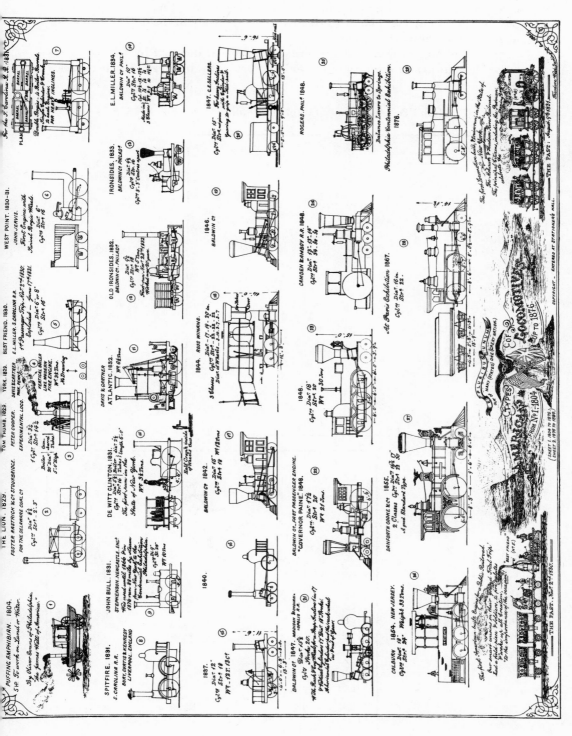

Plate 35. Types of American locomotives from 1804 to 1876. Drawing by T. West. Library of Congress

power. So with the best political intentions he encouraged financial speculation. His intervention was particularly effective in bringing about the decision to set up telegraph lines along the tracks.

The building program of the French railroads, dictated by France's centralized administration, was planned to link Paris with the large provincial cities

FIG. 118.   Development of railroads in France from 1837 to 1856.

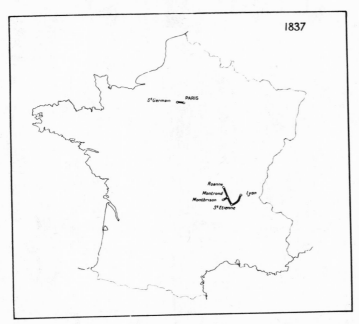

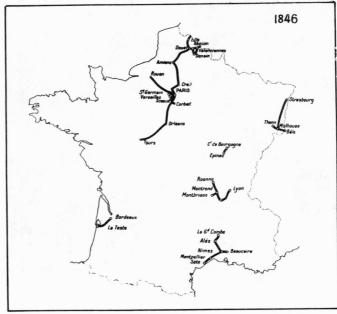

(Figure 118). Thus, the following lines were successively built: Paris-Orléans (1840–1843) with its branch to Corbeil; Paris-Rouen (1843, extended to Le Havre in 1847); Paris-Lille, and several lines in the northern network, particularly those connecting with the Belgian railways (1846–1850); Paris-Chalon-sur-Saône (1848–1851), extended to Lyon in 1851–1854; and Paris-Strasbourg, built in several sections (1849–1852).

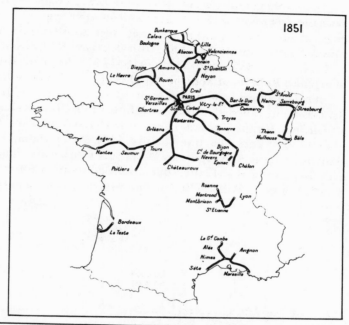

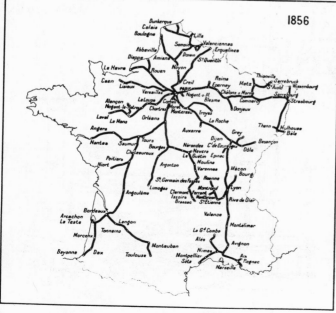

The growth of the total trackage was:

1828	10 miles
1830	18½ miles
1840	264 miles
1850	1,788 miles

By 1855 the French rail network exceeded 2,400 miles. In proportion to the area and population of the country, France was fourth in Europe.

As in other countries, British locomotives were used to open the first rail lines. With the exception of Marc Séguin's locomotive, which had no successors, the first engines put in service in France came from Stephenson's shops, starting in 1832, for the Saint-Étienne-Lyon line; from Murray and Jackson of Leeds (1834), Bury of Liverpool (1836), and Taylor (1837) for the Saint-Germain line, and from Sharp and Roberts of Manchester (1840) for the Versailles line.

French shops soon began to build locomotives, the first being those for the Saint-Étienne railroad in 1838 and those of Le Creusot shops, which in 1838 built La Gironde for the Versailles line. In 1840 Cavé made his debut with La Gauloise, also for the Versailles line (Figure 119). After them, Koechlin at Mulhouse, Hallette at Arras, and especially Derosne & Cail became major builders of locomotives. Beginning in 1842 the Rouen railroad shops at Sotteville were managed by a British engineer, William Buddicom, who developed a particularly sturdy type of

FIG. 119. *La Gauloise*, built by Cavé for the Paris–Versailles line, 1840.

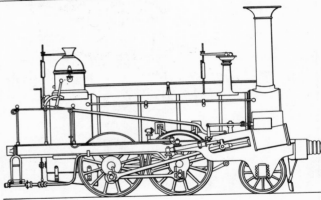

FIG. 120. Locomotive built by Buddicom for the Paris–Rouen line, 1844.

locomotive, some of which remained in service on the Ouest network until the First World War (Figure 120).

By 1842 there were in France 146 locomotives, 88 being of English construction. With the growth of French factories the proportion of locomotives imported from Great Britain decreased considerably in the course of the next 10 years.

Railroads in the United States

The development of railroads began in the United States at approximately the same time as in England and France. In 1830 the United States was still industrially underdeveloped, having only 13 million inhabitants and only 5 cities with a population of more than 25,000 inhabitants. There were no large centers to be linked up that could from the beginning have ensured profitable traffic.

In contrast, immense frontiers were being opened westward to colonization. Construction materials, particularly wood, could be found in place. There were no difficulties to exploiting them, or rules inhibiting builders. Railroads penetrated a back country opened to pioneers with low-cost, rapidly built tracks whose average cost per mile was one-quarter that of European railroads and one-seventh that of British railroads.

Plate 36. Abraham Lincoln traveling to Gettysburg in November, 1863, on a narrow-gauge railroad. (Photo American Cultural Center, Paris.)

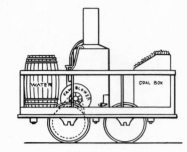

FIG. 121. First locomotive built in the U.S.A., by Peter Cooper for the Baltimore & Ohio Railroad, 1830.

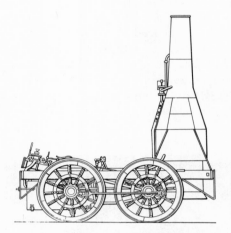

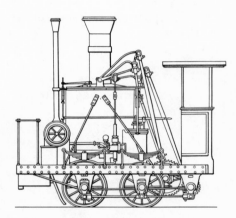

FIG. 122. The Best Friend, locomotive built by Westpoint Foundry Association for the South Carolina Railroad, 1830.

FIG. 123. The Grasshopper, a locomotive built by Cullingham and Winans in 1834 for the Baltimore & Ohio Railroad.

After a rather slow start (only 23 miles were built by 1830, and 2,818 by 1840) railroads became more interesting than canals. (The Erie Canal from Lake Erie to the Hudson had been opened in 1825.) Beginning in 1850, the sale of still unimproved land along the new railroad at low prices of $1.25 per acre encouraged the railroad companies, which resold property at large profits. This windfall triggered feverish speculation and construction between 1850 and 1860. In that decade the total trackage increased from 9,000 to 30,600 miles. The first transcontinental railroad was inaugurated in 1869.

In early years British locomotives were imported into the United States, but American manufacturers soon undertook increasingly more production. European locomotives had not given good results, because of the relatively crude methods used to build tracks over great distances. After a few attempts with prototypes built in the United States (in particular one by John B. Jervis, chief engineer of the Mohawk & Hudson Railway, who invented the first bogie locomotive in 1832), several firms began large-scale construction of them (Figures 121, 122, 123), the first being the West Point Foundry. Shops were also set up by a Philadelphia jeweler named Matthias Baldwin in 1832 and by Thomas Rogers in 1837. Their distinctive locomotives with bogies and funnel-shaped stacks were quickly popularized by pictures.

CHAPTER 5

LIGHTER-THAN-AIR CRAFT: THE FIRST STEPS

I N THE SPACE OF only a few months in 1783 several men succeeded in realizing one dream that had through many centuries made the greatest appeal to the imagination: to leave the surface of the earth and travel through space. This sudden conquest aroused immediate and universal enthusiasm.

Air travel originally appeared as a subject for theatrical exhibition; during a brief episode in the French Revolution it found practical use. Not until the invention of lightweight engines a century later was lighter-than-air flight able to offer the possibility of being a regular means of locomotion.

Hot-air balloons   The circumstances under which aerostation, or lighter-than-air navigation, was born have often been described. The Montgolfier brothers were the first to make use of a long-familiar phenomenon: the lifting ability of hot gases rising above a fire. The traditional story is that in November 1782 Jacques-Étienne Montgolfier (1745–1799), struck by the sight of a piece of cloth inflated by hot air from a fire, conceived of making a small cube of paper that rose toward the ceiling when filled with warm air.

After several other experiments Jacques and his brother Joseph Montgolfier (1740–1810) made a large canvas bag lined with paper, which they inflated with hot air by holding it over a fire of damp straw and wool. The balloon, which had a diameter of 33 feet, rose several hundred yards into the air, where it floated for about 10 minutes. The experiment was performed with proper solemnity on June 5, 1783, before the Estates of Vivarais, sitting in session at Annonay, the Montgolfiers' birthplace near Lyon. Under these circumstances the news spread quickly, and the Académie des Sciences in Paris invited the Montgolfiers to repeat the experiment for its members.

It took several months to make preparations and move the Montgolfiers to Paris. This time was put to good use by the physicist Jacques-Alexandre Charles (1746–1823), who, on August 17, 1783, launched a balloon inflated with hydrogen from the Champ-de-Mars.

Despite the success of Charles's balloon, the demonstrations by the Montgolfier brothers—first in Paris, then at Versailles before the king on September 19—aroused great enthusiasm. The new balloon, which the brothers built in a Reveillon wallpaper manufacturer's factory in the Faubourg Saint-Antoine, was a sphere 46 feet in diameter. A small basket attached to its base carried a sheep, a rooster, and a duck. Like its predecessors, it was inflated over a fire of straw and wool. It rose to a height of approximately 1,640 feet, then came down in the Vaucresson woods several miles from its starting point. This demonstration,

Plate 37. Various balloon ascensions of the 1780s in France. Lithograph by Romanet and Co. Library of Congress

which was as memorable as the first, provided the first study of the behavior of living things in flight.

Fire balloons immediately became fashionable and quickly appeared in numerous cities in France and abroad. They were decorated with elaborate decorative motifs, for they continued to be simply objects of curiosity.

The ancestral dream of being liberated from gravity had such appeal for men that only a few weeks passed until the fire balloon at last gave them the opportunity to achieve it. The first balloonists to leave the earth were Pilâtre de Rozier and the marquis d'Arlandes. The feat took place from the Château de La Muette on

November 21, 1783, using a balloon also made in the Reveillon shop. It had a circular gallery around the lower opening, in which the passengers took their seats. They kept a fire going in a hearth made of iron wire hung under the orifice of the balloon. Several preliminary trials had taken place in October, the balloon being held captive by a rope permitting it to rise to a height of only about 65 yards. During their free ascent Pilâtre and d'Arlandes flew over Paris between La Muette and La Butte-aux-Cailles.

Charles's hydrogen balloon On December 1 Charles made the first ascent in a balloon inflated with hydrogen. Less than six months after the launching of his first apparatus at the Champ-de-Mars, Charles (aided by the Robert brothers Jacques and Nicholas, who were instrument builders and exhibitors at public fairs) had developed a technique for constructing balloons that became generally used.

Charles's first balloon had been launched completely inflated and closed, and its ascent had been more rapid and higher than that of the fire balloons. But because the gas expanded as the altitude increased, the balloon had torn and fallen into fields near the small village of Gonesse, north of Paris.

In order to avoid a similar accident Charles gave his new balloon the shape of an upside-down pear whose lower end was closed off with a sleeve that was left open. In order to control the altitude and descent Charles placed at the top a valve consisting of a brass cap made airtight by a leather gasket. The valve was controlled from the basket by a rope that passed through the balloon. Charles also had the idea of suspending the wicker basket from a net around the balloon. By launching small free-flying balloons before departure he was able to observe the wind direction at various altitudes. He ascended on December 1 with one of the Robert brothers and in 1½ hours traveled, at a height of approximately 2,000 feet, from the Tuileries to Nesle, west of Paris.

Thus, aerostation was born during the span of several months during the year 1783. Fire balloons were now used only for demonstrations at shows. The accident in which Pilâtre de Rozier died on June 15, 1785, while trying to cross the English Channel from Boulogne to Dover in a fire balloon topped by a hydrogen balloon, put an end to the use of fire balloons as passenger-carrying vehicles.

For a long time hydrogen balloons were an extremely popular novelty and provided the means for a number of achievements. On January 7, 1785, Jean-Pierre Blanchard, who later distinguished himself in many ascents, crossed the English Channel from Dover to Calais with an American physician named John Jeffries. Together with Guyton de Morveau, Blanchard was also one of the first to try to guide a balloon through the air with large oars, but these attempts were unsuccessful. Balloons did not become navigable until the second half of the nineteenth century.

The manufacture of balloons The Montgolfier-Charles invention had immediate and unexpected consequences. In 1783 the Académie des Sciences decided to study the best ways to make aerostats. The two principal problems were how to make impermeable fabrics and how to prepare hydrogen in large quantities. The commissioners entrusted these investigations to Antoine-Laurent Lavoisier (1743–1794) and a young engineering officer, Jean-Baptiste Meusnier de La Place (1754–1793).

The tests of fabrics were made by various experimenters, including among others Nicolas Fortin, who became one of the most famous builders of precision apparatus in his time. The fabrics used had to be light and strong. A study was made of the weaving and aging of taffeta, which was coated with varnish to make it watertight. Charles and Robert had used a varnish with a base of boiled linseed oil. Several compounds were tried, including rubber (even though methods of making it suitable for this use were still unknown), wax, glue, and resins. Turpentine and clarified linseed oil were used as solvents. No report on these experiments has survived, but Meusnier, who had followed them closely, gave Coutelle and Conté the benefit of his experience when ten years later it was decided to use balloons to observe enemy movements on battlefields (see Military aerostation, below).

The problem of hydrogen   Work on the preparation of hydrogen (then called inflammable gas) was done by Lavoisier and Meusnier. Hydrogen, the existence of which had been surmised and sensed since the beginning of the century, had been isolated and identified only in 1766, by Henry Cavendish, and its precise nature and chemical properties were still poorly defined. To obtain it, only the traditional laboratory procedure of an acid acting on a metal, specifically sulfuric acid on zinc, was known. Charles and Robert used this method to prepare with some difficulty, large quantities of hydrogen to inflate their balloons. The gas obtained had many impurities.

It happened that in this period the problem of the chemical composition of water became Lavoisier's chief interest. In June 1783 it was learned in Paris that Cavendish had just obtained water by combining hydrogen and oxygen, but the English scientist's interpretation of this reaction was based on the phlogiston theory, so this important discovery contributed no progress to chemistry. Lavoisier, who had at the time formulated his theories of oxidation and the formation of acids and had disproved the phlogiston theory, encountered the problem of the composition of water. With Meusnier he quickly improvised a repetition of Cavendish's experiment and was able to affirm that water was formed of equal weights of hydrogen and oxygen. But, following the method of investigation that he had rigorously applied for ten years, he was obliged to complete the cycle of reactions that would give him an irrefutable demonstration: that is, to decompose water and then synthesize it with the elements collected. Lavoisier persuaded the Académie to study the preparation of hydrogen, for which he proposed to decompose live steam by passing it over red-hot iron. He worked on this problem during the closing months of 1783 and almost all of 1784.

Meusnier was a valuable collaborator. He adapted the sheet-metal bell jars that Lavoisier had built in 1782 for feeding a blowpipe he had used to melt platinum. Meusnier invented an apparatus that changed these bell jars into gasometers capable of accurately measuring the quantities of gas used in the reactions. A first model of a gasometer was built according to his plans by the mechanic Mégnié in 1784, and a second, better model in 1787. Meusnier again assisted Lavoisier in 1784 in putting together the apparatus for the decomposition of water, which consisted basically of an inclined rifle barrel with thin iron strips rolled into spirals. After various experiments, the results of which were presented to the Académie des Sciences during 1784, Lavoisier, surrounded by all the chemists of the Académie and several physicists and mathematicians, performed in late February and early March of 1785 what was perhaps the most important experiment of the century. After decomposing water by using the red-hot iron he collected the hydrogen and weighed the quantity of oxygen fixed in the state of iron oxide. Then he synthesized water in a glass receiver in which the hydrogen was ignited in the oxygen by an electric spark.

This experiment completed Lavoisier's long effort to destroy the phlogiston theory and establish modern chemistry. But it had other results, for it supplied a practical method of preparing economically and with some speed the hydrogen needed to inflate aerostats. This experiment was one of the best examples of the liaison between scientific research and technical innovation, a cooperation still extremely rare in the eighteenth century.

Military aerostation After this brilliant debut aerostation aroused only the curiosity of crowds. Scientists, who had nothing more to contribute to it (and for the moment nothing to expect from it), seemed to lose interest in the subject. Balloons represented only an uncertain way to take aerial excursions, and people could not conceive of establishing regular transportation services with them. Aside from lucrative demonstrations, aerostation aroused a revival of interest only when the Committee of Public Safety decided in 1793, at the suggestion of Monge, to use it for military purposes.

The director of this enterprise was one Coutelle, a little-known former teacher who had been the physics tutor of the count d'Artois. Coutelle found a valuable and ingenious assistant in Nicolas-Jacques Conté (1755–1805), who had acquired great knowledge of science and applied mechanics and had a special talent for invention. Conté, as the guiding spirit behind the Institut d'Égypte, later created for Bonaparte's expeditionary force, cut off from its supply bases, all the means of production indispensable to the active troops of an army occupying a country in which there was no industrial equipment. Although he was the inventor of a large number of ingenious devices, Conté has remained famous especially for combining clay with graphite for pencils to replace pure graphite which was then in short supply because of the blockade.

Coutelle and Conté took up Lavoisier's and Meusnier's method for producing hydrogen. They set up a furnace in the park of the Château de Meudon, which had been turned over to them, and in it heated a series of cast-iron tubes filled with metal filings (Figure 124). Thus they succeeded in producing, in about 15 hours, a quantity of gas sufficient to inflate a balloon. The technique of making envelopes of balloons was also perfected, over several months. Templates were made from

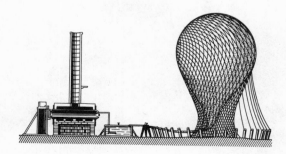

FIG. 124. Preparation of hydrogen for inflating military balloons during the French Revolution.

Plate 38. Illustrations of the centenary of ballooning, reproduced in *Illustrated London News*, January 26, 1884. Library of Congress

which to cut out sections that were glued together to form a balloon, which had been given a spherical shape to simplify operating it. By impregnating both sides of the balloon fabric with varnish Coutelle and Conté succeeded in making it impermeable enough to retain gas for several weeks. A net supported the basket and ropes with which groups of men moved the balloon. There was nothing remarkable in all this except the ingenuity of the operating plan and the speed with which it was completed.

The Meudon aerostation center made only five balloons, four of which were used exclusively by the armed forces: the *Entreprenant* at Maubeuge, Charleroi, and Fleurus, the *Céleste* by the army of the Sambre and Meuse, the *Hercule* and *Intrépide* by the army of the Rhine and Moselle. The *Telemaque* did not take part in military operations. It seems clear that balloons produced a psychological effect more than a tactical one. In addition to the surprise effect on the enemy they symbolized for the soldiers of the Republic the war effort of the Committee of Public Safety. But the Meudon establishment continued to be devoted to aerostation and, more recently, to aeronautical research.

Scientific ascents   After this brilliant episode, ballooning fell back to the level of novelties at public fairs. On two or three occasions balloons were used for scientific observation. On July 18, 1803, a certain Robertson, a Flemish show entrepreneur, with a compatriot named Lhoest, made an ascent at Hamburg during which they reached an altitude of 24,272 feet. They brought back from their ascent a description of various psychological disturbances and an observation of a weakening in the magnetic field and in the functioning of the voltaic pile. In order to verify these facts, which lent themselves to discussion, the science section of the Institut of the Académie des Sciences requested Joseph-Louis Gay-Lussac (1778–1850), who had just demonstrated his qualities as a physicist and chemist, to make an ascent of the same kind. On August 24, 1804, accompanied by Jean-Baptiste Biot (1774–1862), Gay-Lussac ascended from the garden of the former priory of Saint-Martin-des-Champs, where the Conservatoire national des Arts et Métiers had recently been installed, and attained an altitude of only 13,120 feet. A month later, on September 19, Gay-Lussac reached 22,960 feet alone. The thermometric and hygrometric observations he was able to make, and the analysis of his high-altitude air samples, remained isolated observations no different from similar ones already made in the mountains. The data reported by Robertson on electricity and magnetism were not confirmed. The audacity of the aeronauts won them more admiration than the results of their experiments. No similar feats were achieved until July 27, 1850, by Barral and Bixio, who slightly surpassed the altitude reached by Gay-Lussac (Gay-Lussac, 23,-012 feet; Barral 23,121 feet).

CHAPTER 6

THE BIRTH OF THE TELEGRAPH

VISUAL TELEGRAPHY

FOR CENTURIES, and perhaps since the first states were organized, signals transmitted over a distance from person to person made it possible to circulate simple information more quickly than by messengers. Moreover, transmission by sound or sight was not solely a development of civilized communities. But no matter how experienced the operators were in this practice, the circulation of information was slow.

The invention of the first visual signaling system making it possible to transmit long messages in a period of minutes over several hundred miles is credited to Claude Chappe (1763–1805). The history of the Chappe semaphore is well known. In itself the invention did not contribute to technical progress but was rather an adaptation of existing knowledge to meet a new need for rapid information. After a series of tests with several methods over a period of three years, Chappe devised a mechanism consisting basically of a wooden T whose horizontal beam (the regulator) pivoted on its axis, with jointed arms (the indicators) at each end. Since the indicators were weighted at their bases they stayed in a vertical position when at rest. A simple combination of cranks and ropes with reversing pulleys let an operator arrange the beam and indicators in various positions around their axes of rotation (Figure 125).

Such a mechanism could have been built a century earlier by a clockmaker like Abraham Breguet, who built Chappe's device in 1793. But an indispensable accessory was lacking at that time: a telescope with an achromatic objective, which by the end of the eighteenth century had become a practical and widely used instrument of terrestrial observation. Without such an aid it would have been necessary to place the stations so close together that installing a telegraph line would have been too burdensome and the transmission of messages too slow for the invention to be noticeably advantageous for the people of that time.

The originality of Chappe's invention lay in its combining the use of the telescope for long-distance observation with a code of signals quickly indicated in the sky high above all obstacles.

The stations consisted of masonry towers built in open areas so that from any one of them the closest station on either side could be seen. The apparatus, with movable arms regulated from inside, was installed above the tower.

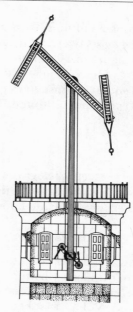

Fig. 125. A station on the French lines of the Chappe semaphore system, circa 1840–1850.

The arms could be arranged in 196 different positions, only 92 of which were used by Chappe for his code. Chappe, assisted by one of his relatives, Léon Delaunay, who as a former consul knew how to encode diplomatic dispatches, composed a dictionary of 92 pages, each with 92 numbered words. Two signals were enough to transmit a word, the first giving the number of the page, the second the number of the word. Transmission was from station to station, word by word, by two station attendants, one observing the transmitting station, the other transmitting to the next station. Coding and decoding were done only at the terminal stations. Later a second dictionary, of common phrases and expressions, was established.

Claude Chappe had begun his experiments in his native Sarthe. When he was certain of his results he came to Paris in 1791 and had the good fortune to obtain the money to build installations for a demonstration. Three stations were established, one on the hill of Ménilmontant, the other at Saint-Martin-du-Tertre 21 miles away, and the third between them. The demonstration took place on July 12, 1793, and Joseph Lakanal obtained from the Convention a decision to build a line from Paris to Lille.

The success of the Chappe semaphore was rapid, thanks to a fortuitous coincidence. The first message sent on the line announced to the Convention the taking of Condé by the Revolutionary army. Several other lines were installed before 1815, and more between then and 1848, the system remaining in service even after the introduction of the electric telegraph. Other systems were suggested later, but Chappe's was the only one developed in France and the one most widely adopted in other European countries.

To a certain extent the semaphore hindered the adoption of the electric telegraph in France. Messages were sent over the lines of the Chappe semaphores at speeds remarkable for that time: from Calais to Paris, 33 posts over 58 leagues took 3 minutes; from Lille via 22 posts over 60 leagues, 7 minutes; from Brest by 54 posts over 150 leagues, 8 minutes; from Toulon over 100 posts covering 207 leagues in 20 minutes.

On November 20, 1844, a first appropriation was voted, at François Arago's request, to install an experimental electric telegraph line along the railway line from Paris to Rouen. The first messages traveled over it on May 18, 1845.

ELECTRIC TELEGRAPHY

Electric telegraphy became feasible after the discoveries of the physicists who during the early nineteenth century studied the phenomenon of electromagnetism and made known their discoveries.

The electric battery The essential condition, if this invention was to become a practical method of communication, was the availability of a continuous, permanent source of electric current. The invention of the electric battery (the voltaic pile) by Alessandro Volta in 1800, which was the result of a controversy with Luigi Galvani, did not immediately ensure its use.

Volta's first battery was a stack of alternating copper and zinc discs in pairs separated by circles of cloth impregnated with brine. It was this arrangement that caused the French to give the device the name *pile* (meaning stack), which was retained, though the stack of discs never reappeared in batteries invented later and used industrially. The cloth separators had the disadvantage that the voltage at the poles disappeared once the cloth was dry. Volta himself contrived a completely different arrangement consisting of a series of containers filled with a salt solution. In each of these a strip of zinc and a strip of copper were inserted, each pair being connected with a corresponding strip in the next container.

The voltaic pile was modified in 1801 by a Scot, William Cruikshanks, who made a series of containers separated by partitions made of sheets of zinc and copper soldered to each other. The salt solution was replaced by acidulated water. This type of battery was used for the first major experiment, that performed by Gay-Lussac and Jacques Thénard at the École Polytechnique, which unfortunately contributed no important results.

In 1812 William H. Wollaston in turn modified Cruikshanks's battery so that the zinc strips, which deteriorated rapidly, could be easily replaced. But he did not succeed in eliminating its most important defect, that after a fairly short period of operation the battery gave no more current. The French physicist Nicolas Gautherot discovered the cause of this phenomenon, which was the accumulating hydrogen gas on the positive pole as the water in the containers decomposed, a phenomenon to which he gave the name *polarization*.

In 1828 César Becquerel eliminated the problem. Each compartment of the battery was divided into two parts by a semipermeable membrane of goldbeater's skin. The compartment into which the zinc strip was inserted was filled with acidulated water; that of the copper strip, with a copper sulfate solution.

Finally, in 1836 the English physicist J. F. Daniell gave Becquerel's two-liquid battery the arrangement that came into general use and was known under the name *Daniell battery* (Figure 126). This was a round glass container in which was placed a circular sheet of zinc surrounding a cylinder of porous porcelain. The inner cell was filled with a copper sulfate solution into which the positive pole, a copper spiral, was inserted. The zinc cell that formed the negative pole was immersed in acidulated water. Numerous changes were made later in the Daniell battery, but in its early form this was the first battery to generate electric current reliably. It made possible the use and development of the first series of telegraphic devices.

FIG. 126.   A set of Daniell piles.

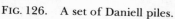

Electromagnetism   The observation that a magnetic needle deviates under the influence of a conductor traversed by an electric current soon led to the idea of using it to transmit agreed-upon signals over a distance.

Experimenters in the eighteenth century had already been impressed by the extremely high speed with which the electrical impulse was transmitted. Several physicists had tried around 1750 to use discharges of static electricity for signaling. A 1774 experiment by Georges-Louis Lesage is the most frequently mentioned one. The apparatus designed by this Geneva physicist consisted of 24 wires corresponding to a letter of the alphabet and through which it was possible to send current discharged from a Leyden jar. Each wire led to an electroscope, the divergence of whose leaves signaled the letter transmitted. Although it did not produce any practical result, this experiment represents the first attempt at an underground telegraph line, the conductors being insulated in glass tubes. Numerous other experimenters, including Claude Chappe in 1790, devoted their efforts during the second half of the eighteenth century to similar experiments. Then, after William Nicholson and another experimenter named Carlyle discovered electrolysis, its principles were put to use in telegraphy, using the same idea of a network of lines for letters. Hydrogen bubbles liberated in the several containers replaced the diverging leaves of an electroscope.

In 1820 André Ampère mentioned the possibility of applying the deviation of the magnetic needle so as to set up an electric telegraph. Several systems were immediately suggested, all involving the complication of providing one line for each letter of the alphabet. The first simplification was conceived of in 1832 by a Russian diplomat, one Baron Schilling, then stationed in Munich. In Schilling's device there appears the first electrical system to use a code making it possible to reproduce the letters of the alphabet. This was done by combinations of six indicators made of disks that were black on one side and white on the other. Each disk, suspended from a vertical wire holding a horizontal magnetic needle, turned one or the other face depending on whether or not the corresponding circuit was traversed by a current. Two additional wires were necessary—one for call signs, the other to return the current.

Several other systems based on the same principle were suggested one after the other in years to come. Each one reduced the number of necessary wires until the system suggested in 1827 by an Alsatian, Carl-August von Steinheil, which had a single circuit. In 1828 Steinheil discovered the possibility of returning current through the ground, which simplified the transmission to its simplest element: a single conductor between two stations.

The first electric telegraphs

In 1837 the first telegraph line was established between Euston and Camden in London, by Sir William F. Cooke (1806–1879) and Sir Charles Wheatstone (1802–1875). The devices invented and used by these two British physicists were of the type just discussed, which was the only one then known— they had five needles and circuits with six wires. The first transmission, which can be seen as the first in the world made on a line under development, was made on July 12, 1837, forty-four years to the day after the first operation of the Chappe semaphore, over a distance of slightly more than one mile between Euston and Camden (Figures 127 and 128). In 1842 the same builders introduced a two-needle instrument (Figure 129), and in 1843 Alexander Bain (1818–1903) built one with a single needle, which was widely employed on the Continent. In France, Louis Breguet (1804–1883) also devised a two-needle apparatus, in 1846, but systems based on electromagnetism were already in use then and for all practical purposes the Breguet system with a magnetic needle was not applied.

During 1820, the year that saw the memorable publication of Ampère's works, François Arago established the principle of the electromagnet, a discovery whose repercussions on industrial civilization were to be considerable after 1850. This principle was first applied only twenty years after Arago's paper. It gave rise to three new types of telegraphic apparatus: the alphabetical telegraph, the electric telegraph with Chappe signals, and the telegraph based on the Morse system. The twenty-year delay in the effective application of the electromagnet seems relatively long, compared with the many suggestions made during this time to use the new knowledge in telegraphy. This was because for some time electromagnets were made with wire of a rather coarse cross section coiled in a small number of turns, since it was believed that the magnetic force was inversely proportionate to the resistance of the conductor. The effect obtained was exactly the opposite of that sought, and these kinds of electromagnets were inadequate to operate an apparatus over a long distance.

Relays

In 1837 Wheatstone invented a device that made it possible to close from a distance the circuit of an electric battery controlling a bell. This was the first relay based on electrochemical action. A U-shaped tube was filled with mercury and a small quantity of acidulated water was placed in one of its sides (Figure 130). When current from the line passed through the water it liberated a small quantity of hydrogen. The pressure of this hydrogen caused enough movement of the column of mercury to close the

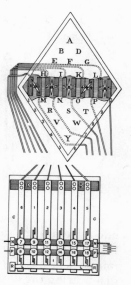

FIG. 127. A diagram of the five-needle telegraph by Wheatstone and Cooke, 1837. *Top:* The receiver. *Bottom:* The transmitter.

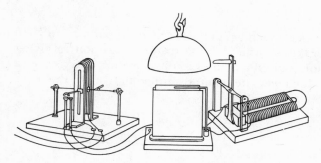

FIG. 128. A diagram of a local circuit of the Wheatstone and Cooke telegraph, 1837. *Left:* A relay. *Right:* The calling device.

FIG. 129. The first electric telegraph transmitting-receiving post built by Cooke and Wheatstone, 1842. *Left:* General view. *Right:* Diagram of the transmitters and their connections.

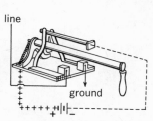

circuit of the sounding device on the other side. A short time later Wheatstone invented another, more effective, relay system consisting of a needle placed in the center of a frame, with a small fork-shaped contact at one end (Figure 131). When current passed from the wire through the frame, the prongs of the fork plunged into containers of mercury and closed the local circuit. Wheatstone immediately had the idea of using current from an electromagnet to operate a switch at the receiving station. The relay closed the circuit of a battery supplying a strong

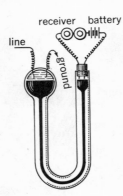

FIG. 130.   Wheatstone's electric relay, 1837.

enough current to activate the electromagnet in the receiving apparatus. In 1840 he devised a telegraph apparatus in which an electromagnet, upon receiving impulses at the receiving station, caused a pointer to pivot around its axis over a dial bearing the letters of the alphabet. The pointer stopped in front of the letter transmitted.

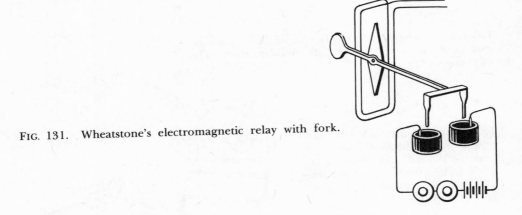

FIG. 131.   Wheatstone's electromagnetic relay with fork.

Alphabetical devices   In its first form Wheatstone's apparatus simply perfected an apparatus devised several years earlier by Cooke, which included a clock movement at each post, with a balance wheel that caused a pointer to turn in jerks. The lever of the escapement had two armatures corresponding to two electromagnets that stopped the mechanism in one oscillation or another when it received an electrical impulse from the transmitting station. Wheatstone's improvement consisted of eliminating the balance wheel of the clock mechanism and controlling the oscillations rather than the pauses of the lever by sending the current alternately through each electromagnet. By 1840 the system had only a single electromagnet, which acted on the pointer by both closing and opening the armature.

An easily operated transmitting apparatus corresponded to the receiving device. This sender included a horizontal dial arranged like that of the receiver. In its center was a crank that the operator turned in order to place it, successively, in front of the letters to be transmitted. During each rotation the crank sent as many impulses as the number of divisions of the dial passed, causing the pointer on the receiving post to advance through the same portion of the circle.

Alphabet devices, of which many variations were developed, quickly replaced needle devices. For about the next ten years they were controlled by batteries and switches. In 1857 Ernst Werner von Siemens (1816–1892) invented an apparatus that included an electromagnetic generator. In 1846 a German named Emil Stöhrer introduced an apparatus with a clock movement controlled by induction currents, but it appears not to have been used. This was true neither of Siemens's apparatus, or the one Wheatstone put in service one year after his German colleague, nor of several other succeeding models.

The first French telegraphic devices — Alphabet devices were not immediately adopted in France, though as early as 1844 Louis Breguet built a model that operated perfectly (Figure 132). The importance of the Chappe semaphore network encouraged Alphonse Foy, then the director of the telegraph service, to have Breguet build an apparatus to use the signals of the Chappe code, in order to avoid retraining his operators.

 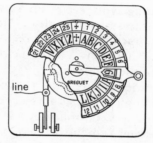

FIG. 132. L. Breguet's telegraph apparatus with dial, 1844. *Right:* Transmitter; *Left:* Receiver.

Breguet's receiving station had two needles, simulating the indicators of the Chappe system. Each was driven by a clock mechanism that could be stopped by an electromagnet, as in Wheatstone's first system. At each mechanical impulse the needles pivoted one-eighth of a revolution. Their simultaneous positions reproduced 64 of the signals in the Chappe code. The transmitting device consisted of two cranks with a simple mechanism making it possible to send over the line, during one complete revolution, four impulses of current separated by equal intervals of rest. At the receiving post these were changed into eight advances of each needle.

The system was put in service on the Paris-Rouen line that opened in 1845. That year Gustave Froment devised an automatic keyboard sender that replaced the crank sender of Breguet's alphabet apparatus and simplified its use (Figure

133). Several additional improvements were made to these devices during the next few years, but after 1850 they were replaced by alphabet systems.

On the public communication networks the alphabet devices themselves disappeared quite rapidly in the face of the Morse system's machines, on which sending was faster. In special cases, however (for example on railroads), they continued in service for almost a century.

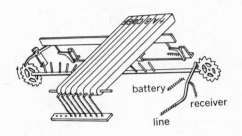

FIG. 133. Froment's keyboard sender for Breguet telegraph machines, 1849.

Printing devices   From the very first use of these telegraph systems attempts were made to develop printing devices. Wheatstone built the first model, using the principle of his alphabet system. The sending mechanism was the same, but the receiver was quite different. The dial and pointer were replaced by a type wheel consisting of a horizontal spindle with 24 radiating arms, each with a letter engraved at its end. The movement of the wheel was controlled like that of the pointer on the alphabet apparatus. The letters called stopped in front of a recording cylinder against which they were pressed by a small hammer. A second circuit controlled the rotation of the cylinder and release of the hammer.

Many ideas were put forward in the next thirty to forty years. In particular, in 1846 an Englishman, John W. Brett (1805–1863), built an apparatus in which the type wheel was controlled by a keyboard, an idea borrowed from Froment. Most other systems kept the dial sender and adapted to the receiver a bobbin holding a strip of paper that unrolled (as in Morse devices) and passed under the type wheel. But these instruments, in which the type wheel had to be located by unequal rotations before printing, worked slowly.

The best solution, found by an American named David E. Hughes (1831–1900), was based on a completely different principle. Instead of regulating the type wheel in discrete movements, Hughes gave it continuous movement throughout the transmission of the messages, each letter being printed as it passed in front of the type (Figure 134). Such a system required two parts turning perfectly synchronized in the transmitter and receiver.

The idea of synchronized machines had been tried before Hughes. The first attempt was by an American, Alfred L. Vail (1807–1859), who in 1845 claimed priority for inventing printing systems, for an apparatus he claimed to have built in 1837. In 1843 Alexander Bain also invented a synchronized system, but the one by Hughes immediately offered major advantages over its predecessors, which seem never to have been developed. The type wheel, under which passed a strip of paper, was connected with a drum containing 28 vertical pins, each capable of

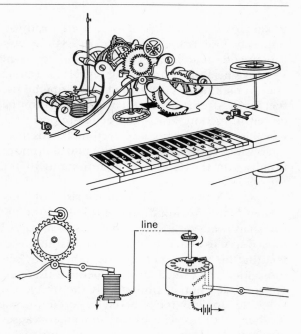

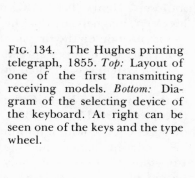

FIG. 134. The Hughes printing telegraph, 1855. *Top:* Layout of one of the first transmitting receiving models. *Bottom:* Diagram of the selecting device of the keyboard. At right can be seen one of the keys and the type wheel.

being pushed slightly downward by a key. An entire set of these keys formed the transmitting keyboard. Above the drum turned a horizontal finger whose movement was synchronized with that of the type wheel of the receiving station. It cleared the drum of the pins corresponding to each letter of the alphabet, in the same order in which the letters of the type wheel passed in front of the printing device. If one of the pins was lifted by the key, the circuit of the line was closed, causing the lever printing at the receiver to move. The Hughes system, put in service in 1856, owed its success to the simplicity of the principle on which it was based. In practice it underwent numerous improvements in the course of time and supplanted all other such devices.

The Morse system

The telegraph invented by Samuel F. B. Morse (1791–1872) is a contemporary of all those discussed above. This American painter, whose curiosity transformed him into a physicist and mechanic, has been the subject of numerous biographies. His artistic activities led him to live in Europe at a time when many minds were occupied with developing knowledge in electrochemistry and electromagnetism. Around 1832 he began to interest himself in a way to apply these phenomena to a telegraph system. It is thought that with the help of the American chemist Charles T. Jackson (1805–1880) he tried to pick up signals from an electric current acting on a strip of colored paper or from the marks left by current passing through the paper. Morse may already have used a bobbin holding a strip of paper unrolled by a clock mechanism.

Several years later he thought of using an electromagnet with an armature holding an inscribing stylus that left long and short marks on the paper as it unrolled. Several years were spent in searching for a satisfactory method of making inscriptions. After first trying a pencil and then a pen, which was difficult to keep constantly inked, Morse used a rod with a round head that marked the signals by embossing the paper. In 1844 he was able to build a bulky device that functioned on an inside circuit but proved useless on an outside line.

Like his European colleagues, Morse ran up against a general lack of experience in making electromagnets. The one he used in his 1844 apparatus was two feet high. After studying the works of his compatriot Joseph Henry (1797–1878) on self-induction, Morse succeeded in perfecting his electromagnets. In 1845 he was able, by employing a relay, to make his instruments function on the first line established between Washington and Baltimore. From here the network spread rapidly over the Continent. Beginning in 1846 the Morse system was adopted in Europe.

Morse's invention is characteristic of most of the inventions born in the United States during the second half of the nineteenth century. His procedure foreshadowed the method that was to make Edison successful. A sure intuition caused him to attack a subject that was "in the air." His quick intelligence and the fact that his mind was little encumbered by scientific notions let him keep only those ideas that seemed of immediate use, and the practical nature of Morse's approach led him to find quickly the simplest solution.

The Morse system is based on two simple ideas: to make signals with a simple mechanical device whose every movement causes similar movements in the receiving device by closing an electric circuit, and to establish a signal code using only two elements, a short signal and a long one. Combinations of no more than four of these were enough to transmit every letter of the alphabet.

The sending device owed nothing to scientific principles—it was simply a manually operated spring lever (Figure 135). Morse did not achieve this simplicity on his first attempt. He first worked out a fairly complex system using characters engraved in Morse code. As in typography, material was composed by aligning the characters in a spiral groove on a cylinder. As it turned, the cylinder controlled the transmission lever. Morse then came around to using the simple hand lever, which could be easily mastered after only a reasonable apprenticeship period by the operators, for the code was very well composed. The common letters were formed from the simplest groups of signs, and the others presented similarities or symmetries that made it possible to learn and use them as easily as letters in the ordinary alphabet.

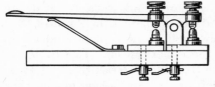 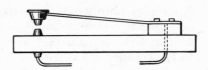

FIG. 135. Morse's manual transmitter. *Right*: With flexible blade (first model); *Left*: Jointed-lever type with reversing spring.

As soon as it became widely known, the Morse type of installation quickly underwent numerous improvements, especially to the receiver. The driving weight of the mechanism that unrolled the paper was replaced by a spring. The problem of inking the printing tip was finally solved. In particular, the construction of electromagnets having evolved, builders succeeded in reducing the bulkiness of the devices. Simplifying the wiring in the sender and receiver further increased the efficiency of the instruments (Figure 136).

In a few years the Morse telegraph supplanted the other systems that had preceded it in Europe. As early as 1854, only ten years after its invention, the Morse telegraph was exclusively adopted for international communication.

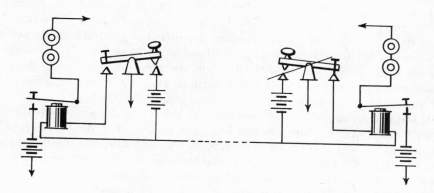

FIG. 136.   Diagram of the connections in the perfected Morse system, 1845.

Telegraph lines   Use of the telegraph as a regular means of communication was possible when many other technical problems were solved. The invention of transmitting and receiving devices was not enough without good solutions for erecting lines and building many instruments, not to mention electric batteries.

For various reasons the first lines were underground. Iron wires strung in the open at first gave poor results, even when galvanized. A decision was made to use copper wires, but in addition to the possibility of adverse effects from storms and meteorological accidents, it was especially feared that such a quantity of copper out in the open would tempt thieves. The first telegraph line, by Cooke and Wheatstone in 1837, was underground. The copper wire was covered with a sheath of cotton and pitch and laid in wooden channels. In the following years every insulating material known at the time—vegetable fibers, glass, glue, gutta-percha, tar, and bitumen—was tried one after the other, and wood, sand, lead, and cement were used to protect the wire.

The experiments were lengthy; even though relatively satisfactory methods were discovered as early as 1860, the insulation problem, including that of submerging lines in the sea and in rivers, was thereafter constantly reviewed. After several short-lived attempts a submarine line was laid by John Brett in 1850 between Gris-Nez and Dover, but the cable broke. It was a copper wire 2 mm. in diameter, insulated by a 6-mm. thick layer of gutta-percha and held down by weights. The overland section was protected by lead sheathing. Builders concluded from this first experiment that underwater cables had to possess specially high resistance to breaking. The cable that was laid in 1851 over approximately the same route was composed of four copper conductors surrounded by an insulating sheath that was already more complex: gutta-percha and tarred hemp fibers, the whole rolled in a mixture of tallow and tar and protected by a strong wrapping of galvanized iron wires. This cable was able to provide regular service from the moment it was laid, and after this success the laying of undersea cables developed rapidly.

Aerial lines had come to be widely used overland. Improvements in galvanizing and soldering made it possible to consider using iron wire, which substantially lowered the cost. The Paris-Rouen line of 1844/45 was an aerial line. Numerous construction problems were left to study. This was the first time it was necessary to make extensive use of tall wooden poles to remain in the ground for long periods. Practice acquired in naval construction and public works provided procedures for preserving wood and securing it firmly in the ground. The posts along the Paris-Rouen line were oak, dried and hardened by slight carbonization. They were anchored in masonry blocks.

It was also necessary to find methods for insulating the wires in suspension (Figure 137). Morse had used simple felt pads. In Germany the wire rested in a notch cut in the top of the pole and coated with glue. The first method used in France was a simple porcelain ring screwed into the post, through which the wire passed. Every quarter of a mile the wire was attached firmly to a stirrup with a wheel and ratchet tightener supported by a porcelain insulator.

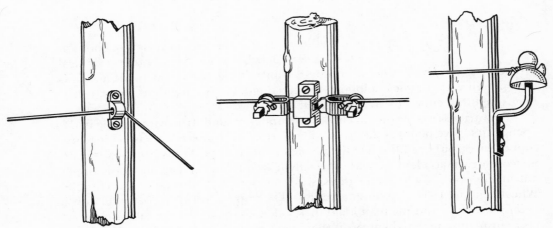

FIG. 137. Poles and insulators for telegraph lines. *Left:* Ring, 1845; *Center:* Insulator with tension devices, 1845; *Right:* Porcelain insulator, 1860.

Glass insulators appeared slightly later in the United States, in a form similar to those that came into use in glass or porcelain in every country in the world. The history of insulating posts and their anchoring systems is in itself quite complex.

Machinery and the electrical construction industry

The history of the telegraph also includes the invention of a quite large number of types of machines and instruments as simple as lightning rods or as complex as commutators, relays, sound devices, galvanometers, and measuring instruments. What has just been said about telegraph lines is only a simple example of the numerous problems that had to be overcome and constantly reviewed, first to establish, then to maintain and extend an increasingly dense network that was in constant service over the surface of the earth.

The most surprising factor in this history is the rapidity (barely ten years) with which technicians in the mid-nineteenth century moved from their first experiments to developing public service. This required transforming physicists into electrical engineers and creating a new industry literally from the ground up. It was one thing to build a few demonstration or research instruments between 1825 and 1835, and quite another to transpose these methods of craft production into a system of industrial production.

Telegraphy brought about the birth of the first electrical industry and obliged it to become a precision industry. In this connection the establishing of electrical telegraphy (perhaps much more than of mechanical engineering, whose transition period occupied at least a half century) was the first symptom of modern industry as we understand the term today. Its progress brought about the birth of numerous other technical fields.

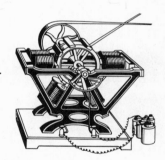

FIG. 138.   Froment's magnetoelectric motor, 1845.

A single example will suffice to demonstrate the importance of this influence: that of the electric motor for industrial use. Hippolyte Pixii's 1832 engine was the first magnetoelectric motor, but the need for electrical transmission brought Gustave Froment's first electric generators and motors into service. This builder, a former student at the École Polytechnique, in 1844 began building various types of electromotors that he used to drive dividing machines in his shops. One of his motors, consisting of eight soft iron hubs attached to a crown that turned in front of four electromagnets, was adapted in 1855 to rewind automatically weights that drove clock mechanisms in certain telegraph machines (Figure 138).

BIBLIOGRAPHY

ARAGON, E. *Ponts en bois et métal.* Paris, 1911. (The author describes numerous ancient bridges but does not indicate the dates of construction.)

AUGUSTIN-NORMAND, Paul. *La genèse de l'hélice propulsive.* Académie de Marine. Paris, 1962.

BERTHOT, P. *Traité des routes, rivières et canaux.* Paris, c. 1895.

BOUCHER, Cyril T. G. *John Rennie 1761-1821. The Life and Work of a Great Engineer.* Manchester, 1963.

CHAPELLE, Howard I. *The Pioneer Steamship "Savannah."* Smithsonian Institution, Bull. 228, Washington, 1961.

DOLLFUS, Charles, et al. *Histoire de la marine.* Paris, 1934.

MONTORIOL, E. *Les systèmes de télégraphie et téléphone.* Paris, 1922.

PANNELL, J. P. M. *An Illustrated History of Civil Engineering.* London, 1964.

PERDONNET, Auguste. *Traité élémentaire des chemins de fer.* 2 vols. Paris, 1856.

SPRATT, H. P. *Outline History of Transatlantic Steam Navigation.* Science Museum, London, 1950. (Extensive bibliography.)

Transports sur rails. Catalogue de Musée du Conservatoire National des Arts et Métiers. Paris, 1952.

VIAL DE CLAIRBOIS, *Marine.* Systematic encyclopedia. Paris, 1783-1787.

PART FOUR
MILITARY TECHNIQUES

CHAPTER 1

FORTIFICATIONS

The persistence of Vauban's techniques

Sebastian Vauban (1633–1707) was the first to conceive of a comprehensive system of fortifications to protect French frontiers in locations with favorable terrain along the lines of natural obstacles. But he had never expounded his principles and his work. His successors, like Louis de Cormontaigne (1697–1752) and Michaud d'Arçon, did not define these principles and were little concerned with a unified system. With them the French turned increasingly to the entrenched camp—a vast area of ground defended by fortified artillery works that offered an appearance of security to an army come to take refuge under its guns.

In conception and construction the works themselves continued to embody the techniques of Vauban's time until the last quarter of the nineteenth century. Bernard Belidor's *Science des ingénieurs* in 1729 did not question the profiles of fortifications used by Vauban but established, using static mechanics, the relations between the weight of masonry components and the thrust of the earth. In structures involving arches Belidor studied their thrust on the heads of piers, which until then had been subject only to empirical rules that were inaccurate and inadequate. He then developed construction methods in masonry, building architecture, gates and forts, barracks, and so on. Belidor's works contain no technical novelties about fortifications, nor did other works until the end of the nineteenth century, because, despite genuine improvement, artillery throughout this period had a range and type of projectiles that were but little improved between 1700 and 1850.

Figure 1 shows the profile of the Paris fortifications built between 1840 and 1841 (to be discussed later). The scarp and counterscarp are masonry. The outer glacis provides the last cover behind the parapet, shielding an outer line of fire capable of stopping attackers at the rampart itself.

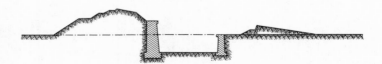

FIG. 1. Profile of the fortifications of Paris, 1840.

The dimensions themselves have changed little since 1700. The masonry parapet is 20 feet high and the moat ranges from 33 to 131 feet in width. The scarp is extremely high (33 feet), as is the slope of the rampart (26 to 33 feet).

We shall see later that rifled artillery introduced few modifications in the defensive plan and that only high-explosive projectiles necessitated more important changes after 1850. Between 1700 and 1850, however, the only effective ranges available to artillery were still 1,750 yards for heavy pieces and 875 yards for field guns.

Hollow shells filled with black powder, the only explosive used, were not very effective against Vauban's fortifications. In order to breach them the attacking artillery had to come quite close to the ramparts and expend many projectiles to make the thick wall of the scarp collapse into the moat.

Organization of protected areas To shelter men, ammunition, and supplies from bombardment, the areas covered in masonry were protected by a layer of earth between 10 and 13 feet thick, which protected the vault and buttressed the piers (Figure 2). Under these conditions this layer of earth was quite sufficient to limit the effects of the largest caliber hollow cast-iron bombs.

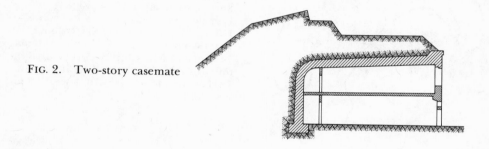

Fig. 2.   Two-story casemate

Casemates sometimes had several stories for barracks in which personnel could sleep safely sheltered. The separate forts of a place, which were rarely threatened except from one side, had casemates turned to present their least exposed side. In isolated forts that could be bombarded from all sides the casemate openings faced on a narrow courtyard. The small courtyard between façades was defiladed by earth embankments atop the quarters. Such casemates were approximately 52 feet long and 20 feet wide, with one or two stories.

These defensive installations persisted in fortifications from the beginning of the nineteenth century down to the wars of the twentieth. Modifications later had to be made to them when rifled guns appeared, around 1850 to 1860, and especially when steel shells loaded with powerful explosives came into use.

Paris fortifications Two attacks on Paris, in 1814 and 1815, had shown that capturing the capital put an end to all possibility of resistance and that this center of communications was too vulnerable if left defenseless. Its fall, quickly achieved by the enemy, had twice decided the fate of the Empire.

In 1835 the government under Louis-Philippe began to give attention to organizing the defense of Paris. In 1840 the danger of war, heightened by events in the Near East, made it absolutely necessary to develop a genuine defensive system for the capital. The work, which took from 1840 to 1844, resulted in fortifications that could at the time be regarded as impregnable.

A twenty-mile-long line of ramparts widely spaced and equipped with 94 bastions enclosed the capital. To better protect this ring against attacks a line of detached forts extended over a perimeter of 42 miles (Figure 3). This line of defense, armed with artillery, was able to prevent the enemy from setting up siege guns within range of the ramparts. Given the range of guns in this period it was sufficient to build outlying forts at distances varying from just under one mile to two miles in front of the ramparts.

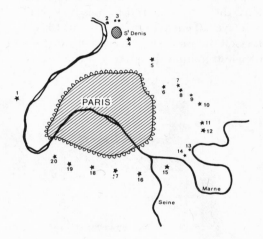

FIG. 3. Plan of the fortifications of Paris and emplacement of the covering forts. 1. Mont Valérien; 2. Couronne de la Briche; 3. Double Couronne du Nord; 4. Fort de l'Est (East Fort); 5. Fort d'Aubervilliers; 6. Fort de Romainville; 7. Noisy Redoubt; 8. Fort de Noisy; 9. Boissière Redoubt; 10. Fort de Rosny; 11. Fontenay Redoubt; 12. Fort de Nogent; 13. Faisanderie Redoubt; 14. Gravelle Redoubt; 15. Fort de Charenton; 16. Fort d'Ivry; 17. Fort de Bicêtre; 18. Fort de Montrouge; 19. Fort de Vanves; 20. Fort d'Issy.

The direction of attacks by the Allies in 1814 and 1815 suggested the zones to be covered: in the north, Saint-Denis (Montmartre being included within the protected ring); in the east, the heights of Romainville and Pantin; in the south, the zone of Ivry-Montrouge, Châtillon, and Charenton. On the west the Seine gave protection, its approach routes being widely covered by the powerful fortress on Mont Valérien.

Such a long defensive system would oblige the enemy to extend his blockade over a distance of 72 miles, which appeared impossible. Thus, a siege of the capital was no longer to be feared.

These fortifications, still in existence without modification in 1870, were besieged though, during the Franco-Prussian War, and determined its result. If the 1840 calculations were then proved inadequate, it was because the range of the artillery had increased with the adoption of rifled artillery between 1850 and 1860 and because the defensive works regarded as complete in 1840 were no longer adequate.

The artillery of the defenders could be considered formidable. It consisted of 2,627 pieces of artillery, including 198 12- and 16-cm. naval guns hastily sent to

Paris as soon as the German threat became apparent. The ramparts were equipped with 805 pieces, the forts with 1,389 pieces, and the forward works with 433 pieces.

The attacking German force of 180,000 men had 672 pieces of field artillery and only 108 heavy guns (50 6-inch guns, 52 5-inch guns, and 6 8-inch mortars) at its disposal. But these guns, whose ranges were longer than those of the defense, were able to annihilate the forts that attacked from the south and to bombard the city within the now ineffective ramparts.

Siege warfare

From ancient times, attacking fortified cities had raised problems that led to the development of a special art — poliorcetics, the study of how to conduct or resist sieges. Demetrius I acquired the surname Poliorcetes (the Besieger) as a practitioner of it, and Flavius Vegetius discussed it at length in his enormously influential work *De re militari*.

Inadequate equipment was used to hurl projectiles on the besieged; it was insufficient to destroy walls. An attacker then tried to reach the tops of the walls with towers, to put him on a level with the defenders. This method was used until medieval times.

Sapping methods were also practiced, which made it possible to dig tunnels to penetrate the besieged place or undermine its walls.

The appearance of artillery and use of cast-iron balls made it possible to attack and destroy fortifications. Large stone artillery balls used by forces under Mohammed II had already opened a breach in the walls of Byzantium.

We have described the evolution in the design of ramparts that resulted from the dangers of attack by artillery using gunpowder. But a siege always required two simultaneous actions: destroying a length of fortification to open a breach and allowing the attacking troops to pass through the breach in a final assault.

The changes in siege warfare were finally described, by Vauban and Cohorn. Vauban formulated its principles in his *Traité sur l'attaque et la defense des places* (1704). Louis de Menno, Baron de Cohorn (1641–1704), a Dutch engineer and general and a rival of Vauban, fortified numerous strongholds like Nijmegen, Breda, Bergen op Zoom, and also published papers on fortification. Whereas Vauban preferred defense by the ramparts themselves, Cohorn relied on numerous outer works.

An attack could be completed only if the attackers arrived at the breach. Once the artillery destroyed the ramparts and opened a breach, the attackers had to penetrate the opening without being overwhelmed and decimated by the defender's fire. Thus, the principal problem was to provide effective shelter to the assault troops to a point not far from the breach.

Sapping

Advancing while taking shelter behind earthworks is an idea as old as siege warfare, as for example during the sieges of Barca in Cirenaica (Libya) by the Persians in 512 B.C. and of Plataea, Greece, by the Spartans.

As early as the thirteenth century a special corps of engineers was assigned to build approach works in sieges. The classic form finally took shape at the beginning of the eighteenth century and lasted until the modern period.

Sappers were directed by attackers toward the objective (Figure 4), using

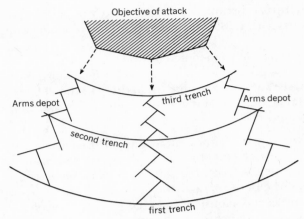

FIG. 4. Plan of saps and trenches in siege warfare.

FIG. 5. Cross sections of saps: single (*right*) and double (*left*).

zigzag approach trenches so that the open trenches would not be raked by the guns of the defenders. Theoretically, three parallel trenches were dug, the first one as far as 650 to 1,100 yards from the objective. The attacking troops assembled in these.

The zigzag trenches were constructed so as to shelter the preceding section from enfilade fire. The parapet was single (Figure 5), assuring protection; but if it was still inadequate, a double parapet was thrown up (Figure 5), covering both sides of the trench.

The third parallel had to serve as a place to assemble the assault troops. Thus, it had to be as close to the breach as possible and have assembly areas where a larger body of soldiers could be mustered. The trenches had firing ledges, either to post snipers or to facilitate climbing the walls when the assembled troops began the assault.

Mining   The classic principle of attacking by mining was to dig a series of chambers and fill them with powder under the enemy's defenses, beginning at the third parallel. By exploding the mines the attackers could either destroy forward works of the defense or even destroy the scarp and counterscarp. And the defense could dig countermines to upset the attacker's approach works.

Until 1885 black powder was the only explosive used in these mines. The practice was to use a simple formula to calculate the charge necessary to produce a given effect. A large enough weight of the charge ("C") exploding at a given depth ("h") in the ground produces a sphere of impact, but the effect does not show on the ground (Figure 6). If the depth "h" is decreased, the explosion sends part of the earth into the sky and produces a round crater of "r" radius, with the soil thrown up forming a rim around it.

The index of the mine chamber is $\frac{r}{h} = n$.

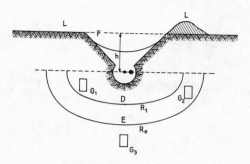

FIG. 6.   Mine chamber.

The effects of different powder charges were determined experimentally and thus a formula was established:

$$C = gh^3 (\sqrt{1 + n^2} - 0.41)^3$$

g is a coefficient dependent on the nature of the ground (1 to 2 in soil, 2 to 4 in masonry work). For $n = 1$ (ordinary mine chamber), $C = gh^3$.

At depth the terrain is compressed by the explosion. At the surface, ellipsoidal zones form—R_1 for a complete break and R_2 for a limited break.

In a countermining operation, to destroy the tunnels G_1, G_2, and G_3 of the enemy, the various coefficients (in particular the one for the depth of the mine chamber for a given distance of countermining) make it possible to calculate under what conditions the destruction of the three mines of the assailants was achieved. In this way it is possible to plan quite exactly the destructive effects desired.

After 1885 it was possible to increase the effects of mining by substituting nitrated explosives (melinite, trinitrotoluene, and so on) for powder. Until then the technique of attacking fortifications remained the same as prescribed by Vauban.

Plate 39. The artillery dock at Balaklava in the Crimea, spring of 1855. Photograph Roger Fenton. Collection André Jammes, Paris.

CHAPTER 2

LAND ARTILLERY

THE LONG REIGN of Louis XIV had been too full of battles and sieges to leave time to modify the artillery system, which dated from the beginning of the seventeenth century. It was not possible to reduce the work of maintaining or building current equipment by introducing even successful innovations, which would have involved delay and additional expense.

It must also be remembered that the wars of the period involved both open battles and sieges, this being an obstacle to separating the two types of matériel required. The two types of strategies contributed to the continued use of calibers that were too heavy because they needed to be powerful.

Eighteenth-century artillery In this period there were few improvements. Gun carriages were pulled by a limber, a pair of low wheels with a shaft attached. It had a pintle that fitted into a hole in the transom at the rear of the gun carriage (Figure 7).

At the beginning of the eighteenth century the guns were still heavy affairs that were difficult to handle on the battlefield. Although the infantry had attempted to equip themselves with the lighter so-called Swedish-style guns that were copies of those by Gustavus Adolphus, these had been abandoned for the time being.

The ammunition supply presented difficulties, for a projectile cast in one province could not be used in a cannon built elsewhere, despite the supposed standardization of calibers.

The customary projectile was a solid ball whose weight in pounds designated the caliber of the piece. The gun denominations of 33, 24, 16, and 12 pounds replaced the old names for French cannons, such as culverins and so on.

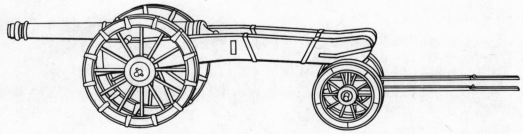

FIG. 7. Gun with forecarriage, late eighteenth century.

Powder was transported in kegs, which along with the necessary tools were brought up to the guns. Powder was scooped out with the lantern, a kind of long-handled trowel with rounded edges, and poured into the gun. At that time the powder charge was two-thirds the weight of the ball. The powder was packed down at the bottom of the bore with a ramrod and was held in place by a plug of hay. The ball was then inserted and held in place by a second plug of hay. Fine powder was packed into the touchhole. The charge could now fire by bringing a lighted wick close to the hole.

The inaccuracy of the firing was compensated for by having the ball ricochet to make a series of bounces, so it could hit the enemy at various points. But to make the ball ricochet it was necessary to reduce the angle of elevation to less than 8°.

When aimed at an angle of 6°, the 6-pounder had a range of only 800 *toises* (about 5,120 feet). The maximum effective range was less than 1,000 *toises* (6,400 feet), and grapeshot was useful only under 300 *toises* (1,920 feet).

Firing was very slow—return the piece to the battery and swabbing, loading, and aiming a very heavy gun required a great deal of time. It was considered genuine progress to fire a 24-pounder 100 times per day or 16- and 12-pounders 150 to 200 shots a day.

Vallière   In 1732 a colonel-inspector named Vallière decided to simplify the calibers and particularly to build guns with more uniform dimensions within the same caliber. The calibers were reduced to five: 4, 8, 12, 16, and 24. All were suitable for "attack and defense of strongholds, and the first three, combined in accordance with the circumstances, were particularly suited to field warfare, so that when necessary the fortified places could help the armies and the armies the places" (*Mémoire* of Vallière the younger).

The regulations on sizes did not apply to the gun carriages, to which each arsenal, retaining its traditions, gave its own proportions. The caliber of the projectiles was fixed, but not the windage, the difference between the internal diameter of the gun and that of the ball.

Plate 40. Officers and soldiers posing along the parapet of Fort Totten, near Rock Creek Church, D.C. The Civil War, which saw the first large-scale use of gun cotton, was fought with iron. U.S. Signal Corps photo No. 111-B-376 (Brady Collection) in the National Archives

The 24- and 16-pounders continued to be heavy—5,400 and 4,200 pounds—because of the power desired. The 12-, 8-, and 4-pounders, intended for field warfare, were longer and still too heavy (3,200, 2,100, and 1,150 pounds).

Cannon cartridges made of heavy paper, parchment, or canvas, which held the weight of powder needed for a charge, had begun to be used. But military authorities still clung to the idea of reserving artillery for sieges, where a slow rate of fire presented no disadvantages, and they forbade the use of cartridges in favor of the lantern. This is the artillery depicted in the plates of the *Encyclopédie*.

The gun barrel used in other countries was no different from the French equipment in either design or production. A few details in the construction of gun carriages had been improved, but it was especially the way they used field artillery that led certain countries to develop artillery of greater mobility. An attempt had been made to lighten the carriages, especially those of the smaller caliber guns, which could thus be brought up more quickly to the line of battle.

Gribeauval   The Vallière equipment had been in use for thirty years when Jean-Baptiste Vaquette de Gribeauval (1715–1789) became inspector of French artillery in 1764. A former artillery officer, he had served since 1757 in Austria and had acquired a deep knowledge of the equipment of other countries and its use. The Seven Years' War had exhausted the stock of French weapons and supplies, which had to be built up again. Speaking of Austrian and French artillery in 1762 Gribeauval wrote that "a well-informed man could select from these two types of cannons an artillery that would decide almost every action in field warfare." In 1764 he himself was called upon to put this reform into effect. His basic idea was to separate equipment according to its purposes for field, siege, fort, or coastal use.

For the field artillery Gribeauval defined new models of the 12-, 8-, and 4-pounders. Longer and lighter, they fired a weaker powder charge, which made it possible to reduce the thickness of the metal and so lighten the pieces.

Ingenious improvements were made in the new weapons: cartridges combining the charge and the ball; a replaceable bead sight of red copper screwed to the metal of the gun, thus avoiding scrapping weapons whose sights quickly deteriorated; the back sight and elevating screw, and the reed quick match, which permitted greater regularity in applying fire.

Guns were made more mobile, with forecarriages mounted on higher wheels supported on iron rather than wooden axles. The introduction of axle dragropes permitted gunners to move guns manually. A trail rope facilitated maneuvering during retreat and when obstacles had to be crossed (Figure 8).

To ensure matching calibers with ammunition, patterns, mandrels, and dies were supplied to the arsenals. An instrument now called a star gauge was invented to measure exactly the internal diameter of the bore. It consisted of movable arms spread by a wedge and pushed through the gun barrel with a long bar.

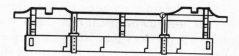

FIG. 8.   Gribeauval ammunition wagon.

The shapes and sizes of the gun carriages and forecarriages and their wheels and axles were strictly regulated so that they could be made interchangeable. Four horses sufficed to pull the 8- and 4-pounders, six for the 12-pounder. A shaft was substituted for the limber and the horses were harnessed in pairs instead of in single file, thus reducing the length of the equipage.

The Gribeauval weapons, which began being built in 1765, were vigorously criticized by supporters of Vallière and were temporarily the loser of these arguments. A 1772 ruling by Vallière the younger required a return to the earlier weaponry. But in 1774 the quarrel was submitted to the marshals, who declared the Gribeauval matériel superior to Vallière's. When Gribeauval became inspector general of the artillery in 1776 he developed the weaponry and had drawings and tables engraved showing it.

The wars of the Revolutionary and Empire periods were fought with this artillery, which proved the worth of Gribeauval's work. Although they remained in service for more than forty years, the guns were still too heavy—the 12-pounder weighed more than 4,400 pounds. The more mobile 4-pounder was therefore the weapon used most frequently in battle, whereas the 8- and 12-pounders were held in reserve until the decisive moment when a mass of artillery could be brought up to overwhelm the enemy.

In 1804 a commission of scientists and generals found that the 8-pounder differed little from the 12-pounder and that the 4-pounder was too weak compared to the artillery of other countries. Only the 6- and 12-pounders were retained, but this equipment had defects, though Gribeauval's had been tried and tested. His was brought back and used until 1827.

An attempt was made thereafter to increase the mobility of French artillery, taking its inspiration from English artillery, which had proved formidable in the Spanish wars. The Gribeauval pieces were retained, but only the 8- and 12-caliber ones, and two 15- and 16-cm. howitzers were developed.

The use of silver fulminate by 1820 brought about the replacement of the portfire stick by a fulminate quick match. Fire was created by friction of a rough copper wire passing through the fulminate composition.

In imitation of English matériel, the forecarriage was connected with a coupling (Figure 9) instead of a fixed connection, which made it easier to haul the

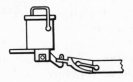

FIG. 9.   Suspension coupling for a gun carriage, 1827.

guns and increased the speed with which a gun could be brought into action. The old munitions chest placed on the gun carriage was replaced by a larger limber box placed on the forecarriage, and the wagon of the caisson held two identical chests. These arrangements made it possible to seat the users on forecarriages and have a "mounted" artillery that could maneuver at a trot over all kinds of terrain and quickly reach a chosen point on the battlefield.

The first experiments with rifled guns The new, modern shell-firing weapons inspired by the Paixhans ships' cannon (1826) belong, in the case of field artillery, to the period after 1850. However, it must be noted that experiments were made just before 1850 that could have led sooner to the adoption of rifled guns, if they had not been held back by red tape. Experiments at this time on handguns with elongated projectiles and rifled bores encouraged artillerymen to adopt the same principles for artillery projectiles.

In 1842 Captain Treuille de Beaulieu drew up specifications for rifling cannons and sent it to the Committee on Artillery, which did not even acknowledge receipt of it. In 1847 a Piedmontese officer named Cavalli designed a heavy-caliber cast-iron gun with a breech mechanism. The bores were rifled and two small diametrically opposed lugs were molded onto the projectiles. Conclusive results were obtained: at two angles of fire the ranges were 2,700 and 3,000 meters for the smoothbore piece and 4,000 and 4,200 meters for the rifled piece.

Treuille de Beaulieu even proposed fashioning rifled guns in steel with a threaded breech having cut off riflings. The twelve guiding lugs of the shell, arranged in two rows, were to be of rolled zinc.

The revolution of 1848 interrupted these studies, which were neglected except for testing 12-caliber howitzers. No other testing was done until 1855. The Crimean War demonstrated the inadequacy of the artillery of the time and the ineffectiveness of smoothbore guns against fortifications. Napoleon III intervened to order that Treuille de Beaulieu's weaponry studies be resumed, but they ended with a compromise: although 1858 model cannons were rifled, they were loaded through the muzzle. Nevertheless, they provided a point of departure for the new artillery.

It must be noted that after the 1848 revolution and until 1850 firearms for all practical purposes wore out but they no longer burst, thanks to improvements in metalworking.

Gun production Jean-Baptiste Colbert provided ships with cast-iron guns, the production of which was distributed among three main centers: Périgord-Angoumois, Nivernais, and Dauphiné. The production of this new design was first perfected at Saint-Gervais-sur-Isère in 1678.

The navy was neglected by the regent, Dubois, and Cardinal Fleury, but Machault and Choiseul undertook to revive it, and the foundries were reorganized by Turgot, Sartine, and the marshal of Castries.

Ruelle was developed from 1750; Indret produced guns from 1777 to 1827. Until 1814 the Liège foundry served the navy, which had established it, and Nevers began operations in 1793.

Gun production methods improved greatly during the eighteenth century. Around the middle of the century cast iron was obtained from charcoal blast furnaces. In 1775 reverberatory furnaces were introduced into France, which were used to remelt pigs cast from a blast furnace in sand channels. It was possible to obtain a larger mass by fusion than by directly tapping the blast furnace, whose hearth was still small.

This remelting process was used at first for heavy-caliber guns after it was

Plate 41.   Rear view of 15″ Rodman Gun, at Battery Rodgers, ½ mile south of Alexandria, showing the revolving mechanism of the center-pintle carriage. U.S. Signal Corps photo No. 111-B-100 (Brady Collection) in the National Archives

Plate 42.   Side view of 15″ Rodman Gun. U.S. Signal Corps photo No. 111-B-353 (Brady Collection) in the National Archives

noticed that reduced metals provided a stronger iron when remelted. Gun manufacturers thus were persuaded to cast all guns in two fusings. By 1825 (or in the case of Ruelle, beginning in 1827), casting guns directly from the blast furnace was practically abandoned. Gun production included making a mold, pouring the metal, and boring the tube.

In 1793 Gaspard Monge published one of his most important works, *L'Art de fabriquer les canons (The Art of Manufacturing Cannon)*. In this treatise he studied the profiles of guns, how to standardize models, and production procedures. He also described molding in clay, which involved first building a clay model supported by a wooden framework around which the clay was tamped down. This mold, approximately 4 inches thick, was then surrounded with iron rings and was finally covered completely with several layers of clay. The model was then broken and removed, leaving the hollow form of the mold, which was lowered into a trench, where dirt was packed down around it.

In sand molding the pattern of the piece to be cast, in either cast iron or bronze, was divided into several sections. Each part was placed in a frame, where sand was packed down around it. Then each section of the pattern could easily be removed. All that remained was to superimpose the framework in order to form a complete mold (Figure 10).

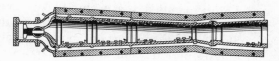

FIG. 10. Sectional sand molding of guns (from Monge).

Direct casting was done at Ruelle until 1827 and later still at Saint-Gervais. Indret, Nevers, and Liège always carried out a second melting. After casting, the piece was left to cool, then was removed from the mold and cleaned of clay or sand.

A gun was thus cast as a solid piece. Then the bore had to be drilled out. A rod equipped with a cutting bar and strong enough not to bend was held against the gun. As it turned, the cutter made a slightly conical hole. The back end of the rod held two mortises in which two steel blades were positioned, which gradually enlarged the hole to bring it up to the caliber desired. Then a more precise borer was used to bring the bore to the exact caliber. The drill cutting the first hole advanced ¾ inch per hour, but the borer moved 1 foot per hour.

The outside of the gun remained in the rough state it had come in from the sand mold. If it had been molded in clay, which left the surface less even, it was machined.

Nineteenth-century methods of manufacturing artillery pieces are clearly differentiated from earlier techniques by improved production methods, better-designed machine tools, and simultaneously increased precision in methods measurement.

CHAPTER 3

NAVAL ARTILLERY

A T THE BEGINNING of the nineteenth century the French regulation dated November 26, 1786, authorizing the use of the Gribeauval models was still in effect in the navy. The Gribeauval guns were thinner and their lengths were rigorously fixed. The calibers used on board ship were 36, 24, 18, 12, long and short 8, and long and short 6.

Guns were now being made exclusively of cast iron. The last ship armed with bronze guns was the *Révolutionnaire,* whose cannons were later installed in the battery below the fortress at Brest. The only bronze guns left were the low-caliber swivel guns intended to arm ship's boats, and mortars used only for high-angle firing of bombs, mortars borrowed from army models.

There was no tendency to modify naval artillery during the Revolutionary and Empire periods, and on land Napoleon fought all his campaigns with the artillery he had known as a lieutenant. He was more concerned with organization and strategy than with technical studies and was almost always hostile to new models.

By a decree dated December 17, 1812, the armament of a 118-gun vessel was to be distributed as follows:

First gun deck	36-pounders
Second gun deck	24- "
Third gun deck	18- "
Fourth decks	12- "

These 118 guns weighed a total of 378 tons.

It is impossible to go into detail here about how a ship's armament was organized. As one example, Figure 11 shows the lashing of a 36-pounder while firing and during a voyage.

Carronades　　A new type of gun, the carronade, appeared. It was based on an English 24-pounder (Figure 12). This was a light, short gun invented by the English general Melville and produced by Gascoyne in 1774 at the well-known Carron foundry in Linlithgow County, Scotland.

Because this gun was light it had relatively thin walls (Figure 13). Used only for short-range combat, it required a much smaller powder charge and thus the initial velocity of the ball was low. Because of its characteristics the gun had only a moderate recoil that could be stopped by a short breech tackle. The gun could be handled by three men instead of seven or eight.

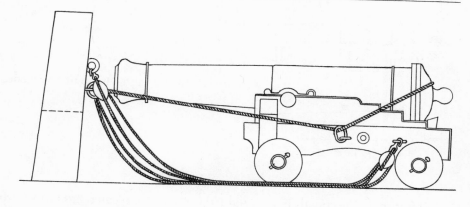

FIG. 11. A 36-pounder in firing position *(top)* and traveling position *(bottom)*.

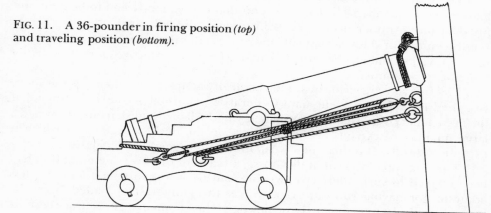

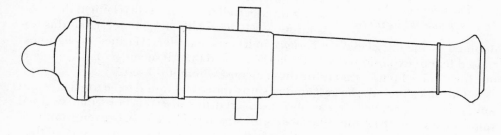

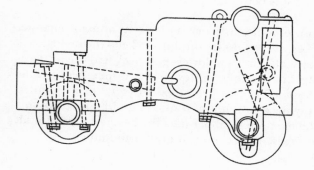

FIG. 12. English 24-pounder and its carriage.

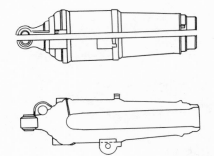

FIG. 13.   English 24-pound carronade.

   This gun had originally been intended for use aboard merchant ships, which had few crew members to man a weapon that consequently had to be light and installed on an upper deck. The British navy adopted carronades in 1779 as reinforcement for ships' armament, and, since at this time the short-range combat tactic prevailed among the British, carronades were effective as well as saving weight and personnel.

   The British were victorious at the battle of Saintes, where their fire was more sustained and effective. Lieutenant-General de Vaudreuil, second in command of the French fleet, reported to Versailles, saying, "All the English men-of-war had a large quantity of carronades or howitzers on the deck, the effect of which is extremely deadly. It is these new weapons that unrigged us on August 12."

   The flagship of the count de Grasse, a victim of this overwhelming fire, had been obliged to surrender. His own fire had been less sustained and also less accurate, for having run out of cartridges the gunners had loaded "with the spoon," that is, by scooping up loose powder. This eliminated all accuracy because of the uneven weights of powder used.

The evolution of naval armament in France   In France the carronade was introduced after 1800, but it was not well received. It was claimed that it hit a target at 240 *toises* (about 1,540 feet), but this was doubted by the *Encyclopédie méthodique* in its article under "Marine." Its lightness caused fear of explosions. Vial du Clairbois noted that "it seems . . . more dangerous for those who use it than for those against whom it is used."

   The 36-caliber, the largest among ships' guns, was found to be too heavy and unwieldy to maneuver. It was also discovered to cause reactions that strained ships' decks. In 1819 the 30-caliber gun was introduced. It became standard armament for a low gun deck and was better adapted for shipboard service than the 36.

   Soon after 1824 the makeup of ships' artillery underwent a major change. The use of various calibers had become necessary on ships to keep the ordnance's center of gravity as low as possible. The first and lowest gun deck had the heaviest guns, with the pieces becoming increasingly lighter in the upper decks. This seemed incomprehensible to Napoleon, who promoted the idea of a uniform caliber in order to simplify supplying ammunition. Builders could not accept this suggestion, because adopting the maximum caliber (i.e., the heaviest guns) for all the upper gun decks would have raised the center of gravity too much.

The solution was found to be to introduce short, and thus lighter, guns. This principle, the one exhibited by carronades, was applied by adopting a different contour for the guns, which made them lighter. Thus, in 1824 short 30-, 24-, and 18-pounders were made obligatory.

A ship's artillery could then be made up of guns of a single caliber, by a law dated February 19, 1829, as follows:

First gun deck	30-caliber guns, no. 1
Second gun deck	30-caliber guns, no. 2
Third gun deck	30-caliber guns, no. 3
On top	30-caliber carronades, 18-caliber guns

The total was 120 guns weighing 325 tons. Guns 2 and 3 were the shortest and lightest.

Howitzers   In the same period a major change was instigated by General Henri-Joseph Paixhans (1783–1854), then a major in the Royal Artillery Corps. In 1822 he began to campaign in favor of heavy-caliber weaponry. He published a tract entitled *Nouvelle force maritime (New Naval Power),* in which he recommended using heavier calibers, the wind resistance being less for heavy calibers.

Paixhans advocated using 80- and 150-pounders (Figure 14), though these could not have been used to fire solid shot, for they would have required enormous powder charges. According to the principle that the powder charge should be ⅓ the weight of the ball, the weight of the gun would have been 200 times the weight of the ball. This would have given guns of 17,600 pounds and 66,000 pounds respectively, which were weights inconceivable and impossible to install on wooden ships at this time.

Paixhans found the solution by using hollow projectiles whose lighter weight required a smaller powder charge (Figure 15). The projectile had a double effect—on the ship's frame from the weight of the ball, and from the explosion of the powder filling its interior.

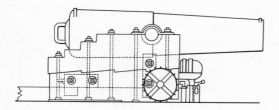

FIG. 14.   The Paixhans howitzer.

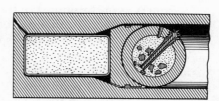

FIG. 15.   Charge of the Paixhans howitzer.

Howitzers were fired with a small charge to give a low muzzle velocity, because at this time these hollow projectiles could be loaded with ordinary gunpowder only. Firing a heavy charge would have created a shock at the departure of the ball violent enough to explode this powder inside the balls before it left the bore of the gun.

The conditions for building howitzers—the invention of a hollow projectile lighter than a solid ball of the same caliber, and use of a lower charge of powder, allowing guns to have thinner walls—thus became attainable, and the weight of these shorter guns made them acceptable. They were adopted in 1827. Because the weight of the hollow projectile no longer had the same relation to a gun's caliber (previously defined by the weight of a solid ball), calibers were now designated by the diameters of guns in centimeters.

Here are some specifications for the new armament:

Regulations effective February 1, 1837

First gun deck	30-caliber guns, no. 1
Second gun deck	30-caliber guns, no. 1 and 22-cm. howitzers
Third gun deck	16-cm. howitzers (formerly, 30-caliber gun)

Regulations effective July 27, 1849

First gun deck	22-cm. howitzers (50-caliber guns) (30-caliber guns, no. 1)
Second gun deck	22-cm. howitzers (30-caliber guns, no. 1)
Third gun deck	30-caliber guns, no. 3 (shorter than the no. 2)
Tops	30-caliber guns, no. 4

These add up to 120 guns with a total weight of 380 tons.

When we compare this with the armament carried by a vessel in 1812, we see that the 120-gun vessel has the same total weight but is considerably better equipped with artillery.

The calibers of projectiles and guns The diameter of a ball was slightly less than that of the gun's bore, so as to leave a certain tolerance (the previously mentioned windage) needed for muzzle-loading. Thus, when each caliber was designated by the weight of the ball, it corresponded with the diameter of the projectile and internal diameter of the gun. For example, a caliber of 4 (4 pounds) corresponded with 2 inches 11 *lignes* 11 points for the ball's diameter and 3 inches 1 *ligne* 3 points for that of the gun. A 12 caliber (12 pounds) corresponded with 4 inches 9 *lignes* 10 points and 4 inches 5 *lignes* 9 points respectively (1 inch = 12 *lignes* = 144 points).

Artillery at the beginning of the nineteenth century had calibers of 4, 6, 8, 12, 18, 24, and 36. The 30 and eventually the 50 were added a short time later.

The table of diameters corresponding to the various calibers was not determined arbitrarily. The diameters of projectiles for each caliber were based on that of the cast-iron ball for swivel guns. This ball weighed 1 pound and had a diameter of 1 inch 10 *lignes* 8 points, or 272 points. The diameter of any projectile was obtained by multiplying the cube root of its caliber, expressed in pounds, by 272, that is, by the formula $\underline{d} = 3\sqrt{\text{caliber}} \times 272$. For example, for the 24 caliber, d = $3\sqrt{24} \times 272 = 5$ inches 5 *lignes* 4 points.

It was also known how to derive the diameter of the bore from the diameter of the ball by multiplying the latter by 1/sine 75°. Constructing a simple graph thus made it possible to find this diameter.

The following table shows the characteristics of all guns in use in France during the nineteenth century.

Caliber weight of projectile	Caliber (diameter of bore, in mm.)	Total length of bore and carriage (in meters)	Length of bore (in meters)	Weight (in kgs.)
Guns prior to 1827				
36 long	174.8	3.276	2.725	3,520
24	152.5	3.065	2.587	2,504
18	138.7	2.876	2.436	2,062
12	121.3	2.678	2.294	1,466
8	106	2.811	2.475	1,166
Guns after 1827				
50	194	3.638	3.094	4,624
30 long no. 1	164.7	3.158	2.641	3,035
30 short no. 2	164.7	2.919	2.458	2,487
30 short no. 3	164.7	2.666	2.250	2,140
Howitzers				
.27 m.	274.4	3.064	2.480	5,200
.22, no. 1	233.3	2.840	2.342	3,636
.22, no. 2	233.3	2.840	2.342	2,722
.16, no. 30	163	2.427	2.075	1,480
Carronades				
30	163	1.787	1.340	1,011
30 with trunnions	163	1.787	1.340	1,051

(The latter was an experimental model of which only a small number were built.)

Later, rifled artillery guns were lengthened, thanks to the use of slow-burning powders. The way they were lengthened was defined by the ratio of the number of calibers (bore diameter) to internal length of the gun. It may be of interest to see what this ratio was for guns from 1800 to 1855.

36-caliber long	=	15 calibers
24- " "		17 "
12- " "		18.8 "
8- " "		23 "
30-caliber long no. 1		16 "
30-caliber short no. 2		15 "
30-caliber no. 3		13.6 "
27-caliber howitzer		9.04 "
22- " "		10.5 "
16- " "		12.7 " (also called a 30-caliber howitzer)
30-caliber carronades		8.2 calibers

Later, ratios of 45.50 and even 55 calibers were achieved in modern guns.

The weight of the pieces was approximately 200 times the weight of the projectile for the 36- and 30-caliber guns, 250 times that for light guns, but only 100 for the 30-caliber howitzer, and it fell to 67 for the 30-caliber carronade.

The velocity and range of projectiles Below are various details on the firing of guns, weights of charges, and velocities and ranges of projectiles. This data is based on tests made at Gâvres between 1830 and 1838 by a commission specially appointed in 1829. At this time experts were carefully studying the firing of weapons and were establishing, from the test results, formulae for velocities and ranges in terms of the weight of powder and other factors.

30-caliber long gun

| Weight of solid projectiles | | 33⅓ pounds |
| Charge (⅓ the weight of the projectile) | | 10¾ pounds |
Angle of elevation	*Initial velocity*	*Range*
0°	420 m.	400 m.
5°	433 m.	1,715 m.
10°	498 m.	2,600 m.

30-caliber howitzer

Weight of solid projectile		33 pounds
Charge		4 pounds
		(.133 of projectile)
Angle of elevation	*Initial velocity*	*Range*
0°	344 m.	280 m.
5°	355 m.	1,360 m.
10°	400 m.	2,200 m.
14°	$\frac{2}{m}$	2,630 m.

30-caliber carronade

Weight of solid projectile		33 pounds
Charge		3½ pounds
		(1/10.5 of projectile)
Angle of elevation	*Initial velocity*	*Range*
0°	311 m.	300 m.
5°	316 m.	1,200 m.
10°	365 m.	2,060 m.
16°	$\frac{2}{m}$	2,756 m.

30-caliber howitzer, hollow projectiles

| Weight of projectile | 23⅓ pounds (with 1¼ pounds of powder inside) |
| Charge | 4½ pounds (ratio: .188 of weight of projectile) |
Angle of elevation	*Initial velocity*	*Range*
0°	411 m.	263 m.
5°	$\frac{2}{m}$	1,329 m.

It was found that with the 30-caliber short gun (no. 2) the results were approximately the same. The powder used until around 1870 was fast burning and small-grained, producing a short explosion. The difference in length between the no. 1 and no. 2 guns had little influence on the velocity of the projectile. Reference to the results of the howitzer firing solid shot shows that the initial velocity increased, but since the weight of the projectile was less, its wind resistance was proportionately greater. With light projectiles the range remains approximately the same as for solid ones.

Various projectiles It should further be noted that with these guns it was possible to fire two balls simultaneously. In this case the departure of the projectile, being slower, tended to allow the pressure of the exploding powder to rise excessively, so the charge was decreased from ⅓ the weight of the projectile as used for the single ball to ¼ the weight.

This type of artillery was used particularly for short-range work, its double shot being intended to sweep the rigging and personnel. It had a lower initial velocity and a shorter range, but it was effective enough on targets less resistant than the thick sides of ships.

Guns could also be loaded with grapeshot, small cast-iron or lead balls in a cluster that spread into a cone shape. This was effective only against groups of men.

Firing the gun Once a gun was loaded, fine, pulverized gunpowder was placed in the vent, a channel in the breech which connected with the bottom of the bore, where the powder had been rammed in. This fine powder was ignited with the linstock, a rod holding a lighted tampion.

Toward 1800 gunsmiths had begun to adapt for artillery the flintlock, which had replaced the lighted wick in handguns. The piece was fired from a distance by pulling a cord that released a cocked hammer that then struck the flint.

In his report, mentioned earlier in this section, Lieutenant-General de Vaudreuil had noted that the English used flintlocks that "permitted them to aim infinitely better than with the linstock." Pierre Suffren had unsuccessfully requested flintlocks for his guns, hoping to improve the firing capabilities of his vessels.

Around 1830 the flintlock system was replaced by a percussion capsule, with the hammer still being released from a distance with a cord. This improvement made firing much more exact.

Tests made on the ranges at Gâvres showed that the results of firing remained the same no matter what system of firing was used.

These various modifications occurred during the period of smoothbore artillery, from 1840 to 1855. Around 1855 this artillery made way for rifled guns permitting the firing of heavier shells with pointed tips, shells that were no longer round but oblong.

During this period when artillery was evolving, ironclad ships began to replace unprotected wooden vessels. Not long afterward, steel became preponderant, which brought about major artillery modifications coincident with the appearance of new types of powder.

CHAPTER 4

PORTABLE WEAPONS

Eighteenth-century muskets

The evolution of portable weapons in the sixteenth and seventeenth centuries led in 1700 to a modern form of infantry weapon. By around 1670 the flintlock (Figure 16) had replaced first the matchlock, then the wheel lock. After 1700 the flintlock rifle (Figure 17) definitively replaced the musket. [The term *musket* was retained in English until rifled barrels were developed, and after, to describe smoothbore weapons, c.f. H. F. Williamson, *Winchester* (New York: A. S. Barnes, 1952, p. 3)]. Cartridges, introduced in the time of Gustavus Adolphus, facilitated loading and standardized firing. Bandoliers worn by soldiers held ammunition for twenty shots. The gun, which was 4½ feet tall and still awkward and heavy, underwent several modifications. Equipped with a bayonet in a socket it made it possible to eliminate pikemen from the infantry as early as 1703.

Gunsmiths experimented quite early with rifled barrels and tested a three-foot carbine so equipped. The problem was to force the bullets into the grooves, a problem hard to solve because the bullet's diameter had to be less than that of the barrel in muzzle-loaded arms. An early solution had been to use a narrower powder chamber, leaving a projection, on the edge of which the bullet rested. The soft-lead bullet could be crushed when the ramrod was struck with a mallet. This weapon, which was difficult to handle, was abandoned, and only the smoothbore weapon remained in use.

FIG. 16. Flintlock musket.

FIG. 17. Flintlock musket and bayonet, eighteenth century.

Plate 43. An assembly room at the Colt Manufactory. From *U.S. Magazine* IV, March 1857. Smithsonian Institution

Weapons gradually became standardized, and as early as 1717 tables describing the obligatory current models appeared. After various modifications the 1777 model flintlock musket became the classic smoothbore portable weapon of France.

At that time troops were armed with five different weapons: the infantry musket, the cavalry pistol, the cavalry musketoon, the dragoon musket, and the artilleryman's musket. These weapons were all designed on the principle of a smoothbore barrel and a flintlock, differing only in their external dimensions and weight. The cavalry pistol was of course the lightest weapon, held in one hand.

The musket had a caliber of 17.5 mm., very close to the 18-mm. weapon already in service in Gustavus Adolphus's army. The bullet weighed approximately 27 grams; "eighteen to the pound," as the expression of the time had it. Loading was done by cartridge, which contained everything needed for firing—the ball, wadding, powder charge, and priming powder—in a paper envelope. To use it a soldier tore open a cartridge with his teeth, poured part of the powder into the pan and the remainder into the barrel. Then he rammed a wad in with the ramrod and inserted the ball, with a second wad to hold it in place.

Well-trained men could fire two shots per minute regularly, which was genuine progress over the speed of earlier weapons. The prescribed loading procedure required twelve motions. The muzzle velocity of the bullet was 1,485 feet per second.

By the very nature of the loading operation the powder charge was irregular. The windage permitted the powder gases to escape. They left a deposit of unburned powder and fouled the barrel. After thirty shots had been fired it was necessary to change the flint in the lock and urinate into the barrel to clean it.

Firing was thus inaccurate. Although the effective range was as high as 270 yards, it was estimated that most marksmen missed a house at 220 yards in two out of three shots. Lacking precision, the musket did not have to be elevated to compensate for a drop in the ball's trajectory. Marksmen were instructed to aim at an enemy's chest at 150 paces, his shoulders at 210 paces, his head at 270 paces, his headgear at 300 paces. Three hundred paces was considered to be the limit of the rifle's effectiveness.

The flintlock, a noticeable improvement over earlier firing systems, made it possible to lower the proportion of misfires. A pan cover protected the priming powder, but this protection was extremely uncertain, and for a long time rain was a major drawback. All the movements required in loading a musket obliged the marksman to remain standing. He could neither lie down nor kneel to take cover from enemy fire.

Infantry fire continued to be ineffectual because of all these problems. Its lack of accuracy and its slowness combined to more or less paralyze the musket in a battle, except when the enemy was at very close range. Thus, hand-to-hand combat with cold steel retained its decisive importance in battles. But even with all its defects the 1777 model rifle served, with several small modifications, in all the wars of the Revolutionary and Empire periods.

Percussion   Radical changes came about in infantry weapons during the nineteenth century. To begin with, percussion priming made firing much safer. Around 1820 the first percussion caps with fulminate of mercury were used in hunting weapons. Fulminate of mercury had been discovered in 1774 by Pierre Bayen. In 1800 a certain Howard discovered for the first time how to use it as a percussion cap by mixing it with saltpeter.

As a result the firelock was modified. A nipple connected with the barrel via the vent was placed near the breech. To the top of this nipple was attached a percussion cap, which was struck by a hammer similar to the one used on flintlocks. This was the percussion lock, which made firing much more regular.

The percussion cap was a small copper capsule containing the mixture of fulminate and saltpeter. It capped the top of the nipple. Priming now became easy and rapid, because of being independent of the powder charge poured into the barrel. Another advantage was that dampness was eliminated and it was now possible to fire in the rain. This improvement was not immediately adopted on infantry rifles, which would have had to be remodeled at great expense. But when threats of war appeared around 1840 the French government decided to have all flintlocks in service remodeled into percussion rifles.

Rifled barrels   The first half of the nineteenth century also witnessed improvements that transformed infantry weapons into rifled breech-loading firearms.

The first attempts to use balls slightly larger than the bore of a rifled barrel showed gunsmiths that helical rifling gave a projectile a rapid spinning movement that improved its firing. If instead of a round bullet an oblong projectile was used, it stabilized in its trajectory, but it was then necessary to use heavy projectiles weighing about 50 grams. If they were fired at the same muzzle velocities as 20- and 30-gram balls the recoil against the gunner's shoulder was too violent. The new rifled guns required reducing the initial velocity, and the advantages and precision won in the low-angle trajectory and penetrating power of the projectiles were lost again. Also, because it was necessary to strike and crush the bullet, the firing rhythm was slower than that of the smoothbore rifle of the same caliber.

There remained only one solution: to insert through the rear of the barrel a bullet with a caliber larger than that of the bore. The expansion of the exploded gunpowder's gases would force the bullet to conform to the grooves. In January 1813, Anne-Jean Savary, the duke of Rovigo (1774–1833), pointed out to the emperor that a gunsmith by the name of Pauly had built a breech-loading carbine that could fire eleven shots in two minutes. Rovigo was enthusiastic about it, and in particular foresaw its application to the cavalry pistols that were so inconvenient for a rider to reload. Napoleon had an examination made of the rifle, but found imperfections in it that would have delayed its adoption. Being perhaps more interested in the problems of his current campaigns that required deploying existing armament than in studies and tests that could produce results only later, Napoleon refused to approve continuing Pauly's work. Pauly's cartridge was primed with potassium chlorate, which was found to be dangerous; this was one reason for its rejection. Moreover, the production of a fragile mechanism requiring precision finishing would have been difficult to organize.

In the same period a Lieutenant Delvigne of the Chasseurs de la Garde built a carbine with a rifled barrel whose powder chamber had a diameter less than that of the barrel. The ball, whose diameter was .3 mm. smaller than that of the barrel, rested against the chamber opening (Figure 18) and needed to be only slightly distorted by several blows of the ramrod to be wedged in and conform to the grooves when fired. A solution first tried in the eighteenth century with a smooth barrel was now applied to a rifled barrel.

A Colonel Pontcharra made a slight improvement in the system with a small greased wooden shoe inserted ahead of the ball, which rested against the opening (Figure 19). With this device the ball could not get into the chamber and pack down the powder. The Delvigne carbine was equipped like this, as was a heavy rifle taken by a battalion of Chasseurs sent to Africa in 1839.

Plate 44. Colt Manufactory Armory Proper—First Division. From *U.S. Magazine* IV, March 1857. Smithsonian Institution

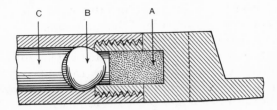

FIG. 18. Cross section of the Delvigne carbine: A, powder chamber; B, bullet; C, ramrod.

FIG. 19. Delvigne bullet as modified by Pontcharra.

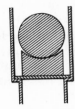

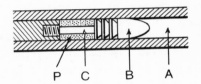

FIG. 20. The Thouvenin-Minié bullet, remodeled by Treuil de Beaulieu and Tamisier. A, forcing rod; B, bullet with grooved base; C, center rod of barrel; P, powder cartridge.

In 1844 a Colonel Thouvenin suggested eliminating the narrow chamber and resting the bullet against a cylindrical pin screwed to the bottom of the rifle. At the same time a Lieutenant Minié, who had assisted in Delvigne's experiments, repeated certain of these tests with elongated bullets. Finally, captains Treuille de Beaulieu and Tamisier designed bullets with grooves in their bases to facilitate forcing them into the threads of the bore (Figure 20). From these experiments came the 1846 carbine, issued to light infantry.

Plate 45. Colt's Patent Fire Arms Manufactory at Hartford, Connecticut. Ca. 1855. Lithograph by Schierholz. Library of Congress

This weapon had defects, however. The presence of the pin made it difficult to clean the bottom of the barrel, and the heavier elongated bullet increased the recoil. The powder charge had to be decreased, and consequently the muzzle velocity fell from 1,650 to 990 feet per second. Firing with the rifled weapon nevertheless proved more accurate and had greater range and penetrating power.

Minié then realized that the pin was unnecessary if bullets with a hollowed-out base were used. The pressure of gases from the exploded powder caused the base to expand, thus forcing the bullet into the grooves. Bullets became lighter, so the recoil was less and at the same time there was no longer any need to force the bullet by ramming.

The rifles currently in use could be remodeled without difficulty. The Chasseurs were equipped with them first, in 1854, followed in 1857 by all the infantry. By 1854 a breech-loading model had been built for the Chasseurs (Figure 21).

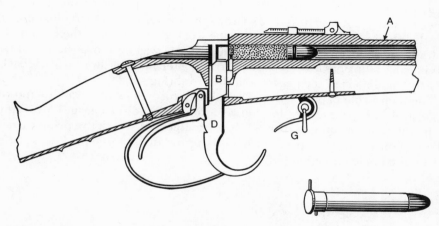

FIG. 21.   Breech-loading musket used by the Guard, 1854. This rifle is loaded with a cartridge with a metal base and cap with pin. The pivoting of D causes the bolt B to slide down and opens the breech of the barrel A for loading. G is used to guide the finger toward D. *Right:* The Lefaucheux cartridge.

The improved firing method, which now appears to be a major advance, aroused objections from conservative schools of thought. They feared that marksmen, encouraged by the ease of rapid firing, would waste ammunition and, since they could not be resupplied during combat, would thus remain defenseless.

Breechloading   Hunting weapons were the first to be given one of the most important improvements: breechloading. The problem was simpler with these weapons, however, since they fired at lower muzzle velocities, that is, with lower internal pressures, reducing the importance of a gastight movable bolt.

In 1832 the Maison Lefaucheux perfected a breech-loading hunting rifle. The difficulty of such a system lay in the tightness of the bolt under pressure from the gases. When applied or held in place with a screw the bolt had to leave no space through which the hot gases could leak under high pressure. Several years later

Lefaucheux found the definitive solution by hinging the barrel at the breech (Figure 22). This method was adopted to manufacture hunting rifles.

One of Lefaucheux's inventions was to place a malleable or elastic copper base on the cartridge. This base expanded under pressure from the gases and thus served as a breech plug, preventing leakage of the powder gases even if there were some play in the parts. The invention of this obturation base made possible a major improvement in priming. The fulminate primer was placed inside the case that could be struck by a firing pin, penetrating the case perpendicular to its axis. The head of the pin passed through an opening in the bore of the rifle and projected slightly. The hammer, activated by gas expansion, struck the projection. All that remained was to strike the exposed primer, as in the earlier percussion rifle.

Military weapons should have quickly adopted this remarkable improvement, but it was not until 1844 that it appeared on a rifle, one invented by a Prussian named Dreyse, an employee of Pauly who had followed up on the ideas of his former employer. As early as 1827 Dreyse had invented a muzzle-loading rifle with a firing pin. For almost forty years he worked at achieving the final design, which was adopted by the Prussian army. Dreyse was no more successful than Pauly in eliminating gas leakage, but by profiling the movable breech at the back of the barrel he deflected the gas toward the front (Figure 23).

The flammable paper cartridge contained the ovoid ball, a wad, the powder charge, and the priming powder, between the wad and the charge. A firing pin held by the movable breech pierced the cartridge and struck the primer against the base of the bullet. This pin, which was long and fine, caused the Dreyse rifle to be given the name *needle rifle.*

FIG. 22.   Lefaucheux gun with pivoting barrel.

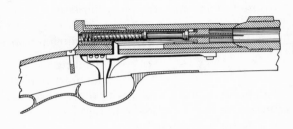

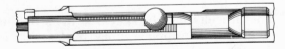

FIG. 23.   Section and plan views of the Dreyse needle rifle with movable breech.

Although still imperfect in respect to the strength of its components, its ballistic qualities, and firing speed, the Dreyse rifle nevertheless brought about a decisive change in infantry firepower. A marksman loaded his weapon simply by inserting a cartridge in the breech and closing it. He could do this standing but also on his knees or lying down and could take shelter to fire. The infantry thereby acquired its full firepower.

In France the advantage of the system was at first doubted, from fear of dangerously wasting ammunition. Not until after Sadowa, where the Prussian victory was attributed to the superiority of the Dreyse rifle over the old rifles in the Austrian infantry, was it suddenly decided to adopt the breech-loading rifle. This was the Chassepot rifle, which was built on the Dreyse principles.

General progress   Pistols had naturally followed the same evolution as rifles, namely the gradual adoption of the percussion system, which greatly facilitated handling this cavalrymen's weapon.

In 1842 France and Switzerland remodeled their old weapons, the change being fairly easy, since the nipple could be screwed onto the barrel and the mechanism of the hammer required only slight modification of the trigger.

Retention of the old weapons meant that the caliber of 18 mm. was not modified, but from now on there was an increasing trend to reducing calibers to 17, 16, and 15 mm. From 1848 to 1851 the 12.5 caliber appeared. At the same time the range of the rifle was increased to 2,640 feet. With the adoption of breechloading the caliber was reduced to 10.4 mm. Given the longer range, the back sight became indispensable for sighting.

The bayonet had been perfected. Instead of the old bayonet hafting, which did not attach firmly to the rifle barrel, the bayonet was held by a small projection locked in place by a spring.

CHAPTER 5

BALLISTICS

T OGETHER WITH astronomy and surveying, ballistics is perhaps the field in which we witness such a close early connection between science and technology that there is no possibility of distinguishing their respective contributions. As soon as firearms became widespread (and perhaps even before), ballistics, which provides the basis for every solution to firing problems, attracted the curiosity of mathematicians, who tried to develop a theory for trajectories of projectiles and to represent its elements by mathematical formulae and graphs. From its origin ballistics was totally confused with conceptions of mechanics. Explanations for the movement of projectiles were sought among the uncertainties of the budding science of dynamics. Before Galileo, erroneous conceptions about slow, strong, movement had paralyzed research. The transition from Aristotle's dynamics to those of Galileo gave a unique explanation to the problem of heavy bodies and movement of projectiles.

First studies on   Volume 2 of the *Histoire générale des sciences* contains
ballistics   a discussion of the ideas of Niccola Tartaglia (1500–1557) in his *Nova Scientia* (1537), which theorized that trajectories were composed of straight lines and segments of a circle (Figure 24). His explanations did not produce a rational theory. His conception of the best angle for the maximum range (45°) was not based on mathematical considerations. He had taken the average between the vertical shot and a horizontal one, both giving a range of zero.

After Galileo, ideas were clarified by Evangelista Torricelli (1608–1647), Marin Mersenne (1588–1648), and François Blondel (1617–1686), and the parabolic trajectory emerged as a logical consequence of Galilean mechanics. Although Blondel had some notion of the effects of air resistance, he considered it

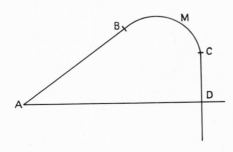

FIG. 24. Trajectory of bullet (from Tartaglia). AB, violent movement, rectilinear trajectory; BMC, arc of trajectory; CD, natural vertical fall.

of negligible importance compared to other causes of firing irregularities, as those produced by differences in the quality of powder, weight of projectiles, and so on.

Ballistics problems were studied at greater length in the eighteenth century. Pierre Varignon's paper written from 1704 and 1707, *Mémoire sur le jet des bombes et en général sur la projection des corps (Treatise on Bomb Propulsion and in General on Propelling Bodies)*, is simply a more detailed study of the parabola, and it did not encourage any progress in artillery. Moreover, those concerned with guns could not profit very much from geometrical speculation alone.

In the same period engineers like Belidor began to analyze more seriously defective matériel, inaccurate aiming, and imprecise loading of powder. Although it was commonly believed that the range of shot was proportional to the weight of the powder charge, Belidor realized this to be erroneous. In 1731 he published *Le bombardier français*, in which he drew up tables from which ranges could be calculated according to angles of elevation.

The first research on curving trajectories of airborne projectiles had been made by Newton, starting from a hypothesis that air resistance was proportional to velocity, then as a function with two terms (V and V^2). Varignon had put forth the same hypothesis and it had been repeated in 1719 by Jean Bernoulli when he considered difficult integrations.

Belidor's 1739 studies on the combustibility of powder had been criticized because the mortars used by the army were not comparable with the one Belidor had used to establish his range tables. The army's powder chambers varied greatly in shape, ranging from cylinders to truncated cones and ovoids. A decreased weight of powder charges would have led to a reduction in the length and thickness of Vallière's guns, of which many military men were unshakable partisans.

Euler reconsidered Bernoulli's data while introducing into the air resistance a term proportional to the fourth power of the velocity. He determined the shape of the trajectory and the differences between the rising and falling portions, establishing a different curve for the parabola. He proved the irregularity of the ranges for angles of fire symmetrical to a 45° angle of elevation and indicated that the maximum range was achieved at angles less than 45°.

The beginnings of experimentation

Euler knew the works of the English physicist Benjamin Robins (1707–1751), which he had translated into German. Robins had introduced an experimental measuring tool, the ballistic pendulum (Figure 25), which began to register when triggered by the shock of a projectile. This device let him compare the ballistic values of different powders. He realized that Newton's law was inaccurate for projectile velocities greater than 990 feet per second. Based on his observations, he accepted mathematics as only an auxiliary technique and a way to represent results.

Robins also noted that there was deviation, or "drift," by the projectile outside the vertical plane of fire, and with great perspicacity he realized the cause of this phenomenon: friction of the projectile in the gun's bore gave it a spinning movement. From this he inferred that to control this movement it would be necessary to use rifled barrels, which should fire not round balls but elongated projectiles.

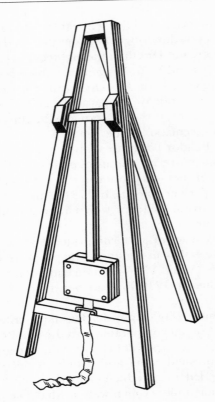

FIG. 25.   Robins's ballistic pendulum.

Robins understood that this phenomenon was similar to the movement of the top and that if the projectile had sufficient velocity the air resistance would maintain its stability on the trajectory, to which it would remain tangent. Robins, an intelligent man ahead of his time, foresaw the advantages of a gun that loaded from the rear through an opening left in the side of the gun and closed by a screw. He declared that the first nation to arm itself with rifled guns would have a decisive superiority over other armies. Robins's works showed, for the first time in the history of ballistics, real penetration and exactness.

Euler refused to accept Robins's theory about drift. Euler's prestige as a great scientist, and the detailed studies we owe to him, led to the neglect of Robins's ideas. One hundred years passed before decisive experiments were able to show the accuracy of Robins's conceptions.

The problem of rifling was difficult to solve with smoothbore guns firing oblong iron projectiles, whereas Louis XIV's reign had witnessed the invention in 1679 of rifled carbines that used a lead ball, making it possible to solve the problem of forcing the ball into the grooves.

A century and a half later, the French navy took from 1844 to 1855 to build the first rifled gun, a 16-cm. howitzer, the 1855 model. A battery of these guns took part for the first time in the siege of Sebastopol. England and Italy were arriving at the same result during this same period.

Until the mid-eighteenth century ballistics had been studied by scientists, physicists, and mathematicians, but then users began to take a direct interest and make more use of experimental research. And when technical services and schools began being organized this provided a new impetus for recognizing the technical character of artillery. Lastly, theoretical progress in weaponry produced more uniform matériel whose less inconsistent effects lent themselves better to establishing firing tables and to organized experiments.

In 1755 a reorganization of the French artillery was carried out. The position of master gunner was eliminated and a single body was formed, the *Corps Royal d'Artillerie,* which soon displayed unquestionably superior education and staff. It was then regarded as the best in Europe and was called the *Corps à talent.* This helps us understand why Napoleon, facing an audience of kings, took pride in having been an artillery lieutenant.

On August 8, 1788, Bonaparte had been made a member of a commission charged with studying how to fire bombs with mortars and guns of various calibers. He was the only second lieutenant on the commission, and it was he who organized the firing and wrote the report, which gave a table of ranges, with clear, precise observations and conclusions.

While the first theories of ballistics were being developed, certain data had been collected on how to use the weaponry in service and on the limits to its use.

Point-blank firing Fixed-charge field guns were fired with a cartridge containing a charge, the projectile being attached to the cartridge. By point-blank firing (Figure 26) was meant the point at which the descending portion of the trajectory intersected the line of fire, as determined by the upper edge of the gun. The average firing distances for field guns were the following:

Caliber	12	8	4
Range	514 yards	503 yards	481 yards

By aiming the gun at a higher angle of fire, extreme ranges of between 875 and 1,100 yards were obtained for 12- and 8-caliber guns and 547 to 984 yards for 4-caliber guns, but firing was inaccurate and difficult to control then. These ranges corresponded to a muzzle velocity of 1,617 feet per second and a powder charge whose weight was equal to one-third that of the projectile.

FIG. 26. Point-blank fire.

Siege firing Heavy 24-, 16-, and 12-caliber guns and 8- and 6-inch howitzers firing variable charges were used to demolish the fortifications of a besieged stronghold. The firing, of the ricochet or enfilade type, was done from the first and second parallels, at 650 and 325 yards. It sought to cut down the parapets of the defense. Siege firing, more skillful than that of field guns, required ballistic knowledge.

Direct fire, with 24- and 16-caliber guns, was done at 650 yards. All these types of firing were done by guns without back sights.

Breaching fire was conducted from the covered way 55 yards from the scarp of the besieged fortification, where the attack force assembled for the final assault. It was done with powerful charges one-half the weight of the projectile giving a muzzle velocity of 1,947 feet per second at the outside, and was continued with charges one-third the weight of the projectile and with a muzzle velocity of 1,287 feet per second.

Mortars

Mortars were long-range weapons whose bombs fell beyond the range of sight, but the explosion's effects could be seen, permitting adjustment of aim. Firing was done at a 45° angle with a variable propelling charge. This type of weapon required a great deal of ballistics knowledge.

Random firing

By aiming 16-caliber or field guns at a 45° angle and using a powder charge one-third the weight of the projectile, experimental random firing was conducted, which was not used in actual battle firing. Ranges were obtained of 4,593 yards with the 24-caliber gun and 4,375 yards with the 16-caliber gun.

Using a 6° angle of elevation for field guns (the maximum that gun carriages permitted), the following ranges were obtained: 1,969 yards with the 12-caliber field gun, 1,367 yards with the 8-caliber field gun, and 1,640 yards with the 4-caliber field gun.

Use of mathematics at the end of the eighteenth century

Ballistics experts of this time held that air resistance was proportional to the square of the velocity, and they were seeking to develop this quadratic ballistics.

Jean-Charles de Borda (1733–1799), an innovator and precursor who dealt with all branches of physics, devoted his first paper, published in 1769, to ballistics; his views appeared the most satisfactory. He paved the way for solving problems by approximating closer and closer to the correct answer, which continued in the works of ballistics experts in the next century. Thus, the history of ballistics at the beginning of the nineteenth century became simply the development and deeper study of Borda's work.

An artillery teacher named Lombard (1722–1794) at the École d'Artillerie of Auxonne, did not distinguish himself by new ideas but had a great reputation among the gunners, and he had the good fortune to be the teacher of Lieutenant Bonaparte, who attended courses at the schools in Valence and Auxonne.

Napoleon's notes from Lombard's lectures have been preserved. They mention Robins and show that Lombard had used Euler's translations of Robins. Lombard's work *Traité du mouvement des projectiles (Treatise on the Movement of Projectiles)*, published posthumously in 1797, summarized the knowledge of the time but particularly introduced the now-well-known theorem about rigidity of the trajectory, which for all practical purposes defines the angle of sight and the angle of elevation.

His work lags behind that of Borda but does contain certain interesting ideas, in particular on the powder charges to be used for the various ranges. He established firing tables for different calibers, which despite their imperfections rendered great service to artillerymen.

Argument concerning the back sight Whether to use a back sight was one element in the Vallière-Gribeauval quarrel in 1765 on the subject of weaponry. Gribeauval's introduction of the back sight was vigorously fought by the supporters of the Vallière system and a bitter argument followed, which appears in the published arguments exchanged by du Puget against the back sight and by Tronçon du Coudray in its favor.

The arguments put forth on each side were based on concepts about the use of guns held by the two parties. Some, like du Puget, felt that errors and the scattering of fire made the search for precision at ordinary combat distances useless. Others, like du Coudray, wished to improve artillery fire further.

What increased the confusion was that the very elements of aiming were not well understood. At this time it still seemed difficult when ranging a gun to separate clearly the angle of sight and the angle of the tangent at the origin of the trajectory (Figure 27).

Lombard must apparently be credited with separating these two elements and facilitating the study of aiming by supposing the trajectory to be rigid; that is, independent of the angle of sight, if the latter remained fairly low, which was generally the case with field artillery. In most cases the angle of the tangent at the origin of the trajectory was 3°, so the trajectory could thus be considered as remaining undistorted by different angles of sight.

The procedures of aiming field artillery in the first half of the nineteenth century remained the same as in Gribeauval's time, but with more precise firing tables the use of the back sight became more effective. However, it must be noted that results were still very approximate. It was still difficult to aim at a moving enemy.

An author in 1816 recommended that gunners practice estimating distances by sight, corresponding to the point-blank range of each caliber. He claimed that in this way they would be more likely to obtain satisfactory results from the very first shots.

In 1852 an eminent gunner named Piobert proposed practical rules for aiming based on an approximate use of the back sight for distant targets.

From the beginning of the nineteenth century on, major improvements based on theory and confirmed by experience put an end to this empiricism. Two distinct sciences emerged: interior ballistics as distinct from exterior, the first being the study of the projectile's movement in the bore of the gun under the effects of pressures from the powder, the second being the study of the trajectory in the air.

Besides Borda, others like Bezout, Legendre, and Gay-Lussac applied themselves to this study, but Poisson, Piobert, and Didion especially contributed new

FIG. 27. Rigid trajectory and angle of sight. S, angle of sight; AMB, rigid trajectory; P, angle of elevation of gun.

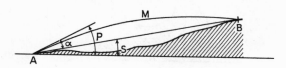

and extensive studies. In 1829 Poisson published his *Formules relatives aux effets du tir d'un canon sur les différentes parties de son affût (Formulae Relating to the Effects of Firing on the Various Parts of the Gun Carriage)* for calculating the extent and duration of recoil. Without knowing the laws about forces of gases from exploding powder or the elasticity of the various parts of gun carriages, which made the problem difficult to solve, Poisson treated the subject completely. He again attacked the problem of external ballistics, upon which General Didion was the first to publish a complete treatise.

Thus the science of ballistics was brought to a high degree of perfection during the first half of the nineteenth century. A path was opened to the more scientific and more detailed studies that followed.

Experimental ballistics: powders

Internal ballistics studies highly complex phenomena—the expansion of the gases that are produced when powder explodes and the movements of projectiles in the bore. Ideas on these questions were still quite vague in the eighteenth century. Investigators had to invent the necessary tools and devise adequate experimental methods.

Chemistry contributed few explanations of the phenomenon of powder combustion. Powders were classified into fine and soft, like flour. As at first used for large firearms, powder was poured into a gun barrel with spoons or lanterns or poured from sacks.

When the corning of powder became common practice, various sizes of grains were tried, to establish a single standard for military gunpowders. By 1818 military authorities had returned to using two sizes of grains, one for artillery, another for muskets.

Until 1775 supply contracts were awarded at auction to a single manufacturer in order to standardize the supply, which gave rise to abuses. In 1775 this system was replaced by a Powders and Saltpeters Authority controlled by artillery officers. Until the French Revolution Lavoisier, one of the four managers, devoted himself to studying saltpeter and its production and how to make gunpowder.

Laws in 1572, 1601, and 1696 had laid down precautions for manufacturing gunpowder. A law in 1686 organized tests in a testing mortar (Figure 28). This bronze mortar had a caliber of 7 inches 9 points, was aimed at a 45° angle, and shot a bronze ball 7 inches in diameter. In 1775 the range required before a weight of powder fixed in 1686 at 3 ounces would be accepted was 90 *toises* (576 feet). In

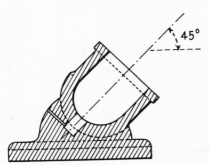

FIG. 28.   Mortar for testing gunpowders.

1822 a range of 248 yards was required with a charge of 92 grams (3 ounces 5 3/9 grains). The powder was refused if the range dropped as low as 220 yards.

Belidor vigorously opposed the idea (which dated from 1530) but was still being supported by Vallière the younger in 1790) that the best range was obtained by a powder charge equal to two-thirds the weight of the ball. He suggested using spherical chambers and a weight of powder equal to one-third that of the projectile. Experiments made at Metz confirmed this theory, but Vallière's stubborn opposition prevented the adoption of this guideline until 1765.

Bigot de Morogues in 1737 and Daniel Bernoulli in 1738 made remarkable contributions to the study of internal ballistics, which served as a basis for studies by Robins and Euler, who were trying to reconcile mathematical theories with experimental data. The seminal works of these two scientists also led to discoveries by d'Arcy (1751), Papacino d'Antoni (1773), Hutton (1773 to 1807), and Rumford (1797), who supplied a formula linking the force of the powder with the density of the charge:

$$P = 1.941 (928.5 \ \Delta)^{1 + 0.3714\Delta}$$

This formula, translated into metric measurements by Piobert, shows P as the pressure per square centimeter and Δ as the density of the charge.

Scientists like Bezout, Laplace, Lacroix, and Legendre gave much assistance and paved the way for future studies. But mention must also be made of the studies written from a practical point of view for the guidance of artillery officers in using the weaponry. For example, a work by J.-J. de Gassendi went through five editions and reached the hands of every army officer.

Outside of France, a *Handbuch für Offiziere* by Scharnhorst (1755–1813), who was known especially for his military and organizational work, was published in 1787. He refers to French scientific efforts in theoretical and experimental studies.

During the wars of the Revolutionary and Empire periods theoretical and experimental research on gunpowder remained dormant, and it was not until around 1820 that this research resumed. This was the work of generals Didion, Morin, Poncelet, and Piobert. The latter established a law of theoretical combustion inferred from the geometrical shape of the grains, but his was only approximate, because he assumed that the speed of combustion was invariable and independent of pressure.

Internal ballistics made no decisive progress during the first half of the nineteenth century. It was after 1850 that thermodynamics contributed the means with which later scientists could establish fundamental principles for the equation concerning the expansion of gases.

BIBLIOGRAPHY

AILLERET, Charles. *Histoire de l'armement.* Paris, 1948.

BETHUYS, G., and MANCEAU, Cl. *L'outillage d'une armée.* Paris, 1892.

BUAT, E. *L'artillerie de campagne.* Paris, 1911.

CHARBONNIER, P. *Essais sur l'histoire de la balistique.* Paris, 1928.

CONTURIE, J. *Histoire de la fonderie de Ruelle (1750-1755).* Paris, 1951.

Encyclopédie méthodique, "Marine" by VIAL DE CLAIRBOIS. Paris, 1783, 1786, and 1787.

FIGUIER, L. *Les merveilles de la science.* t. III.

GESSLER, E. A. *Führer durch die Waffen-Sammlung.* Zurich, 1928.

LACROIX, P. *L'armée depuis le Moyen Age jusqu'à la Révolution.* Paris, 1889.

MAINDRON, M. *Les armes.* Paris, 1890.

PART FIVE

CONSTRUCTING AND EQUIPPING URBAN BUILDINGS

CONSTRUCTION AND ARCHITECTURE

I N THE NINETEENTH century there were three types of architecture: that by
architects trained only in the disciplines of the masters of antiquity or their
Renaissance interpreters, by engineers attracted to applying new materials, and
finally an anonymous architecture derived from an immediate demand for
dwellings, as in wood construction in the United States.

This simplified view should not let us forget that some architects, for example
Henri Labrouste (1801–1875), Victor Baltard (1805–1874), and the Chicago
group, used iron. We shall even see them collaborating with engineers, as did the
architect Charles Dutert (1845–1906) with the engineer Victor Contamin
(1840–1893) in the Gallery of Machines at the 1889 Paris Exposition, and builders
in Chicago. These two examples emphasize that during the period in which we are
interested the art of construction began to be influenced by the pressures of
unrelated techniques.

Furthermore, economic and social factors such as industrial progress, real
estate speculation, and population shifts toward the large cities or new places of
work gave rise to problems of mass housing, and what we now call urban planning
had the task of solving them.

OLD AND NEW TECHNIQUES

*Iron as a
construction material*
When in the eighteenth century the Darbys, ironmasters in Coalbrookdale, Shropshire, succeeded in
reducing iron ore by using coke instead of charcoal,
they opened up a new path leading to the Industrial Revolution. One result of this
discovery was a reduction in prices for iron.

When Abraham Darby III cast the components for the bridge over the
Severn, built from 1775 to 1779, this marked the beginning of the use in construction of cast iron, the form in which this metal first enjoyed great success. In this
bridge, which has a span of 100 feet and a rise of 45 feet, the cast iron distributed
the load by compression, the use for which it is best suited, but the bridge was built
as if made of wood. In contrast Rowland Burdon, perhaps inspired by Thomas
Paine, built into the Sunderland Bridge (1793–1796, now destroyed) a 236-foot
arch with 105 iron sections cast in the form of stone voussoirs.

In these two examples, which caught Jean-Baptiste Rondelet's attention, the new material was first used to substitute for a familiar substance and not in accordance with its own particular qualities, as is done (or should be done) today.

The use of iron in construction can be dated from the Severn 1775 bridge. An attempt to build a cast-iron bridge over the Rhône in 1775 was a failure.

Architecture and traditional construction

In traditional construction around 1750 we do not see the appearance of any really new technical developments outside of minor refinements in stonecutting or slight modifications in hand tools. The strongest lifting devices on building sites were still directly descended from ones used by the Romans. The often quoted "inventions" Claude Perrault used to build the colonnade of the Louvre appear to have progressed little beyond the idea of substituting ramps for ladders in certain cases. Whether a structure was stone, with or without mortar or with lead joints, or of brick, men continued to build as they had for centuries.

It was techniques foreign to construction that tended to modify it no matter what material was used. A major structural improvement appeared between 1624 and 1685 in the invention of the canted flue for chimneys. The result of this practice was that upper stories could be used.

Decisive improvements in the glass industry date only from the mid-seventeenth century (see Volume II, Section Six, Chapter 22), but the fall in the price of this material had architectural consequences. Larger rooms could be lighted by increasing or enlarging bays and using larger pieces of glass with fewer mullions.

As for artificial lighting, neither the perfecting of oil lamps nor the use of kerosene lamps influenced how these lamps were designed. This was not true of illuminating gas, which began to be piped into buildings between 1830 and 1850. Electricity had little influence on the art of building before the end of the nineteenth century. A result of these possibilities for artificial lighting was that architects became liberated from the limitations of natural lighting when drawing up plans.

The changes that came after 1750 were above all formal, but we must trace the origins of the new architectural forms that appeared in traditional construction as they relate to the history of economic, social, and even political factors. A determination to break with the classical and baroque forms that had been repeated until outworn is visible in all the efforts of architects in the nineteenth century. This desire led to a search for examples from remote antiquity, the Middle Ages, or distant (particularly exotic) countries. From this search were born both neoclassicism (a return to antiquity), which appeared almost everywhere between 1750 and 1780 and preferred Greek models to Roman ones, and the less widespread architectural romanticism visible in England after 1785, in the United States after 1800, and in France and central Europe beginning in 1820. Imitation competed with interpretation, in which Claude Nicolas Ledoux excelled (Figure 1), but these movements converged in eclecticism. This term describes the period in which were found, side by side and in every country till 1914 invented styles: neo-Gothic, neo-Renaissance, neo-Byzantine, Louis XIV, Louis XVI, neo-Palladian, Georgian and Elizabethan cottages, and so on.

The qualities of iron are such that in early construction it was cast in the form of Gothic ribs and pillars, resulting in a medieval style. This effect was evidenced

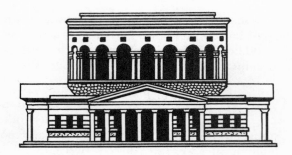

FIG. 1. Designs for tollhouses, Paris. Claude-Nicolas Ledoux, architect, 1780–1788. (From Saint-Victor, *Tableaux historiques et pittoresques de Paris.*)

in the church of Saint Eugène in Paris (1855), the Saint Pancras Station in London (1863–1876), the Lisbon elevator (ca. 1900), and so on. A Renaissance style can be seen in the Harper Building in New York (1854). Art nouveau, no matter how short-lived an episode, had the merit of seeking its inspiration outside the historic models.

Iron's special qualities and industrial production gradually called for a new architectural expression. The period of time separating the first English bridges from Paris's Sainte-Geneviève Library (Labrouste, 1843) is that period when the possibilities of iron were being gradually appreciated. Under the pressure of new demands for railroad stations, market buildings, exhibition halls, and so on, iron made an impact on nineteenth-century construction and made possible the development of the architecture of our time.

THE USE OF IRON

The pervasiveness of cast-iron construction was such in the nineteenth century that there is a tendency to overlook the long use of wrought iron for such purposes as clamps and even to reinforce stones, as in the colonnade of the Louvre (1665) or in that of the Garde-Meuble in the Place de la Concorde (1755–1763). Following Claude Perrault's example, J.-A. Gabriel (1698–1782) assembled the stones of the entablature with clamps, a procedure known since antiquity, but in both colonnades the drums of the columns had a vertical center hole through which passed a rod with horizontal cramps. In 1786 Victor Louis, who had an instinctive knowledge about the moment of inertia before the principle had been scientifically formulated, built the framework of the Théâtre-Français from wrought iron, to avoid the danger of fire associated with wooden superstructures.

The use of wrought iron did not cease; it was employed in conjunction with cast iron, as in the Sunderland bridge, where the arches were of cast iron and the spandrels and rods were wrought iron. Jean-Baptiste Rondelet recommended this practice, in which "the two types of iron are combined in the most advantageous manner: that is, cast iron for supporting, wrought iron for binding." But for many users cast iron seemed to be an all-purpose material.

Cast-iron columns　　Cast-iron columns owed their success to the fact that cast iron works best under compression. One of the first uses of cast-iron columns is contemporary with the appearance of new machines for spinning cotton, which called for greater open areas; iron appeared around 1780, in time to replace wooden posts. According to A. W. Skempton, the use of cast iron for beams appeared in 1796/97 in a Shrewsbury flax-spinning mill.

At the Philips & Lee spinning mill in Salford, Manchester, built by Boulton and Watt in 1801, we find (for the first time, according to S. Giedion) the combined use of cast-iron columns and wrought-iron beams. The mill, measuring 140 feet by 42 feet, had 2 rows of 23 columns each, on each of 7 levels. Wrought iron I beams formed the horizontal framework. The floors were supported from small brick arches springing from the capitals of the columns, a coarse concrete ensuring perfect flatness. The columns had flanges at their bases, which let them be superimposed.

William Fairbairn repeated this system for a refinery built in 1845 on eight levels. In order to provide vertical continuity he fixed small wrought-iron I girders, connected by iron ties, on the cast-iron columns. He also replaced the small brick arches supporting the floors with thin sheets of wrought iron similarly shaped, retaining the cement finish above the sheets.

Meanwhile, cast-iron supports had received quasi-official approval when the confirmed classicist John Nash placed columns in the center of the Red Room and in the kitchen of the Royal Pavilion at Brighton, in 1818–1821. In Liverpool, between 1813 and 1816 two churches—Saint Michael and Saint Philip—were built as cast-iron structures.

It was left to Henri Labrouste (1801–1875) to employ iron architecturally, which he did with an innate sense for good engineering. From this point of view the Sainte-Geneviève Library (1843–1850) in Paris is a major edifice (Figure 2).

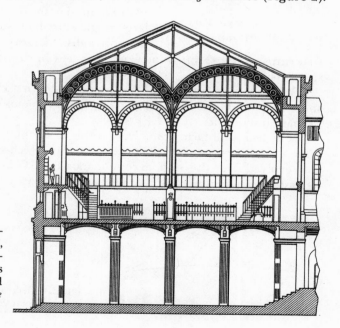

FIG. 2. Sainte-Geneviève Library, Paris. Henri Labrouste, architect. Plan, 1843; construction, 1845–1850. Cross section of reading room and entrance hall. (From *Revue générale d'architecture*, 1852.)

An iron skeleton is enclosed within a stone casing. The building has a vestibule and storage areas on the lower level and a main reading room (278 by 69 feet) upstairs. Cylindrical vaulting 14½ feet high is formed of round cast-iron arches supporting a plastered wire lattice. This vaulting bears on the side walls and on a center row of 18 cast-iron columns 14¾ feet high placed on stone pedestals 8½ feet high. The headroom under the vault is thus 37¾ feet. Seven uprights connect the iron framework above the vaults to the arches.

Labrouste's solution is reminiscent of the one found in railroad station concourses (for example, Euston Station) built in London between 1835 and 1839 by Robert Stephenson. But the architect retained neither the cast-iron spandrels connecting the columns along their axis nor the iron framework with trusses and ties.

The formula was repeated, and expanded, in the reading room of the National Bibliothèque in Paris. Labrouste, its architect, erected between 1855 and 1875 a hall 201 by 122 feet (measured internally), subdivided by shelves and counters so that the actual room was 108 feet square. It is surrounded on three sides by sets of shelves. The fourth is prolonged by a semicircle with a translucent ceiling connected to the enclosing wall by a flat arch, which presents no particular problem.

As in the Sainte-Geneviève Library a metal framework rises between the masonry walls. However, this is no longer a balanced double arch but is rather a vast hangar. Twelve cast-iron columns 11¾ inches in diameter and 33 feet tall from ground to capitals, standing on tall pedestals, demarcate the square in which stand 4 isolated columns supported at their bottoms by masonry pillars. Thus, in plan there are 9 equal squares of 33 feet each. Semicircular wrought-iron arches unite the columns and form a grill that carries 9 ceramic domes 33 feet high each, with an oculus.

Large single-story structures

Iron was used at the time in two types of structures: large single-story halls such as railroad stations, exhibition halls, markets, and large stores, and in structures with an iron framework that tied horizontal components to vertical supports.

Whatever the function of the building, the first kind demands a large open space at ground level with adequate height. Problems of span and thrust were of primary importance.

The technical factors involved in this development were of two kinds. First came a modification of the Polonceau system, which was widely used (Figure 3). This evolved from the original combination in 1837 of wooden rafters supported by cast-iron queen posts or by tie beams in iron replacing those in wood, to

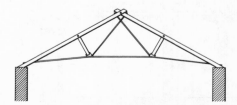

FIG. 3.   Diagram of the first Polonceau truss. (From Planat, *Encyclopédie d'architecture.*)

all-metal assemblies (1845), in which double-T iron beams were substituted for the wooden rafters. The section modulus of these lightweight iron beams provided the maximum shear strength. This system continued to use iron of various kinds—rolled, wrought, or cast.

Metallurgical progress made increasingly daring construction possible by improving the special qualities of the product. Increased production of iron was another factor in its increasingly wide use. It should be recalled that the Bessemer process dates from 1855/56, the Pierre Martin process from 1864, and the Thomas Gilchrist process from 1878/79.

Large single-story structures thus made use of increasingly sophisticated techniques. Cast iron was used for the superstructure of the Church of Saint Eugène in Paris, built in 1855 by the architects A.-L. Lusson and L.-A. Boileau. It was also used for the tall, thin columns of Les Halles (Central Markets) of Paris, built by V. Baltard in 1854–1857, and the Gare du Nord (North Station), built by J.-I. Hittorf between 1861 and 1864.

Plates 46   Photograph taken during the rebuilding of the Crystal Palace in 1852. (Photo Radio Times Hulton Picture Library, London.)

Through their programs the world expositions of the period brought about rapid progress in building large halls. These expositions, between 1851 and 1900, were, because of the pressure of international competition, responsible for improvements in construction techniques and the evolution of an architectural approach by engineers as well as architects. It is generally admitted that France played a special role during this half century.

The Crystal Palace in London (Figure 4) gave, in a sense, the starting signal in 1851. It demonstrated the long experience of the English metallurgical industry. Wood was used for the window sashes and the circular roof beams, but the small beams and bolted cast-iron parts were of iron.

FIG. 4. London, Crystal Palace, 1851 Exhibition. Joseph Paxton, builder. (From Helmut Gernsheim, London.)

Several facts must be noted:

1. Joseph Paxton subdivided his building, which was large for the time (2,583,360 square feet), into small prefabricated sections.

2. The modular dimension was given by a technique foreign to metallurgy, that of the maximum size of glass panel then available, namely, 4 feet long.

3. The glazed area was of considerable importance.

Concerning the last point it will be noted that Paxton had built the tropical greenhouses in Chatsworth (1836–1840), and the relationship of the Crystal Palace to greenhouses, beginning with those in the Jardin des Plantes in Paris (1833, Rohault de Fleury) and continuing with the Châteaux des Fleurs (Lyon, 1845/46; Paris, 1847, Hector Horeau), would seem undeniable were it not for the entire series of galleries and passageways found in Paris as early as 1770. The most interesting of these covered ways was the Galerie d'Orléans at the Palais Royal (Paris, 1829–1831), the roof of which had a semicircular profile.

This then was the dual origin of the exhibition halls, the technical importance of which rivals their architectural interest. The gradual substitution of transparent surfaces for solid roofs and space dividers resulted in enclosures that could be felt but could not readily be seen.

The entire subsequent development of architecture was to proceed, to be sure, from clients' requirements and the technical interpretation of them but also from this revolutionary, if unconscious, new concept of architecture.

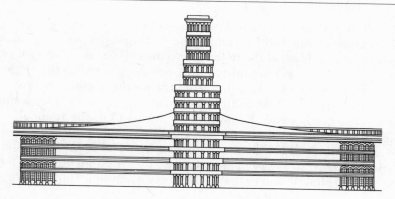

FIG. 5. Project for New York World's Fair, 1853. James Bogardus, engineer. The 300-foot tower was planned for the center of a circular building with four levels. (From *New York World's Fair of 1853: Original and Farsighted.*)

Two years after the Crystal Palace was built James Bogardus (1800–1874) unsuccessfully proposed to the committee for the New York World's Fair a project for an amphitheatre 1,200 feet in diameter, composed of straight girders with a 300-foot tower, to serve as a center support for a suspended sheet-iron roof held up by cables following a catenary curve (Figure 5). The final plans were less pioneering than this project, but progress was observable as one exposition followed another.

In 1855, at the Palais de l'Industrie in Paris, Viel supported the glazed surface (so extensive that visitors were fascinated) on a grillwork of iron beams, partly forged by hand, resting on cast-iron columns. The span of 157½ feet compared with 72 feet at the Crystal Palace but there were no tie beams, the lateral thrust being taken by massive buttresses made of blocks of lead.

In 1867 the engineer and economist Frédéric Le Play (1806–1882), the organizer of the Paris Exposition, put a man named Krantz in charge of construction, and he commissioned Gustave Eiffel (1832–1923) to build the Gallery of Machines. Although the span was some 115 feet, there were no buttresses or tie beams to take the lateral thrusts exerted on the columns. The 92-foot-high columns (which gave an internal height of 82 feet) were connected above the roof, the thrust at the foot being taken by adjacent connected structures. Around the roof ran a platform reached by hydraulic elevators (perhaps anticipating the Eiffel Tower), which permitted the public to inspect the anatomy of the building and see the new manner of organizing space. This was to have important consequences.

The monumental gate to the 1878 Exposition should be noted, for its redundant decoration aroused much criticism but it had a daring glass wall. The Gallery of Machines is also worthy of mention. Shaped like an overturned hull, it was constructed of trusses separately assembled and connected at the top. Oval boltholes were cut every 65 yards to allow for expansion. The form adopted, which resulted from studies on the resistance of materials carried out by de Dion, the builder, made it possible both to eliminate the overhang of columns and to open up the upper halves of the walls.

In 1889 with the Gallery of Machines this evolution reached its peak. This building, by the architect Dutert and the engineer Contamin, was huge: 1,378 feet long, 377 feet wide, and 148 feet high. The principal structure was built of 20 trusses joined at the ridge, at the point where the two elements met (as in 1878), and at the foot. The truss was continuous from the ground to the ridge, which removed all the load-bearing function from the walls and eliminated the capital, the classic dividing point between the load and the support. The connections between the half trusses and the links attaching them to the foundations were made with trunnions (Figure 6). The principle of elastic structure replaced that of rigid structure, as it had already been applied by Eiffel to bridges (notably the Douro Bridge, 1876). Steel had made possible this achievement, which was more important than technical skill in the break with an aesthetic tradition.

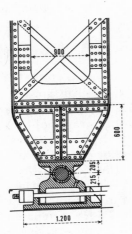
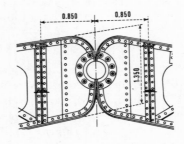

FIG. 6. Paris, Universal Exposition of 1889. Hall of Machinery. Details of the pivot pins of the ridge and foot. (From Planat, *Encyclopédie d'architecture.*)

Criticism was severe, but it did not equal that aroused by Gustave Eiffel's 975-foot iron tower. This symbol of the Exposition presented fewer difficulties for Eiffel and his collaborators (who included Maurice Koechlin) than did straight bridges or those with parabolic arches, the most famous being the Garabit viaduct (opening of the arch: 541 feet; total length: 1,640 feet; 1880–1884). Detailed studies were made to fabricate bridges without scaffolding and to determine soil resistance and thrusts in the construction of the tower. In this rivet holes had to coincide within one-tenth of a millimeter. Because of the difficulty in establishing diagrams for parts situated in oblique planes with variable slopes (Figure 7), a design office was constantly at work. With the help of 1,700 general and 3,600 detailed drawings the tower was built in 2 years, 2 months, and 17 days, of which 1 year, 9 months, and 15 days were required for the actual construction.

The Eiffel Tower is actually a bridge pier that supports nothing. The structure, consisting of four members each composed of four grillwork girders that meet at the top, has only to oppose the wind, which "models" it, in Eiffel's words.

In contrast to large single-level structures, the tower when built had no function. Erecting it was a gratuitous act whose sole purpose was to personify "forever the art of the engineer and the century of industry and science" (*Communication aux Ingénieurs civils de France*, Gustave Eiffel, 1888). But the fame of this

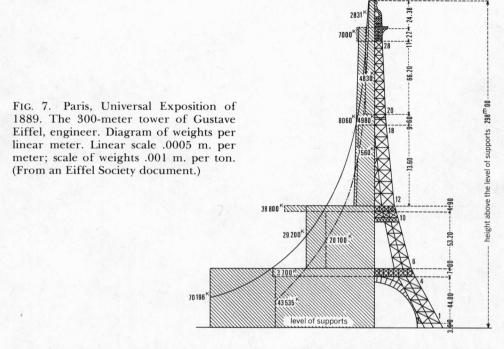

FIG. 7. Paris, Universal Exposition of 1889. The 300-meter tower of Gustave Eiffel, engineer. Diagram of weights per linear meter. Linear scale .0005 m. per meter; scale of weights .001 m. per ton. (From an Eiffel Society document.)

work, the polemics to which it gave rise, and the public success it enjoyed contributed to the development of technology and led to architectural consequences acknowledged by modern contractors who build on many levels.

Structures with steel skeletons

Paralleling the development of large single-level structures, that of multi-level structures in which the framework has horizontal divisions continued under the pressure of the same technical progress.

Rolled railroad rails appeared around 1830. Rolled girders, whose use L.-A. Boileau mentions as starting with the carpenters' strike in 1845 (which came on top of the exhaustion of lumber supplies), were probably old rails. In any event, Boileau wrote in 1871 that "for floors, beams and lintels only the new double-T iron beams are now used in Paris; because of this early use they were at first distinguished among the special irons by the name 'floor beams.' "

At that time, then, builders had available the necessary vertical and horizontal frame members. In 1848 in a five-story factory in New York James Bogardus developed a system that was also used in constructing large stores, warehouses, and commercial buildings, notably along the Mississippi waterfront at St. Louis after the 1849 fire and before the appearance there of the railroad in 1874. These structures, generally anonymous, were built hurriedly with sections that were for the most part prefabricated. This rapid construction was done under the pressure of territorial expansion, St. Louis having become by 1870 the fourth largest city in the United States. The use of metal frameworks later brought about the abolition of façade walls, which were replaced by windows held in the grillwork of the columns and lintels.

Plate 47. The machine section at the Universal Exposition of London in 1862. (Photo Radio Times Hulton Picture Library, London.)

In 1871/72 Jules Saulnier built a factory for the Chocolat Menier Company at Noisiel. Its foundation consists of four pillars placed in the bed of the Marne. The building is raised on four hollow, square-sectioned girders. An iron framework bears the entire weight of the building, universally acknowledged to be the first example of this type of construction. Saulnier used iron wall sections, which he left visible on the outside, with hollow bricks for cladding.

Architectural rationalism   Viollet-le-Duc had recommended such iron wall sectioning in the second volume of his *Entretiens sur l'architecture,* published in 1872, but it is evident that the factory, like the book, was in preparation before the 1870/71 war. Saulnier's application of the idea is so close to Viollet-le-Duc's theory that the relationship is quite obvious.

This is perhaps the basis for the importance attached in the United States to the English-language edition of the *Entretiens* (*Discourses on Architecture,* published 1875–1881). Buffington of Minneapolis, who claims credit (wrongly, according to some authorities) for the invention of the skyscraper, quotes Viollet-le-Duc. And William Le Baron Jenney (1832–1907), who is more probably the originator of the skyscraper, with his first Leiter Building (1879) of Chicago, knew of the Noisiel factory.

The influence of Viollet-le-Duc's *Entretiens,* the first volume of which had been published in 1863, is great. The author formulated French architectural rationalism by violently opposing academicism. His opinions derived from his knowledge of medieval architecture. He thought (perhaps somewhat excessively according to Pol Abraham) he discerned in the diagonal rib system an architecture consisting wholly of ribs. Moreover, he demanded that architecture take into consideration the needs of its time. Ribbed architecture, it seemed to him, could be built with the help of iron (see Volume II). The proof is that in the designs proposed, the cast-iron column replaces first of all the bedded medieval stone column, and an iron framework replaces a wooden one.

The advantage of iron "employed as a rib in masonry is that it makes possible a very light structure, balanced by ties" (*Entretiens* XII). The goal is "to obtain an exterior both of walls and vaults wholly of masonry while avoiding the mass of the material and troublesome points of supports" (*Entretiens* XII). The Chicago skyscrapers meet this definition. He proposed to attain this goal by what he called an organism (Figure 8), a complex system of two cast-iron columns inclined so that one extends out as a result of pressures while the other (thanks to a slope of an equal angle) limits the thrust of the first one. A system of tie beams, cramps, and mortises supplements the principal structure.

In sum, this is the principle of medieval buttressing, restated mathematically and applied to steel, simplifying the lines of force.

Other systems devised by Viollet-le-Duc came from this "organism," such as oblique columns converging at ground level to form a passage under arcades, supports for vaulting (in masonry or light materials) of large halls that eliminated ground supports, and so on. As a culmination of this development Viollet-le-Duc succeeded in designing an iron arch resting on a structure independent of masonry, which became a mere nonsupporting shell. We shall see the importance of this theoretical study in connection with certain buildings in Chicago.

The principles formulated in Volume I of *Entretiens* (1863) can be considered

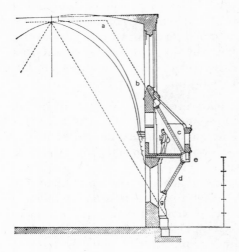

FIG. 8. Design by Viollet-le-Duc, demonstrating "organism," the system of balanced tie beams. The column c, placed in the prolongation of the resultant of the pressures a=b, produces its thrust on the element e. The latter is taken up by the column d and directed to g, where the vertical thrust of the wall provides the counterthrust; a line parallel to a-b-c-e drawn from the keystone of the vault meets the buttress of the wall at ground level. (From Viollet-le Duc, *Entretiens*, vol. II.)

responsible for the architectural revolutions during the end of the nineteenth and first quarter of the twentieth centuries. Viollet-le-Duc wished to apply Cartesian rationalism to architecture, as in the principles of veracity ("it is true that a column is a support and not a decoration"), division (the edifice must be analyzed in order to understand it), increasing complexity ("the first reasons in architecture are none other than the program and the material means"), and general observations ("let the stone clearly appear to be stone; iron, iron; and wood, wood").

If this attempt at a philosophy of architecture (see Volume I, *Entretiens* X) seems at times artificial, the general precepts deriving from it still retain exceptional dynamism. We read, for example, that "any form whose reason for existing cannot be explained cannot be beautiful. The structure must be acknowledged" (*Entretiens* VII); "one must conform to the immutable laws of architecture, which are a matter of common sense" (*Entretiens* VIII); "the simplest structure can be given a style . . . if one knows how to use the materials exactly in accordance with their purpose" (*Entretiens* X).

As the last quarter of the nineteenth century opened, Viollet-le-Duc warned that "by refusing to science the cooperation that she wants only to lend them, architects have played out their role; that of the engineers is beginning" (*Entretiens* XX). This was written sixteen years before the Gallery of Machines and the Eiffel Tower came into being.

The trends in architecture clashed a short time later, at the time of the construction of the Bon Marché department store in Paris, early in 1878. This building satisfied criteria for the new conception of the large store: open promenades at several levels separating the buildings were covered with glass, and in this area metal stairs and footbridges were installed, with the collaboration of Gustave Eiffel and Louis-Charles Boileau. Eiffel's contribution is the steel framework for the roofs, the general structure with its iron pillars, and the stairways and their approaches. Boileau, who was responsible for the general plan, was at the time taken to task for having covered the pillars with plaster.

The system of communicating footbridges can be compared with the one used by Labrouste in the central print section of the Bibliothèque Nationale (1855–1875). Within a rectangular area vertically delimited by the walls (147 by 95 feet and 44 feet high) the architect built two independent cast-iron frameworks. One supports the roof in bays whose centers are spaced at 20 feet; the other supports wooden racks on each side of a central corridor. Traffic moves by balconies and footbridges toward the center and by stairways in the shelf areas, all made of steel grids. The counterbracing role of these elements, in particular the stairs, is by no means negligible. This ensemble, which long remained a model of its kind, is separated from the main hall by only a glass wall, an arrangement that was extremely daring for that period.

In the United States, next to the achievements of James Bogardus and structures in St. Louis, architecture conformed to an eclecticism that rejected no style; following England's example, railroad station concourses were concealed behind traditional structures. These concourses (Figure 9), which vary greatly in type and appearance, were for a long time experimental structures. Some of these edifices have been studied in modern times by Carroll L. V. Meeks. The neoclassic, neo-Gothic, and Italian styles were used in universities, churches, and administrative buildings as well as residences.

FIG. 9.   London, King's Cross Station. Lewis Cubitt, engineer, 1851-1852. At the sides the laminated wood arches are tied to iron stanchions in the stone walls. In the center they rise from a back wall of present arches. The wall receives a portion of the thrust and assures the equilibrium of the system. (From *The Builder*, 20, 1852.)

The Chicago school   All architectural conceptions were challenged in Chicago between 1883 and 1893. A sudden expansion of the city replaced St. Louis as the great market of the Midwest and made rapid construction absolutely necessary. Rising land prices forced contractors to build upward.

William Le Baron Jenney is generally considered the head of the Chicago school. He was trained at the École Centrale des Arts et Manufactures in Paris from 1854 to 1856. Through his office passed the most outstanding of the architects and engineers who built Chicago, notably Martin Roche, William

Plate 48. The building of the Paris Opera House: general view of the construction site, taken on May 10, 1865. Photograph Delmaet and Durandelle. French National Library, Print Collection.

Holabird, Daniel H. Burnham (who went into partnership with John W. Root), and Louis H. Sullivan, who later, in partnership with Dankmar Adler, built in Chicago and many other cities and who trained Frank Lloyd Wright.

The importance of Jenney's work is that he replaced the type of building in which new forms adapted themselves to traditional construction with a completely original metal structure. The framework, originally composed of cast-iron supports and wrought-iron girders, was later built of steel. But from the very beginning the architectonic problem had been solved. The Home Insurance Building (1884/85), now destroyed, had an all-metal structure in which there were several girders of Bessemer steel, apparently the first application of this quality of steel in construction. In the Fair Store Building (1890/91) steel alone was used for the vertical and horizontal elements of the framework (Figure 10).

FIG. 10.   Chicago, Fair Store Building. William Le Baron Jenney, engineer, 1890–1891. The steel skeleton under construction. At the left the nonbearing outer facing is in place. The architectonic model of the skyscraper had now been achieved. (From Goodspeed Publishing Co., 1891.)

These structures, which attained 23 stories before 1893, were only gradually liberated from their nonsupporting peripheral envelopes to become the modern metal frameworks reduced to their fundamental elements and completely glazed. It can be said, however, that all the later architectural elements were present in the tall buildings of Chicago, as exemplified by the Mac Clurg Building built by Holabird and Roche in 1899–1900. In this the externally visible structure is barely covered, windows being the essential element of the façade.

It is important to note that the great Chicago movement was a conscious one. In 1890 John Root declared that the structure of buildings should dictate the choice of external forms. In 1896 Louis Sullivan defined the program and technical functions of the high-rise commercial structure. These principles have remained valid.

WOODEN STRUCTURES

Construction in wood has a long history. By the nineteenth century carpentry had in Europe reached a perfection derived from long centuries of experience. As example we shall mention only the relation between the medieval wooden wall section, certain studies of iron wall sections made by Viollet-le-Duc in *Entretiens,* and the Noisiel factory, built with this process.

The Scandinavian technique of board or log structures continued to follow century-old traditions, but this was not true in the United States. Balloon-frame construction is important because it coincided with territorial expansion (in the beginning it was the only type of dwelling in the West) and because it continued to be used for a long time, at first in its original form, then later for individual houses (Figure 11).

Labor conditions in the United States in the mid-nineteenth century pre-

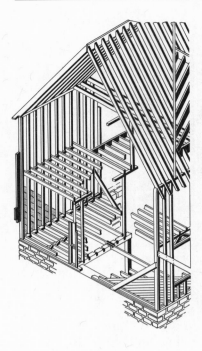

FIG. 11.   Structure of a balloon frame. Isometric view of two-story type. The framework is secured solely by nails. (From Charles H. Singer et al., *A History of Technology.*)

cluded using classic carpentry techniques. The balloon frame is a machine-made framework in which planks are sawed, not worked with tools, and traditional tongue-and-groove joints are replaced by nails. This is obviously genuine prefabrication and, in fact, houses ready to be assembled were shipped every time materials or labor were not locally available.

The technique is simple. Posts are raised on a double footing and are nailed on with toe nails hammered in obliquely. Then a stringer is placed at ceiling level. The roof is supported by a series of rafters placed perpendicular to the posts and reinforced by a stringer. The roof, like the walls, is covered on the outside by overlapping shingles.

What is characteristic is the standardization of dimensions: the baseplates and posts are 4 inches wide and 2 inches thick and the posts are 16 inches apart, center to center. Horizontal pieces naturally form the lintels over openings.

This construction method, of which a journalist wrote in 1855 that "without the balloon frame Chicago and San Francisco would never have changed in one year . . . from small villages to large cities," has not only persisted but has influenced the forms and distribution of housing in the United States, even where wood is no longer the material used.

THE BEGINNINGS OF REINFORCED CONCRETE

After the Paris Exposition of 1889 and the Chicago buildings, iron seemed to be assured of supremacy; but at the end of the nineteenth century a new technique appeared that was to be considerably developed later: reinforced concrete.

Plate 49. The cupolas of the main Reading Room, French National Library in Paris. (Photo Verroust, Paris.)

The fundamental technology involved in construction with reinforced concrete derives from a series of inventions and innovations. First was ordinary cement (Louis Vicat, 1820), then the portland variety (Joseph Aspdin, 1824). Pouring cement in imitation of the cob wall (pisé) technique, as in the building by F. Coignet, 1847 (Figure 12), introducing grids of iron wire into cement and concrete, as in the Lambot barque of 1848, or surrounding lattice containers with cement, as in a flower box by Joseph Monier in 1849, are other innovative steps. Precedents in which iron was surrounded with concrete were already known.

The problem really became important in 1880, when Monier sold his patent for a beam in Germany and Austria. In 1890 Cottancin patented a system of

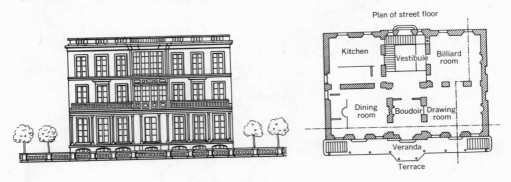

FIG. 12. Saint-Denis, house of poured concrete. F. Coignet, builder, 1853. This house appears to have been the first of its type built in the Paris area. (From *L'Ingénieur*, November 1855.)

barbed links and also a system of reinforced bricks, the latter used by de Baudot at Saint-Jean-de-Montmartre (1897–1902). In 1892 François Hennebique patented a stirrup beam (Figure 13).

By this time reinforced concrete had become a modern material making a liaison between iron and concrete in which each component assumes functions that, although particular to each, nevertheless work together. There is no doubt that the rapid progress and perfection of the new technique came from the experience acquired with large iron buildings. The applied research done by pioneers we have mentioned, and the calculations carried out in France (including

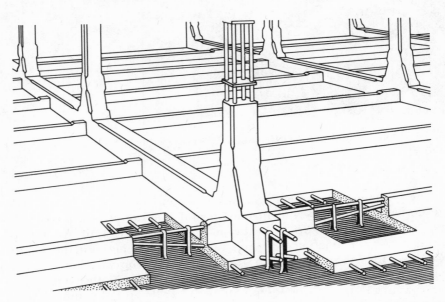

FIG. 13. The Hennebique system. Diagram showing the general principle of the skeleton (first patent, 1892). The strap brace is the new element; in addition, all the features of modern reinforced concrete are already in place. (From Hennebique's records, 1899.)

those by Charles Rabut at the École des Ponts et Chaussées in 1887/88, Edmond Coignet, Louis Considere, and others) as well as in other countries (by Bauschinger, Wayss, Koenen, Bach, and so on) made possible a quick transition from the stage of empirical experience to structures in which reinforced concrete was used, in keeping with its specific qualities (for instance, the building at 25 rue Franklin, by A.-G. Perret, 1903) and which very shortly produced a special architectural aesthetics (as in the Ponthieu garage, Paris, A.-G. Perret, 1905).

A 1906 French regulation concerning the use of reinforced concrete made available to builders a new material and appropriate methods of applying it.

THE ARCHITECTURAL CONSEQUENCES
OF CONSTRUCTION TECHNIQUES

As indicated earlier, three methods of building coexisted in the nineteenth century. It should be added, however, that there were two main intellectual attitudes: fidelity to tradition, and the search for new expression.

Those who wished to break with the past took different paths, some opposing a national (which is to say medieval) tradition to the classicizing tradition, others seeking models in the more recent historical styles (neo-Georgian, neo-Palladian, neo-Renaissance, neo-Louis XIV, and so on), and still others aiming at a renewal of forms through inspiration from the plant world (modern art and art nouveau).

In all cases the influence of the new techniques was small. We have mentioned the use of iron in the Gothic style and, more important for the art of building, its partnership with art nouveau (Figure 14). The use of iron frameworks in structures and the continued use of the balloon frame had architectural consequences, some apparently unintended, others deliberate (as in Chicago).

After the initial surprise of seeing the first large exhibition halls the public seems to have gradually become accustomed, between 1851 and 1889, to these large covered areas into which light flooded through the roof and then through the walls, which from then on were built of transparent materials. The critics and

FIG. 14. Stairway of a house in Brussels, Belgium. Victor Horta, architect, 1893. The cast-iron support is exposed. Its metal decoration is repeated in the painting of the walls and in the mosaic flooring. (From S. Giedion, *Space, Time and Architecture.*)

aesthetes were more reserved, as evidenced by artists' protests against the Eiffel Tower in 1888, but the movement was irreversible. Engineers perfected their techniques and architects became interested in this mode of construction, which reduced the volumes of their buildings to their silhouettes.

Although it was more the end of an evolution than a revolution, the Chicago experience, which was spectacular in its scope, resulted in a profound modification of architectural ideas: function triumphed over form.

Elsewhere in the United States the survival of the balloon frame led to the appearance of an architecture that preferred bare surfaces to decorated ones. This simplicity of appearance was already to be seen in the United States by the beginning of the nineteenth century in brickwork structures with rectilinear forms and bare surfaces, in both urban and rural areas.

It is apparent that the architectural consequences of technology acted on three types of structure: large covered spaces, framework buildings, and individual houses. Furthermore, the influences of Europe and the United States characteristically acted upon each other. In the beginning American architects and engineers came to learn from Viollet-le-Duc or, for example, from Léon Vaudoyer (1803–1872) and Henri Labrouste (1801–1875). Later, when needs similar to those that had caused a new architecture to develop in the United States also appeared in Europe, the Old World went to school in the New and repeated the formula for high-rise buildings. On the other hand, the international style, which began around 1920–1922, seems to owe part of its taste for rectilinear forms, cubic volumes, and bare surfaces to the anonymous wood and brick construction in the United States.

Nevertheless, it cannot be denied that architecture was genuinely challenged by the appearance of reinforced concrete, only the beginnings of which could be mentioned here. Although in the case of high-rise buildings it can be asked whether concrete is preferable to steel and vice versa, it is undeniable that those who build with concrete frameworks benefit (despite the different specific qualities) from experience gained with large steel buildings.

As for the international style, though it is possible to argue about its recent and remote origins, its architectural mode of expression was definitively assured by concrete.

CHAPTER 2

DOMESTIC COMFORT AND SANITATION

O F ALL THE CHANGES during the nineteenth century that resulted from the progress of technology, that of housing conditions is one of the more dramatic. But the historian's attention does not often linger over this phenomenon, for he is more concerned with evolutions in major industries or methods of transportation and communication, which had economic and social consequences of great importance.

Problems of comfort and sanitation in dwelling places and work areas go back a long time. Over the centuries methods of heating, lighting, supplying water, and removing waste water had given rise to installations that in general were dictated by common sense and achieved by fairly common material means. Moreover, the problem concerned only cities of a certain size. As long as the growth of these cities continued to be slow, installations could be modified and adapted without in any way modifying their basic principles.

This was no longer true when the populations of cities began to grow more rapidly or when industrial buildings acquired previously unattained sizes. By the beginning of the nineteenth century London had one million inhabitants and the water supply and sewage systems had become inadequate, but the importance of the problem had yet to be realized, and for a number of reasons no overall solution was imaginable. The various technical problems implied in building a large network of pipes and sewers had never been the object of systematic study. In addition, because the high expenditures that would have been required by such projects would have been nonproductive, communities thus were less ready to authorize them—this society preferred to build railroads rather than sewers.

The appearance of cholera in 1832 was the first warning to create an awareness of the dangers of community pollution, but administrative authorities still had no way to remedy the dangers. The return of the epidemic in 1848 and on several other occasions in the next twenty years contributed to the decision to build the major sewage works that have now become indispensable. The second half of the nineteenth century saw their construction in the largest cities of the countries affected by industrial civilization.

The problem of heating was not within the purview of civil authorities. This was a private concern, whether it was a matter of improving the comfort of a dwelling or of increasing the output of workers in factories by the least costly means. The desire to live better and increase profits brought about the appearance of the first central heating installations as early as the first quarter of the nineteenth century, and they came into general use in the second half of the century.

The improvement of lighting was dealt with in terms of industrial development. Whether it was a question of the manufacture and sale of improved oil lamps or of stearin (tallow) candles, or the distillation of coal and piping of illuminating gas into the home, it was tempting to profit from new inventions and discoveries. The installation and development of networks to distribute gas did not acquire real importance until around the middle of the century. It was necessary to find a satisfactory system to do so, and the trial-and-error period was longer than in the case of the coal distillation process and the purifying and storage of gas.

If we except the inventions of William Murdock, Philippe Lebon, and the works of Eugène Chevreul, it is obvious that the techniques that made it possible to improve comfort and domestic sanitation had a common denominator. They depended not on the emergence of revolutionary inventions but merely on the production of metal pipe and accessory parts with which to standardize and measure the flow of liquids.

The empirical trial-and-error efforts of the first period (until around 1840) were replaced by applying mathematical knowledge to the problems to be solved. The first experiments with equipment gave rise to the first mathematical research on the new problems, and the results of this research then made it possible to develop general solutions. Thus it was possible, between approximately 1860 and 1880, to build the major pipeline systems, wholly or in part.

This field, yet another example of cooperation between science and technology, also gave rise to another important phenomenon. It became (one might even say began so) a field in which to apply modern techniques, and played a part in the creation and rapid development of an almost new branch of industry—the manufacture of metal pipes, industrial plumbing equipment, and metering devices. Although pipes, valves, and faucets had been produced since early times, the industry that emerged in the nineteenth century was totally different from all those preceding it, both by the nature of the products and appliances it began to supply and by the important part it quickly assumed in the development of industrial civilization. New production lines (for example, for steam engines and water turbines) had already given rise in the nineteenth century to the development of industrial piping and plumbing equipment. Water, gas, and heating installations brought these industries a measure of activity completely out of proportion to what they had formerly known.

This subject is very broad and has yet to be studied enough to permit concise summary. By outlining the technical methods through which the conditions of domestic comfort rose in less than one century from a relatively precarious traditional level to that of perfected urban dwellings we shall be able to isolate the chief steps in this evolution.

WATER: SUPPLY AND DRAINAGE

As mentioned, the problem of supplying cities with water was solved in the nineteenth century. This problem was not of course a new one; public authorities had concerned themselves with it in every period. Every possible solution had been availed of before the eighteenth century: wells and cisterns, diversion of streams, canalization of distant water sources, and pumping from streams that ran through cities.

Cast-iron pipes   Pumping from rivers acquired more importance as the construction of pipes and waterwheels improved. The use of heat engines similar to those employed to pump mine water was the only new feature in this period, and even these did not come into use until around the end of the eighteenth century. The cast-iron pipes used for the first time in installations at Versailles were not generally adopted, because in the city conditions under which they were laid they burst under the weight of carriages. The same was true, depending on circumstances, for lead and pottery pipes. Pipes were later buried deeper, and roadways were laid that were more resistant to abuse, after which the use of cast-iron pipe began to become general.

In the second half of the eighteenth century water mains were formed of cast-iron pipes joined together by straps and bolts, or by being fitted into each other. Connecting them with straps had the advantage of permitting the pipes to be taken apart in order to change a damaged part or insert a branch line, but it was difficult to make satisfactory watertight joints, and bolts broke frequently.

Thus, the use of pipes that fitted into each other gradually became more important (Figure 15). Tightness was achieved in the joint by stuffing various materials into the round space left between the two pipes where they joined. In Paris around the middle of the nineteenth century tarred rope and clay were used for this purpose, the joint being finished with a layer of molten lead. However, strapped pipes were never abandoned, because, emplaced at various points, they permitted partial dismantling. In addition, all connections with valves and faucets were made with straps.

FIG. 15.   Water main. Fitted joint.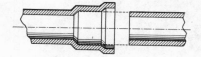

In the eighteenth century pipes were cast in horizontal molds. This method had the disadvantage of producing walls that were not of uniform strength, the weak spots being susceptible to rupture. At the beginning of the nineteenth century production began to increase, and to eliminate defects the molds were placed in an inclined position, a procedure known as side casting. This method had the advantage of ensuring a better flow of the molten metal, the impurities of which rose to the surface and did not remain trapped in the mass. Finally, approximately a half century later, vertical casting of pipes came into practice, as had long been the case for guns, and this process quickly replaced side casting.

After production the strength of pipes was tested with a hydraulic press, then they were coated with oil, tar, or asphalt to protect them from corrosion and ensure their watertightness.

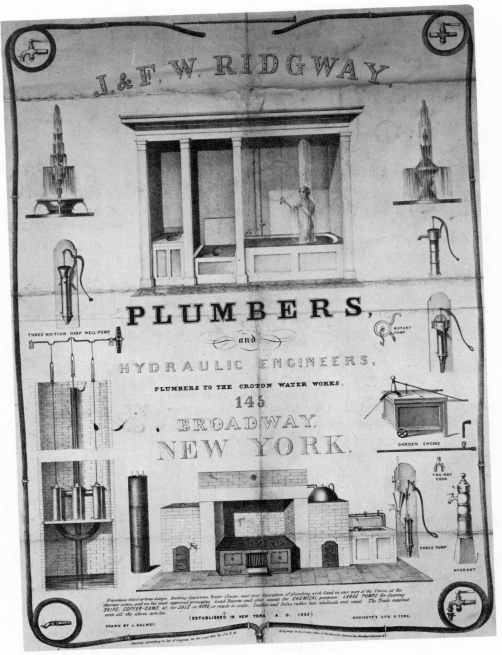

Plate 50. J. & F. W. Ridgway Plumbers and Hydraulic Engineers. Lithograph after J. Calway, published by Endicott, 1844. Library of Congress

Valves and faucets The production of valves progressed with the growing importance of piping installations. No particular difficulty delayed the creation and production of the various types of valves for parts exposed to the open air. The equipment needed to machine the parts existed by the first half of the nineteenth century. This was not true for parts that had to be attached to underground mains. In principle their maintenance and care

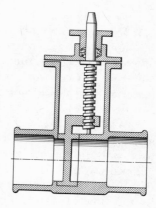

FIG. 16.   Ovid Tupham's screw valve for use in water-piping system. 1837.

required access in an excavation. After 1840 valves were controlled from the surface with a threaded rod protected by a casing covering it completely (Figure 16). The first patent taken out for this improvement is credited to an English engineer, Ovid Tupham, and dates from 1837. The principle was quickly developed and the sluice-valve system was perfected. Cast-iron valves with ordinary valve casings were also made for small mains. They were set in a masonry chamber through which the valve was controlled from aboveground by a key on a stem. Thus, manholes giving access to the various valves and gates for controlling the flow appeared on the sidewalks and roadways.

> *Piping networks*   Modifying and extending the water mains in cities was gradually carried out along guidelines covering all the problems and supplying a definitive solution for them, whatever might be the future needs of the community. In the period from 1860 to 1880 the large water supply companies studied and solved all problems from construction and equipping large reservoirs and laying out the principal mains and branches down to installing meters to measure consumption.

The work of hydraulic engineers from the beginning of the nineteenth century provided a basis particularly to develop formulas appropriate to water mains and how to supply them. In France the Prony formulas were first used. Two equations with four variables (the diameter and the slope per meter of the main, and the volume and velocity of the water) made it possible to calculate two variables when the other two were known or assumed. These formulas were later corrected by water company engineers.

> *Meters*   The equipment for metering the water supplied to the consumer was perhaps the most difficult to provide. To begin with there was an economic difficulty: because water was a product sold cheaply, neither the user nor the supplier were inclined to pay high costs for a metering device. When the major installations were completed, water became abundant in cities, since consumption did not immediately rise in every section to the system's capacity. The water authorities were therefore satisfied to charge a flat rate, either by the so-called open faucet system or by the gauge, a calibrated outlet on the tank of a building.

Metering systems in private installations were inevitable, if only in preparation for the time when consumption reached the capacity of the system and wastage had to be controlled. When the time came, around the middle of the nineteenth century, the technical problem was quite difficult to solve. Because metering devices work under pressure, they had to be watertight and built of materials that would not corrode upon contact with water and air. Finally, their cost had to be as low as possible.

When water flowed without pressure it was possible to use a rising disk whose axle was connected by a crank to the metering device, but this apparatus could be used only in special cases. Where water was distributed under pressure, as it generally was, two kinds of meters—a turbine type and a piston type—were developed. The former, especially in France, consisted of a reel with vanes rotated by the flow of water. The difficulty lay in transmitting this movement to the mechanical metering system. Many designs were tried, including a magnetic device, without obtaining completely satisfactory results. In England chiefly piston meters were constructed, which functioned on the principles of the hydraulic ram. They gave more accurate recordings than did turbine meters and were less fragile, but they cost more. The problem of metering water had not been completely solved even at the end of the century.

Water treatment   During the first half of the nineteenth century authorities began seriously to concern themselves with the quality of public water supplies. Several organoleptic properties, such as flocculation reactions from sulfuric acid, had by the eighteenth century already been used to perform sketchy analyses, but no great importance seems to have been attached to the results. Around 1840 to 1850 the methods of chemical analysis became more precise. Although the action on the organism of the various elements contained in solution or in suspension in the water was still undetermined, their composition, especially of the mineral salts, began to be clearly identified. Between 1850 and 1855 the influence of lime and magnesium salts on water quality was thoroughly studied. The idea of hardness, expressed according to the proportions of calcium and magnesium present, came about thanks to the work of Dr. Thomas Clark (1801–1867) in England and the chemists Boutron and Boudet in France. The idea of bacteriological pollution did not of course play a role until around the end of the century.

The rapid spread of cholera during epidemics had drawn attention to the danger of using for consumption water taken from streams that ran through large cities. The influence of organic matter on the more or less rapid pollution of water began to be realized.

Authorities then undertook to require that water be filtered (especially if it was drawn from streams) through layers of sand and clay. Various arrangements of artificial filters were tried in terms of the output of the beds and the nature of the water to be purified. Despite these precautions, in the period from 1855 to 1860 the water supplies of large cities continued to be of dubious quality. London's was reputed to be the worst—even after filtration it retained a yellowish color. Paris water was taken from the Seine at Chaillot, downstream from the city. Water from this source was "heavily saturated with loathsome matter" (Hervé Mangon).

Plate 51. Main Gallery at the Universal Exposition of Paris, 1878; the metal trusses are being raised. Photograph. Musée du Conservatoire national des Arts et Métiers. (Print by Alain Doyère - Conservatoire National des Arts et Métiers.)

At this time the authorities gave their attention to solving these problems by building vast reservoirs to collect pure water in places distant from the cities. They had available the chemical methods to study the nature of all usable water in the basins surrounding the large cities, and the choice of collecting points could be properly made. These major supply works were carried out for all cities of a certain size during the second half of the nineteenth century, each project continuing over several decades. The first large project undertaken was to supply Paris, plans for which had been drawn up by an engineer named Belgrand in 1855.

Sewer networks   In the same period attention centered on the problems of open sewer networks, the streams that still flowed down the centers of streets, and of draining waste water into streams upriver from the pumping points. With the construction of large multiple-dwelling housing units the problem of how to drain waste water had to be approached on a completely new basis. The per capita and per diem volume of water used began to increase steadily. It was estimated that consumption in London in 1853 rose to 23¾ gallons at a time when only 5¼ gallons were provided for Paris. This was exclusive of the requirements for stables, gardens, street cleaning, and similar purposes.

One factor in the growth of private water consumption was the gradual installation of flush toilets. The principle of these was not new (it had been suggested as early as 1596 by Sir John Harington), but it was not widely used until after the end of the eighteenth century. A toilet with a siphon pan that provided complete sanitation appeared at this time, and its use began to spread during the first half of the nineteenth century.

Sewer networks began to be systematically rebuilt beginning around 1845. Hamburg was the first city to set an example; it had been partly destroyed by fire in 1843. The reconstruction of sewers in London began in 1845 but was not carried out with any great speed until after 1855, by which time two new cholera epidemics had claimed more than 20,000 victims. The system included collecting mains parallel to the Thames, into which they discharged twelve miles below London Bridge. In Paris a new network was established during the urban renewal plan carried out under the direction of Prefect Haussmann. It included a well-known main in the Place de la Concorde that discharged into the Seine. At this time the need to purify waste water before dumping it into waterways became apparent, but practical solutions for the problem were not found until around the end of the century.

LIGHTING

Improved water supplies involved only a relatively small part of the population. In 1858 a city like Paris with approximately 32,000 dwellings had running water in only about 7,000—fewer than one-quarter. The others were supplied by traditional methods, wells or public fountains. Only about ten cities in France were giving any attention to the water problem.

The perfecting of oil lamps

In contrast, progress in lighting techniques rapidly involved the entire population, both urban and rural, and made it possible to put on the market first oil lamps with great illuminating power, then tallow candles. Gas lighting was found only in the largest cities, like London and Birmingham after 1820 and Paris after 1840.

Prior to Chevreul (who invented the stearin candle) the available methods of lighting went back to antiquity. The oil lamp had seen only improvements that added very little to its illuminating power. The principal oils burned in it were from the rapeseed and poppy, both being plants that were widely cultivated in every country; more rarely, olive oil was used. The flame, lighted at the end of a flat cotton wick, remained smoky and strongly colored, and that of tallow candles was not much more satisfactory. Only wax candles gave a relatively bright light, but their price restricted their use to the wealthy.

Improvements in the oil lamp did not result from wide-ranging inventions but were due to the common sense of a Geneva physicist, Aimé Argand, under circumstances described earlier in connection with lighthouses. Differences arose between Argand on the one hand and a pharmacist, Quinquet, and a grocery store owner, Lange, on the other concerning this invention. By 1784 the Argand lamp had found its nearly final form for domestic lighting, and it seems clear that the merits of the devices by his two competitors were limited to several minor improvements and especially to the commercial sale of the device. Actually, this type of lamp could just as well have been invented one or two centuries earlier.

FIG. 17. Argand lamp with glass chimney. The burner is supplied with air through the center pipe and the outer crown.

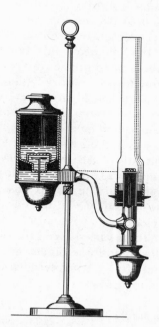

FIG. 18. "Student lamp," in which the wick is kept constantly supplied with oil.

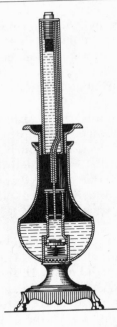

FIG. 19.   Oil lamp with hand pump.

The Argand burner has continued to exist into modern times. It was adapted to gas lighting in the 1840s and then, after 1860, to kerosene lighting (Figure 17).

To ensure even lighting with oil lamps a device was needed to provide a constant supply of oil. A solution was found easily in two different ways. The first consisted of placing the bottom of the oil reservoir level with the burner and constructing this reservoir as a constant-flow supply tank called a Mariotte container. In 1780 the chemist Louis Proust (1754–1826) had suggested this device, which became of greater interest when the Argand burner came into use. In the early nineteenth century Quinquet devised a model that could be attached to a wall on a bracket. Then appeared a model on a stand, which during the nineteenth century came into widespread use under the term *student lamp* (Figure 18).

The second method of supplying oil to the wick was used with lamps whose oil supply was in their base. During the eighteenth century lamps in certain regions were already in use whose reservoir was equipped with a pump that raised the oil. This pump was operated by putting a slight pressure on the upper pipe to which the spindle of the pump was soldered (Figure 19). In 1800 the clockmaker Guillaume Carcel won fame with the idea of operating a horizontal pump by a small clockwork device placed beneath it in a sealed compartment.

In these varied forms the oil lamp became such a common household object that throughout the nineteenth century numerous inventors created variants of these models and many devices to increase their functional regularity and illuminating power.

Lighting and photometry   This period (especially the first half of the century) witnessed the development of photometry methods, in which many physicists took an interest. The invention of the stearin candle and, slightly later, the piping of illuminating gas did in fact greatly draw to these problems the attentions of scientists and technicians. They also studied the nature of flames, that is, gas combustion. The first knowledge about how flames occurred and about the role that ignited solid materials played in their illuminating power was later put to good use, as we shall see. This movement of research into light sources will clearly show how in the nineteenth century the break with traditional methods transformed a banal problem into a technique whose evolution aroused the curiosity of scientists and profited by their contributions.

The later chapter on industrial chemistry shows how Eugène Chevreul's work gave birth to a new branch of this industry, namely that of stearin production and the manufacture of candles. Here it is enough to emphasize the immediate success of this new method of domestic lighting. Its modest cost and ease of use made the stearin candle a new and universally adopted contribution to individual comfort.

Coal gas The gas produced by distilling coal took longer to win acceptance. The history of this invention and the development of early techniques of using it are also included in the chapter on industrial chemistry.

The industrialization of this procedure was attempted in England during the Empire period's blockade because of the considerable increase in the price of oil. The first development company in Paris was founded in 1815 by F. A. Winsor (1763–1830) in partnership with the chemist Friedrich C. Accum (1769–1838). They were joined by Samuel Clegg (1781–1861), an engineer who for the past ten years had been concerned with the distillation of coal and had discovered the first process to purify gas by bubbling it in limed water. The first production and distribution of the gas did not occur until after 1820.

Winsor founded the first such development company in France in 1816, followed by other companies in Paris. Financial difficulties, which almost all of them encountered, obliged them to merge, reorganize, or disappear. The history of all these enterprises is complex until the year 1855 when all the surviving companies combined to form the Compagnie Parisienne du Gaz. The effect of this merger was to make possible standardization of installations and the distribution equipment. In many cities in France development was undertaken, starting in 1830, by English companies.

The first distillation plants were established in the Luxembourg area of Paris around 1817, in the Faubourg Poissonière and at the Saint-Louis Hospital in 1820, then on the Avenue Trudaine. After 1855 all plants in the center of the city were abolished and replaced by the Villette works. The piping network was systematically rebuilt beginning in 1856 at the same time as the large plants intended to replace all those within Paris were built on the outskirts. The last plant built was Le Landy (1889), which at the time was regarded as a model of its type. The production of gas, which in Paris in 1855 was 1.46 billion cubic feet, increased more than seven times in the next forty years.

Distribution equipment This rapid increase was due to the development of equipment needed for distribution. These installations required solving many more problems than did the water networks. With the exception of methods to produce, purify, and cool the gas, the storage and maintenance of a steady supply required the invention of a special apparatus

Plate 52. The shops of the "Compagnie Continentale pour la fabrication des Compteurs à gaz" (Continental Company for the Production of Gas Meters). Engraving taken from Turgan, *Les Grandes Usines,* vol. XVI, Paris, 1885. (Photo Alain Doyère - Conservatoire national des Arts et Métiers.)

(Figure 20). In principle the various devices did not present any difficulties. From the beginning gas meters had been designed that needed only to be enlarged to attain the capacities necessary in the second half of the century. The diving bell was adapted to regulate pressure in the distribution system. Practice and experience made it possible to discover quickly methods to perfect the complete installations, which became more complicated as they became more extensive.

Burners

Among other problems, burners came to the attention of inventors and engineers. It is impossible to review here the many solutions suggested and tried. In England so-called fish-tail

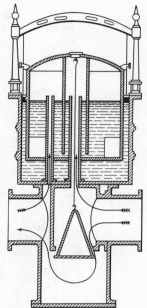

FIG. 20.   Piping illuminating gas. Bell-type distribution control.

burners were used at first that consisted of a pipe with several holes in its end. In France the batwing burner (Figure 21) found the widest use. In 1829 the rue de la Paix in Paris became the first public street to be lighted with gas. Many experiments with devices that could be applied to chandeliers now began, and metal workers sought the most decorative forms. Many difficulties appeared, not the least of which was the cost of producing a design in large numbers. The burner's gas consumption in relation to its illuminating power was also carefully studied. Numerous experiments were made to obtain as complete combustion of gas as possible by improving the distribution of air to be burned. In Paris the end result of this research seems to have been the adoption of the intensive burner, known as the Fourth of September burner because it had been tried in the street of that name in 1878 (Figure 22).

For domestic purposes the batwing burner was widely used for a long time. Studies of flames had shown the desirability of placing materials inside them that could be brought to red or—better—to white heat to increase their illuminating power. After various experiments, for example those by Sellon, who used a wick of iridio-platinum gauze, and by Clamand, who used magnesium powder, the definitive solution was not found until 1885, by the Austrian physicist Carl Auer von Welsbach. His invention (popularized under the name *Auer burner* in France) had a small mantle consisting of gauze impregnated with thorium oxide, to which was added a small quantity of cerium oxide (Figure 23).

Meters　　The industry began to sell gas to consumers on a rental basis, but the need for a metering device at the entrance to each individual installation was soon obvious. Samuel Clegg's invention provided the basic form used until modern times. In an early experi-

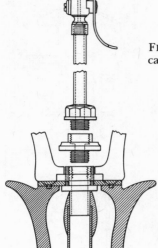

FIG. 21. Connection of a bat's-wing burner with the top of a candelabrum.

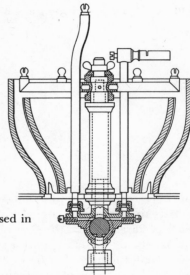

FIG. 22. Intensive burner for street lighting, first used in the rue du 4-Septembre in Paris, 1878.

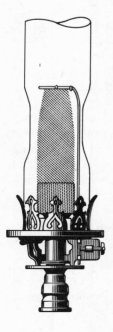

FIG. 23. Auer von Welsbach's incandescent gas mantle for gas lighting. 1885.

ment Clegg had devised a system of two bell-shaped receivers that rose and fell alternately as they filled with gas. They emptied through an upper nozzle with a valve. The oscillating movements made it possible to count the volume consumed in units. In a second arrangement Clegg applied the same principle to a horizontal, compartmented drum turning in a vessel that was half filled with water. When completed and perfected, the Clegg gas meter (Figure 24) was almost universally adopted.

FIG. 24.   Gas meter. Around 1850.

In its classic form the illuminating gas industry attained its technical peak in the first quarter of the twentieth century. It not only helped to improve living and working conditions appreciably, even in small cities, but also (as we shall see in Volume IV) was the origin of the great industry of synthetic chemistry. Developments within this one industry alone have in one century singularly changed the material conditions in all countries of the world, at least to the extent that they have been affected by industrialization.

HEATING

In the first half of the nineteenth century the techniques for heating buildings experienced a highly significant period of change, though the evolution was less rapid than that of the water supply and public and domestic lighting. Central heating installations appeared at the beginning of this period, marking the creation of a new branch of industry whose great development in the second half of the nineteenth century is well known.

Stoves and fireplaces   The major changes in heating equipment were in fact directed especially at classic heating methods. The work of Benjamin Thomson, Count Rumford, carried on between about 1795 and 1800, contributed new ideas on how to build fireplaces and improve and regulate their draft, and how to increase heat transfer between the gases and the surrounding atmosphere. The results were immediately applied, at least in the new houses built for the wealthy urban classes. The Rumford stove was widely adopted. Its trapezoidal base replaced the traditional rectangle and it was equipped with an exhaust pipe that was inclined at its base, an arrangement that made it possible to move the hearth forward into the room. A short time later a Parisian inventor named Lhomond invented the movable device quickly popularized as the hood. Grates for coal, metal mantelpieces that projected out into the room, and similar arrangements appeared in this period.

In most cases the improvements from the first half of the nineteenth century were indirectly suggested by Rumford's work. Besides the first material results, they have retained a certain historical importance because they suggested new ways to study a quite commonplace problem. Although no mathematical approach could yet be taken in these investigations, the new approach to these problems brought unquestionable results in a few decades.

During the first half of the nineteenth century coal began to be used abundantly in cities to heat dwellings and factories. Stove construction rapidly underwent major changes. The hearths, dampers, and heat transfer characteristics were studied. Progress in producing sheet metal industrially and in casting made possible the commercial production of highly developed units. By the middle of the century appeared the first models of stoves with radiating vanes and the slow-burning *poêle*. Once easily maintained home fireplaces of a certain capacity were available, ducts to distribute hot air began to be installed in new buildings.

Finally there was an easy transition to gas heating devices, which began to be manufactured for the kitchen and to heat rooms around the middle of the nineteenth century.

Progress in this field was not as spectacular as, for example, the invention and use of illuminating gas. It was due to many minor inventions that could be applied only because industry had production methods available to it that were completely different from those of the preceding century. But we must not be deceived by this for these new inventions were quite important to a large part of the population. Like the Argand burner, the Carcel lamp, and the wax candle, they transformed the living conditions of most inhabitants in cities of all sizes. In addition, by opening up a new field of industrial activity they caused to appear a new category of specialized technicians unknown until then. Until around the end of the century these technicians had only pragmatic training, but after that the basic knowledge of this profession acquired another character until it now includes highly scientific elements.

The first central-heating experiments

When the first central-heating installations appeared in the first quarter of the nineteenth century, they affected a much smaller proportion of the urban population, but these installations were nevertheless a significant factor in the technical improvements of the time.

The use of coal as a domestic fuel spread as the result of changes in certain industries. With the development of steam engines the problem of industrial heating acquired a new character by the beginning of the nineteenth century. As the result of a scarcity of wood, several industries (for example, chemical products and glassmaking) adopted coal as their fuel. Later, locomotives encouraged a more intensive development of coal mines.

By 1810 to 1815 furnaces and boilers could be built safe enough to encourage the idea of using steam to heat buildings. Cast-iron pipes that met construction requirements were also available.

Steam heating   The first central-heating installation was built in 1817 in a silk factory in Watford, England. It consisted of a generator that delivered steam to the top of the building and a network of pipes through which it descended from story to story back to the boiler (Figure 25). Strictly speaking there is no new invention in this installation. The dimensions of the furnace and boiler were made to fit the use to be made of them; the safety and supply systems were borrowed from familiar designs. Pipes were assembled by being fitted into each other in a technique common by then. Other experiments made in succeeding years in heating greenhouses and workshops were satisfactory and quickly became numerous enough to let the English engineer Thomas Tredgold (1788–1829) publish a short essay on the subject in 1824. It was reprinted the following year and immediately translated into French. The personality of the author, who had devoted much study to steam engines, and the popularity of his work, are quite significant.

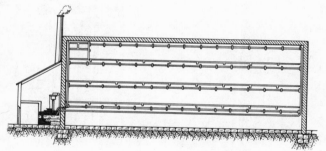

FIG. 25. Steam-heating apparatus installed in the Watford silk mills, 1817. (From Tredgold.)

In England as on the Continent several physicists and engineers began to study the technical conditions for the best installations from the point of view of fuel consumption, heat produced, and, of course, human safety. After Tredgold had publicized the best layout for the furnace and boiler (Figure 26), Péclet in France devoted himself to studying the cooling and condensation of steam and to computing the sizes of piping. The first large installations (for example, the Palais de l'Institut in 1833) were built by the man who was probably the first French specialist in this field, Philippe Grouvelle.

As with water and gas installations, it was necessary to develop a number of special control devices, separators for the condensed water, and so on (Figure 27). A method of making pipes of cast or drawn iron and copper was quite rapidly perfected. The network of pipes itself appears to have been seldom used as a heating element. "Steam stoves" were installed into which the steam was injected and condensed. Characteristically, these devices were given the external shape of coal stoves or classical fireplaces. This respect for traditional forms is frequent throughout the nineteenth century. Later, Etienne Lenoir (1822–1900) gave his gasoline engines the look of steam engines, and Gottlieb Daimler (1834–1900) built his first automobiles to look like horse-drawn carriages without shafts.

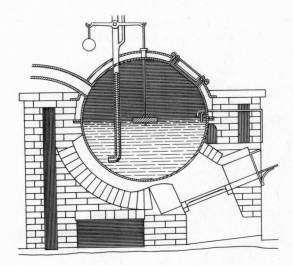

FIG. 26.   Cross section of a boiler for a central heating system. 1824. This is a large boiler made from a metal cylinder. Note the automatically controlled water inlet.

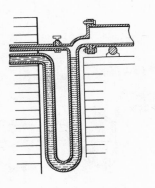

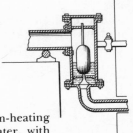

FIG. 27.   *Left:* Siphon for evacuating condensation water in a steam-heating installation. 1824. *Right:* Evacuation chest for condensation water, with valve controlled by a float. Steam-heating system. 1824.

Hot water circulation   Heating by circulating hot water has origins older than the use of steam. As early as 1777 a factory owner in Le Pecq, Bonnemain, built such an installation in his factory, for artificially incubating eggs. It already contained all the elements of later installations: a boiler, a network of tubes, and an expansion chamber. This equipment was well enough designed to remain in service till 1845.

Around 1828 to 1830 this system began to be applied, first in England, then in France. The first patents on this subject were undoubtedly those by the brothers Henry Cruges and Charles Fox Price in England in 1829 and a French manufacturer, Léon Duvoir, in 1834. In these early systems the heating elements were either "water stoves," huge cast-iron containers filled with hot water that circulated from one floor to the next, or the circulation pipes themselves. They functioned at atmospheric pressure (Figure 28).

FIG. 28. Duvoir system of central heating by circulation of water under low pressure.

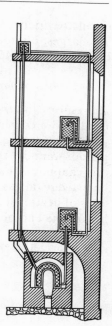

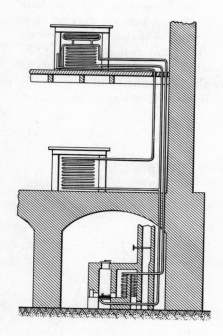

FIG. 29. Perkins system of heating by circulating steam under pressure.

Pressurized steam   Several years later it was decided to close the circuit with a safety valve and distribute the steam under pressure. It thus became possible to decrease the sizes of pipes, meaning economy in the cost not only of the material but also of installing it.

Duvoir adopted the water-stove system, which distributed the steam under pressure. This was not without danger in case the wall of a stove ruptured, an accident that would have been all the more serious because all the stoves were installed in a single, interconnected line. The installation built by Duvoir toward the end of the July Monarchy in the Chamber of Peers operated under a pressure of 5 atmospheres.

The tube arrangement (Figure 29), which anticipates our modern radiators, was recommended and applied in the same period by an Englishman named Perkins. By increasing the steam pressure to as much as 15 and 20 atmospheres Perkins achieved even greater economies. Builders still took the precaution of concealing the coil of pipe in each room under an imitation sheet-metal fireplace in which openings were left for air to circulate.

A combination of water and steam was also used during this period. This system consisted of passing the steam pipes through large containers of water placed in the areas to be heated. The water thus heated then passed through a circulatory network, giving a larger surface area to exchange heat with the air. The largest installation of this type was set up by Grouvelle in the Mazas prison, built between 1845 and 1850.

Ventilation problems   For this building Grouvelle designed a general ventilation system. The problem of ventilating industrial premises and theatre halls had concerned engineers for several years and had produced a considerable literature by the mid-nineteenth century, but no new system had emerged from this research. We shall merely note that these preoccupations were like those that had given rise to all the major innovations discussed in this chapter. An attempt was made to put to good use available mathematical knowledge on gas circulation, the composition of the atmosphere, and the conditions of heating it in closed containers. But no original solution was to come about before the end of the century.

BIBLIOGRAPHY

ABRAHAM, Pol. *Viollet-le-Duc et le rationalisme médiéval*. Paris, 1934.

ACHE, J.-B. *Acier et architecture*. Paris, 1966.

_____. Techniques de construction et formes architecturales," in *Études sur l'art en France au XVIIe siècle*. Paris, 1958.

BOILEAU, L.-A. *Le fer principal élément constructif de la nouvelle architecture*. Paris, 1871.

BUFFET, B., and EVRARD, R. *L'eau potable à travers les âges*. Liège, 1951.

DAVEY, Norman. *A History of Building Materials*. London, 1961.

DEFRANCE, E. *Histoire de l'éclairage des rues de Paris*. Paris, 1906.

FAIRBAIRN, W. *On the Application of Cast and Wrought Iron to Building Purposes*. London, 1854.

GIEDION, S. *Space, Time and Architecture*. 8th ed. Cambridge, 1949.

MARÉCHAL, Henri. *L'éclairage à Paris*. Paris, 1894.

MEEKS, Caroll L.-V. *The Railroad Stations*. New Haven, Conn., 1956.

MORIN, Arthur. *Manuel pratique du chauffage et de la ventilation*. Paris, 1868.

RONDELET, Jean-Baptiste. *Traité théorique et pratique de l'art de bâtir*. Paris, 1802-1805. Numerous revisions.

SKEMPTON, A. W. "The Origin of Iron Beams," in *Actes du VIIe Congrès International d'Histoire des Sciences*, 1956.

TREDGOLD, Thomas. *Principe de l'art de chauffer et d'aérer les édifices et les maisons d'habitation*. Paris, 1825.

VIOLLET-LE-DUC, Eugène-Emmanuel. *Entretiens sur l'architecture*. Paris, t. I, 1863; t. II, 1872.

PART SIX

THE EXTRACTION AND EXPLOITATION OF NATURAL RESOURCES

CHAPTER 1

THE EVOLUTION OF AGRICULTURAL TECHNIQUES

THE REVOLUTION IN CULTIVATION

T HE EIGHTEENTH CENTURY marks a turning point in the history of agriculture so significant that it is possible to speak of it as being a revolution. One of the best contemporary agronomists did not hesitate to write that this was the golden age of agriculture, at least if we are referring basically to the agriculture of Western Europe.

Increased population What gave agriculture this new impetus was above all the growth of population. France, which at the death of Louis XIV in 1715 had had barely 17 to 18 million inhabitants, began demographic growth that gave her 25 to 26 million inhabitants on the eve of the Revolution in 1789. England had fewer than 5.3 million inhabitants at the end of the seventeenth century, but approximately 9 million, less than a century later. This movement was general throughout Europe. A period of relative peace and the end of the civil wars were partly responsible for this increase in the number of mouths to be fed.

In a parallel development, cities were growing. The expansion of trade, which saw the opening of new markets in the West Indies, Africa, and North and even South America, was partly the cause. Advances in industry, which began this movement (of which England and France were the leaders) and which make up the Industrial Revolution, were undoubtedly another factor. Small cities and the larger towns as well as ports and big cities benefited from a prosperity that caused the populations of them all to increase.

This urban thrust, which was particularly apparent in the last seventy years of the eighteenth century, affected the agricultural population. Rural areas, which were more completely separated from cities than they had been until then, had to supply the urban masses, who now produced almost nothing or no longer enough to satisfy their daily needs. The countryside had to supply them with bread, wine, meat, fruit, and some of the vegetables that constituted their usual fare, which undoubtedly had improved, judging by the fact that the mortality rate was falling, a possible indication of a better diet.

These factors alone would not have been enough to bring about the profound revival of agriculture that could be observed almost everywhere. If it had remained tied to its past methods its inadequacies would inevitably have had repercussions on the demographic movement itself, which was what inspired the

474

pessimistic doctrines of Thomas Malthus in 1798. But agriculture developed new methods, beginning with new crops.

For food production there were two crops introduced from the Americas — corn and potatoes. Both had been introduced in Europe before the end of the sixteenth century but made slow progress, and even at the beginning of the seventeenth century they had not yet become important crops. It was perhaps enough for them to have crept into the old agricultural systems at all, not only to contribute to increasing the amount of food but also to introduce into the old systems possible substitutions whose formulas and potential would soon be realized. They were later joined by the sugar beet and leguminous fodder plants in meadows. The stage was now set to practice the new crop rotation, from which a revived agriculture could be expected.

The new enthusiasm for soil cultivation   At the same time a change of attitude was taking place, influenced by the movement of ideas begun in the seventeenth century by Francis Bacon, René Descartes, Pierre Bayle, Bernard Fontenelle, and others. In agriculture this new rationalism replaced the empiricism that had not questioned traditional methods. It was accompanied by a new taste for experimentation and direct observation of phenomena and was combined with a kind of fashion for science in general and the natural sciences in particular, of which agriculture could be considered a branch. As Voltaire wrote in the article on wheat in his *Dictionnaire philosophique*, "Around the year 1750 the nation, surfeited with verses, comedies, operas, novels . . . and philosophical disputes, finally began to argue about wheat."

In France, England, Italy, Switzerland, and Germany we witness an astonishing flowering of writing on agronomy. Whereas the sixteenth century, though rich in this literature, is said to have published only 26 works of this type, the eighteenth century saw more than 1,200. It is true, as Voltaire complacently remarked in his article, that "everyone read them except the farm workers." But "everyone" was the middle-class landowners, the ruined nobles forced to live off their land holdings, or that educated nobility that paid attention to its estates. It was these people who in France and England came to join agricultural societies in which a welter of new ideas acted to lead farming out of its old passivity.

A genuine elite existed then in rural areas, and insofar as it could set an example it would have been a powerful factor in progress, all the more so in that it was encouraged by certain theories. The Physiocrats who followed François Quesnay (1694–1774) urged that the land be considered as the sole source of wealth and declared that agriculture alone could multiply that wealth. Even if these maxims of Quesnay were not always followed they created an atmosphere favorable to innovation. Agronomists promoted such a program, all recommending methods that were to lead to the disappearance of fallow land. This meant abandoning the old crop-rotation patterns and using new combinations of the crops available, which required mass cooperation by farmers if the teachings of the agronomists were to succeed beyond a handful of exceptionally well-managed estates. The way had been silently paved for their rallying to a new agriculture, and a train of events did the rest. All these factors ultimately collaborated in this movement, which deserves to be called the agricultural revolution of the eighteenth and nineteenth centuries.

No theory can be imposed on the peasant world if it is not based on experience — successful experience, needless to say, carried out under real-life conditions in the countryside. Field workers are distrustful of everything they have not tried themselves. Technical advances are spread only by slow influences, starting with tested examples. This is not to say that all curiosity was dead in traditional rural areas. These areas respect tradition and know that they owe their security to it. No one feels the need to investigate adventurous novelties, but it would be wrong to believe that peasants are irrevocably resistant to all change. The kitchen garden is the place where, in a certain sense, they liberate themselves from the weight of common tradition, stereotyped practices, and routine field work. On these small plots they attempt year round to grow some vegetables that are less coarse than those that come from the fields, like carrots, cabbage, garlic, onions, leeks, herbs for soup and salad, and everything for day-to-day use in the home.

Olivier de Serres (1539–1619) devotes an entire book of his *Mesnage des Champs* to the subject of gardening, of which he speaks lovingly. In his garden at Le Pradel he had a vegetable garden, flower garden, herb garden, and orchard. It is easy to recognize the common practice in the orderly description of this gentleman-farmer, even if the sections of the garden are ordinarily less than precisely defined.

Even if a farmer gave less attention to the kitchen garden than did de Serres, without realizing it he received a lasting and seminal education from it. Here he applied skillful and sometimes discerning crop rotations long before he knew the principle; here he investigated methods to improve and fertilize the soil and saw that it could be transformed into artificial compost. Through the garden he also learned the virtue of that patient and precise work that the Flemish built into a kind of doctrine and that made possible the agricultural transformation already described.

But this is not all. Although we have little testimony about the management of kitchen gardens we do have much on formal gardens and are able to say that the former area has always been an experimental one. It was here that the use of new vegetables crept in, rare flowering plants and fruit trees were propagated, and new types of vines were grown. It was here, finally, that new plants were tried out that when introduced to the fields became the essential factors in the agricultural revolution.

Such is the case with the potato. In his garden de Serres planted the *cartoufles* that had come, he said, from Switzerland to the Dauphiné region in southeast France "a short time ago." The potato was received in Berry, too, where it was hesitantly tried. In 1786, at Saint-Benoît-du-Sault, the correspondent of the provincial assembly declared that "a few inquisitive people" were beginning to cultivate it in this fashion. The same was true around the time of 1759/60 at Boussac and Châteauroux, and in Brittany the Société d'Agriculture described similar experiments in its *Corps d'observations*.

Experiments of the same type occurred in England. In Shakespeare's time the potato was still a luxury food. At the beginning of the seventeenth century it was grown only in gardens, together with turnips and carrots. In 1664, at a time when the potato was still regarded as an exotic plant and it appeared only in the gardens of the rich, John Forster was calling upon farmers to cultivate it in fields.

As for corn, also native to America, where at the time of the discovery of the New World it was the basis of the indigenous agriculture in Andean countries and on the Central American plateaus, we do not know how the first experiments to cultivate it were made. We know only that it was introduced first into Spain and Portugal shortly after the voyages of Christopher Columbus. From there it slowly advanced to reach the northwest part of the Iberian peninsula, then the Basque country and Labour, where the first mention of it occurs at Bayonne in 1523. Corn also must have met much resistance. It was tried first in gardens or on very small plots on fallow land, at the same time, no doubt, as the string bean (*Phaseolus vulgaris*), which like it was a native of the Americas and was often grown with corn, the latter serving as a prop for the bean plants.

Plant rows in fields   The introduction of corn and potatoes into large-scale cultivation was encouraged by their suitability for human nourishment and by the relative ease with which the techniques of producing them were learned.

The cultivation of corn met different obstacles from those the potato met. The areas able to accept it were the same regions that had long been cultivating varieties of millet and sorghum, and corn was sometimes confused with these plants. The term *coarse millet* (in Basque, *artho mayro*) was sometimes used to designate corn. In Chalosse in Aquitaine it was called *milhoc*, from the name of the coarse-grained millet. The other French names for corn—*blé de Turquie* (Turkish wheat), *blé d'Espagne* (Spanish wheat), and so on—have no significance other than to indicate its exotic origin, but the use of the appellation *blé* (wheat, *Triticum*) perhaps shows that it was immediately classified among the cereals.

Nor was there any difficulty in introducing corn as food for humans. Its flour was used to make dishes like Italian *polenta*, Rumanian *mamaliga*, and the *millas*, or griddle cakes, of southwestern France. It was eaten in the form of bread, sometimes mixed with wheat or rye, or even used alone. Animals ate it as grain, as they did other cereals. The stalks were used as litter or even to fill the mattresses of the poor.

It was these advantages that led to corn's adoption wherever it found the damp, warm climate suited to it. It was introduced not only into southwestern France but also into parts of the plains along the Rhône and Saône (perhaps by way of the Franche-Comté region, when it belonged to Spain). It reached northern Italy, certain areas of the Balkan peninsula, and the plains of central Europe. In climates with insufficient rain it was grown as an irrigated crop.

The introduction of the potato into fields was more difficult. The technique of cultivating it was a subject for argument and the object of the most conflicting advice. In France the potato appears to be more or less established only by the end of the Revolution. The main difficulty clearly seems to have been its flavor. For a long time the cultivated varieties produced roots regarded in France and England as pigs' swill. For this reason poor countries were the first to adopt it. In the eighteenth century Ireland was saved from famine by its potato crops, and southern Germany was eating it by the seventeenth century. Some mountainous areas of France were growing potatoes as early as the end of the sixteenth century and into the seventeenth century, and a poor harvest there was regarded as almost a catastrophe. The plains areas hesitated longer to plant potatoes. The potato was accepted in France only in response to energetic propaganda by bishops, village clergy, and administrators. The spectacular experiments and writings of Antoine Parmentier (1737–1813) also helped, as did above all the scarcities during the Revolution and the recommendations of the Convention's Committee on Supplies. Cultivation improved the potato, as undoubtedly did empirical selection by peasants and the natural hybridization of one variety with another.

In any event, with corn and the potato two cultivable crops were available. Thanks to them the land was better cleaned of the weeds that spoiled the cereal crops so often that it was necessary to weed them by hand. The latters' yields inevitably increased, and wherever new crop rotations could include either corn or the potato the area of fallow land was diminished by half. As Arthur Young said upon his arrival in southwestern France in 1787 via the province of Quercy, "Quercy is nowhere near as beautiful as the Limousin, but in compensation it is much better cultivated. Let thanks for this be given to corn, which works wonders!" Later, after visiting part of Aquitaine, which was already partly won over to corn, he added, "The corn frontier marks the demarcation line between the good rural economy of the south and the bad rural economy of the northern part of the realm." It is understood that the "good" economy was the one yielding a grain harvest each year, the "bad" being the one that still continued the practice of fallowing. The same thought inspired an agronomist in the Department of Jura 140 years later to say, "The introduction of corn caused a revolution in the agriculture . . . of the inhabitants of the Jura."

The turnip revolution; the sugar beet   Equally far reaching was the turnip "revolution" in England. We have seen that agronomists and large landowners were inspired by the Flemish example. But neither Barnaby Googe in his *Foure Bookes of Husbandrie* (1577) nor Sir Richard Weston (1591–1652), who recommended cultivating turnips in fields and combining them with clover and artificial fodders, had had the slightest success. Not until long after their deaths were they regarded as innovators, and only then was Arthur Young able to say that Weston had been a greater benefactor than Newton.

Resistance by tenant farmers was widespread, partly because the publicity favoring turnips had not always been very skillful. The sometimes ridiculous exaggerations of "desk farmers" like Adolphus Speed in *Adam Out of Eden* (1659) could well have made them suspect in the eyes of better farmers. But in particular the ignorance of many people and the rigidity of the open-field system made it impossible to spread the use of turnips by popular example. Moreover, turnips did not have the prestige that corn and the potato were capable of, and their spread did not bring about an increase in the human food supply—they could encourage only a change in cattle-raising practices. These depended on stubble fields, heaths, and commons, which provided all the resources needed, at least in the eyes of the inhabitants, who sought more to protect this common domain than to change old practices and adapt themselves to new techniques.

This explains why at the end of the seventeenth century progress was not yet very evident. In his *Systema Agriculturae* (1669) John Worlidge was still urging farmers to cultivate new crops. Evidence collected by a Lord Ernle about this period of England's agricultural history shows that Norfolk and Sussex were almost alone in adopting large-scale cultivation of turnips to feed their sheep.

Michael Houghton was apparently the first to cultivate two acres of turnips, around 1700 in Hawsted Parish. By about 1722 Norfolk, perhaps because of its light soil, had extended its turnip fields considerably, and Defoe in his *Tour Thro' the Whole Island of Great Britain* noted that sheep were being fed on them "like horned beasts." Lord Charles Townshend (1674–1738), nicknamed "Turnip," contributed to their proliferation in the same district, as did the Count of Rothes of Aberdeen County, Scotland, whose turnip crops "were an object of wonderment for the neighborhood."

At the same time the technique of cultivating row plants was being perfected. Jethro Tull (1674–1741), who had been impressed by methods used in France for grapevines, recommended sowing in rows and hoeing frequently the surfaces of fields (cultivating, as we would call it today); for turnips "his method was admirable." This did not prevent it from being neglected in England until, it is claimed, it had become successful in Scotland.

A short time later another plant, the sugar beet, underwent this transformation in cultivation methods. It was developed from the mangel-wurzel, or beetroot *(Beta vulgaris)*, that was already widely grown for fodder in crops rotated in eighteenth-century Germany. Its root was sometimes used for human food, and agricultural societies propagated it in England as being likely to furnish an additional source; it was known there as the "root of scarcity." But its real success came from the discovery of its sugar content by the German chemist Andreas Marggraaf in 1747 and the works of his pupil Franz Karl Achard (1753–1821) in 1796. The beet as a sugar plant was introduced into France in 1786 by Vilmorin and into England by Parkins. Its cultivation was greatly encouraged by the Continental blockade, which prevented the arrival of American cane sugar. The first sugar mill was built in Silesia, the first refinery in France; such factories multiplied in the nineteenth century.

Once it had become part of the cycle of European crops, the sugar beet spread rapidly, especially in the alluvial lands from the Paris basin to the Ukraine by way of the flat, fertile areas of Germany. It requires good preparation of the ground, abundant manure, and a great deal of care: thinning out in mid-spring, after the young plants have broken through, and a series of second dressings. Once the crop has been harvested it leaves a loosened soil free of weeds. In the area best suited to it, it becomes a splendid crop in rotation with wheat.

Through corn, potatoes, and sugar beets, the advantages of cultivated (that is, plowed) fallow land became associated with vegetable cultivation when it added its crop to those usually grown on the same lands. This was undoubtedly a change in agricultural production and in some of its techniques. Cereal crops unquestionably benefited by it, and all the foundations of the old agricultural systems were shaken.

Improvement of grasslands   However important this success of vegetables, it in fact represented only a partial improvement of the agricultural systems then used. The agronomists who had long been recommending the improvement of grasslands realized this. The English were thinking of clover, the French and others of clover but also of sainfoin and alfalfa. Only then would farmers be in a position to change the rotated crops, make them richer, more varied, and more capable of adapting to the geographic conditions of each region.

Independent of obstacles created by those opposed to all innovation, the movement in favor of improving grasslands clashed with the idea that agriculture was above all supposed to feed human beings. There was a kind of obsession in the minds of all those who tilled the soil: their daily bread. Did people still remember the appalling famines that had so often sown death during the Middle Ages and whose hideous specter they had seen again during the wars of the sixteenth and seventeenth centuries and after the winter of 1709? In any event, the peasants were suspicious of grassland improvement, and propaganda could not easily persuade them; only example could change them.

This example came from the great landowners, whether they were nobility or middle class; that is, from those who expected their estates to do more than satisfy their families' needs. To create, maintain, and harvest a grassland and to own livestock commensurate with its available fodder thus required investment that the majority of farmers, even if they were owners, could not easily contemplate. They would also have had to accustom themselves to the idea of eliminating the fallow lands used as poor pastures, that is, to accept the transformation of the old rural communities. At worst, beets or potatoes could be grown in a corner of the fallow land, somewhat as in a garden. Wherever it existed, the improved meadow, which was intended to last for several years and which required mowing two or three times a year, could be reconciled only with a total change in the communal system. It is understandable that at first the new grasslands could be tried out only on the large, independent estates, since they were in a certain sense a prerogative of the landowning aristocracy. This is the idea expressed by the farmers to whom Jethro Tull talked: "Let the gentlemen grow clover if they like. We've got to first take care of paying our rent."

Thus, it was the large landowners who established the first improved meadows. The list of those in France who encouraged "good agriculture" (in the words of Arthur Young) and especially wider use of leguminous fodder plants is a long one. Young mentions Auguste Broussonet (1761–1807), secretary-general of the Société Royale d'Agriculture), Chrétien de Malesherbes (1721–1794), de Guerchy, Le Blanc, de Turbilly, de Lazowski, de Faujas de Saint-Fond, François, duke de La Rochefoucauld-Liancourt (1747–1827), and Mme. de Pont; many others should be added. Some were in positions of power, as for example Armand-Joseph de Béthune-Charrost, a peer of France and the king's lieutenant-general for the provinces of Picardy and Boulonnais, of whom Louis XV said that "he has little presence, but he is single-handedly reviving three of my provinces" (the third no doubt being Berry, where the duke had, among other agricultural advances, improved the meadows). There were less aristocratic people—for instance, François-Joseph de Becquay, treasurer of France in the finance office at Bordeaux, who in 1761 introduced crimson clover on his holdings in the Tarn-et-Garonne area, and de Villèle, the father of Louis XVIII's minister Jean-Baptiste (1773–1854), a landowner in the Lauragais region of Languedoc who promoted new crops. There were people who were almost unknown—for example, Delay d'Agier, a wealthy man highly regarded in his little town of Bourg-de-Péage in the Dauphiné, who was daring enough to sow alfalfa on the stony ground of the plains in the Valence area, the success of which was soon copied. Finally, there were men who were often neither landowners nor aristocrats but were in a good position to assist agriculture, such as postmasters in Picardy who encouraged improving the meadows in order to obtain feed for their horses more easily. They all recommended the new fodders, not always successfully and in some cases not without risk, as for instance the marquis de Marbeuf, who under the Revolutionary government was condemned to death for having laid down pasture at a time when the scarcity of grain was causing concern to authorities.

In England the trend was equally strong in favor of clover and other "artificial" fodders. The agronomic value of rotating cereals with row plants and leguminous fodder had been known since the beginning of the seventeenth century. The practice in the Netherlands had been observed and farmers realized that an agriculture based on this combination of crops made it possible not only to have more animals and thus more manure but also (though they could not completely explain why) an increased output of grain. Nevertheless, the use of clover did not become general for nearly two centuries. At the end of the eighteenth century, when Hertford, Suffolk, and Essex farmers had been completely won over to intensive cultivation with turnips and clover, those in Westmoreland were still very hesitant, especially in regard to pastures.

Good farmers and men as important as Sir Richard Weston not only harvested clover but also taught the techniques needed to grow it successfully. Weston demonstrated that properly preparing a moor by cutting down the stubble with a sickle and by good plowing and liming could win it over for clover, and "this crop could be left in place for five years."

In France this propaganda was supplemented by the support of administrators and their aides and by the example of the Sociétés d'Agriculture, as evidenced by an experiment by d'Etigny, the administrator of the Auch district from 1761 to 1767. The Gascony country in southwest France was not favorable to pasturelands, not so much because of any conservation on the part of the peasants (of which one of the administrator's associates complained in a 1763 memorandum) as because of the summer drought to which the country is usually subjected. However, results were obtained: next to the rape turnips (*Brassica napus*) and the traditional turnips (the so-called Navarre turnip recommended by d'Etigny), experiments were made, often successfully, to establish meadows of sainfoin, alfalfa, and especially clover. Another example is that the Estates of Languedoc, starting in 1756, campaigned intensely in favor of alfalfa, sainfoin, and clover, based on excellent results obtained in various places, notably around Carcassonne. The same efforts were made in sections where because of the extent of the moors and the propensity of the countryside to produce grass the fodder crops seemed to be establishing themselves less successfully. An example was Brittany, where the Société d'Agriculture made an effort to have clover adopted, in default of alfalfa. This was less successful because clover requires "preparation of the land, or attention during the first and often the second year of which the ordinary farmers will become capable, it is claimed, only by degrees."

Thus, the battle had not yet been won. The expansion of improved pastures clashed with custom and the major concern, grain production, but experiments increased, the best sowing techniques were investigated, and it was repeated everywhere that the expansion of fodder crops was the necessary condition for agricultural progress. "Without meadows," claimed the Société d'Agriculture of Brittany, "[there is] no pasturage, and consequently no livestock. Everything decays as livestock decreases, and everything is revived by its increase." This became a general cry that was ultimately heard. The attention that had to be given to animals and breeding techniques was thus at the heart of the problems raised by what Arthur Young calls good agriculture and that others called the new agriculture.

Cattle-breeding techniques   It is perhaps no exaggeration to say that most animals, which were associated with agriculture as a necessary evil, were in this period underfed. Many of them had to be satisfied to pasture on vacant lands and commons, on moors, and sometimes almost exclusively along roadsides. It is understandable that peasants fiercely defended such rights of pasturage as they had been able to win in the forest and that in the open-field areas they struggled hard against enclosures.

The most difficult time to provide food for animals was winter, when they had to remain in stables. The supply of hay and fodder was rarely sufficient to keep them in good condition throughout the winter. Cases are mentioned in which scrawny, anemic animals had to be carried out of their stables during the first warm spring days. They voraciously consumed young grass, causing troubles from which the stock died. They also died from all the illnesses for which no cure was yet known: flukeworms, sheep pox, hoof-and-mouth disease, tuberculosis. From time to time epizootic diseases ravaged entire countries, causing losses that the poor could just barely overcome from one generation to the next. The epidemic of 1774–1776 was so serious, from Navarre to Armagnac and in Lomagne, that Administrator Journet, who was charged with neglect, was severely censured and slit his throat in despair. The only measure against livestock epidemics was to prevent the movement of animals.

It is understandable that livestock was generally mediocre of conformation and of low yield. In England at the beginning of the sixteenth century the dead weight of sheep slaughtered for meat probably did not exceed 28 pounds and that of steers 320 pounds. Around Limoges (where, however, good bovine stock was being formed) Arthur Young found that the average weight of steers was no more than 60 to 70 stone or about 520 pounds. (Nowadays, calves sold at the age of 10 months often weigh between 550 and 650 pounds.) In the southern Alps an adult sheep weighed some 65 pounds, which today is the weight of four-to-five-month-old lambs.

This relatively puny livestock was degenerate. To be sure, every region could boast of having its own breeds, but how could they be defined, when each animal was the result of a chance union of Son of Nobody with Daughter of Everybody? While waiting for the day when it would be possible to increase the number of animals, the first task, or at least the first one undertaken, was to improve the animals physically.

The simplest way to do this was to introduce animals of better stock than the local specimens. Flanders began purchasing Dutch cows, Poitou supplied Brittany with good oxen, and Provence received part of its best sheep from Auvergne, which also sent steers and cows. These practices were not devoid of possibilities for degenerating the breeds. In the absence of knowledge about the principles of crossbreeding, these practices could result only in increased breeding chaos.

An attempt by Jean-Baptiste Colbert to introduce Spanish merinos into France appears to have been a more controlled operation. The flock of the royal sheepfold at Rambouillet was theoretically intended to supply thoroughbred animals. The hope was that a breed of sheep with fine wool would thus be created to meet the needs of the wool industry, which was Colbert's main concern. The experiment was not without failures, and attempts of the same type that were encouraged by the administrators had even more mixed results. Caze de la Bove, the administrator of the Dauphiné, had a small flock brought from Segovia in 1788 and entrusted it to the religious order at Aiguebelle, where its existence was soon in jeopardy. D'Etigny in Auch had a splendid flock purchased, which reached the port in 1763, but the result was a failure, although he was able to offer some rams to the Société Royale d'Agriculture, which distributed them in Normandy, Touraine, Berry, and the Île-de-France. One of d'Etigny's successors, Fournier of La Chapelle, repeated the attempt in 1785/86, this time including hundreds of merino rams in the flock. The same idea was behind the importation of horses into France during the Regency (1715–1723) and into England during the seventeenth century, where an extraordinary mixture of breeds was the principal result. And Colbert's regulations for stud farms made it possible to supply breeders with strong stallions.

Horse breeding in France remained confined to the regions where it was traditionally practiced: Limousin and Navarre, the Boulonnais, Franche-Compté, and especially Lower Normandy, which received colts from the Pays de Caux, Perche, Maine, and sometimes Brittany. They were intended for the saddle, the carriage, and the cart, and were used for plowing only in regions with large or average-sized cereal crops, especially in the north and in the Paris area. The poor regions—Ardennes, Brenne in Berry, the Landes Department, La Camargue—bred small horses that were not held in very high regard. Poitou remained the country of donkeys and mules, and to a lesser degree breeders on the Atlantic coast of southern France and in the Pyrenees devoted some of their brood mares to this purpose. Not until the beginning of the nineteenth century did this production acquire some importance, especially after several Spanish purchases.

A new path had been blazed for improving livestock breeds, and the British took the initiative. Robert Bakewell (1725–1795) deserves the major credit for systematizing the selection process by which animals for the slaughterhouse were bred to combine "beauty with utility of form, quality of meat and ease of nourishment." His principal success was the Leicestershire longhorn known as the Dishley from the name of the farm. Although Bakewell carefully concealed the secret of his methods, John Ellman (1753–1832) of Glynde improved Southdown sheep in the same manner and similar results were obtained for Lincolns and Cheviots. Bakewell also improved horses and obtained short, strong animals that were energetic and better suited for pulling than were earlier ones.

Cattle were the next to receive attention. Longhorns, already improved by 1720 by Sir Thomas Gresley at his Drakelow estate near Burton upon Trent and then by a Webster of Cauley near Coventry, were superseded by shorthorn Durhams and then by Kettons named for the farm of the Colling brothers, Charles (1751–1836) and Robert (1749–1820). Other breeds—Herefords and North Devons—took their place among the quality animals. The large landowners competed with each other, and the founding of the Smithfield Club in 1798 ensured continuity for these fruitful efforts. The nineteenth century had only to continue the work of these selectors and ensure their success by defending the purity of their new breeds.

Interesting though these advances in cattle breeding were, they continued to be the work of experiment and intuition, not being based on genuine scientific knowledge. Bakewell defined his own goal as "to obtain animals that are heavy in the best portions and that repay most quickly the cost of the food eaten." He was not a specialist in breeding; scientific animal breeding appeared only in the nineteenth century.

Efforts to improve livestock breeds nevertheless acquired new significance insofar as they were combined with advances in agriculture. Better animals became available for draft, slaughter, milk, and wool only by feeding them better and breeding them for special purposes. Moreover, their number would have to be increased. All the supporters of the new agriculture insisted on this proportional relationship between livestock and the area under cultivation, but the growth of herds not only required time and money but also called for more abundant harvests. Thus, the problem involved a vicious circle all the more difficult to break because it was first necessary to feed human beings, who were more numerous almost everywhere. Even concerning poultry, René-Antoine Réaumur (1683–1757), the inventor of the "chicken oven" (1749), the ancestor of our artificial incubators, had to contend with the argument that an abundance of barnyard fowl would be detrimental to the grain supply.

Clearing land and improving soil
Livestock breeding thus found itself confronted with an obstacle that poor peasants in particular were unable to overcome. It was from the earth alone that they could secure their basic resources, from the earth that, in the words of François Quesnay, "advances all the expenses of cultivation." Thus they were obliged to find new arable land.

Every period of demographic growth has been associated with the clearing of new land, and the eighteenth century did not escape the necessity of this clearing. But no innovations occurred then in this regard. The technique of preparing uncultivated land was based on *le fer et le feu,* iron and fire, or what in France is generally called *écobuer* and *essarter,* burning and grubbing.

The clearing of land was to be seen everywhere in Europe. In his *L'homme et la forêt* P. Deffontaines has given an evocative picture. The empress Maria-Theresa settled German colonists in the Carpathians. Frederick the Great, preferring, as he said, "men to trees," extended the cultivated area at the expense of the German forest, notably in Brandenburg. In Poznán, Poland, cleared and drained lands were spreading, and farms bore the name *Olendry* as a reminder that Dutch methods were sometimes applied there by colonists from Holland. In Denmark, royal decrees in 1723 and 1751 unsuccessfully invited the population to cultivate the great heath of Jutland, and in 1760 this difficult task had to be entrusted to

German colonists. In Polesie (now the U.S.S.R.), in Finland, in the Black Forest, or in the Ardennes plateau—even in the Alps, Savoy, and the Dauphiné—grubbing was an old tradition that was to last almost into modern times. In 1724 it was described in the Isère, where the burned and plowed areas were very profitable but no longer produced crops after two or three years, "so that the peasants abandon the land and go to make a new burning elsewhere." In places in the Ardennes, at the end of the summer heavy fogs called Rocroi fogs appeared. From the burned areas, tilled with *cherbottage*, a light plowing, two or three crops of rye were harvested, after which the land was left to resume its covering of broom that was gradually replaced by trees. Then the cycle was repeated.

Cleared lands seemed so necessary in France that the royal government encouraged them by a 1761 decree of the Council exempting the lands thus put into cultivation from the *taille*, the *vingtième*, and other taxes. Several Sociétés d'Agriculture expressed the wish that the newly cleared lands be exempted from tithes and manorial rights. In 1766 the king abolished the tithe for fifteen years, to their benefit, and several royal proclamations made the decrees' provisions still more favorable. We have no overall picture of what land was claimed or reclaimed, but some evidence is available to estimate the clearing of uncultivated lands in Brittany, Guienne (Aquitaine), and the marshy tracts of the Nivernais. One's impression, however, is that this effort was not as fruitful as had perhaps been hoped. Discussing the Pyrenees in the Ariège region, Michel Chevalier correctly remarked that many grubbings were only temporary and most of them were repetitions of earlier land clearings that farmers hastened to register in order to benefit from the fiscal advantages occurring from clearing new lands. It is true, though, that when de Froidour carried out the major investigation for reforming the Pyrenees forests in 1670–1675, he noted numerous encroachments on the forest demesne. At the beginning of the nineteenth century one Dralet also drew a distressing picture. The truth is that deforestation had been going on, with high and low points, since the first settlement. Although deforestation was intensified in the eighteenth century and especially during the French Revolution, it is difficult to say in what exact proportion.

In any event, it is certain that this attempt at land clearing indicates a lack of new lands to cultivate and is a sign that farmers were not yet able to give the soil enough productive power. At this point we must note that nowhere in Europe had cultivated lands been ruined, not even in the most heavily and earliest populated areas. Nothing happened here to resemble what was later seen in the United States. Centuries ago the European peasant ceased to be a wandering farmer who abandoned his land the moment its yield seriously decreased. By fallowing and hard work the earth's natural fertility had been protected as much as possible. Certainly the price paid had been continual privation and constant frugality in feeding men and animals, and occasional periods of scarcity, famines, and death. With the eighteenth century came perhaps the moment when the miracle of land exploited yet retaining its productivity for more than two millennia was to be exhausted. This was almost universally felt, especially by the large landowners desirous of maintaining or increasing their income.

Many experiments were made to improve and fertilize the land. A first priority was to drain excessively damp low-lying areas where meadows were covered with coarse grasses or reeds, livestock contracted diseases, and cultivation was practically impossible.

Most of the time farmers were satisfied with ditches, but very often the water flowed poorly, and where the land was worked on the open-field system the negligence of a single person was enough to ruin the work of his neighbors. Under ideal conditions trenches were dug and filled with stones and gravel, sometimes with branches mixed with straw. In Essex this type of drainage was sufficiently widespread that it was held up as an example to the other English counties. In fact, only in the nineteenth century did water drainage as an art become applied to cleansing heavy soils or making them productive. An exception, naturally, was when it was a question of reclaiming swamplands, like those operations we have described, or like the act approved by the English Parliament at the end of the eighteenth century concerning the drainage of 20,000 acres of the king's Sedgemoor in Somersetshire.

During the eighteenth century attention was given to land improvement and manures, suggesting that these were, in fact, innovations. But in reality it was the simple desire to obtain more harvests and better yields that guided experimenters, not a real knowledge of soils and their needs. Here and there farmers revived marling, the ancient practice of spreading calcareous deposits, and they began to practice liming, and spread gypsum over meadows. Numerous experiments in England, France, and elsewhere in Europe are mentioned. Arthur Young states that liming alone made it possible to transform 400,000 acres in England into gardens. He found this practice in many areas in France, supplemented by spreading pulverized seashells as well as silt and seaweed in Brittany, near the coast.

Soot, bones, and a variety of composts were also tried, but farmers remained faithful to farm manure. It was reserved for cereal crops, but there was not enough of it, and the ingenuity of the peasants, who rotted leaves, straw, ferns, and furze in their farmyards, could not make good the shortage. The manure was poor stuff, often a dry straw lacking fertilizing ingredients that was spread over fields. Enclosing sheep when this was possible, using pigeon droppings, purchasing or collecting ordure in cities, spreading kitchen cinders, and lastly weed burning were attempts to supplement the supply of manures collected on farms.

All these practices arose only from tradition or in some cases from a more or less fortunate intuition. They could not be changed and the problem of caring for and fertilizing soil was dealt with sensibly (if not immediately solved) until discoveries in chemistry and biology could be applied.

THE NEW AGRICULTURE

The end of the eighteenth century and beginning of the nineteenth opened a new period in the history of agricultural techniques. Throughout Western Europe an effort was being made to give the methods a scientific basis; a genuine agronomy was tending to replace "agromania." The advances achieved originated in practice, though, more than in theory—even today, "science has by no means solved all the problems raised by the exploitation of the soil" (A. Demolon). What triumphed, then, was nothing more nor less than the agricultural revolution as we have seen it taking shape since the end of the sixteenth century.

Theory and practice:
the struggle against
fallowing

The goal of how to transform agriculture had been set unequivocally: basically it was necessary that cereal production, which was still discontinuous in time and space, be made continuous without a rest period for the land. In other words, the struggle to remove what Duhamel du Monceau called "the disgrace of the fallow lands" had begun.

Agronomists all agreed about the necessity of this change. The writings of Arthur Young in England, Albrecht Thaer (1752–1828) in Germany (including his *Möglinische Annalen der Landwirtschaft*, 1807–1814, continued by Körte), Schwerz and Charles Pictet de Rochemont (1755–1824) in Switzerland, Yvart and Morel de Vindé in France, as well as the experiments of Mathieu de Dombasle (1777–1843) at Roville near Nancy and the propaganda and studies of the Société d'Agriculture of Paris (reorganized in 1803/4 and continuing the work of the *Feuille du cultivateur*) all had the same goal: to promote agricultural methods by which production would give higher yields.

At the same time, fundamental discoveries were opening ways to regenerate agriculture down to its foundations by knowledge of soils, the atmosphere, and biology and botany. Antoine Lavoisier's theories and those of Henry Cavendish, Karl W. Scheele, and Joseph Priestley paved the way for the teachings of Sir Humphrey Davy in Great Britain, Jean Chaptal, Jean-Baptiste Boussingault, and J.-B. Dumas in France, and Justus Liebig in Germany. The discoveries of Charles Naudin (1815–1899) in France in 1864/65 and of Gregor Mendel (1822–1884) in Czechoslovakia in 1864 came much later to throw scientific light on practices of plant selection and hybridization. Nevertheless, research like that of Louis de Vilmorin and his imitators brilliantly paved the way for improving plants under cultivation and introducing new varieties. Regarding equipment, farmers were no longer alone in seeking the most sensible forms for tools; mathematics and the machine industry began to become involved in the search for tools capable of intelligently easing the task of cultivators. In short, many ideas and much research were applied to convert agriculture into a science. (We can judge this merely by leafing through the admirable five-volume *Cours d'agriculture* by the Count de Gasparin, the Librairie de la Maison Rustique, 1843–1849.)

But this great effort did not truly bear fruit until the second half of the nineteenth century, when it could be rediscovered, expanded, and popularized, as part of the practices of cultivators. For the moment, agriculturists stuck to experimentation. In 1819 Mathieu de Dombasle founded a school of agriculture at his Roville farm, where his only ambition was to educate farmers who would be free of the deplorable habit of "wanting to solve all questions a priori." Boussingault himself, at his Pechelbronn estate in Alsace, fleshed out his theories with experiments he carried out after 1834. In 1843 Sir John Bennet Lawes (1814–1900), a pupil of Charles G. B. Daubeny (1795–1867) at Oxford, founded (with the collaboration of Davies Gilbert) an experimental station at Rothamsted, Harpenden, in West Hertford, from which significant work later came.

Thus, it was still experience more than science that convinced and converted the best-educated and richest farmers. There were, for example, Bujault, a farmer in Poitou, great English landowners like Thomas W. Coke (1752–1842) of Norfolk, and many others. Their major preoccupations were improving methods and techniques, introducing new crops, popularizing new crop rotations, and, in the words of Arthur Young, liberating themselves from the "abominable yoke" of the fallowing system.

This system did not, however, lack defenders, and its continued existence in many places was not without justification. This was the case where because the climate delayed the ripening of harvests there was no time afterward for new seeding, as in the mountains. In such cases there was forced fallowing. In certain countries where large amounts of land were available, the continued use of fallowing avoided the necessity of making enormous expenditures for fertilizers. Farmers were satisfied with lower yields, so they did not have to invest heavily. This was the practice in certain newly opened lands given over to cereal grain production, as in the American wheat belt, which opened up around 1820 after this principle was applied to extensive agriculture. Although the area is now seeking higher yields and more crop variation, biennial fallowing was for a long time the basis for developing the large landholdings in the prairies of the United States and Canada. In this case fallowing is economic in nature. The same custom is observed in the Argentine pampa and in the dry plains behind Australia's eastern coastal mountains or in Swanland, in the Southwest.

On the other hand, many indigenous producers of cereals in North Africa practice traditional fallowing to this day. They continue to sow their seed after rainfall on lands that have merely been scraped by a few scratches with a swing plow. Often, too, they plow a fallow field; the soil thus loosened is able to hold more moisture than hard, unplowed ground. The same practices are found in the Near East, at least where no irrigation water is available, and they are still frequently observed in southern Italy and Spain, where this routine is justified, as in North Africa and the Far East, by the usual dryness of the climate.

In temperate and notably Western Europe the custom of fallowing had less reason for continued use, but it still kept much of its influence, despite the efforts of those who had shown the possibility of abolishing it. But, as already observed, nothing could be effectively achieved without first changing the agrarian structure. In particular, wherever the open-field system and its requirements survived, there was a need to free the land and those who cultivated it from the heavy oppression of custom. And where crop rotation was not regulated, it was necessary to eliminate the commons and the practice of pasturing on fallow lands. In other words, the technical advances that completed the agrarian revolution in line with principles set forth long before were achieved only through another revolution that was political and social in nature and brought about the triumph of agrarian individualism.

The enclosure movement in England; technical achievements

The struggle for freedom from open-field cultivation was the most tenacious and most lively in England, as seen in numerous acts of Parliament from the sixteenth to the nineteenth centuries. The first significant stage came in an 1801 act intended specifically to simplify the procedures leading to enclosure. Applicable especially to commons, it was complemented by an 1836 act aimed especially at arable open fields and an 1845 act setting up local commissioners of enclosure to replace the parliamentary commissioners.

It is common knowledge that this liberation of lands tilled under restrictions had such important social consequences as to be called sometimes the enclosure revolution. The movement has been accused of decreasing the number of small landholders to the benefit of rich ones and of merchants anxious to invest. More precisely, the elimination of open fields and breaking up of common lands often made the picturesque but uneconomical tangle of small plots disappear. Some owners consented to an amicable redistribution, but in most cases isolated holdings were bought up from poor people for whom the common pastureland was a necessity and who could no longer exist after its disappearance. Since the agrarian revolution coincided with a tremendous growth of industry and a corresponding disappearance of many small crafts, the result was heavy migration from country to city, all of which favored the formation of large estates. These were at the same time sustained by rising prices while small, less favored farmers had to submit to increased taxes and the burden of mortgages if they wished to round out their holdings. In short, the enclosure revolution was cruel to the poor. The period from 1813 to 1835 was a time in which the number of yeomen and copyholders, who had been more favored by the old system than the new, rapidly declined.

On the other hand, agricultural techniques progressed handsomely under enclosure. Efforts were made everywhere to produce more wheat, meat, milk, and eggs. Moreover, circumstances made it imperative to increase yields. The population of England and Wales at the end of the seventeenth century—5.5 million— gradually rose to more than 8.8 million by 1801, reached 10.15 million by 1811, and continued to rise. At the same time, cities witnessed the massing of people being attracted by industry, whom the countryside had to feed.

In this context it was generally accepted that the country should be self-sufficient as far as possible. After 1670 grain laws forbade or regulated export. Grain prices benefited from a sliding scale that was constantly reviewed, and subsidies were distributed to stimulate grain production. This policy enabled England to survive, by one means or another, the years of poor crops from bad weather, namely 1765–1767, 1770–1774, and 1782–1784, not to mention the catastrophic winters of 1708/9, 1739/40, and 1795/96.

External circumstances also favored the progress of the new techniques. Enclosures generally decreased the wheat areas, to the benefit of meadows for cattle grazing. The price increases during the Napoleonic wars and especially during the Continental blockade slowed the movement and led to a search for higher yields by better plowing and applying more fertilizers. The crisis thus served agricultural progress, and England came out of it with greatly improved techniques.

In addition, these techniques had been undergoing constant improvement, especially on the large estates and to a certain extent elsewhere. Enthusiasm for agriculture was still the fashion for the nobility. Younger sons became passionately interested in the art, and even George III himself boasted of his nickname, Farmer George. Certainly by the end of the eighteenth century a new spirit was infusing the efforts of those whom Arthur Young had converted. Agricultural societies were proliferating. Most counties had one and sometimes also an experimental farm. Publications were appearing, some to meet an early death, though others prospered for a long time, as for example the *Farmer's Magazine*. The first issue of this dates from 1800, shortly before the beginning in 1803 of the first six courses in agricultural chemistry given by Sir Humphrey Davy, who had recently been made assistant professor of chemistry at the Royal Institution of Great Britain. Agriculture was thus taking on a scientific hue, and experiments undertaken by societies or well-educated landowners were carried out with a desire for scientific precision.

The large estates were in fact in the forefront of technical progress and served as examples for smaller farmers. Such an example is Coke in Norfolk, who had taken over his lands at Holkham in 1776 and until his death in 1842 was constantly trying fruitful experiments. Through liming he transformed sandy soils that were barely able to produce rye, heavily dressing them with manure and even crushed bones. He thus obtained splendid harvests of wheat and, with beets, rutabagas, clover, and sainfoin supplied a model for those crop rotations that provided abundant harvests without exhausting the soil. At the same time he was able to triple his livestock and, continuing the work of Bakewell, set out to improve their quality. Seeking sheep and cattle best adapted to the Norfolk climate he taught his tenant farmers to feed their animals better by making use of botanical information to create meadows, supplementing their fodder as needed with oil cake, and following the practice of bringing them in for the winter.

Cultivation systems and grazing methods were not the only experimental areas to discover new directions. Coke and other landowners substituted sowing in rows for broadcast sowing of wheat, turnips, mangel-wurzel, and sainfoin. Coke showed that using a seed drill saved seed, increased the crop, and facilitated the work, especially weeding.

Their examples were not in vain. To be sure, there was a great deal of resistance—neighboring farmers regarded innovations by Coke, seen as a young man disobeying the sayings and proverbs of their ancestors, with hostile curiosity. There was much argument about his changes. The potatoes he planted continued to have alleged serious defects. The best said of them was that perhaps they weren't poisoning the pigs. Wheat cultivation as Coke practiced it appeared suspect—it is said that nine years passed before he found someone to copy his techniques. But the prejudice died down and the younger generation gradually dropped the old techniques. In 1809 Arthur Young could write, in a report on the county of Oxford, that they were then in a period of great changes, even if the "civilized enclosures" were still closely fenced in by the "Goths and Vandals."

Adoption of crop rotation in France and Central Europe

France did not undergo such revolutionary changes; advances in individual freedoms and freedom of cultivation occurred erratically, for reasons analyzed by Kareiev, Henri Sée (1864–1936), and Marc Bloch (1886–1944). The enclosure struggle had proved abortive almost everywhere, although it had had the support of Bertin the elder (1766–1841), Daniel Trudaine (1703–1769), the marquis d'Ormesson, and sometimes of the provincial assemblies. Various measures were taken by certain provinces such as Hainaut, Flanders (to protect meadows), and Languedoc (to free vineyards and olive and chestnut groves from community grazing). Elsewhere almost nothing had been possible in the face of resistance by the small farmers whose livestock, though limited in numbers, needed to use fallow lands and have pasture rights.

The Revolutionary government attempted to open debate on the subject. In September/October 1791 the Constituent Assembly proclaimed the right of enclosure, which the Convention confirmed in Article XVII of the Declaration of Rights in 1793. Pasturing rights on fallow land could now be exercised only where they were based on a special claim, immemorial custom, or where authorized by law. The same measures, repeated in the rural code of 1808, reveal a hesitancy later overcome only by experience.

As for commons, another obstacle to the extension of cultivation, we know what happened: the poor were hostile to land distribution, wanting to preserve their common pastureland, and rich landowners accepted it only when carried out in proportion to their holdings. Efforts to eliminate commons had poor results and old practices lingered on.

In the same spirit, a law dated June 5, 1791, established the rights of landowners to choose their crops and use the equipment they preferred, as already requested in 1771 by Abbot Roubaud in the *Journal d'agriculture*. They profited by the law only to the extent that progress prompted them. Wars, requisitions, depreciation of the currency, and a shortage of labor often frustrated the best intentions.

Perhaps the sale of national lands had more favorable results. The smallholder probably profited by it to round off his holding, and the large holding often became still larger. But is it true, as Claude-Henri Saint-Simon claimed in 1824, that new owners proved more capable than the old? It is difficult to say, but in any event progress was hindered by the ignorance of some, the poverty of others, and the disinclination of all to take risks. This is seen indirectly from the efforts made at the beginning of the century to publicize better methods. *Théâtre d'agriculture* was republished in 1804 by Abbot Gregory and François de Neufchâteau. Between 1801 and 1827 the latter wrote many books and articles urging farmers to get instruction and officials to undertake to organize agricultural education, as had already been done in Venice and in Austria, Bavaria, and Saxony. In the same period Jean Chaptal (1756–1832) was attempting to popularize his 1803 work *La Chimie appliquée à l'agriculture (The Application of Chemistry to Agriculture)*, just as he had made an effort in 1811 to lead viticulture and in 1801 the art of winemaking out of their empiricism. But a long road had still to be painfully traveled to attain anything recognizable as modern agriculture.

Changes were nevertheless being made, above all toward causing the disappearance of traditional crop rotation. As in the eighteenth century, this involved first the most extensive estates, for example those of landowners in the Beauce area, "who have been generous enough to sacrifice acres of land and years of harvest to experiments on the rural economy" (i.e., on the new techniques). Similar efforts could be noted everywhere, and progress was observable under the stimulus of a growing national market and the protection of laws defending it after the Napoleonic era against excessive importation of grain and against competition for wool, flax, hemp, and livestock. Basically, however, this progress had to do only with the quantity, not the technique.

Nevertheless, it can be noted that the plants introduced in the sixteenth century, which at first had won only slow acceptance, were ultimately introduced wherever they were likely to give good results. Thus, corn became generally adopted in Franche-Comté, Alsace, and especially the Southwest, where the wheat-corn rotation (sometimes with crimson clover) spread to such an extent that agricultural inspectors reported in 1847 in connection with the use of corn in Castelnaudary near Carcassonne that it had become "the chief cause of the bad system of cultivation that is followed there." To be sure, they were generally content to prepare the ground for corn by *pelleversage,* or winter deep plowing. At the same time, they regretted that this enthusiasm for corn, because of the food it furnished, led to growing it on impoverished lands, using it too frequently, and letting it interfere with improvement of meadows. At least the method of cultivation was now fixed: sowing was done in rows 24 to 32 inches apart; a second dressing or hilling was done sometimes with a swing plow, sometimes with a hoe; tasseling required an ordinary knife or pruning knife; harvesting meant cutting down to the ground with a sickle or pruning knife; ears were dried in a loft, where they were frequently stirred; and, lastly, husking was done on winter evenings with a toothed iron rod.

Corn spread out from the regions where Arthur Young had observed it in 1787. The Charentes provinces made room for it next to their winter wheats and minor grains. In Bresse it was adopted and taken out of the *verchères,* or kitchen gardens, near the houses and put into the fields, where it was combined with other crops. Corn helped to develop the raising of poultry, fowl, and capons. Alsace, which had cultivated it since the seventeenth century, saw it established in Montbéliard near Besançon, where the weather calls for cornmeal porridge.

The potato, for its part, came down out of the mountains and left the poor regions, sometimes to penetrate the plains, where it was often planted on fallow land. It was still accused in Montbéliard of exhausting the soil and making the wheat sown there the next year unable to grow. But the food shortages during the French Revolution assured the complete acceptance of the potato. It was still necessary for cultivation and natural or deliberate selection to permit the cultivation of varieties capable of "sustaining human beings." And it was necessary to improve the techniques of cultivating it, for until the beginning of the nineteenth century the plants were grown too close together, were not hilled up, and were not always given the right amount of manure. Once these advances were made the potato, like corn, revolutionized the old crop-rotation cycle.

The same was true of the sugar beet. After being a government monopoly at the time of the Continental blockade it became an item for individual speculation wherever it had normally been successful. It tended to be the customary partner of cereals on the alluvial lands in the Paris basin and in the north, whereas in Alsace it complemented the range of industrial crops—colza, or rapeseed, flax, hemp, tobacco. The sugar beet had already acquired such importance that it stimulated many experiments in Germany and France. Those by Louis de Vilmorin are famous. On the family estate of Verrières he set forth for the first time in 1856 the principle of genealogical selection that is still rigorously applied, according to Auguste Chevalier. This principle gave agriculture a new species of sugar beet, the experiments being aided by the newly invented saccharimeter.

It should be noted that in the same period improved meadows were expanding, and not only on large estates. (See O. Festy's 1814 analysis, *Statistique agricole.*) Moreover, farmers were learning to enrich the flora of the natural meadows and improve these grazing areas with drains, so it is understandable that cattle raising made new progress in quantity and quality. Scientific animal breeding could now help breeders, and veterinary medicine was making an effort to eliminate catastrophic animal diseases.

In particular we can observe a reduction of fallow and waste land. The statistics suggest that in France the first half of the nineteenth century witnessed a more than 25 percent reduction in the area of nonproductive ground and that the same period marked the triumph of the agricultural revolution as begun in the eighteenth century. Almost everywhere, cultivation continued to replace successfully the old methods of production. Multiple crop rotations were developed, and it is enough to look through a book like *Les Assolements* (*Crop Rotations,* 1862, by Gustave Heuzé) to observe their variety and adaptation to each area of France. The result of this fundamental change in agricultural practices was to give each locality its own characteristic features. Diversity in agriculture can be seen as a consequence of that technical revolution whose development from the sixteenth century until the first half of the nineteenth has been traced.

France and England were not the only countries to benefit from this development. The Scandinavian countries and Finland changed the patterns of their cultivation, which encouraged technical improvements. Denmark set an example: a series of ordinances and laws, particularly those of 1769, 1776, and 1781, brought about the abolition of the *solskifte,* the Danish equivalent of the open-field system, and caused an almost complete redistribution of agricultural land. Enclosures and the formation of small family holdings permitted individual initiative.

In Germany similar changes and the same progress were made. At Hohenheim near Stuttgart an experimenter named Schwerz set the example for new types of crop rotation in which he combined cereals, colza, beets, and clover. His seven-year rotation seemed so well conceived that the French École d'Agriculture at Grignon, near Versailles, founded by Bella in 1829, adopted it without modification. Everywhere at this time the potato and sugar beet were becoming more accepted, and Germany was paving the way for specialized uses of them.

In Switzerland, where the influence of the Physiocrats had made itself powerfully felt, scientific and economic societies propagated their doctrines and, with necessary adaptations, became interested in agricultural progress. The Bernese agronomists Hiezel and Isaak Iselin (1728–1782) led those who expected large landowners to improve their methods of cultivation. Enlightened agronomists and farmers like Jacob Guyer, nicknamed the rustic Socrates, instead recommended experimentation by farmers themselves. Guyer's farm at Wertmetschweil, in the Zurich bailiwick of Greifensee, served as a model not just for Switzerland. Thanks to concerted efforts by both groups, land clearing and swamp draining were actively pursued, whereas the cultivation of potatoes and clover spread and made it possible to reduce the area of fallow lands. The Bernese agronomists successfully recommended the rotation system of potatoes/winter grains/spring grains/clover, which was far superior to rotations customarily practiced.

Technical progress besides large-scale cultivation   Simultaneous with the development of the agricultural revolution, the techniques peculiar to special crops were being modified.

A crop as old as grapes did not escape these changes. Constructing and improving roads, digging canals, population growth, and larger cities favored the consumption of wine, though its price had a tendency to rise. Wine entered more and more into the popular diet, at least among the French. A search for grapes that would yield a great deal of wine led some viticulturists in southern France to adopt the *aramon,* which became the standard vine for quantity production. Other productive varieties replaced traditional vines; for example, *gamays* replaced *pinots.*

The progress of viticulture, especially in Mediterranean regions, largely compensated for the decay of northern vineyards, and the time was not far distant when the latter would be almost completely abandoned. In contrast, Bas-Languedoc and the neighboring regions extended their vineyards to the point of disturbing local authorities, who were still preoccupied with the grain supply. Almost everywhere the parliaments and administrators had sought to slow the movement. A decree on June 5, 1731, forbade new plantations, but around 1750 the authorities relaxed the ruling, and after 1800 viticulture began to enjoy a protection, which accounted for part of its success.

In the same period the prestige of the quality vineyards often declined. The almost universal degeneration of many famous vintages cannot be forgotten in spite of the renown of such names as L'Hermitage or, even more, of champagne, the product of the collaboration of great nobles and abbots, among them Dom Perignon, though he was not its inventor.

The reaction can be understood from the attention given to knowledge about the plants. Elie, the duke of Decazes (1780–1860) assembled more than 1,300 varieties in an experimental vineyard in Luxembourg. Count Odouart published an *Ampélographie* (on viticulture) that anticipated the splendid works of Dr. Guyot in 1866–1868. Everywhere, in Andalusia as in Italy and France and on the banks of the Rhine, agricultural writers described the vines and classified them either by their botanical characteristics or by when the first buds appeared. Viticulture and oenology as well were thus escaping from mere trial-and-error. Vine growers no longer merely mixed plants in their vineyards but instead made increasingly skillful cuttings and began analyzing their degree of alcohol, thanks to Gay-Lussac's testing alembic, or checking the amount of tannin and the nature and quantity of free acids.

The process of cultivating vineyards was becoming much more well organized. Planting was still done with cuttings or rooted plants mostly from vine growers' own nurseries, in holes dug with an iron dibble or in ditches. Vines were renewed by layering them, but the plants were rooted up only when the vine appeared to be exhausted, sometimes after thirty or forty years of production. The vines were planted in groups or in rows on oak, chestnut, or acacia vine props, but sometimes on tall poles and on trellises or on large props or trees. Growers were sometimes satisfied to attach a vine to reeds or to link the shoots of one plant to a neighbor so they would support each other.

Few innovations in these planting methods occurred in the nineteenth century. Experiments were made on the best distance to leave between ridges and thus on the number of stocks to be planted per hectare. Iron stakes and support wires appeared, the result of progress in metallurgy. Similarly, after 1830 to 1840, pruning, which was usually done with a knife, began to be done with shears, the use of which became widespread once toolmakers could produce tools with blades fine enough to make clean cuts.

Almost everywhere, and notably among small proprietors, cultivation continued to be done with the spade or hoe. However, plows were also used, and the appearance of the so-called vine-grower's plow made it possible to attach less importance to manual second dressings. The grape harvest remained, inevitably, faithful to old practices. Grapes were cut particularly by women; but transporting them (sometimes in baskets on one's back), treading in wooden vats, and pressing in the screw press were work for men. An innovation early in the nineteenth century may possibly have contributed to the harvest operations by deliberately delaying them, whether by planting varieties that were slower growing but more productive, or by increasing the number of stocks per hectare. This among other things was a sign that economic conditions had changed and were leading to expanded production.

Other circumstances increased development in silkworm cultivation. At the beginning of the nineteenth century and even earlier Italy and France were the foremost European producers, with Italy having had a longer tradition in the art of raising silkworms than did France. The populous Italian countryside easily supplied the labor needed to breed silkworms and to operate the spinning and throwing mills. In much of Italy the custom of combining mulberry trees with crops had been favorable to the spread of these trees. In France the peasants' hesitancy to introduce them to their lands, which were devoted above all to cereal grain production, had hindered the expansion of sericulture, despite energetic, intelligent, and persuasive propaganda since the time of Olivier de Serres (1539–1619). It was not until the first quarter of the nineteenth century, when the agricultural revolution was beginning to gain momentum, that peasants in the south of France became willing to plant all the mulberry trees needed by breeding farms, which were by now located almost everywhere.

In both Italy and France the techniques of silkworm breeding were now well known, if not exactly followed. France claimed that it produced cocoons of higher quality than Italy, and in his 1885 report Natalis Rondot suggested that this superiority resulted less from the art of the silkworm raisers than from geographical conditions: "Generally produced [in Italy] in the plains and alluvial lands, they are not of such a nature that first-quality silks can be obtained from them." He naturally made an exception for those that came from the hilly regions of Briançon and Piedmont. This geographical factor was perhaps the reason for the excellent cocoons produced in France in the Cévennes, the Bas-Vivarais, the middle Rhône, Provence, and even Mediterranean Languedoc and certain parts of the Garonne basin.

In Italy as in France, silkworm breeding establishments had been perfected. In some places special silkworm nurseries were built to replace the poorly ventilated and maintained rooms, haphazardly equipped, fitted out with tables on which the worms found their food. Thanks to the thermometer perfected by René

Réaumur (1683–1752), the temperature most favorable for incubating eggs and for actual breeding could be determined. But although growers frequently made an effort to achieve these optimum conditions, technical progress in silk production insofar as it was an agricultural enterprise ended there. The spinning and working industries were far more developed.

This was all later challenged after 1850 when silkworm breeding was afflicted by pébrine. Until then the worms had sometimes had flacherie (flaccidity), muscardine, and other diseases. Pébrine was more serious in nature and greatly influenced the development of sericulture. Pasteur discovered its cause between 1865 and 1869 and indicated its remedies by selective breeding. A new era now opened for the silk-breeding techniques and the silk industry.

The needs of another textile industry led to the initiation of a new crop that had no direct connection with the agricultural tradition of the region in which it achieved its fullest development. The plains of the Comtat Venaissin (now largely Vaucluse) became, in the eighteenth and nineteenth centuries, one of the largest producers of madder, said to have been introduced in 1750 by a Persian named Althen. Comptroller-General Bertin proposed establishing it throughout Languedoc and even in Poitou. Farmers in the Comtat, who were well located for trading, ultimately assumed a quasi-monopoly of the product. In order to succeed they planted madder on their alluvial plains, which were drained for the purpose, and sought new fertilizers—it was apparently for madder that they began to use oil cakes. They defined the methods of sowing and planting, the conditions for weeding, hoeing, and gathering seeds, and how to tear out roots with a heavy three-toothed spade known as a *fourcade*. This intensive cultivation not only brought the Comtat's farmers new resources but also prepared them for the techniques of horticulture, in which they later succeeded so well.

The cultivation of chicory came from a completely different source. Chicory's adoption is related to the use of coffee, for the poor people of Switzerland, Germany, and England adopted it first as a substitute for the drink made from the beans of the coffee tree. Chicory was introduced in 1800 near Valenciennes, where it was so successful that it quickly spread to all the neighboring cantons and to Belgium. On polders near Antwerp it was substituted for colza. Here again the farmers had to learn how to grow this delicate crop and prepare its roots. These were cut at the base, split lengthwise, divided into squares called *cossettes,* then dried over a fire and finally roasted like coffee before being powdered under grindstones.

At first a luxury, today a need, the success of tobacco was ensured. Its known history in Europe dates only from the sixteenth century. Snuffed, chewed, and smoked, it has conquered practically the whole world. In the East it is grown in small, widely scattered crops. Western Europe, Belgium, France, Spain, and Switzerland offered the best locations on carefully prepared, richly manured fields. In France, where this crop is subject to strict rules imposed by the government monopoly existing since 1810, techniques of growing tobacco are regulated down to the smallest detail: the number of plants per hectare, the varieties cultivated, the number of leaves retained, disbudding, drying in special sheds sheltered from the sun, packaging in *manoques,* and so on. With this type of crop the producer has little initiative and almost certain profit.

The techniques of growing these products, which after a fashion are marginal, are not themselves very original; they are related to all the techniques a farmer learns in the garden. They testify, though, to his adaptability and the sureness of his intuition. They are the badge of his craft which, even when applied to what is most necessary and commonplace, engages his whole body and mind.

Progress in equipment   When it was taking place, the agricultural revolution had results whose scope we are only now beginning to measure.

Considering only the techniques of agricultural labor, it must be noted that the new agriculture was far more complex than the old. In temperate countries it continued to be based on diversifying crops, with cereal grain cultivation as its essential base. But cultivated plants became more numerous, their rotations acquired a faster rhythm, and the rest period provided by the fallowing system disappeared. From now on the peasant in the first half of the nineteenth century was to be engaged in endless labor. There were still peaks in the rhythm of his duties, but they were more numerous than in the past, when there were only two: plowing and sowing, and harvesting. To the extent that the farmer had remained a manual laborer, having the help only of his draft animals, he was overworked. He had to mobilize all the energies of his family and sometimes seek outside help. He also had to seek out possible new work techniques and abandon, albeit unwillingly, his familiar farm equipment for new tools.

Industry offered him new possibilities for equipment, for it had become capable of supplying him with more effective and stronger tools and eventually machines. The first (or at least the most visible) advances were made in the plow. Thanks to iron and steel, which had become less expensive and of better quality, almost all spades and hoes were of metal. Plowshares and the share of the *aratrum* were no longer simple pieces of wood, and moldboards were made of strong steel already polished in the factory. Iron plows without wheels can be seen, such as the model known as the Dombasle (Figure 1), which was adopted and perfected at

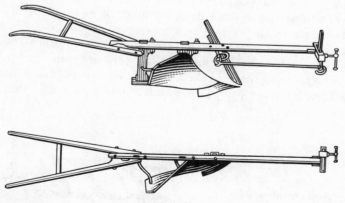

FIG. 1.   Plow of Mathieu de Dombasle. Elevation *(top)* and plan *(bottom)*. This plow, which was rapidly adopted, is characterized by its straight beam with front guide and its arrangement of the plowshare, moldboard, and sole plate *(from right to left)*.

Grignon by an experimenter named Bella. Numerous light, manageable plows that could be easily controlled were produced by English, French, Belgian, and German manufacturers. These new plows were better balanced than the old ones, for the science of mechanics played a role in producing them and could even measure with dynamometers their tractive effort and the conditions that must be met by a train of wheels. The moldboard could now be given the most appropriate shape (Figure 2). A certain Arbuthnot, who modified Walter Blith's 1630 plow,

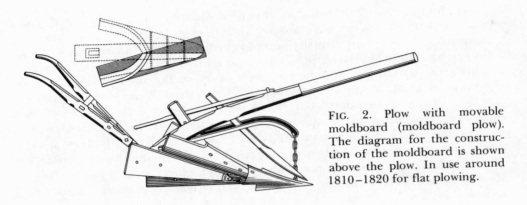

FIG. 2. Plow with movable moldboard (moldboard plow). The diagram for the construction of the moldboard is shown above the plow. In use around 1810–1820 for flat plowing.

provided a theoretical basis for it, and an Italian named Lambreschini solved the same problem. The plows suggested by Hamilton in 1623, Brounecker in 1627, Parham in 1634, and especially those by Norfolk and Rotherham mark genuine advances over the almost monumental plows pulled by six or eight horses that were customarily used in England. From then throughout the eighteenth and to the mid-nineteenth centuries many models of plows appeared—heavy trenching plows, large plows, and light plows adapted to the nature of the soil. Plows with two or more shares were tried, an idea dating from the sixteenth century but never applied before. Adrien de Gasparin (1783–1862) felt that Godefroy's plow, of which he gives a description, had demonstrated all its qualities in actual use. Finally, reversible plows, the immediate ancestors of the modern European Brabant plow (Figure 3), were tested. The use of genuine subsoil plows was even envisaged, but the problems raised by this type were not completely solved. The same advances were being made in the United States. In 1837, at Grand Detour, Illinois, a blacksmith named John Deere built a plow with a steel share.

FIG. 3.   Metal Brabant plow with reversible double plowshare. In use after the middle of the nineteenth century for flat plowing.

Plate 53. John Deere plow, 1838. Smithsonian Institution

Lands plowed with the *charrue* or turned over with the hoe or spade had uneven surfaces and rows, and gaps in the topsoil layer had to be leveled. On small plots this was still done in the medieval way, using a wooden club to crush the clumps of earth. Wooden or stone rollers were also used, but rollers with iron spikes or even with cast-iron disks that had cutting edges were already beginning to appear. Harrowing with a bundle of thorn faggots weighted with stones, or with the primitive harrow, became rare as harrows with metal teeth were built.

Once the soil could be better prepared, the mechanization of seeding became of interest as soon as the superiority of sowing in rows over broadcast sowing was appreciated. In 1634 Ramsay and in 1639 Gabriel Plattes in England tried out seed drills of their own invention. John Worlidge described a machine that could trace furrows and drop in seeds simultaneously with manure. De Gasparin noted around 1845 that "since Tull, the books on agriculture . . . are filled with descriptions and drawings of seed drills." He mentioned one by Feost, perfected by Thomas Coke of Holkham, and those by Locatelli, Dacklet (whose drill was adopted by Thaer), a German named Fellenberg, and one by Hughes, of which he says that "it is one of the most perfect produced to date." He mentioned English seed drills with a seed box carried by the sower himself, used to sow turnips. De Gasparin recalled that Dombasle attempted to overcome the difficulties resulting from uneven ground, as James Smith had done before him in building a seed drill with articulated drills. The ingenuity of builders was active everywhere in this respect, but except on certain large estates the "majestic gesture of the sower" was not abandoned.

Harvesting was done with a smooth or serrated sickle and a scythe. The sickle was almost universally used to allow reapers to cut down the fully mature wheat without large losses of grain. It cut high, and the stubble served as feed for animals and as manure. The scythe saved time, to be sure, but what was the gain of a few hours on small farms where there was no shortage of labor? Large estates easily found reapers from migrant seasonal workers or even from among workers in cities. Once peace had returned at the beginning of the nineteenth century, some of this migrant labor disappeared into the factories. Then propaganda for the scythe became effective and the production in England and France of steels suitable for its manufacture made it possible to furnish scythes rivaling those of Austria and Germany. A single factory in Toulouse turned out 54,000 scythes in 1819 and 120,000 in 1827, whereas another, in the Ariège region, forged 50,000. Even before 1850 the sickle was no longer used for harvesting except by poor people and in mountainous areas, where it is still to be found.

Basically this was a victory for industry, which was preparing to win others by supplying agriculture with the new tools it needed. We shall not discuss minor equipment, in which iron soon replaced wood. Inventors applied their ingenuity especially to reaping and threshing machines. In 1577 Barnabe Googe mentioned a reaper consisting of a "kind of low carriage . . . equipped in front with sharpened sickles," claiming that it cut "everything before it." An engineer named Person was thinking of a similar machine when he presented his "reaping cart" to the Committee of Public Safety on June 28, 1794. Already by 1788 one de Bellenoüe, a lawyer at the parliament of Blois and a landowner in the Beauce region, concerned with the fatigue of his reapers, had presented to the Académie des Sciences a machine that could be pushed by a horse with six revolving scythes that were supposed to cut 1,250 square *toises* per hour (1 *toise* = 6.4 feet). Everywhere attention was being paid to easing the hard task of reapers, and it is obvious that the list of designs would be endless if we note that before 1831 patents had been issued for two French, one German, thirty-three English, and twenty-two American inventions. Those that were built, especially in England, were never completely satisfactory. The first American machines, by Obed Hussey in 1833 (Figure 4) and Cyrus H. McCormick between 1831 and 1834 (Figure 5) proved to be genuinely practical harvesters. By the end of 1850 the firm of Gray & Warner, which was producing McCormick's machines in Chicago, had sold 1,500 in the

FIG. 4.   Obed Hussey's reaper, patented December 21, 1833.

United States, and Hussey had sold approximately 500. The McCormick reaper appeared at the Exposition of the Royal Society of Agriculture in 1849 and at the Great Exhibition in London in 1851 and received the approval it needed by being placed ahead of all the American and European machines shown. The new era of mechanical cultivation had begun.

How to thresh grain made a similar appeal to inventors' imaginations. This operation was still performed with elementary and sometimes ancient methods. Throughout southern Europe the equivalents of the ancient *tribulum* (threshing board) and *plaustellum* were used. They are still found today in Spain, as the *trillo,*

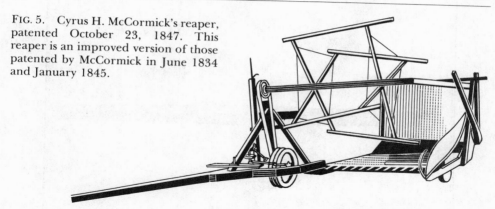

FIG. 5. Cyrus H. McCormick's reaper, patented October 23, 1847. This reaper is an improved version of those patented by McCormick in June 1834 and January 1845.

and in several backward areas in the Balkans. Elsewhere the flail was used, and even now its steady beating can still be heard in a few mountain barns, especially in northern Portugal and northern Spain. Treading was done by animals, especially in the Midi, or with a stone roller drawn by oxen, a horse, or a mule. The ideal form of roller for most effective threshing was still being sought in the nineteenth century.

The difficult and overwhelmingly slow work of separating the wheat from the chaff inevitably encouraged a search for a mechanical means to replace flailing, treading, and rolling. The eighteenth century applied itself to the problem. A Swedish plowman from Niermdal in the province of Madelpapel is mentioned as a pioneer, and the engineer of a king of Poland thought highly of a thresher invented by a Pole. The agronomist Abbot Rozier built a machine in 1766, and Duquet in 1722 and Malanagny a short time later also offered the products of their mechanical ingenuity. In October 1794 the director of the *département* of Loire-Inférieure recalled that he had a thresher in his possession that had been inspired by an invention by a Dane named Foster, of which a description was given in *L'art de battre, écraser, piler, moudre et monder le bled (The Art of Threshing, Crushing, Pounding, Milling and Cleaning Corn)*, published in Paris in 1769. Many other threshers were suggested during the French Revolution period, and under the Convention experiments were made with those of a carpenter-mechanic named Prudon and by one Cessart, the inspector-general of public works in Paris. In 1808 the Bureau of Arts and Manufactures studied an invention by a certain Lepure, a landowner near Nantes. There were other inventions using beaters or chains, generally operated by horse-driven treadmills. None were fully satisfactory, even the one by Mathieu de Dombasle, which soon had a competitor in Ransomme's collapsible model, whose advantages were praised by de Gasparin.

Some of these threshers were already combines, since they winnowed and sifted the grain at the same time as they husked the ear. These were the same functions performed by the modest crank-driven machines with a drum and rakes, a winnowing basket and sieve, that on small farms replaced treading on the threshing floor and winnowing. The latter was now done on a windy day only rarely, by tossing the grain into the air with a scoop, or in a barn by removing chaff by having a drum equipped with floating bags turn around an axle. The use of the reed winnowing basket, the handling of which required skill and endurance, also

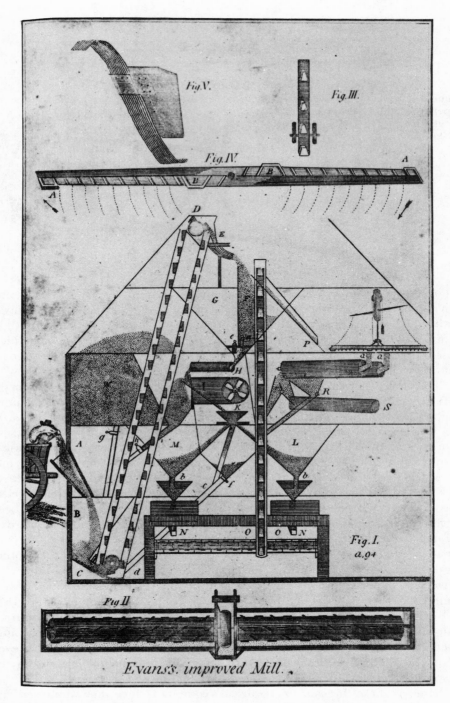

Plate 54. Drawing of Evans's improved grist mill. Smithsonian Institution

declined. The fanning mill, which combined the winnowing operations, is still used today for similar small operations. The application of steam meant that every aspect of this part of agricultural work would soon be revolutionized, which became one of the technical advances in the second half of the nineteenth century.

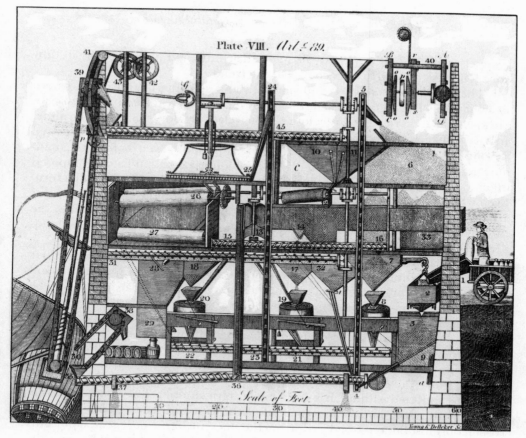

Plate 55.   Photograph of grist mill from Evans's book. Smithsonian Institution

The significance of the agricultural revolution   The first part of the nineteenth century witnessed a new approach to agricultural methods as agronomists tried to define and promote them. Much was accomplished in this period to bring about profound transformations in agriculture, of which the sixteenth century had had a vision and for which the eighteenth had provided the program.

Although it was a question simply of introducing new plants and new crop rotations into the old agricultural systems, the opposition of farmers arose from more than their ignorance. Their constant concern had always been to satisfy the basic needs of existence for themselves and their families by tilling the soil. Production for sale remained almost an exception, home consumption the rule. Such an economy, autarchic in tendency, inevitably brought about closed minds. Those who were liberated from it furnished proof that agriculture, when transformed along the lines advised, did not compromise the essential objective but rather the contrary. Successful experiments always did more for agricultural progress than did abstract teaching. The agronomists of the time were good observers rather than scientists, so their advice was ultimately accepted.

Aided by circumstances and events (among which even the misfortunes of wars played a role), the appearance of new needs and greater ease of moving products encouraged farmers to abandon their inherited passivity. The institutions followed, and officials encouraged the trend.

The increased production and yields within a span of 100 to 150 years were such that it can be said that agriculture had never known their like. In this sense we can speak of an agricultural revolution. The relatively slow changes in farming, and its diffusion, gave it an appearance different from that of the Industrial Revolution, which was achieved in a shorter period—even before the mid-nineteenth century it had accepted the direction that coal and steam imposed upon it. The agricultural revolution had a completely different growth pattern. Even when we can establish its success it was still based on the work of men and animals, and the mowing machine and mechanical reaper (not to mention the thresher) had hardly taken their place in the work cycle, which increased crop diversity made more exhausting.

This relative stagnation of agricultural techniques arose essentially from their objective. At the time when it was undergoing its radical changes industry was still producing and working only inert materials, or at least materials reputed to be inert. But farmers were in the presence of a complex biological environment whose particular reactions they had experienced from the beginnings of agriculture. Because they had domesticated the plants and animals they were unable to treat them as mere things. The farmer formed with them a partnership in which he was only ostensibly the master and which he dominated only when science had revealed their true nature.

Thus confined within fairly strict limits, agricultural activity was necessarily imbued with tradition. It was respectful of the past and seemed able to depart from it only insofar as it freed itself from the stock answers (the legendary origins of some of which were still believed true) that appeared to justify it. The scientific spirit of the nineteenth century led toward liberation, and agriculture, till now an art, gradually took on the character of a science.

Similarly, agriculture fell under the influence of methods and practices in the new industrial world. Industry came to supply it with the equipment that gradually liberated it from manual labor. The call of the cities, depriving agriculture of part of its labor supply, forced it to change its work methods. The broadening of markets opened up by the creation and development of the large industrial cities eventually led agriculture toward a specialization that until the beginning of the nineteenth century it had had only a rather limited experience of, confined to a small part of its output. The technical revolution just described had not fundamentally changed the fairly uniform appearance of those agricultural areas dominated by grain cultivation. These areas' adaptation to economic conditions brought about their gradual diversification. Around the middle of the nineteenth century, then, the entire rural world was on the eve of a series of new revolutions that were more impressive and more profound than the revolution during the century from 1750 to 1850.

CHAPTER 2

THE MINING INDUSTRY

W E HAVE LITTLE INFORMATION on the early stages of the mining industry before the Renaissance, but beginning with this period we possess a considerable mass of written documents and fairly numerous printed sources. However, an inadequate critical examination of this material is a stumbling block to historical research, and moreover, very few mineral deposits exploited in the past have been the object of detailed monographs based on the archives of the old mining companies.

The oldest known publication on mineral deposits, *Ein nützlich Bergbüchleyn,* the first edition of which was published around 1500, was the work of a doctor in Freiberg named Ulrich Rülein von Kalbe, who died in 1533. This book went through eight editions in the sixteenth century and two in the seventeenth, the last appearing in 1698. In 1530 another doctor of German origin, Georg Bauer (1494–1555), better known under the Latinized name of Georgius Agricola, wrote the famous *De Re Metallica,* which for almost two centuries was the most complete treatise for the use of miners and metallurgists. This work, published in Basel one year after its author's death, continued with the same subjects about which Agricola had been publishing since 1530.

De Re Metallica, valuable to the historian because of its 269 plates representing scenes of mining and metallurgical activity, was not completely free of deficiencies, even for contemporary craftsmen. The drawings were not revised by Agricola, and certain figures do not correspond exactly to their descriptions. All of them, however, are remarkable for their realistic portrayal of working situations and a general precision in technical details. In some instances Agricola poorly understood the explanations furnished by his sources and was sometimes even unaware of major technical innovations of his time, as for example the first system of remote control for pumps on various levels. A device to do so using rods operated by a waterwheel was installed in 1550 by Michael Mittelbach near Joachimsthal, only thirty miles from Chemnitz, where Agricola lived. However, the permanent success of his work illustrates the slow evolution of the metallurgical and mining techniques between the sixteenth and eighteenth centuries.

PROGRESS TO THE END OF THE EIGHTEENTH CENTURY

Most methods of mining, including mechanical methods described in sixteenth-century works, were still in use two centuries later. Some devices labori-

Plate 56.   Open-face mining of the zinc mine in Scharlei in Silesia. Engraving taken from Turgan, *Les Grandes Usines,* Paris, 1870. (Photo Alain Doyère - Conservatoire national des Arts et Métiers.)

Plate 57.   Underground mine, early nineteenth century: mining by underhand stoping. Engraving taken from Héron de Villefosse, *De la richesse minérale,* Paris, 1819; frontispiece of the atlas. (Photograph Alain Doyère - Conservatoire national des Arts et Métiers.)

ously developed during the second half of the seventeenth century had been added to this ancient stock of techniques.

Prospecting   Prospecting methods had been only slightly improved by the practices of observing the terrain and examining rocks and vegetation. The hazel dowsing rod in use since time immemorial was far from being abandoned, despite the exhortations of rationalist authors. It was thought that mineral matter regenerated itself in abandoned mines in somewhat the same way that plants grow, fed by moisture that contributed the materials for regeneration. Although this conception was practically abandoned in the eighteenth century as regards metal-bearing deposits, it continued to be generally accepted for coal. Even in the nineteenth century it only very slowly disappeared from the minds of uneducated miners.

Ideas concerning the direction of underground seams and the significance of surface outcroppings gradually acquired some consistency. In the eighteenth century the "iron hat," or rust-colored deposit of oxidized pyrites at the outcrop of a metal-bearing vein (the *eiserner Hut* of Germans, the gossan of miners in Cornwall), had a significance well known to specialists: it was a surface indication that faithfully yielded information on the promise and wealth of the underlying mineral deposit. In the search for veins the principle of deposits running parallel was beginning to prove a useful guide. Practice showed that a known vein was almost always accompanied by parallel ones. Experience also showed that other systems were often joined to a first orthogonal system of fractures, each one corresponding to a given mineral development. As early as the sixteenth century miners working in the Joachimsthal field had already distinguished four major systems.

In coal prospecting another principle, that of the continuity of seams, sometimes provided an extremely effective guide to extrapolating the existence of a seam. For instance, after the border changes in northern France as a result of the Treaty of Ryswick in 1697, shafts were dug in the Valenciennes region to seek the southern extension of the Borinage seam. The search, continued until 1734 by the engineer Pierre Mathieu (1704–1778), led to the discovery of the Anzin bed. Nevertheless, chance still proved in most cases to be the prospector's most valuable aid.

Systematic geological studies were finally undertaken during the first half of the nineteenth century, and documents became available to prospectors that permitted them to narrow down the area of their investigations. In this way a coal bed in Pas-de-Calais was discovered on June 7, 1847, thanks to information collated onto the geological map of that *département* by a mining engineer named Charles du Souich (1812–1888).

Subterranean geometry   The earliest extant printed documents show that geometric surveys were being made in mines as early as the sixteenth century. Their original object was to ascertain that the miners of one company were not trespassing on the domain of a neighboring company. In Germany and Hungary mining concessions were delimited by a fixed perimeter marked off aboveground, and in early times the geometer simply brought these surveys up to date, to scale, and perpendicular to underground operations. This was still being done in the seventeenth century. Mine plans began to be drawn up in Saxony in 1633; a 1667 edict ordered the officer of the large mines in Freiberg to draw up an official government mining chart. In Sweden the survey service, created in 1628, was especially charged with drawing up mining maps. In France technicians from Saxony had disseminated the methods used in their country, but in certain provinces these methods were still unknown in the mid-eighteenth century.

Thus, in the Forez (now in the Loire), where a landowner also owned the mineral rights, numerous challenges led to frequent intervention by surveyors, whose method involved small planks placed at angles in the mine galleries, on which the angles for changes of direction were noted. The galleries were marked off by wires stretched out straight from one plank to the next, the starting direction being found with the help of two plumb lines placed on the overhead timbering of the mine shaft. Once the operation was finished the surveyor folded up the network of wires and spread it out on the surface of the ground in the position noted belowground.

The instruments used in subterranean geometry had evolved little since the sixteenth century. The mine compass, already described in von Kalbe's *Bergbüchleyn*, consisted basically of an adaptation of the Nuremberg model sundial in widespread use for centuries (Figure 6). The hourly graduations of the dial, ranging from 5:00 A.M. to 7:00 P.M., had at first been surrounded simply with a graduation in degrees comprising twelve intervals, each of fifteen degrees. The hourly graduation was then quickly abandoned, but the hour name given to each interval was retained. The mine compass quickly came into general use, with several variations. The types used in Bohemia and Saxony were made so that the zero alignment 12–12 was placed in the direction being sighted, which was marked by noting the position of the magnetic needle on the graduation. The model used in the Tyrol, known under the name of the Alpine compass, had an alidade and, eccentrically, a small compass equipped with a datum line. The plateau was turned until the datum line was under the magnetic needle, at which

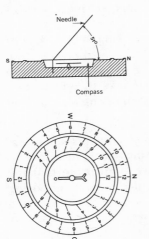

FIG. 6. The mine compass based on the model described in von Kalbe's *Bergbüchleyn*.

point the alidade marked the azimuth of the rope on the limb of the plateau. By the end of the sixteenth century the mine compass became equipped with a suspension device that facilitated its use.

In addition, the geometer used the classic surveying instruments: the half circle, the graphometer, chain, rules for measuring distances, the level, the compass case. Of these only the clinometer, to measure angles in a vertical plane, had been adapted to mine work.

Tools   The miner's tools varied little over the centuries. In addition to the pick and the hammer, which have symbolized the miner's profession until modern times, he used other tools adapted to the various phases of work: a small pick consisting of a short rod of tempered iron, with an eye for hafting and a blunt tip at one end; a two-handed hammer, iron wedges, a crowbar, and a shovel to remove broken rock. The shape and weight of these tools differed slightly from one region to the next. Since it did not derogate from the local methods of working, the traditional shape of these tools underwent no modification. When the quality of steel improved, the form of certain tools (for example, the pick) was changed. By the eighteenth century the point used to split rock was being made of a piece of steel soldered to a square iron that was struck by the two-handed hammer, then blunted and tempered.

In the seventeenth century the use of black powder for cutting introduced a new tool, the drill bit, for drilling mine holes. In the eighteenth century this bit was perfected by the Swedes, who changed its square section to an eight-sided one and gave the cutting edge, whose shape had at first been that of a simple chisel, a slight bulge at its base. These modifications made it possible to remove debris from bottoms of holes and prevented the tool from becoming wedged in the rock. This example shows how the slow improvement of tools sometimes occurred (Figure 7).

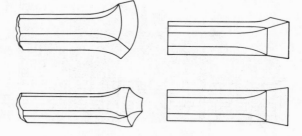

FIG. 7. Faceted cutting edges, by von Torckens. Eighteenth century.

Extraction   After the Renaissance, open-cut mining was finally abandoned in all the mining districts of any size, specifically in Germany, Austria, and Hungary. An orderly subterranean architecture appeared in which vertical shafts driven from the surface gave access to horizontal subterranean galleries. From these galleries, which led to the working areas, were connecting shafts to lower levels of the mine.

In the sixteenth century Hungarian miners developed methods of working veins, where the conditions are more difficult than in sedimentary deposits. They

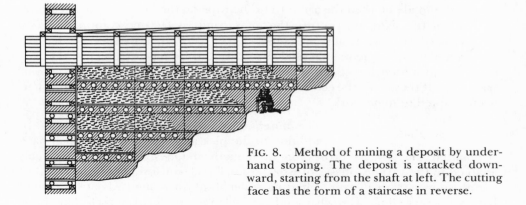

FIG. 8.   Method of mining a deposit by under-hand stoping. The deposit is attacked down-ward, starting from the shaft at left. The cutting face has the form of a staircase in reverse.

abandoned underhand stoping, so-called because ore was removed in a series of broad, descending stopes, or steps (Figure 8). They realized the advantage of dividing the work into stages of from 50 to 66 feet each, which in turn were subdivided into levels attacked one after the other by working upward. At the base of the level to be worked a road was dug to drain off water and haul out the ore. During the skinning off of the first level the workers laid down a bed of planks supported on round pieces of wood, firmly anchored in the walls of the vein and designed to support the fill. This would permit them later to continue working the lower level (Figure 9). This method of overhand stoping was suitable for thin veins. A worker had the impression that he was working under a huge stairway with broad treads.

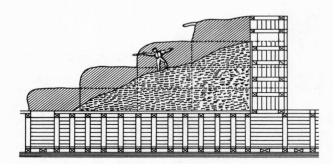

FIG. 9.   Method of mining a deposit by overhand stoping. The deposit is attacked up-ward from the lower horizon-tal gallery. Filling with sterile fill makes possible a large sav-ing in timbering.

Another method of mining thin veins, drift working, appeared in turn (Figure 10). With this technique the miners also worked by sublevel stoping, but on a single horizontal level, whereas in overhand stoping they occupied different levels. At the top of the face the first miner attacked the vein at a height of 6½ feet for a width of 6½ to 10 feet. The other miners were placed at intervals of three cuts. The mining of this section of the vein was begun, timbering was put up, the ore was removed, and the waste was placed to the side of the crosscuts. Once the crosscuts were filled and the props removed, the miners stood in the area between the three cuts that separated them and cut into the first and the third, the one in

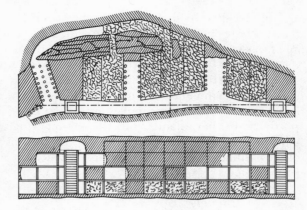

FIG. 10. The drift-mining method. *Top:* Horizontal plan; *bottom:* Vertical cross section. Note the two vertical shafts and the galleries for working and removing the ore, which are filled in as the work progresses.

the center being left for removal later. This method offered many advantages, particularly that of permitting the complete extraction of ore, because none of it had to be left behind to form a pillar.

Timbering and masonry The shafts were in most cases square or rectangular in cross section, to facilitate the installation of wooden coffering when cutting through soil that lacked cohesion. The coffering consisted of oak timber pile planks cut at an angle at one end, driven at a slight deviation from the vertical and held by frames. Contrary to what is often depicted, the coffering did not consist of jointed horizontal frames (Figure 11).

The deepening of workings had made evident the advantages of isolating a section of the mine, to avoid having to drain the water that flowed into it. The wooden works built for this purpose —called cofferdams when placed in galleries

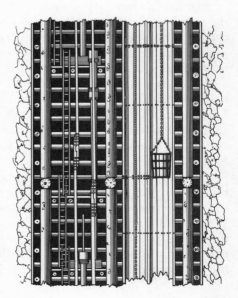

FIG. 11. Timbering of a mine shaft around 1810. *Left:* The shaft with ladders for lowering personnel and with the rods that control the pumps. *Right:* The hoisting shaft.

and plugs when in shafts—had to be watertight under pressure. In the Liège Basin, where the pressures were less than 330 feet of water, a straight compartment was used in narrow galleries and mitered partitions similar to sluice gates in wide galleries. In Saxony, where the pressures sometimes exceeded 330 feet of water, the partitions were shaped like a round cap.

In the eighteenth century an imminent scarcity of wood and a constantly increasing need for it compelled miners to substitute masonry annually in those portions of galleries and shafts whose timbering would have had to be replaced. This practice, which appeared in 1707 in Saxony, spread during the century to other mining basins in the countries in which the wood crisis was becoming more pronounced.

Blasting   From ancient times miners had used fire to break down hard rocks against which the pick was useless. A pile of faggots was set against the working face, whether horizontal or vertical. The miner set it on fire, left the site, then when he returned threw water on the ashes and the face, in which cracks appeared.

During the seventeenth century black powder began to be used instead of fire to attack hard rocks. Around 1625 the use of black powder made its appearance in the mines of Schemnitz (Stiavnica), Czechoslovakia. It was long believed that this powder had been in use in the mines of Freiberg since 1613, but in fact it was not so used up to 1630. A short time later the sale and use of the powder became regulated.

At first black powder was carried in leather horns worn at the belt. The miner poured it into a hole he had drilled and packed it in with the help of a wooden peg. In 1687 a Saxon miner named Karl Zumbe introduced a method of tamping the powder with clay plugs shaped by hand. In 1689 a Zellerfeld, Hanover, bookbinder named Johann Andreas Lufft made the first paper cartridge to hold a powder charge.

During tamping it was necessary to make a channel in the powder for setting the fire. For this purpose an iron priming needle was used at first, but upon contact with rocks this tool sometimes gave off sparks that caused accidents. Zumbe replaced the iron priming needle with one of brass, which made the use of powder safer.

This new method of breaking rock spread very slowly, because of easily understandable prejudices. It was introduced in the copper mines of Ecton, England, in 1638 and in the tin mines of Cornwall in 1689. In Schemnitz the pick continued to be used on hard rock throughout the eighteenth century. Until the end of the nineteenth century fire setting was still practiced in many mines in Europe.

The black-powder method of blasting was improved in the eighteenth century. We mentioned the modified shape of the bit used to drill the blasting hole; the worker also used a scraper to clear the hole of dust that accumulated in it. Where he did not use a cartridge he used a cylindrical tube to pour powder into the hole without spilling it. Tamping was done (after the priming needle had been placed against the wall of the hole) with either clay, a wooden stake, or sand. After the needle was withdrawn a wick was inserted into the hole. This wick consisted of

Plate 58. The copper mines at Falun; the horse engine (or whim) driving the hoisting device. Painting by Peer Hilleström, 1784. Stora Kopparberg, Sweden. (Photo Stora Kopparberg.)

black powder glued to a small coiled strip of paper, completed by a sulfur fuse for igniting.

The problem of pumping   As soon as mines began to go belowground the flow of water into the lower parts of shafts and galleries necessitated important pumping equipment. Between the beginning of the sixteenth and end of the eighteenth centuries this equipment underwent a major evolution that is the most characteristic of all the improvements from which this industry benefited.

In the time of Georgius Agricola several technical solutions were being employed. Bucket chains or hydraulic chain pumps lifted by a drum with spikes were operated by classic methods such as cranks, windlasses, treadmills, squirrel cages, and waterwheels. Piston pumps were already being operated by walking beams. Lastly, simple casks were hung on a chain wound around the drum of a water-driven hoisting machine.

In mountainous areas drainage galleries connected the lowest point in the deposit with the bottoms of neighboring valleys. As the mine increased in depth it became necessary to link up with more distant valleys whose lowest points had to correspond with the lowest level of the mine. Thus, in Hungary a gallery opened in 1494 at Hodritz (later called the Ladislas Gallery, then the Emperor Francis Gallery) was extended to a point where in 1765 it was twenty miles long.

Of all these various methods, piston pumps started the most significant technical developments during this period. In the sixteenth century miners had begun to install pumps in series, one above the other, each pump emptying the water it raised into a vat, from which the next pump took it up to the next level. When the shafts became deeper at the end of the sixteenth and beginning of the seventeenth centuries, the piston rods were connected to a master wooden beam that descended along the entire length of the shaft. Quite early, remote-control devices using a series of jointed tie rods were combined to drive these beams by a treadmill or (at the end of the sixteenth century) waterwheels. By the seventeenth century in particular the carpenter's art made these devices increasingly extensive.

By the end of the seventeenth century the perfection of the construction and the sturdiness of machines being installed at the surface attested to the high level that wooden machinery had reached. The period saw ingenious carpenters installing lines of tie rods extending in some cases for over a mile. A Liège mechanic named Rennequin Sualem (1645–1708) had assembled a device of this type between 1681 and 1684 on the Marly machine described in the preceding volume.

Finally, in the closing years of the eighteenth century the Cornwall mines installed a Newcomen heat engine. (The history of this invention and its developments to the middle of the nineteenth century are described in Part I of the present volume.) We have seen how the use of the steam engine spread quickly in Great Britain and then more slowly on the Continent.

The heavy cost of wood or coal for operating atmospheric steam engines led in certain regions to a search for a less troublesome engine to perform the same services. A Schemnitz mechanic named Jozsef Karoly Hell substituted the action of water for that of steam in a ram that retained the ratchet mechanism and distribution system used by English builders. In 1749 he installed his first hydraulic ram at the mouth of the Leopold shaft in such a way as to connect the apparatus of the drainage pumps directly with the driving piston. Later he fitted up two additional engines with a walking beam identical to that of steam engines. Hell also tried to combine the action of water and air in an engine whose lower tank was filled with pump water that was lifted by the air evacuated from a higher tank when the driving water reached it. The hydraulic ram was seldom used before the end of the eighteenth century, but during the nineteenth it occasionally became an economical replacement for an engine whose maintenance and use were relatively costly. The German mechanic Georg von Reichenbach (1772–1826) improved its performance and so extended its use. Between 1808 and 1817 Reichenbach installed nine of his engines and five waterwheels to transport brine from the salt mines in Salzkammergut. Hydraulic rams were similarly installed in Hungary, Hanover, and in the Finistère area at the Huelgoat mines in 1833 (Figure 12). The latter case involved a Cornish pump with a master rod whose driving cylinder was installed in a shaft at an intermediate level between a main

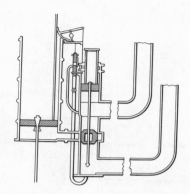

FIG. 12.   Hydraulic ram at Huelgoat. 1833. *Left:* The chamber of the lifting pump; its piston is controlled by the distribution mechanism, which in turn is activated by the stream of water falling down the column. The inlet and exhaust of the water appear at right in the drawing.

and an upper drainage gallery. This engine continued to operate until the mine was closed in 1865.

Hauling and hoisting   Baskets, sledges, backpack baskets, wheelbarrows, and trolleys used in the sixteenth century to transport ore in mines had not by the mid-nineteenth century completely disappeared from certain mines. The trolley, the parent of hauling vehicles, consisted of a box on four wheels: two small ones close together in front and two large ones wider spread slightly behind the center of gravity. At the face, when empty the box was tipped slightly toward the front. For haulage the operator applied light pressure on a handle at the back of the box, which was then supported only on the two rear wheels.

The front of the trolley was soon equipped with a steering bar, the end of which slid between two flat wooden rails secured to the ground. In this way the trolley could travel rapidly through a winding gallery despite the almost total darkness. In addition, since the gallery floor dipped slightly toward the shaft so water could run off, the effort needed to roll the loaded trolley was approximately the same as that required to return it empty.

A variant of this vehicle, the Hungarian trolley, was also used. It had no steering shaft and only a single small wheel in front, with the rear axle placed at the center of gravity.

Mine cars with four equidistant wheels of the same diameter, of which drawings are often seen, were probably used only aboveground. Around the middle of the eighteenth century the two parallel flat wooden rails that formed the hauling platform over the water drain became genuine guide rails.

Mine owners in the Newcastle area were the first to build special roads from the shafts to the barge docks. The first of these roads was undoubtedly laid around 1630 by an English engineer named Beaumont. In 1765 Gabriel Jars described these four-foot-wide tracks formed of square oak planks pegged to crossties. The tip carts were equipped with four spoked cast-iron wheels with flanges and were pulled by horses.

Twenty years later the wooden rails began being systematically replaced by cast-iron ones. When it was reequipped in 1783 the Mont Cenis-Le Creusot mine was provided with a network of cast-iron tracks with switches. Transport on metal

FIG. 13.   Coal mine in Silesia. Around 1810. Surface installation for hoisting and hauling.

rails was quickly set up in all the large mines during the first third of the century (Figure 13). In France the first installations of this type were laid out at Rive-de-Gier in 1824. It is not necessary to repeat here the earlier discussion directly relating this aspect of mine development to the invention of railroads.

Hoisting had long been done (at least in shafts that were not very deep) with an ordinary winch operated by a crank or by a variation of the squirrel cage. For deeper shafts, as early as the Middle Ages horse-powered or water-operated hoisting machines were installed. They were traditionally placed under a conical wooden shed that from a distance appeared to be a vast tent.

The horse-powered hoisting machine was also known as a whim. A treadmill operated a vertical drum around which the two sections of a cable wound alternately. They passed over two large winding pulleys mounted on the headframe and were sent back into the shaft. The cable was so wound that one of its ends reached the surface as the other arrived at the foot of the shaft. The horses were then made to walk in the opposite direction. In the mid-eighteenth century German mechanics replaced the vertical cylindrical drum with two drums shaped like truncated cones that were superimposed so as to decrease the work required of the teams. In Sweden a single biconical drum was adopted.

In the waterpowered hoist a reversible wheel equipped with two sets of flat paddles facing in opposite directions was wedged onto the horizontal shaft of the winding drum of the hoisting cable. By a series of sluices the engine operator could reverse the direction of the wheel's rotation. As shown in Agricola's drawing reproduced in Volume II, waterpowered hoisting machines underwent no notable transformation until their replacement by steam-powered hoists during the first half of the nineteenth century.

The Swedish engineer Christopher Polhem (1661–1751) showed great skill in developing mechanical installations for his country's mines—pumps, pump controls, and hoists. In particular he designed in 1694 a system of two vertical rods that worked alternately in opposite directions from top to bottom. Hooks engaged the buckets of ore and lifted them to the surface. This system was adopted in the

Plate 59. Steam engine for the hoisting of material from a mine, Staffordshire collieries. Early nineteenth-century engraving. (Photo Radio Times Hulton Picture Library, London.)

nineteenth century to raise and lower personnel on a kind of moving stairway. The first installation of this type was by an engineer named Doerell in the Zellerfeld mines in 1833.

The double-acting steam engine was gradually applied to hoisting, to drive the winding drum for the cable, which was mounted on a shaft with a flywheel. A brake with shoes was fitted to the shaft in order to stop the cable from unwinding if necessary. In France the first steam engine for hoisting coal was installed at the Littry mines by mechanic Constantin Périer in 1800.

Before the appearance of hoisting cages, the ore or coal was hoisted in baskets by cable. Iron chains could not be used for two reasons: the links were always likely to open under stress, and corrosion was rapid, especially in the metal mines. Hemp therefore continued to be the preferred material for making mine cables.

Mechanical preparation   Once raised to the surface, the ore had to be prepared prior to the metallurgical treatment.

Dry or wet crushing underwent practically no changes for three to four centuries. In the eighteenth century the iron stamp of an ore-crusher weighed thirty to forty pounds for dry crushing and twice that for wet crushing. A waterwheel or a horse whim turned a camshaft that lifted the catches of the stamps one by one. This was the classic arrangement employed in many other industries, which was replaced only very slowly during the nineteenth century.

The ore had to be washed after crushing. This was traditionally done in inclined wooden chutes equipped with baffles in which the material was subjected to a stream of water and agitated with an iron rabble so as to remove the soil. The arrangement of these ore washers varied slightly with the period and region. In the seventeenth century a similar washer was known to French miners as the English washer.

The washing table was frequently accompanied by a washing cylinder consisting of a box containing a mixer with fins. Six to eight two-foot square sieves were juxtaposed so as to classify by size grains ranging from one inch to less than one *ligne* in diameter. In the eighteenth century a sizing drum of sheet metal with a horizontal axle performed this grading operation.

In the nineteenth century the steam engine became a source of power in ore preparation. The principal improvement in these operations during the first half of the nineteenth century is credited to a French engineer, Aristide Bérard, who in 1833 converted a jugging screen operating in the water into a piston vat, giving a decisive impetus to coal washing. The coal arrived at one end of the vat and the washed coal and schist were evacuated separately at the other. Similar procedures were immediately adopted in other countries.

PROGRESS OF MINING TECHNIQUES TO 1860

The mining industries experienced particular growth thanks to the economic development in Continental Europe that followed the end of the Napoleonic wars.

During the closing years of the eighteenth century major efforts were made in every country to encourage the training of qualified personnel through instruction and specialized literature, and to attract workers from established mining areas to those less advanced. In France the efforts of Gabriel Jars and Guillot-Duhamel after 1756 remain the most characteristic examples. Several mining schools had been opened in Hungary in 1747 and in France in 1767. High-level training began in 1761 in Prague, 1763 in Schemnitz, and 1765 in Freiberg. A royal mining school housed until 1788 in the Hôtel de la Monnaie (Paris Mint) was founded in 1783. After being reestablished in 1794 the École des Mines provided continuous instruction in Paris after 1815. In 1816 a school for miners opened in Saint-Étienne and immediately became a school for engineers. As for publications, in addition to the treatises published in ever-growing numbers after the middle of the eighteenth century, the *Journal* (later *Annales*) *des Mines*, which began publication in 1794, became the indispensable instrument for studying and disseminating new knowledge for this industry.

The developments in mining techniques in the nineteenth century were many and varied. The principal advances were in lighting and ventilation, mechanical equipment, hoisting cages, and, not least, drilling equipment.

The problem of firedamp   Although the danger from firedamp had long been known, a name for it appeared only relatively late, in notes by the French chemist Jean Hellot around 1756. The intensive working of coal mines began only during the second half of the eighteenth century, when explosions became more frequent.

For years the miner's lamp had consisted of a sheet-metal box open on one side to provide slow combustion of a tallow candle or vegetable oil. In massive deposits worked in large chambers the miners lit large candles made of a strip of gauze coated with tallow and rolled around itself.

Open-flame lighting was quickly recognized as a source of danger in coal mines, but no other method could be substituted for it. The question was opened to competition at Liège in 1783 and 1787 and at Mons in 1809, but without success. In England, two firedamp accidents in succession in coal mines led the metallurgist J. J. Wilkinson to decide to found, in October 1813, a society to study methods of preventing explosions in mines. In 1815 the English chemist Humphrey Davy, who had a great reputation at the time, was invited to cooperate in the work of this society, and in less than one month he discovered the principle of the safety lamp. He observed that the explosive flame of a mixture of air and firedamp was not transmitted through small openings. After studying all aspects of this phenomenon, which Wollaston and Tennant had also observed in the same period, in January 1816 Davy devised the lamp with a metal screen that bears his name. It was soon known that George Stephenson, then a modest wheelwright at the Killingworth mine, had invented a similar device at the same time.

Dissemination of the safety lamp   The Davy lamp, which immediately became known in France, was manufactured in that country starting in 1818, and in 1823 its use was made obligatory in mines with a problem of firedamp. This rule transformed practices of individual lighting, which until then had always been left to each miner. Distribution of lamps became a duty of the mine owner, who numbered and assigned them. The installation of lamp rooms facilitated a roll call after each shift returned to the surface.

A large number of models of safety lamps were invented and manufactured during the nineteenth century, but few were in fact used. The Davy and Stephenson lamps, which were the most widely adopted, had a glass tube inside the metal mesh cylinder to protect the flame and act as a fresh-air intake above a crown of perforated sheet metal. This design is reminiscent of the Argand lamp popularized by Quinquet in the closing years of the eighteenth century.

Until 1880 vegetable oil was the only combustible employed in the safety lamps. The lighting obtained was weak and the oily by-products of combustion dirtied the screens and reduced the air supply.

Use of the safety lamp did not prevent firedamp explosions—several disasters occurred in France in 1829, 1840, and 1859. It was finally realized that safety was endangered by air turbulence. Accidents in Welsh coal mines led the British to discover, during the second half of the nineteenth century and long before their Continental colleagues, the explosive properties of air laden with coal dust.

The use of explosives   In explosives one invention and one innovation should be mentioned. William Bickford, a furrier from Tuking Mill in Cornwall, covered a cylinder of priming powder with a sheath of plaited cord and one or several mesh envelopes impregnated with tar. This safety fuse, which he patented in 1831, became named for him and was introduced into France in 1842, where it was manufactured in Rouen.

The innovation mentioned, the Ruhmkorff induction coil, was employed

Plate 60. Miners going down one of the mine shafts of the Le Creusot mines, circa 1855. Photograph. Collection Yvan Christ, Paris.

after approximately 1860 to ignite a fulminate detonator, thus eliminating the use of a flame and permitting simultaneous blasts. This procedure did away with long-burning flames, reduced the number of misfires, and made it unnecessary to wait one hour, which had formerly been required in case of a misfire when a wick was used. The manufacture of electric igniters and perfection of a magnetoelectric exploding device, like the Breguet device built after 1870, assured its wide dissemination in the following years.

Ventilation The problem of ventilation required special attention even when mines were not very deep. The various types of bellows used in metallurgy were adopted for this purpose (Figure 14). Among these the hydraulic blast engines were the most powerful ones available. In the eighteenth century a blast engine fed by a stream of water falling through 10 to 13 feet could force fresh air through pipes for a distance of 1,000 *toises* (6,400 feet). In coal mines, particularly those in the Liège Basin, a coal fire was made at the base of a shallow shaft connected with an air supply that was free of firedamp and with the air-return shaft (Figure 15). The fire method of ventilation offered real advantages because of the simplicity of its equipment and operation, and it was widely used until mechanical ventilation became effective in the nineteenth century.

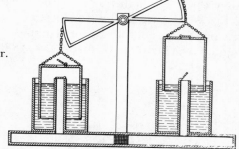

FIG. 14. Harz double ventilator.

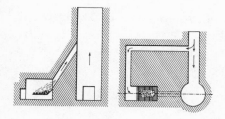

FIG. 15. Ventilation by fire. *Left:* Vertical cross section of the shaft; *Right:* Horizontal plan of the galleries.

Ventilation was given more and more attention during the first half of the century. The nature of air circulation in mines was better understood then, as was the need for circulation from bottom to top at each face. Provision was made for evacuating a mine by the shortest path and through shafts with gastight walls. Among the mining engineers who concerned themselves with these problems, the

Frenchman Charles Combes (1802–1872) published the most useful results, in 1838.

The need to change the air in coal mines was more urgent in Belgium, where the seams worked were thin and deep, the galleries narrow and often subject to firedamp, than in England, where fire ventilation worked satisfactorily for years in beds that were thick and not very deep. The subject was therefore opened to competition by the Académie Royale des Sciences et Belles-Lettres of Brussels. The papers that won the prizes (all of which referred to Combes) stressed the inadequacy of the air-pump ventilators employed until then and encouraged efforts to build "dynamic" fans (see below). In fact, the first analytical theory of fans was established only in 1878 by the French engineer Louis Ser (1829–1888).

Air-pump ventilators were constructed between 1820 and 1840, functioning on the principle of piston or rotative pumps, drawing in air from the mine and forcing it into the atmosphere after raising its pressure enough to ensure its evacuation. In French-speaking areas these were known as *ventilateurs volumigènes*, a name given because at each stroke they extracted a volume of air equal to their own volume. In order to provide a sufficient change of air in mines as they became deeper or more subject to firedamp, these ventilators became so big as to obstruct the openings of mine shafts and block all ventilation if there were a stoppage. In addition, their operation was slow, their output low, their resistance high, and their yield small.

After 1840 research was devoted to building "dynamic" fans, so called because they acted simultaneously on the pressure and velocity of the air being removed. Several designs were suggested but all had various disadvantages. The one that came to be generally adopted in the second half of the nineteenth century was invented by Théophile Guibal (1814–1888) in 1858 (Figure 16). In less than

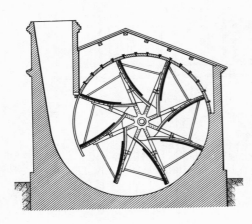

FIG. 16.   Guibal's enclosed fan with vanes, 1858.

twenty years he equipped English, Belgian, French, and German mines, and for many years his invention was employed almost exclusively in the mines of the entire world. In Belgium it continued to be made until 1922.

Guibal's studies of the flow of air in subterranean workings, from which he invented his fan, also led him to postulate that the ventilating conditions in mines were connected with the value of the ratio of the square of the amount of air discharged to the loss of pressure, a ratio he called the temperament of the mine. In 1892 Auguste Rateau named the unit of temperament the *guibal*.

Hoisting cages The first hoisting cage was installed in 1833 by T. Y. Hall in a shaft of the South Hetton colliery in Wales. At the time iron wiredrawing was expanding to meet the needs of the navy and public works, and there began a substitution of iron cables in mines for cables made of aloes, whose round, flat forms had been standardized by John Curr in 1798. Production spread gradually to Germany (1834) and Belgium and France (1841). Steel cables came later.

The first cages were guided vertically on rigid wooden rails, but improvements in wiredrawing made it possible to use flexible cables for this purpose, though the advantages and disadvantages of the two systems were passionately argued in every country.

The installation of hoisting cages required a counterbalancing system that would permit loading and unloading at the various levels simultaneously during a change of shifts. Furthermore, safety mechanisms were needed to forestall accidents in case cables broke. In France two grip gears were invented, one in 1845 by J.-B. Machecourt, the other in 1849 by P.-J. Fontaine; both were successfully installed. Between 1851 and 1859 twenty-nine cable breaks occurred, and on each occasion the grip gear functioned, saving the lives of 150 miners. The grip gears could be installed only on the wooden guides used in France to separate the cages. The grips, withdrawn in normal operation, acted by gradually bearing on the inside race of the guides when the grips were activated by a mechanism triggered by the breaking of the bearing cable. As of 1860 no effective grip gear had been devised for cages guided by cables.

The installation of cages in mines required major investment, so before putting them into general use, French mine owners appealed, around 1850, to the imaginations of their engineers to find an alternative; but none of those tried were satisfactory. Some suggestions were inspired by the system of movable ladders used since the last century, a method that continued in use until around the last quarter of the nineteenth century. There were large numbers of them in the Harz area and, after 1842, in Cornwall, where they were called man engines. In Belgium between 1845 and 1886 they were known as *warocquères,* from the name of their promoter, Abel Warocque. The *warocquère* could raise or lower 160 miners per hour in a shaft 650 feet deep.

Boring equipment We have detailed descriptions of two European drills employed in the eighteenth century. One was a cable drill, built in 1715 by Johann Just Bartels, a chief machinist at Zellerfeld. The origin of this percussion method is very early; it is well described in a Chinese treatise published in 1637 by Sung Ying-hsing. The other drill, contemporaneous with the former, was used in 1718 in Poland to determine the thickness of layers of salt and was described in 1750 by its inventor, Johann Christian Lehmann. In this case an auger was screwed to the end of a column of iron rods that were rotated with a wrench (Figure 17). Around the middle of the eighteenth century this drill was modified into a percussive drill with solid rods.

FIG. 17.   First mechanical drill for mining rock salt.
Poland, middle of the eighteenth century.

The perfecting of drilling tools became a subject for competitions and publications during the first half of the nineteenth century. During this period in France artesian wells began to be dug, for which it was necessary to reach increasingly greater depths.

The most important operation of the time was drilling an artesian well in Grenelle near Paris at the instigation of François Arago. The operation took from December 1833 to February 1841 to reach a depth of 1,797 feet. The bore was drilled by the percussion method. Solid iron rods 26 feet long, screwed or cottered together, were used. To the bottom of them were attached open augers or ball valves, depending on the nature of the terrain to be drilled. One winch was used for setting the tools, another for drilling. Many accidents delayed the progress of the work, which was a resounding success, Arago having predetermined the depth to be reached within a few meters.

Drilling was above all a matter of reconnaissance; it was important to obtain samples of the terrain drilled. The cup valve, used to bring up the rock chippings, was the first sampling device. In 1838 Maximilien Evrard succeeded in cutting out plugs of soil at the bottom of a bore hole, which were the first plugs taken on location in France.

The principal obstacle to deep boring was the vibration that spread through the hole when the bit struck bottom. These vibrations became dangerous below a depth of 1,000 feet. Engineers then thought of eliminating the rigid link between the bit and the drill rod, an idea that led to free-fall devices, the first being Karl von Oeynhausen's jars in 1834. This invention is a milestone in the history of mine prospecting, for from then on it was possible to examine the subsoil at great depths.

In the same period the engineer Pierre-Pascal Fauvelle (1794–1865) invented a process for continuous cleaning of the drill, which he patented in 1845 under the name *hydraulic drill* (Figure 18). The drill consisted of hollow boring rods into which a current of water was sent from above under pressure. The water came out at the bottom through small openings in the bit and returned to the surface in the space between the pipe and the wall of the hole, bringing up with it the debris crushed by the bit. Cleaning by injecting water eliminated the need to replace periodically the bit with a bailer for ordinary cleaning. In addition it improved the effectiveness of the bit, as demonstrated in 1846 when an artesian well in Perpignan was dug at the rate of more than 3¼ feet per hour. From the Fauvelle process derived percussive drilling with a hollow pipe and continuous cleaning and the rotary system, which each had extraordinary success in the petroleum industry after 1900.

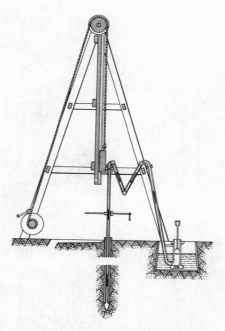

FIG. 18.   Fauvelle's hydraulic drill.

Mechanical drilling   Finally, a major advance was contributed to the mining industry by the engineer Germain Sommeiller (1815–1871), who in 1858 patented the first compressed-air drill. This invention, developed to drill the seven-mile Mont Cenis Tunnel, begun in 1857, is based on an idea by the English engineer Thomas Bartlett. The piping of compressed air, which after 1863 brought mechanical drilling to the mines, constituted the first convenient method of transmitting power over a distance and making it available to every miner.

The advances made in this area between the beginning of the eighteenth and end of the nineteenth centuries were the work more of ingenious engineers than of mine owners. They resulted from the emergence, after the beginning of the nineteenth century, of an increasingly larger group of trained engineers who brought about increased production capacity for an industry on which the whole development of industrial civilization was based. The world production of coal

Plate 61. Le Chaufour pit at the Anzin mines, 1854. Contemporary color lithograph, by N. Leclercq. French National Library, Print Collection. (Photo Ph. Brossé - P. U. F.)

alone which was probably between 15 to 20 million tons in 1800, reached 160 million in 1860 (for France, 1 million in 1820 and 6,850,000 in 1860). These advances also had the by no means negligible result of improving considerably the working conditions of the miner, who for centuries had borne an exhausting and dangerous burden.

CHAPTER 3

THE EVOLUTION OF METALLURGY

BETWEEN 1750 AND 1850 metallurgical technology underwent a profound transformation. The production of iron in particular experienced an almost total technical revolution. In contrast, methods of working other metals evolved quite slowly. This discussion thus deals with iron metallurgy, with a few brief remarks on techniques relative to nonferrous metals.

The stability of ironworking techniques   At the end of the seventeenth and beginning of the eighteenth centuries the techniques of ironworking, a partial summary of which was given in Volume II, had achieved an almost perfect equilibrium. This stability was the result of a technique that related very well the raw materials employed, to the still very limited iron consumption.

The raw materials consisted of relatively widespread fossil fuel, a generously distributed supply of ore, and available waterpower. Iron was thus produced almost everywhere, in small quantities, a system perfectly suited to localized, small consumption. Where a national or even an international market existed, it was because the factories were located near the major trade routes.

Cast iron was produced in blast furnaces, the largest of which were some thirty feet high and were built of a pyramidal masonry bulk with a refractory lining. Alternating layers of charcoal were piled in, with flux added when it was felt necessary. Openings were left to tap both the pig iron and the slag. The blast, forced into the furnace through nozzles called tuyeres, was supplied by blowing machines, generally two bellows driven by waterpower through a mill wheel and operating alternately to supply a continuous blast. The daily output varied between two and four tons. Diderot's *Encyclopédie* gives us exact pictures of the apparatus as it existed in France in the mid-eighteenth century.

The operation of blast furnaces required a great deal of attention. Charcoal was first heated for three to four days, then the charge of ore was gradually placed in the furnace while the force of the blast was increased. The ratio of charcoal to ore depended on the quality of the ore. Swedenborg recommended that the furnace always be given slightly less ore than it seemed to demand. The furnace had to be constantly watched to avoid melting the tuyeres, the problems that arose when ore was poorly mixed and cleaned, and the explosions that might occur if a poorly distributed charge left a vacuum.

The metal was refined into iron. Refining fires were used in which the reduced metal was smelted in a charcoal hearth containing slag that acted as a decarbonizer. There were various methods of refining, like the Walloon, Comtoise, Champenoise, and German, but their differences were often minimal. In the Nivernais and Styrian refineries decarbonization was accelerated by passing a blast of air through the molten, reduced metal. This idea, as we know, was later successfully revived.

Ironworking   The iron thus refined took the form of a spongy mass that was still full of slag and had to be hammered to give it a firmer texture and remove all the impurities. This was done under a hydraulic hammer. The helve of the hammer rested against a horizontal axle on which were cams that raised rhythmically. There were three types of hammers, depending on how the cams functioned:

- With the terminal hammer the cam acted on the helve of the hammer, so the camshaft was behind the housing that enclosed the hammers, generally in groups of two and three.
- With the lateral hammer the cam acted between the pivot axis and the head of the hammer (Figure 19). The camshaft was thus placed parallel to the hammer. This is the type depicted in the *Encyclopédie*.
- With the frontal hammer the cams were located on a rotating drum in line with and in front of the hammer. This obliged the attendant to work from the side (Figure 20).

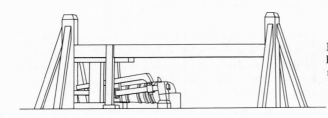

FIG. 19. Housing of a helve hammer. Beginning of the nineteenth century.

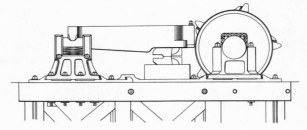

FIG. 20. Model of a hydraulically operated frontal hammer, mid-nineteenth century.

At the end of the eighteenth century only the first two types were used; the frontal hammer was introduced during the first half of the nineteenth century. The terminal type of hammer weighed less (between 110 and 550 pounds); the lateral type, more (440 to 880 pounds). The striking velocity depended on the number of cams and the power of the stream of water. It was possible to change the crown gears bearing the cams and attached to the driveshaft or to regulate the flow of water over the mill wheel. The height of the drop was generally inversely proportionate to the weight of the hammer. Sometimes there was a part acting as a spring, which gave greater power to the hammer. The hammer head, called the helve ring, had a dovetail notch in which various types of tools (the peens) could be attached, depending on the work to be done. The hydraulic hammer thus developed into a very flexible instrument adaptable to all kinds of work.

The hammer performed clearly determined tasks, listed here in the order in which they were performed for working merchant iron:

- Shingling was done to condense the iron and remove slag. At the same time the iron was given the form and consistency that "merited for it the name piece," in most cases an octagonal prism or a rectangular parallelepiped. The product remaining at the end of the operation constituted merchant iron. The lateral hammer was the one most frequently used for shingling.
- Welding was used to combine several qualities of iron. In general this was done with soft irons and case-hardened irons, assembled in fagots and hammered so as to produce a strong and flexible homogeneous metal. This procedure, of German origin, was a trade secret. A heavy hammer had to be used.
- The two remaining operations require no explanation. These were drawing and platemaking, which were done with lighter hammers. Scythes were made by drawing; most iron tools, by platemaking.

Forging thus shaped a major part of the iron to the point where it reached marketable quality. Blacksmiths, farriers, makers of edge tools, and locksmiths generally made use of hammer-forged iron, but there was also other production equipment:

- Rolling mills do not require detailed description. They were used to manufacture sheet metal, a rare and expensive product not very widely used. The adjustment of the rolls was done with screws and nuts.
- Splitting mills were a type of rolling mill having rolls with cutting edges that fitted into each other. With this apparatus the iron was cut into thin rods that were used to make nails, iron wire, rifle barrels, and so on. The iron that was passed through the splitting mill had first been run through the rolling mill.
- Drawing mills produced iron wire. The wire was passed through a series of holes that decreased in size, then was coiled on a bobbin rotated by a mill wheel.

Casting and tinplate   Next to these simple techniques, which mostly dated from the sixteenth century, a certain number of special processes, which we shall not discuss at length, may be noted. One such was casting, much practiced, either by primary or secondary fusion, as for naval guns, bullets, ordinary cast-iron ware, and cast-iron plates for fireplaces. Basically there were two types of casting: sand casting and clay casting. Certain castings required a metal sufficiently fluid to be poured in a relatively thin layer, as for example for pipes.

Another method was tinplate making, probably started in the Nuremberg area at the end of the fifteenth century. It reached the western countries toward the end of the seventeenth. The secret of tinplating, which long remained a difficult operation, was jealously guarded. The sheets were made of soft iron, but they were generally uneven and poorly cleaned. The chemicals with which they were coated in order to effect the tinplating constituted the secret of the operation.

Plate 62.   Interior of a foundry, circa 1790. Painting by Léonard Defrance. Liège, Musée d'Art Wallon. (Photo Buloz, Paris.)

The fuel problem This was therefore a perfectly organized technical structure, with difficulties that were natural rather than strictly technical in nature. Although there was on the whole no shortage of ore, fuel was in contrast a fairly widespread concern. By the eighteenth century some regions had been obliged to abandon iron production for insufficient sources of wood, and others had considerably restricted production. Fuel consumption was in effect very high. One Grignon, an ironmaster from Champagne and the author of numerous works about his craft, estimated the average blast furnace consumption in France to be approximately 1¾ pounds of charcoal for each pound of cast iron, "in methodical and continuous work." Fuel consumption in forging varied greatly, depending on the work to be done. It was still very large for refining and quite high for forging as such, where the work often required several heatings in succession. In 1771 the annual consumption of a 700-pound hammer was estimated at 4,000 cords of wood. A paper written in 1795/96 estimated the consumption of the iron industry in France at 6 million cords annually, which was indeed considerable.

Waterpower, which required equipment that was often very costly, proved in many regions to be extremely erratic. Factories were sometimes obliged to stop operations during periods of low water.

Forest reserves thus had to be restored. The iron industry was not the only one drawing on them, and for reasons of law and order the authorities were careful to see that cities and rural areas, as well as other industries such as naval construction, were regularly supplied. Although there were areas where forges represented the only market for wood, it is possible that elsewhere there was an opposite tendency to restrict iron production. It was not unusual to see factories standing idle, apart from sometimes long seasonal halts, for two, three, or even ten years, in order to give forests time to grow back.

THE ENGLISH TECHNICAL REVOLUTION

In England this situation became catastrophic. Deforestation had been intensive since the sixteenth century, and the number of areas engaged in iron smelting had decreased considerably. To conserve wood for other purposes (and we know the importance of shipbuilding for this country), it became urgently necessary to reduce iron production. At the end of the seventeenth century and throughout the eighteenth England had thus been obliged to look abroad for her iron supplies, first to Sweden, then to Russia after the middle of the eighteenth century. This foreign iron had come to represent approximately 60 percent of the English consumption.

It was probably this special situation that led to changes in some iron smelting techniques. The remedies offered to deal with the problem inevitably upset a long-established technical equilibrium, and a new technical system was therefore urgently needed with the consequent changes in the other steps in iron manufacturing.

Smelting with coke   An immediate solution would be to substitute another fuel for charcoal. It is not astonishing that the first such experiments were made in England, where the scarcity of wood was most keenly felt and where, on the other hand, coal was abundant and already well used.

Coal had already been used in iron production, but solely in forges, for reheating iron. Its use for this purpose is mentioned as early as the fourteenth century, but though in many districts this use was regarded as harmful for the iron, by the sixteenth century it had become widespread. It is reported also in the Forez and Nivernais regions in France, and Agricola in 1556 describes the procedure as being extremely common in Germany.

It was quickly realized that coal could not be charged directly to the blast furnace, because impurities in the coal were transferred to the iron and gave poor quality products. This was true especially of sulfur, which makes iron brittle. The idea persisted that after suitable preparation coal could become a useful fuel in furnaces and experiments were carried out in England starting at the end of the sixteenth century, because in 1558, 1581, 1585, and 1588 severe measures had to be taken to limit the consumption of wood.

We have very little information on the first experiments made in this field. Although we possess patents for using coal to reduce ore, the inventors' specifications were intentionally vague and inexplicit.

A certain Wynston in 1550, and Thomas Proctor and William Petersen in

1589, took out such patents and argued from conclusive experiments about which we have no precise information. The same is true of the patent granted in 1607 to Robert Chandell. And in 1612 Simon Sturtevant was authorized to use pit coal and sea coal in iron production to save on wood, which the foundries were consuming in large quantities. In his *Treatise of Metallica,* published in London in 1619, Sturtevant indicates that he used the coal not in its pure state but transformed it with a preparation "whose purpose is to draw from it everything that could corrupt or alter the metal." He gives no other information.

A similar patent was granted on April 3, 1613, to John Robinson, a man of whom practically nothing is known. Documents recently brought to light show that he probably had been financed by Lord Dudley, the owner of various metalworking establishments. By a contract dated May 25, 1618, Robinson ceded to Lord Robert Dudley that part of his patent concerning smelting iron with crude coal in a clearly demarcated territory. It appears that this method had not yet been completely developed. On February 22, 1622, the patent was transferred to Lord Dudley, who continued his experiments which seem to have involved a mixture of charcoal and crude coal.

In a work called *Metallum martis,* published in London in 1665, Sir Robert Dudley, the son of Lord Dudley, claimed to be the inventor of a process for smelting ore with coal. But a 1635 report mentions that though Dudley had for several years pursued the paternal dream, he had at that date not yet arrived at any satisfactory result.

Other names appear in the history of this research, which became increasingly important for England: Gumbleton; Dr. Jordan in 1620, at the Pensmet blast furnace at Hascobridge in Staffordshire; Buck, who obtained a patent in 1651; Copeley in 1656; Blauenstein in 1677. Nothing came of these numerous experiments, notwithstanding the patents and claims of their authors.

The first experiments by Abraham Darby

We now come to Abraham Darby (1677–1717), who we must note was born in Dudley into a family of locksmiths. He was thus acquainted with the use of iron and forge work. He apprenticed in a malting establishment, where the malt was dried with coke, a point confirmed by *Natural History of Staffordshire,* published at Oxford in 1686. This work clearly states that coal was carbonized in the same way as wood and the product was known as coke. Coke was produced for this use in open piles, yielding by this method approximately 33 percent. In 1702, after being a manufacturer of malt mills Darby founded a copper and brass business. It must be noted again that coke was being used at the beginning of the eighteenth century, for smelting copper and refining lead. The coke used in the malt kilns near Darby was obtained by roasting earth-covered piles of coal in the open. Consequently, it cannot be denied that coke was probably discovered in the second half of the seventeenth century and was used in a number of industries; we have just seen that Abraham Darby had worked at these very industries.

It therefore appeared completely natural that Darby, who by both profession and apprenticeship had a knowledge of ironworking and the existence of coke, and who perhaps had heard about the experiments made by the Dudley family, thought of charging coke to the blast furance. In 1708 he established the Bristol

Iron Company at the old Coalbrookdale furnace near the Severn River, in a region where iron ore had been mined for years. It was located near a coal deposit known as the Motte, which had good coking coal low in sulfur. The furnace was rented in September 1708 and was repaired by January 1709. On January 25, 1709, the first pigs of cast iron were sent to Bristol, and we may suppose that from that moment on the furnace produced cast-iron smelted with coke, according to a statement dated 1775. A 1712 letter shows that though smelting with coke was perhaps not yet completely perfected, it was nevertheless commonly used in Coalbrookdale in this period, perhaps in the production of poor quality castings.

Darby first made cast-iron cookware and other hollow containers. Coke produced a higher temperature and thus gave the cast iron a greater proportion of silicon. This fact, added to the high phosphorous content of the ores used, made possible a very liquid metal, which limited the risk of defects in the castings. Darby's hollow containers, which were of thin metal, were thus able to compete with heavier copper articles.

The method had to be considerably improved in order to become genuinely useful industrially. Improvements were made both in the production of coke and in the operation of furnaces. At first piles alone were used, similar in principle to charcoal heaps, with a vent in the axis and with numerous openings. The coal had to be carefully arranged according to the size of the lumps. Later the baker's oven was used, brought up to red heat with coal and then a charge of coal placed in it for which only a small air hole was left. Genuine coke ovens as we know their principles today came much later. Output was thus gradually improved.

The output of coke, its calorific content, and its resistance to crushing made possible the production of more cast iron with less fuel, although in fact the first coke ovens gave lower yields of no more than about 5 tons a week. A better supply of fuel and a more powerful blast permitted several coke ovens to function together, thus increasing the size of the reduction furnaces and thereby the daily output.

Another problem was that it proved difficult to obtain good wrought iron from cast iron produced with coke. Starting in 1748 Abraham Darby II took up this problem, which he solved by selecting the best local ores, that is, those containing the lowest content of phosphorus.

The slow dissemination of the technique These dates must not be taken as accurate. Darby began to produce cast iron with coke at Coalbrookdale in 1709, but the procedure acquired an industrial rhythm of operation only very gradually. Improvements in coke production and in operating a furnace with a fuel to which workers were not accustomed took time, and it may well be that the first output could be used only to produce a poor quality cast-iron ware or even (as happened around the end of the century at Le Creusot) to produce cast-iron pigs used as ballast in ships. Smelting with coke was still rarely practiced; in 1760 there were only seventeen coke ovens operating in Great Britain, but the second half of the eighteenth century saw the new technique spreading.

The slow beginning of coke smelting is moreover confirmed by the European experience. Although certain Germans had made parallel experiments (for example, Sim Koch in Stolberg factories in 1717, Ehrenberg in 1727, and Rothenburg in 1729), the Continental countries appear to have been far from a solution. Shortly before the middle of the century, probably, the news of the English discovery arrived in France. In 1756 Guillot-Duhamel and Jars were sent to England to find out "if it is true that they are using crude coal in the furnaces of factories to smelt iron ore . . . if it is necessary to remove the sulfur for this purpose and reduce it to what the English call coke." We have no account of their trip, but we do know that Jars' experiments began only in 1768/69, at Hayage in Lorraine, where undoubtedly the first smelting of cast iron with coke in France was effected. Other experiments were made with coal from Le Creusot, by the chemist Guyton de Morveau in 1771. Here, as the result of a vast joint effort, in which the government played a role, and with the assistance of the English ironmaster William Wilkinson, the first French coke blast furnace was built. The first industrial smelting was done in December 1785 (Figures 21 and 22).

Around the middle of the century the prince of Nassau sent a commercial counsellor named Heuss to England. Later, in 1771, a Prussian state counsellor, one von Pfeiffer, unsuccessfully recommended adopting coke smelting in that country. The prince of Nassau took responsibility for all the experiments but did not accomplish anything definitive. In 1799 the king of Prussia ordered the construction of a coke blast furnace at the *Königshütte* (the government mines in Upper Silesia), which was lighted in 1802. However, it must be noted that the natural conditions of the iron industry on the Continent were appreciably different. Wood was not yet in short supply, but transportation remained difficult. Coke smelting in England, having become absolutely necessary by the scarcity of wood, was facilitated by the nearness of coal and iron deposits to each other and by much better transportation facilities. A technical advance is not a goal in itself; it must be capable of adaptation to natural conditions, which is to say it must be integrated into a geographical area.

Puddling The coke method made it possible in the second half of the eighteenth century to produce cast iron in much greater quantity in areas that were not necessarily the old iron-producing regions. A problem was thus suddenly raised: how to refine the iron produced. This was simultaneously a fuel problem—a large quantity of which was still necessary—and a problem of how to treat a mass of molten metal. In this context the old methods of refining were inadequate.

Raw coal could not be used in contact with molten cast iron. English ironmasters were perfectly aware of this, for they encountered the same difficulties with coal that they had experienced earlier with the blast furnace.

Here again there were undoubtedly many unsuccessful experiments. Patents which were granted reveal both the desirability of a solution and the difficulties in achieving one. John Wood in 1760 and John Roebuck (1718–1794), the founder of the Carron ironworks, in 1762 took out patents that led nowhere. An intermediate solution was adopted: the reduced metal was refined in a preliminary coke hearth, and then the partially refined, reduced metal flowed directly into a second, lower hearth, where the refining proper was completed with charcoal.

Together with Richard Reynolds, a son-in-law of Abraham Darby II, the brothers Thomas and George Cranage, who were workers at Coalbrookdale, built

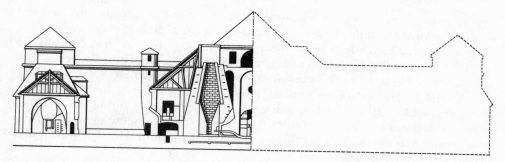

FIG. 21. Arrangement of the blast furnaces of the *Grande fonderie* at Montcenis-Le Creusot, 1785.

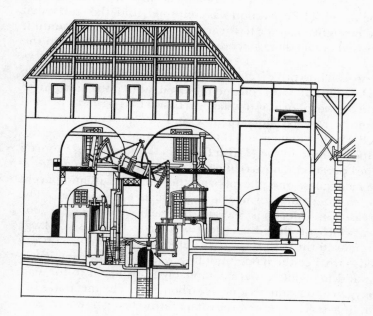

FIG. 22. Steam engine and bellows of the factory at Montcenis-Le Creusot, 1785.

a reverberatory furnace they proposed to use for refining, as of a patent dated June 1766. The metal was thus no longer in contact with the fuel. Their method appears to have been based on the action of oxygen in the atmosphere, which was difficult to control. The iron produced in this way was of poor quality, being brittle when hot because of excessive sulfur.

On May 7, 1783, Peter Onions, a foreman at the Merthyr Tydvil forges, took out a patent describing a process similar to puddling, but the effective development appears to have been by Henry Cort, whose final patent was dated February 13, 1784.

Cort had taken over the business of one of his uncles, a supplier of anchor chains and other iron products to the Royal Navy. In 1780 he signed a contract to supply mast hoops made from the scrap iron supplied him by the admiralty. In 1781 the deliveries of scrap iron were such that changing them into hoops could be done only at a loss, so it was necessary to lower production costs.

A first patent was taken out on January 17, 1783, for a "new process for shingling, soldering, and lastly making iron and steel in bars and in slabs, etc., of good quality and in larger quantities than was permitted by the methods in use until now." Actually, Cort was rolling slabs supplied to him. His only innovation was to substitute the rolling mill for the drop hammer.

As a result of this patent, the British admiralty encouraged Cort to develop a method for refining, the result being the so-called dry puddling process patented on February 13, 1784. For this purpose Cort used a reverberatory furnace and raw coal. The reduced metal was either cast iron or hot metal directly from the blast furnace. A worker stirred the molten mass continuously through side openings in the furance. As Cort observed, a kind of boiling occurred, liberating a gas that burned with a blue flame. The operation was continued until flakes of metal appeared. These were brought together to form a mass that was stirred until it became of a pasty consistency. At that moment the iron was removed from the reverberatory furnace.

The cast iron was broken into pieces, mixed with slag, and refined over a coke fire, which caused it to lose part of its carbon and removed most of the manganese and a larger proportion of phosphorus if the slag was basic. This partially refined cast iron was placed in the reverberatory furnace and ore or scraps from the rolling mill were added. (It should be noted that here we may recognize the two methods of steel production used in the Martin furnace, the so-called scrap-iron and ore processes.) The operation was carried out in an oxygen-rich atmosphere. The remainder of the manganese and phosphorus, the silica, sulfur, and part of the phosphorus were oxidized and formed a slag, which was removed. The temperature was increased in order to accelerate the reaction between the iron oxide and the carbon, which produced a violent boiling of the mass. A large quantity of slag was removed through the furnace door. The metallic bath was then vigorously stirred—whence the name puddling—in every direction with a long iron rod. Silicon and manganese were completely transferred to the slag, which absorbed the oxygen and again became decarbonizing. The metal was in a state of white hot grains that stuck together, the temperature being now too low to maintain the metal in a molten state. Stirring became difficult, the temperature dropped, boiling decreased, and the atmosphere became neutral. The iron now included some slag. A worker lifted and turned the entire mass, to complete the decarbonization. He then divided the mass into four or five portions, being careful not to include the slag in balls, each of which weighed between 66 and 88 pounds. They were then taken to be shingled in order to remove the slag completely.

Cort's reverberatory furnace was lined with fireproof bricks and had a bottom of tamped clayey sand. The materials were heated by direct contact with the flame, but the basic principle was that of separating them from the fuel itself. The furnace included a stokehole. The fusion or reheating of the metal was done in the hearth, 13 feet long by 5 feet wide, which was either inclined or concave, to facilitate thorough stirring of the metal with iron rods. The concave roof reflected the heat from the furnace back onto the hearth. The space between the hearth and the fire, called the furnace bridge, had a height that varied according to whether a high temperature was desired or whether one wanted to avoid oxidation and burning. To avoid heat losses the height of the furnace decreased toward the back, away from the fire. The furnace ended in a chimney, the height of which varied from 50 to 65 feet. Such furnaces, with a few modifications, remained in use until around 1860.

The first puddling furnaces were introduced on the Continent early in the nineteenth century. Some metallurgists appear to have profited by the Peace of Amiens in 1802 to visit England, from which they brought back the new English refining processes. The puddling furnace may possibly have been introduced later in other Continental countries, where this procedure became known through the efforts of one G. Dufaud, an engineer in the Nivernais factories.

Rolling mills   The same difficulty previously mentioned was also present in forging: as soon as increasing quantities of iron became available, the old hydraulic hammers were no longer adequate to work it and convert it into either merchant iron or manufactured products. Another method thus had to be perfected.

A patent taken out by Cort in 1783 for a rolling mill was actually an adaptation of a previously known apparatus. There were several problems, the first of which

Plate 63.   Drawing by Oliver Evans from "The Young Mill-Wright." Smithsonian Institution

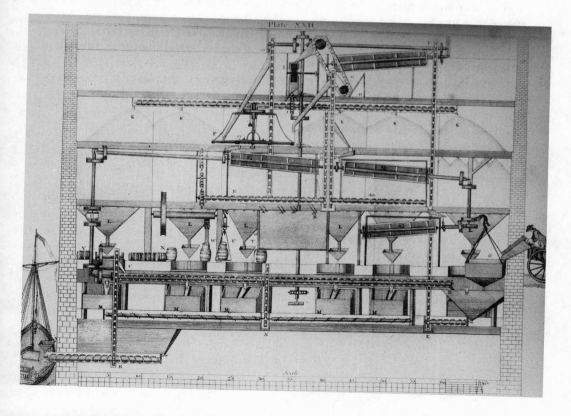

is easily understandable. Unless it was desired to roll sheet metal, smooth rollers could not be used. Actually, grooved cylinders were used (even throughout the entire nineteenth century) that produced what are now called sections. In a work by William Emerson (*The Principles of Mechanics*, London, 1758) we find an interesting picture of a rolling mill (reproduced in an earlier chapter), which with a very few changes must have been the one used by Henry Cort. There are two smooth cylinders 7¾ inches in diameter and two grooved cylinders 11¾ inches in diameter and approximately 4¼ feet long.

Pictures exist of one of the first rolling mills at the Worthey forges in Yorkshire; the original mill is preserved in the Science Museum in London. It is simply a housing carrying rolls with graduated grooves diminishing toward one end, making it possible to reduce the dimensions of its bars with each passage through the mill. Here again, this must have been the common model of the first rolling mills.

A second problem was that of effectively adjusting the rolls. This was an early problem but a less serious one in the old rolling mills. A primitive system of tightening with wedges was followed by a system of screws and nuts (Figures 23, 24, and 25).

The last problem was to give the rolling mill greater strength, which will be discussed later.

The use of Cort's invention spread rapidly. Even by 1789 we find many English plants being equipped with rolling mills to produce iron bars.

The power problem   The problem of power came up in several respects, the first being geographical in nature. With new resources the iron industry could move out of the traditional areas. In England and later on the Continent the new iron industry had almost everywhere moved to the coal fields, but it was then quite possible that the water resources capable of supplying the necessary power might not be adequate or available there. It was therefore obligatory to find means of extending the technical change by finding a new source of energy.

The second problem—the necessity of having more abundant power—was partly related to the first. The blasting engines of the furnaces and rolling mills now required not only more power but also, since coke production could be continuous, steady and reliable power.

At the very moment when the technical changes were being completed in the iron industry, the steam engine, after all Watt's improvements, became a genuinely useful machine. Nothing more was needed to adapt it successfully.

The first uses to which the steam engine was applied were perhaps not the most logical ones. The steam engines first used in the iron industry were still Newcomen engines. The engine installed at Coalbrookdale for the blast was used only to lift water to make it turn a mill wheel. It was no doubt shortly before 1780 that the Darbys adopted Watt's engines and used them directly. In 1784 their yards were already covered by a vast network of cast-iron tracks over which mine trucks rolled. The great ironmaster John Wilkinson, son of Isaac Wilkinson (who in his time had been one of the first to follow the Darbys in coke smelting), ordered a steam engine, from Boulton and Watt, which was the first to be more than a simple pump for the blowing engine of furnaces.

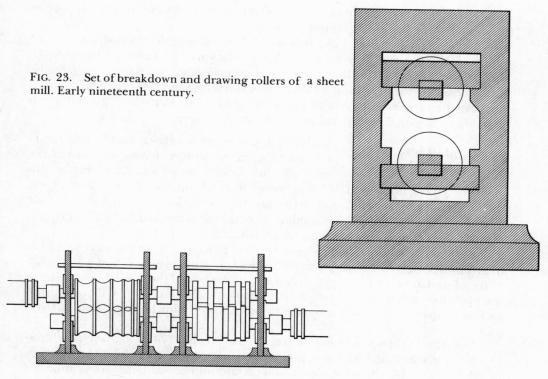

FIG. 23.   Set of breakdown and drawing rollers of a sheet mill. Early nineteenth century.

FIG. 24. Roll train. *Left:* Roughing roll. *Right:* Drawing roll. Early nineteenth century.

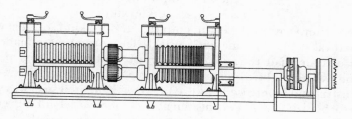

FIG. 25.   Finishing rolls for drawing iron. Construction at the Rybnick Forge, around 1830.

In 1782 Cort was concerned with finding a solution to the problem of power for his rolling mills. In that year he visited Watt's Soho shops to buy a steam engine. Very probably it was because of this engine that Cort was able to develop his rolling mill and obtain his patent the next year.

As soon as the iron industry had the steam engine, which it could feed with the coal over which it was installed, it discovered that it had broken all ties with its earlier supply system, except for ore, which had indeed on the Continent a considerable bearing on the slow adoption of English methods there. It can truly be said that the new iron industry now had no relation to classic iron production as described at the beginning of this study.

To be sure, we should not be deceived, for a complete transformation of industry was possible only when all the innovations had become effective. Although starting in 1770 in England we may note the beginnings of a change in the distribution of factories and in their concentration into a smaller number of increasingly larger units, it was not until after 1785 that the true Industrial Revolution began. The revolution was, however, very rapid.

Machinery for working metal The development of a certain mechanization in ironworking was, to be sure, independent of all the advances just briefly reviewed. An effort in this sector of production could well have been expected independent of a change in the techniques of handling raw materials. It is nevertheless remarkable to note that here again the major dates combine to make the last quarter of the eighteenth century the very first era of technical innovation.

We have little information about the inventions leading to the mechanization of metalworking in the closing years of the eighteenth century. At best it is possible to fix a few dates and a few types of tools. At least one of these machines is due to the inventive genius of an ironmaster already mentioned, John Wilkinson, who had developed a machine for boring cannons, chiefly for boring cast-iron naval guns.

From these early experiments, which dated from 1774, Wilkinson produced in 1776 a machine for boring cylinders that was the first machine tool to work metal. We later see the appearance of a certain number of lathes, the history of which has been described earlier.

Crucible steel The problem of steel was long obscured by a lack of chemical knowledge, the true nature of steel being completely unknown.

Until the later years of the eighteenth century two kinds of steel were made: so-called natural steel and cementation steel. The former were made from ores that manufacturers had learned to distinguish and from which partly decarbonized iron was undoubtedly obtained. The steels from Rives, France, and from Styria in Austria and from Sweden were famous. Cemented steel was obtained by partially recarbonizing iron. For this purpose, a great variety of ingredients were used in addition to charcoal, each of which supposedly gave the steel a special quality. The operation was performed in small converting furnaces, good examples of which can be seen in the *Encyclopédie méthodique*.

René Réaumur (1683–1757) was one of the first to become interested in the theoretical aspects of steel production. He first made as precise an examination as possible of the various qualities of steel known at the time and so introduced the first methods of metallography. The transition to the experimental stage was more complicated. He applied a current theory of salts and sulfurs, leading him to suppose that steel had a sulfur and salt content intermediate between that of cast iron and soft iron. He postulated the existence of a certain substance, an excess or shortage of which prevented an iron product from acquiring the properties of good tool steel. He believed, therefore, that it was possible to make steel by fusing a mixture of cast iron and soft iron. Over a simple forge fire he melted a mixture of scrap metal, nails, and forged iron with molten metal. This procedure indeed had a future, but its inventor found himself unable to pursue his research, which lacked a correct theoretical chemical basis.

An identical idea was taken up several years later by a Doncaster, Lincolnshire, clockmaker named Benjamin Huntsman (1704–1776). His craft required for watch springs very homogeneous steel, which it was difficult to obtain by cementation, a process that in many cases produced only a superficial carburetion. His investigations, continued after 1740 at Sheffield, probably produced no results until around 1750.

To obtain a homogeneous metal Huntsman smelted it at a very high temperature in hermetically sealed crucibles of fireproof clay with small quantities of charcoal and crushed glass to serve as reagents (Figure 26). Crucible steel was originally not so much a new method for making steel as a technique to improve products then in common use. The high temperature enabled Huntsman, like Réaumur to obtain molten steel. The one disadvantage of this method was that only relatively small quantities could be expected, at a high cost.

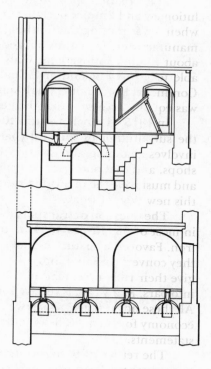

FIG. 26. Huntsman's crucible furnace for steel making. *Top:* Lateral cross section showing the arrangement of the hearth; *Bottom:* Frontal cross section showing the layout of the hearths and crucibles.

The discoveries by Lavoisier and Priestley that established modern chemistry made it possible to give the iron industry a more solid basis, but the basic ideas were not clarified until the end of the century. The works of Berthollet, Monge (1746–1818), and Vandermonde (*Les différents états de fer,* a work that appeared in 1788) appeared after considerable progress had been made throughout the century. Metallurgists and manufacturers had hitherto proceeded by trial and error and blind experimentation, but by the very end of the century scientists had opened new paths that led to new techniques.

THE FIRST HALF OF THE NINETEENTH CENTURY

Production conditions had thus been visibly transformed. The new techniques also had to meet an increased demand and to adapt to favorable dispositions of natural resources, and to an adequate structure of capital.

The economic situation   In England the most favorable conditions existed together. Coal and iron mines were contiguous and transportation was easy in the producing regions, many of which were located near seacoasts. Capital was abundant and a steady demographic growth made it possible to find the necessary labor supply. By 1806 the old method of production dependent on wood had practically disappeared. Major enterprises were dominating an industry whose concentration was already evident.

The situation was much more difficult in Europe. The wars in the Revolutionary and Empire periods cut off the Continent from England at the moment when it was putting the finishing touches on the new processes. The Continental manufacturers were thus obliged to wait for some length of time before learning about English innovations. Only after 1815 were engineers and manufacturers able to go to England and English workers and industrialists to settle on the Continent. It was not enough simply to have a knowledge of English methods; it was equally necessary that the general industrial conditions be favorable.

In 1815 a French manufacturer wrote: "The persons who so casually suggest the substitution of mineral coal for charcoal appear to be unaware that this involves changing almost everything in the furnaces, refineries, machines, and shops, and that one must be near coal mines that supply the proper type of coal and must have the ore within range of the fuel, and that one must train workers in this new type of work."

The question of transportation was equally formidable: "It would be illusory, in most of our forges, to claim to compete with the English in the price of their iron. Favored by nature in fuel and ore, which they find combined in a single pit, they convert the latter into coke and, by means of steam engines and rolling mills, give their rolls a tremendous power sufficient to draw out this primary product into bars. Many canals receive this iron and facilitate its transportation to the sea. All these advantages, which we are far from possessing, are immense sources of economy for them." The German and Belgian manufacturers could make similar statements.

The return of peace brought the fear that England now had an opportunity to conquer the European market. Only the establishment of high tariff barriers in almost all the European countries after 1821 made it possible to secure the investment needed for modernizing an industry that still remained largely conservative in its techniques. The production of cast iron was still to a significant degree dependent on charcoal; even in 1850 less than half was being produced with coke. On the other hand, the English puddling process was quite rapidly

Plate 64. Casting of a very large bronze capital of a column for the Czar Alexander monument in Leningrad by A. Ricard de Montferrand (1834). Lithograph after Fragonard. French National Library, Print Collection. (Photo Documentation Française, Paris.)

established, and iron produced with coal easily prevailed over iron produced with wood. Thus, during the first phase of European economic growth, from 1823 to 1825 and still more from 1835 to 1839, English techniques were permanently introduced.

But these techniques themselves were undergoing major changes.

The hot blast   The idea of using a hot instead of a cold blast in the blast furnace undoubtedly occurred quickly to metallurgists; they could hope in this way to decrease fuel consumption. But practical realization of this idea was not without serious difficulties.

In 1824 a Scottish manufacturer questioned an engineer at the Glasgow Gasworks about a method of purifying the air blown into blast furnaces by adapting the technique used for illuminating gas. It was thought that the excess of sulfur contained in the air in summer was the cause of the erratic operation of the furnaces and poor quality of the metals. James B. Neilson (1792–1865) showed that in summer the air had a smaller proportion of oxygen. It was decided to perform experiments, in which Neilson applied the principle of the expansion of gases by passing the air intended for a blast furnace through a container heated red hot.

The experiments were continued by Neilson and Charles Macintosh (1766–1843). In 1828 the air was still being heated to only 28° above the outside

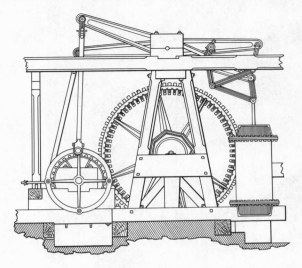

FIG. 27. Althans blowing engine, built at the Lohen factories near Siegen, Prussia, around 1825. *Center:* Waterpowered driving wheel; *Left:* Toothed wheels transmitting motion to the walking beams; *Right:* Blowing cylinders (only one is visible in the drawing).

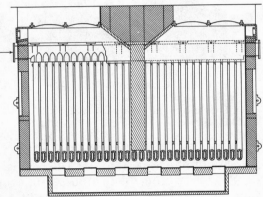

FIG. 28.   Longitudinal cross section of Corngreaves's hot-air stove.

temperature. It was now understood that a higher temperature had to be obtained and that the simple red hot pipe was no longer sufficient. A first patent was taken out in September 1828.

In May 1829 Neilson employed a furnace that brought the temperature up to 93°. In 1830 he obtained a temperature of 315°. Finally he was led to use a tubular furnace, perfected between 1832 and 1833, but difficulties persisted. With the increased temperature of the blast, the point at which fusing occurred dropped constantly inside the furnace. The temperature in the area near the tuyeres increased and threatened to destroy them, a problem dealt with in 1829/30 by John Condie, who cooled the tuyeres with a stream of water. The solution had now been found, and between 1832 and 1834 Scottish and English manufacturers hesitantly adopted the new apparatus.

In adopting the hot blast the English iron producers had several results in view. They hoped first of all to substitute coal for coke. It quickly became evident that even partial operation with coal gave poor results; the reduced metals were very phosphoric and were so high in sulfur that manufacturers could no longer hope to eliminate bubbles during puddling. In addition, working the blast furnace at the fore hearth was made very difficult while the charge fell erratically. With coke alone the operation was clearly better, but because the reduced metal was still full of graphite and phosphorus it proved unsuited for molding.

To these difficulties were added those of the equipment itself. It was impossible to keep repaired the cast-iron pipes in which the air circulated. There were considerable losses of blast, high maintenance costs, and heating stoppages that were disastrous because of the disturbances they created in the operation of the blast furnaces. All the metals obtained by this method were siliceous, so a series of improvements was needed.

The second result of adopting the hot blast was twofold and beneficial: an increase in the average production per furnace and a reduction in the consumption of coal per ton. The second advantage was the more important. The following figures, obtained by Neilson at the Clyde Ironworks, testify to this:

	Coal in tons	Cost per ton
1811	11	£8
1828	8	£4 12s. 1d.
1831	4	£3 5s. 6d.
1832	2.5	£2 12s. 8d.

The economies realized were the subject of discussion for a long time.

Other methods were proposed to solve the various problems raised by the use of the hot blast. The chemist Jacques Thenard (1777–1857) showed that it was highly advantageous to divide the air introduced by the tuyeres into the blast furnaces, using a grill placed in front of the tuyeres. A Frenchman, one Cabrol, the manager of the Decazeville factory, took out a patent in 1834 to which various additions were made in 1838. His method consisted of passing the blast through grills laden with fuel, to obtain "decomposed air and carbon monoxide." The decomposition of the CO_2 lowered the temperature of the gaseous flux to around 280°. Additions to the patent aimed to obtain methodical heating of the blast.

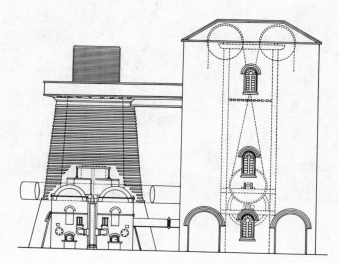

FIG. 29. Corngreaves's blast furnace, Staffordshire. *Right:* Charging tower.

Plate 65. Men and women working together in the English metallurgical industry, around 1855–1860. Photograph G. B. Gething. Collection Société Française de Photographie, Paris.

The adoption of the hot blast by one method or another was gradual, but by about 1850 the new technique was already widespread.

The recovery of furnace gases   For lack of detailed writings, the history of the technique of recovering waste gases is still very obscure. One Aubertot, an ironmaster in Berry, was undoubtedly the first to conceive of using the waste heat of gases from blast furnaces. The experiments must have begun during the Empire period, probably around 1805 or 1806. Aubertot made use of the gases to heat cementation furnaces installed above blast furnaces and to fire bricks. In 1810 Aubertot took out a patent for a reverberatory furnace suitable for cementing steel, remelting cast metals, and making lime and other materials.

The use of these gases was not simple. It was immediately realized that they had to be purified, which was done with quite primitive methods. Moreover, the application of waste heat to devices situated above the furnaces was not very convenient. In a sense the idea had no practical application.

The appearance of the hot blast nevertheless revived the idea of using the heat given off by the furnaces, to heat the blast and even more to supply the blast engines. Experiments were therefore resumed and the process was definitively perfected in 1835, at the furnace of Échalonge in the Franche-Comté. Here again an appreciable economy in fuel was obtained.

As strange as it may seem, the utilization of waste gases worked to the advantage of the traditional rural small-scale metallurgy. Small factories far from coal production areas could now, without additional expenses for fuel, adopt steam engines for blast works and workshops and, when necessary, for the hot blast.

The development of the puddling process   The puddling furnaces used by Cort still presented numerous disadvantages. The bed consisted of tamped argillaceous sand. Silicon in the form of hammer scales overwhelmed the iron oxide as it was in the process of being formed, at the expense of the cast iron. Neutral or acidic silicates were thus

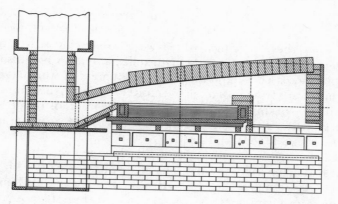

FIG. 30.   Vertical cross section of the Blaina puddling furnace (from Percy).

formed and there was no effect on the various elements in the reduced metal, in particular the manganese, phosphorus, and silicum, which unlike carbon and sulfur could not be eliminated under the direct action of the air. This made necessary preliminary refining in the lower hearth, as long as this problem had not been solved. The principal defect of puddling was the loss of metal, which could reach 25 percent.

From 1816 to 1818 Samuel Rogers of Nantyglo conceived of replacing the sand bed with an air-cooled cast-iron bed. Several years later he recommended installing walls of the same type, the whole being cooled by circulating water. With these changes he estimated that weekly production could be raised from 10 to 20 tons.

The problem of the bed continued to preoccupy metallurgists, and various patents were taken out in England on this subject. In 1822 R. S. Harford thought of protecting the bed of the puddling furnace with charcoal. At this period experiments were also made to run molten metal directly into the puddling furnace, thus avoiding the expense of remelting. Also in 1822 a W. Jones recommended that the puddling furnace be charged with preheated metal.

Most of the difficulties were removed by the discoveries of Joseph Hall, made between 1825 and 1832, for which no patent was taken out. His method was known as pig boiling, or wet puddling. Hall used forge slag (calcined iron oxide) as an oxidizer. This basic lining made it possible to eliminate preliminary refining. The name *pig boiling* comes from the fact that the oxygen from the slag, combining with the carbon in the reduced metal, caused genuine boiling in the molten metal because of the carbon dioxide. The name *wet puddling* derives from the liquid nature of the slag. Hall's discoveries made possible economy in metal and fuel.

Thus the chemical difficulties were solved. Puddling nevertheless continued to be an extremely difficult operation. Stirring the mass with the long iron rods needed was an almost inhuman operation, hence the interest in mechanical stirring. The first patent for a mechanical puddling furnace, granted in 1836, aimed at maneuvering the rods by steam power. The difficulties were overcome only much later. The first rotating puddling furnace appeared in 1857, when the discovery of the Bessemer process for steel production caused the iron production to disappear fairly soon.

The power hammer   The rolling mill provided iron bars in large quantity but it was useless for dealing with pieces in special shapes. To work these forgings, which were needed in increasing numbers, manufacturers still had to rely on the hydraulic hammer, which also had limited power. Despite increased weights and the development of frontal type hammers, certain of which were from now on made entirely of metal, this equipment was no longer suited for working large forgings. The invention of propellers for ships called for large shafts that had to be forged. It was therefore imperative that new equipment be found to meet this need.

The idea of using the steam engine to lift a hammer was an old one. The first experiments had taken a wrong turn. The idea of using steam to lift water, which then fell on a classic mill wheel, had already been conceived. James Watt had already thought up a hammer to be operated directly by a steam engine. A patent dated April 28, 1774, concerned large hammers or pounders "to forge or stamp

Plate 66. Power hammer in operation in the Derosne & Cail shops at Grenelle. Engraving taken from Turgan, *Les Grandes Usines*, Paris, 1865. (Photo Alain Doyère - C.N.A.M.)

copper or other metals and materials without the intervention of rotating mechanisms or wheels, attaching the said hammers and pounders either directly to the piston or to the piston rod of the engine." There was also such a patent by an inventor named Deveral, taken out in June 1806. However, these investigations seem to have been abandoned, undoubtedly because their usefulness was not yet appreciated.

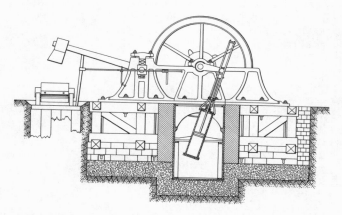

FIG. 31. Trip-hammer operated by a steam engine with an oscillating cylinder, around 1846.

Inventors and manufacturers probably took up the question during most of the early part of the nineteenth century and suggested solutions that gradually put the problem on the road to solution, but the device did not take concrete form until around 1840. It is useful to repeat some details given in an earlier chapter.

Today our sources seem to prove clearly that the definitive idea came simultaneously to two engineers, the Englishman James Nasmyth (1808–1890) and a Frenchman named François Bourdon, in 1839. Nasmyth probably clearly understood in which direction the solution was to be found—his surviving sketch dated November 24, 1839, proves this—but it is only a simple drawing, leaving a certain number of difficulties unclarified. Bourdon's idea also dates from 1839, but he may at the time have drawn up a detailed plan that may have been shown to naval engineers, for it was basically a question, as noted earlier, of a machine to forge the shafts of marine engines. Bourdon's employer, Schneider, is said to have hesitated. Then the two manufacturers made a trip to England in 1840, during which they may have learned of Nasmyth's sketch. Bourdon is believed to have disclosed his plans on the same occasion. In any case, Schneider, struck by the coincidence of the two concepts, encouraged his engineer to build the machine. Bourdon thus built the first power hammer, based on his 1839 plans, at the end of 1840 or the beginning of 1841; the first patent was taken out on July 30, 1841 (Figure 32). Meanwhile, Nasmyth came to Le Creusot and saw the apparatus.

This first power hammer, built toward the end of 1840, had a striking mass ("tup") of 2.5 tons and a fall of 6½ feet. The apparatus consisted of four cast-iron uprights joined by crossbars. A plate acting as an entablature supported the steam cylinder. The whole was supported by four props springing from the angles of the entablature. The shaft and the hammer operated along a slide bar. Later projects simplified the structure of the apparatus, leaving only two braces.

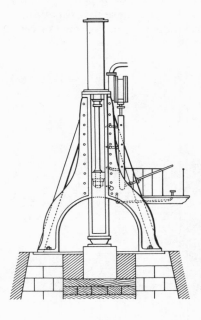

FIG. 32.   Bourdon's steam hammer. Drawing from the patent of July 30, 1841.

These machines now multiplied and their weight rose to 3 tons. In addition, small 1.8-ton hammers were constructed. Bourdon demonstrated that it was impossible to go below 1 ton. The power of these hammers was gradually increased.

In this period metallurgists also thought of adopting the hydraulic press. Sir Charles Fox's 1847 patent was still very vague. In 1851 Guillemin and Minary patented a hammer raised by hydraulic pressure, but the first conclusive experiments were not performed until 1857, by Benoît and Duportail. Bourdon himself in 1852 prepared a plan for a 120-ton hydraulic hammer.

A number of small improvements Besides these major inventions, which appreciably changed metallurgical techniques, the first half of the nineteenth century saw many small advances. We might almost call it a virtually imperceptible evolution of some techniques.

Although ore preparation was modified very little, by 1850 the preparation of coke was, in contrast, completely changed. Production in heaps (which long persisted in certain regions, particularly in Germany) gave way to baker's oven. Thereafter, coke furnaces, which at first were simple rectangular ovens, were constantly being improved. In 1840 Cox took out a patent for a vaulted furnace. Jones introduced a furnace that had a yield of close to 65 percent. In 1857 at the Marquise factory a Frenchman named Appolt invented a furnace composed of

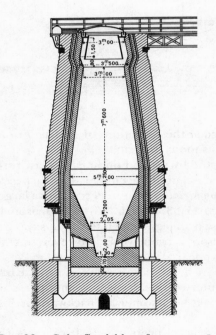

FIG. 33. Coke-fired blast furnace at Le Creusot. Elevation and vertical cross section through the tuyères, around 1865 (from Percy).

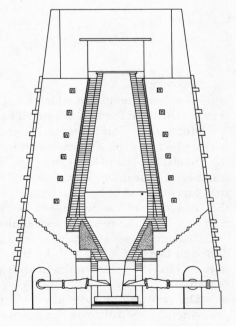

FIG. 34. Blast furnace at Gluwitz in Silesia, around 1830.

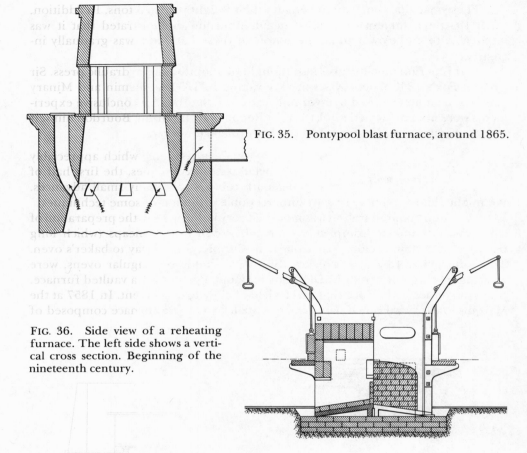

FIG. 35.   Pontypool blast furnace, around 1865.

FIG. 36.   Side view of a reheating furnace. The left side shows a vertical cross section. Beginning of the nineteenth century.

vertical compartments, in which he approached the conditions of retorts. From then on the coke furnace advanced toward its modern form.

Much discussion continued concerning the forms and outlines of blast furnaces, which to some extent determined the descent of the charge. The furnaces were of all shapes and heights; in his *Treatise on Metallurgy* John Percy gives a large number of extremely varied examples (Figures 33, 34, 35, 36). The masonry structures tended to become lighter, and cast-iron legs came into use to support the furnace itself, independent of the masonry framework. However, metal frames to hold the refractories had not yet appeared.

Charging was gradually mechanized. Inclined ramps were slowly abandoned in favor of hoists with hydraulic counterweights or even steam-operated devices. However, the Continent appears to have been somewhat backward in this regard.

The recovery of waste gases still posed delicate problems. In furnaces with permanently open throats the gas was collected around the circumference; in those with closed mouths it was collected in the center. The gases brought out much solid matter, and methods of basic purification were still very incomplete.

The available statistics on the energy used by the iron industry between 1835 and 1844 in France show that the use of waste gases spread quite rapidly. (The figures indicate horsepower.)

	1835	1844
Waterpower	19,217	16,744
Steam (coal)	1,089	1,531
Steam (gas)	$\frac{2}{m}$	2,524
	20,306	20,799

In 1844 the iron-smelting industry in France had 62 engines that were heated by coal as against 92 operating with gas from blast furnaces.

The evolution of the rolling mill has been much less thoroughly studied. Improvements were probably made slowly and almost imperceptibly, particularly in the method of adjusting the rolls and even in how they were produced. The fabrication of rails certainly led to modification in detail which, when accumulated, transformed this technique.

THE NONFERROUS METALS

The advances in the production of nonferrous metals were much less spectacular. Here the evolution was much slower and we cannot speak of a revolution as we can in the case of the iron industry. In this area the most important factor is incontestably the discovery of new metals and how to prepare them, at least in the laboratory, which pertains more to chemistry than to industry.

Progress in the eighteenth century
Few advances were made in the eighteenth century. There could be no question of modifying the practices in use until then, certain of which dated from early antiquity.

Platinum was discovered in 1735 in ores from Colombia by Antonio de Ulloa and Charles Wood. In 1784 Chabaneau succeeded in preparing an ingot of platinum. His method consisted of a treatment with aqua regia and a precipitate of the chlorides, with the exception of that of platinum. In this way a platinum foam was obtained, which was compressed.

Nickel was isolated in an impure state by Baron Axel F. Cronstedt in 1751 and in a pure state in 1775 by Torbern Bergman (1735–1784) and Orfiedson. The same was true of cobalt, prepared in 1735 in an impure state by Georg Brandt and in a pure state in 1790 by Bergman. Actually, these metals were not widely used, and no industrial preparation was begun; they were still scientists' curiosities. Discoveries of metals multiplied at the end of the eighteenth century. Chrome was isolated by Nicolas Louis Vauquelin (1763–1829) in 1797. Carl W. Scheele (1742–1786) discovered tungsten in 1781 and in 1782 Bergman succeeded in preparing this metal. We owe molybdenum to Peter Jacob Hjelm in 1782 and zirconium to Martin Klaproth (1743–1817) in 1789. The chemistry of metals had thus made considerable advances, due in large part to the birth of a new science of chemistry, led by Lavoisier and Priestley.

Four metals were produced on a large scale in this period: lead and copper in particular, zinc and tin to a much lesser degree. Lead and copper were extracted from their ores by roasting, then by reduction, and finally by refining, using methods which had not progressed since the sixteenth century. Lead was rolled and sold in sheets. Copper was often hammered, with hydraulic hammers that bore a strong resemblance to the tilt hammers used in iron production. Copper was also worked, manually, with a hand hammer, particularly for cauldrons and vats. The same was true of gold and silver, which were obtained by amalgamation or cupellation, using very old techniques.

Progress in the nineteenth century   The first half of the nineteenth century did not fundamentally change the look of the metallurgy of nonferrous metals; the period witnessed new discoveries and extremely slow improvements.

The first task was obviously to identify the metals, then prepare them in the laboratory and develop the means to prepare them industrially insofar as an immediate and profitable use could be discovered for them.

The greatest discoveries were of aluminum, by Friedrich Wöhler in 1827; chrome, isolated by Robert W. Bunsen in 1854; vanadium, by Nils G. Sefstrom in 1830; uranium, by E.-M. Péligot in 1841; palladium and rhodium by William H. Wollaston in 1804 and 1805, respectively; osmium and iridium by Smithson Tennant, and ruthenium by Karl Klaus in 1844.

In certain cases easier methods were tried, but they were not adaptable on an industrial scale. For example, for the reduction of aluminum Sainte-Claire Deville used the action of sodium on the double chloride of aluminum and sodium. An ingot was prepared in this way for the Universal Exposition of 1855, and production began on a very small scale at Glacière in 1856 and Nanterre the following year. The cost was so high that jewelry was made from aluminum, which was treated as a rare and expensive metal.

The metallurgy of the classic metals appears to have been considerably modified, but as yet little is known about the exact stages. The metallurgists proceeded by a series of improvements, modifying the equipment rather than the traditional methods, which remained more or less the same.

Copper ore was roasted with coke, as had been done in England from the end of the seventeenth century. In this way a matte of the double sulfide of copper and iron was formed that was again roasted and then treated in a shaft furnace. A variety of methods existed in the large copper-producing regions; the very nature of the ores probably led to these differences. The Welsh method consisted of a series of roasting and smelting operations repeated until a product containing 70 to 75 percent of copper was obtained. This matte was oxidized and roasted ($Cu_2S + 2CuO = 4Cu + SO_2$) in a reverberatory furnace that was very similar to iron furnaces. The German method used the traditional shaft furnace. There was little change in copper metallurgy before 1880.

Lead was smelted by roasting and reduction. The roasting was done in a reverberatory furnace, the reduction in a shaft furnace or water jacket. Few modifications were made either in the methods or in the equipment.

In 1804 a Belgian, the Abbot Duny, developed a new method for extracting zinc. A mixture of ore and charcoal was placed in many crucibles and zinc vapor was distilled off. This method was used particularly at the famous deposits of Vieille-Montagne, between Liège and Aachen. The use of zinc was not yet greatly developed; the almost complete monopoly held by a single firm did not encourage improvements in the techniques of working zinc.

The methods of extracting and refining precious metals were equally static. In 1842 Karl Karsten used the zinc method to reduce silver and obtained crystals of lead, zinc, and silver, which were then distilled. In 1853 Hugh Pattinson tried slowly cooling the lead bath and found that the part that remained liquid was the richest in silver. The operation was repeated a certain number of times in the same manner. Gold was still obtained by amalgamation. Around 1830 a Frenchman named Poisat invented a more developed method of refining gold by separating it from silver. This discovery brought about the recasting of coinage almost everywhere in Europe. In 1848 in England, however, gold was obtained by chlorination.

Lastly, in 1832 Muntz introduced an alloy that was 60 percent copper and 40 percent zinc, an alloy used to sheath vessels. Its advantage was that it could be hot rolled.

By the end of the eighteenth century the technique of iron production had been completely transformed. This evolution brought about two major efforts, quickly in England, more slowly on the Continent, on the structure of this industry.

On the technical level iron now became an important competitor of wood, which until then had been the most widely used material, and its use could now extend far beyond the narrow framework within which it had been imprisoned for centuries. In 1772 the first iron bridge was built over the Severn, at Coalbrookdale, and early in the nineteenth century the first iron vessels were built. Iron framework invaded construction (the Wheat Market, Paris, 1804); Polonceau's invention of the truss made the rapid adoption of the new design possible. Nor should it be forgotten that railroads came to benefit greatly from this technical revolution.

CHAPTER 4

THE RISE OF THE HEAVY CHEMICAL INDUSTRY

THE DEVELOPMENT of the chemical industry during the period studied in this volume presents a certain similarity to the evolution of the iron-smelting industry during the same period. One is struck by the importance of the new methods for transforming raw materials, which made it possible to offer chemical compounds, some of which had been seldom used until then, for sale in industrial quantities.

The shift in chemical activities As in the iron industry, the basic products, around the production of which a heavy industry became built up, were compounds that had been known for several centuries, such as carbonate of soda and sulfuric and hydrochloric acids. The first was obtained, as explained in Volume II, by simple methods from various vegetables, but since it was produced only in certain regions and countries, it gave rise to an important long-distance trade that increased the price consumers had to pay. The two acids were little used; until around the last quarter of the eighteenth century the laborious method of producing them had made only negligible progress. Although the demand for sulfuric acid grew slowly during the eighteenth century, it remained small for hydrochloric acid.

Around 1770 to 1780 the chemical industry gave the impression that its status quo would endure for a long time to come. The production of saltpeter and of nitric acid had led to an original complex of industrial organization that was an early example of vertical concentration. The system remained in existence for approximately a century, with a few gradual modifications arising from the use of sulfuric acid to treat the natural nitrates. The barely modernized production of saltpeter disappeared as an industrial activity only with the closing decades of the nineteenth century, when smokeless powder, as it was then called, based on nitrated cellulose, supplanted the traditional black powder.

Next to manufactures based on the extraction and treatment of nitrates, however, another group of products gradually began to emerge in the closing years of the eighteenth century and first quarter of the nineteenth.

The problem of bleaching The first event that determined the development of this new manufacturing complex was Scheele's discovery of chlorine in 1774 and Berthollet's study of its bleaching properties, the results of which were published by him in 1785. At the time chlorine was not regarded as a simple substance, but in accordance with Lavoisier's theory as an oxygenated muriatic (hydrochloric) acid. In Scheele's method it was obtained by the oxidizing action of manganese dioxide, from either hydrochloric acid or sea salt and sulfuric acid. This error in interpreting the nature of chlorine and the reaction used to prepare it facilitated (by a strange paradox) an understanding of its bleaching action on vegetable products and in particular on flax, hemp, and cotton fabrics.

At that time the bleaching of these textile products was done by repeated washing, soaping, and rinsing action separated by intervals during which the pieces of cloth were exposed for a long time to air by spreading them in the meadows around the factories. The action of the rain, air, and sun could be interpreted by the presence, recently understood and accepted, of oxygen in the air. It was natural to think that the oxygen which, it was believed, entered into the composition of chlorine could replace that in the air.

Spreading out fabrics in meadows made vast stretches of good land, generally located near cities, which greatly needed the space, useless for agriculture and cattle grazing. In addition, the process was an extremely long one. Six months were required to obtain properly bleached linen fabrics: two or three weeks of exposure repeated five times between the washing operations. One and one-half to three months were required for cotton fabrics. The use of chlorine, which could reduce the bleaching operations to a few weeks, thus aroused lively interest.

The production of chlorine required the availability of a large quantity of hydrochloric acid, which in turn could be produced only by sulfuric acid. This was a very expensive compound, and despite the still new and not widespread use of lead chambers, the production methods then known permitted only very small quantities to be produced.

Artificial soda   The second event that determined the development of new manufacturing methods was political in nature: the outbreak of the revolutionary wars and a sudden scarcity of products imported by sea. Among these were the Spanish sodas, indispensable for the dyeing industry. For many years the cost of importing soda had encouraged experimentation to discover a method for preparing alkali or its carbonate from a natural product as common as sodium chloride. In 1776 the Académie des Sciences of Paris opened the question to competition, offering a prize of 2,400 *livres.* This led to work by various chemists, among whom the methods described by a Benedictine, Father Malherbe, and a manufacturer, Carny, began attempts at industrial development. A dozen years later Nicolas Leblanc, a doctor in the service of the duke of Orléans, devised a method that was easier to develop and with the help of a little-known chemist named Dizé succeeded in putting it into usable form. Leblanc's work, begun around 1780, bore fruit five years later and a factory was established at Saint-Denis with capital supplied by the duke of Orléans.

In spite of Leblanc's ingenuity, his method was inefficient because the cost of sulfuric acid was high, and the hydrochloric acid and calcium sulfide produced as by-products could not be used. Moreover the hydrochloric acid caused considerable inconvenience, for it was difficult to remove without causing damage to the surrounding neighborhood. Thus, without the Continental blockade, which stimulated a search for a substitute for natural soda, the production of artificial soda would have encountered great difficulties in establishing itself as a new industry.

After the execution of the duke of Orléans ("Philippe-Égalité"), the factory at Saint-Denis was isolated and closed in 1793. The Committee of Public Safety then began examining the various techniques of producing soda and settled on Leblanc's method, which it ordered published. But the factory at Saint-Denis (then called Franciade) was not put back into operation until five years later, under the government's administration. When the property was returned to Nicolas Leblanc he had to undertake considerable expense to recondition the furnaces and was financially ruined. He died a short time later in 1806 at the age of sixty-four.

The prosperity of the soda factories came after his death. During the forty preceding years, the technique of producing sulfuric acid had been improved to the point where it became a product in common use. At the same time the preparation of bleaches from chlorine obtained by decomposing hydrochloric acid had also developed. All the conditions were favorable for the gradual development of the heavy chemical industry of acids and alkalis. Almost a half century of persevering efforts by the most enterprising manufacturers was still necessary before the cycle of chemically and economically complementary manufactures could come about that made the mineral chemical industry (along with the iron industry) one of the two most important industries in the second half of the nineteenth century.

The production of sulfuric acid

When the Leblanc method of producing artificial soda created a hitherto unknown demand for low-cost sulfuric acid, the method of producing this acid had already seen one important improvement, the system of lead chambers.

It will be remembered that around the middle of the eighteenth century two methods were used to obtain sulfuric acid. The one supplying most of the acid used by the dye industry consisted of decomposing by heat ferrous sulfate distilled in a sort of reverberatory furnace. The acid obtained was known as glacial, fuming, or Nordhausen acid, the latter being the name of the city in Saxony where the largest and oldest factory existed.

Until around the middle of the nineteenth century the acid derived from sulfates continued to be almost the only one used in dyeing, in particular to mix indigo. Even in this period the acid obtained in lead chambers by the oxidation of sulfur dioxide did not fill every need, and concentrating it continued to be a difficult and costly operation. When around 1870 the madder dye industry acquired some importance and required a larger quantity of concentrated acid, the production of Nordhausen acid by the old method experienced a revival, but around the end of the century the production of sulfuric acid by the contact process put an end to the distillation of sulfates.

The other process, equally old, consisted of burning sulfur under a bell jar in the presence of a small quantity of saltpeter. The acidic vapors were absorbed by the water in the bottom of the cupel. The acid content of the product obtained was low, approximately 50° Bé. (the Baumé hydrometer scale). It was used only in the pharmacy, for minor laboratory preparations, or for certain processes in light industry. Thus, in one of the bleaching operations for linen fabrics a process involving soured buttermilk was replaced by a treatment with dilute sulfuric acid, reducing the duration of this operation from several weeks to several hours.

The invention of lead chambers
The first modification of the process, which had been used unchanged for several centuries, was introduced by an Englishman, Joshua Ward (1685–1761), a rather strange individual who served as a model to the painter Hogarth. In 1736 Ward used large glass spheres instead of pottery bell jars to perform the combustion of sulfur. He even had the idea of placing several glass spheres in a series. The use of glass spheres reached the Continent after 1746. Several factories adopted them, first in Berlin, then at Liège, Rouen, and Winterthur.

No matter how large they could be made, the capacity of the glass spheres was limited. Thus, in order to have larger closed volumes available, the manufacturer John Roebuck had the idea of using lead, the only metal that could not be attacked by the acid in this concentration. In 1746 with his partner S. Garbett he had built the first lead chamber in Birmingham. Its capacity was so far no greater than that of the spheres, measuring six feet in each of its three dimensions. Lead was still an expensive material that was just beginning to be obtained in sheets from the rolling mill. The greatest problem was to ensure tight joints between the sheets.

The construction of lead chambers progressed only slowly in England and on the Continent during the second half of the eighteenth century. In 1762 John Holker (1719–1786), who had been granted the title of Inspector General of Manufactures in France, could not attract English workers capable of soldering together the lead sheets, and in 1768 near Rouen his son founded an establishment that used glass spheres; he did not build the first lead chamber in France until 1774.

Lead chambers made possible increased production. The price of the acid had risen in England from 1½ to 2½ shillings per ounce when it was manufactured with the bell jar and the same sum per pound with spheres. But even though it dropped to three or four pence a pound with the chambers, the demand for acid remained stationary, so manufacturers hesitated to devote large sums of money to these installations. Every possible substitute was tried unsuccessfully, and finally the technique of constructing chambers was perfected. Around the end of the century they measured between 23 and 26 feet in length and 16½ feet in height, rested on masonry pilings, and had double-pitched roofs. With the exception of the dimensions, this design was not modified for more than a century.

With the development of the production of artificial soda, between approximately 1810 and 1820, sulfuric acid began to find a large market, and the construction of lead chambers expanded accordingly. Their dimensions increased and a series of three chambers began to be installed on different levels, arranged so that the acid and water in the chambers would flow from the third into the second and from there into the first. It titrated respectively from 15° to 18° Bé., 38° to 40°, and lastly 48° to 50° in each chamber. In 1826 J.-B. Dumas reported that the capacity of the chambers, in cases where only one was used, varied in France from 5,000 to 10,000 cubic feet and in England went as high as 100,000 cubic feet.

While these installations were spreading, manufacturers had to solve three other problems: the combustion of sulfur to produce the sulfur gas, the intervention of nitrous compounds in the oxidation of the sulfur gas into sulfur trioxide, and concentrating the acid in the chambers to raise it from the strength of 50° Bé. to a commercial strength of 66° Bé.

The combustion of sulfur The combustion of sulfur became quite a difficult operation to perform as soon as one increased the scale from bell jars to chambers. There was a risk of either liquefying or sublimating the sulfur, involving losses of raw material, which was relatively expensive since it was imported from Sicily. In the case of sublimation it affected the purity of the acid obtained.

The first operation was performed on the bottom of the chamber, where a mixture of sulfur was placed with between 1/7 to 1/8 its weight in saltpeter. The method was slow, for it was necessary to wait until the combustion gases had been thoroughly absorbed and the chamber ventilated before opening the chamber and replacing the charge. This led to using a wagon, which was loaded on the outside, pushed into the chamber, and removed after combustion (Figure 37). The proper moment to remove the carriage occurred when the vapors in the chamber were no longer white. A worker had to learn this by observation and know how to evaluate the odor and glowing red color of the vapors at the end of the operation, in order to manage the process successfully.

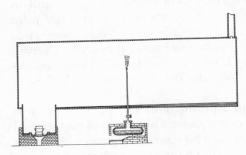

FIG. 37. Manufacturing sulfuric acid. Lead chamber with carriage loaded with sulfur, around 1820.

Sulfur trioxide was absorbed by water in the bottom of the chamber or, as developed by certain manufacturers, trickling down the walls. Finally, in the first quarter of the nineteenth century water was sprayed from jets placed under the roof, a design that later prevailed.

Using a loading wagon meant intermittent combustion, which resulted in an appreciable loss of time, when it was a question of increasing production. At a very early date manufacturers investigated ways to maintain continuous combustion of the sulfur. Holker tried it in 1774 at Rouen and Jean Chaptal (1756–1832) later studied it, being undoubtedly the first to adopt it, at Montpellier. He burned the sulfur in an outside furnace and sent the sulfurous vapors through a pipe into the lead chamber. Around 1800 combustion was also performed inside the chamber, on a sheet of cast iron placed in a corner next to a loading port and heated by an outside furnace. These methods raised the problem of proper draft, solved by using a tall stack, an idea that no doubt led to replacing large-capacity chambers with a series of smaller ones, the stack being placed over the last one.

The role of nitrous products The ventilation problem was linked with that of the role of nitrous products in the oxidation of sulfur gas. It had long been known that the presence of nitric acid or of nitrates was indispensable for the production of sulfuric acid, but it was generally believed that these products played the role of an oxidizer. Thus, a large quantity of them was used and the chambers were completely sealed off to avoid losses of sulfur gas.

In 1793 Nicolas Clement discovered that it was more advantageous to ventilate from the top, since the absorption of the vapors by the water caused an intake of air into the furnace. In 1806 he showed that the nitrous products were only an intermediate stage in the oxidation process. Clement caused the formation of chamber crystals by combining sulfur gas, air, and nitrogen dioxide and recognized that the action of water on these crystals, nitrosylsulfuric acid, produced sulfuric acid and nitrous gas.

This is probably the first example of an application of the new theories of chemistry, which Lavoisier had formed thirty years earlier, to improving an industrial method. Once these ideas had been acquired, the process could be better regulated, but these advances were not generally adopted as a whole before 1820.

At this time the sulfuric acid industry began to expand and all the changes that had occurred since John Roebuck's innovation completely satisfied the manufacturers. In 1828 J.-B. Dumas wrote that "the art of producing sulfuric acid by the present method is sufficiently close to perfection that we can hardly hope for a considerable decrease in the price of the acid by any modifications made in the equipment or its operation." Nevertheless, the forty years that followed led this art to still greater perfection.

Concentrating the acid in the chambers The problem of concentrating the acid in the chambers was an extremely difficult one. Sulfuric acid is a product with very special properties that have always been stumbling blocks for manufacturers. This final portion of the operations had always required heavy equipment.

The acid, at 50° Bé., was collected by draining it out of the chambers, then was first concentrated in lead cauldrons. However, since metal could not withstand such a high concentration, it was necessary to complete the operation in glass or stoneware retorts. An attempt was made in the early nineteenth century to use platinum, but the cost of the equipment led quickly to abandonment of this metal. Manufacturers returned to it later, in the second half of the nineteenth century, after platinum metallurgy had made sufficient progress.

The calcining of pyrites Contrary to Dumas's expectations, the method of producing acid was to undergo further major improvements, involving first the production of sulfur gases from sulfurated ores, then the recovery of nitrous gases at the outlet from the lead chambers. Finally a new production method, based on the catalytic oxidation of sulfur gas, appeared during the second half of the nineteenth century.

The preparation of sulfur dioxide by the combustion of sulfur was an effective but relatively expensive method. The only sulfur deposits abundant enough to be profitably exploited were in Sicily, so that all the countries producing sulfuric acid (Great Britain, France, Belgium, Prussia, and Switzerland) had to import it at great expense. A few experiments were made at the beginning of the nineteenth century to derive sulfur gas from ores formed of metallic sulfurs: iron, zinc, or copper pyrites. The first patent was taken out by two Englishmen, Hill and Haddock, in 1818. Calcining the pyrites in a blast transformed the sulfur from the sulfides into sulfur dioxide, but it left an abundant residue of oxides and metallic sulfates that could not be used. Besides, the pyrites available contained a certain proportion of natural oxides, and their sulfur content was therefore not high enough to make the calcining economically satisfactory.

Experiments had not made much progress when in 1838 a syndicate of French merchants obtained from Ferdinand IV a monopoly for the Sicilian sulfur trade. The cost to manufacturers immediately doubled, so they once again became interested in developing pyrites.

In the previous year a certain Perret, who had just established an enterprise at Saint-Fons near Lyon that later became prosperous, took out a patent for calcining copper pyrites, the first patent industrially developed. The pyrites from French deposits, particularly those near Lyon, had already been used during the Revolutionary and Empire wars to produce sulfur and sulfur gas by crude, low-yield methods. The Perret method was sufficiently satisfactory to permit the Saint-Fons factory to process 2,000 tons of ore in its first year of operation.

Although the sulfur trade monopoly was abolished in 1840, English manufacturers began to exploit the copper and zinc ores of Wales and Ireland, sending the by-products to metallurgical factories. They devoted some ten years to dealing with numerous difficulties before achieving satisfactory results. After 1850 the business of treating pyrites expanded and developed rapidly when in 1860 the processing of ferrous pyrites imported first from Spain and then from Norway began.

From then on the combustion of sulfur rapidly disappeared from European factories. American manufacturers continued to import Sicilian sulfur until around the end of the century. In 1890 they in turn replaced it with the calcining of pyrites, but in 1902 Herman Frasch (1851–1914) introduced a method of extracting sulfur from subterranean deposits in Louisiana by liquefaction. Importation from Sicily was completely cut off, but America continued to produce sulfuric acid by the combustion of sulfur as well as by calcining pyrites.

The recovery of nitrous gases

The gases escaping from the chimneys of lead chambers contained enough nitrogen oxides to be harmful in the areas around factories. Although saltpeter was not expensive, it was advantageous to try recovering part of the nitrous products in order to reintroduce them into the production cycle.

After studying the problem in 1827 and 1828 Gay-Lussac conceived of leading the gases from the chambers into the bottom of a column filled with coke, down which trickled the acid from the chambers. The liquid collected at the bottom of the column was an acid saturated with nitrosylsulfuric acid formed by fixation of the nitrous compounds contained in the gases. In 1835 the Société Saint-Gobain, which since 1806 had been preparing soda by Nicolas Leblanc's method, completed its sulfuric installation with a Gay-Lussac tower, the first one put into operation.

However, the acid in the tower had in turn to be cleared of nitrous compounds, for which purpose it was diluted, to destroy the nitrosylsulfuric acid. These operations imposed new limitations and were troublesome. Although the

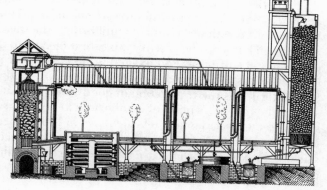

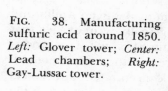

FIG. 38. Manufacturing sulfuric acid around 1850. *Left:* Glover tower; *Center:* Lead chambers; *Right:* Gay-Lussac tower.

Gay-Lussac tower saved two-thirds of the quantities of saltpeter formerly needed, it was so cheap that very few manufacturers adopted the improvement. They began to take an interest in it only when in 1859 the English manufacturer J. Glover took out a patent for a tower to concentrate the sulfuric acid that came from the chambers. This tower, filled with refractory materials like that of Gay-Lussac, received from above a flow of acid from the chambers. The sulfur gases issuing from the furnace at a high temperature concentrated the acid through which they passed, and were cooled (Figure 38).

It was also found advantageous to carry the acid collected at the base of a Gay-Lussac tower to the top of a Glover tower. This acid, which was already titrating at 60° Bé., lost its nitrosylsulfuric acid. The nitrated compounds were volatilized and reintroduced into the chambers with the sulfur gas. Sulfuric acid titrating at 60 to 62° Bé. was collected at the base of the Glover tower.

The use of this combination of cycles spread quickly between 1860 and 1870, and thus the method for producing sulfuric acid acquired its definitive form.

The contact method   This industry was advanced further in coming years by a new method that oxidized sulfur dioxide directly by means of a metallic catalyst. Studies of catalytic oxidation had been begun in the 1830s by various industrial chemists. This was the period when Doebereiner had just invented the Doebereiner "steel," in which gas was ignited by platinum foam. Around 1835 Jacob Berzélius put forward a theory of catalytic reactions and invented this expression, which came to have an extraordinary destiny at the end of the nineteenth century.

In 1837 Peregrine Philips of Bristol became the first to take out a patent for a way to oxidize sulfur gas by using platinum as a catalyst. In France the following year Frédéric Kuhlmann (1803–1881) patented a similar technique for oxidizing ammonia into nitric acid. But the time was not yet ripe for the development of these processes.

In 1875 a German chemist named Klemens Winckler patented a method identical with that of Philips but using platinum chloride as a catalyst. Also in that year the Englishmen Rudolph Messel and W. S. Squire patented the same technique.

The first attempts at development after 1880 were failures. Several difficulties had to be overcome in order to use the sulfur gas obtained by calcining pyrites. Besides, this reaction was one of equilibrium, the theory of which was in this case not yet well known. The gaseous mixture subjected to the action of the catalyst was composed of sulfur gas and oxygen in stoichiometric proportion, that is, according to the classic equation of a total reaction. The firm of Badische Anilin und Soda Fabrik was the first to obtain good yields by using an excess of oxygen that shifted the reaction's point of equilibrium in favor of sulfur trioxide. This processing secret was accidentally revealed only in 1895. Thereafter the contact method, with various catalysts, was widely employed to produce concentrated sulfuric acid and oleum, which synthetic dye factories were beginning to consume in increasing quantities.

The importance of sulfuric acid It seems desirable to discuss details about the history of the sulfuric acid industry because its history between 1750 and 1900 enables us to understand the complex transformation over a century and a half of a craft activity into a major industry. It is obvious that this change was not an easy one, but no effort was avoided in bringing it to fruition, because of the economic importance represented by the growth of production and decrease in cost.

In the early stages experienced manufacturers played the leading part. If we read, for example, Chaptal's *Traité de chimie industrielle* (1806) we see how indifferent to the new chemical theories industry remained. Yet Chaptal was, in the eighteenth century, the first professor to teach Lavoisier's theories. The science of chemistry became a factor in progress for industry only after about 1820.

The new inventions were only very cautiously and slowly adopted by manufacturers because the profit motive was even more dominant in this area, as in the iron industry, than in mechanics. Profits were the basis for the development of the entire heavy industrial chemistry during the nineteenth century, a development that could come about only because of an increasingly close connection between the various manufactures. To be sure, these factors are not peculiar to the chemical industry, but it is in the history of that industry during this period that they are perhaps most clearly visible.

The production of sulfuric acid became industrialized solely by reason of the adoption of the Leblanc method for producing artificial soda. When abundant quantities of acid came on the market it became the essential raw material for new manufactures that in their turn developed into industrial activities of considerable importance. Although the transformation was spectacular between 1820 and 1850, this period was still one of trials and research. The real expansion to a modern scale occurred between 1860 and 1880, when a complex of heavy industry was completed. The annual production of sulfuric acid, like that of steel, then became an index of activity for industrialized countries.

The industrialization of the Leblanc method The extraction of soda from sea salt was already in practice when Nicolas Leblanc began his experiments. The first experiments, for which several attempts at industrial development were made, were inspired by the simple idea of removing soda directly from its combination with hydrochloric acid, using litharge or lime. A mixture of the two compounds was kneaded into a paste that was left to mature in a damp place. In a few days the soda appeared by efflorescence on the surface. Chaptal, like certain English manufacturers, used litharge. The by-product, a mixture of oxide and chloride of lead, could be used as a pigment for paint. The manufacturer Carny used the lime method and later exploited the Leblanc method in his factory at Dieuze, long one of the most important in France.

As we have seen, production based on sodium sulfate required the use of sulfuric acid, which was rare and expensive at first. Even in 1806 Chaptal wrote, "It has been found more advantageous to decompose the sodium sulfate, and Messrs. Leblanc, Dizé, Alban, Bourlier et al. have publicized economical methods in this regard."

The preparation of sodium sulfate, like the transformation of this salt into its carbonate of soda, was done in reverberatory furnaces (Figure 39). For the second operation equal portions of sodium sulfate and chalk were mixed, and half the weight of each of the two products was added in charcoal. The reaction occurred at dark red heat. When the mass became fluid it was poured out on the ground. After it had cooled the mass was broken up and laid in a damp place to permit the sulfurated gases to escape and efflorescence to occur.

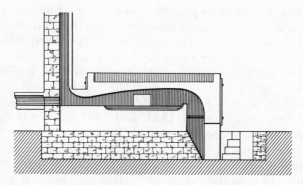

FIG. 39. The first Leblanc method for manufacturing soda. Cross section of the reverberatory furnace for decomposing sodium chloride by SO_4H_2. The bed consists of a lead tank. The hydrochloric acid vapors were evacuated through the pipe at left into a lead chamber. The mixture was then sent into another furnace for the final firing. Later the two operations were performed in the same furnace by shifting the material on the remodeled bed.

The factory sold the crude product, or the crystals obtained from the evaporation of lye in the product, or the evaporated and calcined residue of the mother liquor. This last product, consisting principally of calcium sulfide and lime, had little caustic power.

The process still used at this time by Alban at the Javelle (or Javel) factory, then near Paris, was the one suggested by Father Malherbe in 1778; the reduction of the sulfate was done with charcoal and iron scrap. After washing and crystallization the result of the product of the fusion was pure carbonate. This method was faster than Leblanc's but was more difficult for workers and more expensive for the entrepreneur, so in the early nineteenth century it was abandoned.

In 1806 the Compagnie de Saint-Gobain purchased an old glassmaking plant to produce its own soda, since the qualitative differences of products sold by other manufacturers were too extreme. In France the Chauny soda works later became the largest producer of Leblanc soda in the nineteenth century.

Twenty years later the Leblanc method was perfected by using a double reverberatory furnace. Under a deeply depressed elliptical vault the bed was divided into two compartments. The first, 10 feet long by approximately 8¼ feet wide and sheathed with brick, was used for transforming sodium chloride into sulfate. The second, slightly smaller, was faced with sandstone and used for changing sodium sulfate into carbonate.

The operation, performed with a load of 880 pounds of material, lasted approximately two hours. Stirring the material and caring for the fire in the various phases, especially toward the end of the operation, required skill on the part of the worker, on whom success was completely dependent. This process was used for several decades. Improving the production technique involved particularly the arrangement of furnaces, the method of washing the soda when it came out of the furnaces, recovering the heat to evaporate the carbonate solutions, and mechanizing the stirring operation.

The last point saw the most progress. In 1853 two Englishmen named Elliot and Russel thought of replacing the classic reverberatory furnace with a cylindrical metal one that when placed horizontally could be revolved around its axis. The rotary furnace was used for the first time in England in 1855 by Stevenson and Williamson. Approximately ten years later it appeared on the Continent and its use quickly became general.

Numerous other additions were made to the Leblanc method between 1840 and 1860. For example, between 1851 and 1853 the English manufacturer William Gossage laboriously perfected a method for obtaining solid caustic soda from the carbonate solution.

But two essential problems had to be solved before the production of artificial soda could show real industrial growth, namely, how to recover the two superfluous by-products calcium sulfide and hydrochloric acid.

The recovery of sulfur   All the sulfur introduced in the form of sulfuric acid when producing artificial soda was lost in the form of calcium sulfide. Manufacturers had to get rid of this residue at great cost by submerging it when their plants were in a coastal area, which was the case with many factories near salt marshes. But as many enterprises were located next to deposits of rock salt, in which case the soda ashes were buried in abandoned parts of mines. Major efforts were made to liberate the sulfur from its combination with calcium so as to reintroduce it into the production cycle.

The decomposition of the calcium sulfide could theoretically be done various ways. When treated in solution with carbonic acid the sulfur changed into sulfurized hydrogen, from which state it could be transformed into sulfuric acid. This method was tested in 1838 but could not be used industrially until 1882, when Claus succeeded in decomposing sulfurized hydrogen by using ferrous oxide as a catalyst. Other methods had been tried—for example, changing sulfur

Plate 67. The Forges d'lvry: rolling mill. Engraving taken from Turgan, *Les Grandes Usines*, Paris, 1882. (Photo Alain Doyère - C.N.A.M.)

into hyposulfite, from which the sulfur was liberated by treating it with hydrochloric acid—but this proved too burdensome. During the 1870s an economical method was successfully applied that consisted of adding sulfuric acid to the soda ashes and activating the hydrochloric acid by liberating the sulfur.

Variations in the cost of pyrites and the demand for hydrochloric acid to prepare bleaching products, and the market demand for soda made with the ammonia soda method, gradually and steadily intervened to modify manufacturing methods. It can be said that the problem of recovering sulfur was never satisfactorily solved. When Claus's catalytic method was perfected, Leblanc soda production began to decline.

Hydrochloric acid and chlorine

During the early development of the Leblanc method the hydrochloric acid obtained in the first operation was simply rejected into the atmosphere. But when production began to increase, the damage caused by these vapors became so great that demands were imposed on manufacturers. The absorption of hydrochloric gas by water at first required huge, cumbersome tanks (Figure 40) until shortly after 1830, when the English manufacturer Gossage, who was beginning to experiment with recovering sulfur, conceived of passing the gas through a tower filled with coke in which water trickled downward.

Part of the hydrochloric solution collected at the base of the tower was used to prepare chlorine, but the only known method was Scheele's, so this remained

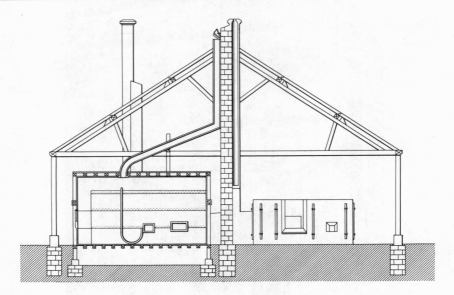

FIG. 40.   Recovery of the hydrochloric acid in the manufacture of soda by the first Leblanc method. *Right:* View of the furnace for transforming sodium chloride into sulfate; *Left:* Cross section of the lead chamber in which the hydrochloric acid vapors were collected.

difficult in the absence of a method to recover the by-products. The demand for chlorine was not very great. Most of the water laden with hydrochloric acid was discharged into streams.

Until the middle of the nineteenth century the production of bleaching products remained very modest, because of its cost. All the manganese used in the form of dioxide, and half the chlorine, was lost as manganese chloride, which was useless. In 1855 C. T. Dunlop suggested decomposing manganese chloride with lime by heating the mixture in solution. The greatest part of the manganese could be recovered, but two-thirds of the chlorine was still lost in the form of calcium chloride, so the method was not profitable enough (Figure 41).

In succeeding years manganese dioxide began to be used in the Bessemer method for steel production and its cost thus began to rise. In 1864 Walter Weldon (1832–1885) succeeded in industrializing the method of regenerating dioxide

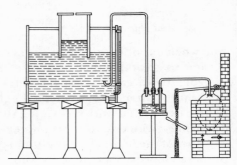

FIG. 41.   Equipment for large-scale manufacturing of chlorine.

discovered by Dunlop by inventing a device that could accomplish the reaction in a blast furnace by reintroducing the nondecomposed products into the cycle.

In the next ten years H. Deacon successfully continued his long effort to decompose hydrochloric acid in water and chlorine, by oxidation of the acid at 450°. He brought about the reaction in a tower lined with porous materials and in the presence of copper chloride, which acted as a catalyst.

The nondecomposed acid resulting from the Deacon method was sufficiently concentrated to be treated economically by the Weldon method. This solved the problem of preparing chlorine under satisfactory economic conditions, and the production of bleaching products then began on a major scale.

Bleaching products   Once the bleaching properties of chlorine were known, manufacturers quickly learned how to prepare it in solution for bleaching linen, hemp, and cotton fabrics. The first industrial preparation of chlorine undoubtedly took place soon after 1785 in the chemical products factory created at Javel in 1777 by a financing company sponsored by the Count d'Artois. Berthollet took charge of this new factory and later his son also had a private enterprise, but he suffered business reverses and committed suicide. At Javel Alban was one of the first, in the late eighteenth century, to produce alkaline hypochlorites by dissolving chlorine in alkaline solutions or limed water. In England in 1798 Charles Tennant (1768–1838), who developed the first great British chemical establishment, dissolved chlorine in limed water. The next year he succeeded in obtaining solid lime hypochlorite, which he sold commercially as bleaching powder.

For twenty to thirty years chemists remained convinced that dissolving chlorine in alkaline solutions weakened its bleaching properties. In 1806 Chaptal, discussing this question, condemned the use of alkaline hypochlorites, saying, "That which is known in Paris under the name *eau de Javel* [dissolved hypochlorite] is nothing more than oxygenated muriatic acid combined with an alkali." He added disdainfully, "It is used in households to remove fruit stains from linen." The first major industrial installation in France, built by Widmer for Oberkampf at Jouy-en-Josas, produced only an aqueous chlorine solution. Lime was added to the bleaching bath to decrease the noxious odor when it was being used.

Twenty years later it had been generally recognized that the instability of the liquid solution was a major defect. The bleaching products then produced consisted solely of alkaline hypochlorites (actually, a mixture of hypochlorite and chloride) in solution or solid form. This production became sufficiently advanced to allow the introduction of chemical bleaching in the largest factories for treating fabrics (Figure 42).

After the mid-nineteenth century the demand for chlorine grew as the production of paper pulp from plant cellulose expanded. At this time the greatest efforts were made to lower the cost of producing chlorine. In 1844 John Mercer (1791–1866) discovered how to treat cotton fibers with caustic soda, a process that became known as mercerizing cotton. Mercerizing did not come into practice until after 1850, and it did not come into wider use until the 1880s. But in the same period the production of paper pulp increased rapidly because of increased world paper consumption, which also used large quantities of caustic soda.

For all these reasons the production cycle of the major mineral chemical

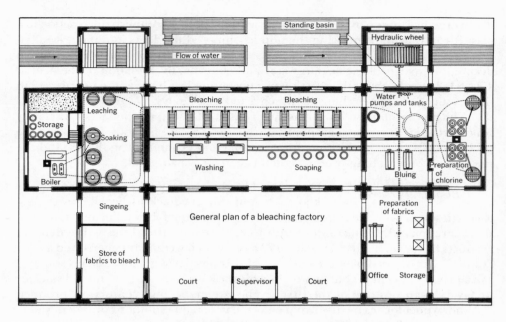

FIG. 42.   A bleaching factory, around 1830–1835.

industry acquired a constantly growing importance. The years between 1860 and 1880 marked the peak period for use of Leblanc soda, which had brought about the creation of this industrial complex. After this time the ammonia soda method gradually displaced the Leblanc method.

The evolution of heavy equipment

In all this long series of inventions the role of chemical discoveries as such is relatively modest. From this point of view only two great innovations can be noted: those due to work by Berthollet and by Leblanc. Practically all the other reactions put into practice had been known before the period of industrialization. The new chemical language made it possible to understand them better and combine them judiciously, but the essence of the development of industrial methods is in the evolution of the basic installations and equipment.

Firing methods made steady progress that is difficult to analyze without going into detail about the techniques of constructing furnaces. At first, like the iron-smelting industry, industrial chemistry derived a great advantage from adopting coal as a fuel in place of wood or charcoal. Then masonry furnaces were better conceived and built in increasingly larger units. The crucible furnace, on which products enclosed in retorts were distilled (for example, nitric acid), the origins of which date from the fifteenth or sixteenth century, was now used only for small-scale production. The reverberatory furnace, which appeared at the end of the seventeenth century in glass factories, was adapted to the various operations in each industry. In particular the shapes of hearths, how to intensify the draft, the shapes of loading ports and vaults, and so on were studied.

Other forms of structures were invented as well as the classic furnaces, boilers, and dissolving and evaporation vats. The first example from this period is perhaps the system vats in series invented by Nicolas Clément-Desormes (1779–1842) at the beginning of the nineteenth century to dissolve Leblanc soda. Then came Gossage's vertical absorption towers for recovering hydrochloric acid and of Gay-Lussac and Glover to produce sulfuric acid, from which derived the devices invented for transforming certain by-products.

Around the middle of the nineteenth century the heavy equipment of the chemical industry became diversified to the point where it was possible to envisage solving problems in the face of which only failures had been thus far experienced. Ernest Solvay's success in extracting soda is due partly to this wealth of methods, which he was able to adapt to a new problem.

Ammonia soda   The idea of removing soda from chloride by ammonia was more than a half century old when Ernest Solvay (1838–1922) began his experiments. It was appealing by its apparent simplicity. By causing ammonia and carbonic gas to act on sodium chloride, sodium bicarbonate is formed while the ammonia changes to chloride. The difference in solubility between the two salts makes it possible to collect the first one to precipitate. Simple heating transforms it into sodium carbonate, and the carbonic gas can then be recovered. The ammonium chloride is easy to decompose with lime to liberate the ammonia.

Plate 68. Furnaces of the Saint-Léonard factories at Liège, belonging to the Société des Mines et Fonderies de Zinc de la Vieille-Montagne. Lithograph by Maugendre. French National Library, Print Collection. (Photo Documentation Jacques Ostier, Paris.)

In practice the realization of this attractive cycle proved beset with difficulties. The first experimenter to concern himself with it was undoubtedly Fresnel, during the Empire period. But since he used solid sea salt and let all the ammonia escape, he obtained no results. After a German named Vogel gave a better description of the principle in 1822 and demonstrated the necessity of using brine rather than solid salt, the first serious experiments were made in England. Several manufacturers expended much time and money, but in vain. Those who came closest to success were, around 1838, H. G. Dyar and J. Hemming, at Whitechapel. They expected to achieve the theoretical yield of 90 percent, but they barely surpassed 37 percent. The losses of ammonia were around 27 percent, but Dyar and Hemming calculated that it was enough to decrease the losses by 10 percent to permit the price of their soda to be brought down to that of Leblanc soda. Despite costly efforts over ten years, they were not successful.

During the same period Deacon pursued similar efforts, which he was obliged to abandon. In France, Théophile Schloesing (1824–1919) and a colleague named Rolland succeeded in establishing, between 1854 and 1858, a method for treating solid salt, a technique put into use in a factory at Puteaux. Despite one difficulty that had earlier stymied Fresnel, namely the high proportion of non-decomposed salt, they continued production until 1870. Their method was then taken over by a manufacturer in Nancy named Ernest Daguin. But the Solvay method was already acquiring a commercial importance that enabled it to replace all the others.

Ernest Solvay's chemical studies began in 1861. The son of a family of industrial chemists, he was in the best possible circumstances to pursue this field. Having learned from the experiments before his own, he carefully and competently studied the installations likely to give the best results, particularly those in which the carbonation and recovery of ammonia were performed. The absorbers in which the carbonic gas was to act on the salt and ammonia laden solution consisted of metallic towers in which the solution circulated from top to bottom through perforated sheets of metal, where it encountered the carbonic gas introduced through the bottom. Ammonium chloride was collected by heating the mother liquor and was then distilled with lime. This final step was well enough conceived to permit the loss of only about 1 percent of the ammonia.

After founding a development company, Solvay began manufacturing in 1863, though he still required several years of tentative experiments to succeed in perfecting his method. But he had the wisdom, and especially the financial means, to refrain from granting concessions, so he benefited fully from all his experience and later from the revenues of his establishment, which rapidly became high.

Several offshoots of the Solvay method arose during the last years of the nineteenth century and were successfully exploited, notably by a French manufacturer named Merle who in 1855 founded the Société des Produits Chimiques, at Salin in the *département* of Gard. Through a series of mergers and partnerships this company gave birth to one of the largest modern French firms, the Établissement Pechiney.

The distillation of coal — It is also to an adaptation of heavy equipment that we owe the success of the coal distillation industry, which was very slow to establish itself during the first half of the nineteenth century. The advantages of coal distribution were publicized only in the very last years of the eighteenth century, but for about a century it had been known that by distilling coal an inflammable gas and tars were obtained. Attempts on several occasions to make use of them did not meet with much commercial success. The preparation of coke for the iron industry permitted all the by-products to be lost.

The first attempt to exploit coal gas when this new industry was being born was due around 1785 to Archibald Cochrane (1749–1831). Then, between 1790 and 1800, William Murdock in England and Philippe Lebon in France simultaneously succeeded in collecting the distilled gases to lead them to a burner. The flame at the end of the burner was used for illumination.

Lebon concerned himself above all with the distillation of wood, for which he took out a patent in 1799 and offered the first demonstration in 1802. His idea was to use to the fullest all the products of distillation —charcoal, acetic acid (for which he provided a method of preparing industrially that was used after him), and, finally, gas for illumination. In addition, heat from the distillation furnace was to be used to heat dwellings. But his "thermolamp," as he called it, disappointed his contemporaries. The apparatus was cumbersome and the flame provided insufficient light and gave off a troublesome odor. After Lebon's death in 1804, wood was no longer distilled for illumination.

Murdock performed his first experiments between 1792 and 1798, then in 1802 installed a lighting system in the Boulton and Watt shops at Soho and in the Phillips and Lee spinning mill at Manchester in 1805. In that same period Samuel Clegg was successfully continuing similar pursuits. The first attempts at adapting gas lighting for commercial use were made in England starting in 1806 by a businessman of Moravian origin, Frederick Albert Winzler (1763–1830), who had anglicized his name to Winsor. In 1810 he established the first development company in London, the Westminster Gas Light and Coke Co., with Samuel Clegg as its chief engineer.

At this time the possibilities of using not only coal tar but also ammonia salts and pitch had been revealed by Friedrich Christian Accum (1769–1838), a German chemist in Great Britain. But the by-products of coal distillation were neglected by developers until around 1830 to 1840, which suffices to explain the difficult beginnings of this industry that a half century later acquired considerable importance.

In the very early stages, coal was distilled in heaps without any precautions and the gas was guided into pipes without any washing, but the equipment was quickly improved. Distillation was first performed in cast-iron classically shaped retorts. Then an attempt was made to simplify the loading and unloading operations, and the shape changed but the name retort remained. These retorts first had a cylindrical shape, then later were elliptical, to provide a greater heating surface.

Between 1820 and 1830 the types of furnaces, retorts, and general equipment evolved toward devices that, after being definitively perfected around 1850, changed very little until the first quarter of the twentieth century. Upon leaving the retort the gas passed through a drum, where it was bubbled in water, which isolated the retort from the rest of the cycle. The gas then passed through a network of cooled tubes in which the tar condensed, then into a vat lined with lime or various materials to purify the gas, which finally was collected in a gasometer.

How to construct gasometers occasioned some discussion but the well-known classical arrangements were adopted almost immediately.

Despite this equipment, the gas supplied around 1830 to cities still had a disagreeable odor of sulfurated hydrogen. It was not until 1849 that Frank Clark Hills introduced ferrous oxide as an effective purifying material (Figure 43).

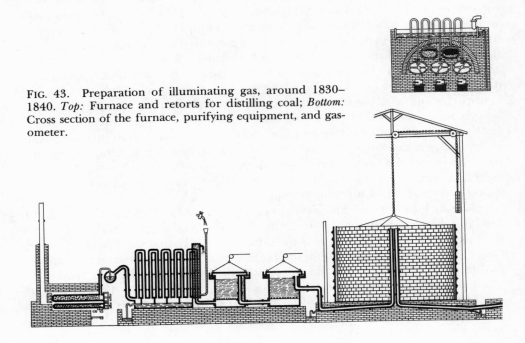

FIG. 43.   Preparation of illuminating gas, around 1830–1840. *Top:* Furnace and retorts for distilling coal; *Bottom:* Cross section of the furnace, purifying equipment, and gasometer.

Concerning by-products, around 1820 tar began to be used for roping and making joints gastight. After 1833 English factories sold small quantities of ammonia and chloride. However, this source was not really exploited until after the middle of the century, when the production of chemical fertilizers began.

The distillation of coal tar was practiced on a small scale starting around 1830. The naphtha derived from it gave Charles Macintosh (1766–1843) in 1823 the rubber solvent that enabled him to produce and successfully market the first raincoats. Creosote began to be used in 1838 to protect railroad crossties, and in the same period pitch found a use for surfacing roadways.

But the light products of distillation—benzine, toluene, and so on—continued to be strictly laboratory products. They had an unsuspected industrial potential. Because the illuminating gas industry made these products readily available to chemists, they completely revised their knowledge and established the first theories about organic chemistry. The entire system of chemistry became profoundly transformed by this development. The second half of the nineteenth century had hardly dawned when Perkins's work gave birth to the new industry of artificial dyes, and coal tar acquired considerable economic value in less than a decade.

Plate 69. Continuous papermaking machine at the Essonnes plant. Engraving taken from Turgan, *Les Grandes Usines,* Paris, 1860. (Photo Alain Doyère - C.N.A.M.)

Mechanization and the papermaking industry   Another important factor in the development of the chemical industry was use of the steam engine to operate stirring, pumping, and tearing machines, which made it possible to increase production rapidly and to extract, under favorable economic conditions, substances that until then could not be used. At the same time the boiler of the driving engine supplied steam to heat production boilers, steamers, and drying cylinders.

The complete change in paper production methods is from this point of view a remarkable example. In the space of some forty years all the operations performed manually since the seventeenth century became completely mechanized. By approximately 1840 vat-made paper had become a rarity that found justification only in producing certain qualities of paper, such as that used for accounting ledgers.

The first step in this direction was by an employee at the Essonne paper works, one Louis Robert, who took out a patent for the first machine to make paper continuously. But his machine, or more precisely those built following along its lines after 1815 to 1820, could be used satisfactorily only when the preliminary operations of preparing the pulp had all been mechanized.

This outfitting of the paper industry was carried out all the more rapidly because the development of industrial machinery in the same period made it possible to build faster printing presses (Figure 44).

It was easy to increase the capacity of vats for washing rags, and the building of machines to break and refine rags presented no great difficulty. These consisted of cylinders equipped with cutting blades and placed in a vat in which water

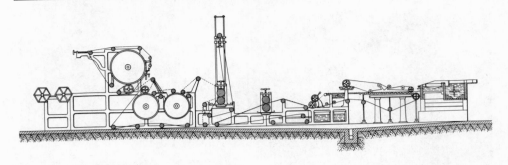

FIG. 44.   Continuous papermaking machine. *Right:* Vat of refined pulp; next to it is the wire mesh, then a series of cylinders and drying equipment. The strip of paper winds on the drums at far left. Dotted line indicates the paper; solid line indicates the wire mesh and the drier felts. Around 1830–1840.

flowed. At one end a funnel caught the torn fibers. Bleaching was done in calcium hypochlorite if white rags were being used, in gaseous chlorine prepared on the spot if the rags were colored. After this a washing operation was performed in the beater, where the sizing was done. Perfecting the sizing operation in the beater required numerous experiments, which were carried out in France by the Société d'Encouragement pour l'industrie nationale and were applied on a large scale for the first time by Canson. The pulp was finally poured into a large vat with mechanical beaters, from which it was guided onto the endless metal mesh of the machine for pressing and drying the paper.

Naturally, this equipment did not eliminate craft skills for every operation. Its widespread use permitted an intensification of production shortly after 1850. At this time wool, flax, and cotton rags became inadequate as raw materials. For several years English producers had held a monopoly on Algerian alfa grass, also called esparto grass. French producers had begun to use straw, but use of such substitutes was still quite limited.

In 1846 a French manufacturer named Voelter invented a method to grind wood pulp mechanically. Several years later, a new method of curing tobacco being in fashion, the pulp of plant fibers (particularly of straw) was employed exclusively for making cigarette paper. But cotton substitutes did not begin to be used in large quantity until after 1870, when chemical methods of removing impurities—the soda method in 1852, the bisulfite method in 1866—were discovered.

Boilermaking and beet sugar — The use of metals in building heavy installations and equipment was quite important. We have seen the use the sulfuric acid industry made of lead, without which it would certainly have been unable to develop. Iron, especially cast iron, was used increasingly, but copper was the material that aided the development of the sugar industry.

The principle of how to extract beet sugar had been described in the eighteenth century by the German chemist Franz Karl Achard (1753–1821). Its industrial use was one consequence of the Continental blockade during the Napoleonic Empire. From 1800 to 1810 fruitless attempts were made to extract from grapes enough sugar to replace that which no longer arrived by sea. At the very beginning of the experiments a chemist named Deyeux demonstrated that it would have been more effective to treat a certain type of beet that was cultivated in several areas. In 1806 certain manufacturers, including Derosne, who later specialized in constructing sugar mill devices, tried to follow Deyeux's recommendations. In 1812 the first lump of sugar was obtained in a Passy factory.

Cultivation of the sugar beet was then intensified. In France there existed a certain number of establishments that refined the raw products extracted from sugarcane imported from overseas. New equipment based on these installations was gradually invented and built.

Mechanical graters using the hydraulic press Périer had just introduced into France were built to extract beet juice. Numerous models of both types of machines were invented, but only a certain number of each came into use. In particular, around 1835 to 1840 the pressure exerted manually on the grater in grating devices was replaced by mechanical pushrods.

Processing beet juice required a series of operations—clarification, filtration,

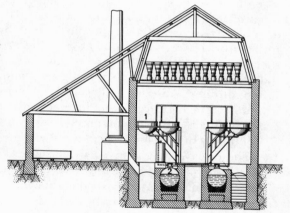

FIG. 45. Beet-root sugarmill, around 1835. *Left:* Building containing the washer, grater, and double-acting hydraulic press (the latter two not shown); *Right:* Double-bottomed boilers for the clarification of the juice (1) and steam generators (2). The operations of concentration, clarification, and filtration through bone black are not shown. The upper story houses containers of syrup in process of crystallization.

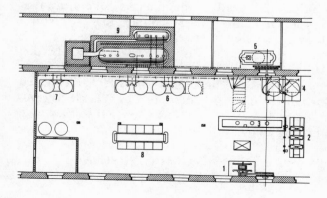

FIG. 46. Extraction and refining of beet sugar, around 1835. 1. Grater; 2. Pumps of the hydraulic presses; 3. Hydraulic presses; 4. Clarification boilers; 5. Steam engine; 6. Concentration pans; 7. Boiling pans; 8. Filters; 9. Generator and boiler.

evaporation, and crystallization—for the needs of which the entire art of boilermaking came into play (Figure 45). Clarification was done by adding either sulfuric acid or lime to the juice. Lime was used only after the adoption of filtration through bone black, whose absorbing and bleaching properties had been discovered in 1811 by Pierre Figuier.

The purified syrup was then concentrated in evaporators, which were quickly perfected by applying mechanical methods to move the agitators and pumps that circulated the liquid. Finally, in the last stage, a steam engine with an oscillating cylinder was even used, to operate the blowing engine of the evaporator (Figure 46).

Although after the Restoration the sugar-beet industry developed only slowly, building and perfecting the many bulky pieces of equipment it required was a primary activity for a whole range of enterprises, and the development of this equipment occupied a large place in the technical literature during the first half of the nineteenth century.

Chemical research and stearin production   We have already seen the part played by chemical research in the development of various industries. We can gain only a very rough idea of the contributions of laboratory chemistry to industry if we limit ourselves to only the major inventions, such as those of Berthollet or Leblanc. In reality, from the early nineteenth century until around 1860 or 1870, when chemical research began to be seriously organized for a specific purpose by the big firms themselves, a large number of chemists, most of whose names are not famous, discovered through their personal laboratory work vast numbers of new facts, many of which led to industrial improvements. After Nicolas Clément and his son-in-law Desormes (often confused with each other), we must mention more or less obscure chemical inventors such as Decroizilles, Pluvinet, Anselme Payen (1795–1871; the discoverer of cellulose), Braconnot, and others who were among the most effective.

Industry in turn made increasingly larger contributions to scientific chemistry. The discovery of iodine by the saltpeter manufacturer Bernard Courtois (1777–1838) in 1811 is characteristic of this period.

During the first quarter of the nineteenth century a new industry was born from pure laboratory research. In 1816 a chemist named Braconnot, a botany professor in Nancy, separated stearin from its two other components, olein and margarine, by treating tallow with turpentine. By saponifying stearin with an alkali or acid he obtained a whitish, solid product at ordinary temperature that could replace wax in candle production. In 1818 Braconnot, together with a pharmacist named Simonin, took out a patent that was never exploited.

The production of candles with stearic acid was undertaken by two French manufacturers, Adolphe de Milly and Mottard, only after long work on fats was carried on by Eugène Chevreul between 1813 and 1823. Chevreul had revealed the composition of fats in which glycerin, already described by Scheele, is combined with organic acids, including stearic acid. In 1825 Chevreul studied with Gay-Lussac a method of saponifying tallow with soda, which de Milly used after 1813, replacing soda with lime (Figure 47).

The first brand of candle put on the market was called *Bougie à l'Étoile*, because of the location of the factory established by de Milly. The production technique applied in this factory derived from Braconnot and Chevreul. Something new was added when the wick, which was of braided cotton impregnated with boric acid, was produced. The wick melted in the flame and vitrified the ash as combustion occurred.

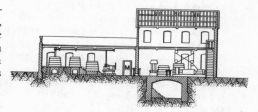

FIG. 47. Shop for manufacturing stearin candles, around 1840. Saponification, treatment, and washing of the soap are performed in the vats in the room at left. The room contains a vertical press for cold-pressing oleic acid, and a horizontal hot press. Molding the candles was done upstairs; the oleic acid was collected in the basement. M: steam engine.

The stearin candle industry developed rapidly, for it contributed a practical, cheap method of individual lighting. A full line of specialized equipment was rapidly created, such as the hydraulic press used to separate solid acids (stearic and palmitic) from oleic acid. In 1841 Auguste Pierre Dubrunfaut (1797–1881) invented a way to purify acids by distilling them through the action of superheated steam. Few production modifications were made thereafter.

Appearance of modern explosives   Toward the end of the first half of the nineteenth century the manufacture of new explosives began, as a result of recent laboratory research. In 1830 the first studies on the action of nitric acid on cotton were published. In 1845 in Basel the German chemist Christian Friedrich Schönbein (1799–1868) succeeded in nitrating cotton by using a mixture of sulfuric acid and nitric acids, and he manufactured the first guncotton. In 1847 trinitroglycerin was obtained for the first time by the Italian chemist Ascanio Sobrero (1812–1888), using a similar method. However, industrial production of these explosives was not undertaken until twenty years later.

In 1864 Alfred B. Nobel (1833–1896) discovered how to make a fulminate detonator, and in 1866 found a method for stabilizing nitroglycerin by attaching it to kieselguhr (diatomite). Under the name *dynamite* the new explosive quickly came into use in mines and for public works. In 1875, when he gelatinized nitroglycerin by dissolving it in a collodion, Nobel took the first step toward producing a complete series of explosives adapted to various uses. Smokeless powder (guncotton) found its first large-scale use during the Civil War in the United States.

At this time the production of artificial dyes in turn began to grow after the work done by Sir William Perkin in 1856, and the chemical industry experienced a new impetus.

BIBLIOGRAPHY

AITCHISON, Leslie. *A History of Metals*. London, 1960. Especially volume II.

CLEGG, Samuel. *Traité pratique de la fabrication et de la distribution du gaz d'éclairage et de chauffage*. Translated from the 3rd edition (1859) by Ed. SERVIER. Paris, 1860.

FAUCHER, Daniel. *Le paysan et la machine*. Paris, 1954.

FESTY, Octave. *L'agriculture pendant la Révolution française*. Paris, 1947.

FLACHAT, E., BARRAULT, A., and PETIET, J. *Traité de la fabrication de la fonte et du fer*. Paris, 1846.

GILLE, Bertrand. *Histoire de la métallurgie*, "Que sais-je?" Paris, 1966. Bibliography with a general orientation.

GUILLAUME. *Instruments aratoires inventés, perfectionnés, dessinés et gravés par*. Paris, 1821.

HABER, L. F. *The Chemical Industry during the Nineteenth Century*. Oxford, 1958.

HASSENFRATZ, J. H. *La sidérotechnie*. Paris, 1812.

HATON DE LA GOUPILLIÈRE, *Cours d'exploitation des mines*. 1885.

HAUDRICOURT, A., and BRUNHES-DELAMARE, J. *L'homme et la charrue à travers le monde*. Paris, 1955.

HÉRON DE VILLEFOSSE, A. *De la richesse minérale*. Paris, 1810-1819. Inquiry into mineral extraction conducted during the Empire.

KARSTEN, C. J. B. *Manuel de la métallurgie du fer*. Metz, 1830.

PERCY, J. *Traité complet de métallurgie*. Paris, 1865.

PILTER, T. H. *Traité des machines à moissonner*. Paris, n. d. (around 1878).

SCHNEITLER, André. *Die neueren und wichtigeren landwirtschaftlichen Maschinen*. 1861.

Sidérugic et croissance économique en France et en Grande-Bretagne (1735-1913). Notebook of the Institute of Applied Economic Science. Paris, 1965. Very extensive bibliography.

TRESCA, Alf. *Le matériel agricole moderne*. Paris, 1893.

PART SEVEN

THE TEXTILE
INDUSTRIES

Plate 70. Original Jacquard loom with his mechanism for patterned fabrics; from the Société d'Encouragement pour l'Industrie Nationale. Paris, Musée du Conservatoire national des Arts et Métiers. (Photo René-Jacques, Paris.)

THE SPINNING OF TEXTILE FIBERS

I T IS DOUBTFUL IF, in the middle of the eighteenth century, any production methods could be found less developed than those of spinning. This essential activity, which survived as a cottage industry in the Middle Ages, when every trade had been organized as a guild, still remained in the hands of peasant women and servants.

The simple spindle was the instrument most widely used in the medieval period. It was of primitive origin and suited to spinning both wool and flax. After the Middle Ages the spindle was gradually replaced by the spinning wheel and (in the case of wool, whose fibers are long) by the spinning wheel equipped with a flyer. The use of the latter spread quite slowly in Central Europe. Of these three devices, the first two embodied the principle of primitive, intermittent spinning, but the latter, in contrast, operated by modern continuous spinning. However, their productivity remained far below that of the earlier and later stages of fabric production, namely preparation of the fiber and weaving.

This anomaly of evolution had serious consequences when textile manufacturing was industrialized, because increased demand brought about a serious shortage of yarn.

It has been estimated that eight or ten spinners working full time were needed to keep up with the output of a single weaver. But when summer agricultural work was at its height this figure became in fact less. Thus it is not surprising that there were early efforts to mechanize spinning or at least to increase its productivity. Leonardo da Vinci left a drawing of a spindle that traveled back and forth to distribute automatically the yarn evenly on the bobbin, and Giovanni Branca left plans for a spinning wheel operated by a waterwheel.

It is worth noting that beginning in the seventeenth century this strangling bottleneck in the technical process helped accelerate the spread of the treadle spinning wheel. The spinner's right hand, now freed, could draw out the fibrous material, improving the output in both quality and quantity.

Here a final attempt at further development of traditional methods should also be mentioned, namely the two-spindle system. It probably appeared in Germany, after initial experiments to make one person spin on two wheels. It was promoted throughout Europe by the mercantile policies of the governments and taught also in the schools. A watercolor by one of the three Saint-Aubin brothers dating from about 1770 depicts a school of this type. This system was still used occasionally in the nineteenth century, but it cannot be considered a contribution to the progress of spinning.

John Kay (fl. 1733–1764), one of the most prolific geniuses of his time, took out a patent in 1733 for a machine used for spinning and sizing yarn, and at the same time patented his flying shuttle, which increased weaving capacity by at least 25 to 30 percent. Although its use spread slowly, after 1790 the flying shuttle considerably increased the weavers' demand for yarn.

In the meantime, applications for patents by the English wool industry had increased. A very special impetus was provided by a competition sponsored by the Society for the Encouragement of Arts, Manufactures and Commerce: a prize of fifty pounds sterling was promised for the best machine that permitted simultaneous spinning of six threads of linen, hemp, or cotton. The simplicity and cost of the machine had to be taken into consideration in awarding the prize.

Such a clearly determined goal plainly indicated what was the critical problem of the period, but strange as it may seem, the starting point of research was the mill for organzining silk, because investigators had the possibility of seeing it in operation before their eyes. The largest installation of organzining mills, the 25,000-spindle installation of the Lombe brothers, John (1693?–1722) and Sir Thomas (1685–1739) was in operation from 1717 close to industrial Lancashire. Some later inventors saw this enormous machine, almost as complex as a clock movement, which simultaneously threw and reeled the silk thread. A single spinner sometimes operated more than 100 spindles. Similarly, round and oval manually operated mills for twisting wool and cotton thread had long been in existence, inspired by organzining mills.

However, the spinning of fibers inevitably involved the operation of drawing out the fibrous mass, which demanded original solutions. Certain ideas were short-lived, such as the six-spindle wheel of H. C. Buckley, the flyer spindle of High and Kay (1767), and the thirty-spindle wheel of a Russian named Rodon Glinkov.

The first success came through an invention inspired not by continuous twisting but by the intermittent method of the primitive spinning wheel. This method had had a development capable of putting inventors on the road to mechanization. This technique of collective spinning was put into operation in this period and in the last analysis may have originated in rope making. In 1745 this method was described in detail by an English author, and it is depicted in an 1887 painting, "The Flax Spinners" by the Impressionist painter Max Liebermann (1847–1935). In a long row along the wall, seated children are operating spinning wheels. The spinners, slowly backing away from the wheels, feed out with both hands the fiber attached to their belts. When they reach the opposite wall the children wind the finished portion of the yarn by slowly turning the spindle while the spinners return to the spinning wheels.

The spinning jenny This is the situation that confronted the weaver James Hargreaves of Stanhill, when around 1764 he built his famous spinning jenny. Because the jenny merely imitates manual operations, the conception represents a dead end. First 8, then 16, 60, and even 100 spindles were attached to the frame and were operated as a single unit by a hand-turned crank. Bobbins of rove were placed at an angle in the lower portion of the frame. A fiber ribbon unrolled from them through two movable battens that could be brought closer together, imitating the movement of the thumb and index finger in hand spinning.

Plate 71. The *"Spinnstube,"* a rural shop for semi-manual spinning. Engraving by M. Liebermann, 1887. (Photo Conservatoire national des Arts et Métiers.)

Plate 72. Industrial spinning with the mule-jenny in England in 1835. Engraving of the period by T. Allom and J. W. Lowry. London, Science Museum. (Photo Science Museum.)

This pair of battens forming a pincers was mounted on a movable carriage that was the heart of the machine. This carriage moved back and forth on two rails, thus performing under the same conditions the operations to which spinners had become accustomed over thousands of years in working with the spinning wheel and spindle:

1. A drawing out by the outward movement of the carriage, in which the sliver is immobilized by the closing of the battens, and simultaneously . . .
2. Twisting by the spindles, then . . .
3. Winding on the same spindles as the carriage returns (Figure 1).

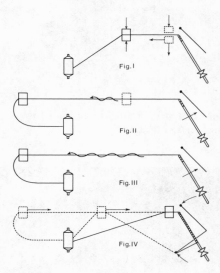

FIG. 1. Operation of the spinning jenny. *(Left)* The bobbin is of drawn sliver. The spindle *(right)* twists and winds. The two bars of the clasp can open and close on the thread and can also move horizontally. 1. Predrawing. The clasp has opened (in position indicated by dotted line) and moved slightly to the left, leaving between it and the spindle a certain length of sliver to be changed into thread. 2. Drawing. The clasp still closed passes from the position indicated by the dotted lines to that at extreme left. During this movement the spindle has begun to revolve. 3. Twisting. The clasp *(far left)* is closed; the spindle revolves and twists the thread. 4. Winding. The clasp moves back toward the right. The spindle, still revolving, becomes filled with thread, which is evenly distributed over the entire spindle by the movement of the special part, drawn at the right of the spindle, which now begins to move.

The jenny became much improved and its use spread rapidly, but it was never employed beyond the limits of domestic industry. In most cases manufacturers rented it to rural weavers; only much later, and then only sporadically, were attempts made to mechanize it. In sum, it was a practical solution to the problem of a multiple-spindle spinning wheel.

The water frame — Continuous spinning was achieved at around the same time. There is a difference in the two operations that depends on the principle itself; only continuous spinning illustrates genuine mechanization.

Initially, continuous spinning relied on water for power, following the example of silk organzining. Hence the term *water frame*. Its construction, patented by Sir Richard Arkwright in 1769, is relatively simple.

The starting point of the operation, as in the jenny, is a sliver of carded cotton, but here the drawing out is done through rollers. The sliver passes between a

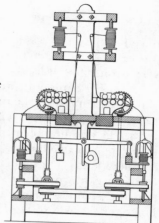

FIG. 2.　Transversal cross section of the water frame. At the top is the sliver of fibrous material, stored on large bobbins. Toward the center are the three pairs of drafting rollers, each pair revolving faster than its predecessor. At the bottom are the flyer spindles, which receive the drawn-out material and give the thread its final twist. The spindles travel upward with an alternating movement, to ensure even winding of the thread. Note the heart-shaped cam and series of levers (*center*) for that purpose.

series of pairs of rollers turning at increasing speeds. The rollers could be adjusted for fineness as desired. The twisting and winding method in no way differed from that of the flying spindle (Figure 2). Hargreaves became obliged to defend himself from attacks by spinners, and his patent, granted in 1770, was annulled because of prior sales of jennies. Arkwright went into partnership with the manufacturer Jedediah Strutt (1726–1797) in 1771 in order to establish a factory in a remote valley. A year later he was able to report results exceeding all expectations, and in 1775 he registered a patent for an improved form of his machine. In this patent he not only described the water frame (among many other inventions) but also gave a description of it so vague that his enemies felt the time was ripe to attack it. But from this period on the Arkwright-Strutt factory worked around the clock, with two shifts of workers. It was only the first of a series of factories that sprang up like mushrooms.

The water frame, produced on an assembly line, was used to establish new factories or was rented out to factories already in existence. The changes brought about in the English cotton industry were much greater and more abrupt than those caused by the jenny. Calico, till then a major import, quickly came to be produced locally.

Cotton calico (in yards)

	English-produced	Imported
1775	56,814	2,111,439
1780	1,143,043	1,071,775
1783	3,578,590	770,922

One can appreciate, on the one hand, the enormous profits this situation brought to cotton manufacturers in return for modest investment and, on the other, extreme misery among spinners, who were suddenly out of work. One child could supervise an output equal to that of ten adults. The exploitation of machines was carried to an extreme. Robert Peel, the future statesman, noted that by operating machines 144 hours per week one had at the time every chance of realizing considerable profits.

The mule-jenny The initial impetus given by this accelerated development met another retarding factor. Yarn produced by the jenny was loosely twisted, and fine grades of yarn could not be spun. Moreover, yarn made by the water frame was very hard, a term still applied to a very strong thread used to form the warp.

In 1774 Samuel Crompton (1753–1827) began experiments to build a machine that combined the two principles, with a view to eliminating the defects of each. In 1779 his mule-jenny achieved its final form, though, as the name suggests, this was an intermediate solution. The drawing mechanism was the water frame, but the machine had a carriage providing a back and forth motion as in the spinning jenny. The bobbins of sliver (the ropelike strand of fiber produced by the card) were drawn through the rollers. The difference in speed between the rollers and the spindles made it possible to obtain a thread of perfect quality and homogeneity whose twist could be varied as desired (Figure 3). The principal quality of this complex machine lay in the possibility of unlimited variations in the speeds of the bobbins of sliver, the drawing rollers, and the carriage. This machine, to which only minor improvements have since been made, is now known by the name *spinning mule*.

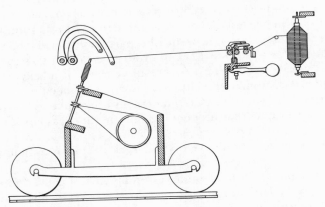

FIG. 3.   Operation of the mule-jenny. The sliver is stored in a creel at top right. Drawing begins between three pairs of drafting rollers, each revolving at a faster speed than its predecessor. The spindles are mounted on a carriage that moves in both directions. Their movement toward the left completes the drawing and twisting process; their movement toward the right does the winding. The mechanism is operated manually by a hand wheel (not shown).

Crompton's poverty prevented him from accumulating the funds needed to register a patent; those who had adopted his invention promised to supply him with money, but they failed to do so. The adoption of the machine spread like wildfire, and improvements followed to make its operation automatic (Figure 4). The problems of quantity and quality associated with spinning had now been solved. The price of yarn fell rapidly, even that of the finest types used to produce muslins. Thus, yarn no. 100, 185 yards of which weighed one gram, fell in a very short time to one-quarter its former value.

FIG. 4. The self-acting jenny. General cross section of the carriage. The mule jenny was only partly automatic. The spindles were turned by a hand wheel operated by a worker. The self-acting machine was similar in arrangement, but all the operations were completely automatic. The various parts were operated and halted by a series of engagements and disengagements of the gears.

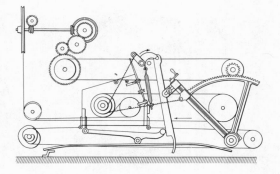

Years	Price	[Index 1786=100]
1786	36s.	100
1790	30s.	83
1792	16s.	44
1801	8s.9d.	24

By 1807 the price had dropped to 6s.9d.; finally, in 1833, it was stabilized at 4s.9d. A single worker could now attend to several dozen spindles. Naturally, the workers, left without work, turned in anger against the factories. In 1777 the water tank at the Cromford factory was maliciously drained, which led to a historic consequence: Arkwright asked James Watt to suggest a method of supplying his waterwheels with water. This was the first example of the use (still indirect) of the new steam engine to give motion to a machine.

In 1779 Arkwright's spinning mill at Birkacre was burned. In 1780 there were further serious disorders and the army was used to guard new factories, though this did not prevent several hundred machines from being destroyed.

The Englishman Robert Owen, himself the owner of a spinning mill, understood the gravity of the problem posed by the living conditions of the working classes. He noted that a working group of 2,500 persons could now produce for society as much as a population of 600,000 individuals could have produced a half century earlier. Thus this question was raised: what becomes of the difference between what is consumed by these 2,500 persons and what the 600,000 could have consumed?

Carding

The invention of spinning machines would not have caused such far-reaching changes if the production phases preceding the final spinning, especially carding and preparation of the sliver, had not also been mechanized. The purpose of carding is to untangle and make parallel the tangled fibers of raw cotton. This is what first caught the attention of builders of spinning machines, for this operation required almost as much work as the spinning itself.

The year 1748 saw the appearance of two patents. One, by D. Bourn, for the first time placed the "card clothing" (i.e., bent wires set in leather) around the circumference of a drum. Here again Arkwright's name was connected with the most successful modification. His second patent (registered in 1775) and the patent that gave rise to the most vigorous opposition described a carding machine

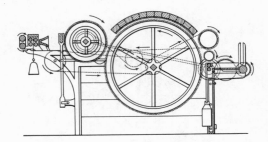

FIG. 5. Ordinary carding machine *(top)* and carding machine with revolving slats *(bottom)*.

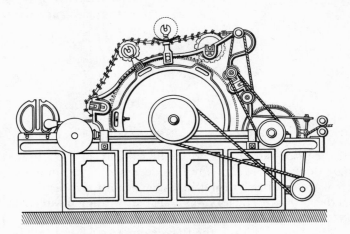

FIG. 5A. In the ordinary machine the material to be carded is drawn between the large cylinder and the cards placed on top of it. The need to clean the cards obliges the worker to stop the machine frequently. This disadvantage is eliminated in the machine with revolving slats, in which the cards form an endless chain that can be moved without stopping the machine.

with a double cylinder, which the inventor quickly developed to meet the needs of his own factories. The end result was a mechanism almost identical with the machines in use today, namely, the card with flats, in which a cover with carding needles covers the cylinder, which is also equipped with similar card clothing. Later Arkwright also tried a device consisting of several small cylinders completely covered with teeth, called a hedgehog card in the cotton industry.

The layer of carded and separated fibers formed between the two sets of needles is removed by a doffer comb, using a back and forth motion. The layer of carded cotton is next gathered up in the form of a roll by passing it through a conical, funnel-shaped passage and is then compressed between two rollers and coiled into the sliver can.

The carded sliver could not be spun as it was, at least not for the finest qualities of yarn. Arkwright solved this problem of preparing the rove by collecting several carded slivers on the water frame, drawing them out together through pairs of drafting rollers—each of which revolved at a greater speed than its predecessor—and then putting them back into a sliver can. The purpose of the method was first to improve the uniformity of the rove and then, during the final draft, to give a slight twist to the rove by slowly turning the can in which it was received for the last time. (For this reason this special conical can was called the lantern can (Figure 6).) Thus, an already slightly twisted rove was spun on the water frame, reducing the risks of breakage.

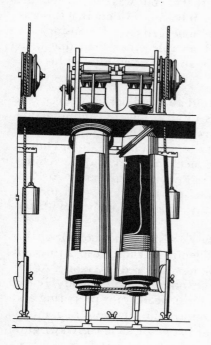

FIG. 6. The lantern can. The sliver of fibrous material comes out of the drafting rollers *(top)* and is drawn into a practically cylindrical box, the lantern. The latter rotates, giving the sliver a slight preliminary twist.

Arkwright's lawsuit   Before analyzing the subsequent development of these devices it is necessary to explain one of the most important reasons for the explosive spread of cotton-spinning machines, even in foreign industries. In 1781 Arkwright brought suit against several manufacturers for infringement of his patents. Those attacked defended themselves by declaring that the description of the patent was deliberately written vaguely so that if one depended solely on the description in the patent it would have been impossible to reconstruct the machine, a point that is the fundamental condition for obtaining a monopoly. Admitting this, Arkwright claimed that he had had only the national interest in view and that he had acted "in order to prevent foreigners from profiting by such an inexhaustible source of wealth." The court was not moved by the patriotism of this argument and annulled the patent.

This first decision effectively accelerated the spread of the spinning machine. Arkwright appealed, calling as a witness in his favor no less an authority than James Watt, who by this time was already famous and esteemed as an inventor and engineer. Watt declared that he was ready to try to build an operative spinning machine, solely from the description that was the object of litigation. Arkwright won the first appeal. The second appeal by his adversaries' attack was accompanied by tremendous publicity. The great manufacturer was now attacked at his weakest point: his authorship of his inventions was challenged. In the public argument on the details of certain mechanisms, the truth ultimately came to light. The debates revealed that the water frame was attributable to Thomas Highs, the carding machine to D. Bourn and Lewis Paul, the drawing mechanism also to Highs, and the lantern can to B. Butler—in short, that anyone was free to acquaint himself with the method of building water frames. It became evident that this was the first major collective invention to have emerged in the history of technology—the owner of the patent assumed no role other than that of a businessman with an enterprising spirit. In other words, Arkwright lost his case and his patents came into the public domain.

The dissemination of spinning frames

The fact that England guarded her borders closely to prevent models or drawings of spinning machines from secretly leaving the country is another question. These efforts were in vain. In 1754, at the risk of his life, John Holker secretly sent to France twenty-four workers, one mechanic, and all the machines needed and founded the cotton velvet industry in France. Significantly, in 1755 Louis XV named him inspector-general of manufactures working with foreign machines. In 1773 his son brought in the first jenny, which was publicly exhibited at Sens, then copied, after which its use spread.

In 1772 the Polish government purchased the English patents, notable on this list is the mill for carding cotton. The improved jenny reached Austria through Baptiste Le Brun in 1776 and in 1785 the machines appeared in Saxony. At the same time both the jenny and the carder were introduced into Hungary, but in 1789 the water frame and other Arkwright machines needed for preparing and drawing out the rove were imported into that country directly from England.

Samuel Slater (1768–1835) began his career in one of Richard Arkwright's factories. The practice of the state of Pennsylvania government of giving premiums for improvements in manufacturing machinery encouraged him to settle overseas. In 1789 he left secretly for the United States and there built from memory a primitive type of water frame with twenty-four spindles. This was the beginning of the cotton industry in New England. The first spinning machines were set up in Prussia in 1791, Russia in 1793, and Switzerland in 1794.

Flax treatment

In the other branches of the textile industry, new inventions were adopted more slowly. Whereas with cotton the spinning technique was already stabilized (with the exception of several improvements, such as the gradual transformation of the jenny into a billy in 1786 and the use of waterpower for the mule in 1790), manufacturers using other raw materials concentrated at first only on mechanizing their technology.

In 1787 J. Kendrew and A. Porthouse modified the water frame so as to prepare flax for wet spinning, a procedure still in use. Flax fibers being longer than cotton ones, the drafting rollers were farther apart. The rove passed over a damp cloth before reaching the spindle. In 1790 Matthew Murray (1765–1826) obtained a patent for a machine for drawing flax in which the fibers were for the first time passed between two broad leather belts. In 1795 Sellers and Standage in turn discovered the principle of drawing by a series of combs, or gills, and shortly thereafter A. Thompson's drawing frame with comb bars was patented. This was the precursor of the intersecting gill (1801) that later became so important in the wool industry.

But these inventions were still not enough to give linen yarn the homogeneity and good quality of hand-spun fibers. For this reason Napoleon opened a competition in 1810, with a prize of one million francs, for a complete solution of the problem of mechanical spinning of flax and hemp. Stimulated by this prospect, Philippe de Girard (1775–1845) submitted his process. Napoleon's downfall deprived him of the prize money, but he nevertheless lived long enough to see the spread of mechanical spinning of flax in France, England, Austria, and even Poland, where he quite successfully undertook to manage the first spinning mills.

The originality of the method lay in passing the flax fiber through a very hot alkaline solution before drawing, which was done on a machine with a series of combs operating alternately (Figure 7). On the spinning machine, which had flyer spindles, the prepared rove was again plunged into an alkaline solution before being twisted.

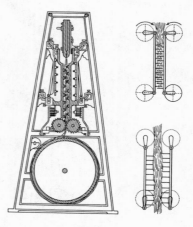

FIG. 7. Philippe de Girard's machine for combing flax. Vertical cross section through the center. The teeth of the comb are mounted on two vertical parallel frames. The strands of fiber are held by the nippers visible in the upper portion. The two additional sketches show the principle of the operation. Note that the combs are operated by cranks that separate and bring them together while moving them up and down alternately. In this way the entire length of flax in the device is combed, even though the teeth of the combs act in a small area.

Wool combing Thus by around 1820 a satisfactory solution had been found for flax spinning. The water frame was well suited for spinning combed wool, provided that the drawing cylinders were spaced farther apart. For carded wool with short fibers, the jenny and its improved version the billy, as well as the mule-jenny, were used. In this case it was rather the combing that presented a problem, wool being, in the length of its fibers, much more mixed than other materials. Cartwright patented a combing machine in 1792, but neither this machine nor those of Wright and Hawksley in 1793–1797, Collier-Godart in 1816, or still less that of Platt-Collier in 1827, with their numerous variants, succeeded in completely supplanting hand work; the comb removed too many long fibers from the sliver.

For example, the Platt-Collier machine consisted of two cylindrical combs turning in opposite directions, on which the worker laid the fibrous material. The combs moved closer together as they revolved until the teeth of each comb reached the fibers lying on its mate. The short fibers fell into the spaces between the teeth, from which they had to be removed by hand.

Realizing the need for a better solution, a Frenchman named Josué Heilmann, who already owned a large number of patents, built a radically new combing machine in 1845. Combining the principles of continuous and intermittent operation, he transferred certain combing phases to a revolving cylinder (Figure 8). This cylinder, placed horizontally beneath the "nippers," was formed of alternating segments, some with rows of comb teeth, the others smooth. A

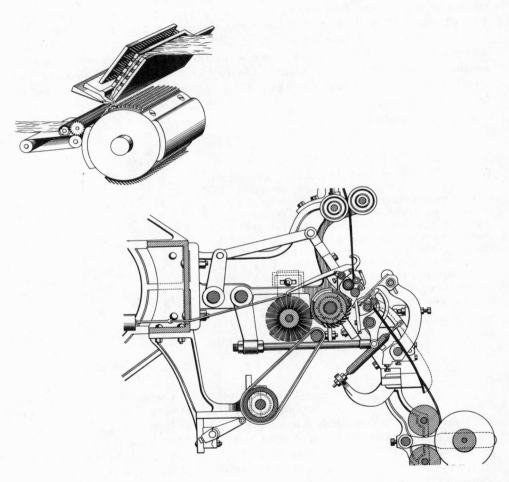

FIG. 8.   The Heilmann combing machine. Cross section view of the entire machine, and detail in perspective of the combing cylinder. In both drawings the textile material enters on the right and leaves the machine on the left. The cylinder has alternating smooth and toothed segments. When a toothed segment comes into position, the material is held between the two nippers (the beginning of this phase is shown in the detail). The smooth surface, coming into position when the nippers open, removes the combed material. A cylindrical brush constantly cleans the combing cylinder (see general view).

length of the sliver of carded wool, gripped in the nippers, was presented to a toothed segment that combed this portion, removing burrs and short fibers from it. When the toothed segment had moved on, the nippers opened and the combed portion now approached two cylinders revolving in opposite directions that grasped the combed strand between them and pulled it through the machine. Meanwhile, the oscillating nippers had drawn in and presented to the combing section of the cylinder another length of fibrous material. The combing cylinder collected short fibers and burrs, which were continuously removed by a cylindrical brush placed in the lower part of the machine.

Use of the Heilmann comber spread rapidly, and it has retained a certain importance into modern times. It must be noted that in the wool industry combers with two or three heads, handling an equal number of slivers, appeared at a very early period.

Cotton machines in the nineteenth century Thanks to the innovations just discussed, as well as to a great number of others it is impossible to discuss in detail, the flax and wool industries arrived, with a time-lag of several decades, at a state of development similar to the cotton industry's. But cotton processing in turn underwent a series of quick improvements that by the second half of the nineteenth century brought it substantially to the level of contemporary technology.

Cotton boles were greatly compressed at the plantation, and breaking them down began to pose a problem by the end of the eighteenth century. Several drum devices with spikes ("willows") were invented for this purpose. The cotton then passed into the opening and beating machines, which completed the cleaning. In 1797 N. Snodgrass invented the first scutcher, a machine that was gradually improved until 1808 in the factories of Arkwright and Strutt, by which time it became practically identical with models still used today. The opening operation that returned the fibers to their original fluffy state was accomplished by the action of the beater, composed of arms turning at high speed and equipped with spikes that vigorously beat the cotton supplied by feed rollers. The seeds, fragments of stalks, and other impurities were thrown out through a grill that formed the lower portion of the machine, and dust was removed by fan suction.

Although a patent had existed in the 1790s for a machine to remove dust created by carding machines, which was harmful to workers, the first practical application came with the machines just discussed.

Following the bale opener and the scutcher (which differs very little from the opener), the lap machine came into use after 1814. This produced a soft roll of felt that could be taken directly to the carding engines.

During this same time the carding machine underwent considerable evolution. The principal problem, cleaning the rows of card clothing, was solved in 1823 by Buchanan and in 1834 by James Smith, with the invention of the card with revolving flats that is still in use (Figure 5). Here again the work became continuous, since stops for cleaning were made unnecessary. The flats were mounted on endless belts, permitting them to be constantly in contact with a cleaning brush.

A considerable change also occurred in preparation of the rove. Upon its exit from Arkwright's drawing frame the still-loose sliver had to be wound on bobbins so it could be spun. This extremely difficult operation was mechanized in England between 1815 and 1825, thanks to the bobbin-and-fly frame. Its principle was no different from that of the water frame, but winding the untwisted rove required a special control system because the diameter of the bobbin increased as new layers were superimposed on it. Both in the United States (by A. Arnold in 1822) and in England (by Green in 1823), inventors strained their ingenuity searching for ingenious devices for differential motions.

The ring throstle   The invention of the ring throstle also provides an opportunity to observe developments in American spinning; first we must outline the structural change that occurred in fine spinning. Around 1780 the water frame was the principal spinning machine in use, but in the nineteenth century discontinuous spinning with the mule came to the fore because of the quality of its output. For example, in England in 1811 there were 5 million spindles in operation: 156,000 on ordinary, manually operated jennies worked in homes, 310,500 on water frames, and 4,600,000 on mule-jennies.

The ratio in favor of the mule increased still further when after continuous improvements it evolved into a completely automatic self-acting machine around 1818 to 1825. This machine was rightly called "one of the most wonderful and most useful automata of modern industry."

With Richard Roberts's 1825 and 1830 patents the cotton and wool industries had a spinning machine which, though they worked discontinuously, functioned almost perfectly and gave a flexible, uniform twist. The self-acting machine did not begin to lose ground until developments in a very recent period.

Under these conditions the last innovation to be discussed here, the ring throstle, came into use somewhat uncertainly. It was the final metamorphosis of the water frame.

In 1828 the American Charles Danforth (1797–1876) took out a patent for a frame on which flying shuttles (Figure 9) were replaced by a tube or cap that moved from side to side. The sliver coming out of the can passed between two rows of drawing rollers, then through the tube, which was kept rotating around its axis, providing the twisting action of the spindle. Upon leaving the tube the yarn wound around a horizontal bobbin. This type of spindle was successful only in the wool industry, because it roughened cotton yarn.

Later an intermediate solution was suggested, though it is unlikely that it was developed. It required turning the metal guide for the thread by a flyer on a ring around the spindle.

Authorities generally agree in attributing the invention of the traveler, which characterizes the ring spindle, to an American named Joseph Jenks. The thread guide, which consisted of an open wire ring, the traveler, slid freely on a circular ring rail around the spindle. This conception, as simple as it was ingenious, assured the ring spindle of unparalleled success. By virtue of its friction on the ring the traveler made fewer revolutions than the spindle, and thus the twisting and winding were done automatically (Figure 10). The invention spread quite slowly at first. Hence, the up-and-down motion of the frame carrying the spindles and the construction of the spindles themselves to permit them being turned at high speeds were not developed as the final improvements to the ring spindle until the second half of the nineteenth century.

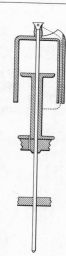

FIG. 9.   The flyer spindle, which simultaneously twists and winds the yarn. Mid-nineteenth century. The flyer *(top)* and the bobbin *(under the flyer)* have the same axle of rotation but revolve at different speeds. The bobbin forms a hollow shaft through which passes that of the flyer. The taut thread arrives at the top and goes through the eyelet visible at the top of the spindle; then it follows the path of the dotted line. The twist results from the rotating movement of the spindle as a whole. The winding is produced by the difference in speed between the flyer and the bobbin.

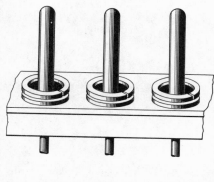

FIGS. 10, 10A.   Ring spindles. The thread arrives at the top. Before reaching the spindle, it passes under the traveler, the small, movable wire clip on the ring around the spindle (see detail, a vertical cross section of this ring). Since the spindle is rotating, the twist in the thread results from the circular movement of the clip on the ring, while the winding of the thread is produced by the difference in velocity between the spindle and the traveler because of the friction of the latter on the ring. *Below:* Detail of the ring and its traveler.

Spinning, the industrial prototype of mechanization   In the space of fifty years the spinning industry, originally one of the most backward of all branches of industry, became a major industry of the most modern type. The organization of factories, from the point of view of buildings and the installation of machines, became a model for other, less-developed, branches of industry. In the fever of the Industrial Revolution, Europe paid admiring tribute to the unique achievements of this branch of industry. In 1823 a friend of the famous German architect Karl Schinkel (1781–1841) wrote him concerning English spinning mills:

> For me, my dear friend, the modern miracles are the machines here, with the buildings which house them, and which are called manufactures. Such a building is eight or nine storeys tall, and sometimes has 40 windows along its facade and often four across its width. . . . The pillars are of iron, as is the framework they support; the inner and even the outer walls are as thin as

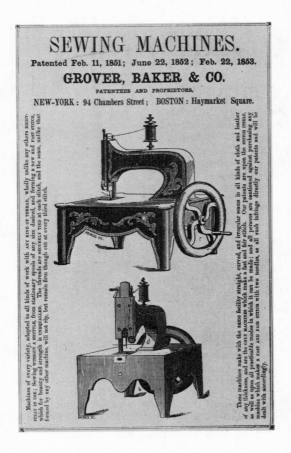

Plate 73. Grover & Baker Sewing Machines. Smithsonian Institution, Collection of Business Americana

playing cards. . . . A certain number of such buildings are located on a very high rise which dominates the vicinity; moreover, a forest of boiler chimneys, still higher up, and which resemble needles. . . . From a distance the whole offers a superb view, especially at night when thousands of windows are brilliantly lighted by the light of gas. You can imagine, indeed, what a strong light is needed, when a single worker must tend 840 threads so fine that 260 hanks of them are needed to make one pound.

Spinning was thus the prototypical model of the modern mid-nineteenth century factory at the very time when the Industrial Revolution was coming to an end, particularly in this branch. The pace of development then slowed, and in the second half of the century spinning gradually lost its influential role.

CHAPTER 2

WEAVING AND MECHANICAL FINISHING

Prior claims by Leonardo da Vinci

It has often been said that a large number of modern inventions are to be found in Leonardo da Vinci's *Notebooks*. For instance, one can find several designs for mechanizing textile machinery that did not, in fact, appear until the eighteenth and even nineteenth centuries. In saying that his contribution to the textile field, when reduced to its correct proportions, is of uncertain value, we do not intend, obviously, to pass judgment on the other branches of his activity as an engineer and scientist, but the textile devices he conceived are indeed of unequal quality.

Organzining mills appeared at Lucca, Tuscany, in the thirteenth century and spread outward from Florence, Bologna, and Lombardy. They were described in 1581 by Montaigne in his *Journal de voyage*. For these mills Leonardo may have invented a device to stop the machine if a thread broke.

The flying shuttle on spinning wheels, which derives from a similar device in organzining mills, had been in existence at least since the fifteenth century. Leonardo made an improvement consisting of a complicated automatic device to ensure uniform distribution of yarn on the bobbin. A similar device did not appear in industry until the end of the eighteenth century.

Leonardo's design for a mechanical weaving loom is not very clear. He seems to propose hand-to-hand passage of the shuttle; that is, passage from one hand to the other without throwing. This sterile formula, though it was later adopted by de Gennes and Vaucanson, never attained the slightest success. Mechanical reproduction of a human gesture has always proved to be a dead end.

Leonardo's idea concerning cropping was not without a certain practical value, since it played a role, though sporadic and temporary, between 1784 and 1835. Cropping machines identical to the one suggested by Leonardo were then being built in twelve European workshops, but their inventors certainly were unaware of the existence of his notebooks of sketches. Several thousand of these machines came into operation, but after 1819 they began to disappear with the development of the Dorr-Collier cropper with spiral blades, a genuine mechanization of the cropping operation. Alcan believed he recognized the principle of spiral cropping in a sketch by Leonardo, but this is an error; it was, in fact, a machine for making springs.

Finally, the gig mills built shortly after Leonardo's death (Volume II, p. 217) are based on a more rational principle than most of the teaseling machines he designed.

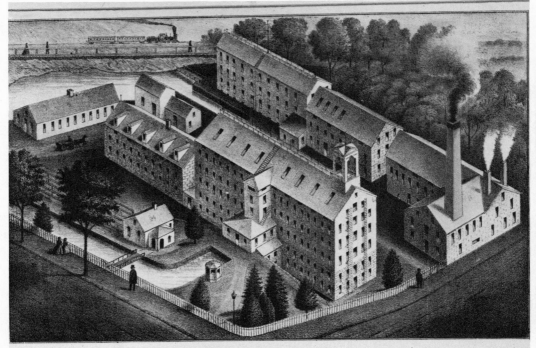

ROCK MANUFACTURING CO'S WOOLEN MILLS, ROCKVILLE, CT.
Established 1821.

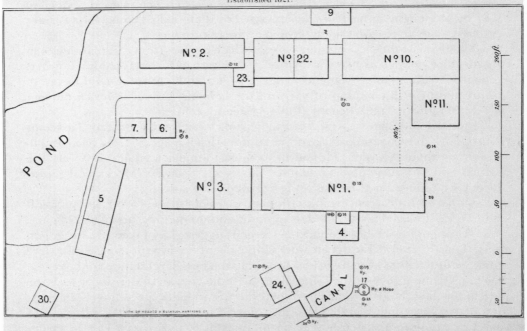

Plate 74. The woolen mills of Rock Manufacturing Company at Rockville, Connecticut, established in 1821. This spinning mill, a prototype of the modern factory of the mid-19th century, was modeled on the English mill. Smithsonian Institution, Peters Collection

Imitating the movement of a bird's wings never led to the invention of a true airplane. Similarly, when inspired by craftsmen's movements, inventors conceived only pseudo-machines which, when introduced into industry for lack of something better, retarded progress: fulling mills with hammers, mechanized cropping tables, and lastly the shuttle loom, the worst of the paleotechnical relics that the weaving industry is still dragging about like a ball and chain.

The balance between spinning and weaving   In the course of the evolution of a technique, increased productivity in a given stage of the manufacturing process never fails to have repercussions on the stage that supplies material to be worked on as well as on the next part of the operation.

The invention of the flying shuttle in 1733 resulted from the impossibility of obtaining fabrics of a certain width without employing a heavy, two-man loom. A single weaver passing the shuttle from hand to hand could weave only widths of fabric limited to the area between his elbows, but the flying shuttle let him weave on broad warps and much faster than before. The spread of this invention, though rather slow in certain areas, had profound repercussions. Since the various operations in an industry are interdependent, their relative speeds must be coordinated. If a technical improvement is made in one of these operations, the rhythm of the entire group is altered and a disequilibrium occurs in the system, so that the ensemble remains unstable as long as the still-backward phases have not caught up with those that have advanced.

We saw earlier that in the old textile industry it was difficult to maintain equilibrium between yarn production and its consumption by weaving looms. A single hand loom provided work for five or six spinning wheels. The result, under normal conditions and in spite of imports, was an almost constant shortage of yarn.

The appearance of the flying shuttle only aggravated this state of affairs. It became imperative to produce yarn as rapidly as it was consumed. This is why the search for a practical method of spinning cotton by machine was so urgently pursued.

Around 1780 a new disruption of balanced production occurred in England. Though spinning machines were already highly perfected, weaving continued to be done manually. Around 1760 it was only with great difficulty that weavers found enough yarn to supply their flying shuttle looms steadily, but thirty years later the situation was reversed: there were not enough weavers for the work. Their salaries climbed rapidly until the general crisis of 1790, which just changed the nature of the problem. In Great Britain the imbalance between the production of yarns and of fabrics had reached such a point that spinners were forced to export, ruining the Continental entrepreneurs of hand spinning and their women spinners.

This was a general crisis, as had occurred during the period preceding the invention of the machine to spin cotton, and it grew with the imbalance that was its cause, reaching its peak around 1800.

At that time prototypes of mechanical looms were already in existence, but they had not yet been sufficiently developed to be put into operation in factories. The crisis of 1800 forced Cartwright's successors to develop for the cotton industry the first mechanical looms that were usable industrially.

The precursors of
mechanized weaving

The idea of mechanical weaving has been attributed to Aristotle, but this is an error in interpretation. Merely reading his *Politics* suffices to prove this.

The spread of the bar loom in the seventeenth century made possible within the foreseeable future mechanizing of weaving fabrics. The principle proved its value in ribbonmaking as early as 1602, and the rest was merely a question of dimensions. But with wide looms new problems of kinetics were to be raised.

Hand-to-hand passage of the shuttle was envisaged by four innovators, none of whom was a weaver: Leonardo da Vinci, J.-J. Becher, and two French mechanics, de Gennes and Vaucanson. The latter's prototype mechanical fabric loom, dating from 1744, was without practical value because of the hand-to-hand passage of the shuttle (Figure 22).

After being applied for the first time, at the end of the sixteenth century, to a small ribbon machine, this hand-to-hand passage had then proved its worth on the bar loom. It is a mechanical loom intended for weaving ribbons. Hand-to-hand passage of the shuttle became impractical as soon as the width of the fabric exceeded the length of the shuttle.

Vaucanson was satisfied slavishly to imitate the action of the weaver's hands. He brought in two sliding bars that simultaneously entered the shed from both sides, one of which pushed the shuttle to meet the other bar. By moving backward the shuttle pulled it toward the other selvage. This loom could no more be put into general use than could de Gennes's around 1678. However, the description of it given by Vaucanson in the November 1745 *Mercure de France* contains (apart from the unfortunate manner of propelling the shuttle) lucid observations that have since been confirmed by the recent evolution of weaving.

John Kay and the
flying shuttle

In order to accomplish in a practical way the passage of the weft through a warp whose width exceeded the length of the shuttle, the shuttle had to be shot in free flight from one selvage to the other and be received in a recoil slide able to return it in the opposite direction (Figure 11). In 1733 John Kay, a thirty-year-old craftsman from Lancashire who at first became successful in making weavers' combs, built such a device, thereby increasing both the production and the capacity in width of the hand loom.

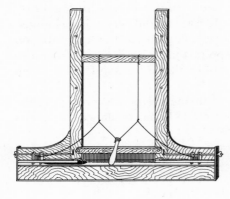

FIG. 11. John Kay's flying shuttle device. The leather drives, or pickers, which drive the shuttle back and forth, move on horizontal sliders. They obey the action of the system of cords, on which the weaver acts by moving the handle visible in the center sharply to the left or right.

Kay was also familiar with the bar loom, for which in 1745 he took out two patents for improvements. Assuredly he did not suspect that the combination of his flying shuttle and the bar loom would in the future make possible the complete mechanization of the entire weaving operation.

Kay installed his device for propelling the shuttle on the batten of the old hand loom. His invention consisted of a shuttle race for passage of the shuttle and shuttle boxes that received it at the end of the throw. The shape of the shuttle itself changed from molded to straight. It was metal-tipped at both ends and equipped with two small wheels that facilitated the travel across the width of the warp.

On each sliding box was a small piece of wood fitted with a leather pad that struck the shuttle in order to propel it. A system of cords controlled these two opposed drivers, cords arranged so as to cushion the reception of the shuttle in the box and prevent it from bouncing back.

In addition to permitting an increase in width, this device considerably improved the rhythm of the work by freeing the weaver's left hand. From now on his right hand never left the handle that controlled the cords propelling the shuttle, while the left hand constantly held the handle of the reed that beat in the weft. In this way reflexes were greatly simplified.

The two-man loom was retained only for fabrics that were exceptionally wide and had a warp too hard for a single man to manipulate with a leg (Figure 12). Such looms existed as relics until 1860 and in some cases even into the 1870s, long after the completely mechanical loom appeared.

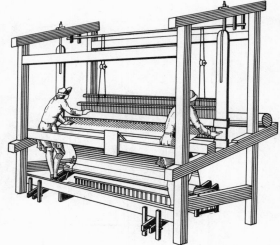

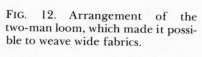
FIG. 12. Arrangement of the two-man loom, which made it possible to weave wide fabrics.

John Kay introduced the flying shuttle into France in 1747, when he was granted a fourteen-year license. Later, shamefully robbed in England by a coalition of manufacturers who were the beneficiaries of his invention, he returned to France, where he worked as an adviser on spinning and weaving for the Inspection des Manufactures. In 1764, having left Troyes to take up a new position at Sens, he disappeared en route.

In 1760 his son Robert invented the multiple-shuttle box, still in use on hand-operated looms, which permitted using several shuttles to produce multicolored patterns.

The pawl-and-ratchet mechanism of the cloth beam for winding up the fabric produced on the loom dates from the thirteenth century (see Volume I, Figure 89, p. 509). At the end of the eighteenth century an English mechanic named William Radcliffe (1760–1841) suggested that it be automated, but not until 1805 did he patent this idea, which consisted of connecting the ratchet wheel with the batten so that the cloth beam would be moved forward by the stroke of the batten.

The advent of mechanical weaving
As remarked in connection with an earlier period (Volume II, p. 215), we can speak of mechanical weaving only when we refer to a loom that, starting from simple rotation, automatically performs the four basic operations of weaving: opening the shed, passing the pick, beating in the pick by the comb, and gradually advancing the warp as the work progresses.

The first advances, by Barber (1774), Cartwright (1785), and Austin (1796), were applied to wooden looms. Some time elapsed before models with cast-iron frames—developed by Horrocks, Roberts, and Hattersley in Great Britain, Heilmann (Figure 13), Koechlin, and Magnan in France, and Schönherr in Germany—were available for factory use. Indeed, the power loom had no future as long as it was constructed with a wooden frame incapable of withstanding the shocks of mechanical motion.

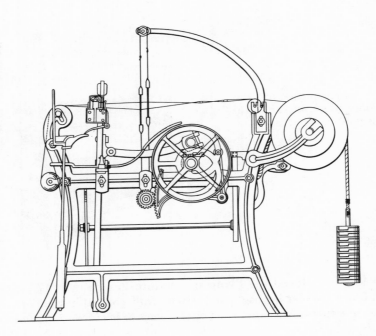

FIG. 13.   Profile view of Heilmann's mechanical loom. *Left to right:* The two shafts, then the reed, and (seen in cross section) the shuttle on the batten.

Mechanization of the loom had to be accompanied by improvements in warping and sizing the warp to make it stronger and so reduce breaks in the yarn caused by the speed of the work, breaks whose consequences become much more troublesome than with the hand loom.

Before power looms could be adopted by industry, it was necessary to devise stop motions, for example in case of a break or failure of the weft, and to block the batten when the shuttle remained caught in the shed. Miller suggested in 1796 the former. Failures in throwing the shuttle increased as mechanical motion was developed.

Width of the first mechanical looms The tens of thousands of mechanical looms adopted industrially in the early nineteenth century, as reported by such enthusiastic statisticians as Sir Edward Baines and one named Barlow, were only light looms for cotton goods. Their width was still narrower than that of the manually operated flying shuttle looms of the period. In 1820 their speed was no greater than 90 picks per minute. One weaver could operate only two looms.

The persistence of light, narrow looms Light looms of this type persisted in a large number of factories, with very minor improvements in detail, until 1930, and even later in certain centers. The looms then sent to the scrap heap were sixty to seventy years old. This serious and anachronistic situation had economic consequences from which certain textile centers did not recover.

Heavy looms The first heavy, wide looms for draperies and tarpaulins appeared in 1823 (Collier & Magnan, Paris), 1830 (Sharp & Roberts, in Great Britain), and 1845 (Schönherr, in Saxony), but their builders experienced difficulties, and the use of such looms did not really begin to spread until around 1860.

Building such looms introduced difficult problems of kinetics. In the early days the shuttle's movement caused a considerable waste of motive power, a disadvantage that has, moreover, never been completely eliminated. The devel-

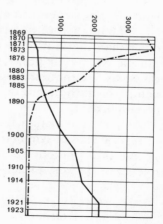

FIG. 14.   Growth of the number of hand-weaving looms (broken line) and mechanical looms (solid line) at Vienne (Isère) from 1869 to 1923.

opment involved very precise adjustments. Absolutely regular power sources were required, something that was particularly difficult to obtain with the means available in the mid-nineteenth century. This explains why manual weaving of carded wool persisted much longer than of combed wool or cotton.

Lastly, during the whole evolution of weaving, hand weavers stubbornly resisted all innovations. They tried with all their power to resist the spread of the flying shuttle and then, during the first third of the nineteenth century, the adoption of mechanical looms. In 1832 the first mechanical looms for combed wool were destroyed at Shipley, and in 1826 in Lancashire repeated destruction of looms occurred. In 1838 there were still 14,000 hand weavers in the city of Bradford.

Controlled design   Patterned fabrics made on the same heddle loom as solid-color fabrics, using no special mechanism, had been in existence since the beginning of weaving. The ad hoc contrivances that were used have only recently been mathematically analyzed, by Delamare and Deboutteville in 1930 and Brandon and Guiguet in 1938.

By making each warp thread independent, the shedding device (discussed later) used for patterned fabrics offered the designer almost total liberty. This is, in fact, a controlled system, obeying rules implied in the use of whole rows of heddles. Obtaining decorative designs by such a method requires, to a greater degree than with figured fabric, a knowledge of the problems of both form and texture. Just as the form of a crystal is a function of its molecular structure, these designs are subject to the rules of weaving with heddles, without their being necessarily symmetrical.

All weaves (ways of interlacing the threads) derive from the simple linen weave, done with two heddles. Other basic weaves such as canvas (French *treillis*, from *tri-licium*, a fabric woven with three heddles) and twill (four heddles) had been practiced in the Bronze Age in China and Europe. Finally came the satins, made with five to eight heddles.

In plain fabrics the warp threads are threaded onto the heddles in consecutive numerical order, but for patterned fabrics the threading sequence follows a complex order corresponding to the order in which the heddles are raised. The result is the production of designs composed of a small number of basic, coordinated motifs, dependent on the number of heddles used.

The method of decorating fabrics by combining such patterns is probably older than the draw device explained below. It flourished especially at certain times and in certain places, notably in ancient China, ancient Peru before and after the Spanish Conquest, among Moorish weavers and table-linen weavers in Silesia before the introduction of the Jacquard loom, and even today in Spain to produce certain bedspreads.

Upon examination, the designs produced by this method generally reveal one or several axes of symmetry. Some experts in ancient fabrics therefore call them geometrical, without appreciating that this characteristic is an essential consequence of the very principle of making designs.

Free design: Figured fabrics are decorated ones produced on a
figured fabrics   loom that makes each warp thread independently, in contrast to the fabrics just described, in which the heddles are maneuvered only in groups. To be precise, the composition of the

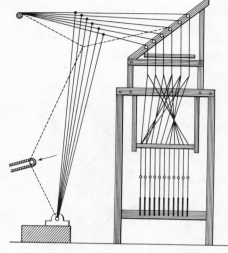

FIG. 15. Operation of the drawloom. With this device the drawboy can now stand beside the loom. He works by pulling on certain of the cords stretched in the vertical position at left (in this case the fourth cord from the left). Solid lines indicate its original position, dotted lines, its new one.

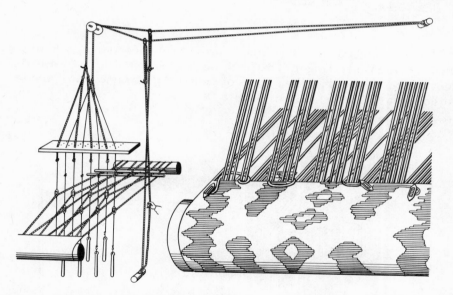

FIG. 16. Principle of the drawloom. The extensions of the warp threads pass through the holes in the bottom board, slide on the pulleys (which form the selecting box), and are then attached to a supporting cylinder; these are the tenter cords. In the center of each is a vertical cord, the simple. When the weaver pulls a simple cord, it acts on the corresponding cord of the tenter, which through the pulley lifts the corresponding warp threads. *Right:* Weaving a multicolored patterned fabric. The length of a pick is divided among several shuttles.

decorations for figured fabrics is not completely free, for repeating the design that forms the fabric's decoration is always limited to a certain extent.

In order to produce figured fabrics, weavers have from the very beginning used the so-called draw device, in which each thread of the design repetition corresponds to an individually adjusted warp thread (Figures 15 and 16). In ancient China a boy perched on top of the loom raised the warp threads, which were preselected in relation to the warp repeat, by pulling on knotted cords (Figure 17). This primitive system, which reached France by way of Italy, continued in use until the seventeenth century.

FIG. 17.   Chinese loom for weaving patterned fabrics (from an eighteenth-century engraving). The drawboy, seated at upper right, selects and pulls the warp threads. The weaving itself is being done at bottom left.

The introduction in 1606 of the improvement known as the selecting box is attributed to Claude Dangon. This is a device that permits a drawboy seated on the floor to operate the shafts by a series of pullies. At the same time it also became possible to weave larger designs (Figure 18).

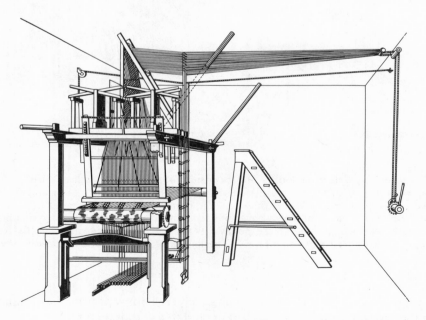

FIG. 18.   Actual arrangement of the drawloom with tenter and selecting box, in the room in which a weaver is working.

A series of minor improvements was made in this draw device during the seventeenth century and early eighteenth, but we shall mention only the simultaneous inventions of Basile Bouchon and one Falcon, the broad import of which went far beyond weaving.

Variable-program control devices   By the early eighteenth century variable-program controls had already been used for two centuries for carillons and astronomical clocks, but for each new tune the pin barrel containing the program had to be repegged. This was also the case on the drawloom, on which the group of leashes corresponding to the design required weeks of work to change.

Bouchon in 1725 and Falcon in 1728 were the first to propose stationary program cards that were instantly interchangeable and could therefore be put in reserve and repeated later without complications (Figure 19). The endless paper pattern suggested by Bouchon was a premature solution, in advance of the state of the art at that time. Inventors returned to this idea in the twentieth century.

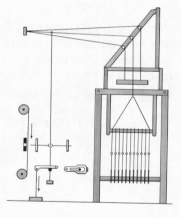

FIG. 19.   The Bouchon loom. The program is entered on a perforated strip of paper (the two rollers at left). Each cord of the loom passes through the ring of a horizontal needle, which is free to move toward the left when it encounters a perforation in the paper. A treadle (bottom) permits the weaver to pull as a unit all the cords selected in this way. Each cord has a bead on it and passes through a hole in a piece of wood that is larger than the bead on the right side and smaller than the bead on the left (drawing in plan view of this element is between the loom and the draw mechanism).

Falcon suggested a string of cardboard rectangles on which the decorative design would be interpreted by rows of perforations, with each cardboard piece corresponding to a pick (Figure 20). The cards were linked together to form an endless chain the length of which corresponded to the number of picks in the warp repeat (that is, the length of the design). This chain of cardboard pieces hung down from the top of the loom. A worker placed them one by one on a perforated piece of wood that was in effect a prism. Then he placed them against the needle board, each needle of which corresponded to a leash. The worker now had only to pull the leashes thus selected. Although this device still required a drawboy in addition to a weaver, it still offered the additional and by no means negligible advantage that the use of this program support was less tiring for the cord puller.

A Falcon loom equipped with a certain fixed number of neck cords (groups of warp threads defining the design element and repeated several times across the width of the fabric) could operate with a large number of varied designs, since to change designs an instantaneous change of cards sufficed, without dismantling

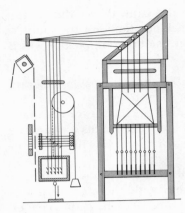

FIG. 20. The Falcon loom. It derives from the Bouchon loom, but here the program is entered on a chain of perforated cards, each one of which corresponds to a single picking action of the loom. The needles are arranged in several parallel rows, which increases the possibilities of the loom.

the loom. This feature permits us to consider the inventions of Bouchon and Falcon as precursors of mid-twentieth century automatic mechanisms.

Vaucanson's contribution Jacques de Vaucanson's attempt to replace the drawboy with an automatic mechanism dates from 1775 and should not be confused with the model of a mechanical loom for taffeta that he built in 1744 (Figure 22).

The 1775 mechanism designed to replace the drawboy automatically coordinates three functions:

1. It applies the perforated program "cards" against a board with flexible needles.
2. It selects these needles as directed by the perforations in the "cards."
3. It forms the shed by providing for raising the warp threads thus selected.

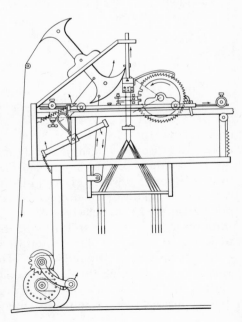

FIG. 21. The draw mechanism of Vaucanson's loom. The program is entered on a perforated cylinder (*top, right*). Horizontal needles rest constantly against the cylinder, penetrating it when they encounter a perforation. In its movement the needle pulls on a vertical hook from which the warp threads are suspended. The hook cannot be raised, since its curved portion is no longer above the pin that is supposed to move it. The cylinder turns automatically at the angle corresponding to a row of perforations at each pick.

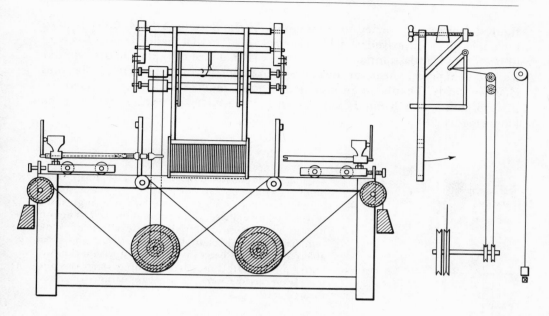

FIG. 22. The movement of the shuttle-throwing mechanism on the Vaucanson loom. In the center is the reed (or comb controlling warp threads) of the loom. The warp threads are perpendicular to the plane of the drawing. To the left and right of the reed are the two arms that hold the shuttle. Each is attached to a traveling carriage. Each arm, moving back and forth, seizes the shuttle at the end of the opposite arm and pulls it through the warp in returning to its original position. Here the shuttle is at left.

Unfortunately, instead of a card Vaucanson suggested a cylinder whose capacity (which was very limited from every point of view) deprived the invention of all practical import. The engineer had taken his inspiration too literally from carillons, music boxes, and automata.

He must have been well acquainted with Falcon's device, for about one hundred of these looms were operating in various shops in Lyon. The card chain could hold a much larger number of holes than could the circumference of Vaucanson's cylinder, a circumference that remained invariable. Falcon could by a simple change in the number of cards vary the warp repeat of the design. Roland de La Platière was therefore correct in saying of Vaucanson that "he worked more as an engineer seeking to be admired by scientists than as an artist who wished to be useful to factories."

A quarter of a century later Joseph-Marie Jacquard (1752–1834) successfully combined the elements introduced by Falcon and Vaucanson. The basic difference between the two pioneers was that though the Falcon loom was in operation in Lyon until 1817, Vaucanson's device proved incapable of any kind of practical application.

Jacquard's synthesis Jacquard first attracted the attention of the Société d'Encouragement pour l'industrie nationale with his machine for making fishing nets (1802). The problem of designing a loom for figured fabrics was opened to competition by the Société in 1804 and Jacquard built at Lyon an improved version of the Falcon loom that made the use of a chain of perforated cards automatic. He had the original idea of replacing the cylinder with a driving mechanism for the perforated prism, permitting the use of Falcon's chain of cards. Thanks to an ingenious arrangement, the carriage pressed the prism holding a perforated card against the needle board at each stroke of the loom (Figure 23).

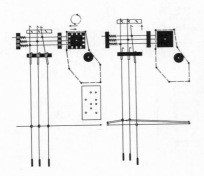

FIG. 23. The Jacquard mechanism. This device combines Falcon's perforated cards and Vaucanson's needles-and-hooks system. The two drawings show two consecutive phases of the operation. *Left:* The top needle has not encountered a perforation; its hook remains behind and cannot be raised. *Right:* The movable part *(top)* has been raised, pulling with it the two hooks at the left; The corresponding warp threads have been raised. *Center:* General appearance of a perforated card.

To this synthesis by Jacquard we owe the final, automatic solution whereby a single weaver of decorated fabrics could pull the leashes for weaving. Jacquard's contribution, which during his lifetime was well known and unquestioned, is now by turns exaggerated or denigrated. Being solely preoccupied with freeing the weaver from needing the assistance of a drawboy, Jacquard never tackled the problem of the mechanization of weaving as such. Hostile critics such as Rodon Font took an unsophisticated attitude to the concept of invention, a controversy mediated with a great deal of common sense by one Usher.

The application of the Jacquard mechanism began in Lyon, then spread abroad with unprecedented rapidity, much faster than the adoption of mechanical looms, showing that it responded to a more immediate economic demand. In Lyon in 1788 there were 14,782 looms in operation, of which only 240 were for figured fabrics, including about 100 of the Falcon type. By 1833 there were 32,000 looms, 20,000 of which had the Jacquard mechanism, and by 1900 there were 60,000 looms, 25,000 of which were Jacquards. It is also important to note that in the initial period of its application—that is, until around the middle of the nineteenth century—the Jacquard mechanism was attached only to manual looms, in harmony with the moderate work rhythm of their still partly wooden construction.

Fulling machines   Throughout the eighteenth century and even later the old fulling mills continued to be used. They acted by kneading, imitating working with the feet. The first continuously acting machines appeared in England and were imported into France around 1838 by Hall fils, Powels et Scott of Rouen. These machines made possible the continuous kneading of a long piece of fabric sewn end to end to form a loop. The fabric was

Plates 75 and 76. Carding and drawing room and mechanical looms; England, 1835. Engravings of the period by T. Allom, J. Carter, and J. Tingle. London, Science Museum. (Photo Science Museum.)

fulled both lengthwise and crosswise by movements under conpression between two adjacent drums.

This machine was developed by Benoît of Nîmes and especially by Vallery and Lacroix of Rouen. They retained the rollers to perform the crosswise fulling, but lengthwise fulling was done by forcing the fabric into a trough formed of three planks, from which it escaped only by separating the planks. An important point is that the pressure of the rollers and planks could be regulated (Figure 24).

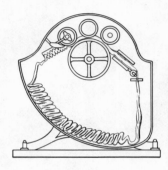

FIG. 24.   A fulling machine. The piece of fabric has been sewn end to end to form an endless chain so that it can be subjected to the action of the working parts *(top)* for an indefinite period of time.

This machine represented the perfection of this technique, though the old fulling mills continued to operate intermittently in certain centers until the end of the nineteenth century. As for fulling with the feet, traces of it could still be found at Lodz, Poland (then still under Russian domination), until the First World War.

Teaseling or napping of fabrics

The teaseling operation consists of raising the surface of the undressed fabric preparatory to cropping. For certain fabrics this was done even before the second fulling. In England teaseling mills, called gig mills, appeared quite early, as seen in Volume II. They were forbidden several times during the reign of Elizabeth I and during each succeeding reign. One of these rotary teaseling mills, which a manufacturer at Heytesbury, Wiltshire, tried to impose on his workers in 1758, was destroyed in a riot. These primitive rotary teaseling machines already made it possible to effect a great economy in time and labor. Work that required 88 hours of manual teaseling could be done by machine in 12 hours, by one man assisted by a child.

This machine was indeed reminiscent of one of the machines conceived by Leonardo da Vinci, although its inventors did not know the drawings by this Florentine engineer. A drum approximately 35 inches in diameter, equipped with teasels, revolved at high speed while brushing the tautly stretched fabric, which passed over several other small-diameter rollers.

Around 1802 to 1806 regulations still forbade the use of mechanical methods for teaseling fabrics. Innumerable documents testify to the workers' resistance to this machine, though its use appears to have been tolerated by the officials.

Wherever shearers were well organized they attempted to resist the use of gig mills by refusing to crop mechanically teaseled pieces of fabric, on the pretext that the preparation was not well done. The workers' resistance gradually ceased; in Yorkshire the number of gig mills rose from 5 in 1806 to 72 in 1817.

In France gig mills were not yet in use in the eighteenth century. A certain Douglas was the first to introduce them, when in 1802/3 he installed his factory to manufacture machines for the woolen industry at the mills on the Île des Cygnes.

After various improvements the machine acquired a more modern form in the hands of one Dubois of Louviers. It had been impossible to find anything superior to teasels for raising the fabric. But the machine was now of metal, equipped with a drum whose surface was formed of frames studded with teasels. An upper and a lower roller received the fabric, which passed from one to the other. An automatic device reversed the direction when the end of the fabric was reached.

The mechanization of shearing

Regarding weaving looms we have noted a slow evolution and the tenacious survival of earlier techniques, with prolonged periods of stagnation. On the other hand the mechanization of shearing experienced a technical revolution comparable with those that occurred in spinning and later with the spread of the Jacquard mechanism.

In spite of the fact that one so-called shearing machine, built in 1758, was not truly designed for shearing, it is clear that shearing machines were in fact being built at the end of the eighteenth and beginning of the nineteenth centuries. They resemble the one sketched by Leonardo (Figure 25) to such a point that the engineers would appear to have been inspired by it. Only the reasoning is identical, however, for by the end of the eighteenth century any mechanic was capable of copying faithfully the gestures of the shearer.

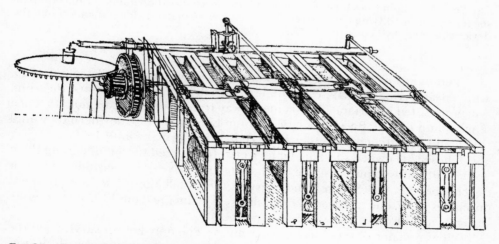

FIG. 25. Project for mechanizing the cloth-cropping operation. (Drawing by Leonardo da Vinci.) Four cropping shears are maneuvered mechanically by rods attached to the ends of the blades. The rods alternately open and close the blades. The fabric automatically unrolls across the table.

Almost simultaneously, between 1784 and 1817, there were in Europe about
a dozen builders who succeeded in having their mechanized shearing tables
accepted by manufacturers. This phenomenon does justice to the memory of
Leonardo, but it is still impossible for his notebooks, buried in archives, to have
come to the attention of engineers (Figure 26).

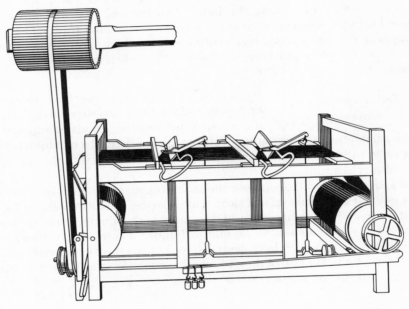

FIG. 26.   A cropping machine that embodies the mechanized operation of the cropping
shears without modifying the structure of the tool. Note that it is almost identical with the
device suggested by Leonardo da Vinci.

Thousands of these crude machines were in operation until around 1835,
with a peak period in 1817. Nevertheless, they did not replace manual shearing,
which persisted in certain fabric centers away from the main economic currents:
England until 1820; Bitschwiller, Sedan, and Linz until 1830; northern Italy until
1850; and Euskirchen and other small centers in Germany until 1870.

Those who owned shearing tables were often forced to continue using them
for lack of funds to purchase the much more expensive spiral machines. Thus, at
Reichenberg in the Sudetenland, despite the installation of numerous spiral
machines, some one hundred manual shearers maintained until 1857 a desperate
struggle against the eviction threatening them.

What remains of these strange machines? The only known survivor, at the
Musée de la Sologne at Romŏrantin, is a pair of shears equipped with devices
showing that it was mounted on a mechanized cropping table.

In connection with these mechanical shearing tables, it is interesting to recall
Napoleon's observation of them. From the steps of the Sedan city hall on August 9,

1803, Bonaparte heard among the voices of the cheering crowd a few that were crying, "Long live the First Consul! Down with the machines!"

Napoleon did not let himself be caught off guard. His minister and friend Chaptal had already had opportunity to submit to him reports on this subject. Rising to the challenge, Napoleon answered, "Your fears are groundless. Since the shearing machines lower the price of fabrics, consumption will increase with the low price at a rate greater than that of the decrease of hands. Moreover, the shearing machines have been installed everywhere abroad: at Verviers, at Aix, and elsewhere. To meet the competition, the manufacturers of Sedan ought in their turn to install them."

The rotary cropper with spiral blades   In 1792 S. G. Dorr of Albany, New York, took out a patent for a rotary machine. Although it had straight blades and therefore no practical value, it was still a first step toward the correct solution.

The machine with spiral blades was invented in the United States by R. Dorr of Kinderhook, New York, around 1807, but he did not attempt to build one. In 1810 its description reached France, where it was patented and then sold by one Jonathan Ellis, regarded by many as its inventor.

After the patent was acquired by the Baron de Neuflize in 1814, systematic experimental work was undertaken in his shop in the rue Richer by the famous Parisian engineer John Collier (Figure 27). Similar machines were built at the

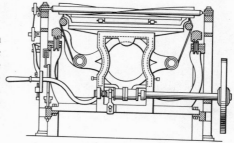

FIG. 27. The Collier transversal cropper with spiral blades; general view from the front. The roller holding the spiral incurved blades is visible at top. Outline of the operation: the fabric to be cropped passes over the lower roller; a stationary blade *(right)* brushes up the nap. The upper roller with the spiral blades performs the cropping.

same time by J. Lewis and by Price in Great Britain. The shearer's use spread in Europe from Paris through Adrien Cochelet, later a diplomat. Shortly thereafter, in 1823, it was introduced into England, thus being probably the first machine imported by that country.

From the moment of its introduction at the Industrial Exposition of 1819, it was a completely modern machine: all-metal, with a brass cylinder, equipped with spiral steel blades, and rolling in antifriction pillow blocks invented specially for this purpose. The position of the cylinder was regulated by micrometric screws.

In the operation of the machine the fulled fabric, the nap of which had first been raised by a rotating brush, passed over a metal spine. The nap, thus in position for shearing, was then caught as in a scissors, between a stationary blade parallel to the cylinder and the rotating spiral blades.

Never before had a textile machine exerted such an influence on other techniques. Thereafter, planing machines as well as lawn mowers were invented based on this model.

Today, after 150 years of use, the shearer can be regarded as the single case of a machine built in final form right from the very beginning. Except for minor secondary improvements, it is still in operation today in its 1819 form, giving full and complete satisfaction.

CHAPTER 3

HOSIERY

I N VOLUME II (pp. 225–46) we outlined the basic features of the two major steps in the technique of knitting, namely:

1. Hand knitting, done, it is believed, on a frame that made it possible to produce a tubular knit, and later hand knitting with two, three, four, or five needles.
2. Knitting with a loom operated by a foot treadle. This stocking frame, invented in 1589 in England by a clergyman, William Lee (d. 1610?), brought about an extraordinary development in knitting technique, not only by considerably increasing the speed of production but also—and especially—by permitting the use of very fine yarns like silk.

Knitting centers of Europe in the eighteenth century During the eighteenth century the system invented by Lee and then developed and improved by Aston spread through France and several other countries, notably Germany. First introduced into Saxe-Weimar, Hesse, Bavaria, and Württemberg in the preceding century by Huguenot refugees who left France after the revocation of the Edict of Nantes in 1685, the looms appeared in Limbach, Saxony, at the beginning of the eighteenth century, then in the Chemnitz region in 1714, and finally in Chemnitz itself in 1728. Sweden learned of Lee's system in 1723 (see Volume II, p. 242). It has been claimed that this system was introduced into Venice in the seventeenth century and from there into Austria, but this information, which to the best of our knowledge is given only by Gustave Willkomm (*Die Technologie der Wirkerei für Technische Lehranstalten und zum Selbstunterricht*) is unreliable. At the beginning of the nineteenth century Poland was still using a drum loom with wooden wedges driven into it spirally, a loom similar to that preserved in the Musée de la Bonneterie at Troyes, dating from around 1750. Russia seems to have been particularly backward, since at the very end of the nineteenth century she had as yet no knitwear industry.

Beginnings of the industry in the United States Information is lacking concerning the other European countries, and what we know of this industry's growth in the New World is also disappointing. In North America the oldest stocking factory operating in New York is mentioned by Milton N. Grass in *History of Hosiery,* as dating from 1744. In an advertisement in the *New York Weekly Journal* of July 14, 1746, its founder, George Cook, claimed to manufacture stockings from every type of yarn: thread, silk, cotton, and combed wool. A contemporary, John Camm, manufactured stockings in Pennsylvania. In 1770 a certain John Morgatroyd, of Wilmington, North Carolina, advertised for a family capable of undertaking the knitting of stockings on a loom. In 1776 Daniel Mause, a hosier, established a plant in Philadelphia to manufacture stockings and other articles. W. Felkin, in *An Account of the Machine-Wrought Hosiery Trade* (London, 1845), estimates that before 1775 there were in the city of Germantown alone 150 stocking looms, the output of which was sold in Philadelphia. Moreover, a factory that later became prosperous was opened in New England around 1771, according to Grass.

The information we have been able to collect on this subject is obviously too fragmentary and incomplete to permit establishing useful production statistics for Europe and America in the eighteenth century, but one point is firmly established: France and England were the only major producers of knitted articles, notably stockings. During 1744 alone, 14 million pairs of stockings were exported by France.

Economic situation in France — Most of the output came from the south of France, in particular from Nîmes, a major center whose origin dates from the seventeenth century. Knitting spread over the entire region, and with almost 9,000 looms produced in 1782 nearly 180,000 pairs of stockings of every quality, mostly for export. Marseille, on the other hand, sold almost its entire output locally. This production was clearly inferior in quantity, but consisted of up to four-fifths silk stockings.

At Aix-en-Provence only ten out of fifty looms were making silk stockings. The cities of Arles, Pertuis, Tarascon, Digne, Lorgnes, Manosque, Draguignan, Salon, and Saint-Rémy had a total of ninety looms, only ten of which knitted silk stockings, whereas the others knitted floss silk.

Further precise information is difficult to find for the rest of France, though we may note that in 1787 the region of Troyes, much more recently developed than Provence and especially Languedoc, had no fewer than 1,715 looms, 500 of which were in the city of Troyes itself and worked a great variety of textiles, chiefly wool.

The distribution of looms in relation to the textiles used, for the entire country of France around the same period, was as follows:

Looms for silk articles		20,000
" " woolen "		25,000
" " cotton "		15,000
" " linen "		8,000

France thus had at the time 68,000 knitting looms. If these figures are compared with those given earlier for productivity (four to six pairs of stockings per day per loom) and those just given for export, it would appear that local consumption was clearly lower than sales abroad. This observation remains valid even when we take into account the inaccuracy of the computations, which include only stockings, whereas many other articles, produced more quickly, were knitted on certain of the 68,000 looms.

Was this success due to very low prices, or was it the reward for exceptional quality? The latter is more probable, for French output has always been recognized for its finish, but it seems certain that France owed her primacy (which she shared with England) to the rarity of knitting shops in the rest of Europe.

Technical improvements   During more than two-thirds of the eighteenth century, the only knitting instrument was the flat knitting machine, the frame machine, as depicted in the *Encyclopédie* of Diderot and d'Alembert. Any improvements made were intended to vary the designs or to increase output by introducing automatic controls. Among these improvements we may note:

1. The presser, applied to William Lee's loom at the beginning of the eighteenth century. Historians disagree on its country of origin. According to Felkin it may have been invented in France, appearing in England only around 1740. It has been claimed that it was first tested in Saxony, but this has not been documented.
2. Rib knitting, invented by the Englishman Jedediah Strutt in 1755, spread rapidly on the Continent, notably in Germany.
3. The so-called catch block mechanism, or tickler, for eyelet holes or net work, which was the subject of several patents, the first of which seems to have been by Morris and Betts in 1764.
4. The device called the eyelet hole, or point net, machine, which made it possible to remove and add loops on the sinkers and thus, by varying loops on the front and back, form designs. According to Felkin, this device may have been invented by Morris in 1781.

Runproof knitting;
appearance of the
warp loom   The most important improvement made to the flat knitting machine was that which made it possible to eliminate a defect in knitted articles: the danger of laddering. The knitted article it produced was made with a single thread, like the hand-knitted article, and breaking this thread in one spot caused the fabric to ladder along its entire length. The invention of the warp loom made it possible to alleviate the problem. This unusual loom produced, instead of a knit fabric formed by continuous looping of a single thread, a genuine web of stitches, each one linked to a warp thread. The result was a cloth comparable with products from the weaving loom.

This was therefore a compromise between two techniques, weaving and knitting. The fabric retained the appearance, elasticity, and flexibility of knitting, but it could not ladder.

According to Felkin, the first warp loom may have been invented in 1775 by an Englishman named Crane, but according to Poppe and Hermbsstädt it may be a French invention dating from 1780. It seems that the first patent may have been taken out in 1791 by an Englishman, one Dawson. The system was introduced into Germany in 1795 by a Berlin manufacturer, Reichel, whence the name *Rachel,* or *Raschel,* loom, by which it is known in France and English-speaking countries (Figure 28).

In France the first patent for the warp loom was taken out in 1829 by Joseph-Auguste Delarothière (1783–1854), a mechanic in Troyes who worked on improvements for the English design and, notably, equipped it with automatic controls.

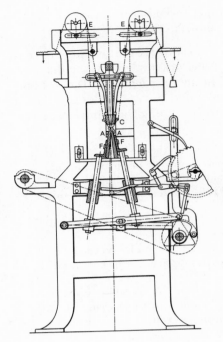

FIG. 28. Rachel rectilinear warp loom. A. Needles slightly inclined to plate F. E. Cylinders with band brakes and counterweights for tensioning the warp.

Briefly summarized, this is the history of the system, which can be regarded as the greatest innovation in the technical evolution of knitting since William Lee.

The Musée de la Bonneterie has a pair of women's nonrun knickers knitted with silk on a warp loom in 1830, and also a warp loom from the same period.

Automatic narrowing — Another giant step forward remained to be taken, affecting "fashioned" hosiery and in particular the manufacture of stockings. This was the automatic narrowing mechanism.

The flat knitting machine, as depicted in the *Encyclopédie*, made it possible to execute a relatively even and fine piece of work, given the technical conditions of spinning and milling at the time. But with fashioned articles its productivity was greatly reduced because workers had to adjust the machines by hand to obtain the decreases necessary for shaping the legs, toes, and heels. This is why output was small in the eighteenth century. Despite all the improvements made to this loom, progress was blocked by this apparently insoluble problem. The talented mechanic Delarothière tackled the problem and solved it by inventing an automatic narrowing mechanism, for which he obtained a patent in 1834. The hosiery industry now became one of the series of high-yield industries that were at that time just beginning their prodigious growth. In the Musée de la Bonneterie can be seen three narrowing machines built by Delarothière himself and bequeathed by him to the city of Troyes, accompanied by his handwritten description, from which we quote:

> Narrowing machine, invented by J.-A. Delarothière, who offered it as a token of esteem to the Museum of his native city of Troyes on January 17, 1849.

Machine no. 1 is the first system he used for this purpose, and for which he was granted the inventor's patent of December 12, 1831.

Machine no. 2, while based on the same principle as the former, nevertheless differs from it by a major modification in the mechanism, which while simplifying it, combines the twofold characteristic of meeting the needs of industry and, moreover, permitting the decreases of the selvage and the heels of stockings, obtained by the addition of a device called slide needles.

It is evident that with the help of this second combination the worker can reduce the amount of work, since he works simultaneously to the right and the left.

This system was to find wide use in the production of silk and yarn gloves. Here we should recall that in his work on knitting (*Die Technologie der Wirkerei . . .*), Willkomm attributes the automatic narrowing mechanism to another Frenchman, Dumont, on the basis of information supplied by Wassermann and Poppe, two German authors from the beginning of the nineteenth century. We have been unable either to confirm this fact or furnish an exact date.

Fully fashioned knitting and the knitting of pieces The flat knitting loom with a wooden housing had been conceived for manufacturing the fully fashioned stocking, but in the seventeenth century it was used to make many other articles. Were such items shaped like stockings, or were they cut out from a single piece of jersey, which it was easy to knit quite rapidly, in a long, uniformly wide strip? The width of the needle row of the loom permitted such individual pieces to be knitted. According to Willkomm, England had in the second half of the eighteenth century mechanical flat machines that made not the shaped article but pieces of uniform width. From here it was only a step to the evolution of a device making it possible to multiply the number of needles and thus the width of the piece of fabric, without however increasing the spread of the needle row or the bulk of the machine. According to certain historians it appears to have been quickly taken up.

Circular machines The origin of the first circular machine is obscure. If we believe Auguste Mortier in *Le tricot et l'industrie de la bonneterie* (Troyes, 1891, p. 43), the first experiments were made in 1769 by the Englishman Samuel Wise, who in the same year patented a mechanical flat knitting machine (Willkomm, op. cit.). In view of the foregoing, was this a cause-and-effect relationship between the two inventions? It would be imprudent to draw hasty conclusions, since there appears to be no serious evidence of existence of the circular machine before 1798, the year in which a Frenchman named Decroix obtained a patent for this type. Four years later it was presented, apparently for the first time, at the Industrial Exposition in Paris, the first of a long series of displays that were to give considerable impetus to the growth of technical research.

The frame that could be seen at the 1802 Exposition was built by Aubert of Lyon, who received a gold medal. It seems certain that in 1818 a Parisian clockmaker named Leroy added the looping wheel with stationary teeth to the mechanism, and in 1821 Andrieux equipped it with divided presser wheels.

What types of articles were made on these early circular machines? We have little information on the subject but might mention that tubular stockings were

produced in England on a circular machine patented in 1816 in the name of Sir
Marc Isambart Brunel (1769–1849). This is undoubtedly the oldest known example of a seamless stocking. This article, sold at a price that challenged all competition, was very successful on European markets. Thus the circular frame had now
found in England a high-output application. In 1830 circular machines of French
origin were operating in Limbach, though in France the factories seem to have
shown some reluctance to adopt it. Rightly or wrongly, it was long regarded as a
flash in the pan, a technical marvel intended, thanks to spectacular demonstrations, to attract crowds at expositions, rather than being intended as a genuine
working tool.

The circular system   The circular machine came into common use in
at Falaise   France only around 1830 at Falaise, where an ingenious mechanic named Lebailly, returning to first
principles, adapted the basic components of William Lee's loom to a circular
design, with the major difference that certain operations were continuous,
whereas in the flat loom they were alternating. (The hosiery center of Falaise
prospered for a long time, specializing in cotton articles of low quality.)

The results of Lebailly's investigations were undoubtedly satisfactory, since
much later, in 1880, a mechanic in Troyes named Hippolyte Dégageux built a
circular machine of this type that was electrically driven (in the Musée de la
Bonneterie).

In another area, at Vonneuil-sous-Biard near Poitiers, a manufacturer
named Vigry was awarded a bronze medal at the Industrial Exposition of 1834 for
cotton hose costing 10 francs a dozen, which had been knitted on a circular frame.
However, the records of the Exposition indicate neither the provenance of the
loom nor its characteristics.

The circular system   Around the same time, mechanics in Troyes at-
at Troyes   tacked the problem of the circular machine and
after years of effort succeeded in building a high-
output machine for all the diameters required in producing a great variety of
articles.

Pioneering this research in the capital of Champagne was, once again a
clockmaker, one Jacquin, who contributed numerous improvements to the system, such as the looping wheel with movable teeth, which is regarded as one of the
characteristics of the Troyes circular loom (Figure 29). By 1837 he had built his
first circular machine of a small diameter, intended for the mass production of
cotton caps. The result was phenomenal, far exceeding the most optimistic hopes
of the builder and knitter, and we are obliged to observe one of the first effects of
the race for output. The rhythm of sales was not keeping up with the increased
production and Jacquin, faced with the problem of disposing of his output, had to
turn his attention to another type of circular machine. He then undertook, at the
request of a third party, to build large-diameter looms intended for manufacturing knitted pieces for ready-made vests and pants, a market then greatly expanding.

The primary preoccupation of this new industry was to avoid, or at least
reduce as far as possible, losses due to cutting. The wider the pieces, the easier it
was for the cutter to find ingenious layouts.

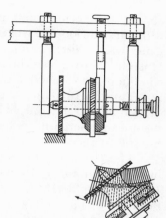

FIG. 29. Jacquin circular loop machine, 1841. Elevation and section. Visible above the needles is the jack wheel that guides the sinkers.

Jacquin was by no means the only builder of circular looms in Troyes. Among his rivals and followers the names of Gillet, Fouquet, Motte, Nogent, and Berthelot should be mentioned (Figures 30 and 31).

In 1853 François Humbert Gillet, who had built his first circular machine thirty years before and, perhaps under the impetus provided by Jacquin, had since then undertaken research into the problems raised by large-diameter ma-

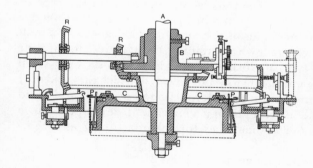

FIG. 30. Berthelot circular machine, Troyes. Vertical cross section showing central shaft A, the disk B integral with the shaft, the bank of movable needles C, the sinkers P, the guide wheels R.

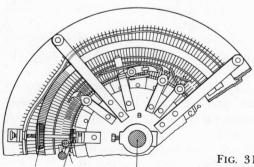

FIG. 31. Berthelot circular machine, Troyes. Horizontal plan; detail as Fig. 30.

chines, constructed a monumental machine 6½ feet in diameter. It was equipped with ten small looping wheels and four cranks, to be operated by four workers. Its gauge was 22 fine; around its circumference it had 3,432 needles. Presented to the Musée de Troyes by its builder in 1860, this mastodon, which is still in operating condition, is exhibited at the Musée de la Bonneterie.

Thus, by 1850 the circular machine had won the race. It was in general use in every diameter, not only in Troyes but in all hosiery centers. We shall see later that the use and then proliferation of motive power contributed to the expansion of its use still further.

The circular frame appears to have returned to England, its country of origin, in the form of a model invented by Fouquet of Troyes and adopted by J. A. W. Pasold (1813–1886), whose descendants still operate a large hosiery business. Fouquet emigrated to Saxony, where he continued his experiments. In 1856 in partnership with one Nopper he took out a patent for a large or "oblique" looping wheel.

Power sources Toward the middle of the nineteenth century the knitting industry took a great step forward, thanks to the introduction of the power loom. The dates of its appearance are, in fact, uncertain. A technical report printed in 1820 says that "for a long time already the English have had hosiery machines, which they operate with steam or water" (Willkomm, op. cit.), though Mortier dates the first such experiments in England from 1828.

Milton N. Grass supplies an interesting piece of information for the United States. The first experiment may have been made on a flat William Lee type of loom purchased in Philadelphia in 1832, to which may have been applied a hydraulic engine designed by an ingenious merchant named E. Egberts and built by Timothy Baily, a skilled cabinetmaker whose training, though, does not appear to have prepared him for this type of work. The two inventors set up a small factory next to a cotton-spinning mill, using its waterpower, to which they had only to connect their machines by transmission belts. It functioned perfectly and could produce four articles simultaneously. This first experiment developed into a successful business with a number of machines for manufacturing undergarments.

In this same year, 1832, an Englishman named John Button emigrated to the United States and established a small manufacturing plant for children's hosiery in Germantown. According to Grass, he too used a foot-treadle machine, which in 1838 he began operating with steam. In 1840 his example seems to have been followed in quite a large number of hosiery plants.

The constantly growing use of the circular frame in the United States quite naturally increased the use of motive power, which after 1850 or 1860 appears to have predominated.

In a major hosiery center like Troyes, France, we find no mention of power prior to 1840 to 1846. The first experiments were made in the factories belonging to Coquet-Vivien, Hippolyte Douine, and Fariat, who operated several looms simultaneously by using a treadmill and later by a hydraulic motor. Several years later, in 1850, steam began to be employed, but here again its use was long in spreading, at least in France, whereas in England, Germany, and, as we have just seen, in the United States, it was already widespread.

Plate 77. Model of Whitney cotton gin. Smithsonian Institution

The use of motive power became general, at least in heavy industry, only around 1880. Of course, electricity was soon to solve triumphantly all the problems raised by propulsion. In 1887 Emmanuel Buxtorf obtained a patent for an electric Jacquard system.

The flat knitting machine with a flywheel

We have discussed at length the beginnings and the rise of circular machines because this invention considerably enlarged the scope of the knitting industry.

Although improvements in the rotary loom assumed increasing importance in investigations by mechanics, the problems posed by the output of the flat knitting loom were, however, not neglected, for only this type could knit fashioned articles.

The foot-treadle-operated machine with a wooden housing was in common use until around 1860 to 1870. An illustration in the *Monde illustré* for 1860 shows a knitting shop in England with numerous operators working in front of such machines in a vast room. This model was later progressively abandoned by large-scale industry, but it remained the craftsman's tool in the city as in villages, and it appears not to have disappeared completely until shortly after 1925.

The appearance of power was followed necessarily by the use of the flywheel.

However, the oldest specimen of the flywheel machine preserved in the Musée de la Bonneterie was hand operated, the movement being transmitted by a camshaft. It was built by one Poivret, a mechanic in Troyes, around 1840. Another flywheel loom, also controlled by a camshaft, was built at Troyes and patented in 1856. This experimental loom with automatic narrowing does not appear to have been mass-produced.

The Paget system   There was soon a genuine revolution in equipment, thanks to the appearance in England of a flat knitting machine with flywheels, a metal housing, and automatic movement, intended for making socks and shaped stockings. It seems to have been invented in 1857 by an Englishman, Luke Barton, then developed a short time later by Arthur Paget (1832–1895), who in 1861, according to Grass, obtained a patent for this invention (Figures 32 and 33). In the following year the Poron brothers of Troyes obtained a license with a view to manufacturing in France this model, which is often called (for reasons we have been unable to discover) the Dutch loom.

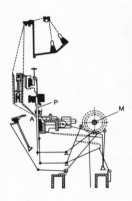

FIG. 32.   Arthur Paget's Dutch machine. Cross section. The two threads are brought from bobbins above the machine to the needle A below the sinkers P. M: Power source.

FIG. 33.   Paget's machine. Cross section showing arrangement of needles and sinkers. A: Needle resting on the blade L during the gathering. B: Sinker bar to which are soldered the sinkers C. These sinkers form a comb that holds the first loops when the needle is withdrawn. The upper part of D gathers and the lower part hooks. The sinkers perform the same work as the plates on a hand machine.

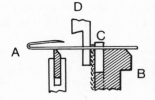

Here is Mortier's description of it:

> This loom, with completely original components, built with a single head and operating at high speed, was the first genuinely practical solution for the stocking loom with continuous rotary movement performing the narrowing operation automatically. . . . Its output was considerable, compared with that of the old loom; it occupied no more space than the latter, and like it could be operated manually; its cost was relatively low considering the advantage it provided. It spread rapidly among home workers. Being also equipped to

operate by motor, it became part of the equipment of the new shops that appeared in Troyes, in the south of France, and in Picardy. Finally adapted to the needs of French manufacturing by a series of improvements (obtaining loop-stitched hems and heels with selvages) it immediately changed the direction of manufacture of the shaped stocking.

Exploitation of the Paget system brought about various small improvements and also the invention of looms regarded as derivatives. It would be tedious to list the inventors in Troyes who between 1878 and 1888 devoted themselves to this inexhaustible field of research and experimentation. Mention should be made, though, to Hubert, who, protected by a patent, undertook construction of a long series of machines. His factory was taken over by Léon Couturat. Several Paget looms and variants, with and without manual control, are preserved in the Musée de la Bonneterie. The Paget machine was still in use at the time of the First World War. The last model of the series, built in 1915 by the Poron brothers, bore the number 4054. From this we see that it had had a long career, although not as long as that of its contemporary the Cotton machine, which is still in use.

The Cotton machine   William Cotton (1819–1887) had worked in the shops of Loughborough, England, of which Arthur Paget was a native and where the first power-operated automatic machines were built. In 1863 he patented a machine that, like his competitor's, was completely automatic but could not be manually operated, and which made it possible to widen as well as narrow (Figure 34). Its speed was the same as the Paget loom's, but since it was built with several knitting heads and could therefore simultaneously knit two, then eight, then twelve shaped stockings, its output was considerable; it was immensely successful in England. It was preferred to the Paget loom because it required fewer workers. The Paget system, also developed but geared toward a

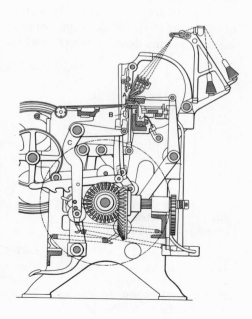

FIG. 34.   Cotton machine. Vertical cross section. A: Vertical needle. B: Needle bar moved back and forth by crank C.

clientele composed above all of craftsmen and home workers, spread rapidly in France and England, whereas the Cotton loom was adopted almost everywhere in England. The Cotton forty-head loom is still in use in large manufacturing plants for shaped articles.

Family knitting machines   While heavy industry was beginning its extraordinary growth in Europe and the United States, around 1860 the "home knitting machine" appeared.

The model offered to housewives during the Civil War or immediately thereafter belonged to the class of circular machines and was built by Herrick and John Aiken. It was a relatively simple, crank-operated machine that could be screwed to the corner of a table.

This machine is mentioned only for the record, as is Lamb's knitting machine invented in 1865 and a system similar to it, the "all-purpose knitting machine for full-fashioned tubes," invented that same year by Emmanuel Buxtorf. The term *full-fashioned* applied to a tubular article will somewhat disconcert the reader aware of the problems posed by the fully fashioned, that is, shaped, article.

Obtaining patterns   In the first half of the nineteenth century there appeared a fashion for stockings in multicolored patterns and with openwork. The Jacquard system for weaving fabrics and rugs in several colors appears to have been adapted to stocking machines quite early, and when in 1887 Buxtorf patented his circular machine equipped with an electric Jacquard device of his own invention, this was simply an improvement of an already existing system (Figure 35). In 1837 warp looms with the Jacquard mechanism were imported from France to Limbach.

The designs on patterned stockings were sometimes quite complicated, composed of three colors. Very often, on the most expensive types, motifs embroidered by hand added additional richness.

Openwork stockings in black and white (in most cases of yarn but sometimes of silk) were veritable prodigies of technique, made with the help of a "point net" mechanism for designs, which could be placed on the flat knitting machine.

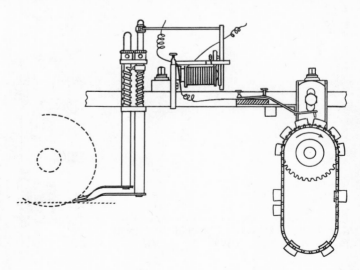

FIG. 35. Electric Jacquard on circular machine, 1887. Control of the electromagnetic drive is provided by a belt carrying projections corresponding to the design to be knitted.

Several patents were taken out for various systems that permitted designs to be executed with mechanical flat knitting machines. In 1872 E. Saupe patented a point net mechanism. In 1875 the Poron brothers adapted the Paget machine to ribbed knitting.

When the use of the rotary machine became widespread, arrangements of needles were sought that would make it possible to obtain designs. Felkin mentions the patent granted to P. Claussen in Brussels in 1845 for pressure wheels varied in circumference so as to produce various patterns, as well as that of Thomas Thomson for a circular rib machine.

Forty years after Gillet built his monumental circular machine mentioned above, Buxtorf invented another bulky unit with a special system of two horizontal needle rows facing each other and with sliding needles having double hooks that could pass from one row to the other. This system made it possible to do fancy knitting, for depending on the position of the needle in one or the other needle row, the stitch appeared on either the right or the wrong side. A loom of this type, built from a Buxtorf prototype dating from 1893, is preserved in the Musée de la Bonneterie.

Manufacturing accessories This account of research and improvements in knitting equipment would not be complete without a word concerning manufacturing accessories, which were also considerably improved during the nineteenth century.

Before the appearance of machine sewing the most important auxiliary was obviously the winding machine. Hand winding continued throughout the nineteenth century in the small craft shops, where it was the indispensable complement of the flat knitting machine with a wooden housing.

The companies that imported the Paget, Hine and Mundella, and Cotton machines also ordered the accessories to complement them. Certain firms, such as Quincarlet-Dupont, Lebocey, Köhler, and Buxtorf, all of Troyes, made this equipment themselves.

The essential element was the binding-off machine, which was used for assembling stitch by stitch the various parts of a full-fashioned article. In most cases they were flat, but they could also be rotary. They could be hand operated, but in most cases they were operated by foot, with two treadles.

Numerous machines were imported from the United States. A chain-stitch machine for sewing cotton bonnets and gloves, American-built in 1846, is preserved in the Musée de la Bonneterie.

The Overlock hemmer, also an American machine (Wilcox & Gibbs were the makers), was used to make hems at the bottoms of tights, sleeves, sweaters, and so on. A model preserved in the Musée de la Bonneterie still has its hem guide with curved needle.

Machines for sewing fashioned stockings appeared around the middle of the nineteenth century. Singers were commonly used. They profited from the use of motive power at the same time as the looms discussed above.

Overall view of technical additions To sum up the developments in hosiery manufacture during the period just studied, slightly more than one century, it should be noted that technical advances were slow until around 1830 to 1850, a period when automatic controls were becoming common, the narrowing mechanism appeared, and the improvement of the warp loom made it possible to ensure good output in the nonrun knitwear industry.

This evolution was paralleled by the development of the rotary machine. Strictly speaking, this was not a new technique but an ingenious application of a system already in existence to a device in a new form.

The major advance, which actually concerned not production but productivity, was the application of power to knitting machines, already done in other industries, notably (in England and North America) in spinning.

The geographical distribution of the manufacturing plants, when lined up with their dates of establishment, shows an obvious imbalance. The first countries to learn and exploit the William Lee system retained an unquestionable advantage throughout the nineteenth century, an advantage that circumstances and certain economic situations helped maintain. England, the first to enter the race, continued approximately twenty years ahead of France regarding improvements in production equipment. With the exception of the mechanism for automatic narrowing, all the major inventions came from England. This superiority of equipment permitted her manufacturing plants to maintain their position in the vanguard of progress. Unfortunately, the possibilities offered by the rotary machine for the production of stockings led many manufacturers to place on the European market, and even to display at universal expositions, products that were quite inferior in quality, like the tubular white cotton stockings that the English and Americans called leg bags. France was able to maintain her predominance throughout the century thanks to the finish of her luxury production. Germany, the third to enter the race, had equipment equal to that of France, but because of the low wage levels could flood the European market with articles that were undoubtedly comparable but that sold at very low prices. Toward the end of the century Germany became a formidable competitor of France, as can be appreciated from the concern expressed in certain articles published in such trade organs as the *Journal de la bonneterie française.*

The United States, as noted, had not entered the race until around the middle of the eighteenth century, and its equipment was borrowed from Europe. Although its production showed a steady increase (from 600,000 pairs of stockings and socks in 1810 to a production in 11 states alone of 22,873,200 pairs in 1860 and 358,697,004 pairs in 1900), at no time does it appear to have succeeded in solving the technical problems. Far from exporting machines, in the second half of the nineteenth century the United States was obliged to purchase Paget and Cotton looms in Germany. Only at the end of the century did it undertake the manufacturing of machines, and American manufacturers also concentrated mainly on developing auxiliary machines for production.

CHAPTER 4

TEXTILE PRINTING

T HE ART OF COLORING fabrics in only certain areas is probably as old as that of weaving. With the help of intaglio- or relief-engraved devices like seals, molds, and wooden or ceramic cylinders it was easy to apply insoluble pigments such as lampblack, ocher, vermilion, crushed indigo, and so on, combined with a viscous base and fixed by drying, or even decoctions of various plants. But these products were not resistant to washing, dampness, or daylight, and they often gave off a disagreeable odor, defects that made them generally unsuited for clothing and furnishings. Several European examples still exist, the oldest of which understandably date from only the end of the Middle Ages.

Starting in the seventeenth century printing, notably maps of cities and geographic maps, was done with copperplates using oil-based inks. In the nineteenth century the lithographic stone was used.

Calico printing   The partial coloring of cotton fabrics, with dyes resistant to air, light, and repeated washings by the so-called Indian method, was achieved in a much more complicated way. Mordants (iron and aluminum salts) were used that of themselves did not dye and that, depending on their degree of concentration and how they were combined, formed a series of insoluble colored lacquers—reds, roses, violets, browns, blacks—permanently fixed on the cotton fiber of fabrics. These fabrics may or may not have been prepared with a vegetable binder (depending on the coloring to be obtained) and fatty matter (buffalo milk) and with Indian madder root.

Indigo blue, in contrast, required no mordant, but because in its natural state it is insoluble in water, it must be prepared by fermentation, discussed later. The fabric was then submerged in a dyebath, the areas that were to remain white being protected by a layer of wax. Wax was also applied when it was desired to obtain particularly fine white or red lines. The design was traced in the wax and the fabric was then treated with the ad hoc mordant, which "took" only on the unprotected areas, the others remaining white.

The only actual pigment applied was yellow, which was obtained from certain plants. Applied on top of blue it gave green, but since it was not washfast it disappeared fairly quickly. This is why in most cases green is practically absent in old calicoes.

Thus, these "painted" fabrics were in reality dyed, accounting for the permanence of their coloring, which accounted for their success.

Iron mordant has a yellowish color, whereas that of aluminum (alum) is colorless. In order to be able to follow his progress, the worker colored the alum red with sappanwood. This stain disappeared in the washing following the application of mordants, and the fabric was white when it was dipped into the dyebath, where the colors immediately appeared, as in a photographic bath. The areas not mordanted and therefore remaining white also took on a reddish color, but this was not permanent, for madder in and of itself does not dye. In India the second bleaching was done in a bath of kid, sheep, and cow dung, the cleansing qualities of which are known.

Printing with molds   Accounts by seventeenth-century European travelers, before the introduction of calico printing into Europe in the second half of that century, mention the production in India and then in Persia of fabrics that were not only painted with mordants but also printed with molds, though the former were always described as far surpassing the latter in quality and beauty. Unfortunately, no specimens of definite dated origins now exist from this inferior product. In the case of resist printing the application of a protective paste or wax on the cloth by a wooden, metal, or ceramic mold offers no difficulty. On the other hand, when it is desired to *print* a mordant, a major problem arises concerning the choice and consistency of the thickening agent. On the solution of this problem depends the success or failure of the piece of fabric, from which, moreover, the mordant must be properly removed before dyeing. The red liquor used in India was alum, a double sulfate of aluminum and potassium. When simply painted on the fabric, alum decomposes on it and relatively easily leaves a maximum of alumina on it, a process that remains incomplete when the mordant is printed in a thickened form. This may explain the mediocre quality of fabrics printed in India and Persia in comparison with those that were painted, if indeed it is not simply because these prints were made with surface pigments.

The fact that in the seventeenth century cotton fabrics were being printed in India at the same time as they were also being painted is confirmed by a 1678 French document in the Bibliothèque Nationale in Paris that apparently remained practically unknown until its discovery, for present purposes, only in November 1965 by the present writer. This document eliminates any doubts regarding the priority of the printing method, attributed to Europe by certain authors (without proof). A certain Roques, an employee at the Surate warehouse of the Compagnie des Indes, was posted to northwestern India in 1678. His report, which includes two chapters on the printing of *chittes,* explicitly mentions engraving on molds (both for outlining the designs and for filling in and backgrounds), iron and aluminum mordants, surface pigments (notably ocher), the use of gum as a thickening agent, indigo, and wax resists for blue and white. The text, often vague, is obviously not that of a man of the arts or a very attentive observer, and cannot be compared with Beaulieu's 1735 work on painting fabrics (see Bibliography). However, as Roques's document stands it is sufficiently explicit for our needs, though it makes no allusion to printing simply the outlines of the designs, with mordants then being painted on the surface (a method described by a mid-eighteenth-century author who does not say exactly where it was done). On several occasions Roques mentions the poor quality of the printing, but he does not state specifically whether it is a problem of poorly placed or defective plates or of unsatisfactory color.

Upon their appearance in Europe at the beginning of the sixteenth century painted Indian fabrics were known as *pintados, chittes,* or *chintz,* terms whose etymology needs discussion. The first name may come from the verb *pintar,* "to paint," or from the adjective *pintado,* "mottled," which has given the guinea fowl its French name, *pintade.* This concept of "mottled" is that of the Mahratti *tchit* and the Hindi *tchint,* derived from the Sanskrit *tchitra,* spotted. These words are the source of the English word *chintz,* the German *Zitz,* and the Russian *sitietz,* words signifying the products of print shops. However, a recent Indian author accepts the root *kship* (throw or hurl), which would likewise have been given as *tchit* in Hindi, *tchint* in Bengali and Mahratti, and *thant* in Gujarati, all used in the sense of throwing drops of water.

There remain two other, strictly manual, methods of partially coloring fabrics, which were not exploited in Europe (except, perhaps, temporarily in England, Sweden, and Hungary), probably because of their slowness and extremely detailed nature. They required a labor supply that European countries would not have been able to supply at competitive prices.

Tie dyeing The first method, tie dyeing, is performed either on the yarn before weaving or on woven fabric, with all types of fibers.

In *ikat* (double-tied resist dyeing, from the Malay word meaning *tie*), certain parts of the yarn are protected against the penetration of a dye by tying or wrapping them. There is a warp *ikat,* a woof *ikat,* and a double *ikat* of warp and woof. After a preliminary dyeing (with or without a mordant, depending on the case), the tied areas that have remained white are dyed a second color, a process repeated until all the desired colors are obtained. The dyed yarns are then woven in a given order, thus producing pleasing effects. This technique is practiced in Asia, Africa, and the Americas.

When the fabric rather than the yarn is tied, a series of dyeings produces a *plangi,* another Malay word, which according to some authorities means *multicolored spot,* to others *reserved spot.*

The work can be done by folding, knotting, braiding, sewing, using small projecting sticks, gluing on patterns, compression *(tritik),* and other methods of protection impossible to list here. The *plangi* technique is undoubtedly very old, but it is impossible to indicate its place of origin; India may have known of it in the sixth century, China and Japan slightly later. The American continents and Africa also practiced (and still practice) it. In India the word *bandhana* (*band* = to tie) is used; the Japanese speak of *shibori* (tied, knotted), and the British call it tie and dye.

Batik dyeing The second method, *batiking,* is based on the Indian method but presents considerable differences in execution, apart from indigo dyeing. In the Indian method the mordant, alum, is applied to the fabric, which is then boiled over moderate heat in a bath of chay *(Oldenlandia umbellata),* whereas the mordant of batik is first prepared with a brew of ashes mixed with oil, generally castor oil. The fabric is then coated on both sides with wax resists—a true batik has no wrong side. Red dyeing is done cold, by rubbing the fabric for weeks on end with *mengkudu* (Indian mulberry, *Morinda citrifolia*) mixed with *djirak* (*Symplocos fasciculata,* a plant containing alum). Brown dyeing is done warm or cold, depending on which observer is describing it, with *soga* (the bark of the tropical tree *Peltophorum pterocarpum,* formerly known also as ferrugineum, indicating the presence of iron) and various ingredients often kept secret. The fixation is done with limed water, though it is not mentioned for red, a sufficient quantity of the indispensable calcium undoubtedly coming from the water used or from *mengkudu,* which grows on calcareous ground. It should be noted that oiling was also practiced in India, either for solid-color red dyeing of cotton threads and fabrics (as described in 1748 and 1756, relating to the Coromandel coast) or in printing, apparently when fabrics with a red background were involved (according to a description of printing at Ahmedabad, north of Bombay, in 1678).

The exact origins and age of Indonesian batik are unknown. The brown color of the *soga,* which apparently has never been attained or equaled by artificial dyes, must be peculiar to Indonesia, since it is said that *soga* is never found in the East Indies.

Origins and spread of calico printing

In the present state of research it is impossible to know where and when the so-called Indian method came to be practiced for the first time and by what route it spread throughout the world, from east to west.

In India itself we find no ancient writings on the subject, because the dyer, though not an outcast, exercised an unclean craft in which notably urine was used. This placed him in a permanent state of impurity and made impossible any marital alliance with most castes. Moreover, even today around Ahmedabad, where craft printing continues to be widely practiced by family associations, one must not count on the natives' knowledge of history in order to learn something about their craft. Everything that antedates their grandparents seems to be lost in time. They know nothing of the origins of their technique. No one remembers the old vegetable dyes; only the synthetic products are known. The idea of saving a printing plate appears to have occurred to no one. When the plates wear out they are thrown into a stream, for religion forbids the destruction of an object that has been used to earn one's living.

Strangely enough, the oldest and most relevant description of partially coloring a fabric with colored mordants comes to us from Pliny the Elder (A.D. 23–79). In Chapter II, Book 35 of his *Historia naturalis* he says that the Egyptians painted garments and veils in an extraordinary manner. On a white fabric they applied not dyes but invisible substances that absorbed dyes. The fabric was plunged into a boiler containing a single boiling dye. When removed it was rich in various shades and resistant to water. All colors were produced by a single immersion; boiling and dyeing were simultaneous.

This description calls for comment. On the one hand, Pliny does not say what textile was used; on the other, the method of blue dyeing with resists is not mentioned. This omission could be explained by the fact that during the period in question apparently only woad, not indigo, was used. Woad, whose dyeing power is inferior to indigo's, required a bath brought up to a temperature in excess of

85°C., too high for any resist. The fabric used could be only cotton or flax. Animal fibers (wool and silk) were also dyed without mordants, because their special affinity for dyes made it impossible to retain white areas after immersion in the dyebath. In the first century A.D. Egyptians may thus have worked with cotton or linen (the latter dyes less easily than cotton), using mordants that were probably colored with madder, without however practicing blue dyeing with resists, for lack of an ad hoc dye. The mordants were painted on, not printed; there is a good reason for emphasizing this fact.

Pliny the Elder's text is the only one of its kind describing the Mediterranean countries of the time as a whole, though in this area dyeing (especially wool dyeing) was widely practiced. It is true that authors took little interest in industrial methods, since for them this was the work of slaves. Where had the Egyptians learned their method of dyeing—did they invent it? In the present state of our knowledge it is impossible to say.

Needless to say, we do not know whether Pliny the Elder personally witnessed what he described or merely repeated what he had heard. We also do not know whether this Latin text, which has so often been printed but apparently has not yet been annotated, has come down to us garbled by the great number of copyists who have reproduced it over the centuries and in a language far removed from that of the author. We are therefore obliged to accept it as it stands and to leave open the question of Egyptian painted fabrics. Translations exist, notably in French, English, and German, and all have the same sense, but the words differ. One says, "In Egypt, even garments are painted by a marvelous method"; another, "In Egypt fabrics are dyed by a most striking method"; the third, "White garments and raiment are painted in Egypt by a marvelous method." Émile Littré, for example, bluntly uses the word "mordant," while others speak only of "substances absorbing the colors."

Leaving aside the Egyptian problem, it can be accepted that the manufacture of painted fabrics spread from India west, first to neighboring Persia, where seventeenth-century French travelers mention it, and from there to Asia Minor, Armenia, and Turkey. For example, the existence (mentioned already by 1547) of printers using surface pigments and others producing chintz, generally Armenians, Persians, and Indians, was observed in Constantinople in 1634. Unfortunately, we possess no information concerning possible printing with thickened mordants.

According to information given in an 1889 lecture in Berlin by a famous chemist dyer on how fabrics are printed among the civilized peoples of Asia, the age-old methods employed in Asia Minor were based on madder and iron and aluminum mordants. The alum was thickened with flour, and the fabric was then left to rest for long months, during which time the alum decomposed and the metal was ultimately deposited as a basic sulfate. The iron mordant was prepared as follows: flour was blended with water to obtain an acid solution after a fermentation period lasting four weeks. Some scrap iron was then thrown in at the time of the new moon, so that the rays of the full moon penetrated directly into the barrel. The liquid was then thickened, also with flour, and printed on the fabric, as in the alum method.

A complete absence of references makes this information practically worthless. As for the story of the full moon, it is found as early as 1742 in a letter by Father Coeurdoux, a missionary in Pondichéry, concerning the manufacture of calico prints. Did the Berlin lecturer take it from this source?

Introduction into France   It appears probable that France was the first European country to introduce Indian methods. At Marseille, where the term *indiennes* was used as early as at least 1580, a contract was signed on June 22, 1648, between a *cartier* (maker of playing cards) and an engraver concerning "the manufacture they have undertaken to dye fabrics to be used for making quilts or chintzes . . . to engrave . . . the proper and suitable models and, that done, to apply them on cloth." An inventory made at Avignon on December 9, 1677, enumerates "a barrel of black color, 22 small pear-wood blocks for engraving and making chintzes, cochineal, madder, Brazil and Pernambuco wood, and berries used for making scarlet color," belonging to a "copperplate engraver and maker of chintzes and Persian fabrics." Although we do not know whether the plates were used simply to trace the outlines of the designs, the mordants being painted in by hand, or whether the mordants were indeed printed on in a thickened form, we have proof that at the times indicated the Indian method was practiced in southern France. The *cartiers* and *dominotiers* (engravers of "histories" and figures on wood blocks) changed their names and became "master craftsman of chintzes." Two of the latter went into partnership on February 1, 1672, and hired two Armenians to "paint fabrics in the style of the Levant and Persia."

Dissemination in Europe   The introduction of calico printing in England dates from 1676, when William Sherwin took out a patent based on the actual manner of printing and coloring fabrics in India. The first printing plant in the Netherlands was established on June 28, 1678, at Amersfoort, with the collaboration of a Turk from Smyrna. It can thus be accepted that the Indian method was introduced into Europe not directly from its country of origin but by way of the Levant, around the middle of the seventeenth century or even earlier.

French and Dutch specialists established calico printing in Switzerland, probably after 1687. The Germans learned of it in Holland around 1689.

Whereas the original Indian method consisted of either painting or printing the mordants, it is generally accepted that in Europe they were printed from the start, though, there being no identifiable specimen or formula from the seventeenth century, the question cannot be answered with certainty. The plates used at Marseille, discussed earlier, could have served merely to trace the outlines of the designs, but it is worth noting the following piece of information. It comes from an anonymous undated manuscript entitled *Manière de peindre les indiennes dont on se servait chez M. le Duc à Chantilly* ("The Method of Painting Chintzes in Use among the Workers of the Duke at Chantilly"): "If fine work is desired . . . it will be drawn with the pen or brush with the colors or mordants which we shall hereinafter discuss. If more ordinary work is desired, it will be printed with blocks." (This Bourbon duke, who died in 1740, a period when making painted fabrics was strictly prohibited in France, did not sell his products but kept them to please friends. He worked as an amateur, so for him the questions of cost and production time did not matter as they did for an enterprise based on profit.)

In France a decree by the Council of State on October 26, 1686, ordered the destruction of all molds and prohibited printing, in order to protect the wool and silk interests, a prohibition maintained until the issue of Letters patent of the king on September 5, 1759. French documentation on the making of printed fabrics is, in consequence, practically nonexistent for this period, and we must turn to other European sources to study this art at its origin. Unfortunately, these sources are scanty, and we must resign ourselves to knowing nothing precise. The oldest-known formulas mentioning mordants, madder, indigo, and gum are probably those in a 1727 Dutch book discovered in Canada before World War II, followed by some Swiss formulas from 1738. The oldest-known and dated swatches of English chintzes, which go back to 1726, are in the library of the New York Historical Society. The oldest-known and dated French and Italian swatches (from Marseille and Genoa), dating from 1736, are part of the Richelieu Collection preserved in the print department of the Bibliothèque Nationale in Paris. Unfortunately, none of these specimens, which also are very small (maximum 3″ × 1½″), have been subjected to a color test. Insofar as can be judged by their appearance, the mordants are printed and dyed. The fact that the French samples belong to the period of the prohibition of calico printing is due to their origin: Marseille had a special manufacturing license for the Guinea trade.

Technical difficulties   By the beginning of the sixteenth century, Europe had learned from the Portuguese navigators about painted fabrics. Her dyers had been famous for centuries. Why then was she so far behind in the partial coloring of fabrics and had taken so long to change from putting the mordant into the dyebath (as is done in solid-color dyeing) to applying it instead to the fabric before dyeing it in order to obtain a colored design. Why did it take so long to apply protective coatings to produce blue and white effects? There are several reasons.

Concerning blue and white articles, it must not be forgotten that before the introduction of indigo only woad was known. As a result of its weak dyeing power the bath had to be brought to a temperature that no resist could withstand. The use of protective coatings became possible only with the indigo bath, with its higher coloring power at a lower temperature. But to protect the cultivation of native woad all European countries introduced restrictions forbidding the use of indigo or permitting very small quantities to be mixed with woad. Not until the end of the seventeenth century or even later could indigo be fermented without the addition of woad.

The application of mordants to be dyed later was a method that would not interest the more numerous dyers of wool and silk, because it was applicable only to plant fibers. We do not know whether cotton and flax dyers made experiments.

In 1768 there appeared in Karlsruhe, Germany, an anonymous work claiming among other things to provide a complete description of the methods of calico printing, kept most secret until then. According to this author, the inventor of textile printing may have been inspired by the fact that spots of rust on fabrics are indelible and moreover that iron salts when combined with tannin give a black color, hence designs intaglio- or relief-engraved on metal plates could be transferred to fabrics treated with tannin with the help of a kind of porridge of iron and flour. So far it has been impossible to confirm this isolated piece of information, but as with the lecturer in 1889, flour was suggested as the thickening agent.

This was only one method for obtaining black. Tannin (gall, sumac, and so on) is perhaps one of the oldest ingredients for dyeing fabrics. The painted fabric industry in India for centuries made black and dark violet dyes with iron and vegetable astringents.

Until the eighteenth century indigo dyers may have had available to them only native fabrics of relatively coarse quality unlikely to give encouraging results. Flax took color with greater difficulty than cotton, and since the bath had to be more heavily saturated, dyers would have had considerable trouble in lightening nonmordanted areas, since they had not had the experience of scouring baths. Moreover, in both cases the problem of the thickening agent would have arisen if the dyers had wished to print the mordants. These technical barriers may explain why it was necessary to await the arrival of Turkish specialists in order to learn how to color fabrics partially.

The preparation of fabrics — Until the discovery, apparently in England, around the end of the eighteenth century of how to print wool without a dyebath by means of steaming, the textile bases used were chiefly cotton, then a combination of a flax warp with a cotton weft, and lastly flax. For a long time good results depended on the use of white fabrics imported from India, the European products being inferior in quality and texture, partly due to the diversity of cottons used. Advances in the spinning of fine cotton, resulting from mechanization, made it possible gradually to do without Indian imports. The nineteenth century saw European, and especially English, fabrics being exported to India.

These white fabrics, sold in Europe by the various East India companies, were prepared with a strong sizing made with rice water. It was therefore absolutely necessary to perform first a complete degumming in wooden vats in which the fabrics were boiled several times. The locally produced gray goods purchased by calico printers were given to a launderer who removed the soiling from spinning and weaving and then bleached them. Since the pieces of cloth had in any event to be bleached again after printing and dyeing, it was less important that they be sparkling white than that they be perfectly free of size and especially of grease. For many years the bleaching of gray goods did not appear on the list of operations of calico printers, who confined themselves to the second bleaching on the meadow. We do not know where and when some manufacturers decided to do their own bleaching. Moreover, it was not until 1837, as the result of major work on fatty substances, that scientific foundations for bleaching cotton in the nineteenth century were laid: liming, treating with hydrochloric acid, and repeated washing with alkaline carbonates.

To complete the cleaning operations, white fabrics were beaten with a flail or in a fulling mill, which was replaced toward the end of the eighteenth century by a beating mechanism, a series of beaters striking on a rotating platform. The washing wheel appeared in England around 1800, followed by a large number of other washing machines with various mechanisms.

Fluff and fibers were then removed from the fabrics by singeing, with an apparatus of uncertain origin invented perhaps around 1774. A red hot metal rod was brought close to the fabric by an appropriate mechanism and was then lightly brushed with a curved metal plate placed on a fire. A revolving hollow cylinder

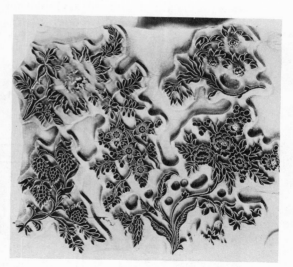

Plate 78. (*top*) Relief-engraved wood plate with brass "pins." (*lower left*) Intaglio-engraved wood plate for the "filling-in" of the color. (*lower right*) Wood plate with strips of brass for the outline of the design. Mulhouse, Musée de l'Impression sur Étoffes. (Photos Musée de l'Impression sur Étoffes.)

heated from within was also used. Later, when illuminating gas appeared in the nineteenth century, the singeing began to be done with gas.

The use of a cropping machine applied to cotton may date from 1787.

Calenders (mangles) were used to smooth the fabrics and make them even and free of creases, a condition necessary for printing. They also served to realign the threads of the fabrics, which were crumpled when they came out of the dyebaths. Calenders consisted of a series of wooden and cast-iron rollers between which the fabric was pressed as evenly and powerfully as possible. They were powered by a man with a crank or treadmill, or by a horse or water.

Before being turned over to the customer, when necessary the fabrics were given a special lustering, like the original chintzes, with the help of a satining machine. They were given a coating of wax, then rubbed with either a stone, a glass, or an agate burnisher, or later, with a piece of polished steel mounted on a pinewood rod, another rod acting as a spring.

This equipment was complemented by presses for wrapping the finished merchandise, boilers for hot dyeing, and vats or boxes for cold dyeing and for scouring the fabrics for passages through bran or cow dung.

Hand and
mechanical printing

In the period under discussion colorfast printing was done by hand, using the method described above, with relief-engraved wooden plates (Figure 36) and later with intaglio-engraved copperplates. The use of the printmakers' press probably began in 1752 near Dublin and in 1756 in England. The printing was later done mechanically (see the patent of a Scot, Thomas Bell, July 17, 1783), with one or several intaglio-engraved copper rollers, accompanied when necessary (in the nineteenth century) by other, relief-engraved wooden rollers. Finally, printing was done with wooden plates operated by the so-called perrotine machine (French patent registered in Paris on July 16, 1832), invented by Louis-Jérôme Perrot of Rouen.

Primitive machines appearing in seventeenth-century engravings have given rise to the statement that roller printing is very old. They were equipped with a wooden relief-engraved cylinder to which the colors were applied with a pad.

FIG. 36. Printing painted fabrics by hand with engraved plates. Mid-eighteenth century.

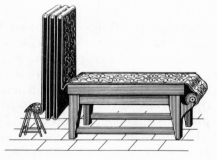

FIG. 37. Printing table. Mid-nineteenth century.

Here we are of course speaking of printing with pigments, and these machines are mentioned only as a matter of record. Mechanization did not require a great effort of the imagination, but the use of a copper roller depended on progress in metallurgy. Still, the perrotine testifies to a remarkably inventive mind.

The entire creative effort of calico printers was concentrated on the chemical aspects of the business, and the success attained in the partial dyeing of fabrics was one of the most splendid that the human mind could have hoped for.

Roller equipment   Soldering engraved copperplates around iron cylinders was unsatisfactory for producing an unbroken repetition of the design. Thomas Bell invented the true roller, which, after its final construction, is engraved and at the same time discovered the indispensable component of the roller, the scraper, or "doctor." The housing, originally of wood, was replaced by one of cast iron. It supported a hollow or solid cast-iron presser roller placed above a copper roller that bore the intaglio-engraved design. Beneath the copper roller was a wooden feeder roller that picked up dye from a trough below (Figure 38). Each engraved cylinder had two "doctors" that traveled back and forth. One removed the color so that it remained only in the sunken

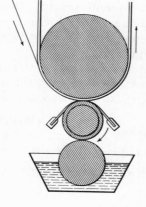

FIG. 38.   Roller printing machine.

portions of the engraving; the other removed any dross left on the roller by the fabric. Theoretically the doctors were of steel, but the composition of the colors (acidic or copper based) might require a mixture of copper, zinc, and tin. They were also made of rubber by 1845, and silver- or gold-plated metal or platinum. The presser roller was separated from the fabric to be printed and from the engraved cylinder by an endless woolen cloth protected by a canvas liner that prevented it from becoming soiled. The finished piece of cloth passed through a dryer, then dropped into a basket. The accompanying liner went into another basket or was rolled up around a can.

The axles of the rollers presented the greatest problem. The rollers were cast and bored, and after the mandrel had been inserted they were turned and engraved. It was found that the rollers slipped on their axle. A square axle was tried, but printers returned to the round axle. The next idea was to lock the axles and rollers together by cutting matching grooves in each, resulting in play between the axle and roller. Finally, a conical steel mandrel was adopted that was forced into the cylinder by a special machine. In the beginning a horse or an ox provided the motive power.

The press for printing copperplate was that used by copperplate printmakers, with only minor modifications. The flat-plate machine had a ratchet wheel on the lower or pressure roller that automatically returned the plate after the printing, which made it possible to adjust the repeats, that is, the lengthwise and widthwise dimensions according to the design.

The perrotine According to its inventor, the perrotine was "a machine for printing in one, two, or three colors, simultaneously, with wooden plates similar to those used by printers." The length of the plates corresponded with the width of the fabric (Figure 39). This machine had certain special characteristics, so it was used for special types of work, especially indigo-resist work, which at that time could not be successfully produced by any other suitable manner. The three-color perrotine could in practice replace a dozen hand printers and a three-color roller machine replace one hundred, in the same working time. Its low output compared with that of the roller machine made the success of the perrotine short-lived; it virtually disappeared during the second half of the nineteenth century, though a few Austrian and Czech plants have continued to use it for blue and white articles. Originally the perrotine was operated by one man, but later a treadmill operated by an ox, a horse, or a hydraulic engine was used.

Mechanical printing and hand printing very often complemented each other. Machine-printed designs were filled in by hand using wooden plates, with additional colors whose number was limited only by the range of dyes available.

The designer Having reviewed the relatively simple equipment used by calico printers, and having described the improvements made during the first half of the nineteenth century, we must emphasize the prime importance of man in the exercise of this genuine art.

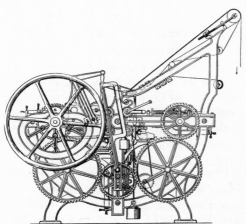

Fig. 39.   Perrot's 1832 machine for printing in one or several colors with a plate.

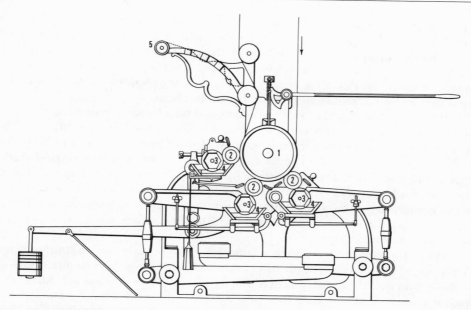

FIG. 40.   Roller printing machine for three-color fabrics. The fabric, carried on a strip of felt, travels around the presser-cylinder (1) and then over the three printing rollers (2); (3) the dye cylinders; (4) the tubs of dye. The printed fabric winds on the cloth beam (5).

The designer was one of the principal people in the business. He had to know engraving and the composition of colors. His design had both to charm the purchaser by its elegance and please the printer by its ease of execution. He had to select only colors that could be successfully printed on fabric. A multicolor design had to be broken down into as many plates as there were colors. The first plate reproduced the outlines of the design in black, then the desired colors were filled in using other plates, some of which might be as small as a simple seal. For large designs there could be a number of fill-ins within the black outlines—far more than 100, and sometimes a multiple of that figure. In other designs each application of a single plate made the repetition, but others were broken up into several plates, the repeat beginning only after each one had been printed. The size of a design had to take into account the ability of the printer to handle the plate. In copperplate work the designs were monochrome and the size of the area selected, which could be as much as one square yard.

Engraving the plates   The engraver, who worked from drawings given him, also had to be skilled in drawing and printing and had to understand colors. In interpreting the colors on the drawing he had to be able to realize the effective possibilities of transferring them to the fabric. He had to be careful not to place his hatchings too close together, since when the plate became wet from the work the wood swelled and the engraving shrank. The plates for china blue (a method of indigo dyeing) and the resists had to be engraved differently from the others, because the oily matter with which they were printed easily overflowed the outlines.

The plates, approximately two inches thick, were made of several layers of wood arranged so that the grain in each layer ran at right angles to the grain in the layers above and beneath it, an arrangement necessary to prevent warping, since the plates were alternately wet and dry. The outer layers, which received the impact of the printer's mallet, were generally of pear or walnut. Boxwood was also used for very small motifs and linden for fill-in plates.

When the design had a "sable" background (i.e., formed of dots), small pegs, or pins, were carved in the wood, but their fragility caused them to break easily. Brass wires were later used for this purpose, forced into the wood with a special tool by women workers called peggers. Iron could not be used because rust would have formed and dulled the reds of the madder bath. Silver pins came into use in the nineteenth century. After a date that is not definitely known but was probably in the last quarter of the eighteenth century, thin brass strips were sunk into the wood, notably for very fine detail. Later, plates were made completely of metal pins and thin metal strips.

When the design was large it was necessary to perform an operation called *chapeaudage,* for a large area of wood takes color unevenly. The design area was hollowed out and filled with pieces of fine felt from old hats *(chapeaux).* After they had been moistened and dried they were scraped down with a pumice stone to the height of the engraving. Pins and the *chapeaudage* process are mentioned in 1760 as being in common use, but their first appearance is not known.

All-metal plates were also made, by stereotyping, notably for blue and white articles, on which were printed a protective coating followed by an indigo bath. The design was engraved on a wooden plate that was then impressed in sand, and a stereotype was made by pouring over the mold a mixture of molten lead and tin. Again, the method was described as early as 1760 but its origins in the calico-printing craft are unknown. Much later (in 1843, probably) a machine was invented that made it possible to work faster and more easily. In a block of wood, generally linden, the outlines of the design were engraved with a steel point gas-fired to red hot. A suitable alloy was then poured into the negative thus formed and the resulting positive was nailed to a plank. This method was much used for reproducing cashmere designs.

Copperplate engraving was done in the same way as engraving for prints pulled on paper. It gave the most remarkable results but required considerable time, sometimes almost a year, which made its use very costly.

Engraving rollers   When roller printing appeared the roller was engraved by hand like copperplates, a long and difficult task, as noted. A mechanical process was then developed, especially for designs with small repeats in which the same design is reproduced a certain number of times over the entire width and circumference of the roller. The design was engraved on a small cylinder of soft steel, which was then case hardened. With a machine this cylinder was pressed against another of soft steel that had the same circumference of a multiple of it, as required. The intaglio design on the small cylinder was thereby reproduced in relief on the second cylinder. This relief was in turn hardened so it could reproduce the design on the copper-printing roller, by a machine that by exerting pressure sank the relief into the copper of the roller. The operation was repeated until the printing roller was completely covered with the design. Needless to say, the circumference of the roller had to be an exact multiple of the model. This was the muller steel plate method, invented by an American, Jacob Perkins (1766–1849), and used for printing bank notes. It was applied for the first time to fabric printing in 1808 in England by one Lockett.

Since engraving a large repeat design could not be done by the muller method because of the excessively large dimensions required for the model, another method was invented, namely, engraving with a pantograph, an instrument used to reproduce designs. It was known in Europe at the end of the sixteenth century. Its use in engraving, credited to an Englishman named Deverill, apparently dates from 1834. The roller was covered with a varnish that was removed by diamond points from the areas to be engraved. The plate was then attacked with acid. An enlarged image of the design was reproduced on a zinc plate, the lines being represented by engraved furrows. A worker followed them with a point linked by the pantograph system to the diamond points, which simultaneously reproduced the design in reduced proportions on the roller. The acid bath caused the intaglio design to appear on the surface of the roller.

The printer's work   Printers and brushers had the task of applying colors to fabrics, which were laid out on a waist-high table, generally of wood, that measured approximately 74″ × 35″ × 8″.

The printer began by examining the condition of the plate. If it was fogged he cleaned it by moistening it on the side of the engraving and then drying the other side in the sun or over a low heat. With calipers he verified whether the four pitch pins, placed in the four corners of every plate to guide the printer in matching the repeats, were equidistant from the center of the plate. After all these precautions the plate was dipped with the right hand in the color frame and was then placed on the fabric and struck with a wood or metal mallet held in the left hand. The operation was repeated until the piece of fabric was completed. In an eleven-hour or so working day, and depending on whether the work was ordinary or fine, a worker could print from 1 to 4 pieces of fabric 15 to 16 Parisian ells long by ¾ of an ell wide (i.e., a piece 35 inches wide by 20 or 21 yards long, the Parisian ell being counted as slightly less than 1⅓ yards).

The color frame, used to apply color to the plate, consisted of a wooden pan approximately 2½ feet long, 2 feet wide, and 7 to 8 inches deep. It was filled with a kind of gum ("false color") collected from cherry trees and dissolved in water to a liquid paste. Over this elastic base was a second frame 2 to 3 inches deep over whose bottom was a tightly stretched fine woolen cloth covered with waxed canvas so the gum and fabric could not come in contact. Coloring matter was poured on the fabric and spread evenly with a piece of old felt or a brush. With china blue the vat was filled with the color itself instead of with gum, and the upper, sliding, pan was lined with fine canvas instead of woolen cloth. The color was able to pass through the holes in the canvas and feed the plate. Cords in the four corners made it possible to hold it at the desired height so it would not penetrate too deeply. (The discovery of this blue, which oxidized rapidly upon contact with the air, is discussed later.)

Each printer had a child assistant, a pull boy, who had to see that the plates were always thoroughly clean, to wash and clean the pans, have his hands always clean, and to apply and spread the color very evenly, a matter of extreme importance. The best printer could do nothing of any value if his assistant was careless or dirty.

When it was necessary to add touches of yellow, blue, or green (the latter by superimposing the first two) to a completed fabric, young girls or women brushers painted the fabric using brushes of various materials, possibly including elder pith or twigs whose ends had been crushed. This was very slow and detailed work. In one week two brushers working together could "illuminate" (to use the trade expression) two to four pieces of fabric similar in size to those above.

This low production explains the considerable number of brushers to be met with in certain factories. But other factories found it faster to illuminate by plate, notably in the case of china blue.

Coloring and mordanting materials   Concerning coloring and mordanting materials, let us first make an important observation: in trade jargon the word *color,* as used until now, indicates strictly a mordant for colorfast dyeing, whereas in the case of noncolorfast dyeing it can also mean a surface pigment, depending on the case. Moreover, a white color corresponded to the application of a resist. So when we read in a formula that, for example, three reds and two violets must be made, this corresponds to applying aluminum and iron mordants to be madder dyed, and not to the application of an actual color to the fabric.

The coloring materials used by calico printers until the beginning of the nineteenth century were of vegetable origin (roots, bark, wood, stems, flowers, seeds, leaves, nutgall), with the exception of cochineal and kermes, which are of insect origin. Turmeric alone could be used in an aqueous solution to dye cotton directly, but not very permanently; the others would not dye in themselves but only through a mordant formed of a metallic salt. This was a soluble compound whose base (the metallic oxide) could be transferred to the fabric in an insoluble state to help fix a colorant on it. The mordant decomposed on the fabric, its acid evaporating if it was volatile or disappearing in the wash after the printing. The metal was fixed on the fiber as an oxide and formed with the color an insoluble lacquer. For madder red, however, a third metal, calcium, was indispensable for successful dyeing. It came either from the water used, from a plant grown in a calcareous soil, or was added by man in the form of chalk. The Indians were ignorant of the latter method, which accounts for the major differences in the quality of their painted fabrics. In Europe the addition of chalk became recognized as necessary, perhaps around 1757 but certainly after 1776.

Iron and aluminum salts were the most widely used, being the only ones that gave fast color with madder. Alum, at first natural but later manufactured, was a double salt of aluminum and potassium known to antiquity and employed in India for painting fabrics, but in a thickened state it gave only mediocre results in printing. Other combinations were tried experimentally, and by an unknown path the industry finally began production of aluminum acetate with the help of lead acetate. This product, which may have been discovered in England before 1754, the date of a known Swiss formula, remained the ideal red liquor down to modern times. Iron mordant continued to be made with scrap iron and with, first, wine and then wood vinegar. It was also made with ferrous sulfate and lead acetate.

Toward the end of the eighteenth century and at the beginning of the nineteenth the ability of other metals, notably tin and copper, to act as mordants on cotton were discovered; we do not know under what circumstances or when. The qualities of chrome as a direct dye with lead salts and then as a mordant were recognized and iron and manganese oxides were successfully produced on fiber. These mordants, employed in a pure state or mixed, supplied the calico printer with quite a broad, colorfast palette, either with madder (starting in 1775), quercitron (derived from the bark of the North American black oak), or, at the beginning of the nineteenth century, with catechu (from the East Indian acacia). With wood and plants of lesser coloring power, and the mordants mentioned above, a color was obtained that was often brighter but unfortunately was generally not fast. It is impossible to give here in lay language more than a general and incomplete survey of discoveries by the first color chemists of printing.

For printing, mordants had to be thickened, the required consistency being different for intaglio printing and relief printing. Gum and starch were the most used; the success of the merchandise depended largely on the method of operation. Once the mordant had been printed the fabric was left to dry for several days under defined conditions of humidity and heat, during which time the mordant decomposed, the metallic oxide fixing itself onto the fabric. When the fabric was dry the foreign substance used for thickening had to be removed as completely as possible, so the cloth was washed and beaten until the water came out crystal clear when the fabric was wrung out. Considerable progress was made when it was realized (probably in the last quarter of the eighteenth century) that the cow dung bath used to scour the fabrics when they came out of the madder bath had a special effect when it preceded the dyeing. The dung protected white areas by preventing the nonfixed portions of the mordant deposited in the bath from affecting the unprinted areas by paralyzing their action, putting them into a state in which they could no longer fix themselves onto the fabric. From then on fabrics were given a dung bath before dyeing and another for the second bleaching after dyeing.

The mordants were colorless or slightly tinted, so in order for the printer to see his work they were colored with lampblack or a redwood decoction that disappeared in washing. A wholly white fabric was therefore immersed in the madder bath, where it simultaneously took all the colors desired.

Surface pigments The partial coloring of fabrics by dyeing was a long and difficult operation, for the mordants had to be applied one after the other and dried after each operation. Calico printers must have made early efforts to find a faster and less burdensome method. One such solution was printing with surface pigments, derived from decoctions and extracts of tinctorial plants and wood thickened with starch, to which a small quantity of aluminum mordant was added. This probably caused some fixation of the oxide on the fiber. The relative permanence of the colors, however, came chiefly from the starch, which did not easily dissolve in cold water but nevertheless did not withstand alkaline washings. This noncolorfast method was used only for inexpensive articles. Steaming (discussed below), introduced into cotton and wool printing at the beginning of the nineteenth century, considerably increased the permanence of the surface pigments. Its use spread spectacularly, first in Great Britain then, around 1830, on the Continent.

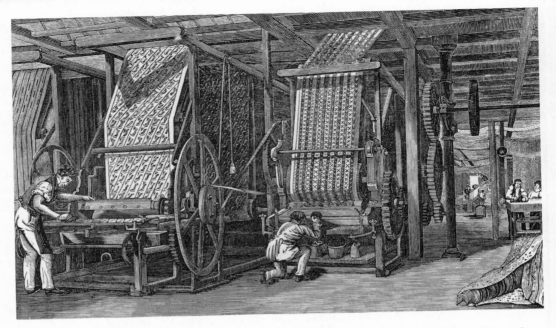

Plate 79 Calico Printing. Wood engraving, 1836, from G. S. White's *Memoir of Samuel Slater, The Father of American Manufacturing.* Smithsonian Institution

Indigo baths   Indigo, not being a mordant color, occupied a special place in the palette of calico printers. This dye is insoluble in water, so it must first be reduced by various ingredients to a state of indigo white (leucoindigo), which is soluble in an alkaline bath. The fabric absorbs it, then when exposed to the air becomes blue as the indigo white oxidizes. The adherence of indigo to the cotton fiber is only mechanical, however, whence the relative evanescence of the blue under friction, in comparison with the maddered colors of painted fabrics, which are lacquers of alizarin-alumina-calcium combined with the cotton fiber.

Articles of blue and white or other colors could be produced only by imprinting resists, protective coatings over the areas where the blue should not take. If the design called for a few touches of blue it was necessary to cover large areas of fabric, then put it through an indigo bath, a slow and costly method. Hence the search for a way to use it also as a surface pigment. From a 1746 formula by a dye merchant in Bremen it appears that for some time he sold, under the name English blue, a product that could be printed on the fabric or applied to it with a brush. The reduction-dissolution of indigo was done with orpiment (a highly toxic arsenic trisulfide), potassium, and lime, gum being the thickening agent. Instead of making a bath of about 120 gallons, only about 5 gallons of water were used. The indigo white was then bottled so it would not oxidize too quickly before being applied to the fabric. The application was done with a plate or brush, in the color frame described earlier. The name suggests that this process was discovered in England, though strangely enough there is no trace of its origin in that country. Indigo white had a considerable influence because of the economy that resulted from it, but printing or brushing on the indigo did not supplant the resist method; one article might require it while another might not.

One disadvantage of the early indigo fermentation bath was that it worked at quite a high temperature, approximately 50° C., which reduced the adherence of the resists. Thus, the appearance of a bath in which cold dyeing could be done was an event of prime importance. Reduction-dissolution was done with ferrous sulfates (vitriol) and lime. The preparation of resists and the manner of controlling the bath were greatly simplified by this process, whose inventor and date (possibly the second quarter of the eighteenth century) are unknown.

Later (but prior to 1766, the year in which the method was published), indigo was successfully reduced on the fiber itself, thus again avoiding the bath and resists. Crushed indigo mixed with ferrous sulfate was printed on the fabric, then the cloth was subjected to the action of a series of ferrous sulfate and lime baths. This blue was called faience blue as opposed to porcelain blue obtained by resists. It was successfully employed for fine intaglio printing, first with the plate and then with the copper roller.

Prussian blue In addition to indigo the calico-printing industry had another blue, Prussian blue, accidentally discovered by a Berliner in 1704 and first used in painting. In 1749 a French chemist named Pierre Joseph Macquer (1718– 1784) demonstrated its possible use in dyeing and printing. Around 1790 the French manufacturer Jean-Michel Haussmann (1749– 1824) succeeded in turning it into a practical surface pigment. Until the appearance of synthetic dyes these two blues formed the base for colorfast green, by imprinting a tin mordant and immersion in a yellow bath.

Another basic method of fabric printing was based on the "corroding" substances. On a fabric completely saturated with mordant ("foularded"), vegetable or mineral acids were printed, preventing the color from acting in areas to which they were applied. The origin of the method is unknown, but it was described in 1766 under the picturesque name of *mordant eater*.

Slightly later (probably not until the nineteenth century) the opposite method was invented: on a solid-color fabric (blue or red, for example) substances were printed that by removal destroyed the color in the desired area. Depending on their nature, not only white but also colored effects were obtained wherever the original color had been removed.

Mordants were also used in the composition of resists. The fabric was then passed through another dyebath, which dyed the mordants. In this way, for example, a red could be obtained that would fit very exactly, without any gap, into a blue ground.

When fabrics came out of the madder bath the nonmordanted white grounds were also covered with color, but this was not permanent. To rewhiten the cloth it was subjected to the "passages" mentioned earlier, the baths of cow and kid dung that scoured it. Then it was laid out in a meadow of firm turf crisscrossed with canals watering it. Here it remained for three or four days while the passages and exposures to water were repeated until the colors reached perfection and the backgrounds a perfect whiteness. Bad weather of course interrupted these operations and made calico printing impossible in winter.

The fabrics were then dried in high towers with characteristic shapes visible in old engravings of printing plants. When finished, polished when necessary, and finally packed in bales, they were delivered to customers.

Printing on animal fibers We have seen that in contrast to plant fibers, animal fibers, because of their special affinity for tinctorial materials, could not be acceptably printed by dyeing. Moreover, the rougher surface of the wool, in comparison with that of cotton, prevented the use of a resist that could easily be removed. Nevertheless, two eighteenth-century methods of printing on wool are known, but they produced only crude or nonwashable fabrics.

The *golgas* (thick flannels), whose surface was made as smooth as possible by twisting the threads enough, were pressed between two wooden forms as wide as the fabric in which a design was engraved. A hot colorant poured over them impregnated only the unprotected portions; depending on the case, unprotected areas might or might not be mordanted. The process probably dates from the first half of the eighteenth century.

The second method was one practiced in France by one Bonvalet of Amiens, apparently beginning in 1755. He used a copper, intaglio-engraved plate covered with a surface pigment of the same type as those used for cotton. This plate was placed on an iron plate that could be heated. Over that was stretched the serge to be printed, covered with a damp woolen cloth, then the whole was placed in a press. The heat and steam released caused a fairly good fixation of the color as well as a waffling of the design, which caused it to appear in relief. The excess color was scraped off. Obviously, the product was not washable. This method was probably of English origin, an ancestor of what became the steaming already mentioned.

Silk was printed like cotton, with mordanting and maddering, but this was one of the most difficult processes to perform successfully, because silk takes color less easily than wool. True whites could not be obtained; the fabric pieces came out of the bath saturated with color, and after a second bleaching the background remained a salmon shade. Dyebaths were now superseded by steaming. Silk was also printed with resists.

At an unknown time it was discovered that nitric acid dyed animal fibers a permanent yellow. A resist was printed, the fabric was treated with the acid, and thus a white design on a yellow ground was obtained. By imprinting a second resist and passing the fabric through an indigo bath, for example, the background became green, with a white, blue, and yellow design. This method was called *mandarinage*.

Wool was not permanently printed until after the discovery at the end of the eighteenth century (undoubtedly in England) of the method known as steaming, which eliminated the dyebath. It consisted of printing a mixture of dye, mordant, and thickener, then exposing the fabric to live steam, a process that provided excellent fixation of colors. Applied later to cotton and silk, steaming was extremely successful, for it considerably simplified operations. The highly detailed dyeing operations were eliminated, and the coloring obtained was satisfactory from the point of view of permanence.

BIBLIOGRAPHY
THE TEXTILE INDUSTRIES

ALCAN, Michel. *Essai sur l'industrie des matières textiles comprenant le travail complet du coton, du lin, du chanvre, des laines, du cachemire,* etc. Paris, 1847.

ASPIN, C., and CHAPMAN, S. D. Ch. *James Hargreaves and the Spinning Jenny.* Preston, 1964.

BALLOT, Charles. *L'introduction du machinisme dans l'industrie française.* Lille-Paris, 1923.

DOYON, André, and LIAIGRE, Lucien. *Jacques Vaucanson mécanicien de génie.* Preface by Bertrand GILLE. Paris, 1966.

ENGLISH, W. "The textile industry. Silk Production and Manufacture, 1750-1900," in SINGER, Charles, *A History of Technology.* Vol. IV, 1958, pp. 308-27.

FELKIN, *History of Machine Wrought Hoisery and Lace Manufacture.* Cambridge, 1867.

GRASS, Milton M. *History of Hoisery.* New York, 1955.

MANN, Julia de L. "The Textile Industry. Machinery for Cotton, Flax, Wool, 1760-1850," in SINGER, Charles, *A History of Technology.* Vol. IV, 1958, pp. 277-307.

MARTINDALE, J. G. "Carding: Evolution and Early Development," *The Journal of the Textile Industry,* 40, 1949, pp. 65-78.

MORTIER, Augustin. *Le tricot et l'industrie de la bonneterie.* Troyes, 1891.

PILISI, Jean. Several articles in the periodical *L'industrie textile;* especially, 1954, 1955, 1956 (mechanization of weaving), and 1967 (controlled ornamentation).

RENOUARD, A. *Traité complet de bonneterie mécanique,* n.d.

———. *Traité complet de la filature du coton.* Paris-Liège, 1865.

———. *Traité du travail des laines.* Paris, 1886.

———. *Traité du travail des laines peignées.* Paris, 1873.

USHER, Abbot Payson. *A History of Mechanical Inventions.* 2nd edition, revised and enlarged. Boston, 1959.

WILLKOMM, G. *Cours technique de bonneterie,* n.d.

PARTIAL COLORING OF FABRICS
PRINCIPAL SOURCES OF OLD MANUSCRIPTS

BEAULIEU. *Manière de fabriquer les toiles peintes dans l'Inde, telle que M. de Beaulieu, capitaine de vaisseau, l'a fait exécuter devant lui à Pondichéry,* Bibliothèque Centrale du Musée d'Histoire Naturelle. Paris, 1734. An absolutely unique document, for it is accompanied by 11 samples representing the successive stages of textiles in process of being manufactured.

ROQUES. *La manière de négocier dans les Indes orientales dédiée à mes chers amis et confrères, les engagés de la Royale Compagnie de France.* Ms. deposited at the Bibliothèque Nationale in Paris, 1678, pp. 155–71, printed at Ahmedabad, in 1678.

RUPIED. *L'art d'imprimer sur toile en Alsace.* Archives Nationales. Paris, 1786. The author, a "student of manufacturing," an inspector of the province of Alsace at Colmar, records his observations on his rounds.

RYHINER. *Traité sur la fabrication et le commerce des toiles peintes.* Bibliothèque de la Société industrielle de Mulhouse, deposited at the Musée de l'Impression sur Étoffes in Mulhouse, 1766. The manuscript, begun in 1766, covers a period from 1738 to 1783, the only known publication of a recognized manufacturer of the 18th century. The author (1728–1790) was the son of the introducer of printed cotton to Basel (Switzerland) around 1716–1717.

PRINTED MATTER

BANCROFT, Edward. *Philosophy of Permanent Colours and the Best Means of Producing Them by Dyeing, Calico Printing,* etc. London, 1794. 2nd ed., enlarged, 1813.

DEGENNES. *Résumé du cours de chimie appliquée aux arts, donné à Mulhausen (Mulhouse).* 1st edition, Strasbourg, 1824; supplements, Mulhausen, Jean Risler & Cie.

DOLLFUS-AUSSET, Daniel. *Matériaux pour la coloration des étoffes.* 2 vols. Paris, 1865. The author was one of the heads of the firm Dollfus-Mieg & Cie of Mulhouse, one of the most important in Europe during this period. Partial reproduction of ms. of Jean RHYINER in book II.

O'BRIEN. *Treatise on Calico Printing, Theoretical and Practical.* London, 1792.

PERSOZ, J. *Traité théorique et pratique de l'impression sur tissus.* 4 vols. Paris, 1846. A fundamental work, of value today. 429 samples inserted in the text of an eminent chemist with long experience in the printing industry.

QUÉRELLES. *Traité sur les toiles peintes dans lequel on voit la manière dont on les fabrique aux Indes et en Europe, on y trouvera le secret du bleu d'Angleterre de bon teint, applicable sur la toile avec la planche ou le pinceau,* by M. Q*** at Amsterdam, Paris, 1760. The first treatise on printing ever published.

Vollständige Entdeckung des bisher so sehr geheimgehaltenen Cotton-oder Indienne-Drucks. Carlsruhe, anonymous, 1768.

English imitations of Indian textiles by DELORMOIS, designer to the king and colonist.

RUNGE, F. F. *Farbenchemie,* 2ter Teil: *Die Kunst zu drucken.* Berlin, 1842. 116 samples inserted in the text of this famous chemist.

THILLAYE. *Manuel du fabricant d'indiennes.* Paris, 1834.

URE, Andrew. *A Dictionary of Arts, Manufactures and Mines.* London, 1840.

VON KURRER, W. H. *Geschichte der Zeugdruckerei.* Nürnberg, 1840 (first work of this type of the 19th century). The author was an expert craftsman.

TWENTIETH-CENTURY SOURCES

BERTHOUD, Eugène. *Traité de la gravure sur rouleaux.* Paris, 1906.

BÜHLER, Alfred. "Plangi," *Les Cahiers C.I.B.A.* Basel, September 1954.

———. "Ikats," *Les Cahiers C.I.B.A.* Basel, July 1951.

CHOBAUT, H. *L'industrie des indiennes à Avignon et Orange (1677-1884).* Avignon, 1938.

———. *L'industrie des indiennes à Marseille avant 1680.* Marseille, 1939.

FLOUD, Peter. "The Origins of English Calico Printing; The English Contribution to the Early History of Indigo Printing; The English Contribution to the Development of Copper-plate Printing," in *Journal of the Society of Dyers and Colourists,* Bradford, May, June, July 1960.

JENNY-TRÜMPY, Adolf. *Handel und Industrie des Kantons Glarus.* Zweiter Teil, Glarus, 1900. (Does not limit itself to Switzerland, but sketches the story of European printing from its beginnings.)

LEIX, A. "Tissage et teinture en Égypte," *Les Cahiers C.I.B.A.* Basel, October 1947.

MAILE, Anne. *Tie-and-dye, as a Present-day Craft.* London, 1963.

PFISTER, R. *Les toiles imprimées de Fostat et l'Hindoustan.* Paris, 1938.

SCHWARTZ, Paul R. "French Documents on Indian Cotton Painting, Part I: The Beaulieu Ms., 1734; Part II: New Light on Old Material," in *Journal of Indian Textile History,* Ahmedabad, II, 1956; III, 1957 (abridged French text in *Bull. Soc. ind. de Mulh.,* IV, 1957, and IV, 1958).

———. "The Roxburgh Account of Indian Cotton Painting, 1795," in *Journal of Indian Textile History,* Ahmedabad, IV, 1959.

———. "Les débuts de l'indiennage mulhousien," in *Bull. de la Soc. ind. de Mulh.,* III, 1950; I, 1951; I, 1952.

———. "Contribution à l'histoire de l'application du bleu d'indigo (bleu anglais) dans l'indiennage européen," in *Bull. Soc. ind. de Mulh,* II, 1953.

———. "Les toiles peintes indiennes, les indiennes et les persiennes," in *Bull. Soc. ind. de Mulh.,* IV, 1962.

Indian fabrics of the Duke of Bourbon (1692–1740) in the château at Chantilly, after two anonymous undated manuscripts, one in the central library of the Museum of Natural History in Paris, the other at the city library of Caen, in *Bull. Soc. ind. Mulh.,* I, 1966.

Printing on cotton at Ahmedabad (India) in 1678, after the *ROQUES* manuscript in the Bibliothèque Nationale in Paris, in *Bull. Soc. ind. Mulh.,* 1967.

STEINMANN, Alfred. *Batik.* Leigh-on-Sea (Essex), 1958.

PART EIGHT
TECHNIQUES OF EXPRESSION

CHAPTER 1

PRINTING

I N VOLUME II we pointed out that the eighteenth century, like the fifteenth, was directly affected by the powerful intellectual tensions of a period rich in every kind of potential. In fact, this movement acquired its full scope only around the end of the century. On the technical level we find the reaction in lively activity, in eager exploration that was often confused by methods revived from the past, in new methods and revolutionary raw materials, as if all the experimenters were already taking the measure of what was to be the mechanistic nineteenth century. We shall offer a rapid survey of all these experiments, to assign them their true significance.

THE GUTENBERG PRESS

In pursuing into the eighteenth century the history of the Gutenberg press, the structure of which changed little after the fifteenth century, we cannot fail to remember Benjamin Franklin. He occupied only an episodic place in this story, but his quality as an individual justifies mentioning him. At the beginning of his career he served an apprenticeship as a compositor and pressman in his brother's print shop. Then in 1725/26 he worked in London in the Watts printing shop and later in Philadelphia, where in 1732 he printed the popular *Poor Richard's Almanac*. Later, when as ambassador to London he found the press whose bar he had so often worked, he gave free reign to his memories during a small party for the pressmen of the printing shop. This historic press is still in existence, preserved at the Smithsonian Institution. But Franklin's work in this area did not stop here; as we shall see later, he maintained an interest in minor problems concerning the graphic arts.

Let us resume the history of the printing press where we left off. As a point of departure, we shall specify that the classic press at this time can be understood from Diderot's picture and description of it in the *Encyclopédie* (Figure 1). Around the middle of the eighteenth century master printers were already trying to eliminate the uprights that impeded the movement of the ropes holding the printed sheets of paper. To do this it was necessary to increase the weight of the base considerably to provide firm support for the apparatus.

In 1772 Wilhelm Haas, a type founder in Basel, built a completely new type of press mounted on a block of stone, which provided much more stability. Its

Plate 80. The Hoe type-revolving cylinder printing press, 1844. Scale model. Musée du Conservatoire national des Arts et Métiers, Paris. (Photo Ph. Brossé - P. U. F.)

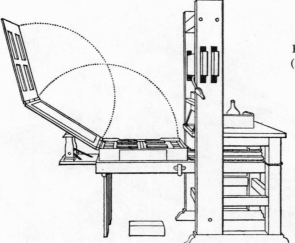

FIG. 1.   Double-acting platen press. (From Diderot's *Encyclopédie.*)

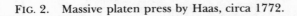

FIG. 2.   Massive platen press by Haas, circa 1772.

principal virtue was eliminating the strong wooden uprights that had until then given the printing press its characteristic silhouette. The upper support of the whole press was a metal arch, through the center of which passed the pressure screw. This was the first press built of metal on such a massive scale (Figure 2).

But the guild of master printers at Basel, using the pretext that Haas was not a member of their brotherhood, succeeded in having him legally restrained from building the press. Around 1787 his son, who was a printer, successfully resumed the project and sold many presses in Switzerland and Germany.

The single-action press   While Haas was developing his press, around 1781, a formidable problem was attacked: the elimination of the old double-action press and its replacement by a single-action one that would appreciably reduce the time of the printing operation. Two famous master printers claimed credit for its invention: Laurent Anisson, director of the Imprimerie Royale, and François-Ambroise Didot (1730–1804), who also gave his name to a new typeface. It is difficult to decide between the two claimants. It is possible that the two engineers completed their work at about the same time. In 1781 a certain Prudon built a press in Didot's shop, "which differed from the old types by its screw." This could well be the first version of the single-action press, but Anisson's request for certification from the Académie des Sciences that the invention of the single-action press belonged to him was granted on May 17, 1783. Pierre Didot objected, claiming that his father was the sole inventor of such a press.

It is not surprising that a controversy of this kind could be provoked by such a complex invention. Special installation of the pressure screw was needed to ensure sufficient pressure on the sheet of paper. In Anisson's 1785 *Mémoires de mathématiques et de physique* he specified that his screw had two threads, superimposed and inclined at different pitches "so that when the screw drops ten *lignes*, the platen attached to it nevertheless drops only a little more than three *lignes*." This made it possible to increase considerably the pressure of the platen on the sheet of paper and thus ensure printing the entire form with no greater effort than in the past.

Plate 81. The press from Watt's Printing House, London, where Benjamin Franklin worked in 1726, is now housed at the Smithsonian Institution in Washington, D.C. Smithsonian Institution

Didot countered this by claiming that Anisson had visited his printing plant in 1781, accompanied by a mechanic, Pagnier, who had measured the thread pitch of the double screw and had thus learned to build a similar press. Moreover, according to Didot, this new press was not as well designed as his own, calling for much more hard work for the pressman.

Actually, it matters little whether the single-action press was invented by Anisson or Didot. Let us simply say that the Imprimerie Nationale still possesses a splendid Anisson single-action press (Figure 3).

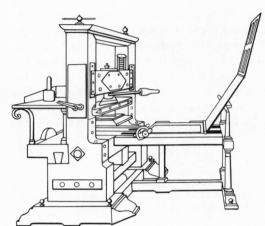

FIG. 3. Single-acting platen press by Anisson, 1783.

In 1784 the printer Philippe-Denis Pierres, assisted by a mechanic named Robert, built a press with no press bar. From descriptions given of it, pressure appears to have been obtained from a horizontal lever placed near the frame, to which the pressman applied strong pressure. A second movement, assisted by a counterweight on the opposite side of the press, freed the form, which could then be removed to prepare another printing. King Louis XVI, to whom this new machine was presented, took an interest in it and ordered one made for his own use, a task entrusted to a mechanic named Baradelle.

Pierres later made various modifications in this first press, especially by considerably lengthening the sweep of the lever. The fulcrum was far to the left under the ink pot, and its movement was toward the extreme right, which permitted the pressman to exert great pressure on the platen through a two-point crank.

In 1784 a locksmith named Genard presented a machine similar to Pierres', except that the two-point crank whose usefulness was not evident had been eliminated. Several models of this machine were supplied to the printing plant of the French royal lottery.

In 1790 a well-known English physicist, William Nicholson (1753–1815) conceived of replacing the inking balls, in use since the days of the first typographers, with a roller covered with a flexible material that would permit easier and, in particular, more even inking. The covering of Nicholson's roller was leather, but in 1819 a French chemist named Jean-Nicolas Gannal used an elastic material made of a glue mixed with molasses, which was softer than leather. The importance of this development of inking equipment was far greater than was realized at the time, since it offered possibilities for mechanizing the inking of mechanized presses later. Nicholson will appear later, involved in other problems concerning printing.

We have now come to the last designs built before the purely mechanical presses introduced to Western Europe by Friedrich Koenig. Around 1795 Charles Stanhope (1753–1816), with the assistance of a mechanic named Walker, built a new press combining the virtues of the various earlier machines. The components of this press, derived from Haas's, were entirely of metal. Thanks to certain improvements, notably in the mechanism that caused the movement of the screw, the pressure of the platen on the sheet of paper was very even and the general operation light, thanks to a set of counterweights in the back. The Stanhope press was thus a mechanical marvel for its time. In various versions, one with a cruciform wooden base, it is still used as a proof press in some typographical shops (Figure 4).

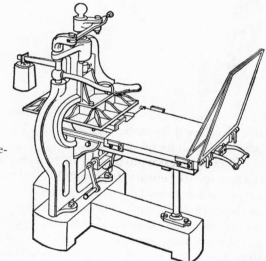

FIG. 4. The Stanhope platen press, derived from the Haas platen press.

From this period on a large number of presses appeared, built completely of iron, then later of cast iron. One of the most interesting is one by George E. Clymer (1754–1834), a mechanic of Swiss origin born in the United States, which appeared around 1797 and was named the Columbian (Figure 5). It gave the printing press a very compact silhouette expressive of great power. Its special feature was that it exerted pressure without using a screw, which was replaced by a series of levers, rods, and joints that interacted to make it possible to bring down the platen forcefully onto the form.

Another press, the Albion, built around the same time, bore a strong resemblance to the Columbian. The Albion was copied in France by Giroudot,

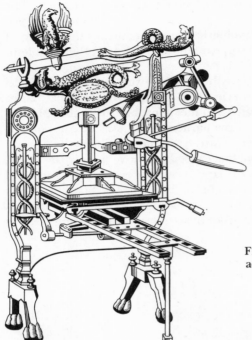

FIG. 5. The Columbian, Clymer's single-acting press, 1797.

under the name Gutenberg press. Another press, also American, the Washington, was developed by Robert Hoe (1784–1833) and was even more compact and powerful than its predecessors.

It is unnecessary to discuss all the presses designed or built at the beginning of the nineteenth century, for it should be obvious by now that under the pressure of events and increased needs for rapid production, if only to ensure the appearance of the periodicals springing up everywhere, the development of printing was to take a completely different direction. The old Gutenberg press, which had made possible so many masterpieces, was doomed, for Friedrich Koenig was already designing equipment that would allow all the operations to be performed mechanically.

PRINTING FOR THE BLIND

Our discussion of printing for the blind (which was in fact very primitive) will be somewhat lengthy, for, as we shall see, it contributed a new tool to the technique of relief printing. It was in operation by 1786 at the Institute for the Blind founded by the Abbot Valentin Haüy (1745–1822), where blind inmates used it to build up their own library.

Haüy himself tells us that on the advice of one Clousier, the king's printer, a locksmith named Beaucher was asked to build such a press on the following principles: unlike common typographical presses, its task was to make a definite

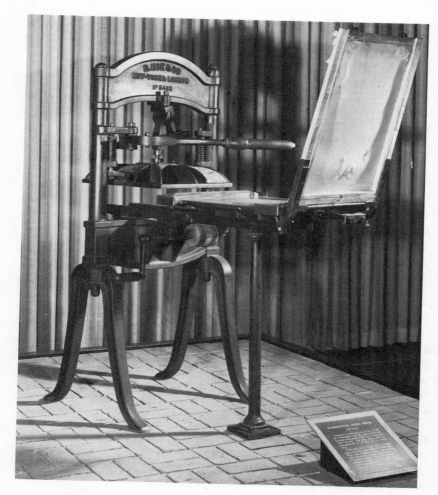

Plate 82. The Washington Hand Press, patented by Samuel Rust of New York in 1829. The Washington was the most widely used hand-printing press in the U.S. during the 19th century. The one shown here was manufactured by R. Hoe & Co., about 1875. The hollow frame construction resulted in a lighter, cheaper, more durable, and more easily assembled press than those made with solid cast-iron frames. Smithsonian Institution

impression that would project on the verso of the paper. The idea came from examining posters that were often printed by hand, using a rubbing pad, on a single side of a sometimes heavily dampened sheet of paper. This method produced an accentuated imprint of the letters on the back of the paper, which a blind person could recognize by touch.

Abbot Haüy, having trained his blind students to read with their fingers, in the school he founded in 1783, then conceived of having a press built (in 1784) by Beaucher. The method used by this machine to apply pressure was extremely simple and required no special precautionary measures. A lever changed the slope of the bed, causing a large roller to move automatically on guides holding the form and attached to the bed. The roller pressed down the sheet of paper, which had been thoroughly moistened then laid over the form. The typefaces penetrated deeply into the paper and projected on the verso. After the paper had been dried the relief could be touched by a blind person's fingers (Figure 6).

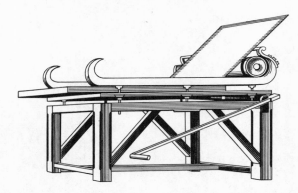

FIG. 6.   Valentin Haüy's first press for the blind, with a striking roller, 1784.

To obtain this result Abbot Haüy had needed special types of a shape that would facilitate the work of composition by the blind. They had to be cast with the face reversed from those used in ordinary printing. In turn, the matrices in which they would be cast had to be prepared with punches whose faces were similarly reversed.

The new contribution to typography made by this crude press was the large cylinder roller that pressed the sheet of paper deeply onto the form. Mechanics appeared not to have immediately recognized the importance of this addition, the cylinder seeming to have no function other than to press its full weight on the damp sheet. However, it was to influence profoundly the future evolution of techniques of typographic printing.

This crude press gave less than complete satisfaction. The uncontrolled movement of the cylinder pulled the paper and blurred the impression slightly. And its passage over the form was too fast to let the pressure of the types into the paper leave a durable trace, as can easily be seen in the pages of Haüy's book, mentioned earlier.

After various experiments with Clousier's presses, the same mechanic, Beaucher, built for the blind a classic platen press that was, however, much more

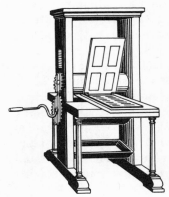

FIG. 7.   The second press for the blind, with two striking cylinders, circa 1820.

powerful than those used by typographic printers, to effect much stronger pressures. An engraving in the Guillié book shows two young blind boys combining their efforts to operate this new press, one pulling and the other pushing, leaving the form under pressure for several seconds so that the recesses made by the letters became deep and permanent.

Around 1820 printers returned to using the cylinder press, developing it along the lines of the copperplate press. Two large cylinders, one above the other, applying the strong pressure needed, were operated by a geared crank. All that was necessary was to cause the movable bed and the form holding the sheet of paper to slide between the two cylinders. To ink the relief impression for sight reading, the sheet of paper could be held by the classic tympan, coated with ink for each impression, which outlined the faces of the relief letters in black (Figure 7).

THE CYLINDER USED IN TYPOGRAPHIC PRINTING

The pressure cylinder had now entered a period of use in typographic techniques, but through a back door. Although it was to revolutionize the functions of the printing press and to lead engineers toward new conceptions from which the mechanical press would be born, several decades passed before mechanical presses could realize the advantages offered by the cylinder press.

The two functions that were later transformed were inking and pressure on the paper. But this was not all: based on the latter improvement, a new conception of the form became possible.

Cylindrical impression   As seen above, the copperplate press had already been equipped with a cylinder that gradually and powerfully pressed the sheet of paper onto the intaglio-engraved copperplate. In the intaglio printing technique the cylinder thus performed one of the essential functions, that of creating a powerful pressure. It is possible that it was this press that Valentin Haüy had in mind when trying to achieve the pressure he needed to obtain a relief on the verso of the sheet of paper.

The appearance of the cylinder in typographic techniques made it possible to eliminate the tympan and frisket and to attach the sheet of paper to the cylinder, which automatically carried the paper to the form. Furthermore, it increased considerably the striking force, since striking was done not by a single pressure over the entire surface of the form but by a cylinder that progressively printed the text on the sheet of paper. Here more than anywhere else we realize the extent to which technicians continued to be obsessed by the demands of their craft. Didot and Anisson, among others, spent money lavishly to modify the striking mechanism of their presses in order to obtain an impression of the entire form with a single stroke of the bar. Yet the copperplate technique had been offering a solution to the problem since the sixteenth century—progressive pressure by the cylinder.

Various attempts were made to adapt the copperplate impression cylinder to typographical printing. We find such references in an 1812 book published in Paris by the Mame printers, successors to Herhan, who, as we shall later see, played a major role in the history of stereography. This *Histoire de l'Ancien et du*

Nouveau Testament (History of the Old and New Testaments), by Royaumont, stated in the frontispiece, "This stereotyped edition [is] decorated with 267 engravings in relief according to the method of M. Duplat and printed *with the text on the copperplate press*" (the last words are in italics in the original). This deliberately obscure phrase can, however, refer only to a typographic impression, since the relief engravings were printed with the text. The novelty was, therefore, that the ensemble was passed under the cylinder of a copperplate press equipped for relief printing. We believe, however, that the tympan and frisket had not yet been eliminated from these presses. Although the method of positioning the paper on the form remained the same, the platen of the single-action press had just been replaced by the impression cylinder, which now made it possible to print the sheet progressively. This was not without its difficulties, which are recorded in complaints by printers who had not succeeded in obtaining as beautiful an impression as before.

The printing cylinder Another way of using the cylinder was to make it the printing element, that is, the form itself. In the eighteenth century the need to print continuous lengths of fabric had caused copperplate printers to reverse the printing procedure; to intaglio engrave the roller rather than the plate, and to print it on the fabric being unrolled flat. This machine, invented by John Bell, was introduced in England around 1780. Christopher Potter (d. 1817) developed it to print in several colors.

Around the turn of the eighteenth century William Nicholson, who had already thought of inking the pages of the form by a roller covered with a flexible material, also became interested in the impression cylinder. He was granted several patents relative to printing, one being concerned with equipping the typographic press with a cylinder on which the types would be held.

The idea was revolutionary but very difficult to put into effect. How could the type pages, whose form was rigorously prismatic, be made to hold on the round, smooth surface of a cylinder? Realizing these difficulties, Nicholson took out a patent but made no attempt to build the machine, simply giving several confusing explanations of the need to "file the types in order to make them more conical toward the foot," and on the construction of "frames adapted to the surface of the cylinder," leaving it to the skill of the builder to solve the other problems posed by his innovation.

THE MECHANICAL PRESS

Inking the cylinder The mechanical press conceived by Friedrich Koenig now made its appearance. The first problem he solved was how to ink the forms. His system, patented in 1810, adapted Nicholson's rollers. Koenig's device was a group of four rollers, one on top of the other, which by moving back and forth carried the ink automatically from a container to the pages of the form.

Friedrich Koenig Friedrich Koenig has been compared with Gutenberg in his display of intelligence and cunning in solving all the difficulties he encountered in his investigations. Moreover, the comparison is justified by the effect of his discovery—an entire evolution in modern printing techniques. Just as Gutenberg was inspired to recognize what was needed first to mechanize a method, Koenig understood with equal genius what would be its final form and invented a press that gradually became automatic by the elimination of more and more human functions.

Koenig built his first mechanical press at Suhl in Thuringia, in 1803. It was not successful. Pressing the sheet of paper on the form was still done by a cast-iron platen that was lowered and raised automatically on the form which, being movable, stopped at the moment of striking. This was still an attempt to mechanize the old platen method. But, as mentioned, the inking was already done cylindrically. With the help of his compatriot Andrew Bauer, Koenig managed to put an improved mechanism into service in Thomas Bensley's London printshop in 1811.

The invention was still not complete, since it retained the impression platen. We do not know if Koenig had learned of the methods of cylindrical impression discussed above and which the Mames were using in 1812, but in that December a new press was completed that was put into service in February 1813. This time an impression cylinder replaced the platen. Its diameter was quite large; its circumference had three impression surfaces, each the same size as the bed of the form. Each impression was thus made by advancing the cylinder one-third. The bed holding the form, previously moved by a large roller operated with a rope, was replaced by a rack with two rows of teeth to advance and return the bed. The rack mechanically linked this movement with that of the cylinder holding the sheet of paper, thus making all the functions of the press interdependent (Figure 8).

So arrived the mechanical press, which radically transformed all printing techniques along the lines required by a world increasingly disposed toward the rapid mass transmission of information.

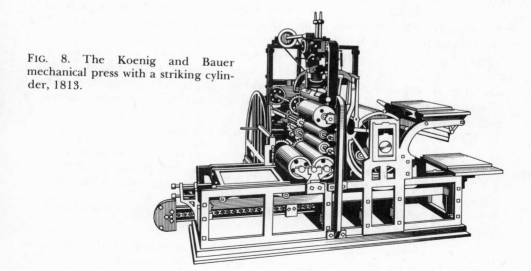

FIG. 8. The Koenig and Bauer mechanical press with a striking cylinder, 1813.

*Rotary printing
of newspapers*

Demand increased remarkably as the result of the proliferation of daily newspapers and especially of the numbers printed, which rose steeply. They were quickly successful, and builders of new mechanical presses were soon overwhelmed with work. Reviving Nicholson's suggestions for a press that would employ a large cylinder on which the type pages for the paper would be held, attempts were made to build one. For this purpose Richard M. Bacon (1775–1844) and Bryan Donkin (1768–1855) tried to overcome the problem posed by the round surface of the cylinder by faceting it, but it was still necessary to file the types so that their face surfaces would have exactly the roundness necessary for the sheets to be printed evenly.

A useful solution was delayed until 1844. Richard March Hoe's type revolving press, like his predecessors' machines, used a center cylinder with a large diameter so as to decrease the curve of its circumference. On the surface of this cylinder Hoe fitted to this curve frames. His type pages were held in the frames by placing between the columns of the newspaper's pages rules whose bases were narrower than their tops, which thus locked the columns against the surface of the cylinder and sides of the frame (Figure 9).

FIG. 9. The tightening wedges of Hoe's press with an impression cylinder.

Around the thick cylinder thus holding the form a series of small cylinders (six, eight, or ten, depending) each brought up a sheet of paper for printing, an arrangement that multiplied the number of copies obtained by a single revolution of the large cylinder. Then, of course, the verso of the sheets had to be printed. The machine was enormous, its operation requiring as many as sixteen workers.

It became evident that this huge circular structure was very weak, being held together only by the miracle of wedges buried here and there between the columns. Under the strain of vibrations by this enormous machine, which operators tried to revolve rapidly, one can imagine the catastrophe that ensued when only one of the wedges came loose. This solution, then, was only a temporary and precarious one.

Two noteworthy improvements were quickly found:

1. Use of a continuous strip of paper, which paper plants had been manufacturing since 1803, so that the reel unrolled as the printing was done, eliminating all the people needed to feed sheets of paper into the jaws of the large cylinder;
2. The use of round type plates, made by molding in a casting machine, which could therefore fit perfectly on the printing cylinder.

In 1845 in France, one Worms, Sr., a printer at Argenteuil, with the mechanic Philippe took out a patent for such a cylindrical machine that printed typographically with round plates on a continuous strip of paper, but problems persisted, especially because of the difficulty of preparing cylindrical forms. Attention was therefore devoted to this problem, and after 1849 plaster casting of the plate for the cylindrical form was abandoned for casting in strong papier-mâché. This new material, much easier to handle, made it possible to obtain perfectly curved stereotypes that fit without difficulty on the printing cylinders of rotary presses.

Around 1863 Nicolas Serrière, a Parisian printer, overcame the final difficulties, and with the help of the builder Hippolyte Marinoni (1823–1904), got into regular operation the first large French rotary press (Figure 10), capable of printing 40,000 impressions per hour, which printed *Le Petit Journal*. After 1868 the rotary press using a continuous strip of paper was generally adopted in all Western Europe and the United States.

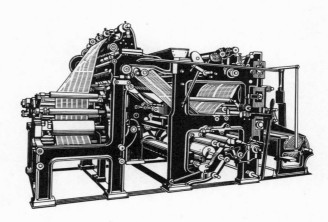

FIG. 10. Marinoni's rotary press with an impression cylinder, 1863.

The need for extremely rapid relief printing existed only in the case of daily newspapers, in which rotary typographical presses proliferated, though usually in shops that were completely independent of those in which books were produced. The book-printing industry was still resisting change, for several reasons. The speed of rotary presses was possible only because the paper was printed from a continuous strip, but book printing, with the exception of a few rare large printings, was done on formats, i.e., on sheets, if only to obtain satisfactory results. Moreover, typography is basically a method of composing texts by means of types; it is a craft in itself, and does not adapt well to complicated equipment involving engravings, acids, and photography. Thus, even today, printing on cylindrical forms does not extend far beyond the domain of the newspaper.

Rotary printing adapted to other methods of graphic expression — The other methods of printing are basically ones using engraving, on either copper, steel, or zinc, so in the rotary printing system printers discovered a new path that met their needs well.

In the preceding survey we discussed the importance of intaglio printing, that is, by copperplate, and later we shall describe another engraving method, using first stone, then zinc, which appeared at the beginning of the nineteenth century and had considerable success. This method, using flat-surface printing, was lithography.

In 1867 Jules Derriey, a builder of machines, designed an intaglio-printing rotary machine in which the recto and verso of the cylinders were hand engraved. The following year Marinoni built his machine, La Diligente, in which a zinc plate prepared by lithography was fixed to an impression cylinder.

But after the appearance in 1893 of photomechanical methods and the possibility of tracing photographic originals on metal, rotary printing presses proliferated in both techniques, and thus photogravure (an intaglio method) and offset (a flat-surface method) became increasingly specialized in the field of large-scale circulations.

CHAPTER 2

METHODS DERIVED FROM TYPOGRAPHY

STEREOTYPING

E NGINEERS did not confine themselves solely to improving the printing press. They reexamined the art of typography itself, which, it was believed, had provided a final solution of the problem of the book. In the seventeenth century, once the enthusiasm for such a miraculous process had cooled, its disadvantages became apparent. To make up and move a form is to realize how difficult it is to handle. How often have young apprentices, and even veteran compositors, inadvertently turned a page into a "pie" or small heap of jumbled types, which then require much time to re-sort into their case? In his famous treatise on printing, Momoro declares that " 'pies' are the ruination of a printing plant." Even today the printer dreads such an accident, known as "making a pie."

Still another disadvantage arises from the difficulty of preserving the pages after printing. It may be convenient to keep the page proofs of an important book in regular use, so that later printings can be made without the expense of recomposing the type for each printing. Piling the pages on shelves required considerable space and constant supervision, for the fibrations caused by creaking presses in a busy shop gradually broke down the sides of the pages, causing their slow deterioration and ultimate destruction. Moreover, all the surviving shop inventories show that the stock of type was limited, so printers could thus be held up by storing composed pages.

Contemporary documents show that the practice of preserving pages permitted some bookstores to sell editions at a very low price, but they also confirm that some stores—notably a certain Athias of Amsterdam, who preserved for several years the pages of a large English Bible—were thereby ruined. Hence the incentive at this time to discover new methods that would facilitate handling and conserving the pages.

Simple stereotyping The Chinese long ago appreciated the need to fix movable characters into a block, after composition, to facilitate printing. Around A.D. 1040 a certain Pi-Ching relief engraved types in fine, glutinous clay and baked them in a furnace. The types were then assembled on an iron plate coated with a mastic of resin, wax, and lime. The plate was heated from below to soften the mastic, and the types were pressed with a flat piece of wood to make the printing surface perfectly even. The type page thus formed a single block and could easily be printed. After use the plate was again heated and the characters were separated, and re-sorted for use in other compositions.

Western use of metal type required slightly different solutions. Johann Muller, a minister from Leyden, is said to have suggested in 1700, soldering typographic pages across the feet of the type. With Van der Mey he tried out his idea around 1700, using mastic and plaster, and later lead. A letter dated June 24, 1801, written by the Luchtmans (Dutch bookstore owners) to A. Renouard, a Paris bookseller, refers to this method in connection with a Bible whose pages, soldered at the beginning of the eighteenth century by Van der Mey, were still being used for printing when the Luchtmans were writing. Camus also speaks of a Dutch Bible by the bookseller Elwe, and of various works dealt with in this manner.

This method was adopted in 1795 by Firmin Didot (1764–1836) in connection with a very special case, a new edition of F. Callet's *Tables de logarithmes.* Mere handling of the pages that had to be kept was likely to shift the types and thus cause inversions of figures and accidental errors. Didot therefore soldered the feet of the composed pages after he had carefully checked the text, thus preserving them. The title page bore the note "Stereotype edition." But this was merely a makeshift and rather poor solution to the problem, and a new technique had to be found.

Polytyping and stereotyping

The words *polytyping* and *stereotyping,* used synonymously in the eighteenth century, covered a variety of attempts to return to the principle of block printing. Printing with blocks, first of engraved wood and then of molded metal, had been the foundation of typography, but their processing was a lengthy job and the technique was irremediably primitive. It was thus necessary to find alternatives, which is what many technicians attempted to do during the eighteenth century.

It should be emphasized that the terms *stereotyping* and *stereography* must be distinguished. Stereotyping is the method used to obtain a printing block from the typographic page, whereas in stereography the block is prepared without the use of the page.

The problem of stereotype molding

The principle of stereotyping therefore required making a mold of the typographic page in a flexible substance, into which the metal—an alloy with a lead base—was poured, thus forming a replica of the page. Because the plate thus obtained was thin it had to be mounted on a wooden or metal base to establish the exact type height.

The most delicate element in this new technique was indisputably the mold. The difficulties of making a correct mold had for several years in the fifteenth century prevented any final solution of the problem of type for books. In the eighteenth century similar problems arose and efforts were made to discover the most suitable materials with which to make molds.

The choice of materials was not easy, requiring continuous research until the early nineteenth century. Three solutions were offered.

The first used soft materials like clay, plaster, or a more complex mixture, which, since it was easily deformed, could not be reused.

The second proposed a mold made with hot metal. Its disadvantage was that either air bubbles were developed in the casting, destroying the shape of the letters, or it was found very difficult and sometimes even impossible to free the mold.

The third solution employed cold metal, into which the letters were punched by a balance press, but in this case the composition punch had to set in a still harder metal so it could be pressed into the cold metal without being crushed.

The study of all these molds is very instructive, for it shows the ingenuity of technicians searching for a material likely to be suitable for a good casting. The Germans preceded the French in this search for suitable molding materials. In 1740 molds were being used in Germany for reproducing and multiplying pictures, vignettes, lamp bases, and so on. These molds were prepared in several ways: from plaster mixed with crushed brick and asbestos, potter's clay mixed with flock, cotton waste and other ingredients like a lye wash made from wood ash or cinders, or from chalk, the whole being brewed up with strong beer.

Molds were also made from molten type metal on which the model to be reproduced was placed after it had been coated with sanguine to protect the wood from the hot metal. Later, in 1780, crushed spar in an ammonia salt solution was used. These molds and castings had not yet been adapted to stereotyping but served simply to make or duplicate engravings for use by printers.

These methods were not used in France until slightly later, but they were adapted directly to reproducing typographic pages. In 1780, at Sélestat in Alsace, François Hoffmann used potter's clay mixed with plaster and combined with a gelatin glue made of gum syrup and potato starch. In 1785 Joseph Carez tried out a mold made of kaolin, which was not successful. In the same year Pingeron reported Hoffmann's new methods, which used a mixture of talc, plaster, clay, Venetian tripoli, and casting sand. In the same year an amateur named Abbot Rochon tried fine sand mixed with coal dust.

In 1787, while developing his press, Pierres used sand molds into which he poured copper. In 1794 Bouvier was still trying to use potter's clay.

In his *Traité de l'imprimerie* (1796), Momoro gives the following formula: take heated German spar and pour a solution of ammonia salt over it several times. Then pulverize the mixture and before using it sprinkle it with reheated pumice stone powder to assist freeing the mold. Bertrand Quinquet, who also published a *Traité de l'imprimerie* (1798/99), confirms that German spar was used to form the matrix.

In 1786 Carez modified his experiments with a mold made from molten metal. At the moment when the metal became covered with a light film, he struck a vigorous blow on the back of the iron chase that held the types, using a block of oak suspended from an iron bar. In 1795 Gatteaux was still using this method.

In September 1798 Pierre Didot, after a year of effort, used a metal mold obtained by pressing the page of type, made of a hard metal, into a softer, cold metal plate.

The all-plaster mold was used in England by Lord Stanhope, with the assistance of Alexander Tilloch (1759–1825) and Andrew Wilson, in 1804. This method reached France in 1818.

In 1846 an attempt was made to replace plaster with sheets of paper coated with whiting and dried onto the type page. We saw earlier that this method made possible the establishment of the shank needed to cast in cylindrical shape the forms required by the modern rotary press.

Stereotyping did not eliminate the time required—and still required—to set up pages in type. On the contrary; allowance has to be made for molding, retouching the flong, and mounting it on a piece of wood or a metal base.

Advantages and disadvantages of the method

Did the advantages of the new process offset the additional work it required? Contemporary reports claimed the following advantages for the process.

First, it facilitated the retention of pages of an entire book for future printings and, better yet, with a greatly reduced volume. The old frames of typographic pages were massive, but the flongs, when detached from their wooden or metal supports, occupied only a limited space.

Second, the castings, as with the typographic pages mentioned above, which were fixed at the base, had the advantage of fixing the composition of the texts in their final form without any possibility of errors creeping into them.

Third, saving the type pages for new editions immobilized large quantities of type, whereas stereotype casting freed the types for further use.

Fourth, repeated printing with the same types, constantly distributed and recomposed, caused rapid wear, whereas in the stereotype method the types were used only as elements for molding and were not actually used to print.

Fifth, the stereotype method made book selling very flexible, since only the number of copies immediately required had to be printed, reprinting following as necessary. Time and paper were saved.

This in turn permitted a limited printing, to test public reaction. Since the pages were preserved, a larger printing could be made when success was assured.

Lastly, in this period not all copies of an edition were immediately bound. Binding was done in small batches, until all the sheets had been used. If it was discovered during the last operation that some signatures were missing, it was easy to reprint them in order to make up the maximum number of copies possible.

Against these advantages—not all of which, however, were real—were there any disadvantages? Contemporary writers made various arguments.

First, the sand mold, whether of earth or clay, shrank during drying, which slightly changed the shape of the letters and sometimes caused the mold to crack and even break.

Second, it was quite difficult to make molten material penetrate all the recessed areas of the mold, whether the latter was of a soft material or metal. This was especially true for page edges, where letters often appeared deformed or clogged.

Third, if one tried to eliminate this disadvantage by pressing forcefully on the molten material at the moment when it came in contact with the mold, there was a great risk of breaking a soft mold.

Fourth, the remedy for this lay in using a metal mold, but then there were other difficulties. If the mold was heat formed it was sometimes impossible, after it had cooled, to remove the type page. If a cold-struck mold was used to strike a matrix, the types used had to be made of an exceptionally hard metal, so the customary printers' types could not be used.

Fifth, in general, in order to have a perfect face plane and thus an excellent striking on the paper, the cast plate had to be rubbed lightly on a bed, which made the face of the character heavier and caused it to lose its original elegance.

If errors were made prior to casting, they could be eliminated only by recomposing the entire page and recasting it.

THE HISTORY OF STEREOTYPING

The discovery of typography had overwhelmingly fulfilled the desires of printers and had given humanism a marvelous tool for communication, knowledge, and propaganda, so it was natural that they made no attempt to discover other printing methods. Although they retained a kind of nostalgia for a time when printing was done with wooden or metal blocks that had been so easy to handle, they appreciated the advantages of the new method.

However, the system of casting that had already appeared in the fifteenth century in the metallographic method was nevertheless not lost. It had to be used only occasionally, especially for preserving and duplicating printing elements, but was also used directly, as we shall see later in the discussion of stereography.

Lottin declares without documentation, that at the end of the seventeenth century Parisian printers were using plates molded in metal to print the calendars found in church books. Firmin Didot owned one of these plates, in copper, which he tells us certainly came from a sand mold and appeared to be of a very crude technique. Camus quotes a compositor to the effect that cast plates were used by the Parisian printer Valleyre before 1735.

All this is quite vague and unproven. Still, we suppose that similar castings — like calendars, for example — must have been made, though not by printers but by specialized molders who, making numerous copies from sand molds, made a business of selling them to printers and booksellers.

This opinion is confirmed by several extant German texts. In 1740 a printer-bookseller from Erfurt, J. Michael Funckter, published a kind of study called *The Art of Heating Plaster, Preparing Sand Molds in Order to Cast Letters, Vignettes, Cul-de-lampes, and Medals, and Forming Matrices of Them.* The existence of such a technique is confirmed at Frankfurt-am-Main, and a typographic manual printed in Halle in 1785 contains an advertisement that at the Slezam shop in Leipzig the reader will find "engravings either of wood or of cast metal."

It is obvious that foundries accumulated a large stock of vignettes, capital letters, and molded decorative elements that were less fragile and deformable than blocks engraved in wood. The idea of applying this technique to conserving texts must have been conceived quickly.

William Ged   William Ged (1690–1749), a goldsmith in Edinburgh, was interested in the printing craft, which one of his relatives practiced in that city. He observed the disadvantages of the typographical technique and looked for ways to obviate them. He perceived in 1725 that the typographic page should be regarded not as the printing element in the chain of work, but as a simple preparatory stage. One must, therefore, use the composition to make a plate that when mounted on wood could be used by itself for printing, with the types being returned to the case even before the printing was done.

His experiments were long and difficult, but successful. He went bankrupt, and came to London, where he entered into partnership with the Fanner brothers, one of whom was a foundryman, the other a bookseller. But, the hostility of printers combined with duplicity by his partners drove him from London, and he returned to Edinburgh. His former partners, using plates prepared by him, then sought to print two small works, including a prayer book that, it was said, "are so full of errors that no one wants them."

Reestablished in his native city, Ged resumed his experiments, financed by several fellow citizens. He apprenticed his son James to a printer and with the help of this son printed in 1739 an edition of Sallust by stereotype, which he had just adapted to book printing. This was therefore the first book correctly printed by this method, and Ged notes in the title, *"Gulielmus Ged, Aurifaber Edinensis, non Typis mobilibus, ut vulgo fieri solet, sed Tabellis seu Laminis fusis, excudebat. MDCCXXXIX."*

Ged died in 1749. There can be no question in our opinion of denying him the honor of introducing stereotyping to book printing, and though he published only a single work done this way, he paved the way for the process. It was revived much later by Alexander Tilloch and Andrew Foulis (d. 1829) of Glasgow, who in 1780 printed a Xenophon, and then by Foulis, who in 1784 printed a Virgil, concealing the method of its production to avoid the jealousy of his fellow printers.

François Hoffmann   In 1784 François Hoffmann, of German origin and a native of Sélestat in Alsace, settled in Paris, intending to practice stereotype printing. He knew the principle of the process, which had been in use in his native region for fifty years. He had examined Ged's Sallust and seen the great possibilities of this method. He began by using a mold with a clay base into which he poured a mixture of lead, tin, and bismuth.

In partnership with his son, Hoffmann immediately became very active. They began by securing an exclusive license to do "intaglio- and relief-engraving by the methods of a new art." Then, at the end of 1784, they launched a prospectus for a polytype journal of the sciences and arts. In January 1785 they received the license for this journal, which was produced by stereotyping and in which they concentrated on information concerning what they called the useful sciences, notably the problems of printing.

Lavoisier took an immediate interest in Hoffmann's process, but he examined it especially from a political and social point of view. In his *Réflexions sur les moyens de faire parvenir aux habitants de la campagne les instructions publiées par le gouvernement (Observations on the Methods of Bringing the Instructions Published by the Government to the Inhabitants of Rural Areas)* he declared that "with this method we have the advantage of being able to preserve the plates as long as is judged suitable, and to print copies only as they are needed. . . . The Administration would keep the plates of the major instructions which it published; it would be able to reprint its works continually and at no cost. . . . It could prepare in advance and keep in reserve all the orders and instructions necessary. . . . Similar plates could also be deposited in the Provincial Administrators' offices, so that at the first signal the information which it desired to spread would be communicated step by step, to the far reaches of the kingdom."

We have already seen from the examples of Haas, Ged, and others the role of conspiracy in the disasters that overwhelm daring inventors and innovators. The Hoffmanns likewise similarly suffered. To protect themselves they applied to the keeper of the seals for an ordinary printer's license under the distinctive title of polytype printer. After two commissioners had investigated the Hoffmanns' shops a decree by the Royal Council dated December 5, 1785, authorized the new printing plant.

The Hoffmanns were thus able to use their process, but they undoubtedly excited formidable jealousy among Parisian printers. Hardly had they finished a three-volume work, L. de Chenier's *Recherches sur les Maures (Investigations on the Moors)* when on February 15, 1787, a new decree was issued by the Royal Council that "prohibits and confiscates the copies of three works concerning the Assembly of Notables, and suspends Messrs. Hoffmann, printers, and Royer & Petit, booksellers, who published them." Hoffmann had imprudently exposed his flank to the attacks of his enemies by publishing texts reputed to be dangerous, and in this way the *Chambre royale et syndicale de la Librairie et Imprimerie de Paris* succeeded in getting rid of him.

Deprived of his printing plant, Hoffmann sought to open new opportunities to use the technique he had just revived, and he reestablished himself in Alsace. He was concerned about the criticisms made of the costs of operating the process. The type page had to be prepared exactly as in the typographic system, so there was no economy of labor. To these expenses had to be added those of casting, retouching the casting, and mounting it on a wooden base. Hoffmann therefore sought ways to eliminate these additional expenses, by doing away with the preliminary typographic composition. On January 21, 1792, he addressed to the Ministry of the Interior a paper from Sélestat (rewritten at Strasbourg on February 6) suggesting a process based on two new principles, which will be discussed later, since at least one of them was of great future importance.

Hoffmann's rivals In 1773 Philippe Pierres also became very much interested in Ged's Sallust, and tried to use the process. Camus tells of having seen an experimental mold made by Pierres. In 1787 he finally succeeded in publishing a book, *Zélie dans le désert (Zelia in the Desert)*, the pages of which had been stereotyped in copper in a sand mold. The result was poor, certain letters being clogged and misshapen.

Abbot Rochon, alert to all new techniques, became interested in Hoffmann's work and experimented with a small number of types. He could compose only four or five lines at a time, so he built up his castings with this number of lines, which were then combined on a single piece of wood to form the page. The result was even poorer than Pierres', but the experiment was still presented to the Académie Royale des Sciences on February 8, 1786.

A certain Joseph Carez, a printer at Toul, received several issues of Hoffmann's *Journal polytype* and, being very interested, began his own experiments in 1785. We have seen that the problem of molds preoccupied him for a long time. After lengthy experimentation he succeeded in producing better results and obtained from the keeper of the seals, on October 17, 1787, an authorization "to print on cast plates" by the method he called homotyping.

Gengembre, who had long worked with Hoffmann, was especially interested in applying these methods to the copperplate process. He will be discussed again later.

The engraver Nicolas-Marie Gatteaux introduced a major modification in the technique. Like many artists and technicians connected with the production of *assignats* (treasury notes) and lottery tickets, he began around 1793 to study the problem of counterfeiting.

The difficulty continued to be producing the casting with molten metal. Great skill was needed to obtain a correct mold from which acceptable plates could be made, and founders had gotten into the habit of preparing several molds of one page to be able to make a choice. After discussing this problem with a brother-in-law named Anfry and with Firmin Didot, Gatteaux stated in a paper that it was necessary to avoid the heat method of making the casting and, instead, to try to press the type page cold into the metal of the matrix by using a powerful balance press. To do this the types themselves had necessarily to be cast with a much stronger metal than that used by printers, so that they could be pressed into the matrix plate without being deformed. A harder material was thus sought; Anfry selected a silver-based alloy. On November 20, 1797, a matrix was successfully

Plate 83.   Hoe's "Web Printing Machine" exhibited in Machinery Hall. Wood engraving after photograph, *Harper's Weekly,* December 9, 1876. Library of Congress

struck without the slightest crushing of type. Herhan and Didot later developed a less expensive alloy that was claimed to give identical results.

A partnership agreement was then made between Louis-Etienne Herhan (Gengembre's brother-in-law), Firmin Didot, and Nicolas-Marie Gatteaux to exploit the three patents they individually registered: the first by Herhan on December 23, 1797, the second by Didot on December 26, and the third by Gatteaux on February 17, 1798. All three then published numerous stereotype editions—a Virgil, a *Phaedra,* etc.—obtained from blocks struck by the cold method and molded in small plates approximately two *lignes* thick called formats, which were then mounted on wooden bases.

STEREOGRAPHY

As noted earlier, the name *stereography* applies to methods that, though similar in principle to earlier methods (that is, they produce a molded printing block), are nevertheless to be distinguished from them by the fact that they do not make use of the typographic page.

One thing is certain: from the start of printing with types and for many and varied reasons, attempts were made to avoid difficulties inherent in the new art. No traces can now be found of many of these experiments. There is, however, a letter by Cl. Fabri de Peiresc dated May 6, 1634, quoting a description by Father Gilles of Loches, of one such process that by chance escaped oblivion and made it possible to reproduce texts in Eastern languages. It describes a wooden plate coated with a varnish composed of linseed oil and lampblack used as a foundation. On this support was placed a small frame as thick as a silver coin; a mixture of hot wax and turpentine was poured into it. When the wax hardened, the text to be reproduced was engraved in the layer of wax with an awl. After the plate was dampened, the apparatus was locked into a second frame two fingerwidths thick, into which was poured a clear paste of barley meal, hardwood sawdust, and crushed brick, the whole being sieved and agglomerated with water mixed with gum. When dry this block formed a solid page containing the text in relief that could be printed on a sheet of paper. After printing, the plates could be broken up, crushed, and again reduced to a fine powder for reuse.

This example is characteristic of the experiments made during the early centuries of printing, but they were only experiments. The stereographic experiment that was rationally tried was performed only with the same stereotyping technique described above when an attempt was made to liberate the process from the long work of composing the pages prior to their being cast. This was in fact a return to the methods that preceded typography, when the metallographic method was paving the way for typography. We remember that to eliminate the long work of engraving required by the woodcut technique, an attempt was made, by driving a series of punches into a copperplate, to create a matrix block from which a relief block was cast, to replace the woodcut. This process was abandoned because striking the punches never became a method capable of producing a perfect face plane on the molded block that would print correctly on the sheet of paper, especially after the printing press had been developed. By the eighteenth century it was believed that the situation had changed. Machinery had been greatly developed and improved, and precise striking could more easily be achieved. We believe that the technicians of this period knew nothing of the old metallographic method but were led to it naturally by their obligation to prepare economically and quickly matrix plates for making the block pages of which they were so fond. This fact had major consequences; if not immediately, then for the future.

The Abbot Rochon and his engraving machine   Once again it was no mechanic who first had the idea for eliminating from the stereotype method the unduly large role played by typographic composition. Rochon has been mentioned for his interest in graphic research. He devoted much time to the problem of preparing the intaglio matrix for texts. With the advantages of technical possibilities in a century beginning to glorify mechanization he designed a machine that would evenly apply, one next to the other in its proper position, all the punches required to form lines and pages in intaglio.

This engraving machine was presented to the Académie des Sciences in 1781, as reported on December 22 of that year by Condorcet and Bossut. A description is in *Recueil de Mémoires,* which appeared in 1783. This text is accompanied by four copperplate illustrations giving a diagram of this ingenious machine as well as a specimen of the work obtained, dated 1782. The sample is completely unsatisfactory because of the poor quality of the letters and especially the unevenness of their edges (Figure 11).

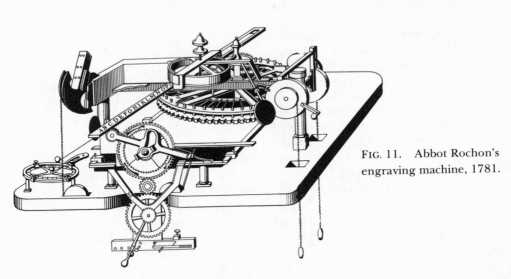

FIG. 11. Abbot Rochon's engraving machine, 1781.

What was the mechanism of this engraving machine? A double wheel of copper turned on its axis in a horizontal plane and steel punches, each bearing a different letter or sign, were fixed around the edge. Each punch could be brought under a pressure screw that forced it into a copper or tin plate. The plate moved in either a sideways direction, so that the punches were struck by aligning the edge with the preceding letter, or up and down, to provide spacing between the lines. A small wheel concentric to the large wheel turned with it and moved a ruler indicating the position of the punch signs on the large wheel. The desired letter was brought under a simple pointer so that the corresponding punch would automatically move under the screw for pressing into the copperplate.

This stereographic machine apparently had no brilliant future but stayed in the laboratory, since, as seen before, by the beginning of 1786 the same Abbot Rochon was experimenting with stereotyping.

François Hoffmann — In 1792 Hoffmann was attempting to eliminate typographic composition from the stereotyping system. His approach to the new problem was as follows: In a lump of clay serving as a mold he made a small furrow with a small plane for emplacing the line. He then pressed into this furrow, one after the other, the punches required by the text. For this purpose he fixed these punches one after the other on a copper block that let him embed them always in an upright position and at the same depth. A copper rule allowed him to move from line to line, down to the bottom of the page. A mold of a page was thus prepared without requiring typographic composition.

Hoffmann had noticed how very difficult it was to obtain perfect letter forms by pouring hot metal into a mold, so he did the opposite. He struck his mold, using a balance press, in cast metal that had not yet completely solidified. This molded block was of a better quality and came to be the method used by Carez after 1786. To be sure, making the mold by setting the punches one after the other into the lump of clay was a long and delicate job, so an attempt was made to obviate partially this disadvantage.

Logotyping — For this purpose Hoffmann became aware of a method called logotype, in which were combined in a single piece of type several letters found together in common French words, such as *-ais, -ettre, -ment*. This procedure was used in 1775 and a brochure published by the Imprimerie Royale stated that it had been discovered in 1774 by Mme. Barletti de Saint-Paul. Hoffmann reported that in 1778 [probably 1783.—Ed.] Henry Johnson published a book entitled *An Introduction to Logography: Or, the Art of Arranging and Composing for Printing with Entire Words, Their Prefixes and Suffixes, Instead of Single Letters,* in which he enumerates the advantages of the method using, for example, the root *consider,* which in English could be expanded into sixteen different words.

Hoffmann thus made up a case with 370 different types, instead of the approximately 150 that formed the normal case. According to him, this enabled him to save a great deal of time in striking the punches in the lump of clay. On February 16, 1792, he obtained a license to practice the polytype and logotype art for fifteen years, but, curiously enough, on November 24, 1793, he assigned it to Jean-Daniel Saltzmann, by an agreement made at Strasbourg.

The disadvantages of the first stage of stereography — In its first form the stereographic method did little to solve the problem, for it had many defects. Moreover, though logotyping theoretically appeared to reduce the labor involved in composition, handling the case of types was complicated enough to slow down the operation, thereby eliminating the hoped-for saving in time.

Casting was still being done in a block of clay, which was fragile and easily deformable. What is more, consecutively striking the type in the material of the mold caused slight distortions in the imprint of the letter and line that had already been struck.

Lastly, consecutively embedding the punches to form a line did not allow the printer to estimate the exact length of the line, and the problem of justifying lines arose again. An evenness of the typographic line had become the golden rule for the aesthetics of pages, and there could be no question of transgression. To be sure, a line could be traced on the block in advance, making it possible to establish the sizes of the spaces for precise justification. But this took time and anyhow was only approximate.

At this point Herhan discovered the principle for the best solution of the problem and, even better, suggested (much in advance of its time) a way of dealing with a major difficulty that appeared during attempts to maximize the composition speed for pages of daily newspapers, by mechanization.

The second step in stereography: Herhan's work

The Herhan-Didot-Gatteaux partnership led the field of block printing, but though they had pooled their efforts each partner had, as we have seen, registered an individual patent in order to protect his invention. The essential feature of Herhan's patent, which he dated from July 1797, consisted of composing the pages from the matrices normally used to cast the types, instead of from the cast types as in the typographic technique. Needless to say, it was necessary to square off the matrices by type sections in order to assemble them in lines, compose them, and thus form a complete page that could then be cast into a mold. Herhan obtained an "inventor's patent to make, use, and supply, for fifteen years, solid formats suitable for printing by following the methods indicated in the description."

The invention was an important one because it involved a revolutionary reconsideration of all the problems raised by stereotyping and stereography. Since the invention of typography, the sacrosanct principle of the technique had been that the types were movable and thus capable of assembly into lines and pages. Herhan had to abandon this 350-year-old doctrine and instead develop the idea that the matrices rather than the type could be the movable elements. Composition consequently had to be done prior to the final casting, not after, as in classic typography. When we consider the traditions of printers and their habit of always thinking conservatively, Herhan's performance can be appreciated at its true value.

However, it should also be mentioned that somewhere between 1792 and 1801 an engraver of music named Fr. Reinhard used matrices in the form of hollow characters to prepare his molds. It seems that the idea of the type matrix was "in the air." It was undoubtedly used at about the same time in all these closely related techniques, which all belonged to stereography.

Herhan prepared his type matrices by first trying to cast each one around its punch, but this operation was unsuccessful because flaws in the metal spoiled part of the production. While building a machine to correct the misprints in his formats (i.e., the stereotype plates) he discovered a solution to the problem.

The machine for correcting formats consisted of a punch that slid vertically between two copper posts and that could remove a defective letter, leaving an exact gap into which a movable type could be slipped and soldered at the foot of the letter.

Herhan substituted for this punch a letter punch with a stop. Exactly beneath it and held between two jaws he placed a small block of lead alloy (later of copper). Then he struck the punch with light taps to cut its imprint in the cold copper down to the desired depth, and corrected any external deformations from the striking with a file. Herhan proposed this invention to the Institut on August 16, 1800, and exhibited at the 1801 Louvre Exposition a duodecimo Sallust that was excellently composed.

In comparison with other stereographic methods Herhan's system had great advantages, which he described in the preface to a volume he printed in 1803 concerning the works of Bernard, which he printed with his new methods. He remarked that before his invention the stereotype plate was the product of three consecutive castings: the normal one of the printing type, the struck matrix made from this first mold, and the cast printing block, taken from the mold of the matrix. With Herhan's method this repeated casting became unnecessary, since the printing block was produced directly from the assemblage of matrices, the page matrices, as he called them. Thus the original purity of the letter forms remained, as in the classic types, which had likewise been made without a series of molds. When we examine the admirable letters in the *Oeuvres de Bernard*, composed in a very fine six-point typeface, we are struck by their perfection.

There were two disadvantages. In stereotyping it was easy to correct composition errors before striking the matrix, but here it was necessary to mold a whole page of matrices before obtaining a proof to read. Herhan answered this objection by saying that the cost of this first casting was minimal and that, moreover, his founders had got into the habit of rereading the texts right in the recess of the matrix block, which presented the text right side up.

Another major disadvantage, which could not be completely eliminated at this stage of development, lay in the fact that the matrices forming a page did not meet exactly and small burrs of lead formed between the letters in the casting, affecting the quality of the printing. This was important enough to prevent Herhan's new method from receiving the credit it deserved. It seems that at the time Herhan was registering his process an attempt was made to eliminate this defect. Around mid-August 1800, one Poterat presented to the Institut a new method of preparing the stereographic matrix, which presented the letters in relief rather than recessed as in Herhan's method. These relief matrices were assembled in order to cast an intaglio matrix block without burrs, from which the page was cast in relief. This proposal, which required an additional casting operation, was never put into operation.

The chief virtue of Herhan's method, which he was already calling monotyping, was that it bore the seeds of one solution for the difficult problem of mechanical composition that arose toward the end of the nineteenth century. It is noteworthy that the word *monotype* was later adopted by Tolbert Lanston (1844–1913) in 1896 to describe the typecasting machine he invented on Herhan's principle, using page matrices held in a movable chase.

*The adaptation of
stereography to
copperplate: polytyping*

Concurrently with the work on stereotyping and stereography just discussed, experimenters were exploring somewhat unusual methods of making intaglio-engraved plates for copperplate printing. These minor experiments are worth discussing first because they were often made by famous people and secondly because they lead up to the production of *assignats*, the notes issued as currency by the Revolutionary government in France, a story extremely interesting from a technical point of view. It should be kept in mind, though, that none of these sometimes picturesque experiments went beyond the experimental stage.

These experiments began no doubt with Benjamin Franklin. Abbot Rochon, a friend of Franklin, tells us that Franklin used the following method: he wrote on a sheet of paper with gummed ink, sprinkled the writing with fine sand or iron dust, then placed this sheet of paper between two plates, one of soft metal (tin or copper), the other of iron. The ensemble was then placed between the plates of a heavy press, which caused the sanded ink to be encrusted in the soft metal. When the sand was removed the sheet of soft metal bore the recessed imprint of this writing, which could thus be printed like copperplate.

Abbot Rochon remarked that the copies were not satisfactory, and he proposed another method. He wrote with a stylus on a varnished red copperplate, then covered the plate with acid, which ate into the metal along the lines of the writing. After carefully washing the plate he inked in the recessed lines and pulled proofs that reproduced the writing in reverse. He then placed blank sheets of paper between the proofs and with a single throw of the press printed the material right side up, by transfer, on the blank sheets.

No invention was involved in this method, which was simply an adaptation of drypoint etching and an investigation into the possibility of rapidly, though crudely, reproducing writing or drawings. These experiments probably date from about 1780 to 1783.

François Hoffmann, of course, became interested in this new process and made his first experiments early in 1784. He wrote and drew on a thick copper slab with what he called an earth color, a dye obtained from crushed earth. Then he pressed on this slab a plate of soft metal that "took" even the finest lines of the design in recess like an engraving. This plate could then be printed by the copperplate method. On March 13, 1784, a representative of the Académie des Sciences who visited Hoffmann's shop made special note of the speed with which the work was done. Camus, relating this visit, assures us that though the writing was recognizable the ink appeared thick and muddy.

Gengembre began his two different types of experiments in 1789, continuing them until the end of 1791. He wrote and drew on the copperplate with a mixture of an iron dioxide and a ferrous compound in quite pure linseed oil. The liquid having cooled, the plate was heat dried. Gengembre made the mold by placing this plate on metal that was beginning to solidify, then passed the whole through a press to form an intaglio plate.

When these first experiments were finished, he went into partnership with his brother-in-law Herhan. As the writing fluid they used emery powder or Cologne ocher crushed in linseed oil. To make the mold, instead of having the pressure exerted horizontally by the movement of the bed under the copperplate cylinder, they used the vertical pressure of a screw press that operated as in the typographic machine.

The advantage of this polytyping was that it permitted rapid production of circulars and printed periodicals. At the end of 1789 a national bulletin appeared in Paris, giving the latest news from all over the country in a rather direct style. This paper was printed by polytyping as on a small four-page quarter. A very well written and printed specimen, dated October 30, 1789, survives.

Replica castings The second method, invented by Gengembre alone, was intended to duplicate intaglio-engraved plates so as to facilitate printing and multiple use. Gengembre intaglio engraved a drawing on a steel plate, which was then tempered. He next prepared a plate of copper hardened by alloying with one-sixteenth part of platinum. This copperplate, placed on the steel plate, was subjected to the powerful action of the balance press and "took," in relief, the intaglio-engraved lines in the steel. Removing the steel plate, he used the hardened copperplate to strike as many plates of resmelted copper as needed. These plates took in intaglio the relief imprint on the hard copperplate. This method came to have a certain importance because of its use in printing *assignats*.

Copperplate engraving on glass It is said that a Nuremberg artist named Heinrich Schwanhard was engraving glass with acid around the end of the seventeenth century. A periodical called the *Breslau Collection* (January 1725) attributes this activity to one J. G. Wigang of Goldingen in Courland, who used "spirits of niter." This type of engraving was then strictly ornamental. In 1771 Karl Scheele specified that this acid could be extracted from fluorspar, that is, fluoric acid, and Antoine François Fourcroy (1755–1809) affirmed that this acid has the property of dissolving siliceous earth.

To use glass for printing plates, which are subjected to powerful pressure on the sheet of paper, may seem absurd. However, this was done by Puymaurin, in 1787, when he presented to the Académie des Sciences an intaglio-engraved glass slab that could be printed like a copperplate. This was not an isolated experiment, since in 1798 William Nicholson published a letter by a Father Wilson of Glasgow who in 1791 had also had the idea of placing these glass plates under the cylinder in a copperplate press, being careful, of course, to put them perfectly in position by setting the bed in a layer of cement.

At the end of 1799 Boudier the younger suggested to the Institut a strange process intended to make it impossible to counterfeit paper money. On the sheet of glass he placed "fragments of a substance that cannot be dissolved by the elements of which its varnish is formed." He then sprinkled drops of a complex fluid on the plate, certain parts of which fixed themselves to the glass to protect it while others evaporated, leaving portions of glass uncovered. Around the fixed areas marbling then occurred that could be cut by fluoric acid and that acted as background for the designs and letters to be printed. The note could no longer be falsified or reproduced, since the marblings were due to chance and were distributed over the entire surface. One difficulty remained, though, in that since the fluoric acid dissolved only the siliceous part of the glass, the poorly supported areas that remained tended to split during printing and to modify slightly the design of the marblings. But even if absolute uniformity of the notes was not obtained it is certain that Boudier's method could prevent the falsification of existing notes.

This method belongs to the technique of intaglio printing and is consistent with the research of this period. The method of spreading over the plate a complex fluid that remained on the glass in certain areas and evaporated from others is strangely reminiscent of the subtle play of nitric acid on lithographic stone just developed by Aloys Senefelder (1771–1834). Moreover, a heavy metal had been replaced by a fragile material for engraving. This is why François, the secretary of the Institut, wrote emphatically in connection with Boudier's invention that "people spoke of engraving in bronze to give the idea of eternal engraving. We can now speak of engraving on glass in the same sense. To make use in this way of the most fragile material for the most durable monuments is a fortunate originality of our century."

The connection with lithographic methods is further illustrated by the process introduced by Poitevin in 1855, which, making use of the first discoveries in photography, used light-sensitive coatings. These discoveries had given birth to a technique similarly based on using a photographically exposed grained glass block. This method is known by the names *phototyping* and *albertyping*.

Assignats The printing of *assignats*, the notes used as currency under the Revolutionary government, began in 1791. The engraving of punches and striking of matrices were begun on November 25, 1790, and the first types were given to the printer Pierre Didot on December 12. The printing of a large number of *assignats* was envisaged from the beginning. A report by a committee on *assignats*, presented to the National Assembly on March 31, 1791, by Leclerc, a Parisian deputy, describes the process.

The paper was ordered from Mme. Lagarde, a partner of Reveillon, at Courtalin. By March 19, 1791, 3,645 reams and 212 sheets had been manufactured, a quantity that could produce almost five million *assignats*, putting into circulation a total sum of 800 million *livres*, secured by public lands.

Of course, the big problem was to make counterfeiting impossible, so it was decided to include a likeness of the king, engraved in copperplate. The remainder of the design was prepared typographically. Because the size of the printing prohibited doing the work with a single plate, the famous engraver Augustin de Saint-Aubin (1737–1807) was therefore asked to prepare 300 copperplates bearing a medallion of the king. Anisson and then Didot were to prepare a similar number of formats bearing the typographic text.

The *assignats* were soon being counterfeited. It was difficult to distinguish the counterfeits, since Saint-Aubin's 300 engraved plates had been individually prepared and were thus not perfectly identical. Gengembre now suggested giving printers as many intaglio-engraved plates as they wanted, declaring that "by a special chemico-mechanical method" these plates would be exactly similar to the initial plate supplied by the engraver. Gengembre was here applying the process he was just then developing, which we have discussed. His proposal was not accepted and *assignats* continued to be counterfeited.

However, to protect their production and surround it with every guarantee the National Convention set up a committee of four persons, by a law of March 1, 1793. Citizen Guillot was named Director of Artists; he was to coordinate the experiments being made by a large number of technicians.

The engraver Gatteaux had already succeeded in engraving steel punches that bore large designs in relief, so this technique was used to supply the decoration to the *assignat* plates.

It was no longer possible to use simultaneously the two major printing techniques to make *assignats*. It was necessary to choose either the copperplate technique favored by Gengembre or return to the relief method of which Hoffmann had been a past master a short time earlier. Director Guillot decided to put both techniques into use, but separately.

Copperplate It was thus perceived that Gengembre's latest discovery was not to be scorned. The engraver Fiezinger experimented along the same lines and it became possible to print 25-franc *assignats*. The original was intaglio engraved. Relief plates ("mother punches") were then made, from which as many plates ("daughter plates") as desired could be made, in intaglio like the original and all exactly alike.

Herhan, who participated in these experiments, was ordered to polytype in copperplate by this method a major portion of the 400-*livre* and 50-*livre assignats*, the production of which had been ordered on November 21 and December 14, 1792. Needless to say, for such a large quantity it was necessary to duplicate the punches and plates, which quickly wore out, and in March-April 1794 Guillot recorded that Herhan struck 5,657 mother punches and cast 9,182 daughter plates for the *assignats* he had been assigned to make.

Relief castings At the same time an attempt was made to cast printing plates in relief. But to make the casting it was necessary to avoid using separate elements. A mechanic named Grassal suggested combining all the parts of the *assignat* in a single matrix, as Guillot noted, and this method was put to use on another block of 400- and 50-*livres assignats*.

Grassal was also entrusted with building the casting machine. On a small table a ram formed of a heavy piece of wood slid between two wooden vertical posts. To it was attached the matrix mounted in a box, which thus fell heavily on a mass of hot metal in a plastic state and which itself was held in a trough of strong paper. The formats, approximately 6 mm. thick, thus came out of the casting machine and were then soldered to a lead base that brought them to the exact type height.

In order to prevent unauthorized removal of a format, Guillot ordered another mechanic, one Augé, to attach to the machine a mechanical counter that through a complex system transmitted the number of blows struck by the ram during the day to a dial in the director's office.

These various methods were also employed to produce the *mandats territoriaux* (notes put into circulation in 1795/96 to replace *assignats)*, with which Guillot's successor Reth (also known as de Servière) was entrusted.

After the abolition of *assignats* and *mandats territoriaux*, the major portion of the printing material was destroyed, but several machines were taken to the Conservatoire national des Arts et Métiers and to the Imprimerie de la République.

THE PRINTING OF MUSIC

Starting in the seventeenth century some engravers and founders began experiments in techniques to improve on the copperplate method of printing music. They followed the two routes already well known, namely overprinting and one-stage printing. For the latter the type was made with both the stave and the note.

In France the Gandos concentrated on developing the overprinting method. To ensure perfect correspondence between the two printings they were obliged to make them consecutively, without removing the sheet of paper from the tympan; that is, they used the same methods already described by Fertel.

B. C. Breitkopf in Leipzig used the single-stage method. To reduce the large number of signs required when the five stave lines and corresponding notes were set on a single type Breitkopf cast five small types, with or without a note, which matched up with each other to form the five lines of the stave. Rosart and Izaak Enschedé used the same method. Fournier the younger, after practicing overprinting, adopted Breitkopf's method, simplifying it slightly.

In order to avoid difficult copperplate work music engravers adopted plates of tin, which were printed in the same way. These were easier to engrave, but they wore out so rapidly in printing that it was difficult to print as many as 800 or 900 copies.

Needless to say, stereography, which was quite in fashion at the time, was also used. In 1801 Dupeyrat described his methods. First the stave lines were engraved in the matrix plate with a lathe. The notes were then struck by steel punches and the whole cast, using the ram, as in Didot's method. Between 1792 and 1801 Fr. Reinhard, the engraver mentioned earlier, developed a method that bore a striking resemblance to Herhan's. He prepared the matrix plate with hollow characters, or matrices, for the notes and texts. Next in two stages he printed first the staves, then the notes and texts, changing the plates without removing the sheet from the tympan.

Pyrostereography Mention should be made of a curious method associated with the technique of relief printing, which was used especially to print music. We have seen that research on molds dominated the history of stereotyping. Around 1852 the procedure used for printing fabrics was applied. On a well-planed block of lindenwood the staves were engraved in intaglio and the block was placed in a burning machine equipped with various steel punches representing the signs, clefs, and notes needed. The machine heated the punches and drove them automatically into the block of wood, gradually to form in it the stereographic matrix that was the basis for the relief block used in the printing.

CHAPTER 3

THE EVOLUTION OF MECHANIZED PRINTING TECHNIQUES

T HE SHORT PERIOD OF hardly half a century, during which major black-line wood engraving, xylography, and metallography culminated in the invention of typography, was followed by a long period of four centuries that showed only slow progress of the craft in the hands of artisans.

Then suddenly all the friends of typography began to look for new methods of graphic expression and busied themselves with methods that appeared to have no particular importance. That they presented stereotyping as the greatest invention in the graphic arts since the birth of typography merely emphasizes that during those four centuries no major invention occurred.

It is clear that the object of mechanics in the eighteenth century was to improve techniques so as to make the work of compositors and pressmen easier and faster. However, it is worth noting in passing that the two discoveries that came to be the basis of rapid mechanization in composing and printing machines, namely Herhan's movable matrix and Abbot Haüy's impression cylinder, went practically unnoticed at the time of their appearance.

The activities of technicians and experimenters of all kinds around the beginning of the nineteenth century were an accurate forecast of the considerable changes that were to appear and completely transform existing practices. The great movement toward machine, the principle of which was contained in the profoundly scientist eighteenth century, was beginning to trouble intellectuals, but it would seem that the technicians were disinclined to go outside the limits of their crafts. It was left to a large number of inquisitive and impatient experimenters to supply the necessary impetus for extraordinary changes in a large number of processes.

Without going too deeply into the story of the explosive age of mechanization, we shall try to show how the way was paved for the Industrial Revolution by minor experiments that led to those major inventions that were to determine its direction.

Prior to this period there were two kinds of printing. One was essentially dominated by book production, but it involved also an engraving technique: wood engraving in relief. The other, reserved for illustration, was the copperplate method, or intaglio printing.

With the beginning of the nineteenth century there appeared a third method of printing, also reserved for engraving, but using neither intaglio nor relief, which we shall thus call flat-surface printing.

This general definition of printing methods will serve to introduce the study of premechanical evolution.

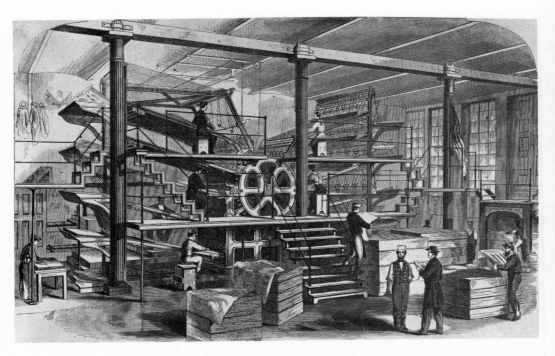

Plate 84. The press room of the New York *Tribune.* Wood engraving from *F. Leslie's Illustrated News,* July 20, 1861. Library of Congress

RELIEF PRINTING

Black-line engraving on end-grain wood
During the eighteenth century the techniques of engraving changed little. The immense success of copperplate and the elegance of the process, the enthusiasm of the public for pictures engraved in this way, and the use of acid by the great masters of painting to express themselves directly, all had relegated wood engraving to "the good old days" and had diverted metal engravers from developing their art. Thus, just as xylography had been abandoned earlier in favor of typography, xyloengraving had given in to the quality of copperplate work, while no one thought that wood could be worked except in the direction of the grain.

But xyloengraving had not spoken its last word. Its practitioners began engraving hard, close-grained woods, like boxwood or pear, perpendicular to the grain. This new technique resulted in an extremely delicate picture quite comparable with copperplate. As a result the wood engraver abandoned the tools used on long-grain wood and adopted the burin.

J.-B. Papillon, who during the eighteenth century attempted to revive the craft of engraving on long-grain wood, speaks with a certain disdain of a man named Foy of Lyon, an engraver for the taxing authorities and the government playing card monopoly, who around 1760 engraved with the burin on end-grain wood, claiming to work quite rapidly by this method. Papillon objected violently to this "technical heresy," which nevertheless became important during part of the nineteenth century.

Around 1771, as the result of a contest sponsored by the Society of Arts in London, Thomas Bewick (1753–1828) similarly began to engrave on end-grain wood (Figure 12). Charles Thompson (1791–1843), a pupil of his, set up a school for engravers in Paris, and thanks to him the technique of end-grain wood engraving had some success in France.

The eighteenth century had already enriched the printed page with numerous vignettes that contributed a note of gaiety to the severity of earlier books. In this period vignettes were engraved in wood and polytyped in copper. At the beginning of the nineteenth century, however, the vogue for vignettes on end-cut wood became irresistible. Joseph-Gaspard Gillé declared in 1808 that French printing establishments had a stock of 80,000 varied motifs, and Firmin Didot, Thompson, Durouchail, Pasteur, Gallay, the General Foundry, Porret, and Lacoste published major collections of vignettes and culs-de-lampe.

FIG. 12.   Proof of an end-grain wood engraving by Bewick, who followed this technique in 1771.

Artists themselves now took over this technique and increased their contributions to numerous small magazines, illustrated newspapers, and a variety of books. The romantic woodcut had been born and with it a period enabling a large number of nineteenth-century artists to express themselves with brilliance and almost complete freedom, either by this technique or by lithography.

Black-line engraving on stone

Black-line engraving on stone, as well as on metal, is simply an adaptation of relief engraving on wood. A brief mention will suffice. In 1810 Duplat took out a patent for a method of relief engraving on stone, described as follows: After being heated the stone was coated with a varnish on which the design was traced. The white portions were then removed with the point. The stone was then attacked by an acid, thereby creating a low relief that was increased by cutting with a burin along the traced lines. Castings for printing were then taken from the engraved stones. Numerous book illustrations were made by this method. The first, in 1811, decorated a two-volume La Fontaine, whereas in 1812 others were made for Royaumont's *History of the Old and New Testaments* spoken of in connection with the typographical cylinder press.

In 1831 Louis Tissier of Lyon experimented with replacing the large plates for wallpaper with stones relief engraved by chemical substances. He met with hostility from manufacturers and, changing his tactics, turned to making small stone engraved pictures for book illustration. In 1839 he published the first proofs of typographic vignettes made in this way. In 1841 he established in Paris a shop for typographic engraving on stone, and that August he published an *Album tissiérographique* presenting these vignettes, which had been engraved on the Bavarian stone Senefelder had used for his first lithographs. Tissier engraved these stones by strictly chemical methods, avoiding all work with the burin. At the Exposition of 1844 he exhibited his process under the name *tissiérographie,* while Auguste Dupont of Périgueux showed similar engravings under the name *clichés-pierre* (stone castings).

All these experiments were destined to be only short-lived, the time had arrived for major inventions. On the one hand classic lithography was beginning to evolve, and on the other photography was soon to make possible an ease of tracing that would outmode any evolution of manual methods, at least for rapid multiplication of graphic material.

Chemical engraving (photozincography)   One cannot overemphasize the beneficial effects on the evolution of graphic arts of both the etching method, which gave engraving a chemical agent capable of replacing the work of the craftsman, and the discovery of photography by Niepce.

The history of engraving methods after the end of the seventeenth century is pervaded by the influence of this chemical agent. Abbot Rochon had already used it to prepare his copperplates, it had been the starting point for Senefelder in his discovery of lithography, and Duplat and Tissier had used it to engrave their black-line stones. In 1845 Loire, Michelet, and Quinet carried out experiments with chemical engraving that on March 21, 1850, bore fruit in a patent taken out by Firmin Gillot for a method called *panéiconographie,* soon called *gillotage* (zincography). Gillot, as a lithographer, proposed to apply the technique of lithographic tracing to any kind of metal or stone by tracing the picture to be reproduced, then to raise it in relief by an acid until it was high enough to print typographically with the text. The subsequent intervention of photography was to permit automatic tracing and lead to the modern technique of photogravure.

Firmin Gillot died young, but his son Charles continued his work, opening in 1876 in the rue Madame in Paris the first photogravure establishment to operate in France. He then attempted to add the halftone to the new method. In 1877 he used a waffled card that was treated by scraping, the scratch board, which made it possible to obtain an entire series of halftone shadings.

Thus began the development of the halftone process, which with a dotted screen secured all the values of photography.

Typometry   Somewhat apart from this evolution toward photo-engraving we find a method that made it possible to compose and print vignettes and patterns, geographical maps, geometric drawings, and other tracings of the same type by assembling movable type. Maps had been printed since the fifteenth century, but they were then black-line engraved on wood or intaglio engraved in metal.

The first experiments in typometry were carried out between 1770 and 1775 in Basel by Wilhelm Haas, whom we have already met in connection with the development of the classic press, and in Leipzig by J. G. Breitkopf, who also printed music. The former printed a map of the Canton of Basel, the latter a map of the environs of Leipzig. The results were not convincing, nor were those achieved by Firmin Didot between 1818 and 1830.

In 1839 a map of the Austrian Empire was printed in Vienna by Raffelsberger, using typographic equipment he had had specially prepared. Carrying this technique to its ultimate conclusion he printed these maps in several colors, using a separate plate for each tone. In 1840 he established a large typometric printing establishment in Vienna that was extremely successful.

In 1844 E. Duverger of Paris exhibited at the Universal Exposition geographic maps made with small typographical copper fillets embedded in a lead slab, the small cast pieces bearing the names of the countries and cities being soldered to the lead plate. The whole plate could easily be passed under the typographic press.

Such a method of obtaining a picture by assembling fillets, vignettes, and typographic letters was not new. In the eighteenth century very curious pictures representing façades of temples, arches of triumph, and other motifs were printed by this method (Figure 13). Enthusiasm for these pictures grew in the nineteenth century, and the industrial expositions in Paris following that of 1844 offered for visitors' attention many complex, and often monumental works of assemblage that had no particular use or application but were nevertheless in a sense masterpieces (a carry-over of the old craft-guild practice) of certain typographical compositors. At the Universal Exposition of 1889 a yard-wide typographical construction was exhibited representing the façade of the Parthenon.

FIG. 13.   Eighteenth-century vignette composition.

Electrotyping   In 1837 Thomas Spencer in England and Moritz Jacobi (1801–1874) in Russia, working independently, discovered the capability of an electric current from the voltaic pile to fix particles of copper detached by the current's action into the grooves of a copperplate coated with varnish and prepared by etching. The accumulation of these particles produced a very definite relief on the copperplate, which could be printed typographically.

In 1838 this method became known in both England and Russia and was used to reproduce intaglio- or relief-engraved plates. A relief or intaglio copy, depending on the individual case, was made by wax molding, which was then galvanized, care being taken to prevent the electrolytic plate from adhering to the relief or intaglio copy. This was achieved by various methods, but in particular by a preliminary application of silver iodide. The electrolytic plate was then detached, reproducing perfectly the initial plate in relief or intaglio. This method attracted the attention of master printers, and in 1848 the Firmin-Didot establishment used it to print 100-franc notes, which had to be printed quickly.

This method was also used to obtain castings of typographic pages, which constituted another form of stereotyping. These pages were molded with wax or lead and were electrolyzed with copper sulfate to obtain a copper shell .2 or .3 mm. thick. This shell was pulled away from the mold if it was of lead or was detached by heating if it was of wax. All that was then needed was to reinforce this thin shell by pouring an alloy of lead and antimony over the back. The base thus obtained could be attached to a block of metal or wood to obtain the proper type height.

Mechanical composition and casting machines   It is of interest to examine the experiments carried out in the book printing trade to liberate printing from the ancestral methods of hand composition. At the beginning of the nineteenth century, when the number of periodicals was growing, it became necessary to find a mechanical method for rapid composition. We have seen that during the last quarter of the eighteenth century there were attempts at logotyping. By grouping several letters on a single piece of type it was hoped to save handling time, but the complication, cumbersomeness, and weight of a composing frame that could contain up to 400 boxes of type more than offset the time saved in handling the individual types. It was therefore abandoned.

The scene of major inventions now tended to shift to the United States, where mechanization was beginning to develop on a large scale, while Europe tended to retain manual practices. The first experiments with mechanical composition were made on the types themselves, by William Church of Boston in 1822. His mechanical composers grouped the types, sorted by characters in magazines, and upon pressure from a keyboard released them in the desired order for assembly in lines. The justification was then done by hand. At the same time Church used a character casting machine that supplied the magazines of his composing machines.

From that moment on, models proliferated despite inventors' numerous failures. The result of these experiments was that the use of a keyboard became indispensable. The type still had to be returned by hand to the case after use. To save this time machines for redistributing the type into the cases were invented and constantly modified until a definitive solution was found. At the 1855 Exposition Adrien Delcambre of Paris exhibited one of his composing machines, which he called a pianotype compositor, and its complement, the mechanical distributor, both of which could be operated by women (Figure 14).

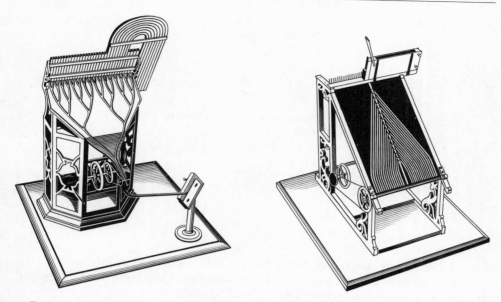

FIG. 14. *Left:* The pianotype compositor; *Right:* Delcambre's distributing machine.

These composing machines could not, however, be truly effective as long as the types themselves were being used to feed them. Sooner or later it would be necessary to adopt Herhan's system and to replace printing types with matrices assembled mechanically so that composition could be done before casting. The composing machines would then become casting machines as well and eliminate distributing machines.

In 1845 appeared a name well known in another field, but surprising to find in the present context. The poet Gérard de Nerval (1808–1855) on January 6 registered at the Institut National de la Propriété Industrielle a patent application for a "machine for printing by means of movable alphabetic rows, called a stereograph."

This was actually a machine for composing and casting, an ancestor of the linotype and monotype. It was supposed to operate by superimposed movable discs each holding around its edge the matrices of all the graphic signs. By turning the individual discs the letters or signs of the text were brought into a single line and cast in lead alloy in relief.

Nerval never built his projected machine, but forty years before technicians concerned themselves with the problem, he had a vision of the path they should take to solve the problem of mechanical composition. All modern composing machines, whether used for block lines or individual types, were to be derived from the principle of movable matrices suggested by Herhan (Figure 15). In order of appearance these were the Mergenthaler linotype (1886), the Rogers typograph (1888), Scudder's monoline (1892), and Lanston's monograph (1896), which adopted even the name of Herhan's method.

To finally replace typographic printing another, equally remarkable, inven-

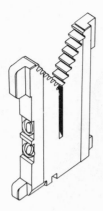

FIG. 15. Linotype matrix-type, 1886. Its principle is derived from Herhan's stereography.

tion was needed: photography. More than a century ago photography invaded the graphics system and transformed its bases; numerous methods were developed that have virtually buried pure typography. Today it is the centuries-old typefaces that we wish to eliminate. Purely photographic composing machines are beginning to appear, among them lumitypes. They assemble the letters and photograph them in succession, justifying them on film, which are then used to make plates or impression cylinders for printing in offset or photogravure.

INTAGLIO PRINTING

When eighteenth-century copperplate printers began to print on fabrics with the cylinder press they had started on the way to mechanization. But since engravers were essentially artists, or at least craftsmen with the burin, the point, and acid, the customary hand methods survived.

The great Senefelder, to whose importance we shall return, became interested first in copper engraving and experimented by inscribing his patterns on the impression cylinder of the textile printers with acid. But when he invented lithography, artists enthusiastically adopted the new method of graphic expression and abandoned the copperplate. The latter's evolution suffered and technicians relaxed their efforts toward mechanizing their cylinder presses. They did develop the so-called doctor, the flexible blade that caused excess ink on the impression cylinder to fall back automatically into the inkpot, but it was as late as 1877 before Guy built a rapid cylinder press capable of printing 1,000 copies an hour.

Engraving machines:
the Collas method

The continuing pressure of new needs stimulated the search for a means to satisfy them. Abbot Rochon, always the pioneer, had tried to supply the stereographic technique with an engraving machine, but aside from the fact that it was unsuccessful, it was limited to the reproduction of texts. At the beginning of the nineteenth century one of the most important needs was to transfer to paper the exact, and therefore mechanical, image of certain objects. The problem was later solved by photography, but before its appearance a large number of machines were designed or built for this purpose.

For a long time efforts had been made to shorten the labor of reproducing material by hand onto plates, by using a device that appears to have derived from the pantograph. This device, invented in 1611 by Christopher Schreiner, made it possible to reproduce material on a smaller or larger scale or to its exact dimensions.

In any case, the first engraving machine, built by Conte in 1803, was derived from the parallel ruler and obtained engraving effects by means of these parallel lines. Moreover, the guilloching lathe had been used for almost two centuries to decorate the surfaces of certain jewels and the covers of snuffboxes.

The guilloching lathe was now used by Achille Collas for his "Collas method," which is in fact mechanical etching. This method, introduced in 1816, was intended to reproduce mechanically low-relief objects such as coins and medals. The first book to contain such plates, *Trésor de numismatique et de glyptique (Treasury of Numismatics and Glyptics)*, appeared in Paris in 1836 with forty remarkable illustrations.

The engraving device had a long arm jointed like the pantograph. One end of this arm "examined" the entire surface of the object to be reproduced by means of a blunt point that followed all the curves of the original by very close and perfectly even parallel lines. At the other end of the arm was a cutting point that traced on the surface of a varnished copperplate lines corresponding to those the first point was following on the original. But unlike the latter these lines were not parallel and even; they undulated, following the relief of the original, and so copied exactly the contours of the object to be reproduced on the flat surface of the copperplate. The plate thus prepared was then subjected to the action of acid as in the etching technique.

Photogravure and photography
The search for exact reproduction now took a still more effective direction. At Chalon-sur-Saône Joseph-Nicéphore Niepce (1765–1833) tried after several experiments with lithography to pull proofs on tin plates with lithographic crayons. His experiments then led him to reproduce engravings mechanically by a completely new method.

The process was as follows: Niepce varnished the verso of a print to make it transparent and placed it face down on a tin plate varnished with bitumen. The black areas of the engraving blocked the light rays; the transparent portions permitted them to pass. The rays bleached the layer of bitumen, which made it possible to obtain an exact copy of the plate. The plate was then washed in oil of lavender so that the layer of bitumen not affected by the light—the black areas of the image—was washed away, exposing the picture. All that remained was to plunge the plate into an acid, as in the etching technique.

In 1827 Niepce made five engravings by this method, but their results were not satisfactory. He then tried to secure an exact "copy of nature," using this method, in William H. Wollaston's camera obscura. For this purpose he placed a bitumen plate in this darkroom to collect on the sensitive plate the light rays coming through the lens of the instrument. In this way a design could be obtained in which the light areas were protected by bitumen and the shadows were represented by the bare areas of the metal.

Louis Mandé Daguerre (1789–1851) had done considerable study on the effects of light with the diorama, which he invented, and he too had undertaken to fix images in a darkroom. On December 14, 1829, he signed a partnership agreement with Niepce. Daguerre replaced Niepce's bitumen with lavender resin, which was more sensitive to light, but the savings in time was minimal. Chance then led the two inventors to use iodine on a silver plate, the first step toward the final solution of the problem, which Daguerre provided five years after the death of Niepce, in 1838.

Charles Nègre perfected the method by exposing a coating of bitumen through the photographic plate. He exhibited his results at the expositions of 1855 and 1867.

Thus out of research engraving the extraordinary invention of photography was born, an invention vaguely anticipated by all the technicians of the time and one that was to change the world, especially the graphic arts.

Meanwhile, the technicians pursued these methods in their search for new methods of engraving. Around 1842 A. Fizeau succeeded in using Daguerre plates to make copperplates from the photographic image with the use of chemicals, so he may be regarded as having paved the way for the photomechanical process. This complicated method was taken up by numerous investigators, notably Beuvière, Charles Chevalier, Dr. Heller of Vienna, and especially Niepce's cousin of the same surname, from Saint-Victor, who spent a fortune on everything connected with engraving, both relief and intaglio. These experiments were often combined with electrotyping, which made it possible to reinforce the engraving plate.

From these experiments, and those on chemical engraving, which were converging toward the same goal, were born all the photoengraving methods needed to duplicate mechanically exact images of objects that (especially in the commercial sense) were to be brought to consumers' attention.

Fox Talbot, in 1852, made use of the light sensitivity of a coating of gelatin glue combined with potassium bichromate spread on a metal plate. He placed a piece of gauze on the plate, set an object on top of that, then exposed the plate to light. Its development in the sun removed the glue from the unexposed areas and the object appeared under a grid pattern produced by the gauze. After an acid bath a picture could be obtained by printing. In 1859 he made use of fine resin powder. Thus began photogravure, which was developed around 1875 by the Viennese painter Karl Klietsch.

Electroplate facsimiles   At this time all attempts at reproduction, from Collas's to Fizeau's, through Niepce's experiments and the daguerreotype, had one essential aim: to reproduce exactly objects or nature. This was the direction of the mechanical development itself, which was moving toward the discovery of a method of automatic and exact reproduction that would soon be provided by photomechanical methods.

For a long time people tried to make the printing plate that was to duplicate them from the objects themselves (if they were flat and lent themselves well to this process). In the sixteenth century and throughout the seventeenth, mechanical copying had been employed to fix images directly on a sheet of paper, of plants coated with a mixture of verdigris ink and pulverized charcoal. In the eighteenth century these methods were developed and modernized. Then, with the appearance of new printing methods in the late eighteenth and early nineteenth centuries these methods were abandoned until, upon seeing experiments made in London, Aloys Auer in Vienna took up the method, improved upon it by adding electroplating, and named it *Naturselbstdruckes* (natural printing).

This technique consisted of using any inanimate material—plant, flower, insect, fabric, lace, cloth—which, as in the Franklin and Rochon methods for sanded writing, was pressed between two plates, one of copper or steel, the other of lead, securing on the lead plate an intaglio impression that could be printed. To reinforce this engraved plate, which would not have withstood the pressure of printing, it was electrolytically galvanized by exposing it to a voltaic current.

On June 28, 1852, Auer took out a patent at the Austrian ministry of commerce to ensure his monopoly of this method of natural printing. In 1854 he published *Die Entdeckung des Naturselbstdruckes; oder, die Erfindung von ganzen Herbarien (The Discovery of Natural Printing; or, the Invention of Complete Herbaria)*, which offered numerous examples of this "natural" printing expressed in the exact colors of the objects depicted.

FLAT-SURFACE PRINTING

Aloys Senefelder soon entered into legend. This extraordinary man with a universal curiosity was born in 1771 in Prague, which he eventually left for Munich. He began as a dramatist and actor but later became a writer, having occasion to frequent printers' establishments in connection with the production of his works. Being curious about their methods, he first made experiments in stereography, so popular in that period. Then, looking for a way to print quickly and cheaply, he repeated the writing experiments of Abbot Rochon and, to obtain like him etched impressions on copper, forced himself to write his texts backward on the plate to eliminate transferring. Again for reasons of economy he soon replaced his copperplates with flat stones he collected on the banks of the Isar and polished. In July 1796 he discovered by an unforeseen conjunction of circumstances that by writing with his chemical ink on one of these stones, which consisted almost exclusively of calcium carbonate, the text resisted application of the acid, which in contrast ate away all the rest of the stone and made those parts capable of retaining moisture and thus of rejecting the ink, which remained only on the written areas.

Lithography A completely new technique had suddenly appeared that made it possible in a strange way to obtain a black-and-white impression of images directly from a smooth surface that did not have to be engraved in black-line or intaglio. This method, as strange as it was unexpected, could only win adherence and arouse enthusiasm, which is exactly what happened.

This process worked as follows: using an ink composed of tallow, soap, resin, and other bases, which had the property of adhering to stone, Senefelder drew a picture on a stone and thus prepared a solid printing base. Attacking the stone by a dilute solution of gum arabic and nitric acid he increased the strength of the image, giving it a slight relief due to the action of the acid on the uncovered areas. The pores in the open area could moreover be saturated with water by keeping them in contact with a damp surface. Thus the ink from the roller adhered only to the image and was repelled elsewhere, provided they were kept constantly in contact with rollers of damp flannel throughout the printing.

In France, Pierre-Frédéric André, the first to become interested in this method, secured on February 11, 1802, an import license for a new method of engraving and printing. In 1816 Count Charles de Lasteyrie and G. Engelmann opened lithographic shops in Paris, in the rue de Four-Saint-Germain and the rue Cassette, respectively.

The appearance of the process was opportune. The extreme delicacy of the medium facilitated the illustrator's work. There was in effect no further need for engraving or for the skill of the human hand working with etching needle or various burins. Acid had already permitted the easier expression or translation of a plastic work by "drawing" with the point, but except in the hands of a genius the results were often crude when dealing with a resistant material. The new technique restored to the hand all its flexibility and former brilliance. Thus, by a novel detour, the craft of copyist and draftsman regained the importance it had had in the Middle Ages, in the days when master writers and illuminators dominated the entire field of the image and the book.

The artist was required, though, to draw in reverse on the lithographic stone, and for texts this was very difficult. Therefore, in 1817 Senefelder extended his process by introducing a transfer stage that made it possible to draw normally on a sheet of paper with a chemical ink that was transferred to the stone.

Around 1836 Auguste Dupont, a printer at Périgueux, mentioned earlier in connection with black-line engraving on stone, accidentally discovered near Châteauroux a quarry with stone quite similar in texture to the Bavarian stone used by Senefelder. Furthermore, in 1839 he perfected a model of lithographic transfer that made it possible to transfer directly onto the stone old prints, which could thus be reproduced in a great number of examples. Using this process he published some important volumes.

The new art became fashionable and was taken up by society people like Mme. Tallien (née Theresa Cabarrus), the duchess of Berry, and the princes of Orléans, following the example of Ingres and Prud'hon.

The process was developed at the same time as that of end-grain wood engraving. The illustrators' palette now became extremely broad and perfectly adapted to the delicacy and flexibility demanded by the current fashion. This fashion, coming after the triumphant popular revolutions, encouraged ironic and merciless criticism. It excited the vindictive imaginations of both genre painters and caricaturists, who in certain satirical papers, like *La Caricature* and especially *Le Charivari,* delighted an ever-growing public. The most well known of these were Monnier, Boilly, Decamps, Grandville, Gavarni, Daumier.

However, with the Second Empire the ferocious laughter of the humorist, muzzled by censorship, died out, and with it the great vogue of lithography as an expression of thought. A new era was about to be born.

Lithography had several disadvantages. The stone was heavy, difficult to handle, fragile, costly, and, in the case of large sizes, slowed up the printing. Senefelder had already studied the problem and observed that under certain conditions metals were also capable of retaining the oil-based ink in confined areas. In 1823, after several experiments, he exhibited in Paris prototype presses that used tin plates. In 1822 Josef Trentsenky of Vienna obtained a license to replace the stone with a lead plate. In the same period one Knecht, Senefelder's nephew and partner, tried to establish the principle of this zincography.

It has already been noted that in France the great builder Marinoni invented in 1868 and built a press, the Diligente, which printed with a sheet of zinc that had first been grained and possessed all the qualities of porous stone.

COLOR ENGRAVING

It was natural that typographical printers attempted from the very beginning to print books in more than one color, to resemble as far as possible the original. Some of their achievements over the centuries have been noted above.

In the field of the print, various artists (particularly Lastmann, Schenk, and Taylor) attempted during the seventeenth century to make color proofs from etchings. They used a single engraved plate on which they applied their colors and which they printed with a single throw of the press. This is often called the dabber method.

Four-color copperplate printing   But a much more interesting process, the basis for a major machine industry, appeared during the second quarter of the eighteenth century. A Frankfurt painter named Jacques Christophe Le Blon was the first to use the mezzotint engraving method to reproduce in color paintings by the masters. He was granted a patent in England in 1719 and, having exploited the process in London after 1720, began the practice in Paris in 1735.

Le Blon prepared three, or rather four, mezzotint plates in metal, using the rocker, thus creating on the plates a close grid that served as a support for the combination of colors. He drew the design on each plate, being careful to match one plate exactly to the other. Then he treated them, choosing at each stage the significant primary colors (blue, yellow, red), the overprinting of which would reproduce the color shades in the original work. He also prepared in the same manner a gray that outlined the shapes and intensified the shadows. The plates were matched to each other in the printing, thus reproducing the original in all its colors. If certain details were not precise, the corresponding plates were retouched. Transparent colors were of course used. Around 1730 Le Blon brought out in English a book entitled *Il Coloretto or the Harmony of Colouring,* which described his method. A French translation (*Art d'imprimer les tableaux*) appeared in 1756. The father-and-sons establishment of Gautier Dagoty in Dijon took over the license from Le Blon and continued his practice.

The process gave a general tonality that was dark and dull, and the coloring varied somewhat from one print to another, but for the period the result was a remarkable advance. Using this method the Dagotys published highly valued works, notably (starting in 1751) a series of volumes entitled *Observations sur l'histoire naturelle, sur la physique et sur la peinture* (*Remarks on Natural History, Physics, and Painting*), decorated with remarkable four-color illustrations.

In the following century this process became a major factor in the radical transformation of the techniques of color printing. After the very interesting experiments of Ducos du Hauron, protected by a patent in 1868, photography began to select the colors of an original through a screen that behaved like the grid prepared by the rocker in mezzotint engraving. In this way the four zinc plates of contemporary four-color printing could be prepared.

English experiments with color printing *The Congreve method.* Around 1830, in England, printers began to use a two-color process called the Congreve method, after the printer who reinvented it after having studied the large capital letters of the psalter printed by Peter Schoeffer in 1457.

This process employed two wooden or metal black-line engraved plates separately inked, each in one color, then carefully matched before being printed with a single throw of the press. The work was then completed by a kind of embossing already used by sixteenth-century binders for decorating book covers in leather or parchment.

Baxterotyping. In 1837 George Baxter in England used a complex method of engraving on steel complemented by wood engravings to do color printing. In 1850 he took out a patent in France to develop the process.

RELIEF PRINTING (EMBOSSING)

Embossing was done by a wooden or metal plate on which letters, decorations, and drawings had been intaglio engraved, being firmly attached to the bed of the press. The tympan of the press was then coated with wax so that the first throw of the bar formed in the wax a mold of the ornaments or letters. This mold was then covered with a light paper. The flat surface of the plate was now inked, and with a throw of the press the sheet of paper was caught between the plate and its mold, which created the desired embossing. The subjects thus appeared in relief and in white on the dark ground of the impression.

This method was employed for the first time in England, but in 1834 the Bauerkeller brothers of Karlsruhe, Germany, applied it to typography. After settling in Paris, where they set up a shop with Gutsch for color embossing, the name being derived from the fact that the relief and recessed areas desired were obtained by pressure. The process made it possible to print maps in various colors and in relief. The Bauerkeller brothers were the first to print such maps, notably a map of Paris of 1846, under the name *geomontography.*

The process was immediately adopted for teaching the blind. Laas d'Aguen, a supervisor at the Institut des Jeunes Aveugles (Institute for Blind Youth) had geographic maps made in this way that his pupils could easily finger read. To make these maps perfectly stable and strong he complemented the embossing techniques as follows: the metal baseplate having been engraved and the mold made of wax or plaster, the sheet of paper (which had been printed beforehand) was embossed as described. Then, without removing the sheet from the platen, other blank sheets were added, embossing them successively. This process "soldered" the sheets together and thus formed a more or less rigid cardboard.

CONCLUSION

What conclusion can be drawn from this rapid examination of the evolution of printing techniques from the origins of printing to the dawn of the mechanical revolution?

It was said earlier that during the eighteenth century graphic techniques seemed to crystallize around crafts, without developing in them the elements of a viable evolution. This leads to an observation that to be sure is not peculiar to graphic techniques but is perhaps more obvious here than in other crafts. In general, the major inventions were the achievements not of craftsmen themselves but of outsiders curious about the secrets of the profession. This should not astonish us, for the inventor is a very special kind of individual who belongs only incidentally to any given element in the chain of work; he lives off his eternal curiosity and his talent for discerning the problem as a whole and solving it almost instinctively. From the small pitchman down to the great scientist we find him, busy and sleepless, interested only in enigmas and disdaining ordinary solutions. Leonardo da Vinci was incontestably the most magnificent of inventors, but we can say that his spiritual father was named Gutenberg.

How many problems had Gutenberg studied before tackling that of the printing arts? Just before becoming involved with printing, he had interested himself in polishing mirrors. Observing the efforts of xylo engravers to prepare their plates, he must have become interested in the nascent study of metals and, as a goldsmith, must have quickly seen ways to remove defects of the technique. But his unusual intelligence, constantly alert, suggested to him that the problem of printing had to be studied as a whole and not only at the level of the preparation of pages. To continue to print them by rubbing was to render absolutely ineffective any improvements that could be made in the method of composition. So, no doubt abandoning his early work, he tried to solve this new problem, that is, to make the work of printing itself more mechanical. To do this he had, in effect, to take up the craft of carpentry and construct a completely new device, the printing press; next, returning to his earlier work, he perfected typography.

Then Gutenberg printed, to be sure, but not like a craftsman confined to his daily task, with a concern for his own welfare as much as with his art. He neglected to sign a single book, and he probably so soon lost interest in a technique that had then become established that certain historians of printing have asserted that Gutenberg himself never printed a single book.

We shall leave the Gutenberg problem only after noting that the first partnership founded in the Western world to solve the problem of the book was, in fact, a particularly effective team, composed of the following:

- Johann Gutenberg, the inspired inventor, the indispensable personality, the *deus ex machina* of the partnership.
- Johann Fust, said to be the prototype of Faust, a kind of banker-humanist who contributed the money needed for building the equipment, purchasing raw materials, and smoothing the operation of the enterprise.
- Peter Schoeffer, the technician, the mechanic (to use a word from a later age), who dealt with the numerous minor problems of development, managed the technical side of the business, making it even more effective, and improved some of the tools.

It is worth lingering over Gutenberg's attractive personality, because he is characteristic of the odd sources for development in the graphic crafts. Maso Finiguerra conceived of copperplating while doing niello work, and Lieutenant Ludwig von Siegen (1609–1676?) put mezzotint engraving on a firm basis. Wilhelm Haas, a type founder, transformed the classic press with its tall wooden beams. William Nicholson, a physicist, discovered the advantages of the inking roller and proposed a rotary printing press. Lord Stanhope established the final form of the platen press. Abbot Valentin Haüy was the first in the history of typography to use a cylinder to bring pressure on the relief. Benjamin Franklin played the role of jack-of-all-trades in engraving and printing. William Ged, a goldsmith, printed the first stereotypic book. An army of small mechanics, working alone or in large shops, in every part of the world, advanced the techniques of stereotyping and stereography. Abbot Rochon, a member of the academies of the sciences and of the navy, turned mechanic and invented an engraving machine. John Baskerville, a writing master and stone engraver, discovered (in addition to a new form of letters)—as might be expected—a method of making a paper better suited to printing than the old laid or wove paper. Finally, it was the "buffoon" Aloys Senefelder who invented and perfected the subtle technique of lithography.

In the field of printing, then, as many investigators came from the liberal arts as from the emergent mechanical arts and even from the intelligentsia. They became interested in the evolution of printing techniques and sought new methods of making them still more effective.

This gave this period of transition the character of a search that was both feverish and disorganized, the importance of the time not always being recognized at first glance. But it inspired and directed the work of an army of mechanics and prepared them for the great adventure of mechanization.

To be sure, this adventure could not be fully realized until a new source of power could free man from all the restrictions of the past. Until then, an army of artisans working at simple crafts with primitive machines were dependent on mills working at the pleasure of winds and streams. With the appearance of the steam engine all this changed and the great adventure began. First in England and then in France, industry began to concentrate around cities and near sources of raw materials and natural markets. Factories, small at first, then larger, were established and their activity became intense. In the new work centers everything was transformed and adapted, and new rhythms evolved. But it can be said that it was the unseen cooperation of workers in past ages that made it possible for mechanization to be adopted almost instantaneously in the various sectors of this nascent major industry.

The first Industrial Revolution attacked the craft techniques of the past, during a nineteenth century whose achievements established it as the most astonishing and extravagant age in history. The leisurely practices of the craftsmen of the past suddenly seemed to be totally destroyed. In the world of printing, new and hastily created typefaces appeared, replacing both the splendid roman characters inherited from a distant past and the austerely designed Didot. Driven by the suddenly expanded needs of printing and the press, technicians were constantly creating new machines, new methods, new means to greater speed. What became of aesthetics in this upheaval? It lost all its virtue and, from one fall to the next, in printing as elsewhere, it finally reached the level of the abominable designs in the modern style that, even to the extent of sometimes omitting the apostrophe, still continues to disturb the spirit of today's typographers.

BIBLIOGRAPHY

[1] *Essai sur l'éducation des aveugles.* Paris, 1876, book partly printed on a press for the blind.

[2] MOMORO.*Traité élémentaire de l'imprimerie.* Paris, 1796.

[3] GUILLIÉ. *Essai sur l'instruction des aveugles.* Paris, 1820.

[4] Cf. Book II of the present work, p. 633.

[5] For these descriptions of the first mechanical presses, we have used the work of NEIPP, Lucien. *Les machines à imprimer depuis Gutenberg.* Paris, 1951.

[6] *Journal polytype des sciences et des arts.* Paris, 1786. A.-G. CAMUS. *Histoire et procédés du polytypage et du stéréotypage.* Paris, 1802.

[7] FUNCKTER, J.-Michel. *Kurze doch nutzliche Anleitung von Form und Stahlschneiter,* 1740.

[8] LOTTIN, A.-M. *Catalogue chronologique des libraires et des libraires-imprimeurs de Paris.* Paris, 1780.

[9] CAMUS, *Op. cit.*

[10] FUNCKTER. *Op. cit.*

[11] *Journal polytype des sciences et des arts,* May 17, 1786.

[12] JAMMES, André. "Arts graphiques," *Brevets d'invention français (1791–1902).* Paris, 1958.

[13] Bibliothèque Nationale, *Choix de manuscripts . . . exposés . . . au Congrès des Orientalistes, September 1897,* Leroux, 1897, no. 47.

[14] ROCHON, Abbé. *Recueil de mémoires sur la mécanique et la physique.* Paris, 1783.

[15] HAMMANN, J. H. Herman. *Des arts graphiques.* Geneva, 1857.

[16] *Journal polytype des sciences et des arts,* May 24, 1786.

[17] "Rapport sur les travaux des citoyens Herhan. . .," by A.-G. CAMUS, in *Mémoires de l'Institut national des Sciences et des Arts,* t. V, an XII.

[18] *Œuvres de Bernard,* Paris, stéréotype d'Herhan, XI, 1803.

[19] ROCHON, Abbé. *Op. cit.*

[20] FOURCROY, *Elémens d'histoire naturelle et de chimie.* 1786, t. II: *Système de connaissances chimiques.*

[21] Compte des travaux du premier trimestre de l'an VIII, rendu à la séance publique du 15 nivôse. Cf. *Décade philosophique* du 30 nivôse an VIII.

[22] This entire section is indebted to A.-G. CAMUS, *Histoire et procédés du polytypage et du stéréotypage.*

[23] Memoir of citoyen Guillot, dated 16 frimaire an III (December 1794).

[24] See our earlier examination in book II of this work, p. 650.

[25] For all that concerns engraving on wood, cf. Marius AUDIN, "Les étapes de la gravure sur bois," in *Bulletin officiel de l'Union syndicale des maîtres imprimeurs de France,* December 1933.

[26] HAMMANN, Herman. *Op. cit.*

PART NINE
THE SPREAD OF TECHNICAL PROGRESS

During the second half of the eighteenth century the movement called the Industrial Revolution radiated outward from Great Britain and spread over the European continent in approximately a century and a half and, in a different form, over the North American continent during the same period. The preface to this volume outlined the reasons why the Industrial Revolution as such has not been studied in the preceding chapters. However, the phenomenon of the spread of modern techniques, starting from an innovating center that for more than a half century held a virtual monopoly on invention, could not be completely ignored in this work. In addition to the evolution of the economic and social structure of the geographical areas involved successively in the phenomenon, the acquisition and development of the classic techniques must be included among the conditions indispensable for such a transformation. In a given milieu, progress toward a new stage is possible only if a certain technical maturity has been achieved. This state of maturity is then surpassed not only under the influence of general factors that remain almost unchanged from one region to another but, even more, under the influence of special factors peculiar to each of them.

Within the framework of a general study it was not possible to trace the history of this diffusion in all the countries industrialized around the end of the nineteenth century. Moreover, in preceding chapters we have on many occasions been able to see how various techniques, whether those of the mining industry or of mechanical construction, for example, penetrated several European countries (when these countries did not themselves play a role as innovators) and North America. In this last section of this volume we have sought merely to assemble and coordinate a certain number of facts relative to the technical maturity of Eastern Europe and Russia on the one hand and the United States on the other.

The reader will understand why these two regions have been chosen as the subjects of the two succeeding chapters, given that we are unable to deal with others whose contribution to the general technical progress we nevertheless are not underestimating. First, each of them now enjoys an incontestable dominance, and for this reason the acquisition of the first elements of modern technology, which put them in a position to attain this superiority at a later stage, should more particularly interest us. These two surveys, short outlines though they may be, help us to understand the nature of the periods of transition in the countries industrialized during the nineteenth century. In this connection they form a transition to the next volume, in which we do not intend to return to the process of geographical diffusion in studying the genesis of the technical bases for industrial civilization.

CHAPTER 1

THE DEVELOPMENT OF TECHNOLOGY IN RUSSIA (1700–1850)

A T THE BEGINNING OF THE eighteenth century, Peter the Great, appreciating the need for major reforms to develop Russia economically and promote her international situation, exerted much effort to overcome the general backwardness of the country. Seeking to expand maritime trade, he had to strengthen not only the army and navy but also the merchant fleet and port installations. This had to lead to the development of heavy industry, the extension of manufactures, and the introduction of new techniques, especially in the mining industries, in metallurgy, and in the transformation of metals.

The absolutist feudal regime, in full strength at this time, had to solve these vital problems. Thereafter, the economic and industrial development of Russia took place under the influence of the changes accomplished at the beginning of the eighteenth century, but the evolutionary process was slow, and at the end of that century the country was still essentially agricultural.

After the War of 1812 some changes began to appear in commercial and industrial activity, leading to the appearance of new social strata in the production structure and to regional specialization. Domestic and international markets began a new expansion. With this development some major changes in production techniques appeared in Russia with the adoption of new forms of machines and steam engines, but only after the reform of 1861 did feudalism begin to give way to a bourgeois state and the development of technology to make remarkable progress. Craft production was replaced, toward the second half of the nineteenth century, by factories and by a system of modern industrial production.

The mining industry   The way was paved for these changes by the development of the mining and metallurgical industry, started at the beginning of the eighteenth century. Peter the Great understood the importance of these industries and paid special attention to them; during his travels in various foreign countries he studied their mining installations. In 1700 he created in Moscow a government organization charged chiefly with directing the prospecting for new deposits. In Russia, as in the other European countries at the time, new needs for metals were making themselves felt in order to keep up with the progress of industry. Prospecting spread, especially in the Urals, and new sources of coal and ferrous and nonferrous ores were found. In 1719 Peter the Great founded the Berg Company, with authority to grant licenses to develop the mining industry and prospect for and extract ores, not only on private but also on public lands. The license could be granted to a person to exploit lands that did not

709

belong to him. These measures considerably increased the interest taken in Russia in the mining industry.

The scientist and great statesman Ia. V. Brious (1670–1735), placed in charge of the company, quickly improved the techniques for extracting and treating ores. He created a laboratory for mining analysis and research and also encouraged the development of a mining profession by such means as the publication of specialized literature by such men as V. N. Tatishchev, V. I. Guenin, M. V. Lomonosov, I. A. Chlatter, and K. D. Frolov.

V. N. Tatishchev (1686–1750), the closest collaborator with Peter the Great, was in charge of the largest industrial zone in the Urals. Under his direction mines were opened and metalworking factories were built. He founded the first mining schools in the Urals, schools that produced Frolov and I. I. Polzunov, as well as other well-known specialists. In 1735 Tatishchev developed the first nation-wide statutes for the mining industry, which remained in force until the beginning of the nineteenth century.

V. I. Guenin (1676–1750) was called from Holland by Peter the Great, who knew how to discover men of talent. For a long time Guenin directed industry in the region of Olonetski and later in the Urals. He introduced major improvements in the production of cast iron and cannons, continuing also the work of Tatishchev.

After he had climbed all the rungs of the hierarchy in his profession and had in his turn become president of the Berg Company, I. A. Chlatter also exerted a great influence on the development of this industry. His work *Detailed Course of Instruction for the Mining Industry,* published in 1760, discusses the problems of geology, mineralogy, and prospecting, the sinking of shafts for extracting ores and, in general, the state of contemporary mining mechanics in Russia and in the other large industrial countries. It contains chapters on the exploitation of coal deposits and use of steam engines for pumping water.

The great scientist M. V. Lomonosov (1711–1765) occupied a leading place in the science and technology of his century. One of his works, *The First Foundations of Metallurgy and the Mining Industry,* was of great influence and was widely referred to in Russia. It is especially noteworthy for Lomonosov's perception that fossil coal is of plant origin and for his theory concerning the natural ventilation of shafts, for which he suggested several machines of his own invention. In addition, all aspects of mining technique were studied in great detail and with a new approach that placed mining development on the level of the leading industries.

New methods of exploitation were widely applied in Russia. The pumping of brine from Permian salt deposits called for drilling increasingly deeper shafts. By 1606 a depth of 328 feet was reached, and with improvements in the technique of drilling in the eighteenth century, shafts were taken as far as 650 feet (Figure 1).

The greatest advances were made in methods of timbering and in hydraulic installations. K. D. Frolov (1726–1800) built a magnificent and successful complex of hydraulic installations in the mines of Kolivano-Voskressen in the Altai (Figure 2), where deep deposits of silver ores began to be exploited about 1770. The old installations for pumping and draining out water were inadequate. Between 1783 and 1789 Frolov and his colleagues built a dam 57½ feet high and 420 feet long, with a width at the base of 302 feet and at water level 48 feet. The

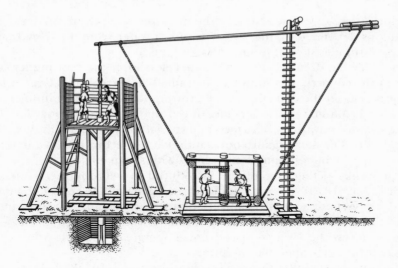

FIG. 1.   Machine for drilling salt wells. Eighteenth century.

water passed through an underground flume to operate a sawmill that supplied the planks used for timbering, whence it was carried in two tunnels to the Preobrajensk and Ekaterina mine. At the latter a waterwheel hoisted the ore from levels of 150 feet and 335 feet. In one hour 12 tubs, each weighing 1,076 pounds, could be raised from a level of 335 feet, with 12 workers feeding the hoisting machine. The water then passed to another waterwheel 56 feet in diameter, which operated drainage pumps from a depth of 699 feet. Finally the water went on to the Voznessen mine, where it operated the hoisting and drainage installations. In

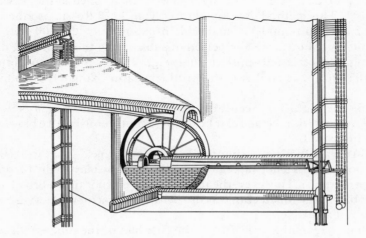

FIG. 2.   Hydraulic installation by Frolov in the Kolivan-Voskressen factories.

this mine one tub was used to hoist the ore from a depth of 197 feet. All these installations depended on the same current of water from the dam, thanks to a network of tunnels several hundred yards long.

In 1773 the Mining School of Saint Petersburg, the first higher technical school in the country, was founded. It trained an increasingly large number of specialists to meet the demands of the growing Russian mining industry.

At the beginning of the nineteenth century the organization developed by Tatishchev was completely reformed by a special committee under A. F. Deriabin (1770–1820). The new organization continued the technical development of the mines, especially by replacing waterwheels with steam engines.

The double-acting engine was introduced in 1803 by the mechanic F. F. Sobakin (1746–1813), the first installation being in the Berezovo gold mines. The Tcherepanovs, both good mechanics, built various machines for the mines of the industrialist Demidov. The pumping machines they installed in 1827–1830 in copper mines in the Urals replaced horse-operated treadmills with which 224 horses had formerly operated the pumps.

Ventilation was also the subject for invention. In 1832 A. A. Sablukov (1783–1857) made the first attempts to use centrifugal force for both ventilation and water pumping. His first centrifugal fans were installed in the Tchaguir mine in the Altai. This invention was an extremely useful advance; until then mines had to be shut down between May and October because of the accumulation of gases during this season. After 1838 Sablukov's fans were completely successful.

The end of this period was marked by the publication of *Course of Instruction in the Mining Art,* by A. I. Uzatis (1814–1875), one of the world's leading specialists in this industry. His work was a course in theory, with a mathematical approach. The course was widely adopted at the Mining Institute (which had succeeded the Mining School of Saint Petersburg) and by established engineers.

Metallurgy The first blast furnaces in Russia were built in 1670 in the Urals and in 1673 at Toula and Kachir. The first refining furnaces for producing iron were established at the Nevian factory around 1701. This method developed rapidly: in 1718 Russia produced 284,000 *puds* (one *pud* = 36 pounds) of malleable iron and only 230,000 *puds* of iron by direct reduction of the ore. The period of substituting the reduction method for the refining method lasted approximately eighty years, until the beginning of the nineteenth century, when Russia was producing approximately 10 million *puds* of cast iron.

During the eighteenth century the capacity of blast furnaces, which were circular chambers with rectangular bosh, grew continuously. The blowing engines were also improved.

In 1805 blast furnaces using the heat from furnace gases were built at the Kussin factory. In 1829 hot air began to be used for the blast in the furnaces and in the smelting cupolas. However, the use of hot air did not find a broad application in the first half of the nineteenth century because refractory materials and suitable fuels were not available.

Puddling began in Russia during the first half of the nineteenth century. In 1854 the metallurgist A. A. Iossa (1810–1894) established puddling furnaces and gas welding in the Votkinsk factory. In 1849/50 the first experiments with puddling by coal were made in Kertshin and Luga factories. The development of rolling was connected with that of puddling, since after 1828 rolling mills equipped with wrought-iron rolls appeared in the Urals.

As in other countries, in Russia in the second half of the eighteenth century and at the beginning of the nineteenth steel was made by the cementation of iron method described by Réaumur. The iron obtained by reducing ore was heated on a bed of flaming charcoal. During this operation the surface of the iron was carburized and the surface layer was tempered by plunging the mass into water. Through repetition of this operation the iron was transformed into a bar of cemented steel. This method survived in Olonetski province until the beginning of the nineteenth century. Since malleable iron was cheap, it supplanted blast furnace iron in all its uses and particularly in the preparation of steel.

In 1808 S. I. Badayev (1778–1847) was successful in making crucible steel at a surgical-instruments plant in Saint Petersburg. This method of production was developed by the metallurgist P. P. Anossov (1797–1851), who in 1830 established the production of crucible steel at the Zlatoustovo factory for the production of scythes and side arms. Anossov also made studies, published in 1841 (Figure 3), on cementation steel for the manufacture of Damascus steels.

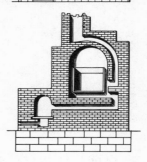

FIG. 3. Resmelting furnace for making Damascus steel. (From drawings by P. P. Anossov.)

Russia had been producing nonferrous metals since early times. In the middle of the eighteenth century the production of copper rose to 180,000 *puds*. The best-known copper foundries were those in the Urals and Siberia. In the second half of the eighteenth century the technique for treating cuprous ores made several advances, thanks to the development of reverberatory furnaces, which consumed less fuel and supplied a better quality copper.

The production of lead in Russia was begun at the same time as that of silver. Around the middle of the nineteenth century more than 60,000 *puds* of lead were cast. The largest silver and lead factories were those of Kolivano-Voskressen (1729), Nertshin (in the second half of the eighteenth century), and the Altai.

At the beginning of the eighteenth century silver ore was sent to Moscow for separation of the silver and gold. Refining the silver was done by the wet method with "Czar water." The gold was refined by a dry method, either by cementation or by fusion with antimony, from which it was then separated by air blasting into the liquid material. In 1859, 1,084 *puds* of pure silver were produced in Russia.

Major transformations in gold refining occurred after 1814, the year in which L. I. Brusnitsin (1786–1857) developed a technique for direct washing of auriferous sands. The amalgamation method was also used. Lomonosov had already shown a great interest in this technique. In 1808 amalgamation became an industrial method at the Mint of Ekaterinburg (now Sverdlovsk), thanks to the works of A. A. Agte and I. I. Varvinskii (1797–1838), and applied slightly later in the Ural and Altai factories.

In 1819 a new metal, platinum, introduced into Europe from South America in the mid-eighteenth century, was discovered in the Ural mines. Platinum metallurgy was rapidly perfected, and by 1828 it was possible in Russia to coin money and make small articles from platinum (Figure 4). Russian research into methods of producing malleable platinum influenced the development of powder metallurgy. The works of P. G. Sobolevskii (1780–1841) had a great influence on the development of this branch.

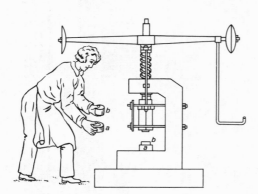

FIG. 4. Screw-type balance press for working platinum. P. G. Sobolevskii.

The making of cast-iron objects by molding reached a high technical level at quite an early period in Russia. Russian founders had acquired a great reputation for their skill in casting cannons and bells. They excelled in casting bulky objects distinguished by their high artistic quality.

A 130-ton bell, the "czar bell" for the Uspen Cathedral of the Kremlin, was cast in 1654. It is no longer in existence. In 1735 Motorini and his son cast a second "czar bell," which weighed 200 tons. During the fire of 1737 this bell cracked and could not be hung in the tower. It is preserved in the Kremlin.

The founders used various techniques to prepare molds for large objects. They cast cannons and balls either in sand or cast-iron molds, the latter being reusable several times. The great technician I. I. Polzunov (1729–1766) also contributed to the development of the technology, especially in high-precision castings of complex shapes. The Russian masters were noted for their skill in casting hollow objects with thin walls. Thus, in the first half of the nineteenth century, at the Berda factory, the figure of an angel was cast for the triumphal column for Palace Square at Saint Petersburg. The British government ordered the bells destined for the tower of Westminster Abbey from Moscow.

Power production   The classic sources of mechanical power— windmills and waterwheels—were still widely used in Russia (as everywhere in the nineteenth century), Russia having more than 200,000 windmills at this time.

Regarding waterwheels, the widely used undershot wheels were gradually replaced after the middle of the eighteenth century by overshot bucket wheels. As the hydraulic engine developed, so did the technique of building dams, with Frolov playing an important role as we have seen. He introduced to Russia the system of articulated transmission that made it possible to transmit the movement of the waterwheel to the principal areas of power use inside the factory.

The dam built for the Votkin factory by Moskvin in the second half of the eighteenth century, almost a half mile long and about 30 feet high, served as a model for many projects.

The work of Leonhard Euler (then a member of the Academy of Saint Petersburg) on the hydraulic engine was discussed earlier in connection with the invention of turbines. His ideas were applied fifty years after their publication. In Russia the first experiments in building hydraulic turbines are credited to I. E. Safonov. An early model built by this engineer was installed in 1837 at the Alpayevo factory in a rolling mill for sheet metal. It developed a power of about 36 kw. with an efficiency of 70 percent, surpassing that of water wheels by 20 percent. Another turbine was installed by the same engineer in 1841 at a factory in Neivo-Chaitan. In 1839 the works of A. I. Uzatis provided the Russian public with the theoretical bases of the construction of turbines. In 1856 V. P. Rojkov (1815–1894) built a double hydraulic turbine with a horizontal axle and two suction pipes (Figure 5). The use of this type of turbine spread widely in the Ural factories at the end of the nineteenth century.

The atmospheric steam engine was introduced into Russia in the first half of the eighteenth century. It was built and improved chiefly by I. I. Polzunov, who in 1764 installed a blowing engine blast furnace at the Barnaul factory. This machine replaced 24 small bellows by 2 large cylindrical bellows and developed a power of 32 hp. The boiler deteriorated rapidly and the engine was abandoned.

Watt's double-acting engine was known in Russia before the end of the eighteenth century, and its use began to spread at the beginning of the following century. This was the classic walking-beam low-pressure model. In 1820 S. W. Litvinov (1785–1843), the owner of Barnaul, was the first person in Russia to

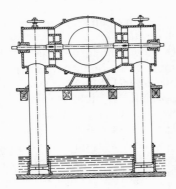

FIG. 5.   Hydraulic turbine by Rojkov, 1856. The stream of water comes in through the central pipe, passes from one end to the other of the distributor and the rotor, and descends through the suction pipes that have closing gates at the bottom, controlled by the wheels at the top.

design a high-pressure boiler. In this the water was heated in one boiler and superheated in a second, where it was transformed into steam at high pressure. The project did not pass the design stage. Steam engines penetrated Russia only very slowly, because of the political structure of the country. In 1840 the steam engines in operation in the country represented a total power of no more than 20,000 hp. Only during the second half of the century did steam come into wide use.

Applications of electricity   The study of electrical phenomena was particularly active in Russia during the second half of the eighteenth century as regards both static electricity and natural atmospheric phenomena. Lomonosov gave a theoretical explanation of the formation of electricity in the atmosphere, by the movements of air masses with different moisture contents, an explanation anticipating contemporary theories.

The works of the physicist G. V. Richman (1711–1753) marked the beginning of quantitative research on electrical and magnetic phenomena.

Shortly after Volta's discovery, V. V. Petrov (1761–1834) became the first Russian physicist to work (in 1802) on the electric battery. In particular he built a large stack of 2,100 copper-zinc elements. He studied the formation of the electric arc in its practical application for lighting and as a source of high temperatures for smelting metals, and he explored the uses of electricity for chemical analysis. He performed major research on electric discharge in a vacuum and on the use of fatty materials as insulators. These latter experiments were made with high tensions of the order of 1,700 v. The results were later applied in making cables.

In the medical field, around 1803 A. T. Bolotov (1738–1833) studied the effect of electrical current on the human organism, with a view to therapeutic applications. He founded an establishment for electrotherapy in which some 500 patients were treated in two years. His work laid the first foundations for galvanotherapy.

In another area, P. L. Schilling (1786–1837) was responsible for applying electricity to the detonation of mines. Schilling solved the problem of firing explosives by using a cable and a primer formed by a double resistor that grew hot upon the passage of an electric current. In 1812 he exploded mines laid in the

Neva with this device. His work was later extended by M. M. Boreskov, V. S. Sereyev, and B. S. Jacobi.

The most important contributions in the field of electricity were those of Jacobi (1801–1874), which became internationally known. In 1834 he was one of the first physicists in the world to build an electromagnetic motor. This motor consisted of two groups of magnets, one stationary and the other installed on a rotating disk. A commutator composed of four rings and four metal brushes that caused alternate inversion of the poles was fed by a battery of sulfate piles Jacobi built. Later he made more powerful engines, installing one of them, which developed a power of ¼ hp., on a small boat. This was the first electrically propelled craft to navigate on the Neva, which it did on September 13, 1838, at a speed of approximately .6 or .7 knot. In the following year Jacobi installed an electric motor on another boat that could carry ten to fourteen passengers. Jacobi also applied himself to building electromagnetic generators for producing current. In 1848 he succeeded in building an electric generator along the lines of the one by Clarke, but better designed and giving a current of a higher voltage. This generator was used by the Russian army for igniting primers in mines. In 1844 Jacobi invented an automatic percussion detonator for mines, which in addition to the explosive charge had an electric pile whose mercury closing was activated by shock.

Jacobi invented electroplating, a discovery he made in 1837 and published in a work entitled *Electroplating* published in 1840. The method was first applied in the execution of metal copies of various objects such as coins and medals. In the same year Jacobi received the Demidof prize for this invention, which immediately met with general success in Russia as well as in every other country.

Toward the middle of the nineteenth century advances in electromagnetism encouraged the construction of devices for various uses. In 1842 the inventor K. I. Konstantinov (1817–1871) built an electromagnetic chronoscope for measuring very short intervals of time. Two years later he invented an installation of the same type to measure the speed of cannonballs. The ball crossed two screens spaced at a known distance and linked by an electric circuit, by means of which the times of impact were recorded on graph paper rolled on a revolving cylinder.

The building of machinery   Industrial progress in mining and metallurgy, as well as in the production of power, governed the development of a new industry, the building of machines to transform metals from forge to finished product.

As in every country, forging was one of the oldest industries. Its development was linked to the use of the hydraulic hammer. A new stage began with the introduction into Russian factories of the steam hammer, invented as described in another chapter. The first power hammers were established in 1848 in the machine construction shop of Ekaterinburg and in the Votkin factory. The means to forge large parts for steam engines and machine tools were now available.

Drop stamping which appeared around 1819 in arms manufactories, made possible the improvement of the technical qualities of the parts made and helped to solve the problem of replacement parts.

Among the traditional machines for working metals were the saw with a horizontal disk, and the vertical drill. The latter was used particularly for boring solid-cast guns, a method used in Russia until around 1840. In 1712 Guenin built for the Olonetski factories a horizontal drill to ream guns which was installed along the lines of the classic model. This machine, which ensured greater precision in metalworking than did the vertical drill, was used in making blowing cylinders and pumps for steam engines.

The reamer, derived from the vertical drill, made its appearance in Russia in 1827. This early machine, powered by a waterwheel with power transmission by a gear train, was built in the Alexandrovo weapons plant at Petrozavodsk. Tcherepanov and his son manufactured all-purpose borers inspired by the manual drills in Viino's machine shop.

The building of copying lathes began in the sixteenth century. Peter the Great built a large machine shop in Saint Petersburg and placed the famous mechanic A. K. Nartov (1694–1756) in charge of it. Nartov built several models of copying lathes equipped with mechanical toolholders. During a sojourn in Paris in 1719/20 he gave a demonstration of his art as a turner before the Académie des Sciences.

Industrial lathes appeared in Russian industry at the beginning of the nineteenth century. In 1812 the mechanic of the Tula armament factory, N. D. Zakavo (1779–1839), built a special lathe for turning the barrels of firearms. This appears to have been the most automated lathe of the period. It had a mechanical feed, a toolholder, movable poppet, and an automatic stopping system. The tool was cooled by a trickle of water, a method that did not come into common use until much later.

Around the middle of the nineteenth century control by a threaded screw was introduced into the building of machine tools. Around the same time planing machines with the same control device began to be used; the Tcherepanovs invented a model of this machine in which the workpiece moved in front of the stationary toolholder.

Milling machines also appeared in the factories. By 1724 Nartov had built the first milling machine used in Russia for cutting toothed wheels. During the first half of the nineteenth century this industrialized machine found wide application in all the Russian metallurgical factories, especially the weapons plants. All-purpose milling machines equipped with a series of interchangeable cutters were developed.

Lifting and handling devices underwent an evolution of the same order as the machines used in working metals. In 1734 the Ekaterinburg factory had a double elevator for loading cast-iron pigs on ships. In 1770 F. D. Golovin, the builder of the Tomski factory, replaced the rotary movement of the jib crane with the gantry having an up-and-down movement for lifting and loading. The advance in the technique of lifting devices had major repercussions on the foundry industry. In the 1820s the first elevator for transferring molten metal to cupolas was built, in the Alexandrovo foundry at Petrozavodsk. There also the cranes with cast-iron bases were installed for the first time in Russia. In this same period the Saint Petersburg arsenal was equipped with a hydraulically controlled mobile crane to move heavy loads. Soon after 1840 traveling cranes were installed in the Ekaterinburg machine factory.

High-precision machinery was developed during the eighteenth century by mechanics like I. P. Kulibin (1735–1818), especially for making watches and astronomical instruments. A musical pendulum clock with automata built by Kulibin is preserved in the Hermitage Museum. Numerous astronomical instruments by him still exist. Kulibin combined the mechanic's knowledge with the artist's talent. He excelled in making optical instruments, and he built reflectors with spherical mirrors capable of increasing by 100 times the illuminating power of a flame. Kulibin, a fertile inventor, was the first to use graphite to lubricate screw elevators. He also made artificial limbs.

Transportation   The mechanization of transport preoccupied Russian inventors quite early. In 1760 L. L. Shamshurenkov built a four-wheeled carriage operated mechanically by human muscle power that was able to transport two passengers. This vehicle, the first mechanical device in the country, with a belt transmission and a free wheel, was presented to the Court of the Empress Catherine. Toward the end of the eighteenth century Kulibin also built a similar light four-wheeled carriage with a gear-shifting device and friction brakes. Like many pioneers of the period he also thought of using the steam engine to propel the vehicle.

Concerning transportation of freight, one of the most famous exploits in the world at the time was the transportation in 1782 of a block of granite for the pedestal of the statue of Peter the Great. This solid block was a meteorite weighing 1,500 tons that was transported along the shores of the Gulf of Finland on a specially built track formed of two parallel channels carrying copper ball bearings. The block, lifted by levers, was placed on a timber platform that was pulled by winches over the ball bearings. Transportation by water was effected on a pontoon placed between two ships.

After the turn of the century the authorities concentrated on building good roads, which were indispensable to cover the great spaces of Russia. In 1825 Guriev suggested surfacing the roads with a wooden pavement, which was used for the principal streets of Saint Petersburg.

The first railroad tracks were built by Frolov starting in 1820. The first of these tracks had cast-iron rails and linked the Zmeino mine with the cleaning plant six miles away. The ore-laden wagons were pulled by horses.

Then came the steam locomotive. In 1833/34 the Tcherepanovs built the first locomotive, at the Nijne Taguil factory. For use in the plant, it could pull a 3.3-ton train at a speed of 10 miles per hour. Its boiler was equipped with fire tubes. In 1835 the Tcherepanovs built a second locomotive that could pull 16 tons.

The first railroad in Russia for transporting passengers was built in 1837, connecting Saint Petersburg with Tsarskoe Selo and Pavlovsk, over a distance of twenty-one miles.

The industrial production of steam locomotives began in 1838 at the Pojevo factory, which was then moved to Saint Petersburg. The first of the locomotives was exhibited in 1839 at the Industrial Exposition of Russia.

In 1851 a double-track line was built between Saint Petersburg and Moscow under the direction of the engineers P. P. Melnikov (1804–1880) and N. D. Kraft (1780–1857). This produced the first great achievements of civil engineering in the age. The engineers D. I. Juravski (1821–1891), S. F. Krutikov, and several others drew the plans and made the computations for numerous suspension bridges.

The first steamboat to be built in Russia was the *Elizabeth,* in 1815, which made the trip between Saint Petersburg and Kronstadt. Two other steamboats, designed for river navigation, were built in the same year at the Pojevo factory. The larger of the two was equipped with a 36-hp. engine and sailed on the Kama. A fourth steamboat, the *Vsevold,* was built for navigation on the Volga as far as Ribinsk.

Communication   Various optical telegraph systems were installed in Russia after the end of the eighteenth century. As early as 1795 Kulibin built by order of Catherine II a semaphore for which he invented an original signal code. In 1815 Poniukhayev proposed a telegraph system with seven lanterns arranged in a circle, which could be uncovered in accordance with a fixed system of combinations. There were still other systems, credited to P. Chistiakov in 1827, Shchegorin in 1829, and Butakov in 1833. In 1824 Lieutenant-General Kozen installed a line between Saint Petersburg and Shlisselburg, which remained in service for ten years. Later a Frenchman, Pierre Chateau, installed Chappe optical telegraph lines in Russia, a system that was also used for communication on the first Russian railroads.

To make up for the lack of optical telegraphs, electromagnetic methods of transmission were tried in Russia as soon as they became known. In 1832 P. L. Schilling demonstrated a device with two wires and a single needle, the various positions of which corresponded to a signaling code. He then built, on the principle of the Wheatstone telegraph, a six-needle telegraph equipped with a keyboard transmitter and a line of seven wires designed for the Latin alphabet. Then he built a five-needle apparatus for the Cyrillic alphabet in 1835.

After Schilling's death, Jacobi continued in Russia the study of electric telegraphs, trying to make their manipulation more convenient and to decrease the number of wires in the line. In 1841 he invented a telegraph model that included a key of the Morse type and an inscribing device consisting of a vertical sheet of glass moved in front of a needle by a clockwork mechanism. An electromagnet caused the needle to move and inscribe a broken line on the glass sheet. This model included a two-wire electric line that was installed between the Winter Palace and army headquarters. In 1845 Jacobi built a telegraph model inspired by Breguet's telegraph with an alphabet dial. He built several different models of this kind of telegraph, which were installed on a line between Tsarskoe Selo and Saint Petersburg, and for other communications.

Jacobi's studies on underground cables were of great importance in the development of the first telegraph installations. In 1843 he suggested the use of relays with the help of supplementary batteries, which made it possible to remedy losses of load on the line and to increase its length. The principle of the retransmission of telegraph signals found extensive application in modern telegraphy. Around the mid-nineteenth century several long-distance telegraph lines existed in Russia; for example, Saint Petersburg-Moscow, Kiev-Odessa, and Saint Petersburg-Warsaw. In 1855 the total length of the lines was 4,680 miles; in 1860, 10,560 miles.

Jacobi was not satisfied with his work on dial telegraphs. Around 1850 he built a telegraph printing apparatus characterized by the periodic synchronization of the impulses given to the type wheel, under which a strip of paper unrolled. An electromagnet caused the letter to be printed each time the type wheel stopped.

Jacobi's work obviously falls in the same line of research as that by inventors in other countries who, independently of him, devoted themselves to inventing printing telegraphs.

In this discussion we have seen that around the middle of the nineteenth century all the major technical inventions that made possible the rise of the industrial nations were the objects of work done by Russian scientists and engineers.

CHAPTER 2

THE INTRODUCTION OF MODERN TECHNOLOGY IN THE NEW WORLD

THOSE WHO COLONIZED the North American continent from Europe brought with them the techniques not only of their native lands but also of their localities. A general description of them here would then require reference to the arts and crafts peculiar to each group, which space prohibits. Despite the considerable geographical barrier of the Atlantic, the isolated colonies nevertheless maintained closer relations with the Old World than they did with each other. The result was that their traditions were maintained until the union of the colonies in 1776, and even until the beginning of the nineteenth century.

The first colonial establishment From the very establishment of the colonies it was a question of survival. The need for weapons, absolutely necessary for hunting as well as for keeping the Indians in check, took precedence over shelter and clothing. Emphasis should be placed on the importance of the musket, a tool of primary necessity in the exploration of the continent, which is at the origin of the basic transformations of the American industrial technology. In the beginning the only capital available to the colonists, aside from small, speculative European investments, consisted of the human energy saved as the result of favorable harvests. The availability of manpower (at first from a kind of indenture arrangement and later from the importation of slaves) made possible the expansion of the physical "capital," but progress remained slow until after the Revolution, when economic independence became attainable.

As late as 1820 more than 70 percent of the labor force was involved in agriculture, and almost all the specifically American innovations arrived at in this period belong to this area. These improvements were imposed on the colonists by natural conditions themselves. The axe, indispensable for clearing the land, immediately underwent major changes, as seen with the American broad axe with its broad cutting edge, a model characteristic of the modifications made in this period to the shapes of handle and blade. In general the hoe sufficed for preparing the soil for essential products such as maize, tobacco, and, later, rice. With the first two the colonists followed methods learned from the Indians. We find examples of the use of the plow after 1632, but this was rare, for the agricultural system was concerned not with commercial production but simply with satisfying the needs of local communities.

Plate 85. "By Industry We Thrive"—"Progress" Our Motto! This print attempts to depict all aspects of American industrial progress. Foreground: a baker reading *Scientific American;* a man, sitting, with a gear and cutting tools; a white collar worker, standing, with paper and plans in hand. Center, standing around a statue of Benjamin Franklin are men each with different tools: a trowel and leveling triangle, a mallet and chisel, a tri-square and saw. At right: a man working on a monumental base with wooden mallet and chisel; a miner in helmet and dress with pick; a blacksmith with hammer and anvil; a wheelwright with wheel and divider. Background from left to right: a factory with smoking chimneys; a train crossing a bridge; a man sawing; a harbor with steamships, sailing vessels, and a lighthouse; a house being built; a farmer plowing; two surveyors; telephone poles; and a church spire. Note the additional designs around the border. Smithsonian Institution

Metallurgy   The adaptation of European tools to colonial needs, done largely by individuals, was achieved by local blacksmiths. The local forge thus formed the core of the iron industry in America. Next to certain attempts to establish plants on a relatively large scale (for instance at Lynn, Massachusetts, in 1640), simple small-capacity forges using local sources of ore, including bog iron, sufficed for the inhabitants' needs. Until an effective transportation system could be built up industrial expansion was practically impossible, because the small industries continued to be scattered. The growing importance of small forges, under the pressure of regional demand, brought about the application of waterpower to forge bellows and trip hammers. The first bellows furnace was built in 1720 by Thomas Rutter at Colebrookedale, Pennsylvania, but this did not indicate a major revolution in the technical organization of the iron industry. The colonies of course exported pig iron to England from 1730 until the Revolution, but though we recognize the quality of the American product, this phenomenon must be regarded as a political aberration emphasizing the inadequacy of the American transportation system. These facts notwithstanding, by the time of the Revolution the American iron industry, consisting of many small local establishments, had reached third place after Russia and Sweden in terms of total production, which at this time amounted to 14 percent of world output.

Steel production was of secondary importance until the Civil War. In 1867 the production of iron in pigs was 1.5 million tons. In contrast, steel production did not exceed 20,000 tons, consisting for the most part of cementation steel. American industry had become accustomed to using minimal quantities of steel—it was possible, for example, to solder a steel strip to the moldboard of a plow to form the share. Despite this economy of material it was necessary to import half of American steel requirements at the time of the Revolution.

Tools used in the construction of homes and farm buildings testify to original American solutions, but lack of space prevents a discussion of these. There remains the problem of clothing.

Textiles   Until the Revolution the textile industry was a family business carried on in every home. However, in some more highly developed regions another practice was common: an entrepreneur gave out what could nowadays be called home piecework. He supplied the raw material to private individuals and when the order was worked up he accepted delivery of the merchandise ready for sale.

Although the Hargreaves jenny (1763) had been introduced into the United States before 1765, it was not introduced into a factory until around 1775. The colonists made an interesting innovation in their use of cotton for the warp. This practice marked the origin of the use of cotton waste in cheap quilts, which replaced the much more expensive woolen blankets.

Energy sources   The colonists used the waterwheel or horse power. The abundance of water resources, especially along the main line of falls in the East, retarded the installation of steam engines, bringing major repercussions on the economy and the industrial organization of the United States. The application of waterpower to sawmills was one of the first achievements to make possible a reduction in human labor and an increase in the production of wood, of which much use was made for construction. Then followed a characteristic invention, that of the gang saw, before the Revolution. Gristmills, like sawmills, also used waterpower, and constituted the first large enterprises in the United States. Several steam engines were imported from England, the first of which was a Newcomen engine installed in 1753 in a copper mine at North Arlington, New Jersey. But even in 1786 the number of steam engines was insignificant.

This quick summary of the introduction of European techniques into the United States makes insufficient mention of the improvisations of certain individuals, forced by circumstances to economize on labor and raw materials. The characteristic trait of the Americans, nowadays called Yankee ingenuity, has its origin in the difficulties encountered by colonists in the pioneer era. Invention is generally considered to be the product of the brain of a thinker or an inspired application of a scientific discovery, but in most cases necessity (or rather convenience) is the mother of invention. This is the origin of the American system. After the organization of a transportation network and the expansion of capital during the first fifty years of the nineteenth century, the need for improvisation decreased, but frustrations persisted and continued to influence American technology.

THE ESTABLISHMENT OF THE FIRST LARGE INDUSTRIES (1800–1850)

There exists a growing tendency among Americans to identify the first half of the nineteenth century with the complete achievement of the American system and of production according to the concept of interchangeability through standardization. The latter is the production of a large number of separate parts for a machine by using special tools and, later (as a single and separate operation), the assembling of all the parts needed for a complete machine. Two conditions precede the undertaking of an assembly-line production of this type: first, the existence of machine tools capable of extreme precision and high production, and second, a system of administration in the factory to prepare a plan and to maintain the pace without unnecessary expense. In these conditions we recognize a simple description of today's system of production, but it must be asked whether the formation of this incontestably American contribution was completed before the Civil War, regardless of the success of the articles exhibited at the first Universal Exposition in London in 1851, where for the first time the Americans demonstrated on the international market their existence as a potential new industrial force.

The economic circumstances The fact is that several circumstances combined after the Revolutionary War, and even after the War of 1812, both to stimulate and to retard the development of the system of interchangeability.

Some of the positive forces stimulating this development were an understandable desire to replace foreign (especially English) imports brought in after both wars because of general scarcity in the United States, and a shortage of trained craftsmen, due to the attraction of the West. It was necessary to economize on labor and increase the productivity of workers. In the first half of the nineteenth century the growth of immigration caused the market for the products of hunting and agriculture to expand and naturally to encourage development of methods of transportation.

On the other hand, forces retarding this growth were, first, restrictions on the exportation from England of certain machines, which delayed knowledge of the new practices in use in that country. This law, finally abrogated in 1843, had fallen into disuse by the end of the decade 1825–1835, but its effects continued to be felt.

Second, there was a partial restriction on the emigration from England of certain specialized workers, which retarded the circulation of information ("know-how") of techniques. This restriction lost its importance before 1830.

Plate 86. At American centennial celebration President Grant and Don Pedro of Brazil start the Corliss engine. Wood engraving from a sketch by T. R. Davis, *Harper's Weekly*, May 1876. Library of Congress

Toward the end of this period qualified workers began to emigrate from England, and later from Germany, in large numbers.

Third, there was a genuine shortage of capital from which the new country suffered from its beginning, a situation in which the banks, themselves poorly organized because they were local and generally small, could not help. The difficulties of American industry in accumulating an amount of capital sufficient to permit it to keep pace with the geographical development of the country influenced the policy of businessmen, for example in the exploitation of inventors' patents.

Fourth, a large part of the scanty funds available were absorbed by the railroads, of which more than 30,000 miles were built before 1860. This represented an expenditure of more than $800 million, a heavy burden on the new economy. Consequently, and despite the importation of capital and equipment from England, there occurred a disproportionate concentration of resources in this one area of economic development.

Technical circumstances   It is difficult to evaluate even approximately the extent of the adoption of new techniques prior to 1855. We know, for example, that Baldwin, the famous locomotive builder, did not achieve a system of interchangeability until 1860. Until then his installations had only primitive tools and, as Charles H. Fitch says, "In order to plane the cast iron for these locomotives, one must clean, file, and plane by hand." At the same time it must be remembered that around 1840 American locomotive builders were exporting a substantial proportion of their production to Europe.

There was exceptional progress in the industries that met the needs of pioneers for clothing and weapons. Three individuals at the origin of this development were at once genuine pioneers and engineers with inventive minds: Samuel Slater (1765–1835), Oliver Evans (1755–1819), and Eli Whitney (1765–1825). Slater has been called the father of the textile industry in the United States. A former employee in Arkwright's concern in England, Slater emigrated to the United States in 1790 and set himself up in Pawtucket, Rhode Island. Equipped with complete information on the spinning machine invented by Richard Arkwright (without, however, possessing the plans for it), Slater succeeded in building machines that replaced the other copies of English models, and in three years he established a cotton spinning mill with seventy-two spindles.

Slater continued to modify and adapt these machines, but the possibility of developing a large cotton industry became realizable thanks especially to an invention concerning the raw material (cotton seeds), that is, the Whitney cotton gin. The first model of this machine, built in 1793, succeeded in ginning a quantity of cotton double that produced by the Indian-type roller machines used until then. Aided by the initiative of Francis Lowell (1775–1817), who conceived of designing a factory so that all the operations contributing to the production of cotton cloth could be undertaken under a single roof, and of Paul Moody (1779–1831), who built a weaving loom—the American cotton industry dominated the national economy after 1825.

Oliver Evans, like Slater a symbol of America's declared independence, set up a shop for building steam engines in Philadelphia in 1802. His high-pressure engine can be favorably compared with the machines of Boulton and Watt, except perhaps regarding cost. The Evans machine's lightness and convenience gave a foretaste of typical American solutions. Evans and perhaps Whitney both give evidence of a talent now regarded as an American specialty: a particular skill in organizing industrial production. Evans's flour mill (1791) is an extraordinary combination of mechanical genius and production planning. Forty barrels of flour could be milled with two workers, an operation formerly requiring four men and one child. Consequently, after 1850 the United States became a major exporter of flour. Evans's manual, *The Young Mill-Wright and Miller's Guide,* constituted a reference work for builders of mills throughout the United States.

Oliver Evans's achievements foreshadowed the development of American technology that later influenced the general technique of steam engines. We refer to the stationary engines of George Corliss (1817–1888) and of Charles T. Porter and John F. Allen, and to the experiments of Ericsson. General adoption of these new steam machines was delayed by the massive use of waterpower and wood fuel and also by the economic conditions outlined above, so that by the end of this period their use was relatively modest, but still they testify to the enterprising American spirit immediately recognized by foreigners. The Corliss engine, whose principal characteristic was its distribution system, was copied in England, France, and Switzerland. The Porter-Allen engine, distinguished by its high speed, was built by licensees in England. Both engines made a great impression in Europe around the middle of the century.

Interchangeability American tradition accords to Whitney the honor of inventing the system of interchangeability already defined. Historians who study this period have reason to believe that other arms manufacturers rival Whitney in this claim. Thomas Jefferson, who was well known to Whitney, appears to have known of H. Blanc's work on weapons production published in 1790, in which it is evident that by 1788 this French engineer was applying this production system in a much more advanced manner even than Whitney. In England, Switzerland, and Sweden we find indications of attempts to systematize production by the end of the eighteenth century. In the United States the Springfield arsenal, whose archives of this period are unfortunately lost, began after 1799 to use machines, to economize on labor. It is even possible that this factory was the source of Whitney's ideas. In addition, Whitney's famous milling machine, described as the first American machine of this type, could have been preceded by similar machines in the national or private arsenals.

Still, Whitney's milling machine has become a symbol in studies on the problem of high-precision machines, whose origins are genuinely American. (A drawing of this milling machine can be seen in Chapter 5, on machine tools.)

A distinction must be made between a machine built for a fixed purpose and a multipurpose machine. The United States has made its unique contribution in the latter category.

Precision machine tools We find the first model of a multipurpose machine in the carpenter shops of national arsenals. Invented in 1818 and built for the Springfield armory as a tool to shape rifle stocks, Blanchard's stock machine proved to be a pattern lathe that could turn shoe lasts and other irregular shapes (Figure 6).

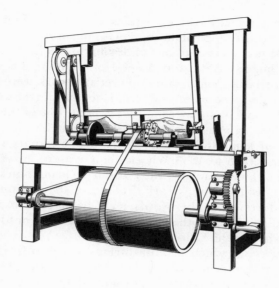

FIG. 6.   Blanchard's copying lathe for duplicating irregular shapes.

The demands of the rifle market, especially for the pioneers in the West, stimulated a great expansion of production and consequently a continuous search for methods to decrease the cost. The national arsenals at Harpers Ferry and Springfield became the base of operations for this demand and the private arms factories the source of specialized machines for this industry. Firms like the Ames Manufacturing Company (1829), Robbins and Lawrence (1838), Woodruff and Beach (1821), Brown and Sharpe (1833), and Jones and Lampson (around 1840) in New England, and William Sellers (1845) and S. V. Merrick (around 1836) in Philadelphia concentrated on this problem. The dates attributed to the principal machines simply indicate the termination of long periods of study and development. We note, for example, the vertical turret lathe of 1854 by Robbins and Lawrence, the milling machines of F. W. Howe (1822–1891) in the same firm in 1848 and 1852, the horizontal turret lathe by Fitch (1845), and the famous Lincoln milling machine of 1855. The effectiveness of these machines can be realized thanks to the development of exact methods of measurement that made possible the construction of the dividing engine by J. R. Brown (1850), the first American machine for automatically tracing graduations. In the following year Brown developed a set of calipers, applying the principle of the vernier, with which highly precise measurements of internal dimensions became possible for the first time.

In this period new weapons factories were established: the Colt factories (1853–1855) and those of Smith and Wesson (1857). As Joseph Wickham Roe says, the revolver belongs to Colt, but the realization of this type of production can be credited especially to Elisha K. Root (1808–1865). Root, head of the Colt factory, is known for his own contributions to the development of specialized machines and for his mandrel lathe and slotting machine.

Despite the importance of these weapons for machines and tool production we note an expansion after 1850 of the market for precision machines. Succeeding years saw the unexpected appearance of sewing machines by Allen B. Wilson (1850), Isaac M. Singer (1851), and Amos Howe (1853). These machines for domestic and industrial use, which required precision work, were perhaps the first articles of assembly-line production aside from the rifle and the watch. Production figures for Wheeler and Wilson permit us to evaluate one of the most important manufacturers of sewing machines and the degree to which invention preceded the development of a machine-tool industry that could turn out specialized equipment. Around 1853 to 1855 Wheeler and Wilson's production averaged fewer than 1,000 machines annually, but it rose to 8,000 machines in 1858. Output rose to 50,000 units by 1866, clearly indicating the beginning of genuine assembly-line production. In other words, it can be said that during the first ten years following the initiation of the industry, the source of production machines was the machine shop of the factory itself.

The introduction of watch manufacturing by Aaron L. Dennison (1812–1895) in 1848 gave rise to new demands for tools. It must be noted that this industry offers a good example of the importance of the private machine shop and of the great difficulties facing anyone interested in the technological history of the United States. The fact that the Patent Office's archives have a complete record of every innovation is most useful, but unfortunately they can give a completely deceptive impression. Struggles over marketing at this period forced businessmen to keep every advantage over their competitors a secret. Even hiring a skilled worker could be an extremely confidential matter. The result was that projects for developing machines were carried out in a private machine shop, access to which was forbidden to everybody except the owner. Any patent taken out had to be

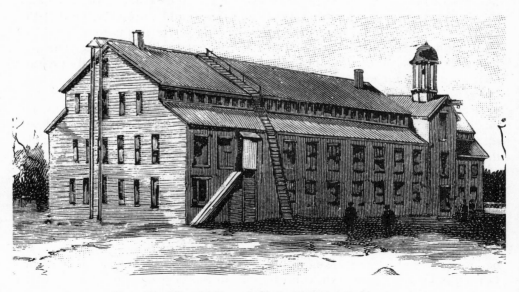

Plate 87. The old Slater Mill. Smithsonian Institution

capable of leading a competitor astray. This is why the statistics of patents in the United States testify, during a period of great fertility to an extraordinary lack of growth until the end of the Civil War. Modern research is concentrated on a reexamination of the history of this period in the hope of a more precise determination of the actual growth of specialized-machine production.

Railroad construction   The industry of the greatest importance for the expansion of the United States was that concerned with the production of locomotives and railroad carriages. We have already noted that although American locomotives were exported to England starting in 1838, the production methods depended on primitive tools. Gradually, around 1860, the large Baldwin enterprise adopted the system of interchangeability. In spite of this, it must be remembered, Americans soon discovered that local geographical conditions and extremely tolerant laws encouraged the development of a type of locomotive better adapted to narrow curves and to track of a very light cross section. Until around 1860 only iron rails were available to American railroads. The first steel rails were imported from England. Wheels with tires of steel surrounding a cast-iron center were developed also, around 1860, but even these were imported. We find the explanation for this in the history of steel production in the United States.

The evolution of metallurgy   Until the end of the Civil War the iron industry continued to develop largely within the local framework. In Europe technical progress was stimulated by a decrease in charcoal resources, and forges emigrated toward the coal measures. In the United States, in contrast, iron-ore deposits were widely dispersed and were always near forests. Until 1860 small forges and furnaces were typical of America. Water was generally the power used.

After the introduction of rolling mills in Pennsylvania around 1817, puddling furnaces began to appear, with coal as the fuel. The first steps were taken toward a greater concentration of the industry. In 1856 more than half the production of rolled iron came from Pennsylvania.

Raw material continued to arrive by waterway, coming chiefly from small forges in forest areas. In 1860 only 10 percent of the cast iron produced came from ore in the Lake Superior region, an area opened up by the construction of the Sault Sainte Marie canal in 1855. Although David Thomas (1794–1882) had introduced the large blast furnace at Lehigh in 1840, with a view to using coke, the great importance of the agricultural market, which preferred iron made with charcoal, retarded the expansion of this method of production. However, around the Civil War period the urgent requirements of railroads outstripped those of agriculture.

The steel age arrived in the United States after the Civil War, thanks particularly to Alexander Lyman Holley (1832–1882), who introduced the Bessemer method and adapted it to American needs. The small production of steel (less than 20,000 tons even in 1867) compared with a production of almost 1.5 million tons for cast iron and consisted for the most part of cementation steel.

In 1831 it was claimed that American steel for agricultural forging "is not first-quality, although it is the most frequently used, and American steel is com-

pletely equal to that of England for the same use. The American competition
completely kept out ordinary English blast steel. The only type of steel imported
from Great Britain was of a different and better quality." In this period production of crucible steel was begun, but very great difficulties were encountered when
an attempt was made to produce crucible steel, because of the lack of a clay suited
for making the crucibles. A crucible steel of trustworthy quality was not produced
until 1852, by a Pittsburgh company. This enterprise failed after two years of
production, a failure due partly to the alleged bad behavior of workers imported
from England, an explanation that must be taken with reservations. According to
Fitch, production of crucible steel was not completely established until around
1865, when the great revolution in the steel industry had already begun in
Europe. The Civil War was waged with wrought iron.

A general view   This study of a transitional period is merely an
                          outline to suggest the extent of the research remain-
ing to be done. Thirty years ago the history of American technology had only two
or three works as sources, which were quite important but not sufficient for the
modern historian. We refer especially to the famous report by Charles H. Fitch
(1883), the general history by Victor S. Clark (1916), and that of J. Leander Bishop
(1864). As supplements to these works we have several documents whose importance varies from one extreme to the other: on the one hand official studies
and reports from the Bureau of the Census, on the other more or less romantic
biographies of inventors and businessmen. Little or no interest was taken until
comparatively recently in the archives of the firms responsible for the development of American industry. It goes without saying that there is a pressing need for
a complete review of nineteenth-century history in the United States. This review
has already begun, with the help especially of studies of those private archives that
have survived. The point has not yet been reached where it is possible to assemble
all these histories in a complete work. Consequently, unduly conclusive gener-
alizations must be considered in discussing the conditions that were to be the
foundations of the later industrial predominance of the United States.

    We have seen that the circumstances under which the nation was founded in
1776 furnished a motive for inventions and at the same time retarded their
realization. It is at least possible to say that until 1850–1860 the roots of the
American industrial technique, in all its originality, were well established in
general in private machine shops, but that with certain exceptions that were
important even on the international scale, any general expansion did not occur
until after 1865. The industrial world was forewarned of the pressure of the
American system, but because all efforts were devoted after the Civil War to the
expansion of U.S. frontiers toward the West, Europe was not able to experience
their true significance until World War I.

BIBLIOGRAPHY

GENERAL WORKS

BISHOP, J. Leander. *A History of American Manufactures from 1608 to 1860.* 2 vols. Philadelphia: Edward Young and Co., 1864.

CLARK, Victor Selden. *History of Manufactures in the United States, 1607–1914.* 3 vols. Published for the Carnegie Institution of Washington by McGraw-Hill Book Co., Inc., New York, 1929.

U. S. Bureau of the Census, *10th Census of the United States, 1880.* Washington, D.C., 1883 / 84. The narrative of Charles H. Fitch is the first extensive description of the American system in official sources.

ON THE DEVELOPMENT OF THE AMERICAN SYSTEM

ROE, Joseph Wickham. *English and American Tool Builders.* New Haven: Yale University Press, 1916.

RECENT STUDIES

HINDLE, Brooke. *Technology in Early America.* Chapel Hill: University of North Carolina Press, 1966.

KRANZBERG, Melvin, PURSELL, Jr., Carroll W., and others. *Technology in Western Civilization.* Vol. I, New York, 1967; vol. II, New York, 1968.

Although grievously insufficient, the statistics of this period are found in convenient summary in:

U. S. Department of Commerce, Bureau of the Census, *Historical Statistics of the United States, Colonial Times to 1957* (prepared by the Bureau of the Census with the cooperation of the Social Science Research Council), Washington, D.C., 1960.

LARSON, Henrietta M. *Guide to Business History.* Cambridge, Mass.: Harvard University Press, 1950.

WOODBURY, Robert S. *History of the Great Cutting Machine* (1958); *History of the Grinding Machine* (1959); *History of the Milling Machine* (1960). Cambridge, Mass.: The Technology Press.

GENERAL BIBLIOGRAPHY

The reader is referred to the general bibliography in book I, page 574. See also the bibliographies for each part of this volume III, pages 89, 231, 390, 430, 472, 580, 653, 705, 733.

ARTZ, Frederick B. *The Development of Technical Education in France 1500-1850.* Cambridge, Mass., and London, 1966.

ASHTON, T. S. *La révolution industrielle.* Paris, 1955.

BALLOT, Charles. *L'introduction du machinisme dans l'industrie française.* Paris, 1923.

Brevets d'invention français (1791–1902). Catalogue d'exposition "Un siècle de progrès technique." Paris, 1958.

BURSTALL, Aubrey F. *A History of Mechanical Engineering.* London, 1963.

DUNHAM, (Arthur, Louis). *La révolution industrielle en France (1815–1848).* Paris, 1953. Extensive bibliography, but several technical weaknesses.

FIGUIER, Louis. *Les merveilles de la science,* 1st ed. 1867-1891; last ed., 1909-1910. To be used with care. Accurate enough for the fields that were developed at the time this author worked.

FINCH, James Kip. *The Story of Engineering.* New York, 1960.

Industrial Archaeology, The Journal of the History of Industry and Technology. Has appeared since 1964; vol. IV, 1967. The title was first *The Journal of Industrial Archaeology.* Revision: Kenneth Hudson, Bath University of Technology, Claverton Dawn, Bath, Somerset. Edition: David and Charles, South Devon House, Railway Station, Newton Abbot, Devon.

KLEMM, Frederic. *Histoire des techniques.* Paris, 1966. For a good introduction.

LABOULAYE, Ch. *Dictionnaire des Arts et Manufactures.* Paris, 1st ed., 1845-1861; 6th ed., 1886. (One can follow in detail progress over 40 years through the different editions.)

LE BLANC. *Recueil de machines.* Paris, 3 vols. (from 1819 on).

LÉON, Antoine. *Histoire de l'éducation technique, "Que sais-je?"* Paris, 1961.

MANTOUX, Paul. *La révolution industrielle au XVIIIe siècle.* Last ed., Paris, 1959.

SINGER, Charles, and others. *A History of Technology,* vol. IV: *The Industrial Revolution,* Oxford, 1958. Important. Extensive bibliography.

Transactions of the Newcomen Society. Annual report (vol. XXXVII, 1964-1965). Published by the Newcomen Society for the Study of the History of Engineering and Technology. This society whose headquarters is in London at the Science Museum in South Kensington, was founded in 1919 on the occasion of the centenary of the death of Watt.

USHER, Abbott Payson. *A History of Mechanical Inventions.* Boston, 1959.

Industrial expositions both national and international have yielded reports and literature that become very extensive after the middle of the century. These publications constitute sources of great interest that generally have been little used till the present. We cite, for example, the relevant reports for the following expositions: expositions of the products of French industry: year VI (Sept. 1798), year IX (1801), year X (1802), 1806, 1819, 1823, 1827, 1834, 1839, 1844, 1849. World expositions: London, 1851, Paris, 1855. Introduction to the general reports for the World expositions of 1878, 1899, 1900 in Paris.

INDEX

Note: page numbers in italics refer to illustrations

Abraham, Pol, 443
Académie des Sciences, 203,
    223, 330, 369, 557
    aerostation and, 371-73
    metric system and, 204, 205
    steamships and, 299, 300
Accum, Friedrich C., 463, 573
Achard, Franz Karl, 479, 576
Achromatic objectives, 218
Acquitaine, 478
Adding and subtracting machines:
    Pascal's, 168, 170-71, *171*
    Roth's, 175, *175*
    Schickard's, 168-70, *170*
Adolphus, Gustavus, 399
Aeolian mills, 22-23
Aerostation, 371-75
    Académie des Sciences and,
        371-73
    military, 373, 375
    See also Balloons
Agier, Delay d', 480-81
Agricola, Georgius (Georg
    Bauer), 505, 516, 531
Agricultural equipment, 487,
    497-504
    plows, 497-99, *497-99*, 722
    reaping and threshing
        machines, 500-2
    rollers, 499
    for seeding, 499
    sickles and scythes, 499-
        500, 529
Agricultural measures, 200
Agriculture (agricultural
    techniques), 2, 474-504
    clearing of new land, 484-85
    crop rotation, 475, 478,
        490-93
    enclosure movement in England,
        488-90
    in England, 475, 487-90
    fallowing, 485, 487-88
    in France, 475-85, 490-96
    grasslands, 479-82, 492-93
    growth and, 474-75
    land reclamation, 485-86
    new crops, 475-77
    rationalism in, 475
    scientific basis for, 486-87
    significance of the revolu-
        tion in, 503-4
    in the United States, 488,
        722
    See also specific crops
Agte, A. A., 714
Aguen, Laas d', 702
Ahmedabad, 636
Aiken, John, 77, 630
Alban, 565, 569

Albert, Charles, 76, 105
Albertyping, 686
Albion mills, *66*
Albion press, 661-62
Album tissiérographique, 692
Alcan, Michel, 599
Alembert, Jean d', 21
Alexandrian engineers, 178
Alfa grass, 576
Alfalfa, 479, 481
Alfonsine tables, 329
Alphabetical devices for tele-
    graphs, 382-83
Alpine compass, 508-9
Alsace, 492
Althans blowing engine, *544*
Althen, 496
Alum, 633-34, 637, 648
Aluminum, 554
American colonies, 722-24
American Revolutionary War
    (1775-1783), 111
Ames Manufacturing Company,
    729
Amiens, 276
Ammonia, soda manufacturing
    method using, 571-72
Ampélographie (Guyot), 494
Ampère, André Marie, 11, 93, 94,
    379
Amsler-Laffon, Jakob: plani-
    meter, 241
Amsterdam, 289
Anchor escapements, 190
    modern form of, *186*
    Mudge, *186*, 187
    recoil, 185, *185*
Anchor forge at Bristol, *173*
Anderson, Sir James Caleb, 265
Anderson, John, 45
André, Pierre-Frédéric, 700
Andrieux, 623
Anfry, 678
Angles, instruments for meas-
    uring, 214
Anisson, Laurent, 659, 686
    printing press by, 659-60,
        660, 665
Annealing, 100
Anossov, P. P., 713, *713*
Anson, George, 331
Antoni, Papacino d', 429
Anzin collieries, 76, 77, *526*
Appliances, household, 161
    See also specific appliances
Appolt, 551-52
Aqueducts, 251
Arago, Dominique François
    Jean, 283, 378, 524
    electromagnet and, 380

railroads and, 357, 359, 362
Arbuthnot, 498
Archimède (steamship), 314, *314*
Architectural rationalism,
    443-45
Architecture:
    cast-iron columns, 435-36,
        435, 443
    Chicago school, 445-47, *447*
    large single-story structures,
        436-41
    ribbed, 443
    steel-skeleton structures,
        441, 443
    traditional construction
        and, 433-34
    in the United States, 445,
        452
    Viollet-le-Duc's views on,
        443-45
    wooden structures, 447-48,
        448
    See also Construction tech-
        niques and materials; *and
        specific types of struc-
        tures*
Architecture hydraulique
    (Bélidor), 6, 28, 30, 71
Arçon, Michaud d', 392
Ardres mill, 32
Argand, Aimé, 283, 461-62, *461*
Ariège region, 485
Ariel (battleship), 325
Aristotle, 602
Arithmaurel, 175-77
Arithmometer: Thomas de
    Colmar's, 172-74, *174*, 177
Arkwright, Sir Richard, 589-
    92, 595
    carding machine by, 589-92,
        590, 595
    patent infringement suit by,
        591-92
    water frame by, 586-87, *587*,
        592
Arlandes, Marquis d', 370-71
Armengaud, Charles, 29, *32*, 38,
    78, 117
Ar-Men lighthouse, 288
Arnal, Abbot of, 74
Arnold, A., 596
Arnold, John, 187, 190, 197,
    330
Artesian wells, 524
Artillery:
    calibers, 399, 410-12
    carronades, 406-9, *407*, *408*
    eighteenth-century, 399-400,
        399
    firing mechanisms, 413

fortifications and, 393-96
by Gribeauval, 401-2
howitzers, 409-10, *409*
land, 399-405
naval, 406-13
production of, 403, 405
types of projectiles, 413
by Vallière, 400-2
velocity and range of projectiles, 412-13
See also Cannons
Art nouveau, 434, 451, *451*
Ascension Island, 331
Aspdin, Joseph, 449
Asphalt, 242
Assignats, printing of, 684,
686-87
Astrolabe, 215, 329
Astronomical clocks, 193, 195
Astronomical instruments, 4,
719
reflecting, 218-20
Athias, 671
Atmospheric engines, 39-44,
40, *42*, *43*, 71-72, 82
with automatic control
valves, 41
boiler of, 40, 42-44, *42*, *43*
calculating power of, 83
consumption of coal by, 84
cylinders of, 40, 44
double-acting, 52
early models of, 40-41
in Russia, 715
for ships, 299
use of, 41-42
See also Newcomen's steam
engine
Aubert, 623
Aubertot, 547
Auer, Aloys, 699
Auer burner, 465, *466*
Auer von Welsbach, Carl, 465,
466
Augé, 687
Austin, 604
Austria, 619
spinning machines in, 592
Automatic machines, early
origins of, 177-78
Automation, 178
early examples of, 180-81
mechanization and, 177
Automobiles, steam-powered,
267-68
Auzout, Adrien, 217
Avignon, Laurent d', *290*
Axe, 722
Axial water turbines, 35-38,
36
Axles, 257
of textile roller printing
machines, 643

Babbage, Charles, 176
Back sight, 427-28
Backstaff, 215, 329
Bacon, Richard M., 668
Badayev, S. I., 713
Badische Anilin und Soda
Fabrik, 564
Baily, Timothy, 626
Bain, Alexander, 380, 384
Baines, Sir Edward, 605
Bakewell, Robert, 483, 484
Baking, 161
Balaklava, artillery dock at,

398
Balance, Fortin's precision,
204
Balance press for working
platinum, *714*
Balance wheel, compensating,
189-90
Baldassare Capra of Padua, 213
Baldwin, Matthias, 112, 350,
359, 368, 727
Bale opener, cotton, 595
Ballast for railroad tracks,
336-37
Ball bearings for water turbines, 31
Ballistics, 422-29
back sight and, 427-28
beginnings of experimentation
with, 423-25
first studies on, 422-23
internal, 428-29
mathematics and, 426-27
mortars, 426
point-blank firing, 425
powders, 428-29, *428*
random firing experiments,
426
siege firing, 425-26
Balloon-frame construction,
447-48, *448*, 451, 452
Balloons, 369-75
fabrics for, 371-72
hot-air, 369-71, *370*
hydrogen, 369, 371-73, *373*,
375
scientific ascents on, 375
Baltard, Victor, 432, 437
Baradelle, 660
Barber, Robert, 604
Barber, Thomas, 604
Barfleur, lighthouses at, 285,
286
Barges, 271, 272
iron, 324
See also Flatboats
Barker, 31, *31*
Barletti de Saint-Paul, Mme.,
681
Bar loom, 602, 603
Barlow, 605
Barnes, 314
Barral, 375
Barrel organ, 178, 181
Barrels, rifled, 414, 416-19,
423-24
Bartels, Johann Just, 523
Bartlett, Thomas, 525
Barton, John, 65
Barton, Luke, 628
Basacle mills, 30
Baskerville, John, 704
Basse-Chaîne Bridge, 256-57
Bataille, E. M., *50*, *51*, *53*,
64, 88
Batik dyeing, 635-36
Battery, electric (voltaic
pile), 378-79, 716
Battleships, *see* Warships
Batwing burner, 465, *466*
Baudry, Stanislas, 259
Bauer, Andrew, 667, *667*
Bauer, Georg (Georgius
Agricola), 505, 516,
531
Bauerkeller brothers, 702
Baxter, George, 702
Baxter, Samuel, 312
Baxterotyping, 702

Bayen, Pierre, 416
Bayeux, 243, *244*
Bayonet, 421
Beams:
cast-iron, 435
stirrup, 450, *450*
wrought-iron, 435
Beam scales, 228
Beaucher, 662-65
Beaumont, Élie de (Duke of
Decazes), 494
Beaunier, 346
Becher, J.-J., 602
Becquay, François-Joseph de,
480
Becquerel, César, 378
Beet, sugar, 479, 492
production of, 576-78, *577*
Beighton, 82
Bélanger, 94
Belgium, 223, 236, 496
mining in, 522
railroads in, 359-60
Belgrand, 460
Bélidor, Bernard Forest de,
6, 28, 30, 71, 392, 423
Bell, Henry, 305, 318
Bell, John, 666
Bell, Thomas, 642
Bella, 498
Belleville multiple-tube ex-
plosionproof steam gener-
ator, 79, *79*
Bell lighthouse, 286-88
Belts, 99, *99*
Belt tightener, 99, *99*
Bements' mortising machine,
133
Bending machines, 156-58, *157*
Benoît, 226, 551, 614
Bensley, Thomas, 667
Bentham, Jeremy, 106, 126
Benzine, 574
Béranger, Joseph:
scale by, 228, *229*
weighbridge by, 230, *230*
Bérard, Aristide, 518
Berg Company, 709-10
Bergès, Aristide, 35
Bergman, Torbern, 553
Bergstrom, 176
Bernard, 683
Bernoulli, Daniel, 21, 25
Bernoulli, David, 299
Bernoulli, Jean, 423, 429
Berthelot, circular looms by,
625, *625*
Berthollet, Comte Claude Louis,
541, 556, 569
Berthoud, Ferdinand, 134, 187,
193, 330
chronometers of, 196, *196*
Berthoud, Louis, 331
Bertin, Louis François, 490,
496
Bertrand, 147
Berzélius, Jacob, 563
Besson, Jacques, 115
Best Friend locomotive, *368*
Bétancourt y Molina, 11
Béthencourt, Marquis de, 58,
74, 78, 94
Béthune-Charrost, Armand-
Joseph de, 480
Betts, John, 621
Beuvière, 698
Bewick, Thomas, 690-91, *691*
Beyer, Peacock and Company, 118

Bibliothèque Nationale (Paris), 436, 445, *449*
Bickford, William, 519
Bicycles, origin of, 268-70
Big Ben clock, 194
Bimetallic compensating device, 188-89, *189*
Binding-off machine, 631
Biot, Jean-Baptiste, 347, 375
Bird, John, 220, 221
Birds, singing, 179
Birembaut, M., 207
Birmingham-London railroad, 359, *361*
Bishop, J. Leander, 732
Bitumen road surface, 242
Bixio, 375
Black, Joseph, 43, 45, 46, 49, 56
Blackfriars bridge, 248
Black powder for blasting mines, 512
Blake, Francis, 43
Blakey, William, 146
Blanc, H., 728
Blanchard, Jean-Pierre, 112, 179, 371
copying lathe by, 728, *729*
Blanking press, 144
Blast furnaces, 527, 551-52, *551, 552*
Corngreaves', *545*
hot, 543-45, *544, 545*
in Russia, 712
in the United States, 731
Blauenstein, 532
Bleaching (bleaching products), 556-57, 568-70
for calico printing, 640
See also Chlorine; *and specific fabrics*
Blenkinsop, John, 339, *340*
Blind, the:
printing for, 662-65, *644*
writing machines for, 165
Blith, Walter, 498
Bloch, Marc, 490
Blois, bridge at, 243, *244*
Blondel, François, 422-23
Blowing engine, Althans', *544*
Blucher locomotive, 335, *335*, 337, 341
Boats, packet, 296
Bobbin-and-fly frame, 596
Bobbins, 595-96
of flyer spindle, 596, *597*
Bodmer, Johann, 107, 120, *120*
planing machine by, 130
Bogardus, James, 439, *439*, 441
Boileau, Louis-Charles, 437, 441, 444
Boilermaking, bending machines for, 157
Boilers:
of atmospheric engines, 40, 42-44, *42, 43*
Belleville's multiple-tube, 79, *79*
fire-tube, 345-47, *345, 347*
French, 63, 78-79, *79*
high-pressure, 58, 63, *63*
Lancashire, 63
for locomotives, *79*, 345-46, 349, 351, 352
marine, 318-20, *318*
of Newcomen's steam engine, 40
of steam carriages, 265, 267-

68
for steam heating, 469, *470*
Bolinder, 131-32
Bollée, Amédée, 267 *268*
Bolotov, A. T., 716
Bolton and Leigh railroad, 342
Bolts and nuts, threading machines and tapping machines for, 121-22
Bon Marché department store (Paris), 444
Bonnemain, 470
Booth, Harry, 342
Booth, Henry, 345
Borda, François, 331
Borda, Jean-Charles de, 26, 28, 33, 205, 209, 426
reflecting circle by, 219, *220*
repeating circle by, 204, 330
Borers, 105
Boreskov, M. M., *717*
Borgnis, 21, 94
Boring equipment for mining, 523-25, *524, 525*
Boring machines (or mills), 4, 49, 73, 112, 122-23
Cave's, 124
for cylinders, 103
Decoster's, 124
Smeaton's, 123
vertical, 123
Wilkinson's, 103, 123, *123*
Bosfrond, 71
Bossut, Charles, 26
Bouch, Thomas, 288
Bouchon, Basile, 180-81
looms by, 609-10, *609*
Boudet, 458
Boudier the younger, 685-86
Bouguer, Father Pierre, 326
Boulton, Matthew, 49, *56*, 58, 63, *66*, 72, 73, 82, 103, 144, 263, 435
horsepower as a unit of power and, 85
measurement of consumption of coal and, 84
Bourdon, François, 550
power hammers of, 147-49
Bourn, D., 589, 592
Bourne, William: *A Regiment for the Sea*, 328
Boury, 77
Boussingault, Jean-Baptiste, 487
Boutmy, G., 148
Boutron, 458
Bowsprit, 292, 293
Bowsprit gallant, 292
Brabant plow, 498, *498*
Braccio (fathom), 199-200
Braconnot, 578
Brahe, Tycho, 217
Braithwaite, John, 345
Brakes of locomotives, 355, *355, 356*
Bramah, Joseph, 105, 106, 126, 134
hydraulic presses of, 151
Branca, Giovanni, 583
Brandon, 606
Brandreth, Thomas, 339, 345
Brandt, Georg, 553
Brass, 101
for astronomical instruments, 220

machines to cut, 104
Brault, *36*
Brazil, 223
Breakers, lighthouses and, 288
Breakwaters, 278-79, *278, 280*
Breast wheel, 25, *25*, 27-29
Breechloading, 419-21, *419, 420*
Breguet, Abraham-Louis, 190-92, 330
telegraph systems by, 380, 383, *383*
Breitkopf, B. C., 688
Breitkopf, J. G., 693
Bresse, 492
Brest, 276
Brett, John W., 384, 387
Brezin, 262
Bridges, 242-57, 440
cast-iron, 250-53, *250-53*, 432-44
flow of rivers and, 245-46
Gauthey's, 247-48
iron, 253-57, *254-56*
of London, 248-51, *249*
of Paris, 251-53, *251-53*
Perronet's, 245-47, *245-47*
railroad, 343
stone, 242-45
suspension, 254-57, *255, 256*, 719
Telford's, 250, 251, 254-55, *255*
truss, 253
wooden, 242, *243*
Bridgewater, Duke of (Francis Egerton), 274
Brindley, James, 274
Briot, Nicolas, 144
Brisson, 205, 209, 349
Bristol, anchor forge at, *173*
Bristol Iron Company, 532-33
Britannia Bridge, 154, 253, *254*
Brittany, 476, 481-83
Brius, Ia. V., 710
Brougham carriage, *258*
Brouneckar, 498
Broussonet, Auguste, 480
Brown, J. R., 729
Brown, Samuel, 105, 158, 254
Brown and Sharpe, 729
Browne, Charles, 305
Bruned, M. I., 26
Brunel, Isambard Kingdom, 253, *254*, 307, 312, 314-16, 325, 337, 350
Great Western Railway and, 359
Brunel, Sir Marc Isambart, 105, 106, 624
Brunton, *341*
Brusnitsin, L. I., 714
Buchanan, Archibald, 595
Buck, 532
Buckley, H. C., 584
Buddicom, William, 366-67, *366*
Buffington, 443
Buffon, 284
Bujault, 487-88
Bullets, 415
rifled barrels and, 416-19, *418, 419*
Thouvenin-Minié, 418, *418*
See also Ballistics
Bunsen, Robert W., 554
Burdin, 30, 32-33, *33*
Burdon, Roland, 250, 432
Bureau of Longitudes, 330
Burgundy Canal, 272-73

Burners, 464-65, *465*
Burnham, Daniel H., 446
Burns, Thomas, 334
Burrill, E., *287*
Burstall, Timothy, 345
Burt, William Austin, 165
Bury, Edward, 349
Bushnell, David, 312
Butakov, 720
Butler, B., 592
Button, John, 626
Buxtorf, Emmanuel, 627, 630

Cables, 100, *100*
  bridges suspended from, 255-57, *255, 256*
  mine, 517, 523
  telegraph, 387-88
Cabrol, 545
Cachin, Baron, 280
Cadiat, 35
Cail, 111, 133, 352
Caillon's planing machine, 125-26
Calash, *257*
Calcium sulfide, soda production and recovery of, 566-67
Calculators (calculating machines):
  difference engines, 176-77
  Roth's, 175, *175*
  Schickard's, 168-70, *170*
  See also Adding and subtracting machines; Arithmometer; Multiplying machines
Calenders (mangles), 641
Calibers of cannons, 201
Calibers of guns and projectiles:
  naval, 410-12
  standardization of, 399
Calico printing, 587, 633-34, *650*
  coloring and mordanting materials, 648-49
  designers, 644-45
  dissemination in Europe, 638-39
  engraving plates, 645-46
  engraving rollers, 646-47
  in France, 638, 639
  hand and mechanical, 642-43, *642*
  indigo baths, 650-51
  origins and spread of, 636-38
  preparation of fabrics for, 640-42
  printer's work, 647-48
  Prussian blue, 651
  roller printing, 642-44, *643, 645*
  surface pigments, 649
  technical difficulties, 630-40
  See also Textile printing
Calipers, 158, 729
  outside, *212*
Calla, Étienne, 80, 108, 303
Calla, François, 108-9, 139
  punch shears of, 153, *153*
Calley, John, 40, 45
Callon, 35
Calway, J., *456*

Camm, John, 620
Cam profile, musical devices using, 179
Camus, A.-G., 95, 672, 675, 677, 684
Canada, fallowing in, 488
Canal du Centre (Charolais), 272
Canals, 272-76
  in England, 273-74
  in France, 272-73
Candles, 461
  stearine, 462-63, 578-79, *579*
Canne, 199
Cannons:
  boring, 73
  bronze, 406
  calibers of, 201
  carronades, 406-9, *407, 408*
  cartridges for, 401
  cast iron for, 403, 405
  drills and borers for, 105
  howitzers, 409-10, *409*
  production of, 403, 405
  rifled, 403
  sand molding of, 405, *405*
  Whitworth, 108
  See also Artillery
Canson, 576
Canvas, 606
Cape Horn, 331
Cape of Good Hope, 331
Carbine, Delvigne, 417, *418*
Carbonate of soda, *see* Soda
Carcassonne, 481
Carcel, Bertrand Guillaume, 283, 462
Carcel (lighting unit), 283
Carcel lamp, 283
Cardan joint, 100
Carding, 589-92, *590*, 595
Carding and drawing room, *613*
Carez, Joseph, 677, 681
  stereotyping by, 673, 677-78
Carlyle, 379
Carnot, Sadi, 11, 78, 94
Carny, 557, 565
Carriages, 257-58, *257, 258*
  steam-powered, 260, 263-65
Carronades, 406-9, *407, 408*
Carter, J., *613*
Cartier, gear-cutting machines of, 142-43
Cartridges:
  for blasting mines, 512
  gun, 414, 415, 420
  cannon, 401
Cartwright, Edmund, 53, *53*, 65, 76, 593, 604
Casalis, 77
Casemates, 393, *393*
Cassini, Jean-Dominique, 205, 207, 220
Castelnaudary, 492
Casting machines, 694, 695
Cast iron:
  atmospheric engines, 42
  blast furnaces for, *see* Blast furnaces
  bridges, 250-53, *250-53*, 432-33
  casting of, 529, *543*
  coke smelting of, 533-34
  columns, 435-36, *435*, 443
  loom frames, 604
  pipes, 455, 469
  rails, 332-33
  refining, 527-28, 534

reverberatory furnaces for, 403, 405, 534-36, 570, 714
  in Russia, 714-15
  steam engine framing, 63-64
  in the United States, 731
  water valves, 457, *457*
  See also Iron
Catechu, 649
Cattle-breeding techniques, 478, 482-84
Caustic soda (sodium hydroxide), 569
Cavalli, 403
Cavalry pistol, 415
Cavé, François, 65, 69, *69*, 110-11, 139, 152, 272
  bending machines of, 157
  boring mill of, 124
  locomotive by, 366, *366*
  power hammers by, 147, 148
  punch shears of, 153
  riveter built by, 155
Cavendish, Henry, 372, 487
Caze de la Bove, 483
Cécile, 78
Célérifère, 268
Cellini, Benvenuto, 144
Cembalo-scrivano of Ravizza, 167-68, *168*
Cement, 449
Cementation steel, 540, 713, 731
Center lathe, 117
  simple, 117
Centesimal weighbridge, *229*, 230
Cercle hollandais (Dutch circle), 216, *216*
Cessart, 501
Chabaneau, 553
Chaillot foundry, 73-74
Chaillot steam pump, *71*, 72-73
Chains:
  bridges suspended from, 255-56, *256*
  Vaucanson, 103-4
Chaléat, Rev. R., *186*, 187, *187*
Chaley, 255
Chalk, 648
Châlons school, 108
Chancellor Livingston (steamboat), 305, *305*
Chandell, Robert, 532
Chapeaudage, 646
Chapman, William, 342, 350
Chappe, Claude, 376-77, 379, 720
Chaptal, Jean, 487, 491, 560, 564, 565, 569, 617
Charcoal for blast furnaces, 527
Charentes provinces, 492
"Charlemagne stack," 205-7
Charles, Jacques-Alexandre, 369, 371, 372
Charles-Philippe (steamship), 271-72
Charlotte Dundas (steamship), 302-3
Chassepot rifle, 421
Chasseurs, 417, 419
Chateau, Pierre, 720
Châtellerault munitions factory, 108
Chaulnes, Duke of, 221
Chemical engraving (photozincography), 692
Chemical fertilizers, 574

Chemistry (chemical industry), 556-79
  beet sugar production and, 576-78, *577*
  bleaching, *see* Bleaching
  coal distillation industry, 572-74
  explosives and, 579
  heavy equipment in, 570-71
  industrialization of, 564
  of metals, 553
  papermaking industry, 575, *575*, *576*
  soda, *see* Soda
  stearin production and, 578-79
  sulfuric acid, *see* Sulfuric acid
Chenier, L. de, 677
Chepstow Bridge, 253
Cherbourg, 277-81
Cheret, 145
Chevalier, Auguste, 492
Chevalier, Charles, 698
Chevalier, Michel, 149, 485
Chevreul, Eugène, 11, 463, 578
Chézy, Antoine de, 246, *246*
Chicago school, 445-47, *447*
Chicago skyscrapers, 443
Chickens, 484
Chicory, 496
Chile, 223
Chimneys, canted flue, 433
China, stereotyping in, 671-72
Chintzes, 638, 639
Chirk aqueduct, 251
Chistiakov, P., 720
Chlatter, I., 710
Chlorine, 556-57
  manufacturing of, 567-68, *568*
Chocolate, 161
Chocolat Menier Company, 443
Choiseul, Duc Étienne François de, 262-63, 403
Cholera epidemics, 453, 458, 460
Chopitel, 150
Chrome, 553
Chrome mordant, 649
Chronometers, marine, 195-97, *195*, *196*, 330-31
  by Berthoud, 196, *196*
  by Le Roy, 196, *196*
Chronoscope, electromagnetic, 717
Church, William, *287*, 694
Cigarette paper, 576
Circular knitting machines, 623-26, *625*, 628, 629, 632
Circular saw, 105
Cities, population growth in, 474
Civil War (American), *400*, 579
Clamand, 465
Clapeyron, 94, 349
Clarence carriage, *258*
Clark, Thomas, 458
Clark, Victor S., 732
Claus, 566, 567
Claussen, P., 631
Clegg, Samuel, 357, 463, 465, 573
Clement, Joseph, 103, 106, 118
  planing machine by, 126-27
Clement, William, 185
Clément-Desormes, Nicolas, 561, 571
Clermont (steamboat), 106, *304*,

305
Clichéspierre, 692
Clippers, 296-97, *297*
Clock factory of Frédéric Japy, 182-83
Clockmaking (clocks), 4, 160, 178
  astronomical, 193, 195
  compensating for heat, 188-90, *189*
  early techniques of, 183-84
  escapements, 184-88, *185*, *186*, *188*
  factory production of, 182-84
  isochronism, 190
  machines for, 104-5
  observatory, 194
  pendulum, 192-94
  planetary, 193
  public (monumental), 194-95
  regulators, 192-94
Clousier, 662
Clover, 479-81
Clutch for transmission shafts, 99, *100*
Clymer, George E.: printing press by, 661, *662*
Coal:
  consumption of, 83
  distillation of, 572-74
  heating with, 468
  measurement of, 83, 84
  mining for, 507
  washing of, 518
Coalbrookdale:
  bridge at, 250, *250*
  cast-iron rails in, 332-33
Coal gas, 463, 573
  See also Gas lighting
Coal mining, prospecting, 507
Coal tar, 574
Coastal navigation, 295-96
Cobalt, 553
Cochelet, Adrien, 617
Cochrane, Archibald, 573
Cockerill, John, 360, 362
Coeurdoux, Father, 638
Coffee, 496
Cofferdams, 511-12
Coffering, 511-12
Cohorn, Baron de (Louis de Menno), 395
Coignet, Edmond, 451
Coignet, F., 449, *450*
Coining of money, 144
Coke, iron smelting with, 531-34, 542, 551-53
Coke, Thomas W., 488, 490, 499
Colbert, Jean-Baptiste, 328, 403, 483
Collado: *Manual de artilleria*, 105
Collas, Achille, 697
Collet, Anton, 112
Collier, George, 605
Collier, John, 593
  cropping machine by, 617, *817*
Collier, William, 593
Colliers, 296, 297
Colliery railroads, 332-35, *334*, *335*, 339
Colling, Charles, 484
Colling, Robert, 484
Colombia, 223
Color engraving, 701-2
Colt's Patent Fire Arms Manufactory, *415*, *417*, *418*, 729

Columbian press, 661, *662*
Columbus, Christopher, 329
Columns, cast-iron, 435-36, *435*, 443
Combes, Charles, 522
Combines, 501
Combing machines:
  for flax, 593, *593*
  for wool, 593-95, *594*
Comet (warship), 305, *305*, 307, 318
Committee on Preparatory Research (France), 224
Communication, *see* Telegraphs
Compagnie Continentale pour la fabrication des Compteurs à gaz (Continental Company for the Production of Gas Meters), *464*
Compagnie de Saint-Gobain, 566
Compagnie des Eaux, 73, 74
Compagnie des Indes, 277
Compagnie du Chemin de fer de Saint-Étienne à la Loire, 346
Compagnie Générale des Omnibus, 260
Compagnie Générale Transatlantique, 312
Compagnie Parisienne du Gaz, 463
Comparator, 202
  Hartmann's automatic recording, 203
  Lenoir's, 205, 210-11, *210*
  for revising standard meter, 223, 224
Compasses, 329
  Alpine, 508-9
  mine, 508-9, *508*
  reducing, 212, *212*
Composing machines, 694-96, *695*
Compressed-air drill, 525
Compressor roller, 241-42, *241*
Comptoir d'Escompte (Discount Bank), 109
Comtat Venaissin, 496
Concrete, reinforced, 448-51
Condensers:
  steam-engine, 46, *48*
  for steamship engines, 319-20
  See also Condensing engines
Condensing engines, 44-50, *47*, *48*, *50*, 82
  double-acting, *see* Double-acting engines
  financial agreements and lawsuits involving, 49-50
  in France, 72-73
  industrial construction of, 49
  origin of Watt's work on, 45-46
  principle of the condenser, 46
  1769 patent taken out by Watt on, 48-49
  Watt's experimental model, 46, 48, *48*
  See also Steam engines
Condie, John, 544
Condorcet, Marquis Marie Jean Antoine de, 204, 205
Congreve method, 702
Considere, Louis, 451
Construction techniques and materials:
  architectural consequences

of, 451-52
cast-iron columns, 435-36, *435*, 443
iron, 432-41, 443, 451
large single-story structures, 436-41
reinforced concrete, 448-51
steel, 440-41, 443, 446
steel-skeleton structures, 441, 443
traditional, 433-34
wood, 447-48, *448*
wrought-iron, 434, 435
See also Architecture; *and specific types of structures*
Consumption of coal, 83
by steam engines: measurement, 83, 84
Contamin, Victor, 432, 440
Conté, Nicolas-Jacques, 372, 373, 375, 697
Conti, Pietro, 165
Control valves, in atmospheric engines, 41
Cook, James, 296
Cook, George, 619-20
Cooke, Sir William F., 380, *381*, 382, 387
Cookware, cast-iron, 533
Cooper, Peter, *368*
Copeley, 532
Copper, 553-55
in Russia, 713-14
Copper mines at Falun, *513*
Copperplate impression cylinder, 665-66
Copperplate printing, four-color, 701-2
Copperplates:
stereography, 684-88
for textile printing, 642-44, 646
Copper sheathing of hulls, 326
Copying lathe, 112, 718, 728, *729*
Coquet-Vivien, 626
Coradi, 241
Cordier, 77
Coriolis, Gaspard Gustave de, 21
Cork-making machine, 161
Corliss, George Henry, 79
Corliss engine, *727*, 728
Cormontaigne, Louis de, 392
Corn, 475, 477, 492
Corngreaves' blast furnace, *545*
Corngreaves' hot-air stove, *544*
Cornish engines, 66-68, *67*, 87
Corse (steamship), 314, 315
Cort, Henry, 150, 535-39
Corvettes, 294, 309
Cottancin, 449
Cotton, 591
bales of, 595
bleaching, 640
carding of, 589-92, *590*, 595
machines for manufacture of, 595-96
mercerizing, 569
printed, *see* Textile printing
See also Spinning of textile fibers
Cotton, William: knitting loom by, 629-30, *629*
Cotton gin by Whitney, *627*, 727
Coulomb, Charles Augustin de, 21, 209, 239

Counter, 87
Counter (counterweighted) scales, 228-29, *229*
Courrejollet, 77
Courtois, Bernard, 578
Coutelle, 372, 373, 375
Couturat, Léon, 629
Cows, *478*, 482-84
Cox, 551
Coysevox, 179
Crampton, Thomas R., 352, *352*
Cranage, George, 534-35
Cranage, Thomas, 534-35
Crane, Josiah, 621
Cranes, 718
Creosote, 574
Crimean War, 403
Crompton, Samuel, 588
Cronstedt, Baron Axel F., 553
Cropping (shearing), mechanization of, 615-18, *615-17*
Cropping machines, 599
Crop rotation, 475, 478, 490-93
in France, 491-93
Cross-staff (Jacob's staff), 214, *214*, 329
Crown-wheel escapement, 184-85
Crozat, 276
Crucible furnace, 570
Crucible steel, 541, *541*, 713, 732
Cruges, Henry, 470
Cruikshanks, William, 378
Crushing of ore, 517
Crystal Palace (London), *437*, 438-39
Cuba, 223
Cubitt, Lewis, *445*
Cugnot, Nicolas Joseph, 72
steam-powered wagon of, 260-63, *260-62*
Cullingham, *368*
Culs-de-lampe, 691
Cunard Line, 312, 325
Cup valves, 524
Curr, John, 333
Currier, Nathan, *273*
Cutoff valve of double-acting engines, 55
Cutters, milling, 142
Cutting tools, 105
Cuvillier, *169*
Cycloped, 345
Cylinder escapement, 186, *186*, 187
Cylinders:
of atmospheric engines, 40, 44
boring machine for, 103
of condensing engines, 46, *48*
steam engines with oscillating, 68-69, *69*
Cylindrical impression, 665-66
Cylindrical inch foot, 83-84

Dacklet, 499
Dagoty, Gautier, 701
Daguerre, Louis Mandé, 698
Daguin, Ernest, 572
Daimler, Gottlieb, 469
Dallery, Charles, 312, *314*
Dalton, John, 58, 78
Damascus steel, 713, *713*
Damiron, 161
Dams in Russia, 715

Danforth, Charles, 596
Danfrie, Philippe, 215
Dangon, Claude, 608
Daniell, J. F., 378-79
Daniell battery, 378-79, *379*
Daracott, G., 144
Darby, Abraham, 250, 332, 532-33, 538
Darby, Abraham II, 533, 538
Darby, Abraham III, 432
Darcet, Jean Pierre Joseph, 209
D'Arcy, 429
D'Artigues, 218
D'Artois, Count, 569
Daubeny, Charles G. B., 487
D'Auxiron, Joseph, 299-300
Da Vinci, Leonardo, 583, 614
Notebooks, 599
shearing machine by, 615, *615*, *616*
weaving and, 599, 602
Davis, John, 329
Davis, T. R., *727*
Davis quadrant, *214*, 215, 219, 329
Davrainville, 178
Davy, Sir Humphry, 487, 490, 519
Davy lamp, 519
Dawson, William, 621
Deacon, H., 569
Deadbeat escapement, 185-87, *185*, 709
Deane, Sir Anthony, 324, 326
De Baudot, 450
De Bellenoüe, 500
Deboutteville, 606
Debray, Henri, 224
Decameter, 226
Decazes, Duke of (Élie de Beaumont), 494
De Cessart, 278, *278*, 279
Decimal system of weights and measures, 223
Decimal weighbridge, *229*, 230
Declination, 329
Decoster, Pierre, 109, 121, 122
boring mills of, 124
drills of, 139
gear-cutting machines by, 143-44
milling machines by, 135-36
shaping machines by, 132-34, *132*
shears of, 153-54
slide lathe prototypes built by, 119
Decoudun, 89
Decroix, 623
Decroizilles, 578
De Dartein, 243
Deere, John, 498, *499*
Deffontaines, P., 484
Defoe, Daniel, 236, 479
Deforestation, 485, 531
Defrance, Léonard, *530*
De Froidour, 485
Dégageux, Hippolyte, 624
De Gasparin, Count Adrien, 487, 498, 499, 501
De Gennes, 602
De Guerchy, 480
De La Bretonnière, 278
Delachaussée, Mme., 144
Delamare, 606
Delambre, Jean Baptiste Joseph, 205, 207
Delamolère, 22

De La Morinière, 122
  planing machine by, 127-28
De La Platière, Roland, 611
Delarothière, Joseph-Auguste,
  621-23
Delarue, Thomas, 161
Delaunay, Léon, 377
De Lazowski, 480
Delcambre, Adrien, 694-95, *695*
Delisle, 315
De Lôme, Dupuy, 317, 322
  iron ships and, 325
Delvigne, Lt. Henri Gustave,
  417
Delvigne carbine, 417, *418*
Demarne, 234
Demetrius I, 395
De Milly, Adolphe, 578
Demologos (steamboat), 305,
  305, 306, *306*
Demolon, A., 486
Denison, Edmund Beckett (Lord
  Grimthorpe), 194
Denmark, 484-85
Dennison, Aaron L., 730
Deparcieux, Antoine, 28
De Pont, Mme., 480
Deriabin, A. F., 712
De Rivaz, Isaac, 264, *264*, 301
Derosne, 111, 133, 352
Derosne & Cail, 157, 366
  power hammer of, *549*
Derriey, Jules, 670
Désaguliers, 28, 31, *31*, 41, 82
Desblanc, 301, *301*, 303-4
Desbordes, 89
De Servière, 687
Detached escapement of Le Roy's
  chronometer, 196, *196*
Detent escapement, 187-88, *188*,
  190
D'Etigny, 481, 483
De Turbilly, 480
Deveral, 549
Deverell, William, 146
Deverill, Hooton, 647
De Villèle, 480
De Voglie, 243
De Wendel, Charles Alexis, 333
Deyeux, 577
Diaz, Bartholomew, 327
Dickinson, H. W., 39-42, *48*
Diderot, Denis, 105, 134, 146,
  150, 171, 183, 201-2, 527,
  528, 656, *658*
Didion, Gen., 427-28
Didot, Firmin, 672, 675, 678,
  693, 694
Didot, François-Ambroise:
  printing press by, 659-60,
  665
Didot, Pierre, 659, 679, 686
Dietz, Charles: steam car-
  riages by, 265, *265*
Difference engines, 176-77
Digges, Leonard, 216
Digges, Thomas, 216
Distillation, *see under*
  specific materials
Divider, proportional, 212-14,
  213
Dividing engine, 729
Dividing machines, 221-22, *221*
Dizé, 557
Docks, dry, 281-82
Dodds, Ralph, 341
Doebereiner, 563
Dollond, John, 218

Dombasle, Mathieu de, 487, *497*,
  499, 501
Dombasle plow, 497-98, *497*
Donkeys, 483
Donkin, Bryan, 668
Dorr, G., 617
Dorr, R., 617
Double-acting engines, 47, 50-
  59, 70-71, 74, 76, 77, 103,
  712
  cutoff valve of, 55
  experiments leading to, 52-53
  governor of, 55, *55*
  for hoisting coal, 517
  parallel motion and, 54, *54*
  planetary gear of, 54
  principle of, 53-54
  in Russia, 715-16
Double-expansion engines, 77
Douglas (textile mfr.), 6155
Douglas, Sir James, 288
Douine, Hippolyte, 626
Douro bridge, 440
Dowsing rod, 507
Draft of horses and horsedrawn
  vehicles, 239-40, *240*
Drainage of land, 485-86
Draisienne, 268, *269*
Drais von Suerbron, Baron, *165*,
  166, 268
Dralet, 485
Draperies, looms for, 605
Drawbench, 145-46
Drawing mills, 529
Draw loom, 607-9, *607*, *608*
Dredges, 289-90, *290*
Dreyse, Johann Nikolaus von,
  420
Dreyse rifle, 420-21, *420*
Drift mining, 510-11, *511*
Drill bit, 509
Drilling machines (drills),
  105, 119, 136-39
  compressed-air, 525
  cutting speeds of, 139
  horizontal bow, 104
  hydraulic, 524-25, *525*
  mining, 523-25, *524*, *525*
  radial, 111, 138-39, *139*
  in Russia, 717-18
  vertical, 137-38, 717-18
  Whitworth's, 138, *138*
Drop hammer, 145
Drop stamping, 717
Dry docks, 281-82
  See also Graving docks
  at Brest
Dubied, 111
Dubois, teaseling machine by,
  615
Dubois, Guillaume, 403
Dubrunfaut, Auguste Pierre, 579
Du Buat, 245-46
Ducommun, 111
Du Coudray, Tronçon, 427
Dudley, Lord Robert, 532
Dudley, Sir Robert, 532
Dufaud, G., 537
Du Fay, Charles François de
  Cisternay, 203
Duhamel-Dumonceau, Henri
  Louis, 294, 487
Duillier, Nicolas Fatio de,
  190
Dujardin, 167
Dumas, Jean-Baptiste André,
  487, 559, 561
Dumont, 623

Dumotiez, Francois, 210
Dumotiez, Joseph, 210
Dundas, Lord, 302-3
Dunlop, C. T., 568-69
Dunlop, John Boyd, 270
Duny, Abbot, 554-55
Dupeyrat, 688
Dupin, François Pierre Charles,
  239
Duplat, M., 666, 691
Dupont, Auguste, 692, 700
Duportail, 551
Du Puget, 427
Dupuit, 239-41
Duquet (du Quet), 312, 501
Durenne, Antoine, 156
Dutch circle, 216, *216*
Dutch loom, 628-31, *628*
Dutert, Charles, 432, 440
Duverger, E., 693
Duvoir, Léon, 470, 471, *471*
Dyar, H. G., 572
Dyeing:
  batik, 635-36
  in Egypt, 636-37
  sulfuric acid used in, 558
  tie, 635
  See also Textile printing
Dyes, 579
Dynamite, 579
Dynamometer, 239-40, *240*

Earnshaw, Thomas, 187, 190,
  197, 330
East India Company, 324
Eclecticism in architecture,
  433
École des Ponts et Chaussées
  (School of Bridges and
  Highways), 235, 245
École Polytechnique, 94
École Royale d'Arts et Métiers,
  108
Ectot, Mannoury d', 32, *32*
Eddystone lighthouses, 282,
  286, *287*, 288
Edgeworth, Richard Lovell, 139
Edwards, John, 62, *62*, 77
Egberts, E., 626
Egerton, Francis (Duke of
  Bridgewater), 274
Egypt, textile printing in,
  636-37
Ehrenberg, 533
Eiffel, Gustave, 444
  Eiffel Tower by, 440-41, *441*
  Gallery of Machines (1867)
  by, 439
Eiffel Tower, 440-41, *441*
Elastic structure, 440
Electrical industry, telegraphy
  and, 389
Electric battery, 378-79, 716
Electricity, 433
  in Russia, 716-17
Electric power, 100
Electromagnetic chronoscope,
  717
Electromagnetic generators,
  717
Electromagnetic motor, 717
Electromagnetism, 11
  telegraph and, 379-80
Electroplate facsimiles, 698-
  99
Electroplating, 717

Electrotherapy, 716
Electrotyping, 693-94
Elevator, 718
Elise (steamship), 272, 310
Ell, 199
Elliot, Obadiah, 265, 566
Ellis, Jonathan, 617
Ellman, John, 483
Embossing, 702
Embroidering machine, 161-62
Emerson, James, 150, *150*
Emerson, William, 538
Emery wheels, 140
Enclosure movement:
    in England, 488-90
    in France, 490-91
Engelhard, Otto, 112
Engelmann, G., 700
Engerth, Wilhelm: locomotive
    by, 362, *362*
Engineering, 93
    mechanical, 4-5
Engineers:
    Alexandrian, 178
    bridge and highway, 235-37
Engines, *see* Internal-
    combustion engine by de Rivaz;
    Steam engines
England, 248
    agriculture in, 475, 487-90
    calico printing in, 638
    canal network in, 273-74
    clover in, 479-81
    enclosure movement in, 488-90
    horses in, 483
    iron and steel industry in,
        531-45, *546*
    land improvement in, 486
    livestock in, 482-84, 490
    population growth in, 474
    potato in, 476, 477, 490
    road-building in, 236-38
    steamship experiments in,
        302-3
    sugar beet in, 479
    turnips in, 478-79
    See also Great Britain;
        London
English blue, 650
Engramelle, Rev., 179
Engraving:
    automatic, 180
    black-line on end-grain wood,
        690-91, *690, 691*
    black-line on stone, 691-92
    chemical (photozincography),
        692
    color, 701-2
    See also Intaglio printing
Engraving machines, 696-97
    by Rochon, 680-81, *680*
Enschedé, Izaak, 688
Envelope-folding machines, 161
Epidemics:
    cholera, 453, 458, 460
    livestock, 482
Ericsson, John, 312, 314, 315,
    315, 345
Erie Canal, 275
Ernle, Lord (Rowland Edmund
    Prothero), 478
Escapements, 184-88, *185, 186,
    188*, 194
    of Le Roy's chronometer, 196,
        196
    of watches, 190
Esparto grass, 576
Essonne paper works, 575, *575*

Établissement de constructions
    mécaniques, 111
Établissement d'Indret, 322
Établissements Cail & Cie,
    157, 366
Établissements Pechiney, 572
Euler, Leonhard, 21, 28, 423,
    424, 429, 715
Europe:
    iron industry and economic
        situation in, 542
    knitting centers in, 619
    railroads in, 360, 362
    See also specific countries
Evacuation chest in a steam-
    heating installation, *470*
Evans, Oliver, *502, 503, 537*
    steam engines by, 59, 61, *61*,
        265, 727-28
Evrard, Maximilien, 524
Explosives, 579
    electrical detonation of,
        716-17
    for military mines, 396-97
    in mining, 519, 521, 716-17
    See also Gunpowder
Expositions, 438
    See also specific expositions
Eyelet holes, machines, 621
Eyepieces, precision instru-
    ments with, 217-18

Fabrics:
    bleaching, 557
    coloring, *see* Textile print-
        ing
    figured, 606-12, *607-11*
    fulling of, 612, 614, *614*
    patterned, 606
    teaseling or napping of,
        614-15
    See also Textile industry
Fabri de Peiresc, Cl., 679
Fabroni, Giovanni Valentino
    Matteo, 205
Face lathe, 117, 120
Factories, 2, 100
Fairbairn, William, 118, 253,
    431
    riveter of, 154, *154*
Fair Store Building (Chicago),
    446, *447*
Falaise, circular knitting
    machines in, 624
Falcon, 180-81
    looms by, 609-12, *610*
Fallowing, 485, 487-88
Fanning mill, 502
Fans for mine ventilation, 522,
    712
Farcot, Joseph, *78,* 79
Farcot firm, 225
Farey, John, *44, 48, 56,* 82, 83
Fariat, 626
Farming, *see* Agriculture
Fasteners, 161
Fathom, 201, 203
    braccio, 199-200
    toise, 199, 200
Faucets, 456-57
Faujas de Saint-Fond,
    Barthélemy, 480
Fauvelle, Pierre-Pascal, 524-
    25, *525*
Favier, 240
Favre, Antoine, 179

Fayolle, 150
Felkin, 620, 621, 631
Fellenberg, 499
Fenbach, 38
Fenon, Auguste, 194
Fenton, Roger, 339, *398*
Feost, 499
Ferrand, 162
Ferrous oxide for purifying
    illuminating gas, 574
Fertilization of soil, 485-86
Fertilizers, chemical, 574
Festy, O., *493*
Fiezinger, 687
Figuier, Pierre, 578
Figures, automatic, 179
File, slotting, 104
Finiguerra, Maso, 704
Firebox of atmospheric engines,
    42, 43
Firedamp explosions, 518-19
Fireplaces, 467-68
Fire-tube boiler, 345-47, *345,*
    347
Fishing nets, 611
Fish-tail burners, 464-65
Fitch, Charles H., 727, 729,
    732
Fitch, John, 302, 303
    propeller-driven boat of,
        312, *312*
Fitzgerald, Keane, 52, 151
Fizeau, Armand Hippolyte Louis,
    224, 698
Flachat, Eugène, 349, 358
Flad, M., 175
Flail, 501
Flamsteed, John, 330
Flanders, 482, 490
Flatboats, *273,* 274
    See also Barges
Flavius Vegetius: *De re mili-
    tari,* 395
Flax, 592-93, 640
Fleury, Cardinal André Hercule
    de, 403
Flint, 218
Flintlock rifle, 414-16, *414*
Flintlocks for naval artillery,
    413
Flour mill, 74
Flying shuttle, 601-6, *602, 603*
Flywheel, knitting machine
    with, 627-28
Focq, Nicolas, 72, 101
    planing machine by, 125, *125*
Fodder, 482
Fodder plants, leguminous, 480,
    481
Font, Rodon, 612
Fontaine, P.-J., 523
Fontaine-Baron, 35-37, *36,* 38
Foot (measurement), 198-99
Forfait, Pierre-Alexander
    Laurent, 326
Forge hammer, 146
Forges in America, 723-24
Forging, 529, 530, 717
Forster, John, 476
Fortifications, 392-97
    organization of protected
        areas, 393
    of Paris, 392-95, *392, 394*
Fortin, Nicolas, 206, 210, 222,
    372
Fort Totten (United States),
    400
Foster, 501

Foucauld, Pierre, 167
Foulis, Andrew, 676
Foundry, *530*
Fouquet, 626
Fourché, 210
Fourcroy, Antoine François, 685
Fourneyron, Benôit, 33-35, *34, 35,* 37
Fournier (sheep breeder), 483
Fournier, Rev., 328
Fournier the younger, 688
Fourth of September burner, 465
Fox, Sir Charles, 551
Fox, James, 107, 152
  planing machine by, 126
  slide lathe by, 118, *118*
Foxlow, 74
Foy, Alphonse, 383, 690
France:
  agriculture in, 475-85, 487, 490-96
  bridges in, 242-48, 251-53
  calico printing in, 638, 639
  canals in, 272-73
  corn in, 477, 492
  crop rotation in, 491-93
  enclosure movement in, 490-91
  grasslands in, 480-81, 492-93
  horse breeding in, 483
  iron industry in, 542, 553
  knitting industry in, 619-21, 624-26, 632
  land clearing in, 485
  livestock in, 482-84
  machine-tool industry in, 107-11
  metric system in, 203-11, 222-26
  mining in, 507, 508
  naval artillery in, 408-9
  navy in, *see* Navy, French
  population growth in, 474
  potato in, 476-78, 492
  railroads in, 346-49, 351, 357-59, 362-67, *364-66*
  railroad track gauge in, 338
  road-building and highways in, 235-37, 239
  silkworm breeding in, 495-96
  spinning machines in, 592
  steam engine in, 70-80
  steamship experiments in, 299-301
  sugar beet in, 479, 492
  telegraphs in, 380, 383-84, 388
  tobacco in, 496
  vineyards in, 494-95
  water turbines in, 29-30
  See also French Revolution; Paris; *and specific topics*
Franche-Comté, 492
François, 480, 686
Franco-Prussian War, 394-95
Frank, A., *287*
Franklin, Benjamin, 656, *659,* 684, 704
Frasch, Herman, 562
Fraunhofer, Joseph von, 218
Frederick the Great, 484
Frémont, 145-46
French boilers (Lancashire boilers), 63, 78-79, *79*
French Restoration, 77-78
French Revolution, 73, 74, 204
Fresnel, Augustin-Jean, 283, 572
  lens system developed by, 284-85, *284, 285*
Fresnel, Léonor, 288
Fribourg, bridge at, 255
Frigates, 294-97, 309, 324
Frisius, Gemma, 195
Frolov, K. D., 710-11, *711,* 715, 719
Froment, Gustave, 383-84, *384*
  magnetoelectric motor by, 389, *389*
Fulling machines, 612, 614, *614,* 640
Fulton, Robert, 106, 108, 274, 302-6, *304-6,* 312
Fulton I (warship), 306-7, *306*
Funckter, J. Michael, 675
Furnaces:
  blast, *see* Blast furnaces
  for chemical industry, 566, 570-71, *571*
  crucible, 570
  puddling, 536-37, 547-48, *547,* 731
  reverberatory, *see* Reverberatory furnaces
Fust, Johann, 703

Gabriel, Jacques, 243, *244,* 434
Galapagos archipelago, 331
Galerie d'Orléans (Paris), 438
Galileo Galilei, 213, 331
Galleries, 438
Gallery of Machines (1867), 439
Gallery of Machines (1878), 439
Gallery of Machines (1889), 439-40, *440*
Galvanotherapy, 716
Galy-Cazalat, 89
Gambey, 216, 222, 223
Gando, 688
Gang saw, 724
Gangways, 292
Gannal, Jean-Nicolas, 660-61
Gap lathes, 120
Garabit viaduct, 440
Garbett, S., 559
Gare du Nord (Paris), 437
Gas, illuminating, *see* Gas lighting
Gas burners, 464-65, *465*
Gascony, 481
Gascoyne, 406
Gases, recovery of: iron production and, 547, 552-53
Gas heating, 468
Gaskell, Holbrook, 147-49
Gas lighting, 461
  burners for, 464-65, *465*
  distillation of coal for, 573, *574*
  distribution equipment for, 463-64, *465*
  ferrous oxide for purifying, 574
  meters for, 465, *467*
  in Paris, 463, 465, *466*
  in railroad coaches, 354, *354*
Gas meters, 465, *467*
Gasometers, 372, 573-74
Gassendi, J.-J. de, 429
Gatteaux, Nicolas-Marie, 673, 678-79, 687
Gaudry, Jules, 108, 111

Gauge:
  with circular vernier, *202,* 203
  screw-type, *202*
Gauge Act of 1846, 337
Gautherot, Nicolas, 378
Gauthey, Émiland-Marie, 247-48, 272
Gauthier, Abbot, 299
Gautier, Commander, 331
Gavioli brothers, 181
Gay and Silver milling machine, 135
Gay-Lussac, Joseph-Louis, 11, 375, 378, 494, 562
Gay-Lussac tower, 562-63, *563*
Gear-cutting machines, 141-44
  Cartier's, 142-43
  Decoster's, 143-44
  platform machines, 142
  speed and cost of work, 143
  Whitworth's, 143
Gear-milling cutters, 105
Gears:
  bevel, *97*
  helical, 96, *96*
  herringbone, 96
  making of, 95-96
  stepped, 96, *96*
  Watt's planet, 54, *54*
  Watt's sun, 54, *54*
  windmill, 20
Gear teeth:
  epicycloidal, 96, 97
  geometrical study of, 95-97
  involute, 96, 97, *97*
Gear transmission, *see* Transmission
Ged, James, 676
Ged, William, 704
  stereotyping and, 675-76
Genard, 660
Generators, electromagnetic, 717
Gengembre, 119, 678
  stereography by, 684-87
Gensanne, 72
Geodesic Association, 223
Geological studies, mining and, 507
Geometric surveys, 507-9
Geomontography, 702
George III, King of England, 489
Germany, 484, 619, 638
  mining in, 507-9, 516
  railroads in, 359-60, 362
  sugar beet in, 479
Gerstner, 239, 281
Gething, G. B., *548*
Gig mills, 599, 614-15
Gilbert, Davies, 487
Gillé, Joseph-Gaspard, 691
Gilles, Father, 679
Gillet, François Humbert, 625-26
Gillot, Charles, 692
Gillot, Firmin, 692
Gillotage, 692
Gingembre, 161
Girard, Philippe Henri de, 593
Giraud scale, 229
Giroudot, 661
Givry, 331
Glass, 433
  copperplate engraving on, 685-86
  optical, 218

Glass spheres for production of sulfuric acid, 559
Glidden, 166, 167
Glinkov, Rodon, 584
Glover, J., 563
Glover tower, 563, *563*
Gluwitz, blast furnace at, *551*
Godart, 593
Godillot, Alexis: factories, *176*
Gold, 555
  drawing of, 145-46
  in Russia, 714
Golovin, F. D., 718
Gooch locomotive, 337
Googe, Barnaby, 478, 500
Goss, John, 175
Gossage, William, 566, 567
Gouet, 122
Gough, Nathan, 265
Gould, Commander, 196
Governor of double-acting engines, 55, *55*, 79
Gradients of roads, 237, 241
Graham, George, 185, 188, 203, 220, 221
Grand Surrey Iron Railway, 333
Grand Trunk Canal, *273*, 274
Grant, Ulysses S., *726*
Grapes, 494-95
Graphometer, 215-16, *216*
Grass, Milton N., 619, 620, 626, 628
Grassal, 687
Grasse, Admiral François Joseph Paul de, 331
Grasshopper engines, 68
Grasshopper locomotive, *388*
Grasslands, 479-82, 492-93
Graving docks at Brest, 276
Gray & Warner, 500
Great Britain, 236
  American industry and, 111-12, 725, 727
  atmospheric engines in, 41-42
  Industrial Revolution in, 8
  machine-tool industry in, 106-7, 158
  navy of, *see* Navy, British
  railroads in, 274, 359-60
  railroad track gauge in, 337
  steam engines in, 56
  See also England; *and specific inventors and topics*
Great Britain (steamship), 314-16, *316*, 319
  construction of, 325
  engines for, 321, *321*
Great Exposition of 1851 (London), 107, 128, 223
Great Western (steamship), 310-12, *311*
Great Western Railway, 311-12, 314, 337, 359
Green, John, 596
Greenhouses, 438
Greenwich Observatory, 330
Gregory, Abbot, 491
Gresley, Sir Thomas, 483
Gribeauval, Lt. Gen. Jean-Baptiste Vaquette de, 262
  artillery by, 401-2, *401*, 427
  star gauge by, 201
  Tables de construction, 202
Grignon, 530
Grimthorpe, Lord (Edmund

Beckett Denison), 194
Grinding machines (or mills), 140-41
Grist mills, 724
  Evans's, *502*, *503*
Groignard, 282, *282*
Grouvelle, Philippe, 469, 472
Grover, Baker & Co., 164, *597*
Grubbing, 484-85
Guadry, J., 139
Gueldry, 225
Guenin, V. I., 710
Guibal, Théophile, 522-23, *522*
Guiguet, 606
Guilhiermoz, 198
Guillemin, 551
Guilloching lathe, 697
Guillot, 687
Guillot-Duhamel, 518, 534
Guilmet, André, 269
Guinand, P.-L., 218
Gunboats, iron, 325
Gun carriages, 399-402, *399*, *401*, *402*
Gun forecarriage, *399*, 401, 402
Gunpowder, 400
  Bélidor's studies on the combustibility of, 423
  experiments with, 428-29
  in mining (military), 396-97
Guns, *see* Artillery; Cannons; Rifles
Gurney, Goldsworthy, 265
Gutenberg, Johann, 703-4
Gutenberg press, 656, 658-62
Gutsch, 702
Guyot, 494
Guyton de Morveau, Louis Bernard, 371, 534

Haas, Wilhelm, 693, 704
  printing press by, 656, 658, *658*
Hachette, Jean Nicolas Pierre, 77, 78, 94, 108, 239
Hackworth, Timothy, 340, 342, 343, 345, 350
Haddock, Uriah, 562
Hadley, John, 219
Hairspring:
  compensating for heat with, 189
  isochronism of, 190
Halftones, 692
Hall, Joseph, 548
Hall, Samuel, 320
Hall, T. Y., 523
Hallette, 19, 111, 152, 154, 366
  boiler by, 79, *79*
Hallette shops as Arras, *169*
Halley, Edmund, 328, 330
Hall fils, Powels et Scott, 612
Halm, Matthäus, *71*
Hamburg, 460
Hamilton, 498
Hammer:
  drop, 145, 157
  forge, 146
  ironworking, 528-29, *528*, 548-51, *549*, *550*
  mechanical (or tilt), 146-47
  power (steam), 107, 147-48, *148*, 157, 717
  side, 146
Hancock, James, 265

Hanson, John, 265
Hardouin-Mansard, Jules, 243
Harford, R. S., 548
Hargreaves, James, 584, 587
  spinning jenny of, 584, 586-89, *586*, 724, 727
Harington, Sir John, 460
Harley, 312
Harper Building (New York), 434
Harpers Ferry, national arsenal, 729
Harrison, John, 188, 189, 330
  marine chronometers of, 195-97
Harrowing, 499
Hart, Rev., 112-13
Hartmann, Richard, 112, 203
Harz double ventilator, 521
Haswell, 152
Haton de La Goupillère, 93, 94
Hattersley, 604
Hauling vehicles for mines, 515-16
Haussmann, Baron George Eugène, 460
Haussmann, Jean-Michel, 651
Haüy, Abbé René Just, 205, 207, 209
Haüy, Abbot Valentin, 662-65, *664*, 704
Hawkins, John, 95-97
Hawsley, 593
Hay, 482
Heat-compensating devices for clocks, 188-89, *189*
Heating, 453, 467-72
  central, 468-72
  by circulating hot water, 470, *471*
  by pressurized steam, 471-72, *471*
  stoves and fireplaces, 467-68
  ventilation problems, 472
Hedley, William, 340, *340*, 344
Heilmann, Josué, 161, 594, *594*, 604, *604*
Hell, Jozsef Karoly, 514
Heller, 698
Hellot, Jean, 518
Hemmer, overlock, 631
Hemming, J., 572
Hemp, 517
Henderson, James, 161
Hennebique, François, 450
Henry, Joseph, 386
Henry, William, 299
Herhan, Louis-Étienne, 679, 695, *696*
  stereography by, 682-85, 687
Hermbsstädt, 621
Herrick, 630
Herringbone gears, 96
Heuss, 534
High-pressure engines, 58-63, *61-63*, 65, 77, 263, 727-28
Highs, Thomas, 592
Highways, 235
  railroads and, 242
  See also Roads
Hill, Edwin, 161
Hill, Thomas Irving, 562
Hilleström, Peer, *513*
Hills, Frank Clark, 574
Hindley, Henry, 221
!ittorf, J.-I., 437
Hjelm, Peter Jacob, 553
Hodgkinson, Eaton, 253

Hoe, Richard March:
  printing press by, 668, *668*
    722
  web printing machine by, *678*
Hoe, Robert, 662, *663*
Hoffmann, François:
  stereography by, 681, 684
  stereotyping by, 673, 676-77
Hoisting, in mines, 516-17,
  517
Hoisting cages, 517, 523
Holabird, William, 446, 447
Holker, John, 559, 560, 592
Holland, *see* Netherlands, the
Hollerith, 181
Holley, Alexander Lyman, 731
Home Insurance Building (Chicago), 446
Homfray, Samuel, 338
Hooke, Robert, 39, 96, *96*,
  185, 188, 218
  coupling by, 100
Horizontal drill, Vaucanson's,
  137, *137*
Horizontal engines, 69, *70*
Hornblower, Jonathan, 61, *62*,
  70
Horrocks, William, 604
Horsedrawn vehicles, 257-60
  draft of, 239-40, *240*
  railroad wagons, 332-33, 339
Horsepower:
  nominal, 86-87
  as the unit of power, 85
Horses, draft (pulling power)
  of, 239-40, *240*
Horta, Victor, *451*
Hosiery, 619-32
  patterned and openwork, 630-
    31
  tubular (seamless), 623-24
  See also Knitting
Hot-air ballooms, 369-71, *370*
Hot-air stove, Corngreaves, *544*
Hot water heating, 470, *471*
Houel, 157
Houghton, Michael, 479
Houldsworth, Thomas, 161
Household appliances, 161
  See also specific appliances
Howard, 416
Howe, Amos, 730
Howe, Elias, Jr., 163, 164, *164*
Howe, Frederick W., 135, *136*,
  729
Huelgoat mines, hydraulic ram
  in, 514-15, *515*
Hughes, David E., 384-85, *385*,
  499
Huguenin, Simon, 111
Hulls:
  designs and diagrams of,
    326-27
  of *Great Britain*, 315-16
  iron, 322, 324-27
  of sailing vessels, 291, 294-
    95, 297
  sheathing, 326
  studding, 326
  of warships, 291-92, 322
Hulls, Jonathan, 52, *52*, 298-
  99
Hulot, 105, 134
Humphreys, Edward, 320
Hungary:
  mining in, 507-10, *510*, 514
  spinning machines in, 592
Hunt, Walter, 163

Hunting weapons, 419-20
Huntsman, Benjamin, 541, *541*
Huot, 35
Hupeau, 243, *245*
Hussey, Obed, 500, *500*
Hutton, 429
Huygens, Christian, 182, 188,
  330
Hydraulic drill, 524-25, *525*
Hydraulic hammer, 528-29, *528*,
  548
Hydraulic press, 151-52, *151*
Hydraulic ram, 514-15, *515*
Hydraulic turbines, *see* Water
  turbines
Hydrochloric acid, 556-57
  chlorine production and,
    567-69
  soda production and recovery
    of, 567-68, *568*
Hydrogen, preparation of, 372,
  373
Hydrogen balloons, 369, 371-73,
  373, 375
Hypochlorites, alkaline, 569

Illuminating gas, *see* Gas
  lighting
Imison, John, 95
Inches, 199
India, 277, 322
  textile printing in, 633-38,
    640
Indicator, 87
Indigo baths, 650-51
Indigo blue, 633, 639, 640
Indonesian batik, 636
Indret factories, *98*
Induction coil, Ruhmkorff, 519,
  521
Industrial design, 64
Industrial machinery, *see*
  Machine industry; Machine
  tools
Industrial machine tools, *see*
  Machine tools
Industrial mechanization, *see*
  Mechanization
Industrial Revolution:
  chemical industry and, 564
  concept of, 7-8
  technical revolution and, 8-9
Ingold, Pierre-Frédéric, 184
Inlet mechanism, Watt's, 50-51,
  50, *51*
Instruments, large, 216-17
Insulators for telegraph lines,
  388, *388*
Intaglio printing, 669-70,
  696-99
  See also Copperplate impression cylinder
Interchangeability, system of,
  728
Internal-combustion engine by
  de Rivaz, 264, *264*
International Bureau of Weights
  and Measures, 201, 223
International Commission on
  the Meter, 223-24
Intersecting gill, 593
Iodine, 578
Iossa, A. A., 712-13
Ireland, 477
Iridium, 554
  in alloy for standard meter,

  223-25
Iron (iron industry), 101
  bridges, 253-57, *254-56*
  as a construction material,
    432-41, 443, 451
  drawing of, 146, 529
  fuel problem and production
    of, 530-31, 534
  hammers for working, 528-29,
    528, 548-51, *549*, *550*
  hot-blast, 543-45, *544*, *545*
  hulls, 322, 324-27
  production of, 106
  puddling, 534-37, 542-43,
    547-48, *547*
  recovery of furnace gases,
    547, 552-53
  refining, 527-28
  rolling mills, 6, 149-51,
    150, 529, 537-39, *539*, 713,
    731
  in Russia, 712-13
  sheet, 151
  smelting, 531-34, 542, 551-53
  steam engines in, 538-40,
    548-51, *549*, *550*
  in the United States, 723-24,
    731
  warships, 325-26
  windmills, 22
  See also Cast iron; Wrought
    iron
Iron mordants, 633-34, 637,
  648
Ironworking, 527-30
  hammers for, 528-29, *528*,
    548-51, *549*, *550*
  mechanization of, 540
Isabey, Eugène Louis Gabriel,
  307
Isochronism, 190
Italy, 223
  silkworm breeding in, 495-96
Ives, James Merritt, *273*
Ivry bridge, *243*

Jackson, Charles T., 385
Jacobi, B. S., 717, 720-21
Jacobi, Moritz, 693-94
Jacob's staff (cross staff),
  214, *214*, 329
Jacquard, Joseph Marie, 181
  looms by, *582*, 611-12, *612*,
    630, *630*
Jacquet-Droz, Pierre, 151, 165,
  179
Jacquin, 624, 625, *625*
Jamain, 151
James, William Henry, 265
Janety, Marc-Étienne, 210
Janvier, Antide, 193
Japy, Frédérick, 104, 184
  clock factory of, 182-83
Japy, Louis, 146
  stamping system of, 157
Jars, Gabriel, 515, 518, 534
Javelle (or Javel) factory,
  565, 569
Jayet, Jean, 175
Jecker, 210, 222
Jefferson, Thomas, 728
Jeffries, John, 371
Jeker family, 161
Jenks, Joseph, 596
Jenney, William Le Baron, 443,
  445-46, *447*

Jenny, spinning, 584, 586-89,
    586, 724, 727
Jervis, John B., 368
Jessop, William, 334
Jet propulsion, 302
Jibs, 292, *293*
Johnson, Henry, 681
Joinville, Prince de, 322
Jones, W., 548, 551
Jones and Lampson, 729
Jones brothers, *257*
Jonval, 35, 37, *37*, *38*
Jonval-Koechlin turbines, 37,
    37, *38*
Jonveaux, E., 147
Jordan, 532
Jouffroy d'Abbans, Marquis
    Claude François Dorothée
    de, 72, 271, 300-1
Journet, 482
Juravski, D. I., 719

Kalbe, Ulrich Rülein von, 505,
    508
Karmarsch, 140
Karsten, Karl, 555
Kay, John, 584
    flying shuttle by, 602, *602*,
    603
Kay, Robert, 604
Kendrew, John, 592
Kepler, 169
Kilogram, 205-7, 210, 211, 222,
    225
    See also Metric system
Kinematics, 94, 95
King's Cross Station (London),
    445
Kintzing, 178, 179
Kitchen gardens, 476
Klaproth, Martin, 553
Klaus, Karl, 554
Klietsch, Karl, 698
Knaus, 165
Kneader, 161
Knecht, 701
Knitting (knitwear industry):
    European centers of, 619
    in France, 619-21, 624-26,
    632
    fully fashioned, 623-30
    of pieces, 623
    rib, 621
    runproof, 621-22
    in the United States, 619-20,
    626, 632
    See also Hosiery
Knitting looms (or machines):
    accessories for, 631
    with automatic narrowing
    mechanism, 622
    circular, 623-26, *625*, 628,
    629, 632
    by William Cotton, 629-30,
    629
    flat, 621, 622, 626
    flat, with a flywheel, 627-28
    flat, for patterned and open-
    work stockings, 630-31
    in France, 620
    for home use, 630
    by Paget, 628-31, *628*
    power, 626, 632
    warp, 621
Koch, Sim, 533
Koechlin (textile manufactur-

ers), 604
Koechlin, André, 37, 366
Koechlin, Maurice, 440
Koenig, Friedrich: printing
    press by, 666-67, *667*
Kolivano-Voskressen, mines of,
    710-12, *711*
Konstantinov, K. I., 717
Körte, 487
Kozen, Lt. Gen., 720
Kraft, N. D., 719
Krantz, 439
Kremer, Gerhard, 327-28
Krutikov, S. F., 719
Kuhlmann, Frédéric, 563
Kulibin, I. P., 718-20
Kutsch, 210

Labeleye, Charles, 248
Laboulaye, Charles de, 20, 93, 94
Labrouste, Henri, 432, 435,
    435, 436, 452
Lacaille, Nicolas Louis de,
    204, 205
La Condamine, Charles Marie
    de, 204
Lacroix, 614
Lagarde, Mme., 686
La Gauloise locomotive, 366,
    366
La Gironde locomotive, 366
Lagrange, Joseph Louis, 205,
    209
Lagrous, 175
La Hague, lighthouse at, 288
La Hève, lighthouses at, 285,
    286
La Hire, Philippe, 24, 239
Laird, John, 325
Lakanal, Joseph, 377
Lamb, 630
Lambreschini, 498
Lamps:
    Argand wick, 283-84, *284*
    Davy (miner's), 519
    of lighthouses, 282-85, *284*,
    285
    oil, *see* Oil lamps
    of railroad coaches, 354, *354*
Lancashire boilers, 63
Lancashire Witch locomotive,
    342
Lancaster locomotive, *350*
Land areas, measures of, 200
Land clearing, 484-85
Land distances, measures of,
    200
Land drainage, 485-86
Land reclamation, 485-86
Lange, 461-62, *461*
Languedoc, 481, 490-91, 494
Lanston, Talbert, 683
Lanston's monograph, 695
Lantern can, 591, *591*, 592
Lanz, 94
Lapidary's mills, 140
Laplace, Marquis Pierre Simon
    de, 209
La Rochefoucauld-Liancourt,
    Duke François Alexandre
    Frédéric de, 480
Lasteyrie, Count Charles de,
    700
Lathes, 101, 113-21
    American, 728-29
    automatic, 120, 179

center, 117, 120
copying, 112, 718, 728, *729*
cutting speed of, 119-20
cutting tools for, 105
face, 117, 120
first French builders of,
    108, 109
gap, 120
guilloching, 180, 697
invention of, 102-3
Lincoln, *121*
Maudslay's, 115-17, *116*, 120
naval, 119
reproducing, 180
screw-cutting, *see* Screw-
    cutting lathes
Senot's, 115
simple center, 117
slide, *see* Slide lathes
vertical, 120, *120*
watchmaking, 104
wheel, 120-21
Wilkinson's, 116-17
Latitude, calculation of, 329-
    30
Laurent, 281
Lavoisier, Antoine Laurent,
    205-7, 428, 487, 541, 564,
    676-77
    hydrogen preparation and,
    371-73
Lawes, Sir John Bennet, 487
Lead, 553-54
    in Russia, 714
Lebailly, 624
Le Blanc, 480
Leblanc, Nicolas, 557, 564
    soda manufacturing method
    of, 564-67
Le Blon, Jacques Christophe,
    701
Lebon, Philippe, 11, 573
Le Brun, Baptiste, 592
Leclerc, 686
Leclercq, N., *526*
Lecreulx, 247
Le Creusot factories, power
    hammers built at, 147-49
Le Creusot foundry, 73-74, *76*,
    78
    coke-fired blast furnace at,
    551
Le Creusot region, 272
    mines at, *520*
    railways in, 333-34, *334*
Ledoux, Claude Nicolas, 433,
    434
Lee, Edmund, 19
Lee, William, 619
Lefaucheux, 419-20
Lefaucheux cartridge, *419*, 420
Lefèvre-Gineau, 205-7, 209
Leguminous fodder plants, 480,
    481
Le Havre, 276
Lehmann, Johann Christian, 523
Lemaître, Louis, 152
    riveting machine by, 154-56,
    155
Lemire, 104
Lemoyne, 284
Lendersdorfer, rolling mills
    of, *167*
Lenoir, Étienne, 204, 219-20,
    330, 469
    comparator built by, 205,
    210-11, *210*
    repeating circles by, 207,

208, 219-20
Lenses:
   Fresnel, 284-85, *284*, *285*
   See also Optical glass industry
Lepaute, Jean-André, 193
Lepaute, Jean-Baptiste, 193
Lépine, 171
Le Play, Frédéric, 439
Lepure, 501
Le Roy, Julian, 188
Le Roy, Pierre, 187, 189-90, 330, 623
   marine chronometer by, *195*, 196, *196*
Lesage, Georges-Louis, 379
Leschot, 179, 202
Les Héaux-de-Bréhat, lighthouses at, 285, *286*, 288
Leupold, Jakob, 52, *52*, 58, 65, 93
Levers:
   of watches, 185
   weighing instruments and, 228
Lewis, J., 617
Lhoest, 375
Lhomond, 468
Liddell, Richard, 289
Liebermann, Max, 584-85, *585*
Liebig, Justus, 487
Lifting devices in Russia, 718
Lighthouses, 282-88
   effects of swell and wind on, 288
   masonry, 285-88, *286*, *287*
   optical devices for, 283-85
Lighting, 454, 460-67
   gas, *see* Gas lighting
   photometry and, 462-63
   of railroad coaches, 354, *354*
   See also Lamps
Light machinery, origins and importance of, 160
Lightships, 289
Liming, 486
Limoges, 482
Lincoln, Abraham, *367*
Lincoln lathe, *121*
Linear measures, 198-203
   agricultural, 200
   for land and ocean, 200
   precision of, 201-3
   standards of, 201
   surveyor's, 199
   textile, 199-200
   See also Meter, standard; Metric system
Linen, 606
Linotype:
   matrix-type, *696*
   Mergenthaler, 695
Lithography, 670, 686, 692, 696, 699-701
Littré, Émile, 637
Litvinov, S. W., 715-16
Liverpool-Manchester railroad, 342, 343, 349, 354, 360
Livery carriage, *258*
Livestock, 478, 482-84, 490
Livingston, Robert R., 303, 304
Locatelli, 499
Lock, Bramah's, 105
Lockett, Joseph, 647
Locomobiles, 266, *266*
Locomotion locomotive, 342
Locomotive Act of 1861 (England), 266
Locomotives, 265, 338-54

American, *363*, 368, *368*, 727
Blenkinsop, 339, *340*
Blucher, 335, *335*, 337, 341
boilers for, 345-46, 349, 351, 352
brakes of, 355, *355*, *356*
Crampton, 352, *352*
driving wheels of, 352
Engerth, 362, *362*
evolution of, 349-50
French, 366-67, *366*
Gooch, 337
injection of exhaust steam, 346
long-boilered, 351, *351*
North Star, 351, *351*
Northumbrian, 349
Novelty, 345, 346
outline of the growth of, *75*
Patentee, 350
Planet, 349-50, *350*
Puffing Billy, 340, *340*, *344*
rack, 339
Rocket, *344*, 345-46, *345*, 349
   in Russia, 719
speed of, 350-52
steam distribution in, 352-54, *353*
Stephenson's, 335, *335*, 337, 338, 342, 348, 349
   on Stockton-Darlington railway, 342-43
Trevithick's, *59*, 338-40, *338*, 346
Log, ship's, 328
Logotyping, 681, 694
Loire River, navigation on, 271
Lombard, 426-27
Lombe, John, 584
Lombe, Sir Thomas, 584
Lomonosov, M. V., 710, 714, 716
London:
   bridges of, 248-51, *249*
   sewer network in, 460
   water supply of, 453, 458
London-Birmingham railroad, 359, *361*
London Bridge, 248, 250
London Engineer (steamboat), *309*
London Exposition (1851), 107, 128, 223
London Exposition (1862), *442*
Longitudes, determining, 330-31
Longridge, Michael, 342
Looms, 599-606, 727
   bar, 602, 603
   by Bouchon, 609-10, *609*
   with cast-iron frames, 604
   Chinese, 608, *608*
   cloth beam of, 604
   draw, 607-9, *607*, *608*
   Dutch, 628-31, *628*
   by Falcon, 609-12, *610*
   for figured fabrics, 606-12, *607-11*
   with flying shuttle, 599, 601-6, *602*, *603*
   heavy, 605-6
   by Jacquard, *582*, 611-12, *612*, 630, *630*
   knitting, *see* Knitting looms
   mechanical, 604-12, *613*
   for patterned fabrics, 606, *608*
   persistence of light and narrow, 605

Rachel, 621-22, *622*
   with selecting box, 608-9, *608*
   two-man, 603, *603*
   with variable-program control devices, 609
   by Vaucanson, 602, 610-11, *610*, *611*
   warp, 621-22, *622*
   width of, 605
   See also Weaving
Lorient, 277
Lottin, A.-M., 675
Louis, Victor, 434
Louis XV, King of France, 480, 592
Louis XVI, King of France, 660
Louis XVIII, King of France, 78
Louvre, 434
Lowell, Francis, 727
Lowry, J. W., *585*
Luchtmans, 672
Lufft, Johann Andreas, 512
Lumitypes, 696
Lusson, A.-L., 437
Luxembourg, 223

McAdam, John Loudon, 236-37
Macadam roads, 236-37, *237*, *238*
MacClurg Building (Chicago), 447
McCormick, Cyrus H., 500, *501*
McCormick reaper, 500, *501*
Machault d'Arnouville, Jean Baptiste, 403
Machecourt, J.-B., 523
Machine, definition of, 93
Machine Age, 158
Machine industry (machine-tool industry), 92, 101
   in Germany, 112-13
   in Russia, 717-19
Machine tools, 4-5, 93, 105-59
   first, 103
   first American builders of, 111-12
   first English builders of, 106-7
   first French builders of, 107-11
   first German builders of, 112-13
   in Russia, 718
   in the United States, 111-12, 159, 189, 728-30
   See also Machine industry; *and specific tools*
Macintosh, Charles, 543, 574
McKay, Donald, 297
MacLaurin, Colin, 21
Macomber, R., 144
Macquer, Pierre Joseph, 651
Madder, 496, 648
Magnan, 604, 605
Magnetoelectric motor, 389, *389*
Magnin, Jean Marie, 162-63
Mail carriage, *257*
Malanagny, 501
Malbec, 140
Malesherbes, Chrétien Guillaume de, 480
Malherbe, Father, 557, 565
Mallet, Anatole, 357
Malthus, Thomas, 475

Mame printers, 665
Manby, Aaron, 68, 324-25
Manchester-Liverpool railroad,
  342, 343, 349, 354, 360
Mandarinage, 652
Mandats territoriaux, 687
Manganese dioxide, 568-69
Mangles, 641
Mangon, Hervé, 458
Manometers, 88-89
Mantes bridge, 243, 245, *245*
Mantoux, Paul, 7, *8*
Manual foot, 199
Manure, 486
Maps:
  embossed, 702
  printing of, 693
  See also Navigation charts
Marbeuf, Marquis de, 481
Marbot, Baron de, 236
Marchiennes au Pont, blast
  furnaces at, *180*
Marggraaf, Andreas, 479
Maria-Theresa, Empress, 484
Marine astrolabe, 215, 329
Marine charts, 327-28, 331
Marine chronometers, 195-97,
  195, 196, 330-31
Marinoni, Hippolyte, 669, *669*,
  670, 701
Mariotte, Edme, 25, 122, 128
  tilt hammers by, *147*
Mariotte container, 462
Marling, 486
Martin, Ernst, 165
Martin, Louis, 76-78
Masonry:
  lighthouses, 285-88, *286, 287*
  for mines, 512
Masts of sailboats, 292-93,
  292, 293
  scarcity of wood for, 323-24
Mathematical calculations,
  mechanizing, 168-77
Mathematical instruments, 211-
  14
  See also Precision instru-
  ments
Mathematics, ballistics and,
  426-27
Mathieu, Pierre, 71, 507
Matthey, 224
Maudslay, Henry, 4, 102, 105,
  136
  lathe by, 115-17, *116*, 120
  machine tools by, 106
  standardization of threading
  of bolts and nuts and, 121-
  22
  steam engines by, 65, 68, *68*,
  320
Maudslay, Joseph, 69, 136
  steam engines by, 320
Maugendre, *571*
Maurel, François Marie, 175
Maurepas, 281
Mause, Daniel, 620
Maxwell, James Clerk, 226
May, Charles, 71
Mayer, Tobias, 219
Mayer and Cie., J. J., 154
Meadows, 482
  drainage of, 485-86
  See also Grasslands
Measurement:
  of angles, 214-16
  linear, *see* Linear measures
  universal system of, 203-4

See also Metric system
Measurement of mechanical
  power, 81-89
  calculating power, 85-86
  consumption of coal, 84
  counter, 87
  horsepower, 85-87
  indicator, 87, *88*
  manometers, 88-89
  Newcomen's rule, 81-82
  pressure on the piston, 82
  round in, 82
  Smeaton's calculation of
  output, 83
  Smeaton's table, 83-84
Measurement of speed, in
  navigation, 328-29
Measurement of time, 182-97
  See also Clockmaking
Measuring instruments:
  evolution of, 226-30
  for navigation, 328-31
Measuring rods for triangulation of the meridian, 207,
  208
Méchain, Pierre François André,
  205, 207, 209
Mechanical engineering, 4-5
Mechanical power, measurement
  of, *see* Measurement of
  mechanical power
Mechanisms, study and classifi-
  cation of, 94-95
Mechanization (industrial
  mechanization), 1, 101-59
  automation and, 177
  expansion of, 92, 100
  of professional and domestic
  activities, 160-61
  See also specific topics
Medhurst, 357
Medicine, electricity and, 716
Medina, 329
Mediterranean Sea, 331
Meeks, Carroll L. V., 445
Megevand, 182
Mégnié, 222, 372
Melnikov, P. P., 719
Melville, Alexander, 406
Menai Strait, bridge across,
  253-55, *255*
Mendel, Gregor, 487
Menno, Louis de (Baron de
  Cohorn), 395
Men-of-war, *see* Warships
Mercator, Gerardus, 327-28
Mercer, John, 569
Mercerizing of cotton, 569
Mergenthaler linotype, 695
Meridian, triangulation of the,
  207-9, *208, 209*
Merino sheep, 483
Merklein, Jean, 210
Merle, 572
Merrick, S. V., 729
Mersenne, Martin, 422
Mersey Canal, 274
Mersey lighthouses, 283-84
Messel, Rudolph, 563
Metal lathes, *see* Lathes
Metallography, 540
Metallurgy, 527-55
  in Russia, 712-15
  in the United States, 723-24,
  731-32
  See also Metals
Metals:
  nonferrous, 553-55, 713-14

  precious, 555
  See also specific metals
Metal wire, 100
Metalworking:
  mechanization of, 540
  See also Metallurgy
Metcalf, John, 236
Meter, standard:
  international convention on
  the (1875), 225, 226
  modern definition of, 226
  revision of (1869-75), 223-26
  shape of, 225, *225*
  See also Metric system
Meters (metering devices):
  gas, 465, *467*
  water, 457-58
Metric system, 4, 203-11
  Académie des Sciences and,
  204, 205
  creators of, 205
  difficulties of, 222-23
  diffusion and revision of,
  222-26
  French laws concerning, 222-
  23, 226, 227
  international standards for,
  224
  kilogram, 205-7, 210, 211,
  222, 225
  official standards of 1799,
  210-11
  principle of the natural unit
  and, 204
  provisional standards for,
  205
  results of applying, 228
  shapes of weights, 226-27,
  227
  standardization of meters and
  their multiples, 226
  standardization of weights,
  226-27
  triangulation of the meridian
  and, 207-9, *208, 209*
Meusnier de La Place, Jean-
  Baptiste, 371, 372
Meyer, Henry, 71
Meyer, Philip James, 269, *269*
Mezzotint engraving method,
  701, *704*
Michaux, Ernest: velocipede by,
  268-69, *269*
Michelin removable pneumatic
  tire, 270
Michelson, Albert Abraham, 226
Micrometers, 217-18
  Palmer, 203
Midland Railway, 337
Mile, nautical, 328, 329
Military aerostation, 373, 375
Mill, Henry, 165
Miller, *315*
Millet, 477
Milling cutters, 105, 134, 142
Milling machines, 134-36, *135*
  Decoster's, 135-36
  of Gay and Silver, 135
  of Robbins and Lawrence, 135,
  136
  in Russia, 718
  in the United States, 728,
  729
  Whitney's, 134, *135*, 728
Mills, *see specific kinds of
  mills*
Mimerel, 147
Minary, 551

Mine cars, 332-35, *334*, *335*, 515-16
Mine compass, 508-9, *508*
Mine plans (or maps), 508
Minié, Lt. Claude-Étienne, 418
Mining, 505-26
  blasting techniques, 512-13
  boring equipment, 523-25, *524*, *525*
  coal, *see* Coal mining
  explosives in, 519, 521, 716-17
  extraction techniques, 509-11
  firedamp explosions, 518-19
  geometric surveys, 507-9
  hauling and hoisting, 515-17
  hoisting cages, 517, 523
  mechanical preparation of ores, 517-18
  military, 396-97, *397*
  prospecting, 507
  pumping, 513-15, *515*
  in Russia, 709-12, *711*
  safety lamp, 519
  schools of, 518
  timbering and masonry, 511-12, *511*
  tools, 509
  ventilation in, 521-23, 712
Mining Institute (Russia), 712
Mining railroads, 332-35, *334*, *335*, 339, 346, 515-16
Mining School of Saint Petersburg, 712
Minot's Ledge lighthouse, *287*
Mittelbach, Michael, 505
Molard, 263
Moldboards of plows, 497, *497*, 498, *498*
Molds, textile printing with, 634-35
Molybdenum, 553
Momoro, 671, 673
Monceau, Durhamel du, 326
Money, paper: printing of, 685-87
Monge, Gaspard, 94, 105, 405, 541
Monier, Joseph, 449
Monotyping, 683
Montaigne, Michel Eyquem de, 599
Montcenis-Le Creusot, *535*
Montferrand, A. Ricard de, *543*
Montgolfier, Jacques-Étienne, 369
Montgolfier, Joseph, 369
Moody, Paul, 727
Morand Bridge, 242
Mordant eater, 651
Mordants, 633-34, 637-39, 648-49, 651
Morel de Vindé, 487
Morgatroyd, John, 620
Morin, Arthur, 38, 239-40, *240*
Morogues, Bigot de, 429
Morris, John, 621
Morse, Samuel F. B., 137, 385-87, *386*, *387*
Mortars, 426
Mortier, Auguste, 623, 626, 628-29
Mortising machines, *133*, 134
Moskvin, 715
Motel, 330
Motive power, theory of, 93-94
Mottard, 578
Moura, 72

Mudge, Thomas: anchor escapement of, *186*, 187
Mud mills, 289
Mule-jenny, *585*, 588-89, *588*, *589*
Mules, 483
Muller, Johann, 672
Muller, William James, *173*
Muller steel plate method, 647
Multiple-shuttle box, 604
Multiplying machines:
  arithmaurel, 175-76
  Leibniz's, 171-73, *172*
Munster, Sebastian, 214
Muntz, 555
Murdock, William, 11, 573
  steam engines and, 66, 68, 70
  steam-powered carriage by, 263, *263*
Murray, Matthew, 64, 66, 126, 339, 592
Musée du Conservatoire National des Arts et Métiers, 134
Music, printing of, 688
Musical devices, mechanical, 178-81
Music boxes, 179-81, *179*
Music recording, 179
  See also Phonographs
Muskets, eighteenth-century, 414-16, *414*
  See also Rifles
Mylne, Robert, 248

Nails, machines for making, 104
Naphtha, 574
Napier, David, 320
Napoléon (steamship; later the *Corse*), 313-15, *313*, 317, 322
Napoléon Bonaparte, 272, 280, 406, 408, 417, 425, 426, 593, 617
Napping of fabrics, 614-15
Narrowing mechanism, knitting machines with, 622-23
Nartov, A. K., 180, 718
Nash, John, 435
Nasmyth, James, 103, 107, 108, 550
  power hammers by, 147-49
  shaping machine by, 131
Nassau, Prince of, 534
Naturselbstdruckes (natural printing), 699
Naudin, Charles, 487
Naval artillery, 406-13
Naval construction, *see* Shipbuilding
Navier, 21, 28, 33, 239, 248
Navigation, 327-31
  coastal, 295-96
  correcting geographical errors, 331
  determining a course, 329
  latitude, calculation of, 329-30
  longitude, determining, 330-31
  measurement of speed, 328-29
  plotting courses, 327-28
  by sail, 297-98
  steam, *see* Steam navigation
  See also Ports
Navigational instruments, 214-15, 219-20

Navigation charts, 327-28, 331
Navilly, bridge of, 248
Navy, British, 306, 307, 322-24, 326, 408, 536
Navy, French, 403, 406, 408-9, 424
Needle rifle, 420, *420*
Nef, John U., 8
Nègre, Charles, 698
Neilson, James B., 543-44
Neoclassicism in architecture, 433
Nerval, Gérard de, 695
Netherlands, the, 223, 360, 481, 638
Neufchâteau, François de, 491
Neuflize, Baron de, 617
Neuilly bridge, 246, *246*, *249*
Newcastle area, cast-iron rails in, 332-33
Newcomen, Thomas, 39-41, *40*, 45, *57*
Newcomen's rule, 81-82
Newcomen's steam engine, 39-41, *40*, 70, 72, 299, 724
  See also Atmospheric engines
Newspapers, rotary printing of, 668-69
Newton, Sir Isaac, 25, 218, 329, 423
New York Tribune, press room of, *690*
New York World's Fair (1854), 439, *439*
Nicholson, William, 379, 660, 666, 685, 704
Nickel, 553
Niepce, Joseph-Nicéphore, 697
Niepce de Saint-Victor, Claude Félix Abel, 698
Nillus, 136
Nitric acid, 556, 579, 652
Nitroglycerin, 579
Nitrosylsulfuric acid, 562, 563
Nitrous products, production of sulfuric acid and, 560
Nobel, Alfred B., 579
Nollet, Abbé Jean Antoine, 203
Nominal horsepower, 86-87
Nopper, 626
Norfolk, 498
Normand, Augustin, 313-15, *313*
North, Simeon, 134
North Africa, 488
North Star locomotive, 351, *351*
Northumbrian locomotive, 349
Norwood, Richard, 328
Novelty locomotive, 345, 346
Nuts and bolts, threading machines and tapping machines for, 121-22

Oak, 322, 323
Observatory clocks, 194
Océan (warship), 291, 323
Ocean distances, measures of, 200
Octants, 219, 329-30
Odhner, 175
Odouart, Count, 494
Oenology, 494
Oeynhausen, Karl von, 524
Offset, 670
Oil, 152
Oil lamps, 354
  Argand, 461-62, *461*

for lighthouses, 283-84, *284*
perfecting of, 461-62
student, *461*, 462
Omnibus, 259, *259*
Onions, Peter, 535
Oppikofer, 241
Optical devices for lighthouse, 283-85
Optical glass industry, 218
Optical instruments, 719
Ore-crusher, 517
Ore washers, 517-18
Orfiedson, 553
Organism, Viollet-le-Duc's, 443, *444*
Organizing mills, 599
Organizing silk, 584
Organs:
  barrel, 178, 181
  hydraulic, 178
  mechanical, 178-79, *179*
Ormesson, Marquis Louis François de Paule Le Fèvre d', 490
Oscillating-cylinder engine, 68-69, *69*
Osmium, 554
Outside calipers, *212*
Overhand stoping, 510, *510*
Overlock hemmer, 631
Overprinting method, 688
Overshot wheels, 27-28
Owen, Robert, 589
Ozanne brothers, 295

Packet boats, 296
Paddle wheels, steamships with, 298-99, 304, 309, 311, 312, 315, 320
Paget, Arthur, Dutch loom by, 628-31, *628*
Pagnier, 660
Paine, Thomas, 251
Paixhans, Gen. Henri-Joseph, 409, *409*
Palais de l'Industrie (Paris), 439
Palladium, 554
Palmer, Jean, 158, *202*, 203
Panéiconographie, 692
Panemonian mills, 22
Paper, cigarette, 576
Papermaking industry, 575, *575*, *576*
Paper money, printing of, 685-86
Paper pulp, 569
Papillon, J.-B., 690
Papin, Denis, 39, *57*, 298
Parallel motion, Watt's, 54, *54*
Parent, Antoine, 20-21, 25
Parham, William, 498
Paris:
  bridges of, 251-53, *251-53*
  fortifications of, 392-95, *392*, *394*
  gas lighting in, 463, 465, *466*
  sewer network in, 460
  water supply of, 460
Paris Exposition (1834), 108, 110
Paris Exposition (1849), 111
Paris Exposition (1855), 38, 223
Paris Exposition (1867), 223, 439

Paris Exposition (1878), 439, *459*
Paris Exposition (1889), 439-40
Paris mint, 145
Parkins, 479
Parmentier, Antoine, 478
Pasold, J. A. W., 626
Pastures (grasslands), 479-82, 492-93
Patentee locomotive, 350
Patterson, W., 314
Pattinson, Hugh, 555
Paul (designer of milling machine), 136
Paul, Lewis, 592
Paulin, 147
Pauly, Jean Samuel, 417
Paxton, Joseph, 438
Payen, Anselme, 578
Payen, Jacques, 174, 300
Peasants, 497
Pease, Edward, 342
Pébrine, 496
Péclet, 469
Pecqueur, Onésiphore, 265, *265*, 266
Pedometers, 170
Peel, Robert, 587
Peiresc, Cl. Fabri de, 679
Péligot, E.-M., 554
Pendulum, 184
  compensating, 188-89, *189*
  of regulators, 193
Pendulum clocks, 192-94
Penn, John, 69, *318*, 321, *321*
Penzoldt, 145
Percussion capsule:
  for infantry weapons, 416
  for naval artillery, 413
Percy, John, 552
Perdonnet, Auguste, 349, 359
Perforated card, 180-81
Perforated disk for musical device, 180
Périer, Augustin Charles, 72-74, 76, 151, *151*, 304
Périer, Jacques-Constantin, 72-74, 76, 77, 151, *151*, 299, 300, 304, 517, 577
Perkins, Jacob, 104, 112, 471, 647
Perrault, Claude, 433
Perrelet, Abraham-Louis, 191
Perret (chemist), 562
Perret, A.-G., 451
Perronet, J.-Rodolphe, 243, 247-48, *245-47*
Perrot, Louis-Jérôme, 167, 642, 644, *644*
Perrotine machine, 642, 644, *644*
Perseverance locomotive, 345
Persia, 637
Person, 500
Petersen, William, 531-32
Peter the Great, Tsar of Russia, 709-10, 718, 719
Petrov, V. V., 716
Pfeiffer, 534
Phanzeder scale, 229
Philippe, E., 156, 258, 668-69
Philippines, the, 223
Philips, Peregrine, 563
Philips and Lee spinning mill, 435
Phlogiston theory, 372, 373
Phonographs, 180
Photography, 692, 696, 698
Photogravure, 670, 692, 698

Photometry, 462-63
Phototyping, 686
Photozincography, 692
Physiocrats, 475
Pianos, player (pianolas), 181
Pianotype compositor, 694-95, *695*
Piat, 142
Picard, Jean, 204, 218
Pi-Ching, 671
Pick, miner's, 509
Pickard, James, 52, 54
Pictet de Rochemont, Charles, 487
Pierres, Philippe-Denis, 660, 677
Pig boiling, 548
Pigment, 633
Pihet, 142, 153
Pilâtre de Rozier, Jean François, 370-71
Pile de Charlemagne, 205-7
Pillow blocks for locomotive wheels, 342
Pilon, 147
Pin barrel, in musical devices, 179-80
Pine wood, 323-24
Pingeron, 165, 673
Pinions for clocks, 105
Pins, brass, 161
Piobert, 427-29
Pipes, 457
  cast-iron, 455, 469
  for steam heating, 469
Pistols, 421
  cavalry, 415
Piston rings, 65
Pistons:
  of atmospheric engines, 40, 44
  of condensing engines, 46, *48*
  of Newcomen's engine, 40
  pressure on, 82
Pixii, Hyppolyte, 11, 389
Place de la Concorde, Garde-Meuble in, 434
Planetary clocks, 193
Planet locomotive, 349-50, *350*
Plangi technique of tie dyeing, 635
Planimeter, 241
Planing machine, 101, 102, 105, 112, 125-30
  Bodmer's, 130
  Caillon's, 125-26
  Clement's, 126-27
  cost of using, 129-30
  cutting speed of, 129
  De La Morinière's, 127-28
  first English builders of, 106, 107
  first French builders of, 108-11
  Focq's, 125, *125*
  Fox's, 126
  with movable tools, 127
  Roberts's, 126
  sizes and characteristics of, 129
  Whitworth's, 128-29, *128*
  See also Shaping planer
Platemaking, 529
Platform machines, 142
Platinum, 553, 714
Platinum-iridium alloy for standard meter, 223-25
Platt, John, 593

Plattes, Gabriel, 499
Player pianos, 181
Pliny the Elder, 636-37
Plotting courses (navigation), 327-28
Plows, 497-99, *497-99*, 722
Plugs (mining), 512
Plumbing, 454
  cast-iron pipes, 455
  meters, 457-58
  networks of, 457
  sewer networks, 460
Pluvinet, 578
Plymouth, 280-81
Pneumatic railroads, 357-58, *358*
Point-blank firing, 425
Point net machine, 621
Poisat, 555
Poisson, 427, 428
Poitevin, 686
Poitou, 482-83
Poivret, 628
Poland, 236, 484, 619
  spinning machines in, 592
Polarization, 378
Poleni, 175
Polhelm, Christopher, 12, 516-17
Polishing machine, 140
Polonceau, 241, 251-52, *252*
Polonceau truss, 436-37, *436*
Polytyping, 672, 684-85
Polzunov, I. I., 715
Pomone (frigate), 295, 315
Poncelet, Jean-Victor, 21, 38, 93, 94, 96, 147, 151
Poncelet's wheel, 26-27, *27*, 38
Poniukhayev, 720
Pontcharra, Col., 417
Pont d'Austerlitz, 251, *251*
Pont de la Concorde, 247
Pont de Neuilly, 246, *246*, *249*
Pont des Arts, 253
Pont du Carrousel, 251-52, *252*
Ponte Vecchio (Florence), 247
Pont-Gibaud mills, 32-33, *33*
Pont-Royal bridge, 243
Pontypool blast furnace, 552
Poppe, 621, 623
Population growth, agriculture and, 474-75
Poron brothers, 628
Porthouse, Thomas, 592
Ports, 275-81
  breakwaters for, 278-79, *278*, *280*
  Brest, 276
  Cherbourg, 277-81
  dry docks for, 281-82, *282*
  Le Havre, 276
  Lorient, 277
  Plymouth, 280-81
Portugal, 477
Post-mill, 20
Potatoes, 475-78, 490, 492
Poterat, 683
Potter, Christopher, 666
Potter, Humphrey, 41
Poultry, 484
Power, *see* Horsepower; Measurement of mechanical power
Precision:
  of linear measures, 201-3
  mechanical engineering and, 4
Precision instruments, 211-22, . 718-19
  astronomical, 216-20
  dividing machines for, 221-22,

221
  eyepieces adapted to, 217-18
  geodetic, 218-19
  mathematical, 211-14
  for measuring angles, 214-16
  reflecting, 218-20
  for triangulation, 207-9, *208*, *209*
Presses, *see* Printing presses
Pressure:
  indicator, 87, *88*
  manometers for measuring, 88-89
  on pistons, 82
Price, Charles Fox, 83, 470
Price, Stephen, 617
Priestley, Joseph, 487, 541
Priming needle, 512
Printing, 656-705
  of *assignats*, 684, 686-87
  for the blind, 662-65, *664*
  chemical engraving (photo-zincography), 692
  color, 701-2
  electroplate facsimiles, 698-99
  electrotyping, 693-94
  embossing, 702
  flat-surface, 699-701
  intaglio, 669-70, 696-99
  lithography, 699-701
  mechanical composition and casting machines, 694-96, *695*
  of music, 688
  of paper money, 685-87
  relief, 690-96
  rotary, of newspapers, 668-69, *668*, *669*
  textile, *see* Textile printing
  typometry, 692-93
  vignettes, 691-93, *693*
  See also Stereotyping
Printing devices for telegraphs, 384-85, *385*, 720
Printing presses:
  by Anisson, 659-60, *660*, 665
  for the blind, 662-65, *664*
  by Clymer, 661, *662*
  cylinder, 665-66
  by Didot, 659-60, 665
  double-action, 656, 658, *658*
  Gutenberg, 656, 658-62
  by Haas, 656, 658, *658*
  by Hoe, 668, *668*, *678*
  inking the cylinder, 666
  by Koenig, 666-67, *667*
  mechanical, 666-70
  for newspapers, 668-69, *669*
  by Pierres, 660
  single-action, 658-62, *658-62*
  by Stanhope, 661, *661*
  from Watt's Printing House, *659*
Printing table for fabrics, *642*
Proctor, Thomas, 531-32
Progin, Xavier, 166, *166*
Prony, Baron de, 209, 246
Prony formulas, 457
Propellers, 312-16
  transmission system for, 320-22, *321*
Proportional divider, 212-14, *213*
Prospecting, 507
Prothero, Rowland Edmund (Lord Ernle), 478
Proust, Louis, 462
Prudon, 501, 659

Prussia, 236, 592
  See also Germany
Prussian blue, 651
Public transport, 259-60
  See also Railroads
Puddling, 534-37, 542-43, 547-48, *547*, 712-13
Puddling furnaces, 536-37, 547-48, *547*, 731
Puffing Billy, 340, *340*, *344*
Pull boy, 647-48
Pulley blocks, 99-100, *99*, 106
Pulleys, 99, *99*
Pumps, 455
  for mining, 513-15, *515*
Punches, 137
  hollow, 104
Punching machine, Cavé's, 111
Punch presses, 137, 144
Punch shears, 153-54
Puymaurin, 685
Pyrenees, 485
Pyrites, calcining of, 561-62
Pyrostereography, 688

Quadrants, 217, 218, 220
  Davis, *214*, 215, 219, 329
  with shadow scale, 214
Quercitron, 649
Quercy, 478
Quesnay, François, 475, 484
Quinette de Rochemont, 288
Quinquet, Bertrand, 283, 461, 462, 673
Quintenz, Aloïse, 229-30, *229*

Rabut, Charles, 450
Rachel loom (warp loom), 621-22, *622*
Rack locomotives, 339
Radcliffe, William, 604
Radial drill, 111, 138-39, *139*
Raffelsberger, 693
Rags, in paper production, 575-76
Railroad bridges, 343
Railroad cars (wagons):
  horsedrawn vehicles, 332-33, 339
  passenger coaches, 354, *354*
Railroads, 332-68
  braking systems, 355, *355*, *356*
  cost of constructing, 359
  development of, 359-68
  in Europe, 360, 362
  in France, 346-49, 351, 357-59, 362-67, *364-66*
  in Great Britain, 274, 359-60
  highways and, 242
  horsedrawn, 332-33, 339
  in Le Creusot, 333-34, *334*
  mining, 332-35, *334*, *335*, 339, 346, 515-16
  passenger carriages, 342, 354, *354*
  pneumatic, 357-58, *358*
  Rainhill competition (1829), 343-46
  roadbed and ballast for, 336-37
  in Russia, 719
  signaling systems, 355-57
  stationary engines (winches) for, 339, 343, 348
  track gauge, 337-38
  tracks, 332-38, *334*, *336*
  traction methods for, 339
  tunnels for, 359

in the United States, 242,
359, 367-68, 731
Railroad station concourses,
445, *445*
Railroad switches, 356-57,
356, 357
Rails:
cast-iron, 332-33
evolution of, 334-36
for mine cars, 332-35, *334,
335*, 515-16
shape of, 334, *336*
wooden, 332, 515
Rainhill competition (1829),
343-46
Ram, hydraulic, 514-15, *515*
Ramsay, 499
Ramsden, Jesse, 4, 177, 216,
217, 220
dividing machine of, 221-22
Ramus, 77
Ransomme, 501
Rateau, Auguste, 523
Rationalism:
agricultural, 475
architectural, 443-45
Rattler (steamship), 315, 320
Raulin, 89
Ravenhill, *314*
Ravizza, Giuseppe, 167-68, *168*
Razees, 295
Razors, cast-steel, *141*
Reaction turbines, 37, *37, 38*
Reaction wheel, 31-33
Read, Nathan, 265
Read, Samuel, 203
Reamer, 718
Reaping machines, 500-1
Réaumur, René Antoine Ferchault
de, 12, 484, 495-96, 540-41
Recoil anchor escapement, 185,
185
Recoilless (deadbeat) escape-
ment, 185-87, *185*
Recording of music, 179, 180
Red Flag Act of 1865 (England),
266
Reducing compass, 212, *212*
Reed, Jesse, 104
Reefs of sails, 293, 294
Reflecting circle, Borda's,
219, *220*
Reflecting instruments, 218-20
Reflectors for lighthouses,
283-84
Regulators, 192-94
Reichel, 621
Reichenbach, Georg von, 514
Reichenbach, Baron Karl von,
216, 222
Reinhard, Fr., 682, 688
Relays in telegraphy, 380-82,
381, 382
Relief castings, 687
Relief printing, 690-96
See also Embossing
Remington, E., and Sons, 166-68
Renaissance style in architec-
ture, 434
Renkin, Swaim, 12
Rennie, George, 126, 250, 307,
314
Rennie, John, 26, 248, *249,*
250, 307, 314
Rennie, John, Jr., 250
Repeating circles:
Borda's, 204, 330
Lenoir's, 207, *208, 219-20*

Replica castings, 685
Reservoirs, 272
Resmelting furnace, *713*
Ressel, Joseph, 313, *313, 314*
Restoration, French, 77-78
Reth (de Servière), 687
Retorts for coal distillation,
573, *574*
Reuleaux, Franz, 93-95
Reverberatory furnaces, 403,
405, 534-36, 570, 714
for soda manufacturing, 565,
565, 566
Revolution counters, 170
Reynolds, Richard, 534-35
Reynolds, William, 332
Rhodium, 554
Rhône River, navigation on, 272
Rib knitting, 621
Richard, 89
Riché, 222
Richman, G. V., 716
Ridgway (J. & F. W.) Plumbers
and Hydraulic Engineers,
458
Rifled barrels, 414
of infantry weapons, 416-19,
423-24
Rifled cannons, 403
Rifles, 419-21, *419, 420*
breechloading, 419-21
Chassepot, 421
Dreyse, 420-21, *420*
flintlock, 414-16, *414*
hunting, 149-20
See also Muskets
Ring throstle, 596, 598, *598*
River navigation, 271-72
Rivers, bridges and flow of,
245-46
Riveting machines, 154-56
Roadbed, railroad, 336
Road foundations, 237, 238, *238*
Road roller, 241-42, *241*
Roads, 235-44, 515, 719
deterioration of, 236
gradients of, 237, 241
late eighteenth-century, *234*
laying out and building,
240-42
macadam, 236-37, *237, 238*
paved, 235
profiles of, 237, *237, 238,
241*
research methods on, 238-39
Telford's system of surfac-
ing, 237-38, *238*
vehicles and, 239-40
Robbins and Lawrence, 729
milling machine of, 135, *136*
Robert, Gen., 147
Robert, Hubert, 249
Robert, Jacques, 371
Robert, Louis, 575, 660
Robert, Nicholas, 371
Roberts, Richard, 103, 106,
118, 133, 266, 596, 604,
605
planing machine by, 126
Robertson, 375
Roberval scales, 228, *229*
Robin, Robert, 193
Robins, Benjamin, 423-24, *424,*
426, 429
Robinson, John, 532
Robinson, Joseph, 260
Roche, Martin, 445
Rochon, Abbot, 677, 684, 692,

699, 704
engraving machine by, 680-81,
680
stereotyping by, 673, 677
Rocket locomotive, *344,* 345-46,
345, 349
Rock Manufacturing Co., *800*
Rodman gun, *404*
Roe, Joseph Wickham, 102, 148,
729
Roebuck, John, 49, 534, 559
Roemer, Olaus (Oles), 217
Rogers, Samuel, 548
Rogers, Thomas, 350, 368
Rogers typograph, 695
Rojkov, V. P., *715, 716*
Rolland, 572
Roller printing of fabrics,
642-44, *643, 645*
Rollers:
agricultural, 499
road, 241-42, *241*
Rolling mills, 6, 149-51, *150,*
529, 537-39, *539,* 713, 731
at Forges d'Ivry, *567*
of Lendersdorfer, *167*
Romanet and Co., *370*
Roman foot, 198
Roman weighbridge, 230
Romilly, 150, 182
Rondelet, Jean-Baptiste, 432-34
Rondot, Natalis, 495
Root, Elisha K., 729
Root, John W., 446, 447
Ropes, 98-99
Roques, 634-35
Rosa, 103
Rosart, 688
Rotary engines, 52-53, *52, 53*
See also Double-acting en-
gines
Rotary furnace for soda pro-
duction, 566
Rotary printing, 668-70, *668,
669*
Rotating engines, 69-70, *70*
double-acting, 74, 76, 77
Roth, 172
adding machine by, 175, *175*
calculator by, 175, *175*
Rothenburg, 533-34
Rotherham, 498
Rothes, Count of, 479
Roubaud, Abbot, 491
Rouffet, Achille, 122
Round inch, measurement of
mechanical power, 82
Roussin, 331
Rove, 595-96
Royal Albert Bridge, 253
Royal George locomotive, 342
Royal William (warship), 310,
323
Royaumont, 665-66, 691
Rozier, Abbot, 501
Ruhmkorff induction coil, 519,
521
Rumford, Count (Benjamin
Thompson), 58, 239, 429,
467-68
Rumsey, James, 302, 303
Russel, 566
Russia, 338, 531, 619, 709-21
electricity in, 716-17
machine industry in, 717-19
metallurgy in, 712-15
mining industry in, 709-12,
711

power production in, 715-16
spinning machines in, 592
transportation in, 719-20
Rust, Samuel, *663*
Ruthenium, 554
Rutter, Thomas, 723-24

Sablukov, A. A., 712
Safety lamp, 519
Safonov, I. E., 715
Sagebien, 28-29
Sailing vessels, 291-98
  Atlantic crossing by, 309
  colliers, 296, 297
  construction of, 294-95, 297
  corvettes, 294
  frigates, 294-97
  hulls of, 291, 294-95, 297
  masts of, 292-93, *292, 293,*
    322-24
  packet boats, 296
  sails of, 292-94, *292, 293*
Sails, 292-94, *292, 293*
  steam-powered battleships'
    use of, 317, 318
Sainfoin, 479, 481
Saint-Aubin, Augustin de, 686
Saint-Dié, bridge of, 247
Sainte-Claire Deville, Henri
  Étienne, 224, 554
Sainte-Geneviève Library
  (Paris), 435-36, *435*
Saintes, battle of, 408
Saint-Étienne-Lyon railroad,
  347-49
Saint-Eugène Church (Paris),
  434, 437
Saint Helena Island, 331
Saint-Léonard factories, fur-
  naces of, *571*
St. Louis, Missouri, 441
Saint-Louis bridge (Paris), 253
Saint-Simon, Claude-Henri, 491
Saint-Valéry, 276
Salou River, 276
Saltpeter, 556, 558, 560
Salt wells, Russian, 710, *711*
Saltzmann, Jean-Daniel, 681
Samuda, 357
Sandstone grinding wheels, 140
Sané, 295
Sans Pareil locomotive, 345
Saponification of tallow, 578
Sapping, 395-96, *396*
Satins, 606
Saulnier, Jules, 109, 119, 142.
  443
Saupe, E., 631
Sauvage, Frédéric, 312-14, *313*
Savannah (steamship), 310, *310,*
  319
Savary, Anne-Jean (Duke of
  Rovigo), 417
Savary des Bruslons, 6
Savery, Thomas, 39, 41, *57,* 298
Saw, circular, 105
Sawmills, 109, 724
Saxton, Joseph, 97
Scales:
  beam, 228
  Béranger, 228, *229*
  counter (counterweighted),
    228-29, *229*
  Fortin's, 206, *206*
  Giraud, 229

Phanzeder, 229
Roberval, 228, *229*
Scharnhorst, 429
Scheele, Karl W., 487, 553,
  556-57, 567, 685
Schemnitz (Stiavnica), Czecho-
  slovakia, 512
Scheutz, Edvard, 176-77
Scheutz, Georg, 176-77
Schickard, Wilhelm: calculating
  machine of, 168-70, *170*
Schierholz, *418*
Schilling, Baron, 379
Schilling, P. L., 716-17, 720
Schinkel, Karl, 598
Schinz, 89
Schloesing, Théophile, 572
Schneider, Eugene, 147-49, 550
Schneider brothers, 147-49, 156
Schoeffer, Peter, 702, 703
Schönbein, Christian Friedrich,
  579
Schönherr, 604, 605
Schreiner, Christopher, 697
Schütz, Carl, *167*
Schwab, 144
Schwanhard, Heinrich, 685
Schwertz, 487
Schwilgué, Jean-Baptiste, `194,.
  239
Science, technology and, 10
Scoop wheels, water turbines
  with, 30, *30*
Screw-cutting (or -threading)
  lathes, 102, 115-20
  first English builders of,
    106, 107
  Maudslay's, 103
  Senot's, 102, *102*
  Wilkinson's, 112
  See also Slide lathes
Screw press, 104, 144-45, 158
Screw propellers, 312-16
Screws:
  drawing bench used for im-
    proved, 146
  wood, 120
Screw taps, 105
Screw-threading lathes, *see*
  Screw-cutting lathes
Scudder's monoline, 695
Scutcher, 595
Scythes, 499-500, 529
Sea distances, measures of, 200
Sée, Henri, 490
Seed drills, 499
Seeding, mechanization of, 499
Sefstrom, Nils G., 554
Segner, 31
Séguin, Camille, 255
Séguin, Marc, 255, 256
  fire-tube boiler by, 345-47,
    345, 347
  locomotives by, 348, *348*
  Saint-Étienne-Lyon railroad
    and, 347-49
Seine River, navigation on,
  271-72
Selecting box, 608-9, *608*
Sellers, William, 592-93, 729
Sellon, 465
Semaphore, 376-78, *377,* 720
Senefelder, Aloysius, 686, 692,
  696, 704
  lithography and, 699-701
Senot's lathes, 102, *102,* 115
Ser, Louis, 522
Sereyev, V. S., 717

Sericulture, 495-96
Serpollet, Léon de? 267, 268
Serres, Olivier de, 476
Serrière, Nicolas, 669
Service of Weights and Measures
  (France), 223
Severn River:
  Coalbrookdale bridge over,
    250, *250,* 432
  Telford's bridge over, 250,
    251
Sew-embroiderer of Thimonnier,
  162-63, *162, 163*
Sewer networks, 460
Sewing machines, 161-64, *162-64*
  double-thread, 163-64
  Grover, Baker & Co., *597*
  Singer's, 631
  in the United States, 730
Sextant, 219, *219,* 330
Shadow scale, 214-15, *214*
Shamshurenkov, L. L., 719
Shaper, 107
Shaping machine, 130-34
  Decoster's, 132-34, *132*
  with a movable carriage and
    stationary table, 131
  Nasmyth's, 131
  output of, 132-33
  with a stationary carriage
    and movable table, 131, *131*
  vertical, 133-34
Shaping planer, 109
Sharp, John, 106, 108, 131
Sharp, Roberts & Co., 106
Sharp, William, 605
Sharp & Company, 139
Sharpe, Lucien, 105, 158
Shchegorin, 720
Shearing, mechanization of,
  615-18, *615-17*
Shears, 153-54
Sheathing of hulls, 326
Sheep, 482, 483, 490
Sheet iron, 151
Sheet metal, bending machines
  for, 156-58, *157*
Sheet-metal machines, 152
Shephard, Lathe and Co., 112
Sherrat, 52-53
Sherwin, William, 638
Shingling, 529
Shipbuilding (ship industry):
  metal used in, 324-26
  sailing vessels, 294-95, 297,
    322-25
  sheet-metal machines for, 152
  wood used for, 322-24
Ships, 291-318
  electric, 717
  lightships, 289
  sailing vessels, *see* Sailing
    vessels
  steamships, *see* Steamships
  warships, *see* Warships
  See also Hulls; Navigation
Sholes, 166, 167
Shops, 100
Sicily, sulfur from, 561, 562
Sickles, 499-500
Siege firing, ballistics and,
  425-26
Siegen, Lt. Ludwig von, 704
Sieges of Paris, 394
Siege warfare, 395-97
Siemens, Ernst Werner von, 383
Silesia, coal mine in, *516*
Silk:

organzining, 584
printing on, 652
Silk stockings, 620
Silk-throwing machine, 115
Silkworm breeding, 495-96
Silver, 555
  drawing of, 145, 146
  in Russia, 714
Simmons, F. W., *361*
Simonin, 578
Singeing of fabrics, 640-41
Singer, Isaac Merrit, 730
  sewing machines by, 631
Singer (I. M.) & Co., *164*
Singing birds, 179
Siphon in a steam-heating
  installation, *470*
Sisson, Jonathan, 46, 203, 220
Sizing, 640
Skempton, A. W., 435
Skerry Were, 288
Skyscrapers, 443
Slater, Samuel, 592, 727
Slater Mill, *730*
Slide lathe, 4, 101-2, 113-19
  cutting speed of, 119-20
  Decoster's, 119
  first English builders of,
    106, 107
  Fox's, 118, *118*
  improvements on, 118-19
  Vaucanson's, 113-15, *113,
    114*, 117
  See also Screw-cutting lathes
Slide valves, 66, 77
Sliding square, 214
Slitting mills, rolling and,
  150-51, *150*
Slotting file, 104
Slotting machines, 134
Smeaton, John, 10, 19, 21, 25,
  26, 28, 289
  boring mill by, 123
  calculating power of, 83
  lighthouses by, 283, 286,
    287, 288
  measurement of consumption
    of coal by, 84
  steam engine research by, 43-
    44, *43, 44*
Smeaton's table, 83-84
Smith, Francis Pettit, 314, *314*
Smith, James, 499, 595
Smith, Percy, 312, 314, *314*
Smith and Wesson, 729
Smithfield Club, 484
Snail, 178
Snodgrass, N., 595
Sobakin, F. F., 712
Sobolevskii, P. G., 714, *714*
Sobrero, Ascanio, 579
Société d'Encouragement à
  l'Industrie Nationale,
  29-30, 33, 35, 74, 76, 122,
  146, 576
Société des Produits Chimiques,
  572
Société Pajol, 272
Société Royale d'Agriculture,
  481, 483, 485, 487
Société Saint-Gobain, 562
Society for the Encouragement
  of Arts, Manufactures and
  Commerce, 584
Soda (sodium carbonate), 557,
  564
  ammonia method of manufactur-
    ing of, 571-72

Leblanc's method for manu-
  facturing, 556-58, 564-67
Sodium hydroxide (caustic
  soda), 569
Sodium sulfate, soda produc-
  tion and, 565, *565*
Solar time, 193
Solférino bridge (Paris), 253
Solvay, Ernest: soda manufac-
  turing method of, 571
Sommeiller, Germain, 525
Somme River, 276
Sorghum, 477
Soulé, 167
Southern, 88
Southwark Bridge, 250, 251
Souzongno, R., *186*
Sowing, mechanization of, 499
Spain, 223, 338, 477
Spars of sailing vessels, 293,
  204, 324
Speed, measurement of, 328-29
Speed, Adolphus, 478
Speed governor, Watt's, 55-56,
  55
Spencer, Thomas, 693-94
Sphinx (corvette), 308-9, *308*
Spindle, 583
  flyer, 596, *597*
  ring, 596, 598, *598*
Spinning jenny, 584, 586-89,
  586, 724, 727
Spinning mills, 74, *600*, 727
Spinning mule, *585*, 588-89,
  588, 589
Spinning of textile fibers,
  583-98
  Arkwright's lawsuit, 591-92
  carding, 589-92, *590*, 595
  cotton machines, 595-96
  dissemination of spinning
    machines, 592-93
  flax, 592-93
  as industrial prototype of
    mechanization, 598
  ring throstle, 596, 598, *598*
  water frame, 586, *587* 592,
    596
  and weaving, 601
Spinning wheel, 583
Splitting mills, 529
Spring detent, 185
Springfield National Arsenal,
  729
Spritsail, 292, *292*
Square inch, 82
Squire, W. S., 563
Stagecoaches, 259, *259*
Stamping, *176*
  bending by, 157-58
  drop, 717
Stamp press, 144
Standage, Peter, 592-93
Standardize threading, 121-22
Stanhope, Charles: printing
  press by, 661, *661*, 704
Star gauge, Gribeauval, 201
Steam engines, 2, 5, 18, 39-40,
  92
  atmospheric, *see* Atmospheric
    engines
  boilers of, *see* Boilers
  cast-iron framing for, 63-64
  condensing, *see* Condensing
    engines
  consumption of coal by, 83,
    84
  cornish, 66-68, *67*

design of, 64
double-acting, *see* Double-
  acting engines
double-expansion (compound),
  61-63, *62*, 77
dredges using, 290
by Evans, 59, 61, *61*, 265,
  727-28
in France, 70-80
French research on, 78-79
high-pressure, 58-63, *61-63*,
  65, 77, 263, 727-28
for hoisting coal, 517
horizontal, 69, *70*
improvements on general design of, 63-64
industrial uses of, 56
in the iron industry, 538-40,
  548-51, *549*, 550
machining of parts and development of, 64-65
Maudslay's, 65, 68, *68*, 320
naval, 110
Newcomen's, 39-41, *40*, 70,
  72, 724
oscillating-cylinder, 68, 69,
  69
portable, 43
Porter-Allen, 728
for pumping mines, 514
with reciprocating cylinders,
  110
reversal of operating principle of, 51-52
rotary movement, 52-53, *52,
  53*
rotating, 69-70, *70*
science and, 10-11
for ships, *see* Steamship engines
Smeaton's research on, 43-44
steam supply of, 65-66
thermodynamics and, 81
triple-expansion, 77
in the United States, 724,
  728
valves and valve gear for,
  65-66, *65-67*
variable-expansion, *78*, 79
See also Double-acting engines; Locomotives; Measurement of mechanical
  power; Watt's steam en-
  gines
Steam hammer, 107, 147-49, *148*,
  157, 717
Steam heating, 469, *470*
  by pressurized steam, 471-72
Steam inlet mechanism, Watt's,
  50-51, *50, 51*
Steam locomotives, *see* Locomotives
Steam navigation, 271-72
  commercial, 309-12
  early progress in, 305-6
  See also Steamships
Steam-powered dredges, 290
Steam-powered vehicles, 260-68
  Cugnot's wagon, 260-63, *260-
    62*
  by Dietz, 265, *265*
  experiments with, 263-65
  by Pecqueur, 265, *265*, 266
  prejudices and controls on,
    266
Steamship engines, 68, 69
  atmospheric (Newcomen), 299
  boilers for, 318-20, *318*

of the *Clermont*, 305
condensers for, 319-20
de Lôme's, 322
of the *Demologos*, 306
evolution, 318-22
for the *Great Britain*, 321, 321
for the *Napoléon*, 322
power of, 316-17
of the *Sphinx*, 308, *308*
of Stevens' steamboat, 306
water supply of boilers for, 319
Watt's engine adapted for use as, 320
Steamships (steamboats), 79, 296, 298-327
American and English experiments with, 302-3
Atlantic crossing by, 310
Desblanc's, 301, *301*, 303-4
engines of, *see* Steamship engines
first experiments with, 298-99
French, 308-9
French experiments with, 299-301
Fulton's, 303-6, *304-6*
iron, 315-16
Jouffroy's, 300-1
paddle-wheel, 298-99, 304, 309, 311, 312, 315, 320
propeller-driven, 312-16
Russian, 720
speed of, 316-18
See also Steam navigation
Stearin, production of, 578-79
Stearin candles, 462-63, 578-79, *579*
Steel, 77, 101
cementation, 540, 713, 731
as construction material, 440-41, 443, 446
crucible, 541, *541*, 713, 732
Demascus, 713, *713*
natural, 540
Réaumur and, 540-41
in the United States, 724, 731-32
Steel, Henry William, 296
Steel plates, 151
Steelyard arm, weighbridge with, 230, *230*
Steelyards, Roman, 228
Steeple engine, 320
Stehelin, 111
Stehelin & Cie, 152
Steinheil, Carl-August von, 380
Stenotype machine, 166
Stephenson, George, 334-35, *335*, 337-38, 340-47, 349-50, 519
first achievements of, 340-41
Manchester-Liverpool line and, 343
Rocket locomotive by, *344*, 345-46, *345*
Stockton-Darlington railway and, 342-43
Stephenson, Robert, 154, 253, *254*, 436
long-boilered engine by, 351, *351*
Rocket locomotive by, *344*, 345-46, *345*
Stephenson locomotives, 348, 349

Blucher, 335, *335*, 337, 341
Lancashire Witch, 342
Northumbrian, 349
Patentee, 350
Planet, 349-50, *350*
Rocket, *344*, 345-46, *345*
speeds of, 351
steam distribution system in, 353
Stockton-Darlington railway and, 342-43
See also Stephenson, George; Stephenson, Robert
Stereography, 679-87
copperplate, 684-88
copperplate engraving on glass, 685-86
defined, 672
disadvantages of the first stage of, 681-82
by Herhan, 682-85, 687
by Hoffmann, 681, 684
logotyping and, 681
for music, 688
pyrostereography, 688
relief castings, 687
replica castings, 685
by Rochon, 680-81, *680*
Stereotyping, 671-79
advantages and disadvantages of, 674-75
defined, 672
history of, 675-79
of music, 688
molding materials and techniques, 672-75
simple, 671-72
See also Stereography
Stevens, Col. John, 305-6
Stevens, Robert L., 305-6, 312
Stevenson (soda manufacturer), 566
Stevenson, Robert: Bell lighthouse by, 286-88
Stewart, John, 52, 131
Stirrup beam, 450, *450*
Stockings, *see* Hosiery
Stockton-Darlington railway, 342-43
Stöhrer, Emil, 383
Stone, black-line engraving on, 691-92
Stone, Thomas, 161
Stoves, 468
Strasbourg Cathedral, clock in, 194
String bean, 477
Strutt, Jedediah, 587, 595, 621
Stuart, Robert, 55
Studding of hulls, 326
Studding sails, 294
Sturtevant, Simon, 532
Sualem, Rennequin, 514
Suffren, Adm. Pierre André de, 331, 413
Sugar beet (beet, sugar), 479, 492
production of, 576-78, *577*
Sulfur:
combustion of, 560
soda production and recovery of, 566-67
Sulfuric acid, 556-67
calcining of pyrites as source of, 561-62
combustion of sulfur and production of, 560
concentration in lead cham-

bers, 561
contact method of manufacturing, 563-64
eighteenth-century methods of producing, 558
importance of, 564
lead chambers for producing, 559, *560*, 561
nitrous products and, 560
recovery of nitrous gases from production of, 562, *563*
ventilation in production of, 560
Sulfur trioxide, 559, 560
Sullivan, Louis H., 446, 447
Sully, 182
Sunderland Bridge, 251, 432
Sung Ying-hsing, 523
Suriray, Jules, 270
Surirey de Saint-Rémi, 202
Surveying instruments, 4, 215-16
Surveying for mining, 507-9
Surveyor's circle, 216, *216*
Surveyor's measures, 199
Surveys, topographical, 240
Suspension bridges, 254-57, *255*, *256*
Suspensions:
of carriages, 265
for locomotives, 341
Swamplands, reclaiming, 486
Sweden, 508, 509, 516, 531, 619
Swedenborg, 150, 527
Switches, railroad, 356-57, *356*, *357*
Switzerland, 362, 638
spinning machines in, 592
Symington, William, 69, 302, 318

Table engine, 68, *68*
Tacks, wire, 104
Talbot, Fox, 698
Talleyrand-Périgord, Charles Maurice de, 204
Tallow, saponification of, 578
Tallow candles, 461
Tamisier, Capt., 418
Tannin, 639-40
Tapping machines, 121
Taps, 122
Tar, 574
Tarpaulins, looms for, 605
Tartaglia, Niccola, 422, *422*
Tatishchev, V. N., 710
Taton, Renée, 81
Taylor, 351
Tcherepanov, 718, 719
Teak, 322
Teaseling fabrics, 614-15
Technical revolution, myth of, 8-9
Technicians, 11-12
Technology, science and, 10
Telegraph lines, 387-88
Telegraphs, 11, 376-89
alphabetical devices for, 382-83
Breguet system, 380, 383, *383*
electromagnetism and, 379-80
first, 380, *380*
in France, 380, 383-84, 388
Morse system, 385-87, *386*, *387*

optical, 720
printing devices for, 384-85, *385*, 720
railroads' use of, 357
relays and, 380-82, *381*, *382*
in Russia, 720
visual (semaphore), 376-78, *377*
Telescope, Chappe semaphore and, 376
Telford, Thomas, 238, 248, 250, 251, 254-55, *255*
Temporary Committee on Weights and Measures, 205
Tennant, Charles, 569
Tennant, Smithson, 554
Terrible, HMS (frigate), 309, 319
Terror, 73
Tewkesbury bridge, 251
Textile industry, 1-2, 6
in the United States, 724, 727
See *also* Fabrics; Hosiery; Spinning of textile fibers; Weaving
Textile measures, 199-200
Textile printing, 633-52
on animal fibers, 651-52
batik dyeing, 635-36
calico, *see* Calico printing
designers, 644-45
in Egypt, 636-37
engraving plates, 645-46
engraving rollers, 646-47
hand and mechanical, 642-43, *642*
in India, 633-38, 640
with molds, 634-35
with perrotine machine, 642, 644, *644*
printer's work, 647-48
roller printing, 642-44, *643*, *645*
on silk, 652
tie dyeing, 635
wood plates, *641*, 642
on wool, 652
Thaer, Albrecht, 487
Thénard, Baron Jacques, 158, 378, 545
Theodolite, 216, *217*, 219
Thermodynamics, 81, 94
Thermolamp, 573
Thiers, Louis-Adolphe, 362
Thimonnier, Barthélemy: sew-embroiderer of, 162-63, *162*, *163*
Thiout, 183
Thomas, David, 731
Thomas de Colmar, Charles (Charles Henry Thomas), 172-74, *174*
Thompson, Archibald, 593
Thompson, Benjamin (Count Rumford), 58, 239, 429, 467-68
Thompson, Charles, 691
Thompson, Francis, 52
Thomson, Robert William, 270
Thomson, Thomas, 631
Thoresby, Ralph, 236
Thouvenin, Col., 418
Threading machines, 121-22
See *also* Screw-cutting lathes
Threshing board, 500
Threshing machines, 500-1
Thurber, Charles, 166

Tickler for eyelet holes, 621
Tie dyeing, 635
Ties, railroad, 336
Tillet, 205, 207
Tilloch, Alexander, 673, 676
Tilt hammers, 146-47
Timbering of mines, 511-12, *511*
Time, measurement of, 182-97
See *also* Clockmaking
Time equation, 193
Tin, 554
Tingle, J., *613*
Tinplate, 529
Tires of carriages, 258, *258*
Tissier, Louis, 691-92
Tithe, 485
Tobacco, 496
Toise (fathom), 199, 200
Toluene, 574
Tools, machine, *see* Machine tools
Topgallant sails, 292
Topographical surveys for road building, 240-41
Torckens, *509*
Torcy reservoir, 272
Torricelli, Evangelista, 422
Toulon, 281-82, *282*
Tournon, bridge at, 255, *255*
Tours, bridge at, 243, *244*
Townshend, Lord Charles, 479
Toynbee, Arnold, 7
Tracks, railroad, 332-38, *334*, *336*, 719
gauge of, 337-38
Transmission (mechanisms or systems), 98-100
for steamship propellers, 320-22, *321*
Transmission shafts, 98-100
Transportation, 236
iron industry and, 542
public, 259-60
in Russia, 719-20
See *also* Horsedrawn vehicles; Railroads; Roads; Ships; Steam-powered vehicles
Treadmills, 24
Tredgold, Thomas, 42, *42*, *52*, 56, *63*, *68*, 88, 239, 469, *469*
Trentsenky, Josef, 701
Trésaguet, Pierre, 235, 237
Tresca, 89, 225
Treuille de Beaulieu, Capt., 403, 418
Trevithick, Richard, 58-59, *59*, 67, 77, 290
locomotives by, 338-40, *338*, 346
steam-powered vehicle by, 263-64, *263*
Triangulation of the meridian, 207-9, *208*, *209*
Trigonum, 214
Trinitroglycerin, 579
Triple-expansion engines, 77
Trolley (mining), 515
Troughton, Edward, 222
Troyes, circular knitting machines in, 624-26, *625*, 628-30
Trudaine, Daniel, 235, 246, 490
Trudaine, Philibert, 235, 246
Truing machines, 141
Truss bridges, 253
Tub wheels, water turbines with, 30-31, *30*

Tugboat, 110
Tuileries bridge, 243
Tull, Jethro, 479, 480
Tungsten, 553
Tunnels, railroad, 359
Tupham, Ovid, 457
Turbines, water, *see* Water turbines
Turgan, *178*, *180*, *464*, *549*, *567*, *575*
Turgot, Anne Robert Jacques, 204, 235
Turmeric, 648
Turnips, 478-79, 481
Turri, Pellegrino, 165
Twill, 606
Typometry, 692-93

Ulloa, Antonio de, 553
Underhand stoping, 510, *510*
Undershot turbine, 35
United States:
agriculture in, 722
architecture in, 445-47, 452
economic conditions in, 725, 727
fallowing in, 488
immigration of workers into, 725, 727
iron in, 731
knitwear industry in, 619-20, 626, 632
large industries in, 725-32
locomotives in, *363*, 368, *368*, 727
machine tools in, 111-12, 159, 189, 728-30
metallurgy in, 723-24, 731-32
railroads in, 242, 359, 367-68, 731
steamship experiments in, 302-3
system of interchangeability in, 728
waterways and navigation in, 274-75
wooden structures in, 447-48, *448*
Uranium, 554
Usher, 612
Uzatis, A. I., 712, 715

Vacheron, 202
Vail, Alfred L., 384
Vallée, *244*
Vallery, 614
Valleyre, 675
Vallière, Lt.-Inspector, 400-2, 427, 429
Vallière the Younger, 400
Valves:
cutoff, of double-acting engines, 55
steam engine, 65-66, *65-67*
water, 456-57
Vanadium, 554
Van der Mey, 672
Vandermonde, 541
Variable-expansion engine, *78*, 79
Varignon, Pierre, 423
Varvinskii, I. I., 714
Vauban, Marquis de (Sébastien Le Prestre), 278, 392, 395
Vaucanson, Jacques de, 4, 101,

103, 105, 134, 179
horizontal drill of, 137, *137*
looms by, 602, 610-11, *610,
 611*
slide lathe by, 113-15, *113,
 114*, 117
Vaucanson chain, 103-4
Vaudoyer, Léon, 452
Vaudreuil, Marquis de (Louis
 Philippe de Rigaud), 408,
 413
Vauquelin, Nicolas Louis, 553
Vegetius, Flavius, 395
Vehicles:
 horsedrawn, *see* Horsedrawn
 vehicles
 roads and, 239, 240
Velocipede, Michaux's, 268-69,
 269
Venice, 619
Ventilation:
 heating and, 472
 in mining, 521-23, 712
 production of sulfuric acid
 and, 560
Verge escapement, 178
Vérité, Auguste-Lucien, 194-95
Verniers, 202
 gauge with circular, *202*, 203
Vial de Clairbois, 323, 408,
 540
Vicat, Louis, 449
Victoria-type warships, 317-18
Viel, 439
Vignettes, 691-93, *693*
Vignier, interlocking system
 by, 356-57, *356, 357*
Vigry, 624
Viino, 718
Villarceau, Yvon, 189
Villefosse, Héron de, *506*
Villons, 125, 134
Vilmorin, Louis de, 479, 487,
 492
Vineyards (viticulture), 494-95
Viollet-le-Duc, Eugène Emmanu-
 el, 443
Vivian, Andrew, 59, 263, *263*,
 338
Voelter, 576
Vogel, 572
Volta, Alessandro, 378
Voltaic pile (electric bat-
 tery), 378-79, 716
Voltaire, 182, 475

Wade, Gen., 236
Wagon, Cugnot's steam-
 powered, 260-63, *260-62*
Waldeck, 122
Walker, 661
Walschaerts, steam dis-
 tribution system of,
 353-54, *353*
Walter, Joseph, *311*
Ward, Joshua, 559
Warfare, siege, 395-97
Warocque, Abel, 523
Warp loom, 621-22, *622*
Warships:
 artillery for, 406-13
 converted to steam
 propulsion, 316-17
 corvettes, 294
 de Lôme's ideas on, 317
 engine power of, 316-17
 first steam-powered, 306-7
 frigates, 294-95

hulls of, 291-92
 iron, 325-26
 razees, 295
 Victoria-type, 317-18,
 325
Washbrough, Matthew, 52, 151
Washington press, 662, *663*
Washing wheel, 640
Wassermann, 623
Watchmaking (watches):
 Breguet's, 191-92
 cylinder escapement for, 186
 factory at Waltham, Mass., *183*
 history of, 190-92
 machines for, 104-5
 repeating, 190
 in the United States, 730
Water:
 chemical composition of,
 372-73
 hardness of, 458
Water frame, 586, *587*, 592,
 596
 for flax, 592
Waterloo Bridge, 248, *249*
Water mains, 455, *455*
 networks of, 457
Water meters, 457-58
Waterpower, in U.S., 723,
 724
Water pumps, 712
Water stoves, 470, 471,
 471
Water supply, 454-60
 treatment of, 458, 460
Water turbines, 29-38
 Burdin's work on, 32-33,
 33
 early development of, 35
 Fontaine-Baron's axial,
 35-37, *36*, 38
 Fourneyron's, 33-35, *34, 35*
 Jonval-Koechlin reaction,
 37, *37, 38*
 limited distribution of, 38
 reaction wheel principle
 applied to, 31-33, *31-33*
 in Russia, 715, *716*
 with scoop wheels, 30, *30*
 with tub wheels, 30-31, *30*
Waterwheels, 24-29, 38, 73-74
 breast, 25, *25*, 27-29
 metal, 29
 overshot, 27-28, *27*
 Poncelet's, 26-27, *27*
 in Russia, 711-12, 715
 Sagebein's, 28-29, *28*
 theoretical research and
 tests on, 25-26
 undershot, 26-27
 in U.S., 724
 See also Water turbines
Watt, James, 5, 10, 18, 44-
 58, 63, 146, 260, 263,
 435
 Arkwright and, 591
 counter by, 87
 horsepower as unit of
 power and, 85
 indicator invented by, 87,
 88
 measurement of consumption
 of coal and, 84
 nature of work of, 56-58
 parallel-motion work of,
 54, *54*
 See also Watt's steam
 engine

Watt's planet gear, 54, *54*
Watt's Printing House, 656,
 659
Watt's steam engines, *66*, 70,
 82, 319, 589, 591
 condensing engine, 44-50,
 47, 48
 double-acting engine, 53-
 58, *54-57*
 experimental model of condensing engine, 46, *48*
 in France, 72-74, 77
 French license for, 72, 73
 governor, 55-56, *55*
 industrial construction of,
 49
 in iron industry, 538, 539,
 548-59
 operating principle of
 steam engine reversed,
 51-52
 piston developed, 65
 rental of, 49-50
 in Russia, 715-16
 1769 patent for, 48-49
 for ships, 309, 320
 steam inlet mechanism, 50-
 51, *50, 51*
 See also Watt, James
Watt's sun gear, 54, *54*
Waves, lighthouses and, 288
Wax candles, 461
Weapons:
 hunting, 419-20
 portable (infantry), 414-
 21, 728-29
 See also specific weapons
Wear River, bridge near
 Sunderland over, 250-51
Weaving, 599-606
 figured fabrics, 606-12,
 607-11
 fulling machines, 612, 614,
 614
 mechanical, 604-12
 patterned fabrics, 606, *808*
 precursors of mechanized,
 602
 and spinning, 601
 See also Looms
Webster, 484
Weighbridges, 229-30, *229*
Weights, shapes of, 226-27,
 227
Welding, 529
Weldon, Walter, 568-69
Wells, artesian, 524
Welsbach, Carl Auer von,
 465, *466*
West Indiamen, 296
Westinghouse, George: brake
 control by, 355, *356*
Westminster Bridge, 245, 248
Westminster Gas Light and
 Coke Co., 573
Weston, Sir Richard, 478, 481
Westpoint Foundry Association,
 368, *368*
Wheatstone, Sir Charles, 380,
 387
 telegraph, 720
Wheeler and Wilson, 730
Wheel lathes, 120-21
Wheels (of vehicles):
 bending machines for
 shaping, 156
 bicycle, 269-70
 carriage, 257-58, *258*

radius and width of, 239
Whim, 516
White, G. S., *650*
White, James, 96, *96*, 104
Whitney, Eli, 727
  cotton gin by, *627*, 727
  milling machine by, 134, *135*, 728
  system of interchangeability of, 728
Whitworth, Joseph, 103, 106, 107, 136, 139, 158, 159
  automatic lathe of, 120
  Calla and, 108
  gear-cutting machines by, 143
  lathe of, 118-19
  planing machines by, 128-29, *128*
  shaping machines of, 131, *131*
  vertical drill of, 138, *138*
Whitworth proportions, 122
Wick lamp, 283, *284*
Wick of stearin candles, 579
Widmer, 569
Wigang, J. G., 685
Wilcox and Gibbs, 631
Wilkinson, David, 4, 102, 112
  lathe by, 116-17
  screw-cutting lathe, 112
Wilkinson, Isaac, 538
Wilkinson, J. J., 519
Wilkinson, John, 4, 49, 250, 540
  boring mill by, 103, 123, *123*
Wilkinson, Orziel, 144
Wilkinson, William, 534
Williamson (soda manufacturer), 566
Williamson, H. F., 414
Willis, Robert, 93, 94, 96-97
Willkomm, Gustave, 619, 623, 626
Wilson, Father, 685
Wilson, Allen B., 730
Wilson, Andrew, 673
Wilson, Manby, 77

Wilson, Robert, 342
Winans, Ross, *368*
Winches, 339, 343, 348
  mining, 516
Winckler, Klemens, 563
Wind, lighthouses and, 288
Windmills, 19-24
  Aeolian, 22-23
  with cogwheels and crank-shaft, 24, *24*
  Dutch, 21
  with La Hire gear, 24, *24*
  nineteenth-century development of, 21-24
  Panemonian, 22
  with revolving body, 20, *20*
  with revolving cap, *19*, 20
  with self-regulating device, 22-24, *23*
  Smeaton's experimental research on, 21, *21*
  theoretical research on, 20-21
Windsor Bridge, 253
Wines, 494
Winnowing basket, 501-2
Winsor, Frederick Albert (Winzler), 463, 573
Wire:
  drawing of, 145-46
  metal, 100
  See also Cables
Wire tacks, 104
Wise, Samuel, 623
Wist, T., *75*, *363*
Woad, 636-37, 639
Wöhler, Friedrich, 554
Wolf Rock lighthouse, 286
Wollaston, William H., 378, 554, 697
Wood:
  distillation of, 573
  as fuel for iron production, 530, 531
  for shipbuilding, 322-24
Wood, Charles, 553
Wood, John, 534
Wood, Nicholas, 339, 342
Woodbury, R., 97
Wood engraving (woodcut), 690-91, *690*, *691*

Wooden structures, 447-48, 448
Wood pulp, for papermaking, 576
Woodruff and Beach, 729
Wool, 483
  combing of, 593-95, *594*
  printing on, 652
Woolf, Arthur, *57*, 62, *62*, 63, 67
Wool industry, 584
World expositions, 438
  See also specific expositions
Worlidge, John, 478, 499
Worms, Sr., 668-69
Worthey forges, rolling mills at, 538
Wright, Edward, 328
Wright, Henry, 593
Writing automata, 165
Writing machines, 165-68, *165*, *166*, *168*
Writing tympanum of Ravizza, 167-68, *168*
Wrought iron, 64, 732
  beams of, 435
  in construction, 434, 435
Wyatt, John, 228
Wynston, 531-32

Xyloengraving, 690-91, *690*, *691*

Yards, of sailing vessels, 293, 294
Yellow, pigment, 633
Youf, 141
Young, Arthur, 235, 236, 478, 480, 482, 486-88, 490
Yvart, 487

Zakavo, N. D., 718
Zinc, 554-55
Zinc mine, *506*
Zincography, 701
Zumbe, Karl, 512